Graphis Inc. is committed to celebrating exceptional work in Design, Advertising, Photography, & Art/Illustration internationally.

Published by **Graphis** | Publisher & Creative Director: **B. Martin Pedersen**

Chief Visionary Officer: **Patti Judd** | Design Director: **Hee Ra Kim** | Senior Designer: **Hie Won Sohn**

Associate Editor: **Colleen Boyd** | Publisher's Assistant/Designer: **Yuan Zhuang** | Account/Production: **Bianca Barnes**

Interns: **Diamanté Maldonado, Jacqueline Salazar Romo**

Published by:
Graphis Inc.
389 Fifth Avenue, Suite 1105
New York, NY 10016
Phone: 212-532-9387
www.graphis.com
help@graphis.com

ISBN 13: 978-1-954632-28-8

We extend our heartfelt thanks to the international contributors who have made it possible to publish a wide spectrum of the best work in Design, Advertising, Photography, and Art/Illustration. Anyone is welcome to submit work at www.graphis.com.

Printed in China

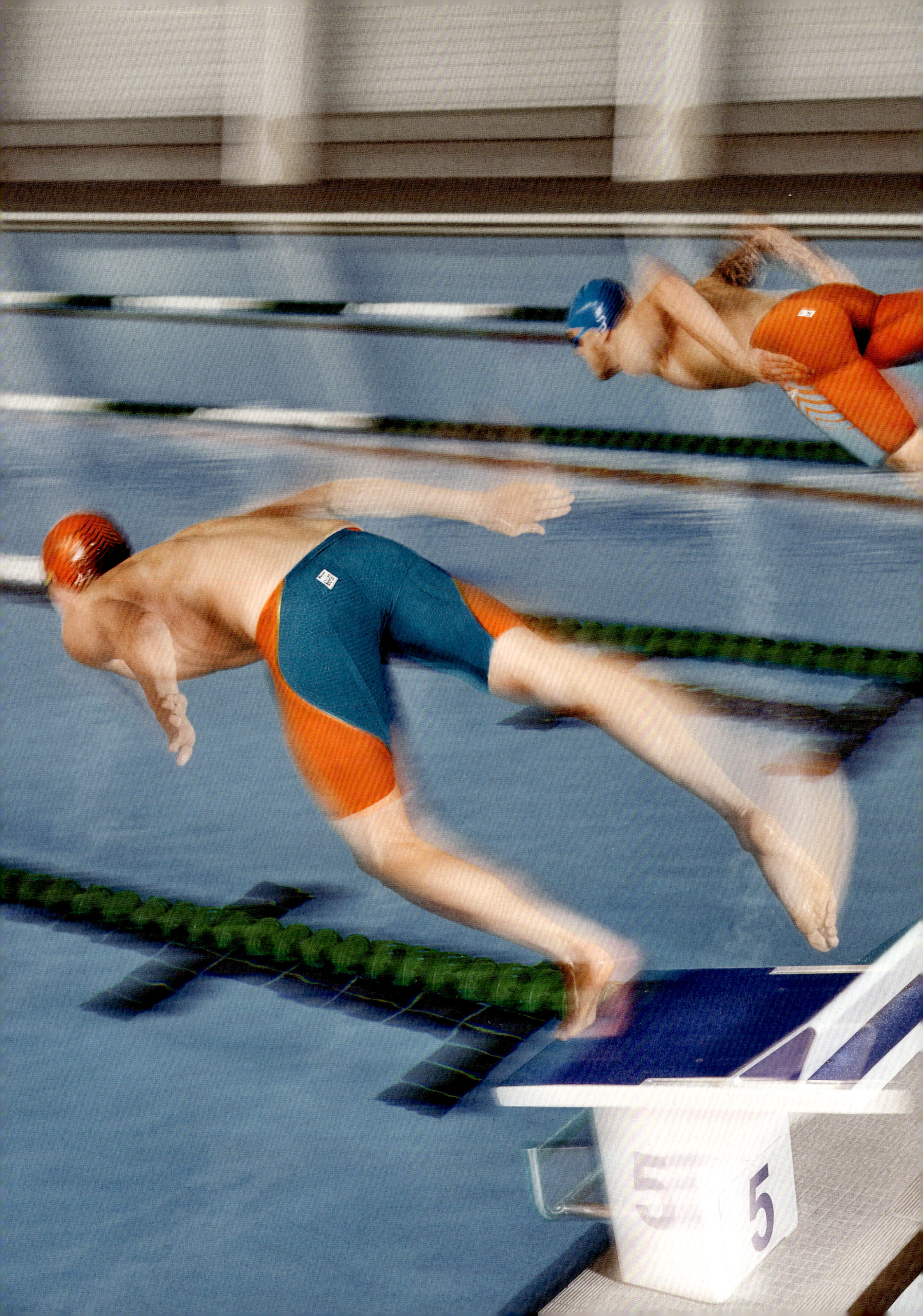
5
5

Contents

Page 3: *"Speedo Fastskin Campaign,"* by Beetle Rhind
Page 4: *"Lips - Zadig and Voltaire,"* by Michael Winokur

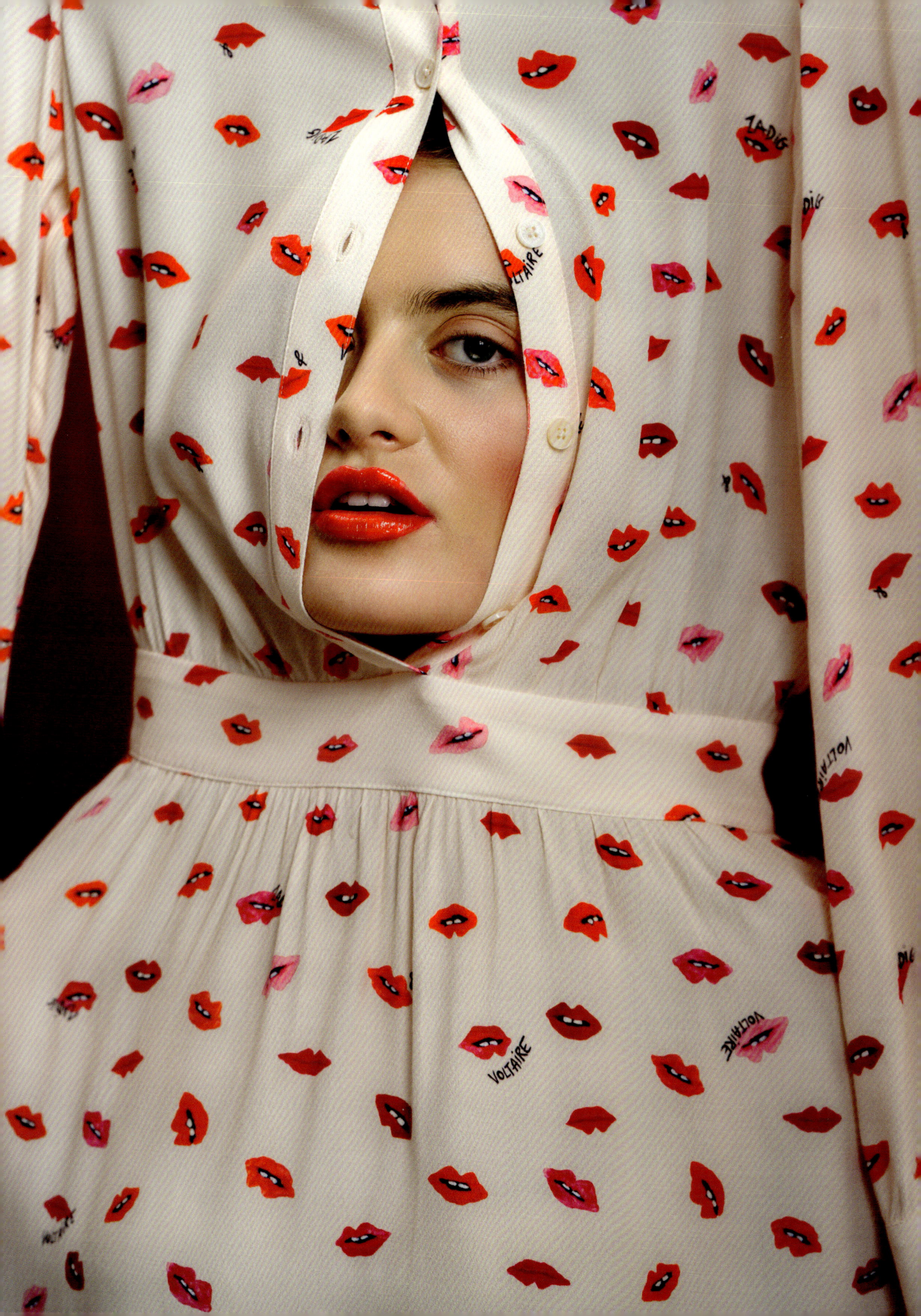
VOLTAIRE

In Memoriam

The Americas

Melvin Thomas Ames
American Photographer
1934 – 2023

Amos Badertscher
American Photographer
1936 – 2023

Jay L. Baker
American Photographer
1959 – 2023

Neal Boenzi
American Photojournalist
1925 – 2023

Kwame Brathwaite
American Photojournalist & Activist
1938 – 2023

Loren Cameron
American Photographer, Author, & Activist
1959 – 2022

Patricia Caulfield
American Photographer
1932-2023

Terence Dickinson
Canadian Astrophotographer & Amateur Astronomer
1943 – 2023

Frederick Eberstadt
American Fashion Photographer
1926 – 2023

John Fielder
American Landscape Photographer & Nature Writer
1950 – 2023

Roland L. Freeman
American Photographer
1936 – 2023

Carl Fischer
American Art Director & Photographer
1924 – 2023

Linda Gregory
American Photographer
1954 – 2023

Henry Grossman
American Photographer
1936 – 2022

Patrick Hamilton
American Photojournalist
1949 – 2023

Larry Haynes
American Surf Photographer
1962 – 2023

Mick “Hutch” Hudson
American Music Photographer
1965 – 2023

Mikala Jones
American Surfer & Photographer
1979 – 2023

Simpson Kalisher
American Photojournalist
1926 – 2023

Emory Kristof
American Photographer
1942 – 2023

Les Leverett
American Music Publicity Photographer
1927 – 2023

Camille Maheux
Canadian Photographer & Filmmaker
1946 – 2023

Reginald Dwayne Mess
Canadian Portrait Artist & Commercial Illustrator
1963 – 2023

Peter Miller
American Photographer
1934 – 2023

Louis “Skip” Perez
American News Photographer, Executive Editor of The Ledger
1962 – 2023

Bryan Randall
American Portrait & Landscape Photographer
1967 – 2023

Bruce Roberts
American Photographer & Author
1930 – 2023

Cervin Robinson
American Photographer & Author
1928 – 2022

Reno Salvail
Canadian Photographer, Artist, & Author
1947 – 2023

Dave Schubert
American Street Photographer
1973 – 2023

Richard Settle
American West Hollywood Photographer
1946 – 2023

Brian Shul
American Aerial Photographer & Air Force Major
1948 – 2023

Herb Snitzer
American Photographer
1932 – 2022

Lisl Steiner
Austrian-American Photographer, Photojournalist, & Documentary Filmmaker
1927 – 2023

Tony Vaccaro
American Photographer
1922 – 2022

Julian Wasser
American Photojournalist
1933 – 2023

George S. Zimbel
American-Canadian Documentary Photographer
1929 – 2023

Europe & Africa

Dorothy Bohm
German-British Photographer
1924 – 2023

Christian Aaron Boulogne
French Photographer, Actor, & Writer
1962 – 2023

Leroy Cooper
Jamaican-British Photographer
1960 – 2023

Mik Critchlow
British Photographer
1955 – 2023

Henri Dauman
French Photographer
1933 – 2023

Marie-Laure de Decker
French Photographer
1947 – 2023

Paolo Di Paolo
Italian Photographer
1925 – 2023

František Dostál
Czech Photographer
1938 – 2022

John Goto
British Photographic Artist
1949 – 2023

Paul Ickovic
Czech Photographer
1944 – 2023

Alain Lacouchie
French Photographer, Poet, & Illustrator
1946 – 2023

Jean-Claude Lemagny
French Photography Historian & Library Curator
1931 – 2023

Erwin Olaf
Dutch Photographer
1959 – 2023

Garrick Salisbury Palmer
British Photographer, Painter, & Wood Engraver
1933 – 2023

Claude Ruiz Picasso
French Photographer, Cinematographer, & Visual Artist
1947 – 2023

Margherita Spiluttini
Austrian Photographer
1947 – 2023

Marilyn Stafford
American-British Photographer
1925 – 2023

Stanislav Tereba
Czech Photojournalist
1938 – 2023

Algimantas Žižiūnas
Lithuanian Photographer
1940 – 2023

Asia & Oceania

Hideo Haga
Japanese Photographer
1921 – 2022

K. Jayaram
Indian Photographer
1949 – 2023

Kim Jung-man
South Korean Photographer
1954 – 2022

Robert McFarlane
Australian Photographer & Photographic Critic
1942 – 2023

K. V. Srinivasan
Indian Special News Photographer
1967 – 2023

Wesley Stacey
Australian Photographer & Co-founder of the Australian Center for Photography
1941 – 2023

Rob Tucker
New Zealand Photographer & Photojournalist
1948 – 2023

Ans Westra
Dutch-New Zealand Photographer
1936 – 2023

Richard Woldendorp
Dutch-Australian Aerial Photographer
1927 – 2023

Opposite page: *“Wired Flowers,”* by Robert Tardio

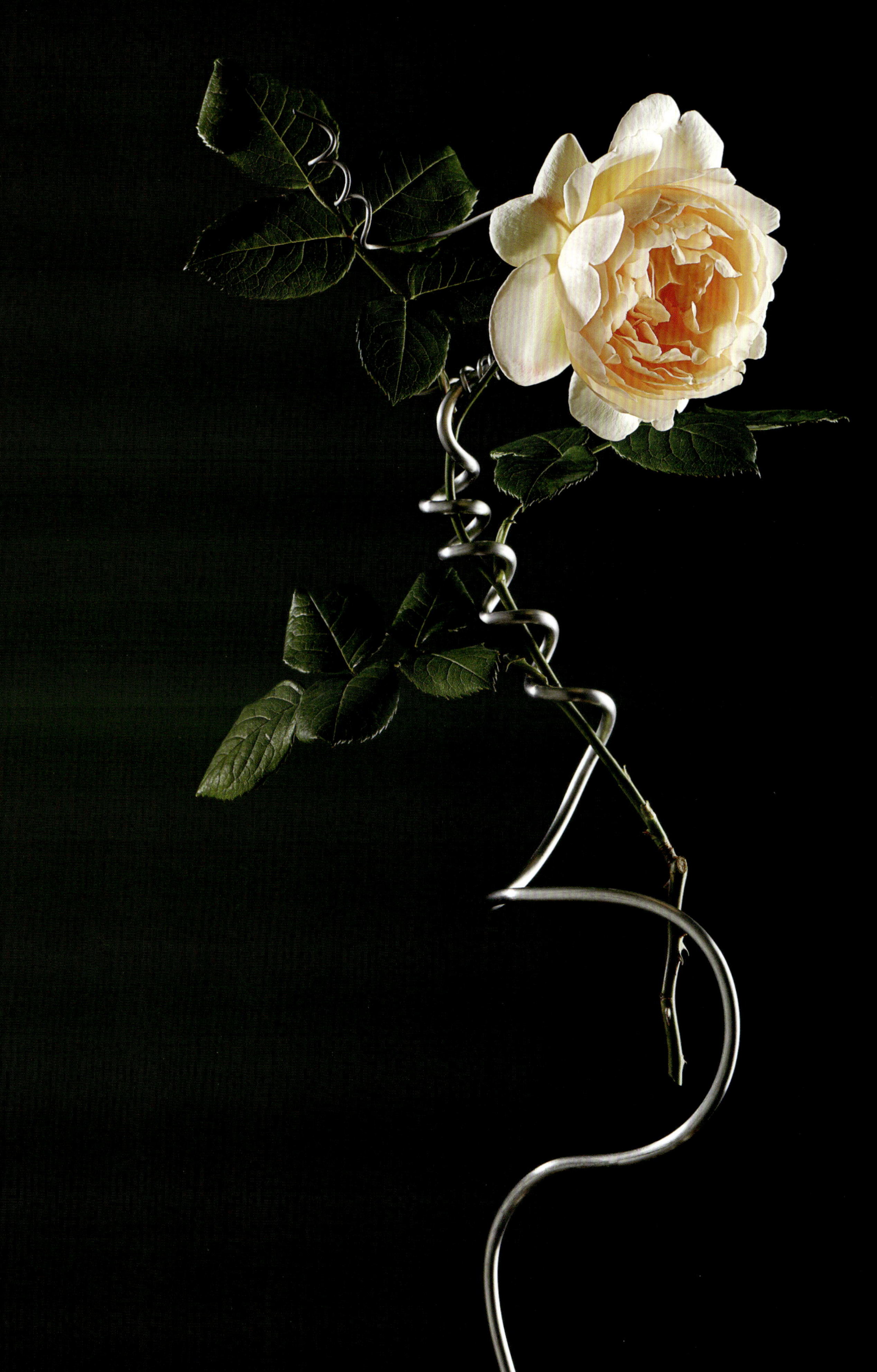

THE AMERICAS

Aperture
www.aperture.org
548 W. 28th St.
New York, NY 10001
United States
Tel +1 212 505 5555

Benrubi Gallery
www.benrubigallery.com
529 W. 20th St., Floor 8
New York, NY 10011
United States
Tel +1 212 888 6007

Center for Photographic Art (CFPA)
www.photography.org
San Carlos & 9th Ave.
Carmel-By-The-Sea, CA 93921
United States
Tel +1831 625 5181

Centro de la Imagen
www.ci.cultura.gob.mx
Plaza de la Ciudadela 2
06000 Cuauhtémoc, CDMX
Mexico
Tel +52 55 4155 0850

Colorado Photographic Arts Center
www.cpacphoto.org
1200 Lincoln St., Suite 11
Denver, CO 80203
United States
Tel +1 303 837 1341

Detroit Institute of Arts Museum
www.dia.org
5200 Woodward Ave.
Detroit, MI 48202
United States
Tel +1 313 833 7900

Foley Gallery
www.foleygallery.com
59 Orchard St.
New York, NY 10002
United States
Tel +1 212 244 9081

Fototeca Nacional del INAH
www.difusion.inah.gob.mx/sinafo/fototeca-nacional.html
Casasola s/n, Centro
42000 Pachuca de Soto, Hidalgo
Mexico
Tel +52 771 714 3653

Fraenkel Gallery
www.fraenkelgallery.com
49 Geary St., #450
San Francisco, CA 94108
United States
Tel +1 415 981 2661

George Eastman Museum
www.eastman.org
900 East Ave.
Rochester, NY 14607
United States
Tel +1 585 327 4800

Gitterman Gallery
www.gittermangallery.com
3 E. 66th St.
New York, NY 10065
United States
Tel +1 212 734 0868

International Center for Photography
www.icp.org
79 Essex St.
New York City, NY 10002
United States
Tel +1 212 857 0003

Intuit: The Center for Intuitive and Outsider Art
www.art.org
756 N. Milwaukee Ave.
Chicago, IL 60642
United States
Tel +1 312 624 9487

Jackson Fine Art
www.jacksonfineart.com
3122 E. Shadowlawn Ave. NE
Atlanta, GA 30305
United States
Tel +1 404 233 3739

Light Work
www.lightwork.org
316 Waverly Ave.
Syracuse, NY 13210
United States
Tel +1 315 443 1300

Museo Archivo de la Fotografía
www.cultura.cdmx.gob.mx/recintos/maf
Republica de Guatemala 34,
Centro Histórico
Alcaldía Cuauhtémoc, CP 06010
CDMX
Mexico
Tel +52 55 2616 7057

Museu da Fotografia
www.museudafotografia.com.br
R. Frederico Borges 545
Varjota, Fortaleza -CE, 60175-040
Brazil
Tel +55 85 3017 3661

Panopticon Gallery
www.panopticongallery.com
502c Commonwealth Ave.
Boston, MA 02215
United States
Tel +1 781 740 1300

Pier 24 Photography
www.pier24.org
24 Pier
San Francisco, CA 94105
United States
Tel +1 415 512 7424

São Paulo Museum of Image & Sound
www.mis-sp.org.br
Av. Europa 158
São Paulo, CEP 01449-000
Brazil
Tel +55 11 2117 4777

SepiaEye
www.sepiaeye.com
31 W. 103rd St. A
New York, NY 10025
United States
Tel +1 917 704 1757

Sous Les Etoiles Gallery
www.souslesetoilesgallery.net
16 E. 71st St.
New York, NY 10021
United States
Tel +1 646 329 6679

SPAO: Photographic Arts Centre
www.spao.ca/gallery
77 Pamilla St.
Ottawa, ON K1S 3K7
Canada
Tel +1 613 562 3824

Steven Kasher Gallery
www.stevenkasher.com
166 2nd Ave. 3A
New York, NY 10003
United States
Tel +1 917 922 6861

Studio391
www.studio391.net
3102 Ocean Drive
Gualala, CA 95445
United States
Tel +1 707 884 9065

The Huntington Library, Art Museum, & Botanical Gardens
www.huntington.org
1151 Oxford Road
San Marino, CA 91108
United States
Tel +1 626 405 2100

Themes+Projects
www.themesandprojects.com
1275 Minnesota St., Suite 205
San Francisco, CA 94107
United States
Tel +1 415 732 0300

The Morgan Library & Museum
www.themorgan.org
225 Madison Ave.
New York, NY 10016
United States
Tel +1 212 685 0008

The Museum of the City of New York
www.mcny.org/exhibitions/photography
1220 Fifth Ave.
New York City, NY 10029
United States
Tel +1 212 534 1672

Yancey Richardson
www.yanceyrichardson.com
525 W. 22nd St.
New York, NY 10011
United States
Tel +1 646 230 9610

Yossi Milo Gallery
www.yossimilo.com
245 10th Ave.
New York, NY 10001
United States
Tel +1 212 414 0370

EUROPE AND AFRICA

Belfast Exposed Photography
www.belfastexposed.org
23 Donegall St.
Belfast BT1 2FF
United Kingdom
Tel +44 28 9023 0965

Ben Uri Gallery and Museum
www.benuri.org
St John's Wood
London NW8 0RH
England
Tel +44 20 7604 3991

Bensusan Museum of Photography and Library
www.sahistory.org.za/place/bensusan-museum-photography-and-library-johannesburg
121 Lilian Ngoyi St
Newtown, Johannesburg 2033
South Africa
Tel +27 11 833 5624

Berlinische Galerie
www.berlinischegalerie.de
Alte Jacobstrabe 124-128
10969 Berlin
Germany
Tel +49 30 789 02 600

Centro Portugues de Fotografia
www.cpf.pt
Largo Amor de Perdição
4050-008 Porto
Portugal
Tel +351 220 046 300

Elipsis Gallery
www.elipsisgallery.com
Hoca Tahsin Sokak No. 16
Karaköy 34425
Turkey
Tel +90 212 249 48 92

Fabian und Claude Walter Galerie
www.fabian-claude-walter.com
Rämistrasse 18
8001 Zürich
Switzerland
Tel +41 44 440 40 18

Finnish Museum of Photography
www.valokuvataiteenmuseo.fi
Kaapeliaukio 3
00180 Helsinki
Finland
Tel +358 9 6866 360

Fotografiemuseum Amsterdam (FOAM)
www.foam.org
Keizersgracht 609
1017 DS Amsterdam
Netherlands
Tel +31 20 551 6500

Fotografiska
www.fotografiska.com/sto/besok/
Stadsgårdshamnen 22
Stockholm, Sweden
Sweden
Tel +46 8 509 005 00

Fotomuseum Winterthur
www.fotomuseum.ch
Grüzenstrasse 44-45
8400 Winterhur
Switzerland
Tel +41 52 234 10 60

Galerie F5,6
www.f56.net
Ludwigstraße 7
80539 München
Germany
Tel +49 89 28675167

Galerie Julian Sander
www.galeriejuliansander.de
Bonner Str. 82
50677 Köln
Germany
Tel +49 221 1705070

Galerie Magnum Photos
www.magnumphotos.com
68 Rue Leon Frot
75011 Paris
France
Tel +33 1 53 42 50 00

Galerija Fotografija
www.galerijafotografija.si
Levstikov Trg 7
1000 Ljubljana
Slovenia
Tel +386 1 251 15 29

Hamiltons Gallery
www.hamiltonsgallery.com
13 Carlos Place
London W1K 2EU
United Kingdom
Tel +44 20 7499 9493

House of Photography of Marrakech
www.maisondelaphotographie.ma
Rue Ahl Fes, 46 Rue Bin Lafnadek
Marrakech 40030
Morocco
Tel +212 5 243 85721

LA Noble Gallery
www.laurannoble.com
133 Attlee Terrace, Prospect Hill
London E17 3EH
United Kingdom
Tel +44 7999 099975

Le Grand Palais
www.grandpalais.fr/en/contacts-rmn-grand-palais
3 Av. du General Eisenhower
75008 Paris
France
Tel +33 1 44 13 17 17

Le Lavoir Numérique
www.lavoirnumerique.grandorlyseinebievre.fr
4 Rue de Freiberg
94 250 Gentilly
France
Tel +33 1 49 08 91 63

Les Douches la Galerie
www.lesdoucheslagalerie.com
5 Rue Legouve
75010 Paris
France
Tel +33 1 78 94 03 00

Maison Européenne de la Photographie (MEP)
www.mep-fr.org
5/7 Rue de Fourcy
75004 Paris
France
Tel +33 0 1 44 78 75 00

MultiMedia Art Museum
www.mamm-mdf.ru
St. Ostozhenka 16
Moscow, Russia 119034
Russia
Tel +7 495 637 11 00

Musée de la Photographie
www.museephoto.be
Av. Paul Pastur 11
6032 Charleroi
Belgium
Tel +32 71 43 58 10

Museo Nacional Centro de Arte de Reina Sofía
www.museoreinasofia.es/en
C. de Sta. Isabel, 52
28012 Madrid
Spain
Tel +34 917 74 10 00

Museum Folkwang
www.museum-folkwang.de
Museumsplatz 1
45128 Essen
Germany
Tel +49 201 8845000

Museum Für Fotografie
www.smb.museum
Genthiner Str. 38
10785 Berlin
Germany
Tel +49 30 266 42 42 42

Museum of Contemporary Photography
www.mufoco.org
Villa Ghirlanda, Via Giovanni Frova 10
20092 Cinisello Balsamo, Milan
Italy
Tel +39 02 660 5661

Museum of the History of Photography Walery Rzewuski in Krakow
www.mufo.krakow.pl
St. Rakowicka 22A
31-510 Krakow
Poland
Tel +48 12 395 70 42

National Museum of Asian Arts Guimet
www.guimet.fr
6 Pl. d'Iéna
75116 Paris
France
Tel +33 1 56 52 54 33

Open Eye Gallery
www.openeye.org.uk
19 Mann Island
Liverpool L3 1BP
United Kingdom
Tel +44 151 236 6768

OstLicht. Gallery for Photography
www.ostlicht.org
BROTFABRIK, Staircase 3
Absberggasse 27, 1100 Vienna
Austria
Tel +43 1 996 20 66

Palazzo Martinengo Colleoni—Center of Italian Photography
www.macof.it
Via Moretto 78
25121 Brescia
Italy
Tel +39 366 3804795

Photology
www.photology.com
Via Berengario da Carpi 33
40141 Bologna BO
Italy
Tel +39 051 444425

PhotoSynthesis
www.magazin.photosynthesis.bg
Vasil Levski Blvd. 57
1000 Sofia Center
Bulgaria
Tel +359 88 802 4999

Prague House of Photography
www.ghmp.cz/en/buildings/house-of-photography
Revolucni 1006/5
110 00 Prague 1, Staré Město
Czech Republic
Tel +42 0 702 283 922

Priska Pasquer
www.priskapasquer.art
Konrad-Adenauer-Ufer 83
50668 Köln
Germany
Tel +49 170 4230636

Russian Museum of Photography
www.fotomuseum.nnov.ru
9a Piskunova Str.
Nizhny Novgorod
Russia
Tel +7 831 437 37 43

Sala Canal de Isabel II
https://www.comunidad.madrid/centros/sala-canal-isabel-ii
Calle de Sta Engracia 125
28003 Madrid
Spain
Tel +34 91 545 10 00

Stredoeurópsky dom Fotografie (SEDF)
www.sedf.sk
Prepoštská 4
811 01 Staré Mesto
Slovakia
Tel +42 1 2544 182 14

Tate Modern
www.tate.org.uk/visit/tate-modern
Bankside
London SE1 9TG
United Kingdom
Tel +44 20 7887 8888

The Museum of the History of Photography
www.mif-spb.ru
Ulitsa Professora Popova 23
197376 St. Petersburg
Russia
Tel +7 812 346 18 50

Thessaloniki Museum of Photography
www.momus.gr
21ist Kolokotroni St,
Moni Lazariston
56430, Stavroupoli
Greece
Tel +30 231 056 6716

The Walther Collection
www.walthercollection.com
Reichenauerstr. 21
89233 Neu-Ulm
Germany
Tel +49 731 1769143

TORCH Gallery
www.torchgallery.com
Lauriergracht 94
1016 RN Amsterdam
Netherlands
Tel +31 20 626 0284

ASIA AND OCEANIA

Asia Camera Museum
www.asiacameramuseum.com
71 Armenian St.
10200 Georgetown, Penang
Malaysia
Tel +60 11 1859 9878

Blender Gallery
www.blendergallery.com
Shop 2, 682 Bourke St., Redfern
Sydney NSW 2016
Australia
Tel +61 04 1232 3727

Erawan Museum
www.erawanmuseum.com
99/9 Moo 1, Bang Mueang Mai
Subdistrict Mueang Samut Prakan District
Samut Prakan Province 10270
Thailand
Tel +66 02 371 3135 6

Fujifilm History Museum
www.fujifilmsquare.jp
9-chōme-7 Akasaka
Minato City, Tokyo 107-0052
Japan
Tel +81 3 6271 3350

Ginza Graphic Gallery
www.dnpfcp.jp
7-chōme-7 Chuo City, Ginza
104-0061 Tokyo
Japan
Tel +81 3 3571 5206

Hiroshi Senju Museum Karuizawa
www.senju-museum.jp
815 Nagakura, Kitasaku District
Nagano 389-0111
Japan
Tel +81 267 46 6565

JCII Camera Museum
www.jcii-cameramuseum.jp
JCII Ichibancho Bldg. 25
Chiyoda 102-0082
Japan
Tel +81 3 3263 7110

Mori Art Museum
www.mori.art.museum
6-10-1 Roppongi
Minato City, 106-6150 Tokyo
Japan
Tel +81 50 5541 8600

Museum of Australian Photography
www.maph.org.au
860 Ferntree Gully Rd.
Wellers Hill VIC 3150
Australia
Tel +61 3 8544 0500

Red Dot Design Museum
www.museum.red-dot.sg
11 Marina Blvd.
Singapore 018940
Singapore
Tel +65 6514 0111

Taka Ishii Gallery
www.takaishiigallery.com
123 Yadacho, Shimogyo Ward
Kyoto 600-8442
Japan
Tel +81 75 366 5101

The Kiyasota Museum of Photographic Arts
www.kmopa.com
3545-1222 Takanecho Kiyosato
Hokuto, Yamanashi 407-0301
Japan
Tel +81 551 48 5599

The Museum of Photography
www.photomuseum.or.kr
Hanmi Tower, 45 Bangi Dong
Songpa-Gu Seoul 138-724
South Korea
Tel +82 2 418 1315

Tokyo Photographic Art Museum
www.topmuseum.jp
1-13-3 Mita
Meguro-ku, Tokyo 153-0062
Japan
Tel +81 3 3280 0099

Additional Museums:
If you are a museum that collects photographs and are not listed above, please contact us for inclusion in our next annual at help@graphis.com.

A Decade in Photography: 11 Platinum Winners from 2014

Title: Behave | **Client:** Self-initiated

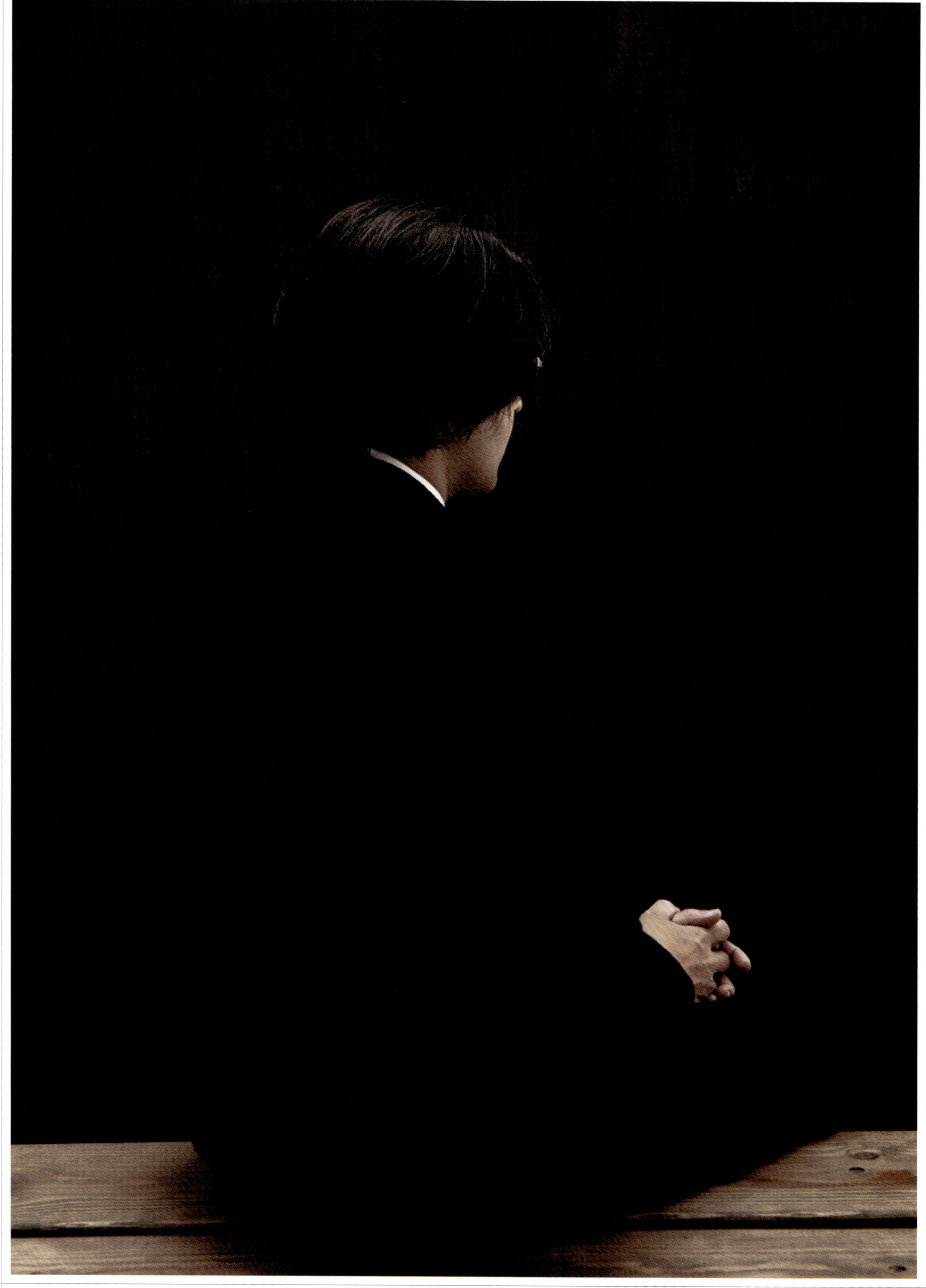

Title: Away | **Client:** Self-initiated

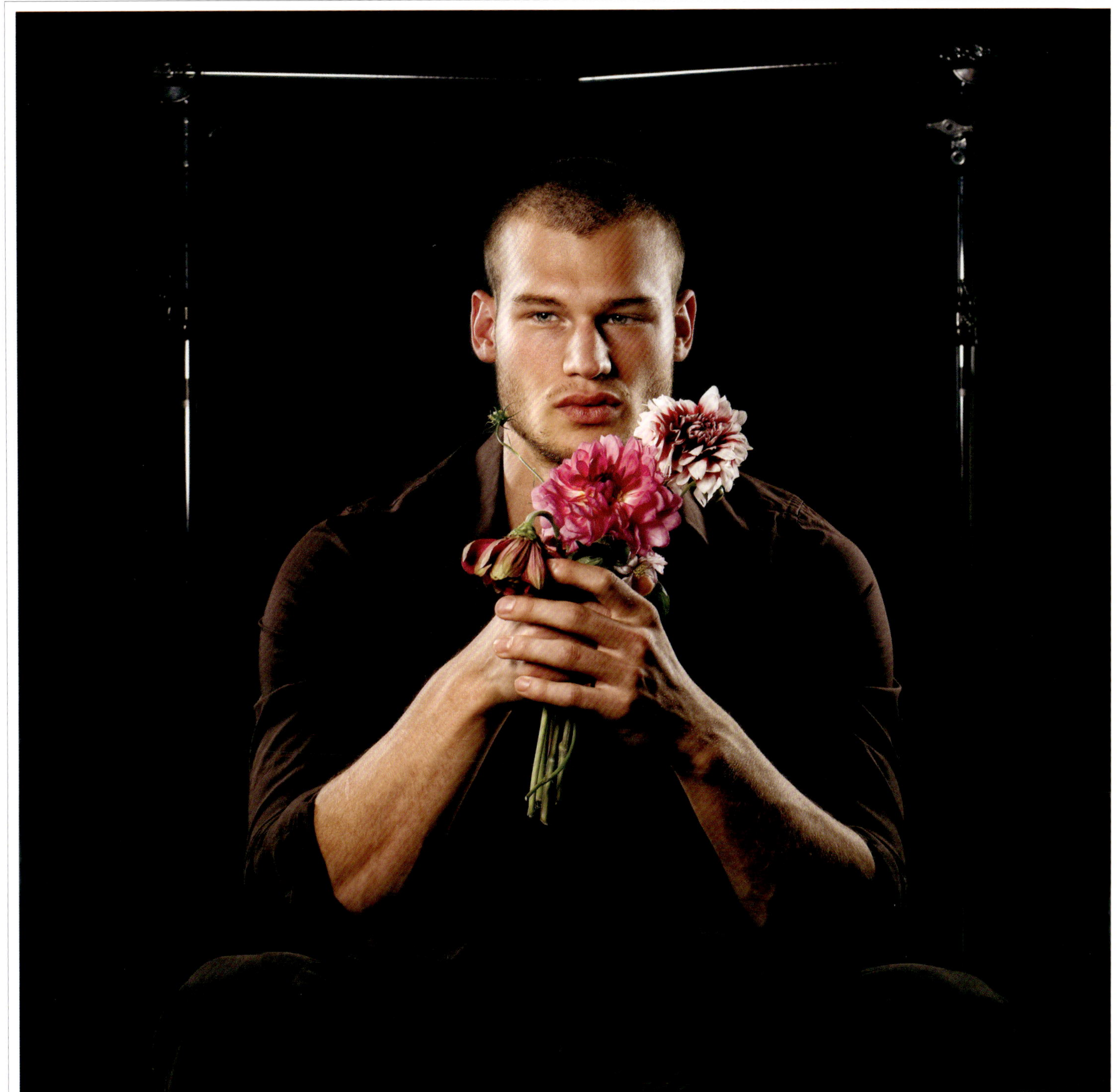

Title: Joel | **Client:** Self-initiated

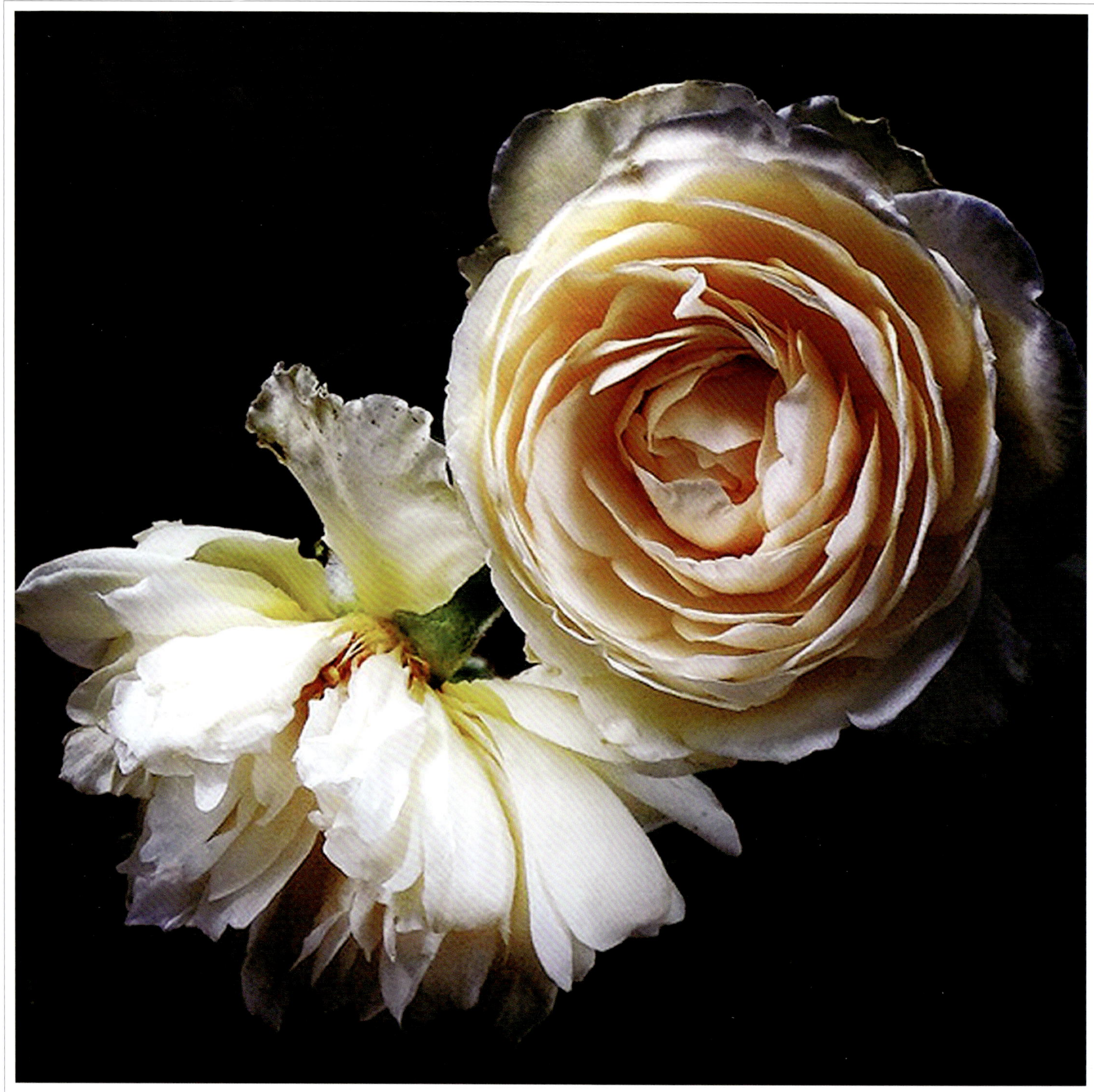

Title: Rose Ballerina | **Client:** Self-initiated

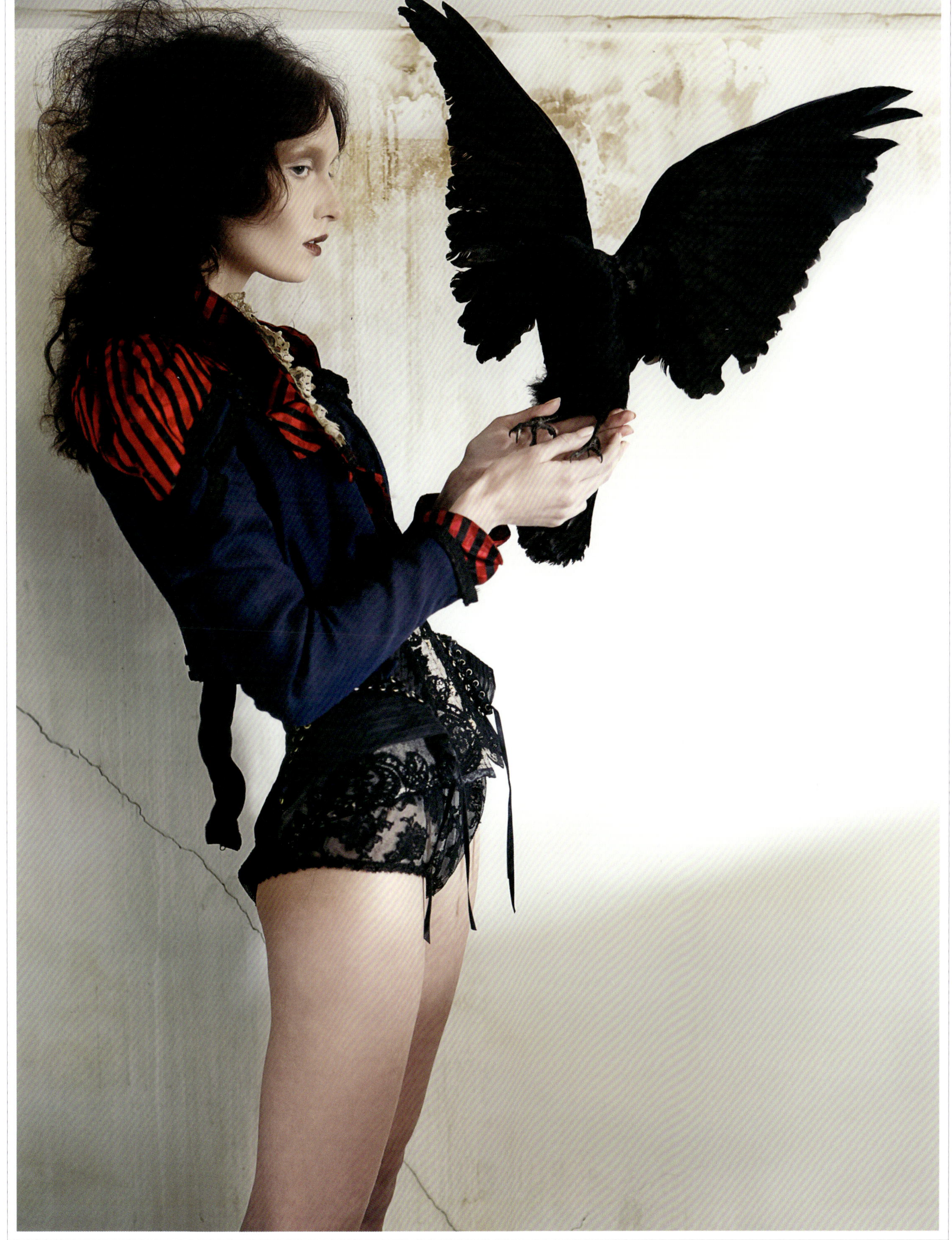

Title: The Whaling Widow | **Client:** Four Magazine

 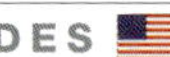

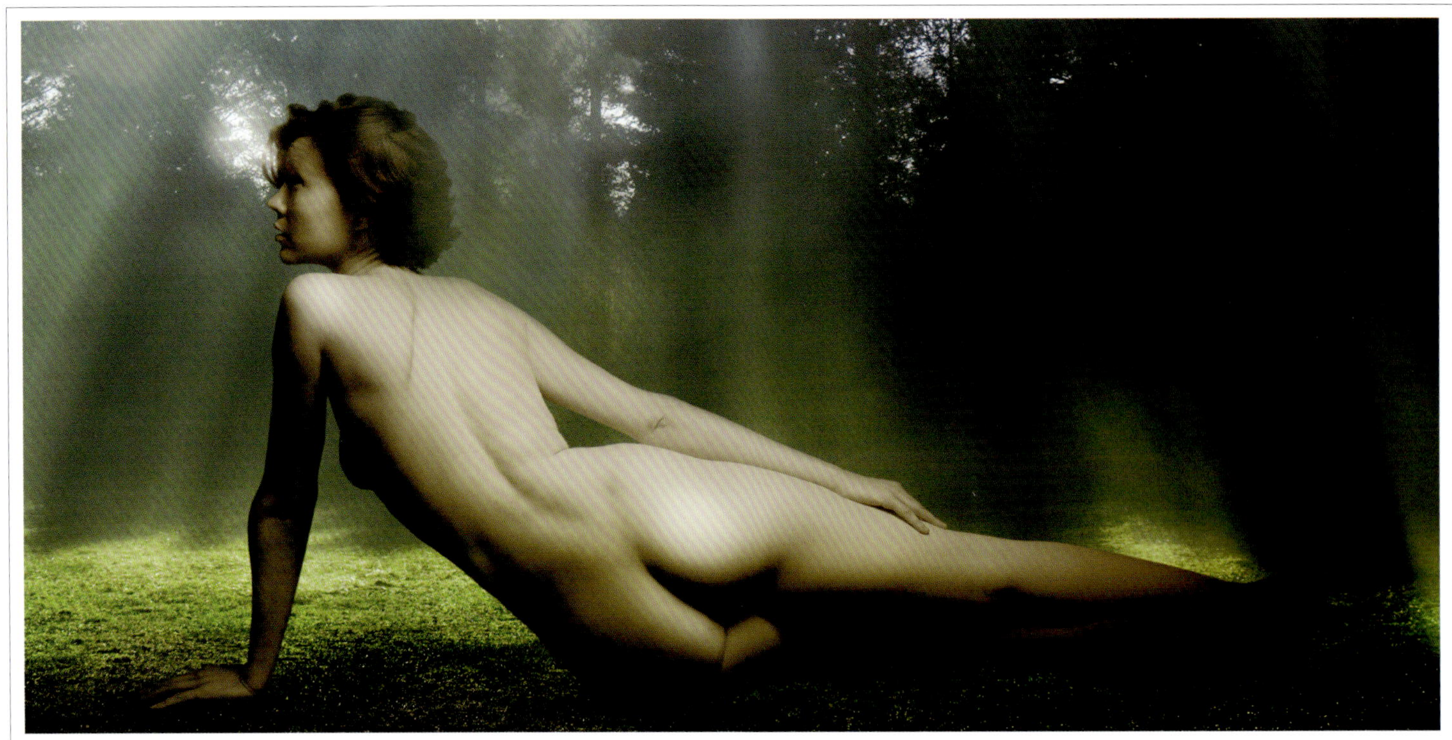

Title: Horse | **Client:** Self-initiated

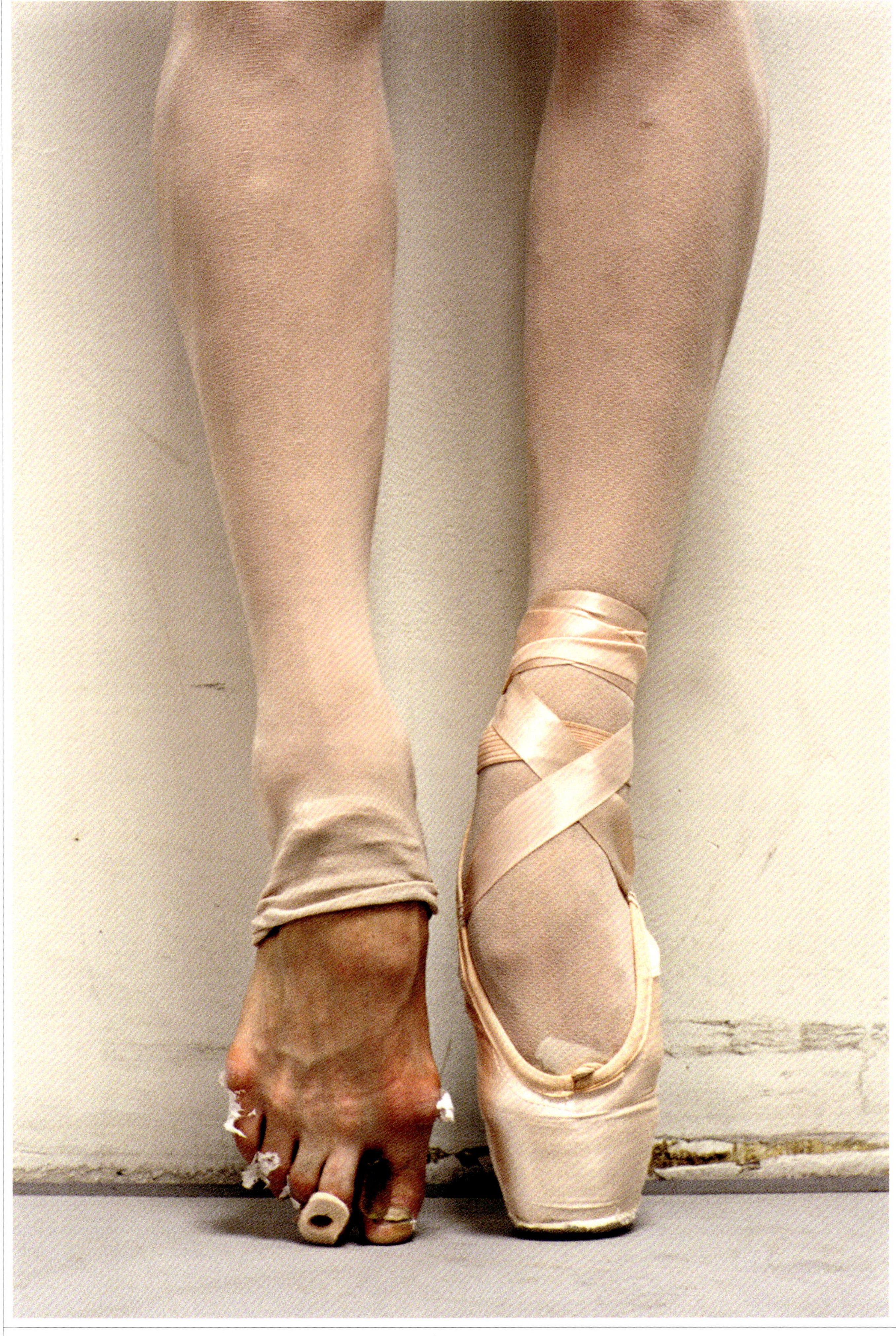

Title: Megan LeCrone | **Client:** New York City Ballet

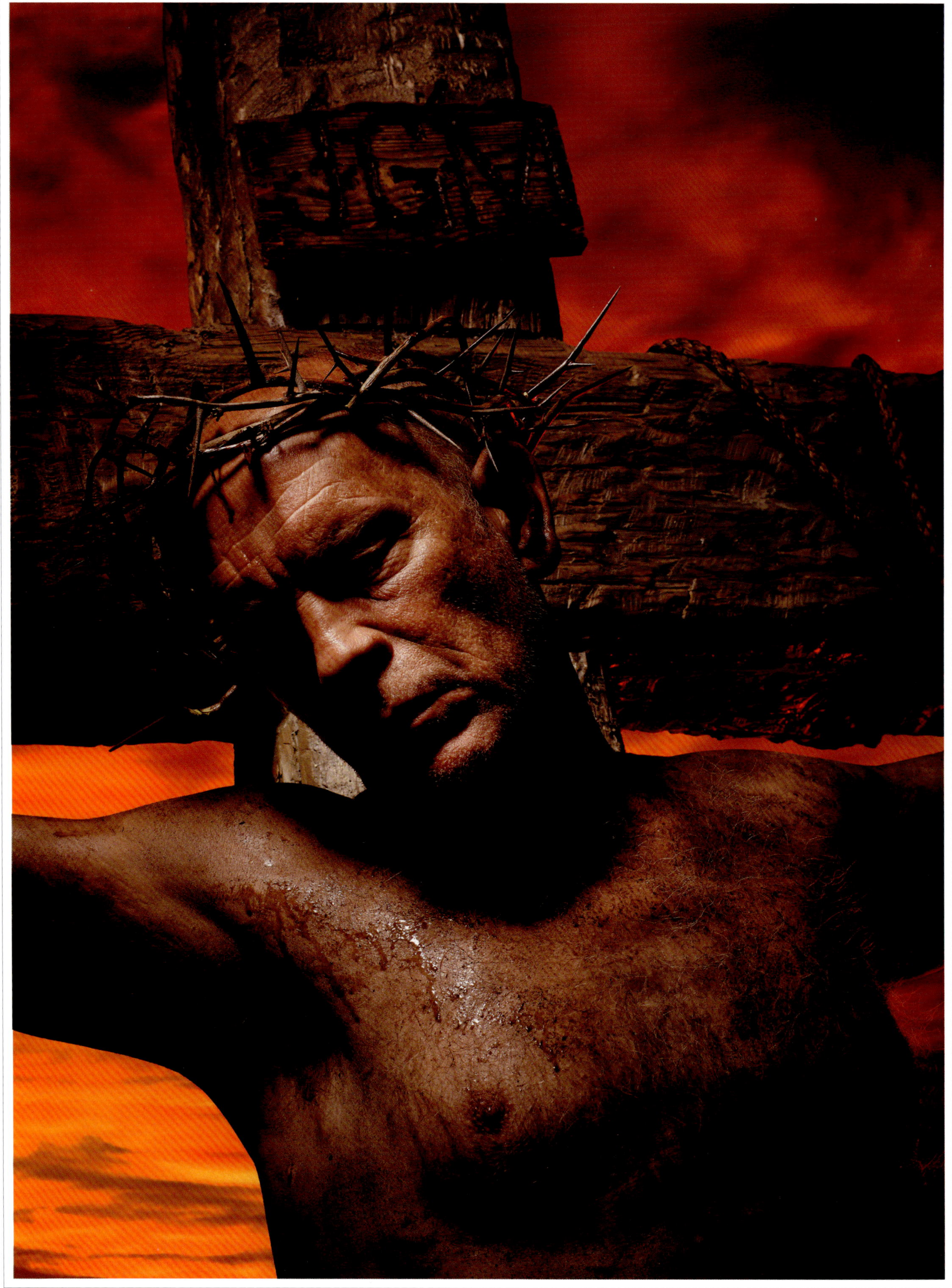

Title: Malkovich Sessions | **Client:** Self-initiated

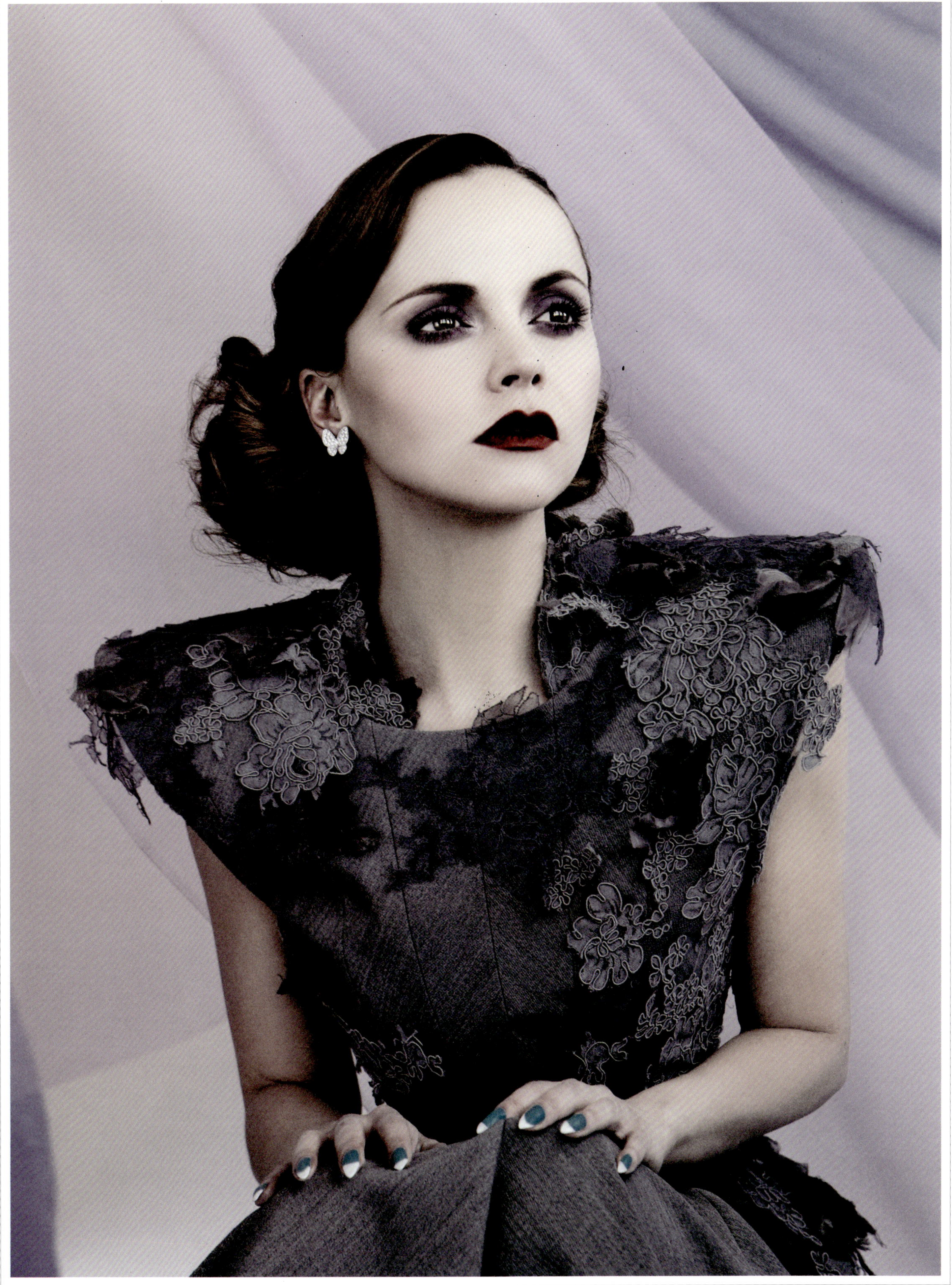

Title: Christina Ricci | **Client:** AS IF Magazine

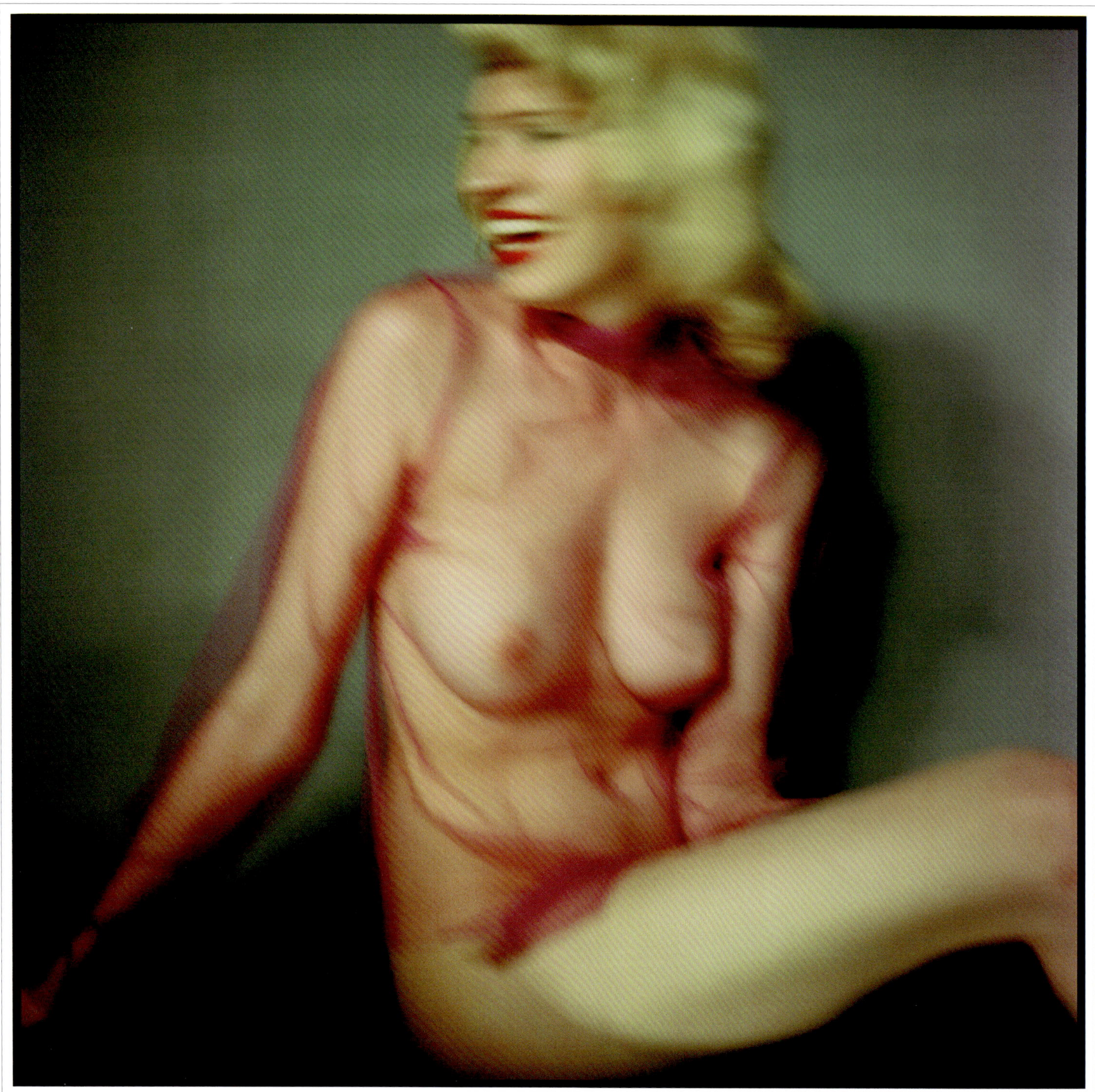

Title: Pinhole Nudes | **Client:** Camera Works

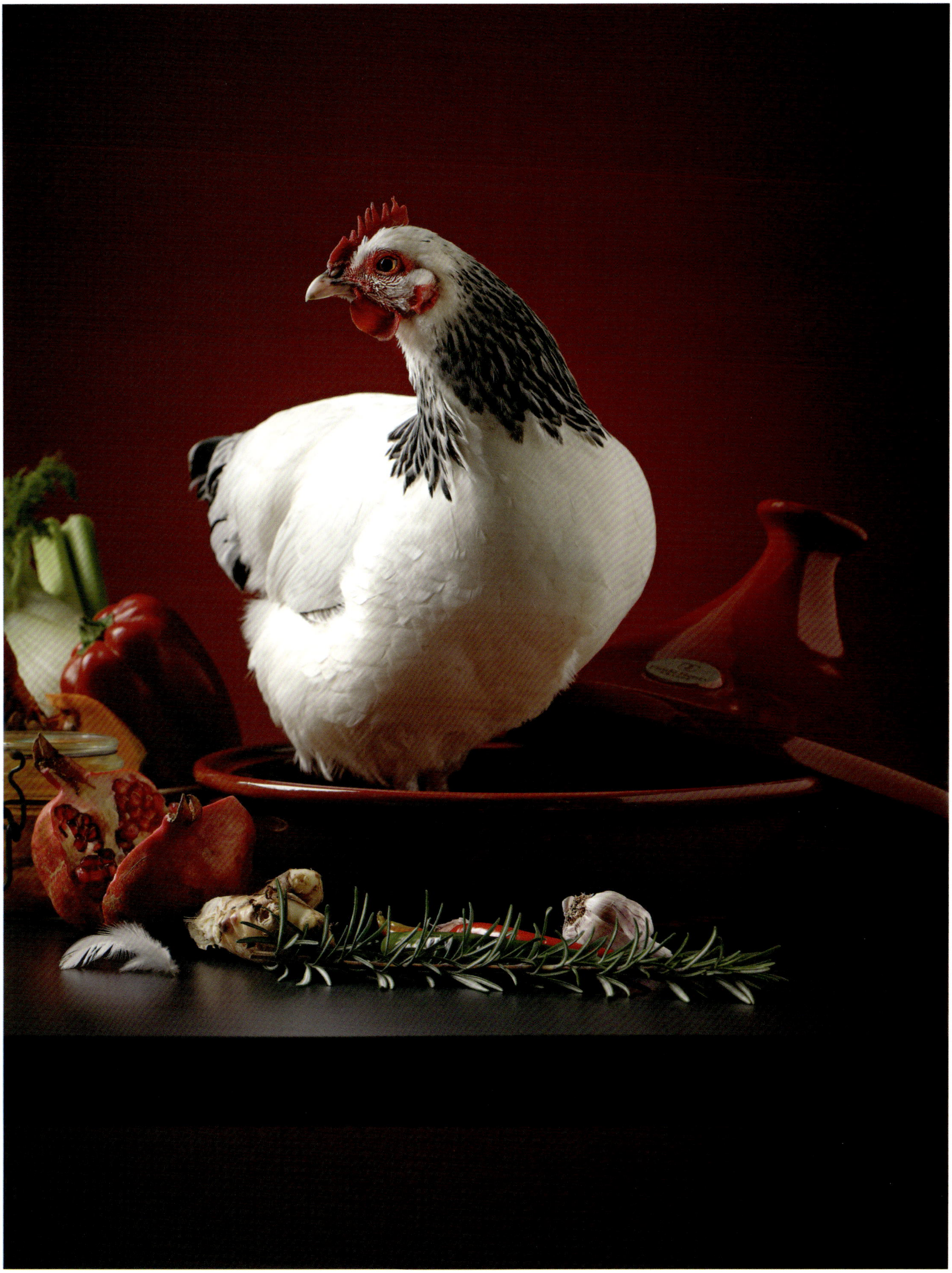

Title: Chicken Tagine | Client: Norman & Dann

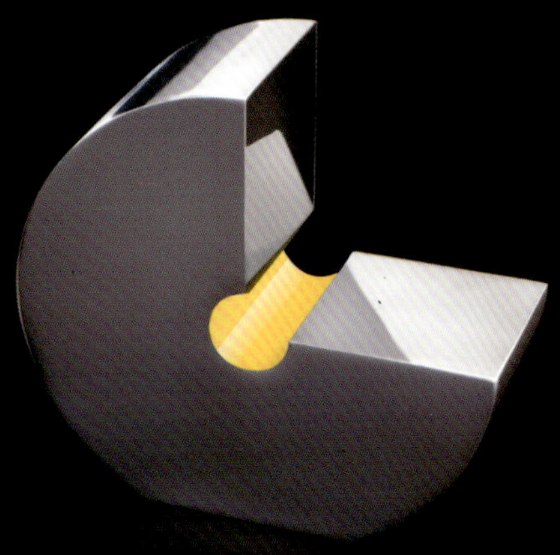

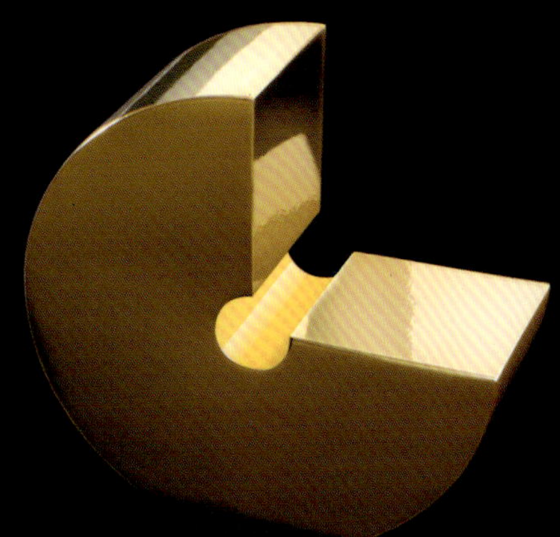

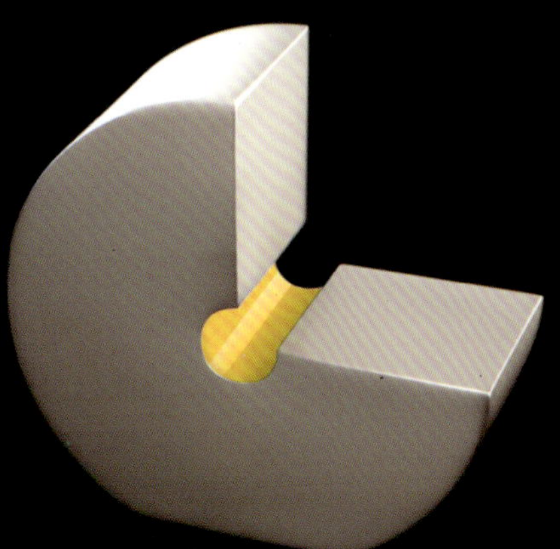

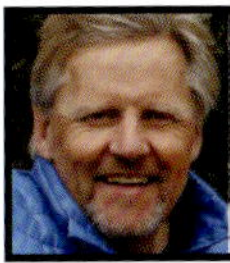

Per Breiehagen | www.breiehagen.com

Biography: Per Breiehagen grew up in a small town in the mountains of southern Norway before settling in the US. His love for the outdoors and location photography has led to advertising and editorial assignments around the world, including the North Pole, Antarctica, and plenty of warmer places in between. He has been fortunate to work with many great people on amazing assignments for clients that include *National Geographic*, *Outside*, *The New York Times Magazine*, Disney, Sony, Samsung, AT&T, Patagonia, The North Face, Asics, and Gore-Tex, to name a few. An early highlight of Per's career was joining and shooting the Trans-Antarctica Expedition: a 3,741-mile-long epic dogsled expedition across Antarctica led by explorer Will Steger. Primary sponsors for this groundbreaking expedition were *National Geographic*, ABC Television, and The North Face. As an avid skier, paddleboarder, and mountain biker, Per brings an understanding of motion, realism, and a creative fine arts feel to his work. Per has won numerous international awards for his work from organizations such as Graphis, Communication Arts, and the International Photography Awards. He currently lives in Minneapolis.

Commentary: It's been a great honor and a real treat to go through this year's Graphis Photography Awards entries. The level of creative talent and awesome photography clearly shows that this is a collection of some of the best in the industry. It is inspiring to see such fresh and unique images from truly talented artists. We are in an age of great changes and turmoil in our field, so to see true craft and creativity on full display is very encouraging. Keep the passion alive, and thank you for letting me be part of the judging process for this year's Photography Awards!

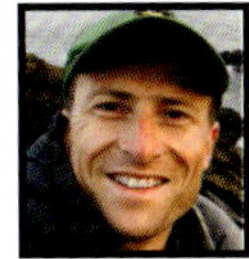

Nick Hall | www.nickhallphotography.com

Biography: Nick Hall is a photographer and director from England, now living on an island near Seattle. He is renowned for his human-nature documentary projects and cinematic global advertising campaigns. Originally a wildlife scientist and biodiversity conservationist, Nick blends his passion for the natural world with the specific needs of global brands and advertising clients, including American Airlines, Barclays Bank, BMW, Four Seasons, Intel, Nespresso, and Uber. Known throughout the industry as a gentle and immersive photographer, Nick brings an inclusive and thoughtful energy to all his projects, allowing him to capture deeply emotional and arresting imagery celebrating our connections to one another and the world around us.

Commentary: The range of themes and styles in the photography I reviewed was inspiring and refreshing. It's exciting to know that there are so many artists out there pushing themselves, their talent, and their craft to create compelling and meaningful work. In a world where we now digest thousands of images daily, it's reassuring to know that top talent is still able to rise to the surface and be visually arresting.

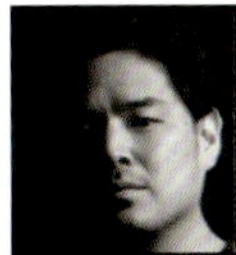

Takahiro Igarashi | www.igarashiphoto.com

Biography: Takahiro Igarashi is a still life photographer based in New York City and Tokyo. He believes in the power of simplicity: to communicate an idea in a moment. Emphasizing the essence of an object while expressing its character through a minimalistic yet dynamic style has led him to work with some of the most respected agencies and brands. He finds his inspiration through timelessness, heritage, and craftsmanship.

Commentary: It was a pleasure to see everyone's viewpoints. Photography has become a tool that's widely available for everyone, especially with the recent advances in technology. Even with the advancements, projecting the message through creativity and technicality to show the vision is the key to a powerful photograph. Oftentimes, one is stronger than the other, and to me, it was very evident who has mastered both and who is still working towards it.

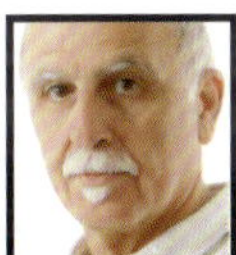

RJ Muna | www.rjmuna.com

Biography: From his studio in San Francisco and various locations around the world, RJ Muna has produced acclaimed photographic images. He has won over 150 national and international awards, including the International Center of Photography's Infinity Award, the Clio Award, and the Lucie Award. His work has appeared in numerous photography competitions, including the Graphis Photography Awards, American Photography, Lürzer's Archive 200 Best Ad Photographers, Communication Arts Photography Awards, and PDN Photo Annual. RJ's images have been featured in several industry publications such as Graphis, *Black & White Magazine*, *Camera Arts Magazine*, Communication Arts, Lürzer's Archive, and many other international publications.

Commentary: I was very impressed with not only the overall quality of the work, but the diversity of styles and concepts. It's really fulfilling to see so many images that make you think, as well as a good number that make you feel. And then there are those that rise above their intended purpose and do both.

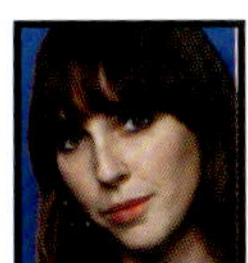

Hadley Stambaugh | www.scad.edu

Biography: Hadley Stambaugh combines her fascination with the human spirit and the natural world to create a unique sense of movement and light in her photography. Her work has a wide range of subject matter, from portraits of A-list actors and fashion icons to still life, everyday students, and their creations. After graduating from Savannah College of Art and Design, she split her time between her hometown of Pittsburgh, PA, New York City, and Savannah, GA. The time spent between city and rural landscapes has allowed her to cultivate a unique aesthetic mixing the urban fashion influences of New York City and the calming beauty of the low country and her current home, Savannah. Currently, she is the creative director of photography for her alma mater, but will forever have the eye and heart of a photographer.

Commentary: Having had the privilege of showcasing my work in past editions of the Graphis Photography Competition, I am continually inspired by the high caliber of talent that the competition attracts. The judging criteria, which seem to reflect a keen understanding of the nuances of visual storytelling and artistic expression, have not only provided a fair evaluation of my submissions but have also contributed to the overall growth of the photographic community. The transparency and professionalism displayed during the judging process are commendable. Such attention to detail fosters an environment where photographers are motivated to challenge themselves, experiment with new concepts, and evolve their craft. Reflecting on my past experiences with showcasing work in the Graphis Photography Competition, I am grateful for the exposure and recognition it has afforded me. The platform has been instrumental in connecting me with a broader audience and fellow creatives, as well as fostering a sense of community that is invaluable in the world of visual arts. The commitment of the Graphis team to celebrate and elevate the art of photography does not go unnoticed, and I am excited to be a part of this creative journey. The feedback received from previous exhibitions has been instrumental in shaping my approach to photography, encouraging me to refine my skills and explore new horizons within the medium.

For judges who were also entrants and winners, special care was taken to insure that they did not judge their own work.

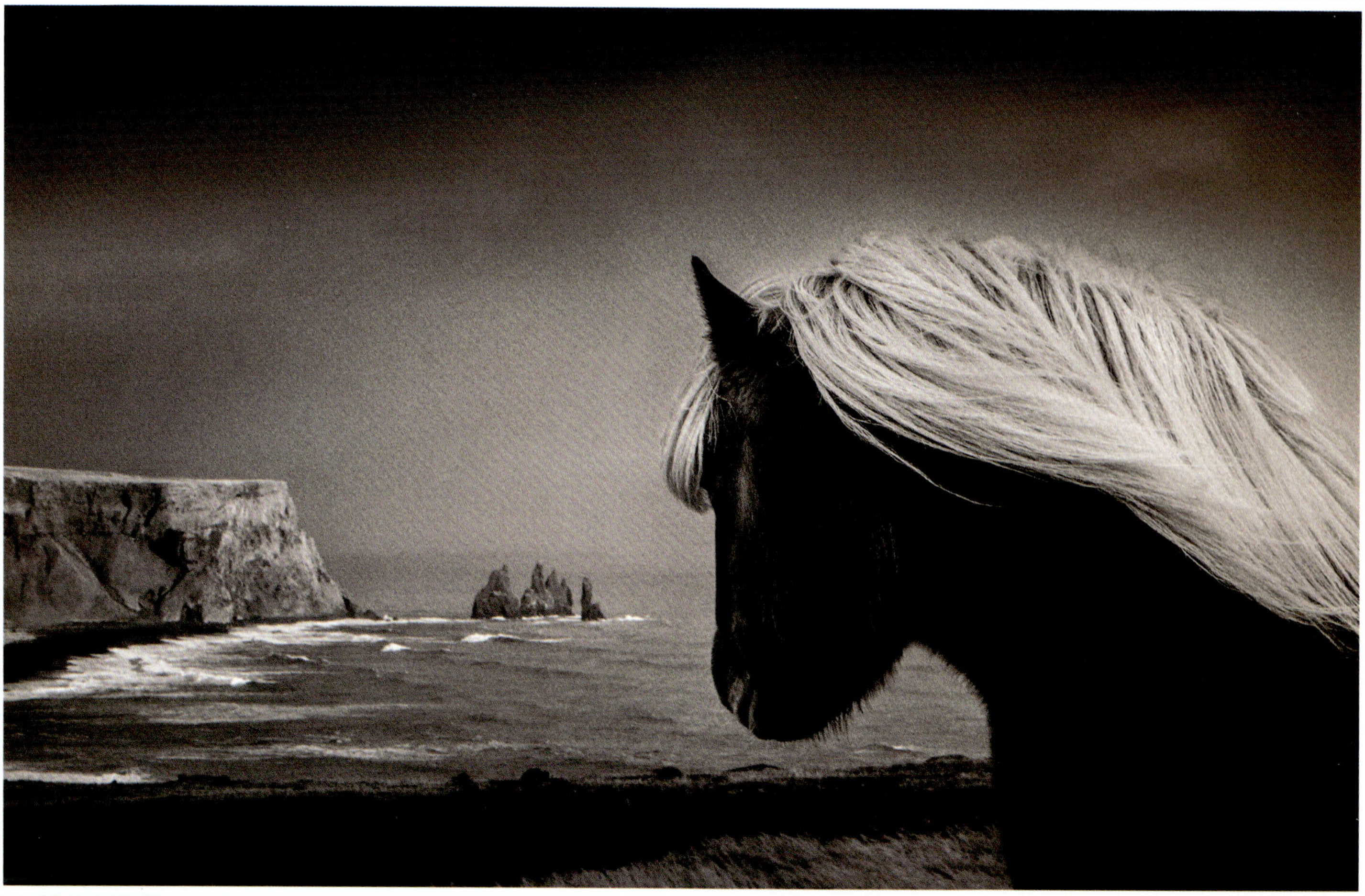

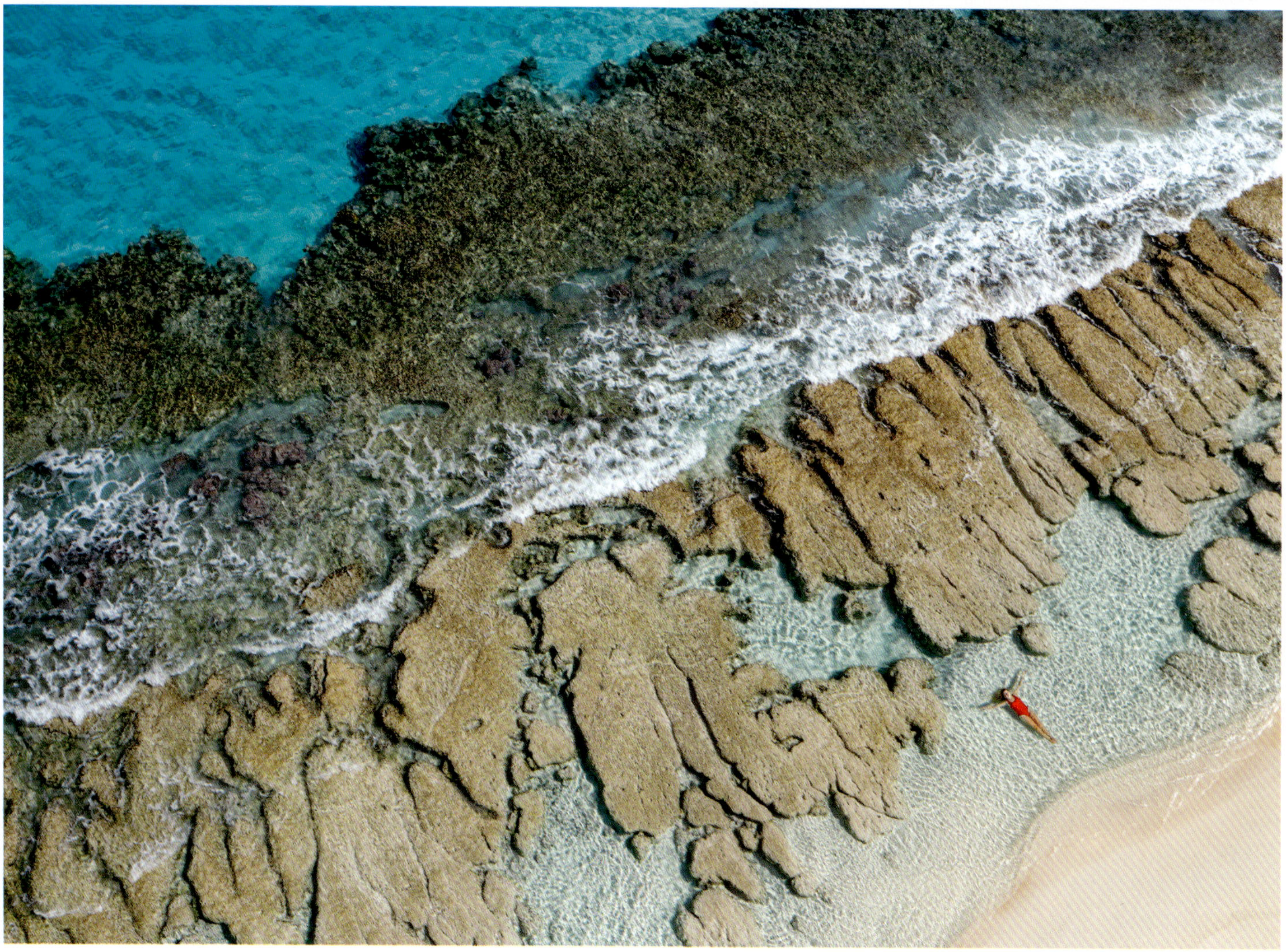

Titles: A Viking Horse Looking Towards Reynisdrangar (The Three Petrified Trolls) in Vik, Iceland, Floating with Stromatolites in Exuma | **Clients:** Self-initiated

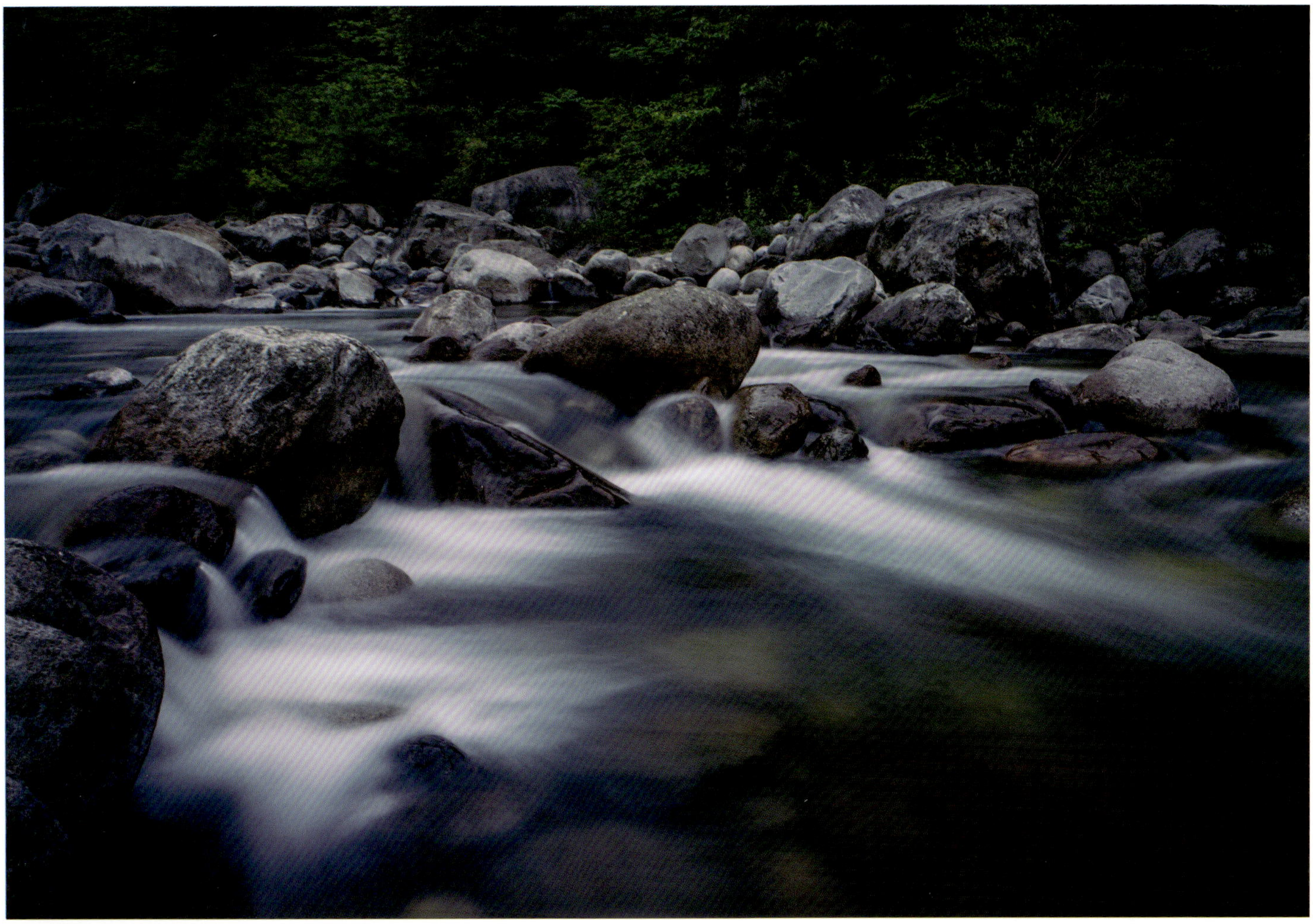

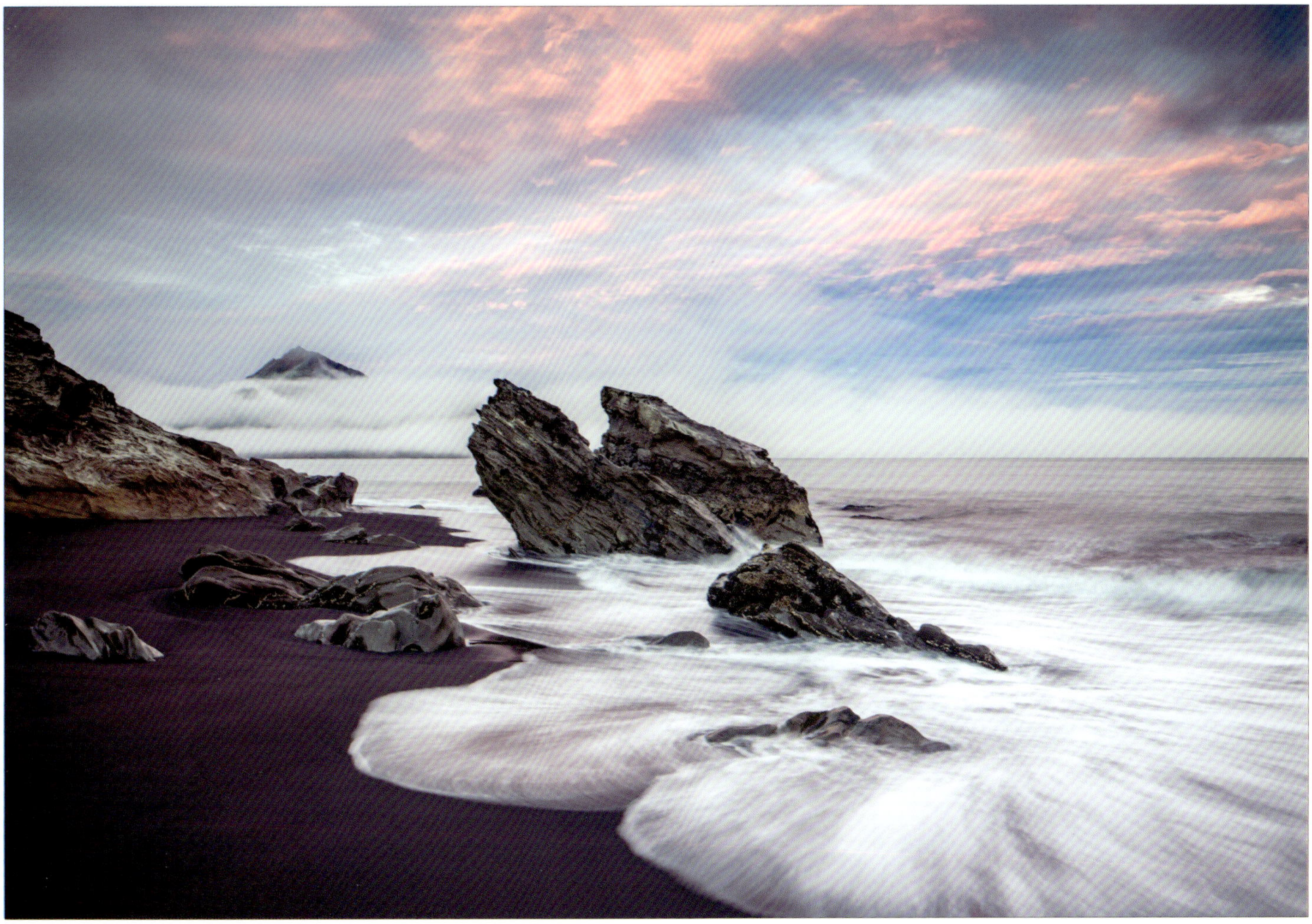

Titles: Searching for Panda, Perryville, AK | **Clients:** The Nature Conservancy Magazine, Bristol Bay Native Corporation

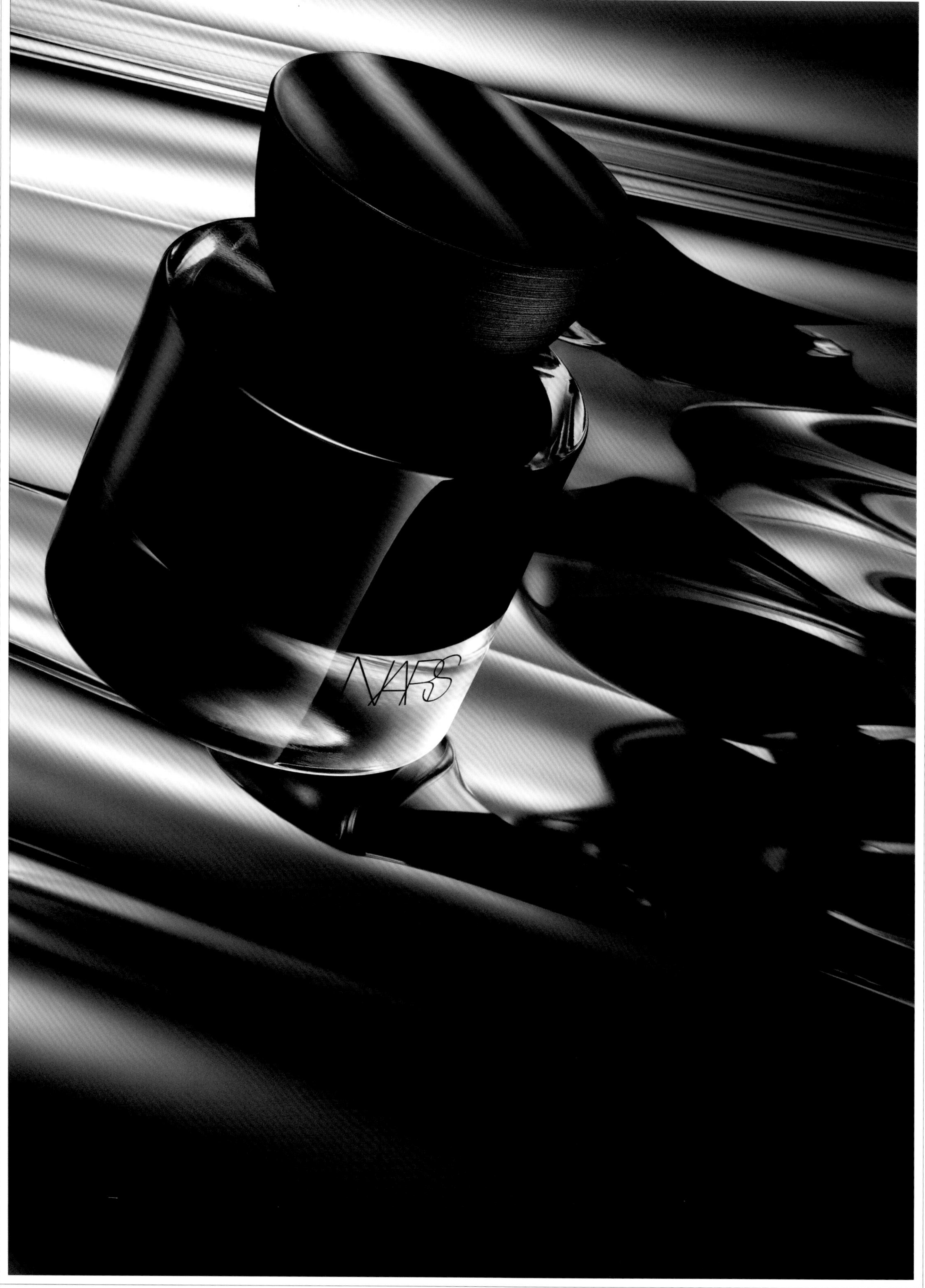

Title: Essence of Audacity | **Client:** Nars

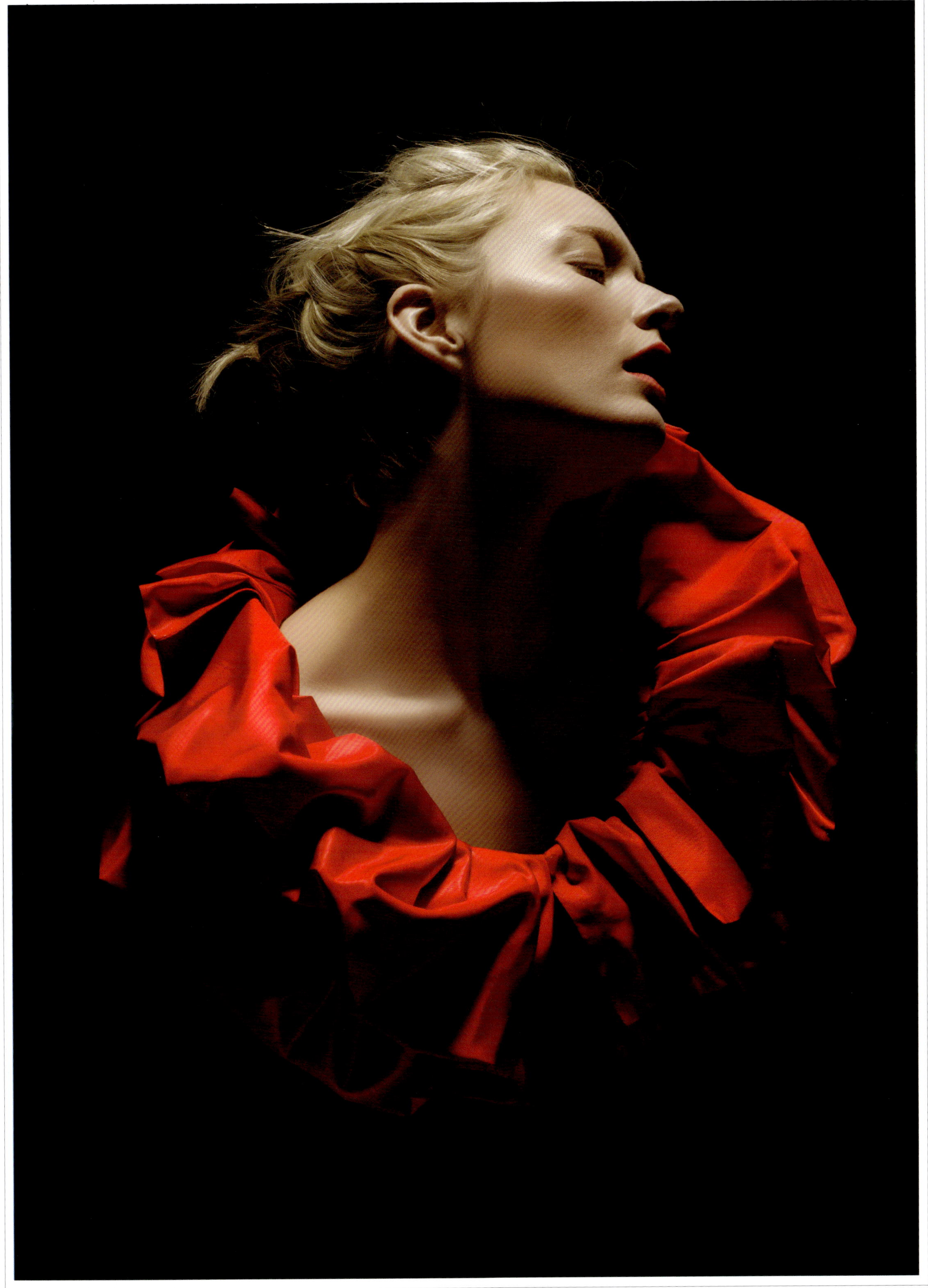

Title: Heather | **Client:** Self-initiated

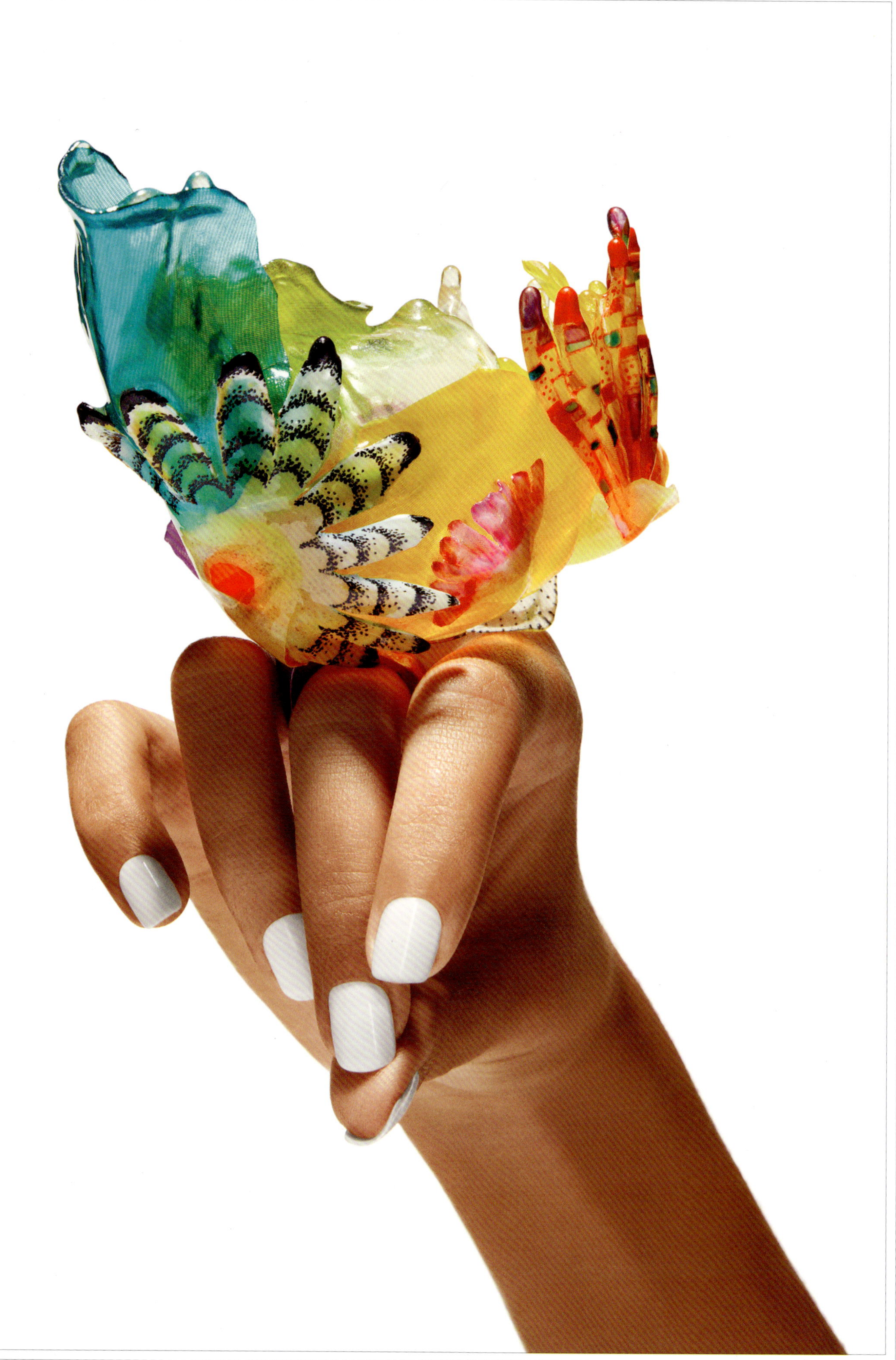

Title: Ring Redux | **Client:** SCAD

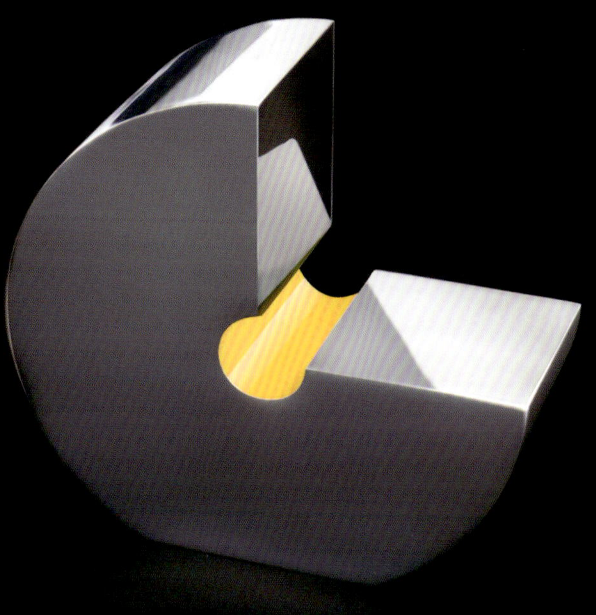

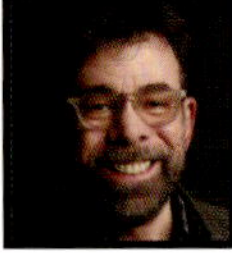

Peter Samuels | Pages: 32, 33 | www.petersamuels.com

Biography: Before moving to San Francisco in 1999, Peter was classically trained as a product and still life photographer at Orange Coast College in Costa Mesa, CA. His clients included notable clients such as AT&T, Toyota, Nissan, and Visa, among others. Then, in 2009, a change occurred when he got his first dog, a doxie/min pin mix named Leica, who soon became his muse, and a new passion emerged as he began to focus on photographing animals. Oddly enough, his technical experience in lighting products became the foundation of his approach to photographing animals and brought a level of production that's become a cornerstone of his visual style. He says, "It's certainly more difficult to photograph a moving subject rather than a product, but the essential formula and the basis of how I use light in my work is the same." And it seems to be working, as work and accolades are coming in like never before, and "it's been very exciting!" While his time with Leica was sadly cut short, she lovingly inspired a new direction in his career: good dog! His clients now include animal brands and related work for Clorox Kitty Litter, Nature's Recipe, Virgin America, Hush Puppies, the SPCA, Amazon, Zynga, and others. In addition to his commercial imagery, artwork sales have also become a growing part of his work.

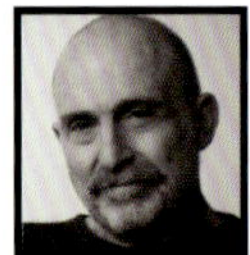

Howard Schatz | Pages: 34, 35 | www.howardschatz.com

Biography: Howard Schatz has received international acclaim for his work and is one of the most sought-after photographers working today. Over 30 years, 23 books of his work have been published. His most recent, *Pairs*, published last fall, and *Kink*, focused on San Francisco's annual Folsom Street Fair, follow on the heels of the magnificent two-volume retrospective, *Schatz Images: 25 Years*. Others include *Caught in the Act: Actors Acting*, *AT THE FIGHTS: Inside the World of Professional Boxing*, *NudeBodyNude*, and three landmark books of underwater imagery: *H20*, *Pool Light*, and *WaterDance*. He has won virtually every award in photography and has had over 100 museum and gallery exhibitions worldwide. Howard has made extraordinary images for advertising clients such as Ralph Lauren RLX, Escada, Sergio Tacchini, Nike, Reebok, Wolford, Etienne Aigner, Sony, Adidas, Finlandia Vodka, MGM Grand Hotel, Virgin Records, and Mercedes-Benz. Howard's fine artwork is represented in galleries in the United States and abroad.

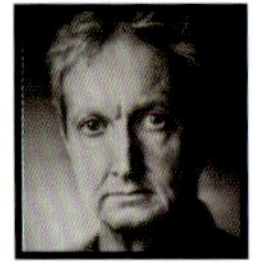

Jonathan Knowles | Pages: 36, 37 | www.jknowles.com

Biography: Jonathan Knowles is an advertising photographer and filmmaker who creates extraordinary imagery for the world's most established brands. He specializes in still life, drinks, beauty, and special effects. For the last two decades, he has consistently featured in the *200 Best Advertising Photographers Worldwide* books, with his image on the cover of the 2020 edition. He has won awards for both moving images and stills from Graphis, PDN, D&AD, the Art Directors' Club of New York, Communication Arts, the Association of Photographers, Campaign, New York Festivals, the Globals, Oneeyeland, and others. In 2019, he won the Advertising Photographer of the Year award for a series of images shot for Dior, with a ceremony at Carnegie Hall in New York City. In 2020 and 2021, he won in the Advertising Film category of the same competition. Today, Jonathan neighbors the Thames River in his London studio, capturing still images and films that will reach people across the globe. It was here that he created the iconic O2 bubbles, and brands such as Coca-Cola, Vodafone, Facebook, Nescafé, Chopard, Graff, Johnnie Walker, Glenfiddich, and many more have sought out Jonathan's distinguished and timeless style.

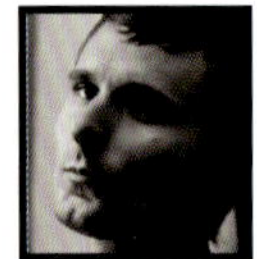

James Minchin III | Pages: 38-40 | www.jamesminchin.com

Biography: James Minchin III began his career in photography in 1993 upon graduating from the School of Visual Arts in New York City. Shortly thereafter, Motown Records moved James to Los Angeles to build and run their photo department. From there, James spent the next decade documenting the world of American music. Word of James' unique perspective quickly spread beyond the music industry. He now competes on a global level, delivering commercial campaigns across a variety of markets. For the last decade, James has been at the forefront of award-winning advertising and has earned many gold, silver, and bronze Key Art Awards for his hero campaigns. James is continuously sought for his distinct vision, his ability to direct and evoke the unexpected from his subjects, and the unfolding narrative he reveals for every project. Collaboration and thoughtfulness are his primary tools, which are seen on every set and in every finish. His commercial endeavors take him around the world, shooting for premium clients such as A24, Paramount, FX, Netflix, HBO, Sundance, Showtime, Rolling Stone, Warner Brothers, Universal, and Sony Music, just to name a few.

I was very impressed with not only the overall quality of the work, but the diversity of styles and concepts.

RJ Muna, *Photographer, RJ Muna Pictures*

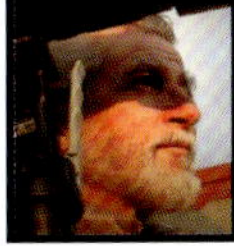

Paco Macias Velasco | **Page: 41** | **www.pacomaciasvelasco.mx**
Biography: Paco Macías Velasco was born in Mexico City in 1951. After graduating from the Mexican Institute of Photography (IMF) in 1970, he took a course at the London Institute of Photography in 1971. In 1996, he earned a diploma in advertising from the Universidad Anáhuac del Norte, Mexico City. He also earned a diploma in institutional communication and political campaign design from IIS, UNAM, in 2015. As a photographer, he shoots many different specialties such as portrait, landscape, automotive, product, food and beverages, hospitality, industrial, architectural, and author photography. After more than four decades of being dedicated to photography, Paco is known for his signature photography and his work in Mexican advertising. His photographs have been shown in various exhibitions and publications, and he has won many national and international awards. He is a producer of photographic projects and concepts. He currently lives and works in Mexico City.

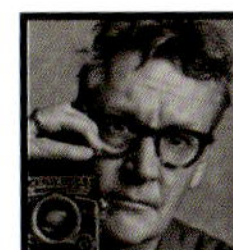

Craig Cutler | **Pages: 42, 43** | **www.craigcutler.com**
Biography: Craig Cutler's meticulous combination of craft and style brings an element of art to his work as a director and photographer. Conceptual thinking lays the foundation for both his print and film approach. Each of his projects, editorial or commercial ads, begins with concepts that initially take shape as sketches and evolve through a series of revisions and additions until a final direction is honed. Craig's work is further differentiated by his focus on lighting. He strips each piece of its setting and uses lighting to evoke the message integral to his concept. A frequent recipient of awards, Craig blends his experience with contemporary vision to create timeless art. He frequently collaborates on projects with his creative agency, CutlerBremner.

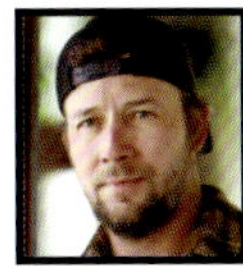

Artem Nazarov | **Pages: 44, 45** | **www.nazarovphoto.com**
Biography: Artem Nazarov grew up in Penza in Western Russia. Given his first Canon camera at eight years old, these early experiences stirred his curiosity about the medium and sparked his passion for visual storytelling. In 2003, after specializing in intellectual property law at the Moscow School of Social and Economic Science, Artem immigrated to the United States. He relocated to Atlanta in 2008 to continue his education at the Portfolio Center, majoring in photography. Artem believes that photography is a beautiful way to explore the world and hopes that his work influences others to travel, immersing themselves in other cultures. In every locale, he seeks the most authentic experiences of the indigenous population, chronicling their unique customs and conventions. He teaches visual storytelling at Miami Ad School and is a board member of Good Thinking Atlanta. His work has been recognized by American Photography, Communication Arts, the ADDY Awards, the Dallas Society of Visual Communication, Graphis, and the SEED Awards. Artem's clients include Coca-Cola, CNN, Getty Images, Google, and *The New York Times*.

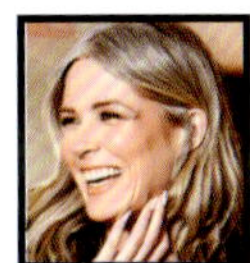

Lindsey Drennan | **Page: 46** | **www.lindseydrennan.com**
Biography: Lindsey is a commercial photographer from Toronto, Canada, represented by Coup&Co. Highlighting a photography career spanning over 19 years, she has curated a portfolio with an extensive array of Canada's premier brands, esteemed publications, leading agencies, and prominent production houses. Her career started in 2005. While pursuing her studies, she became the first-ever international student to secure an internship at the iconic *Vogue* magazine in New York City. Since then, Lindsey has dedicated her expertise to commercial product and beauty photography, setting unparalleled standards of creativity and excellence.

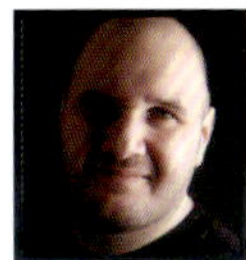

John Surace | **Page: 47** | **www.johnsurace.com**
Biography: John Surace is a creative director and still life photographer with a focus on hierarchy, form, and palette. His images are informed by a simple and graphic layout. An emphasis on purposefully arranged props and artfully shaped light serves to tell intriguing stories across his photographs. John trusts the precision of a Sinar P2 view camera to help realize his work. Deliberate lens movements and the Scheimpflug principle ensure critical focus and distortion correction in one exposure, which affords him more time on-set, crafting composition and light. The images are captured in the large pixels of a Phase One P25 digital back, which enables the use of large format film lenses designed to the highest standard of optical clarity, color, and contrast. As a preference, John is committed to in-camera still life photography.

It's been a great honor and a real treat to be a judge and to look through this year's Graphis Photography Awards entries.

Per Breiehagen, *Photographer, Per Breiehagen Photography*

Visit our Credits & Commentary section in the back of the book to read the full assignments, approaches, and results from this year's Platinum Winners.

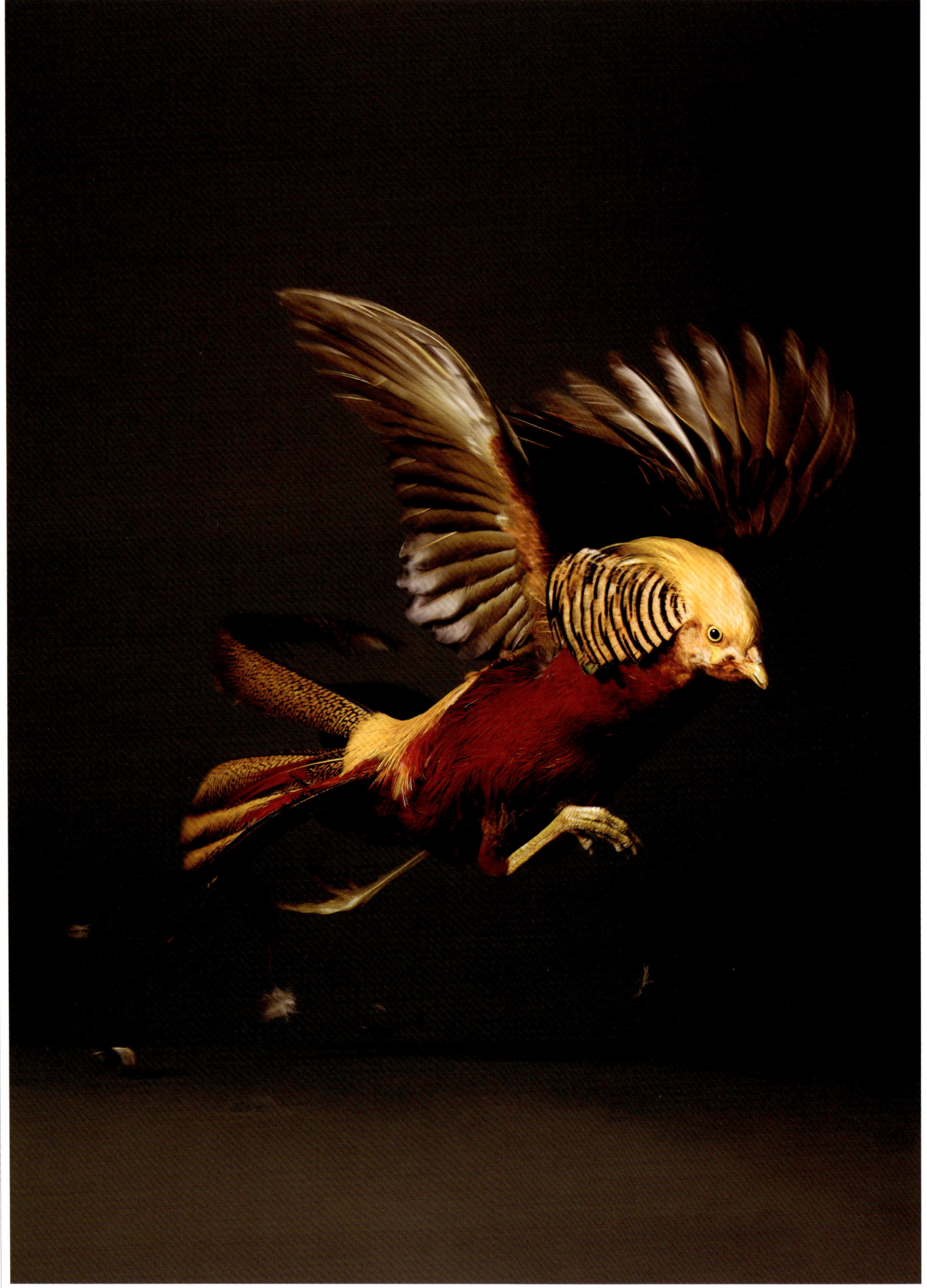

Title: Pheasants and Peafowl | Client: Private Commission

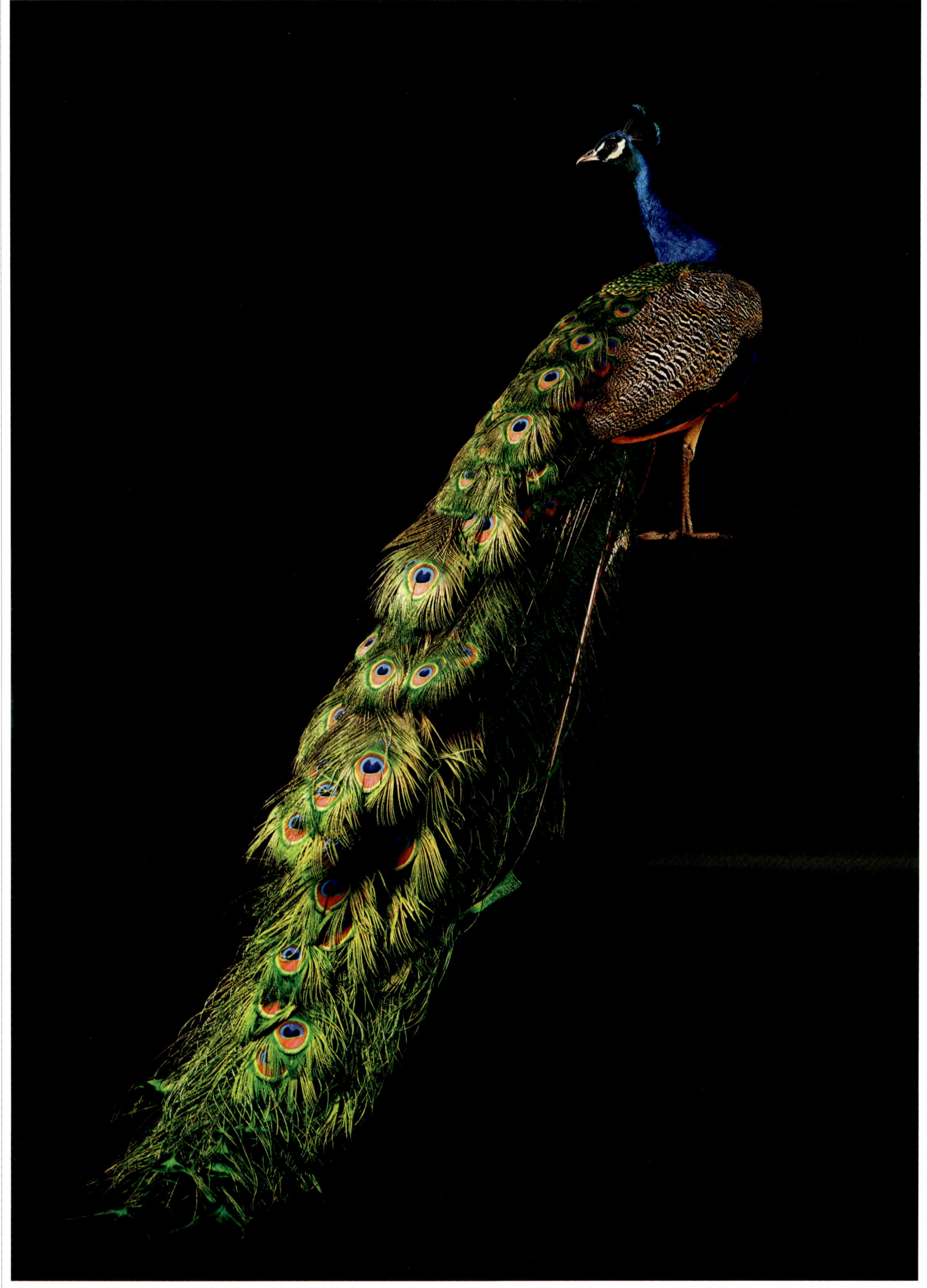

Title: Pheasants and Peafowl | **Client:** Private Commission

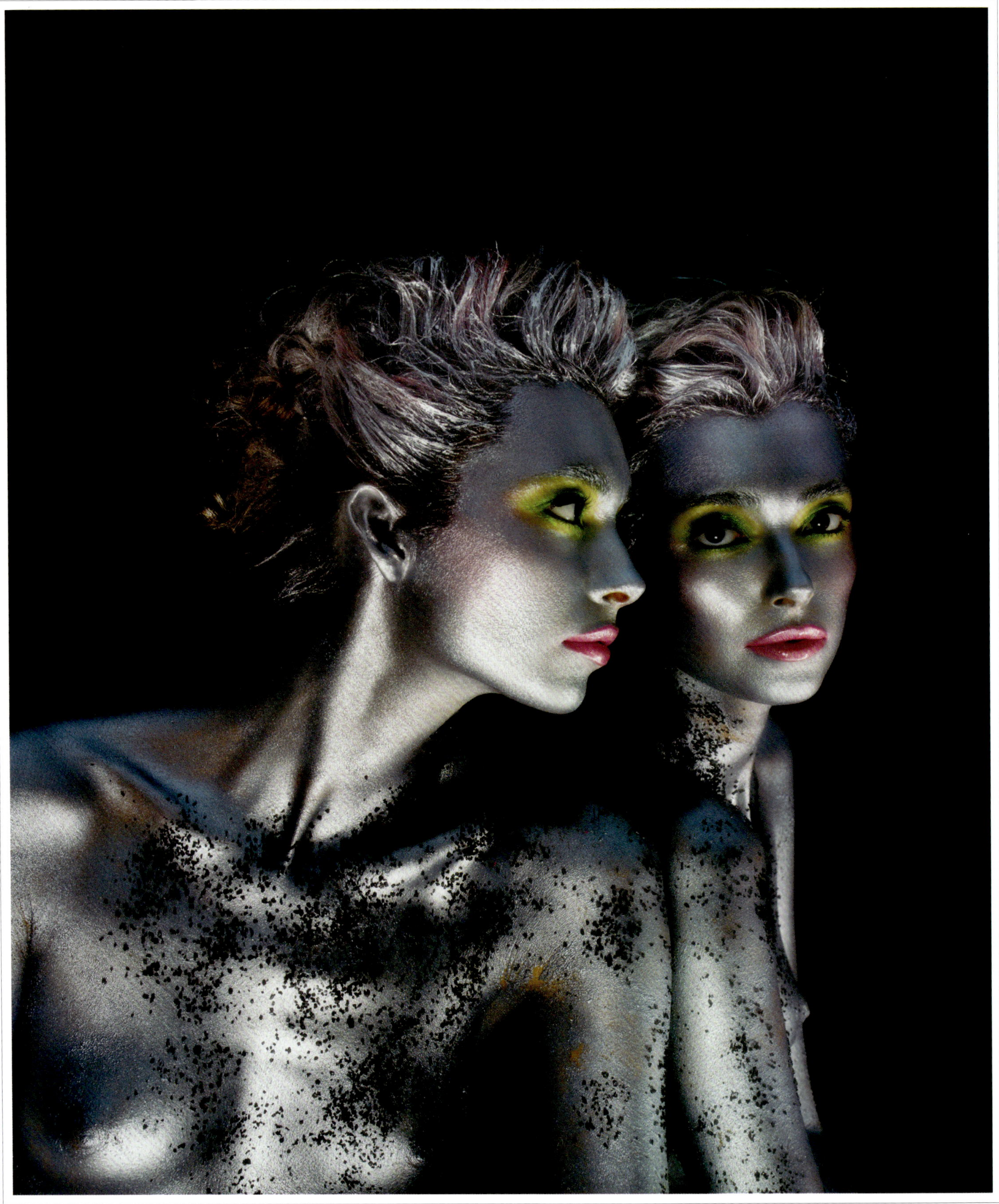

P232: Credit & Commentary

Title: Beauty Study #1299: Model Natalia Costa | **Client:** Self-initiated

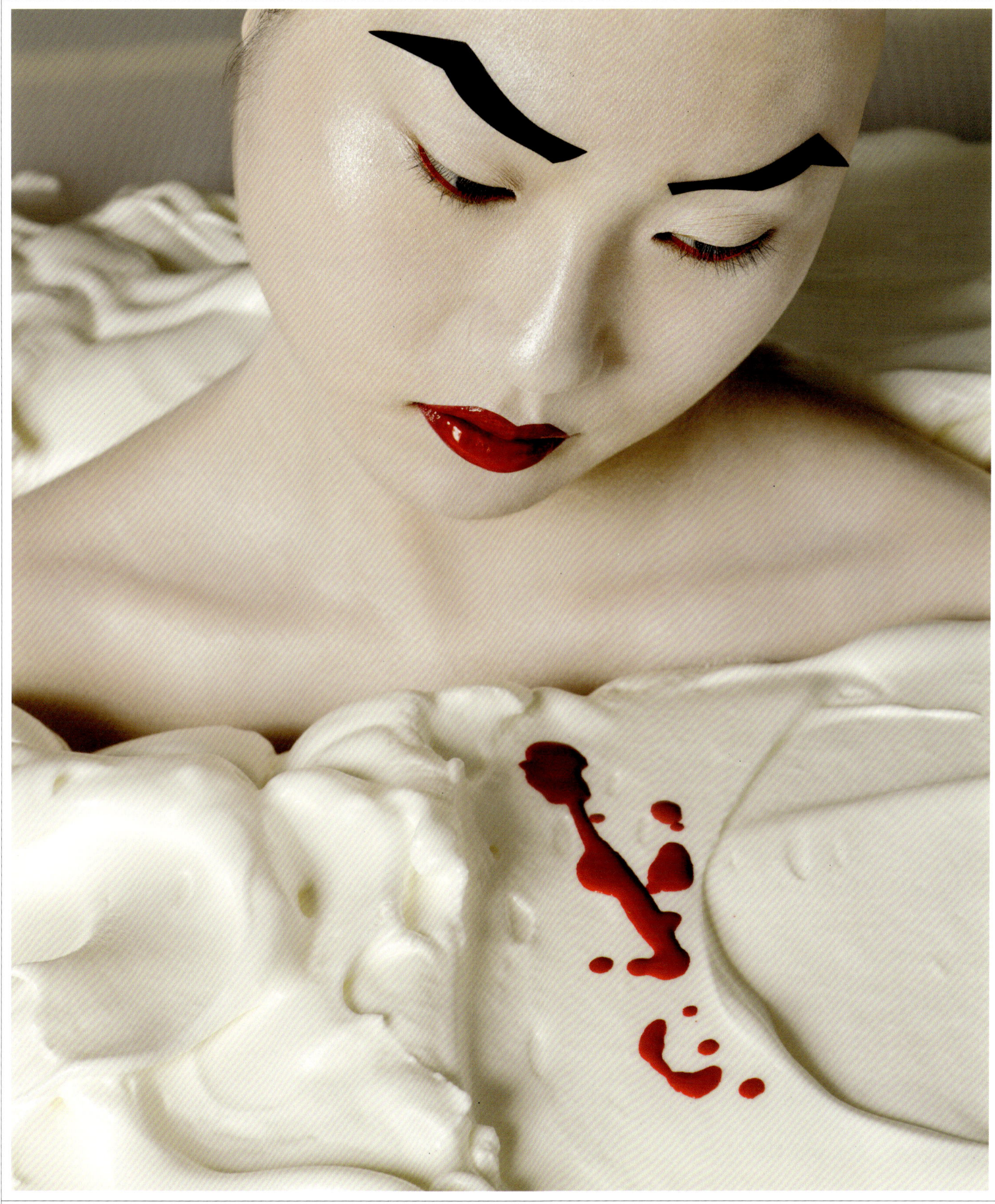

P232: Credit & Commentary

Title: Beauty Study #1392: Reiko Yamanaka | **Client:** Self-initiated

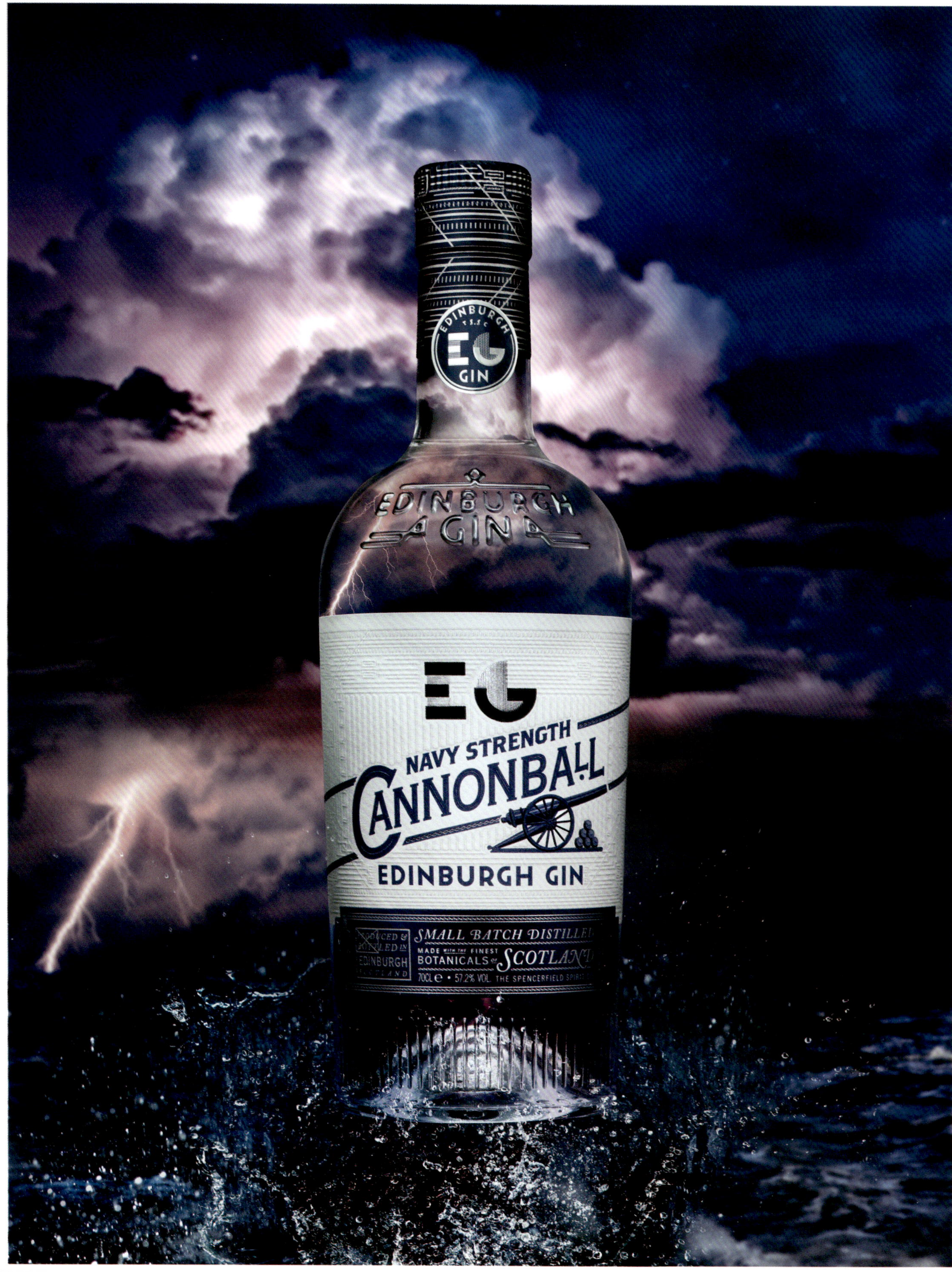

P232: Credit & Commentary | Title: Edinburgh Gin - Filled With Wonder | Client: Edinburgh Gin | Image 1 of 4

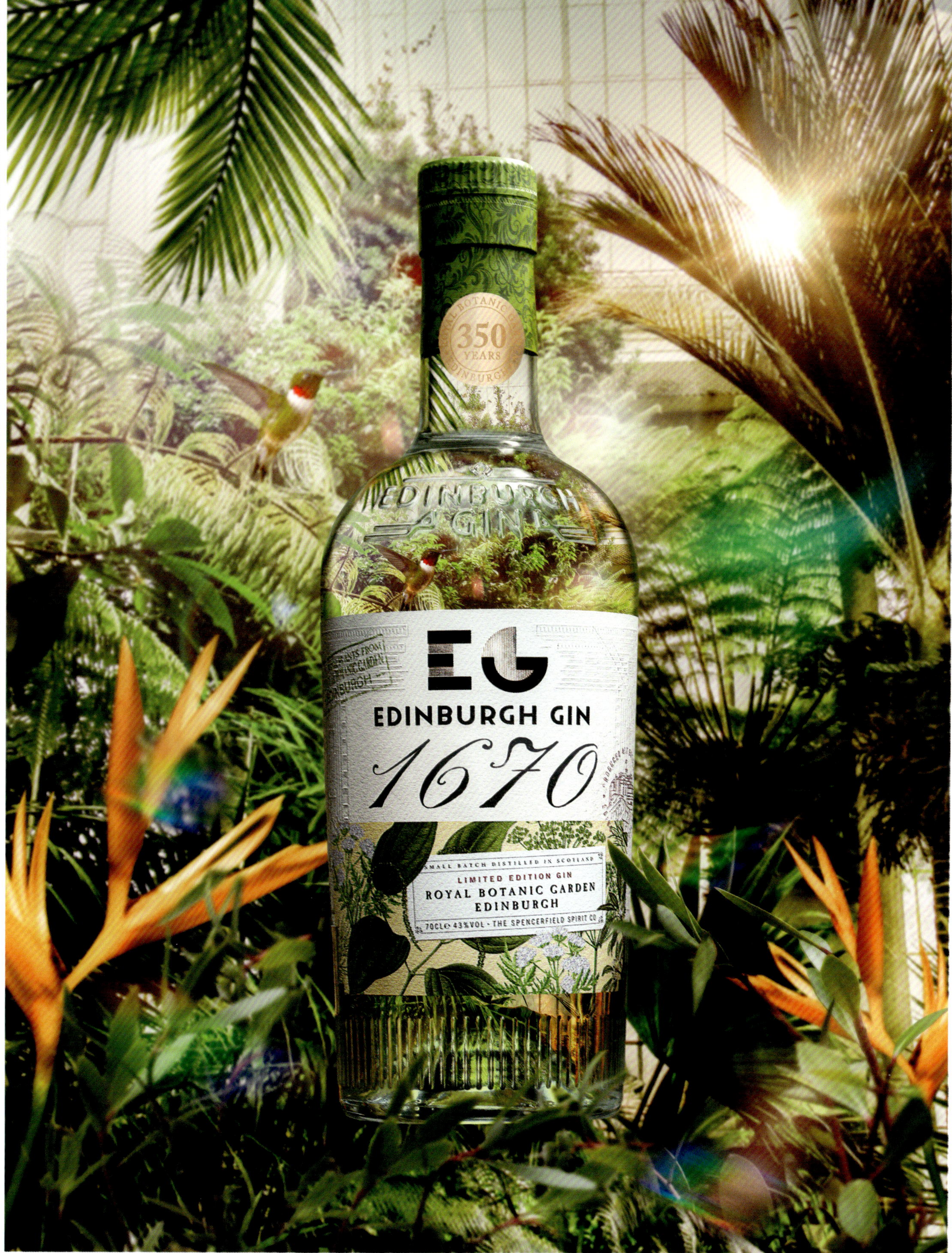

P232: Credit & Commentary

Title: Edinburgh Gin - Filled With Wonder | **Client:** Edinburgh Gin

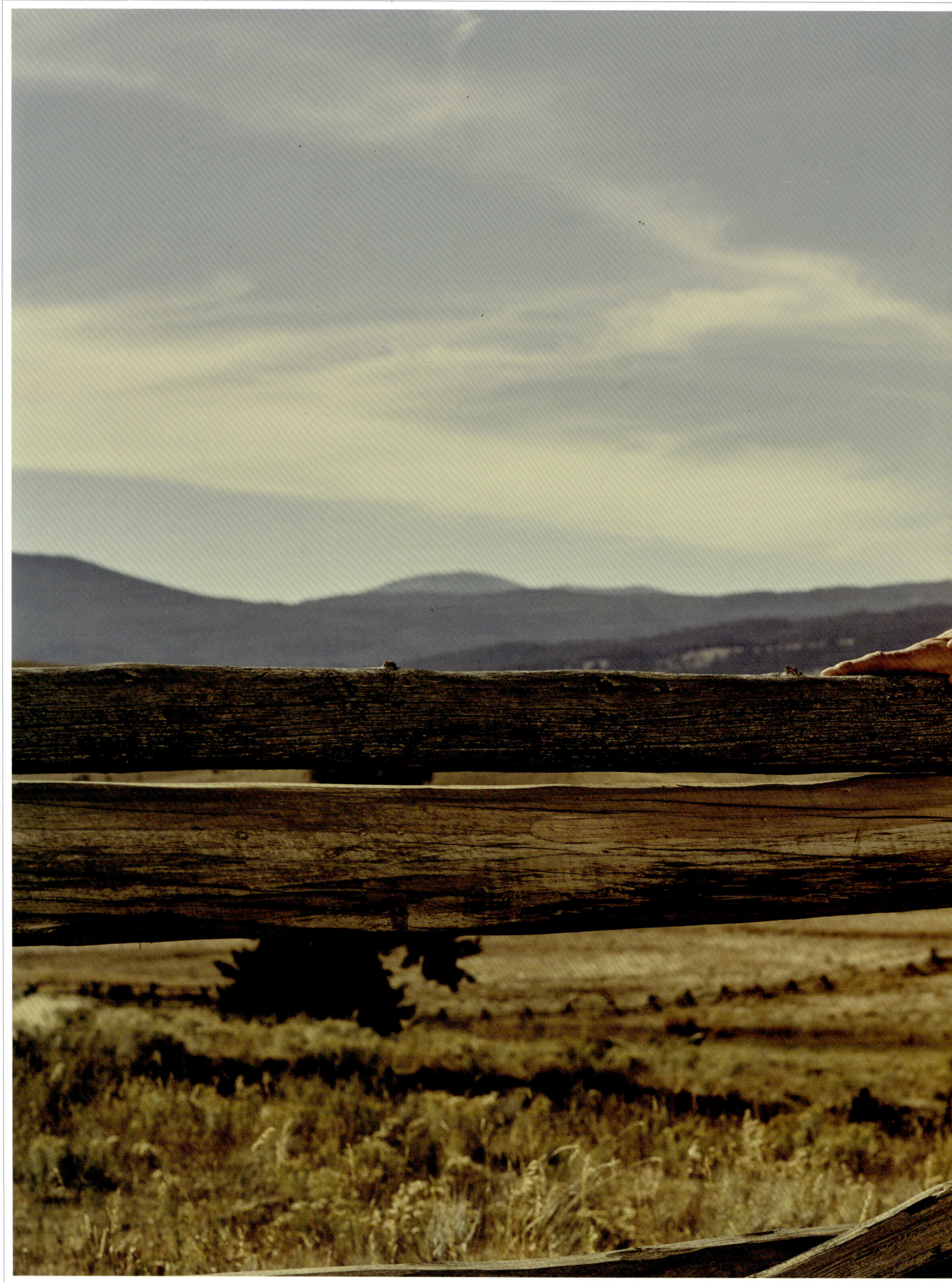

P232: Credit & Commentary

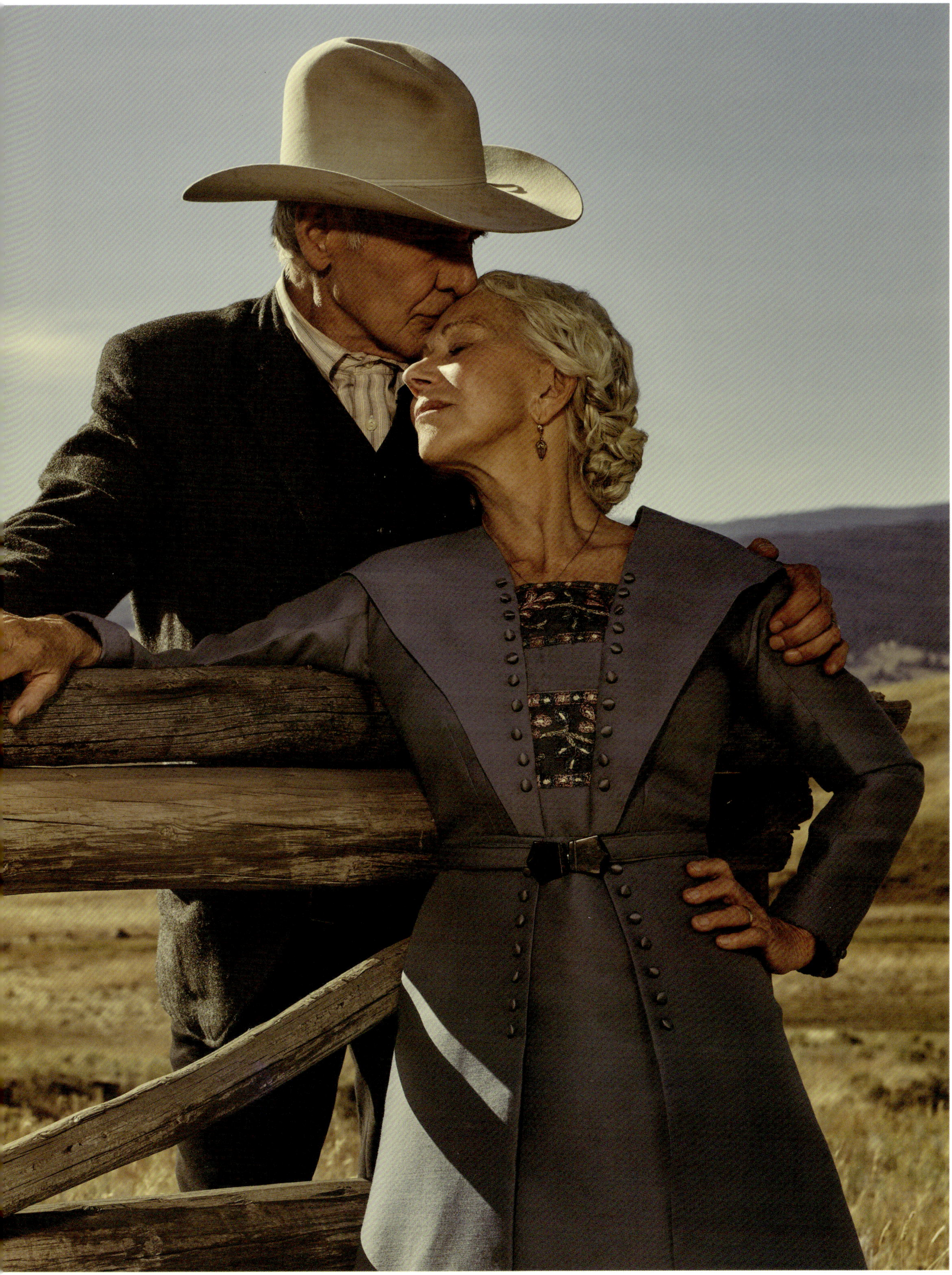

Title: 1923 Environmental Portraits | **Client:** Paramount+

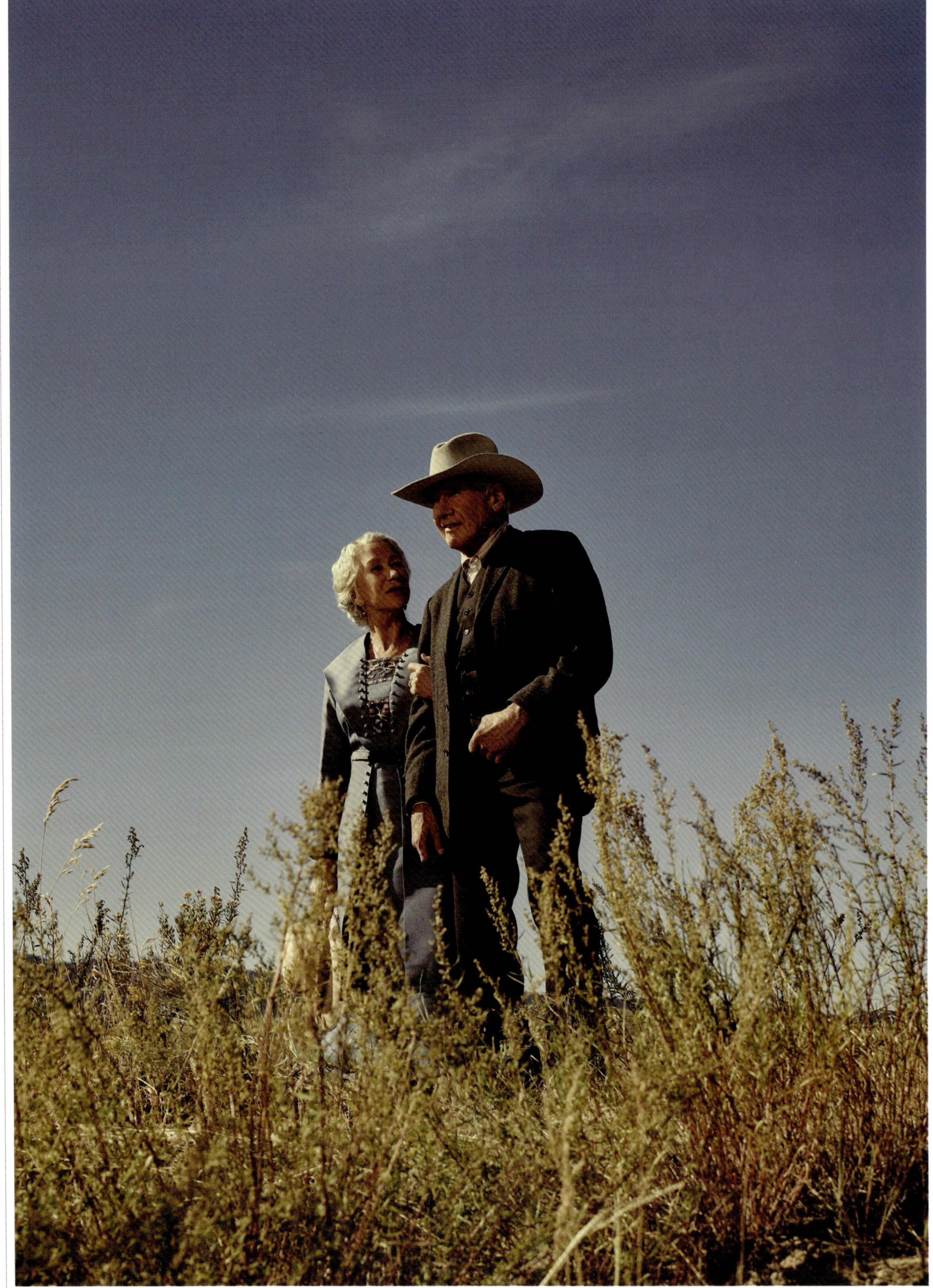

P232: Credit & Commentary **Title:** 1923 Environmental Portraits | **Client:** Paramount+ Image 2 of 7

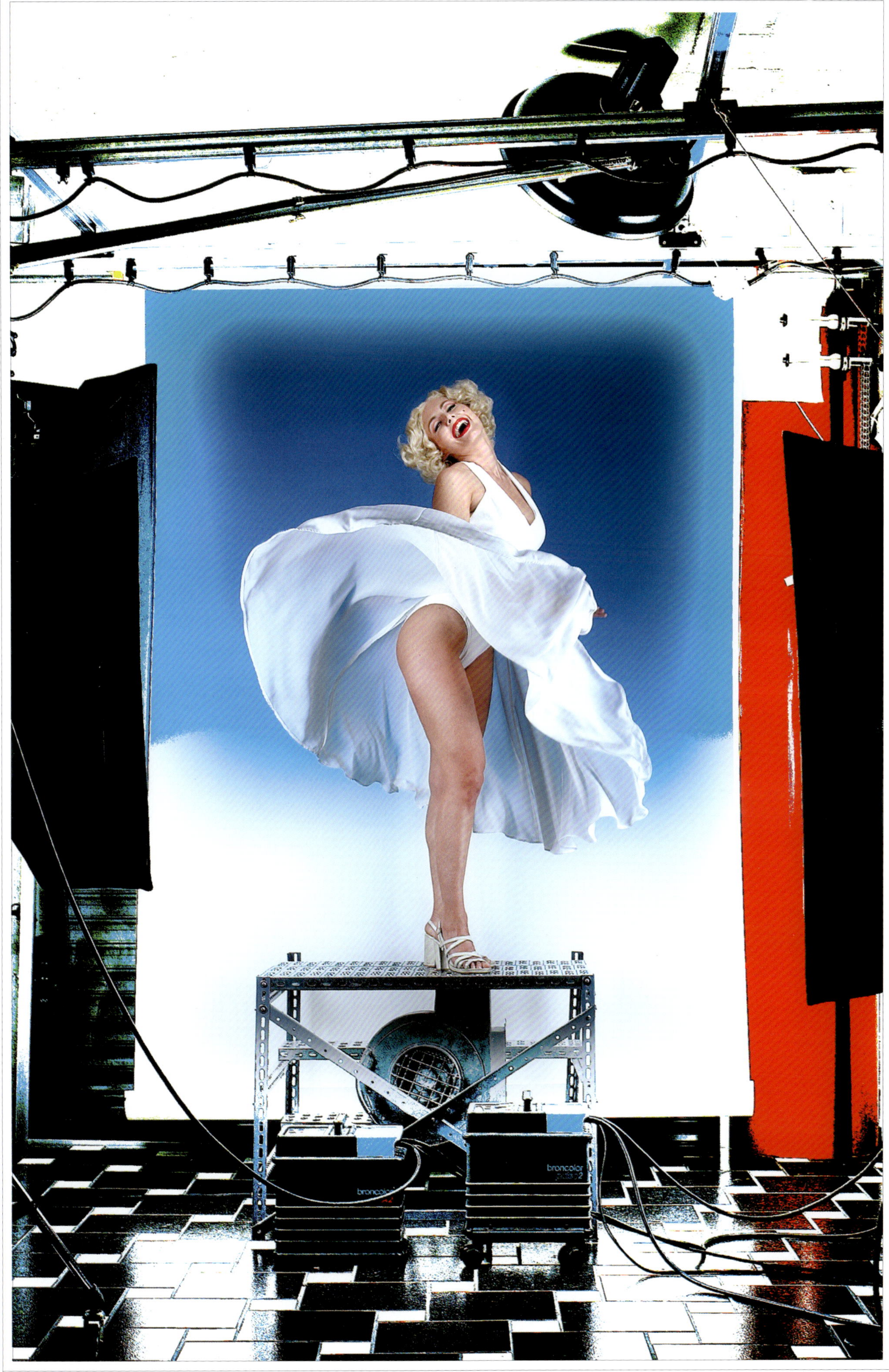

P232: Credit & Commentary **Title:** The Spirit of Marilyn Monroe Visited My Studio | **Client:** Self-initiated

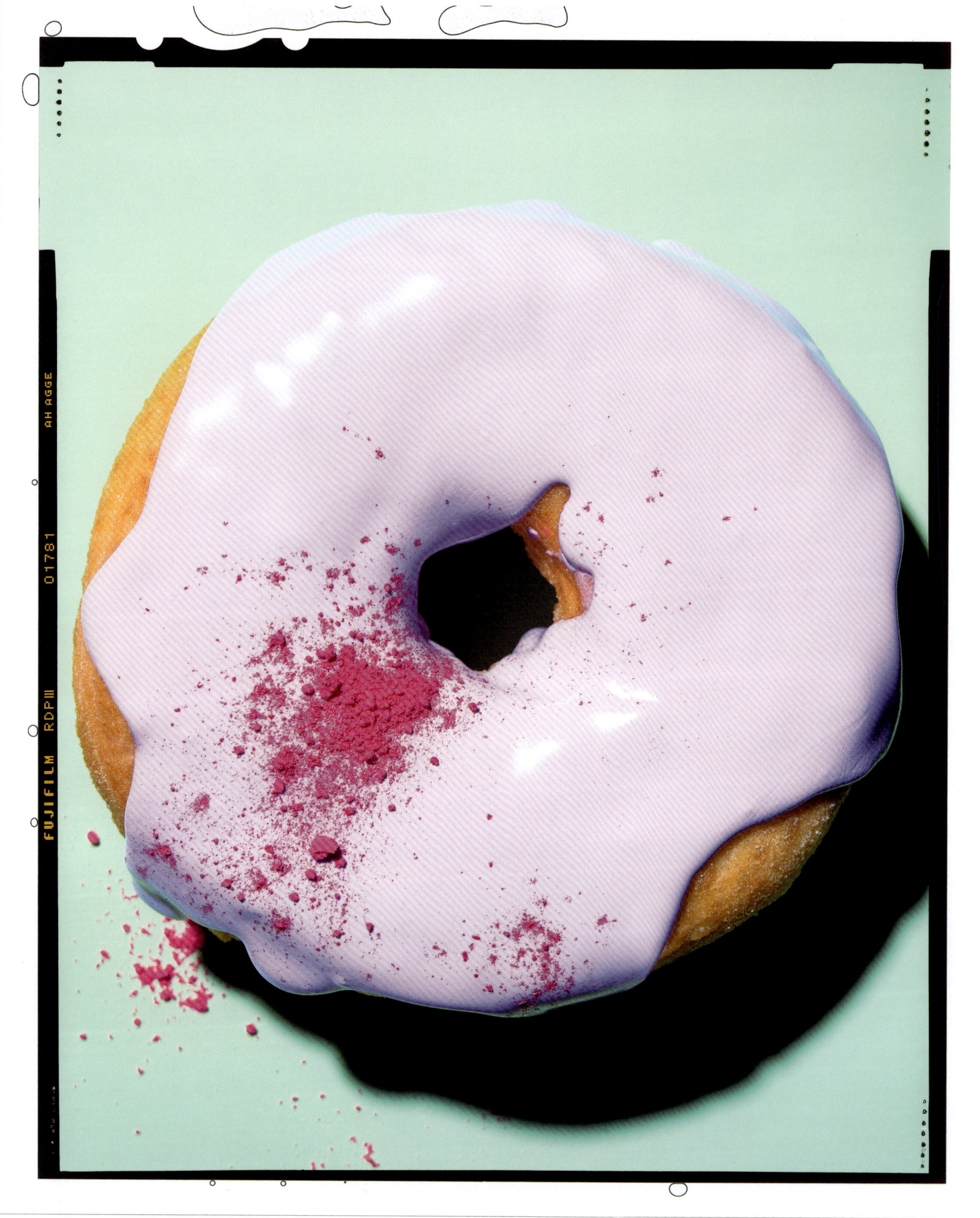

P232: Credit & Commentary

Title: Doughnuts | **Client:** Self-initiated

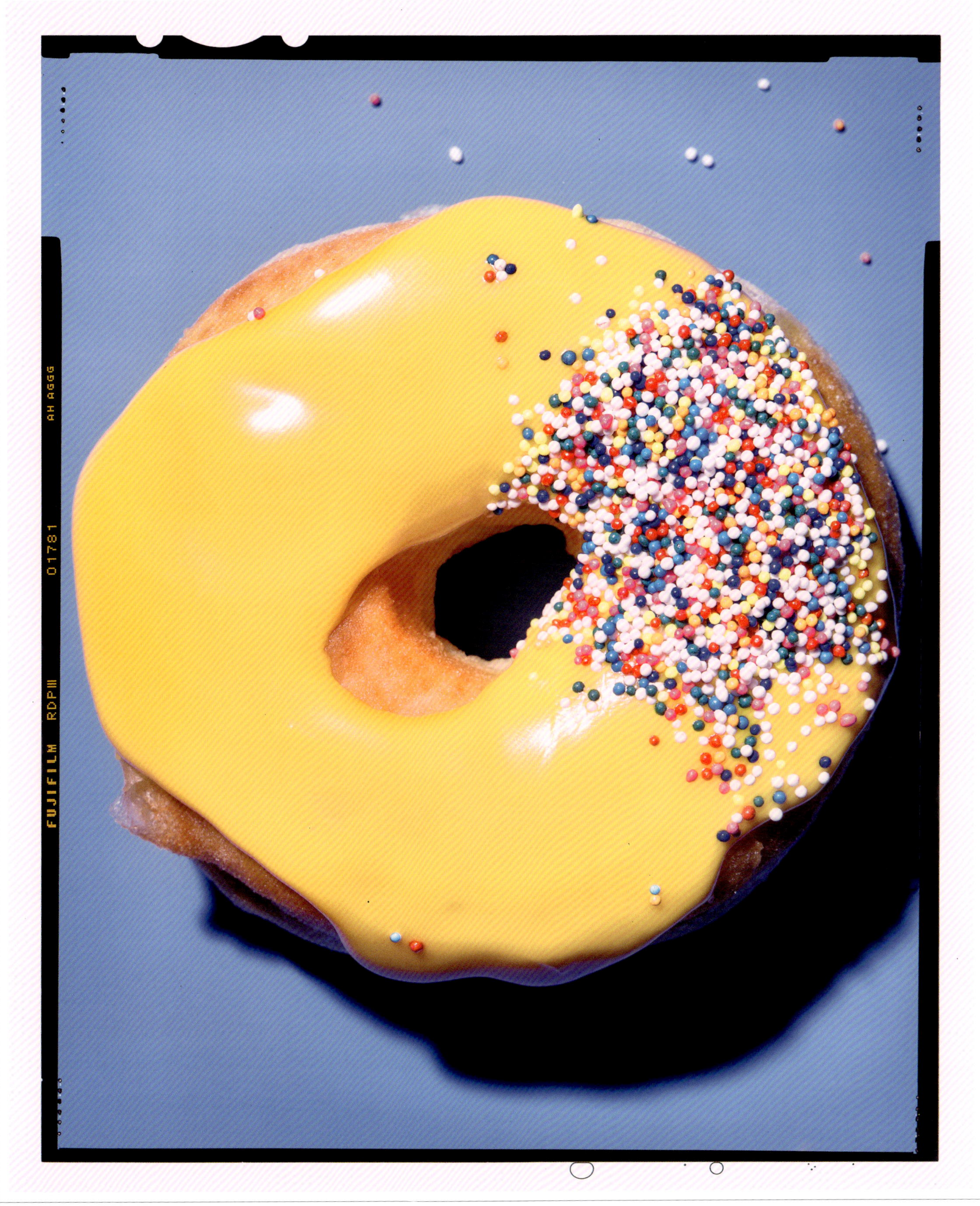

Title: Doughnuts | **Client:** Self-initiated

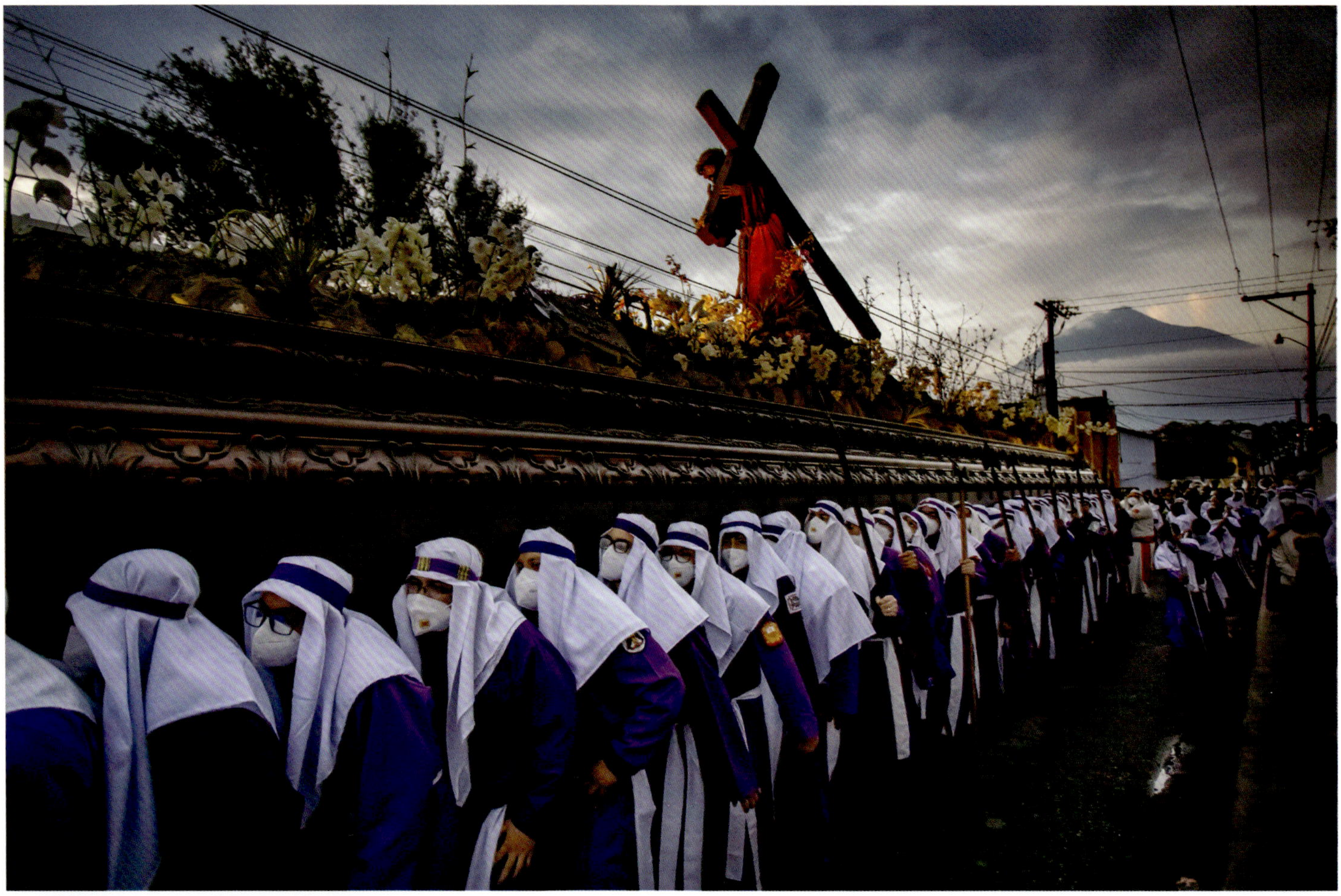

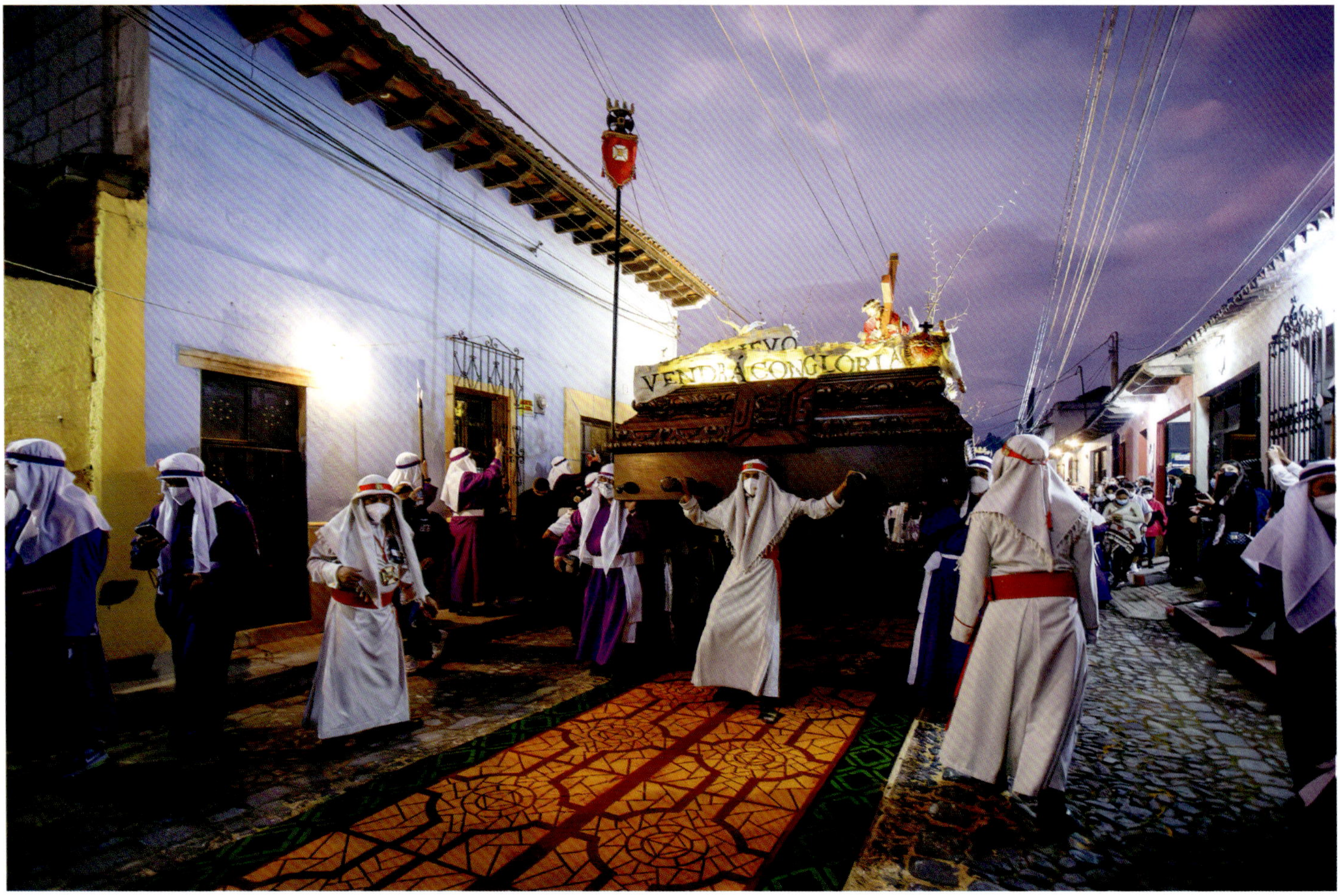

Title: Cucuruchos: The Holy Week | **Client:** Self-initiated

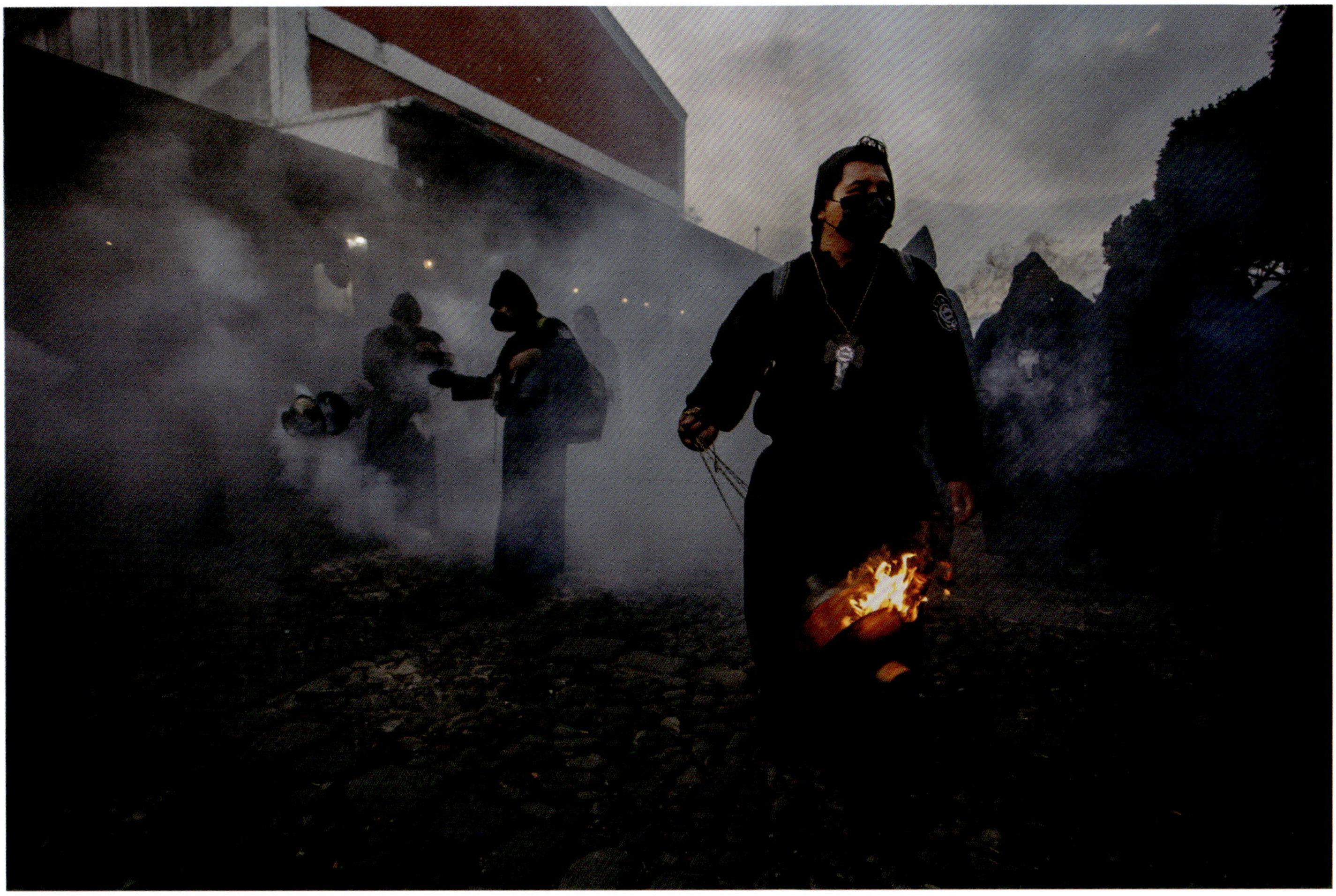

Set in Antigua, Guatemala, “Cucurochos: The Holy Week” is part of an ongoing project focused on the religious syncretism unique to Central and South America that blends Roman Catholic traditions with indigenous religious traditions.

Antigua hosts one of the most historic and elaborate Semana Santa (Holy Week) celebrations in Latin America. Cucuruchos weave through the city carrying ornate andas, sacred floats depicting the Stations of the Cross. While carrying them, the disciples traverse over alfombras, elaborately decorated carpets painstakingly created with colorful flowers, leaves, and fruits that depict both Catholic and Mayan themes; for example, butterflies symbolize the indigenous population’s esteem for them and represent the cyclical nature of life and the afterlife. As they head towards the cathedral, the cucuruchos float above the alfombras as turibulos release incense, the burning of which symbolizes purification.

Through vivid visuals and insightful narratives, this project immerses viewers in the essence of a tradition that continues to evolve, resonating with echoes of devotion across generations.

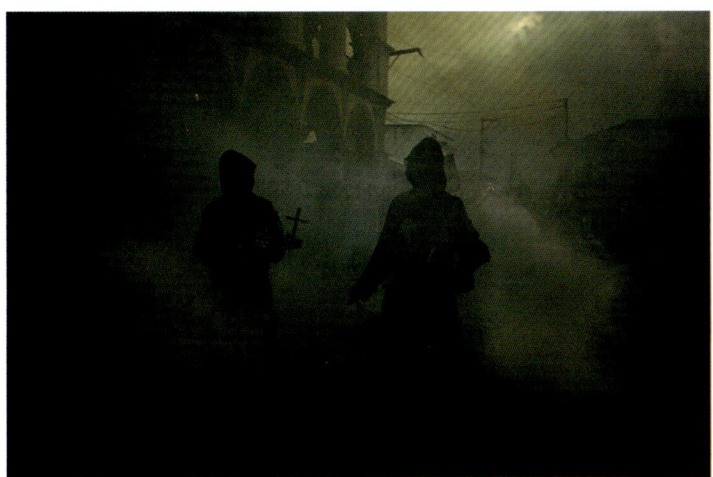

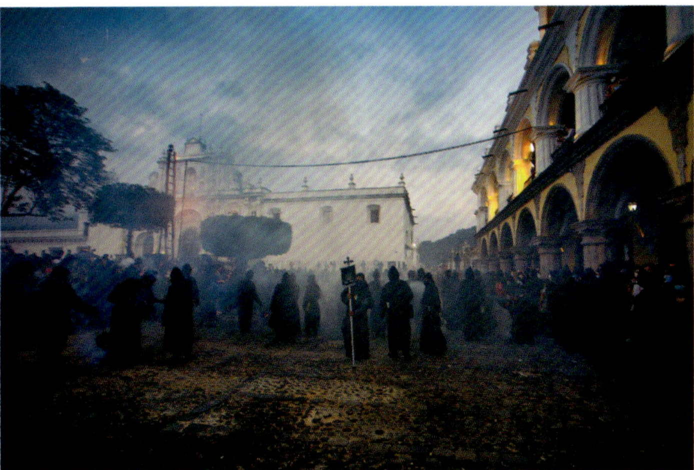

Title: Cucuruchos: The Holy Week | Client: Self-initiated

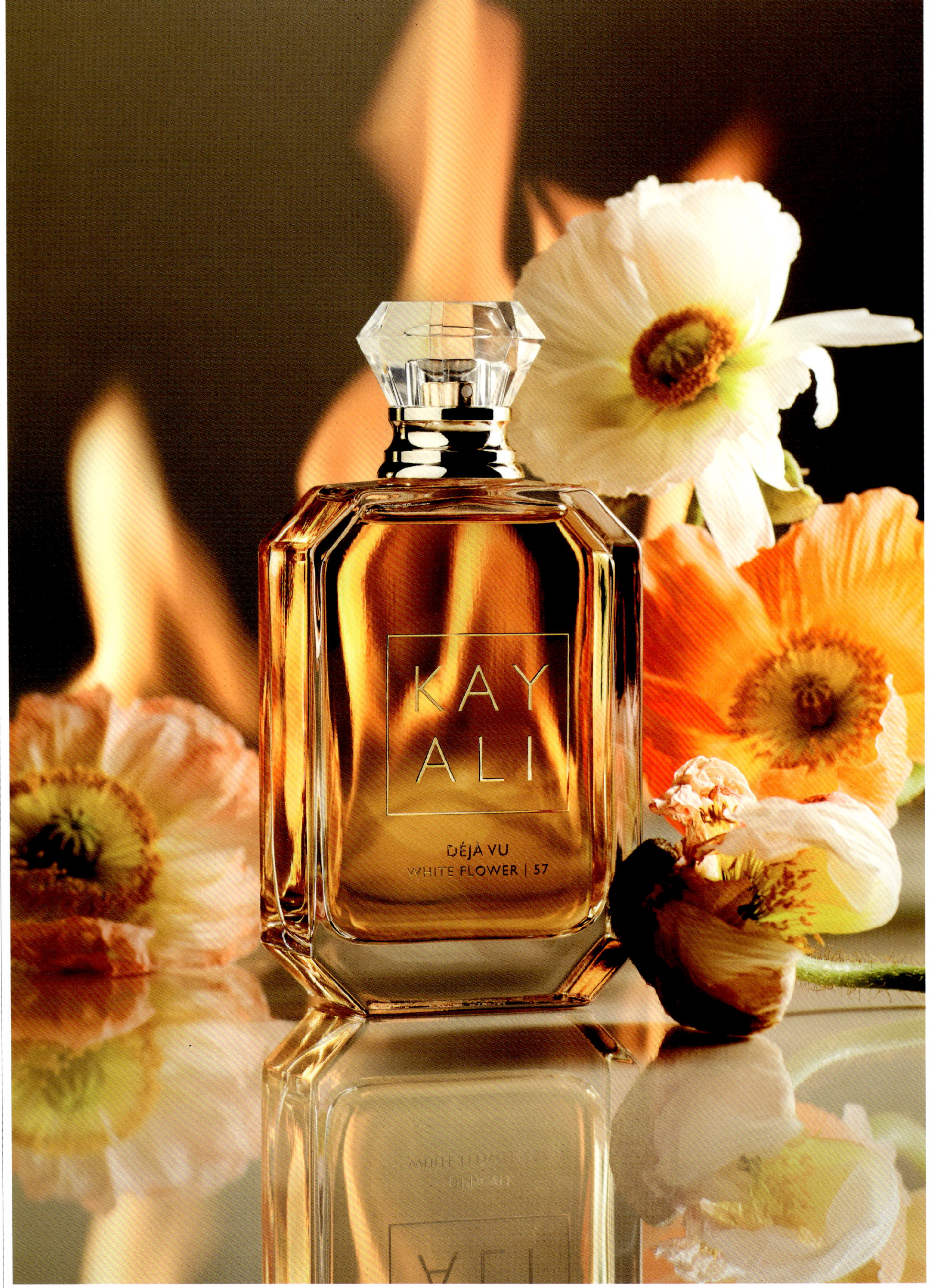

P232: Credit & Commentary **Title:** Fragrance on Fire | **Client:** Self-initiated

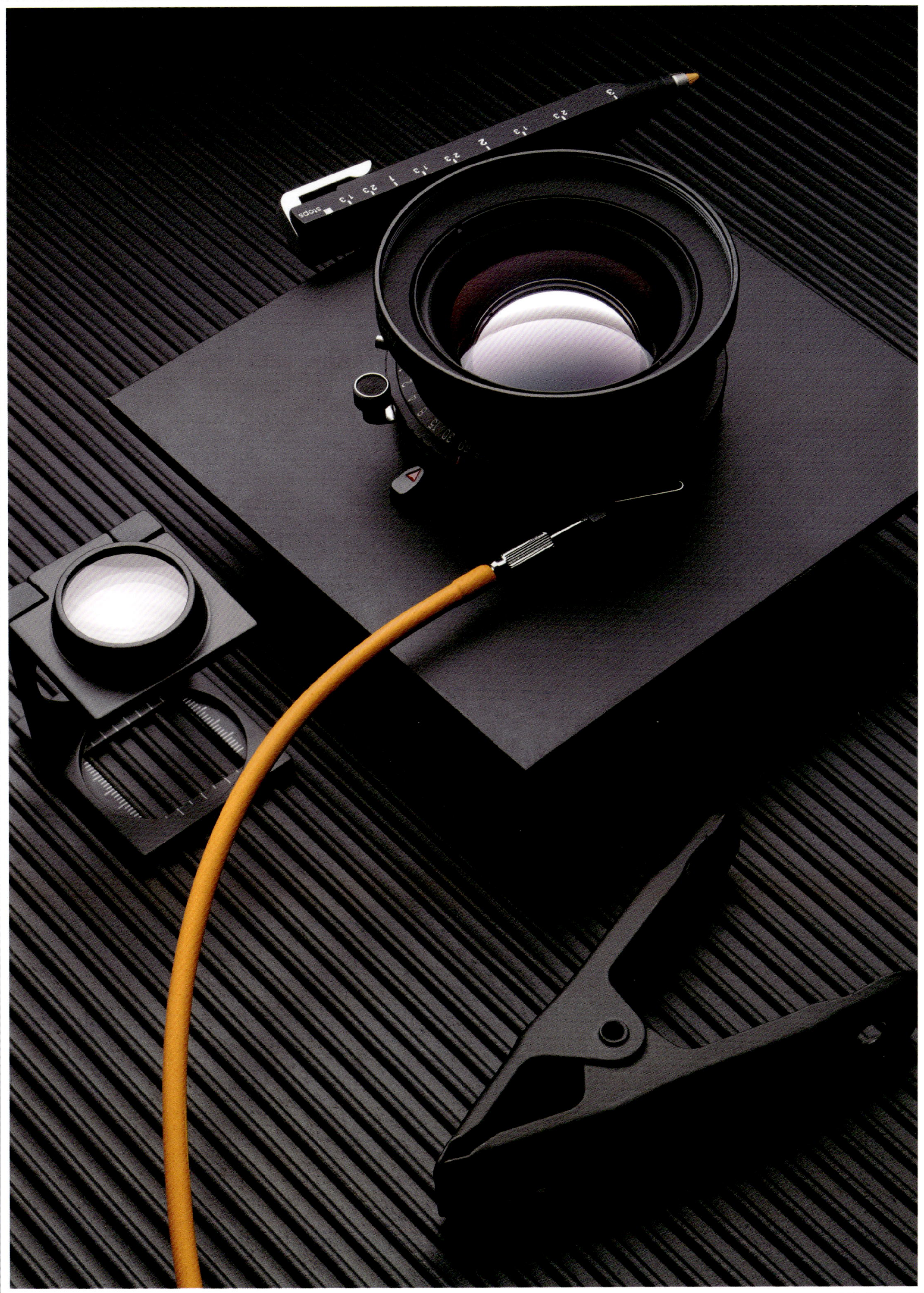

P232: Credit & Commentary

Title: Accoutrements | **Client:** Self-initiated

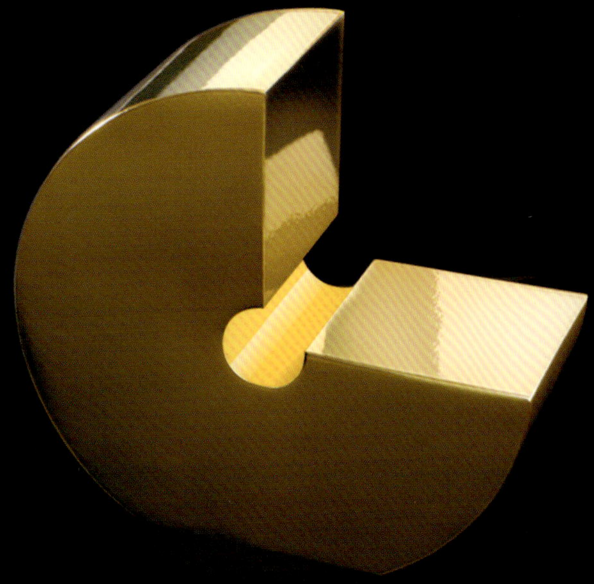

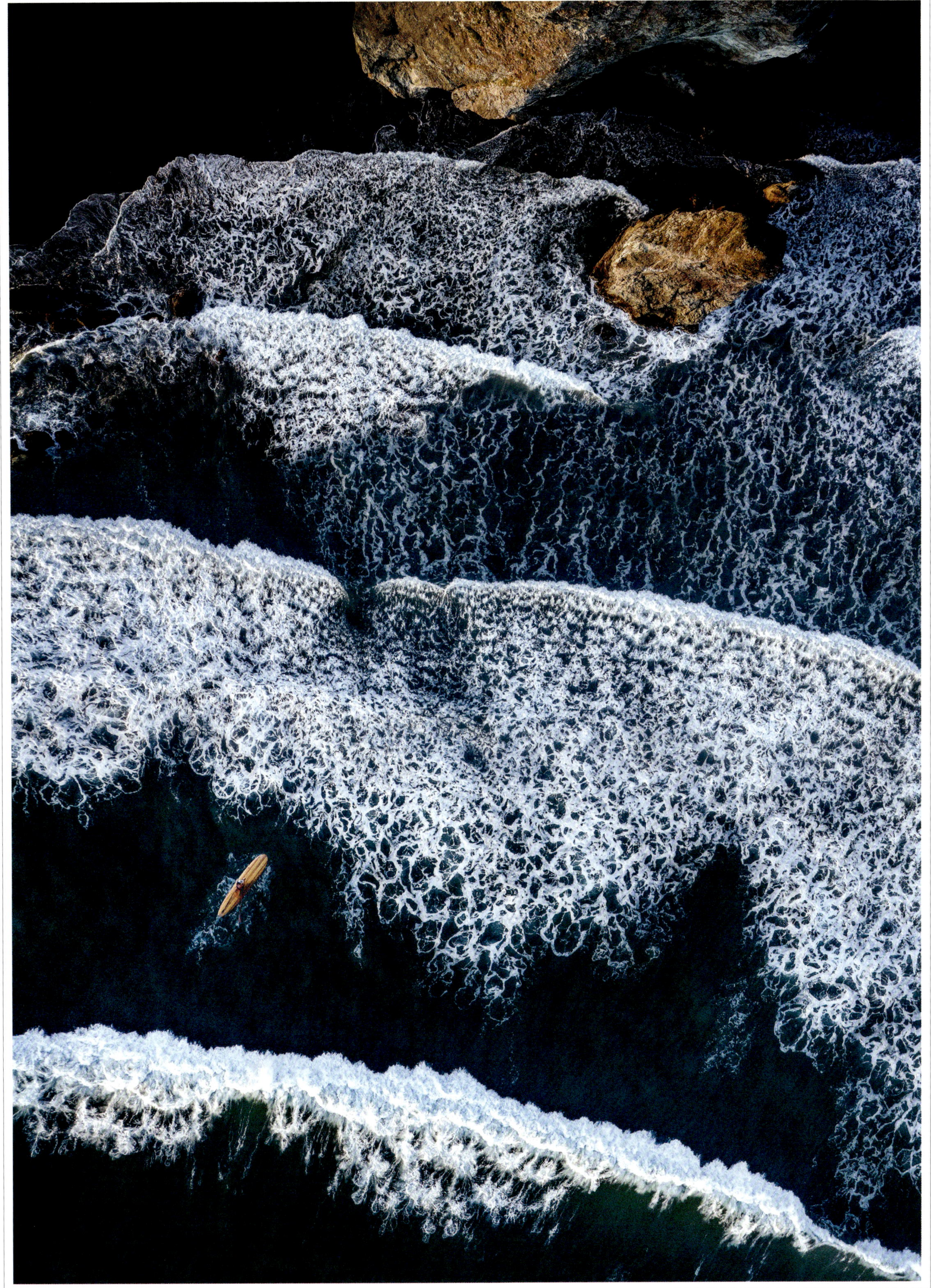

P232: Credit & Commentary

Title: Paddling Through the Oregon Breaks | **Client:** Self-initiated

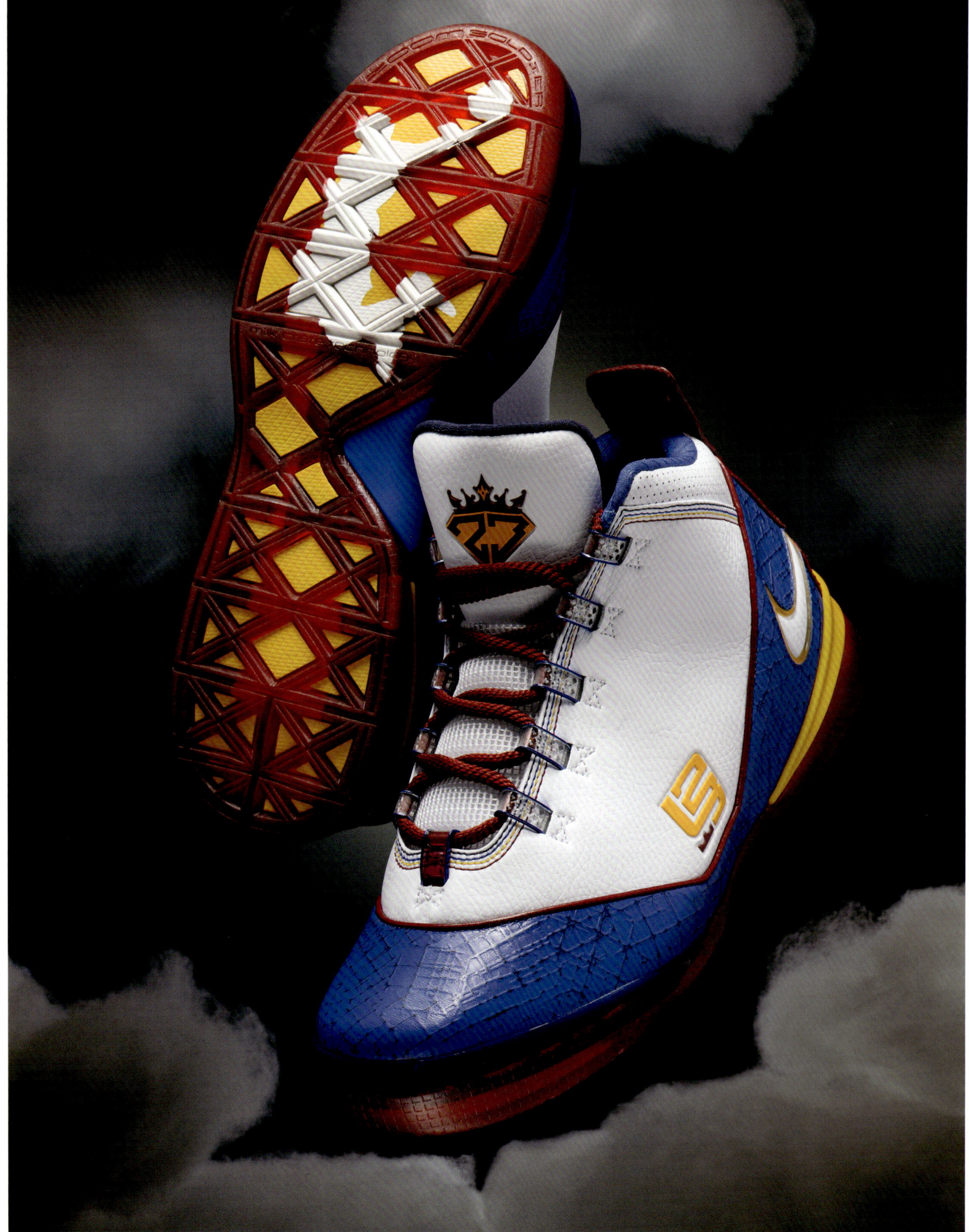

P232: Credit & Commentary

Title: Nike Zoom Soldier II "Superman" Akron Look See | **Client:** Heritage Auctions

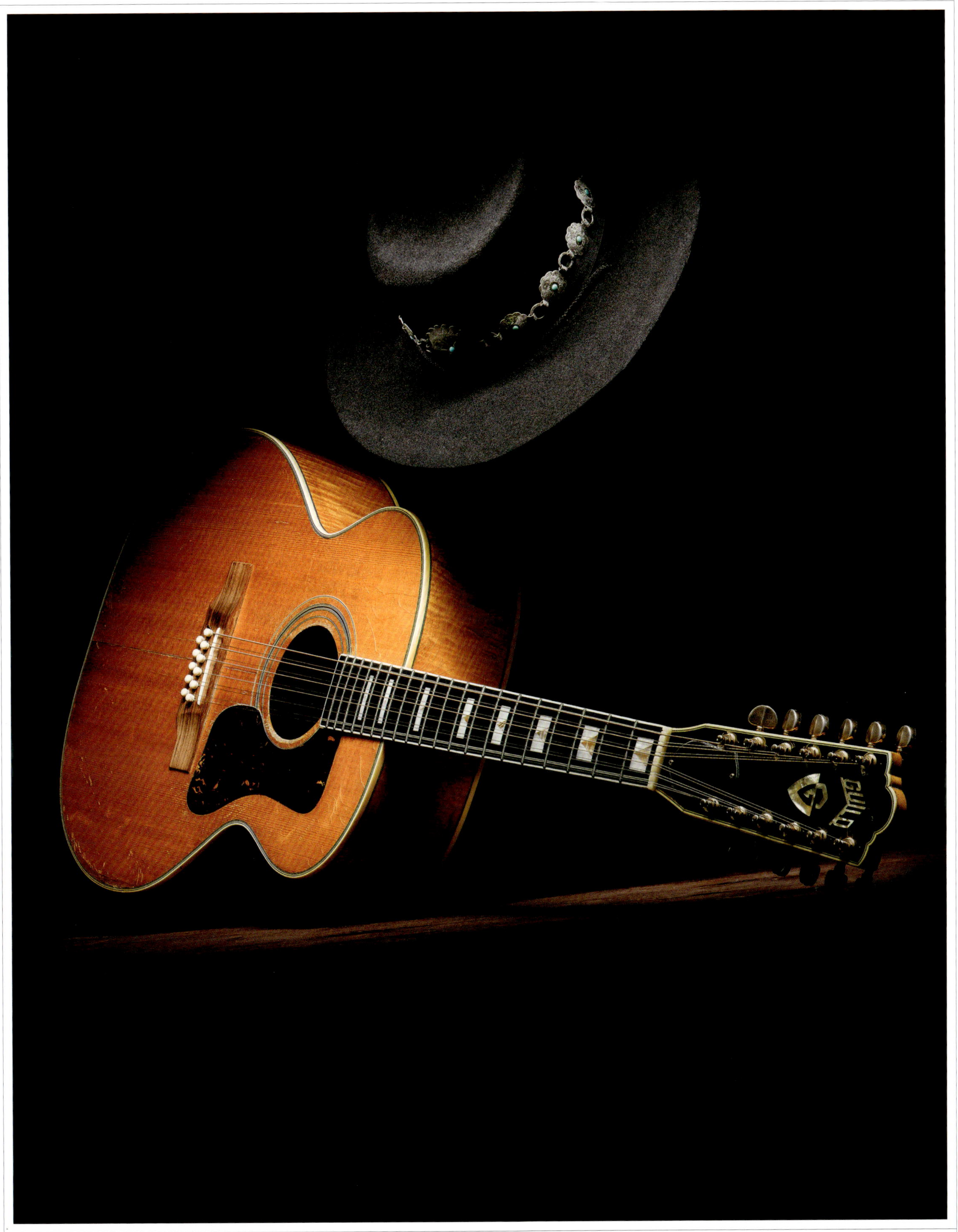

P232: Credit & Commentary **Title:** Stevie Ray Vaughan MTV Unplugged Guitar | **Client:** Heritage Auctions

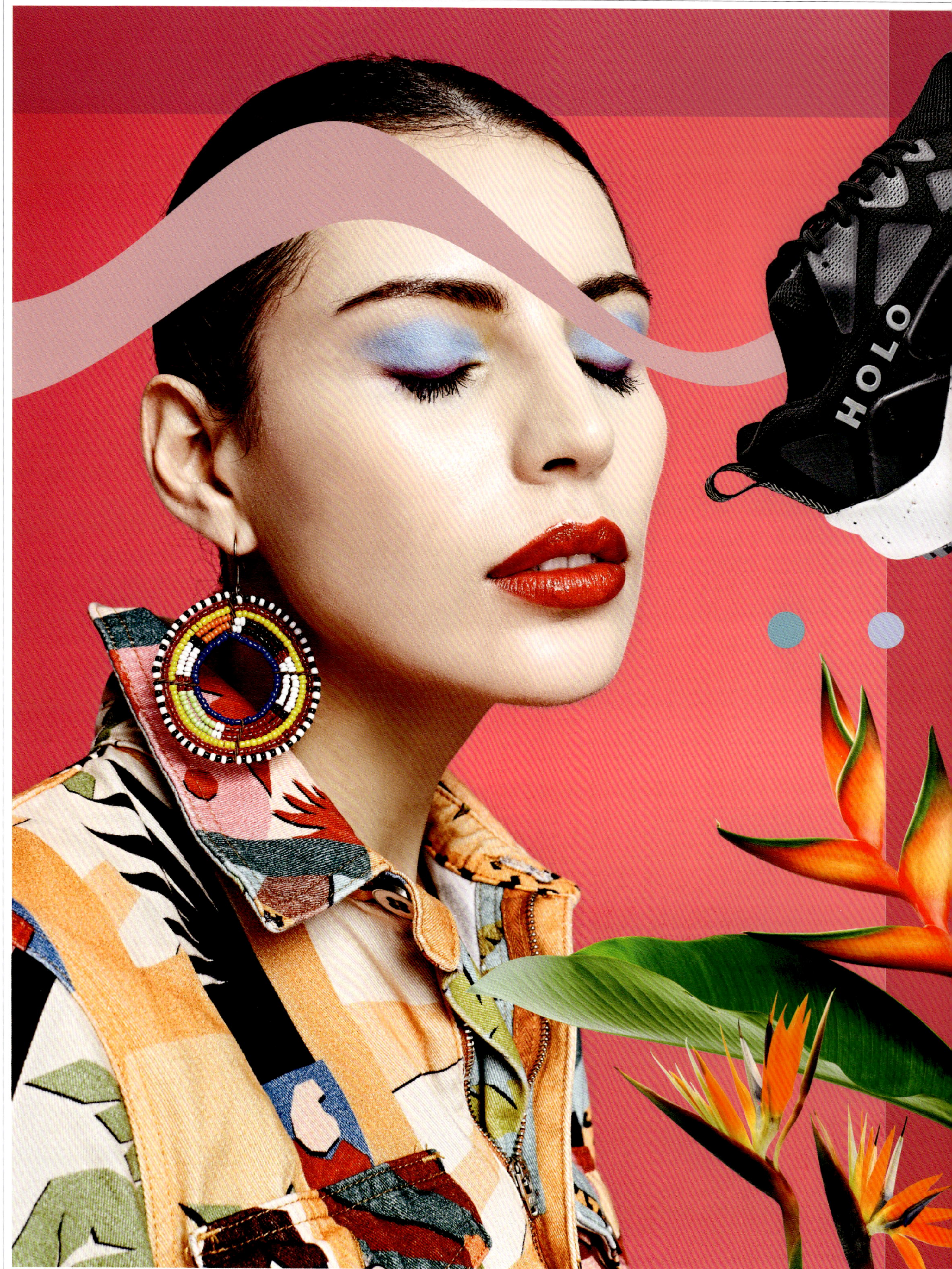

P233: Credit & Commentary

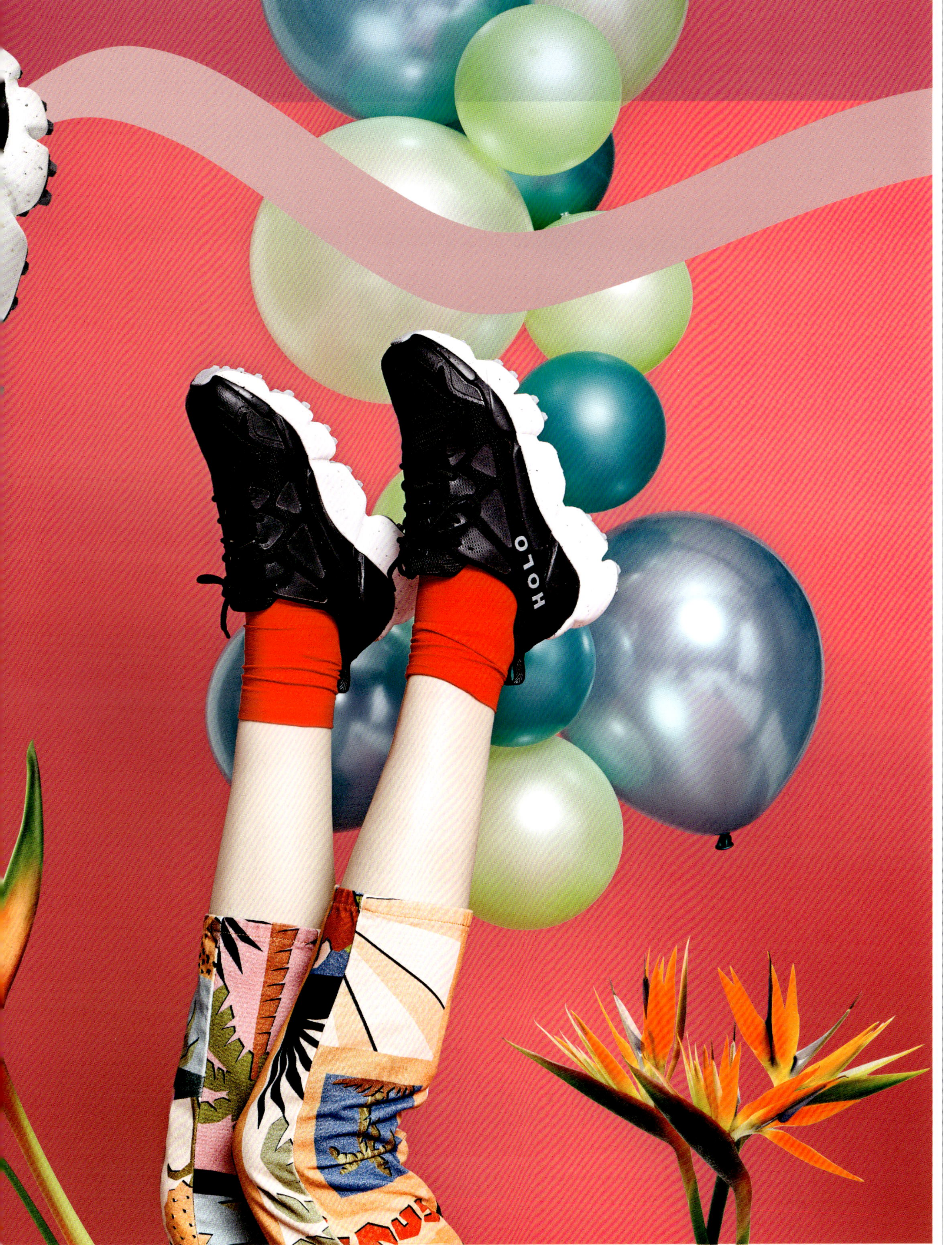

Title: Holo Footwear Ad Campaign | **Client:** Holo Footwear

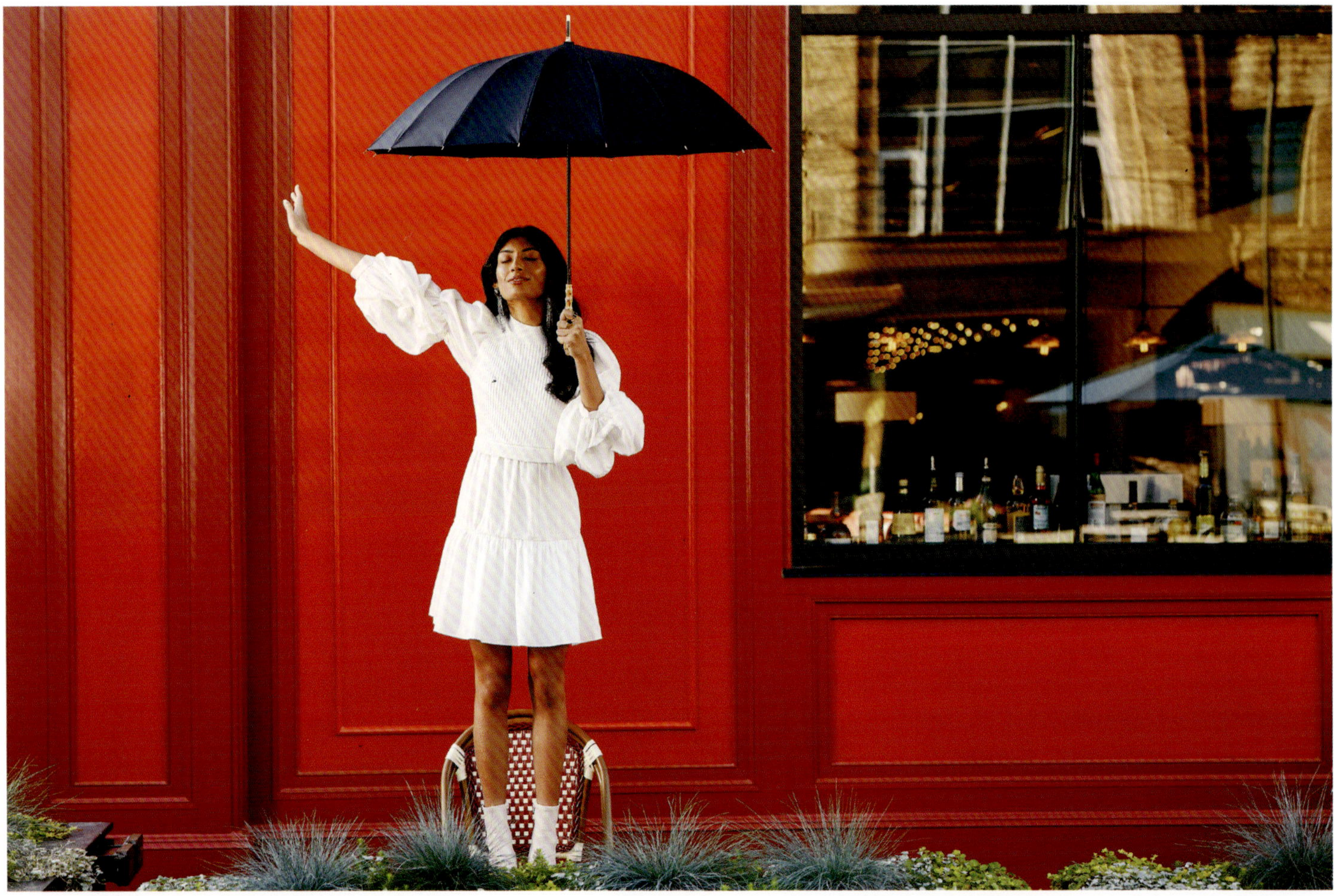

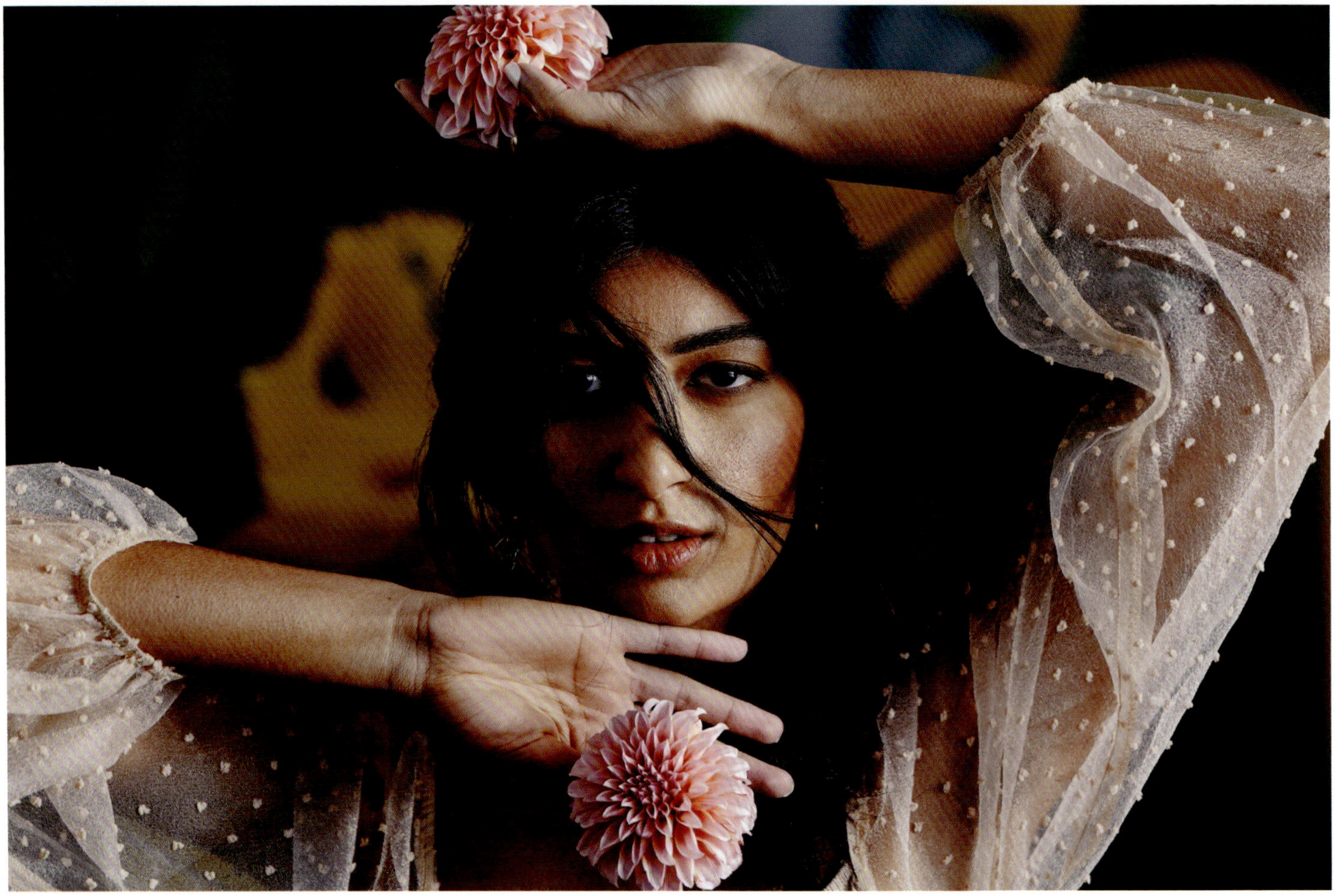

P233: Credit & Commentary

Title: Fenton | **Client:** House of Current

Images 1, 2 of 7

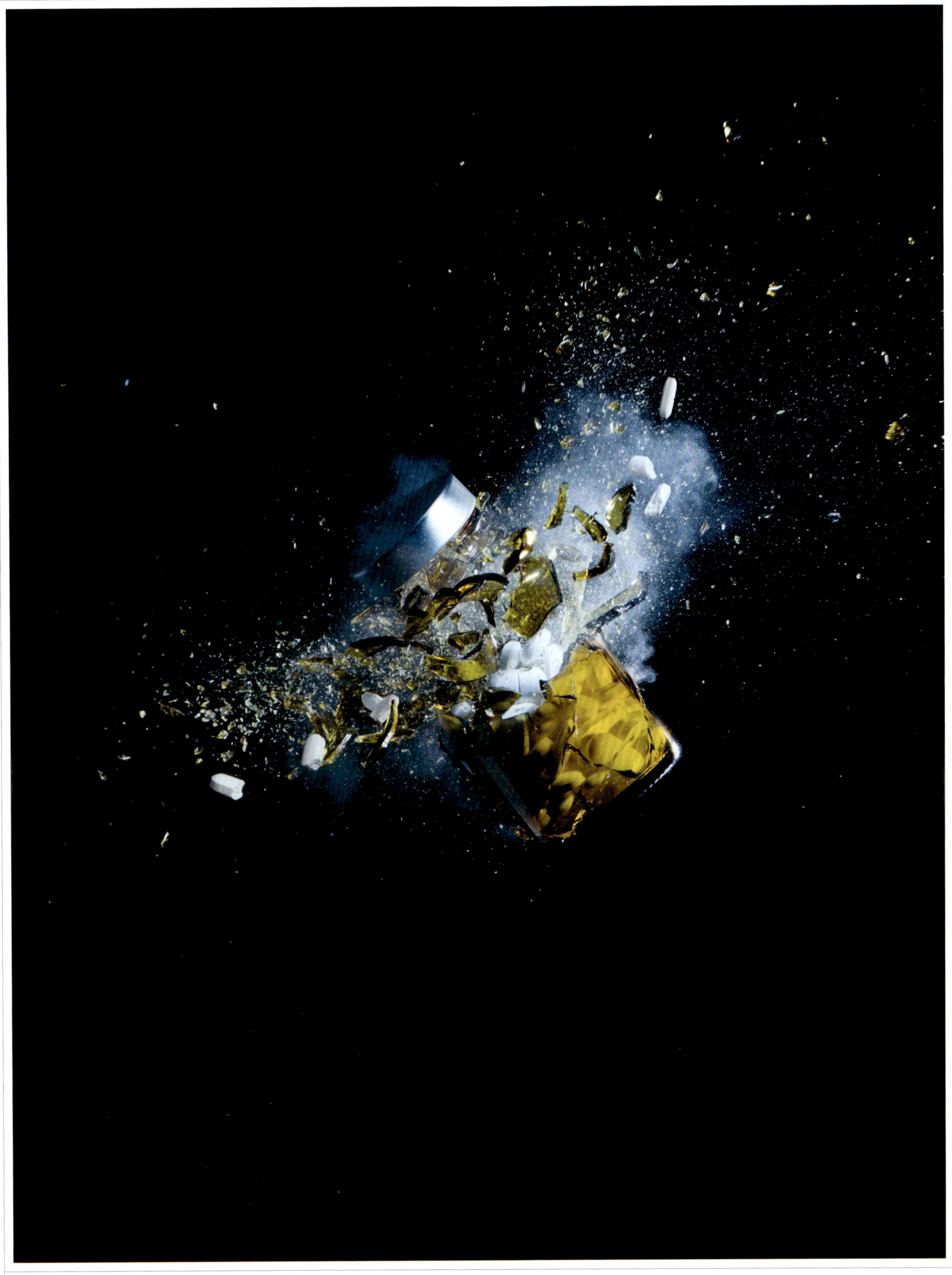

P233: Credit & Commentary

Title: Malpractice | **Client:** ITV

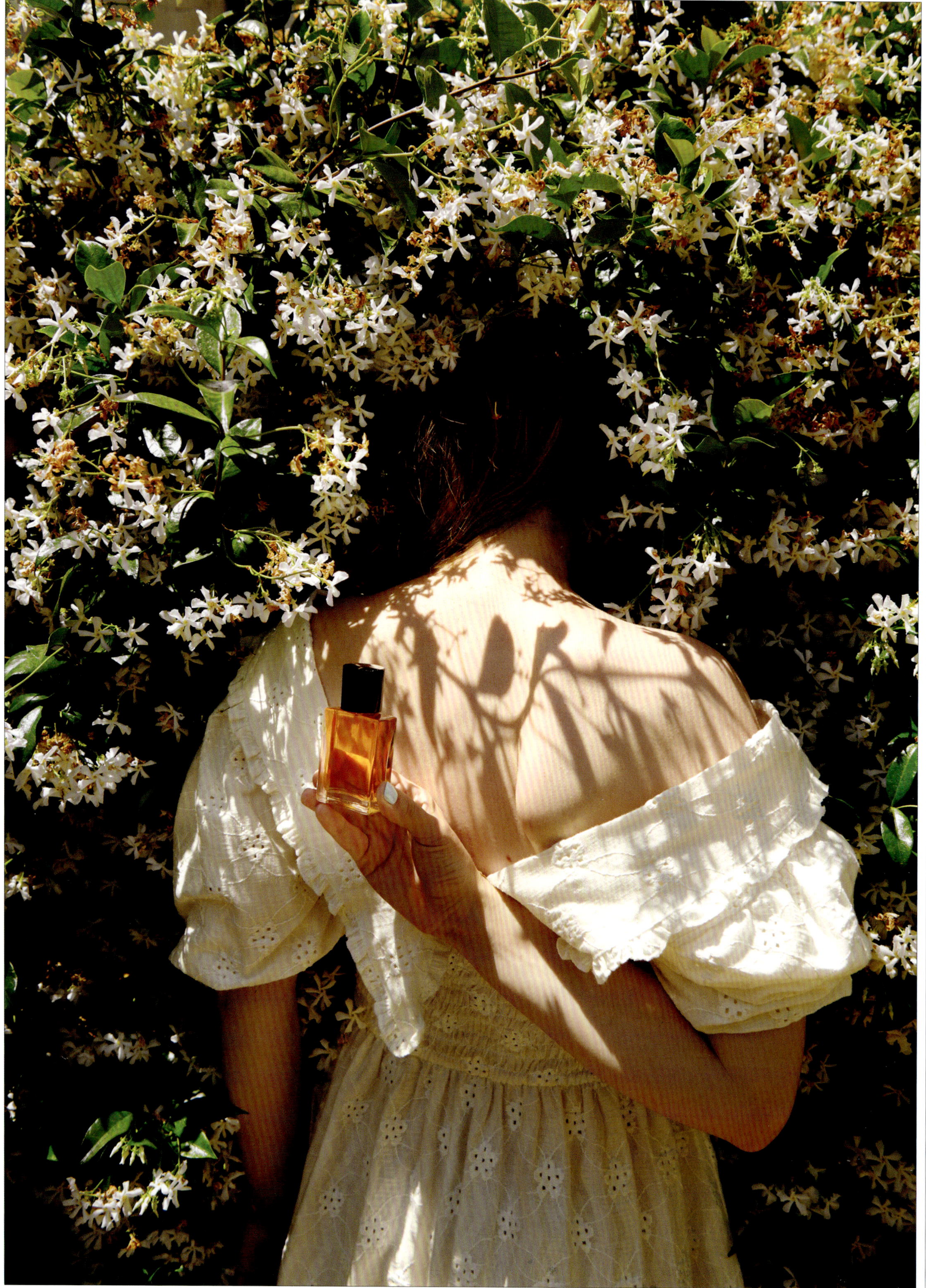

P233: Credit & Commentary

Title: FLWRs | Client: FLWR

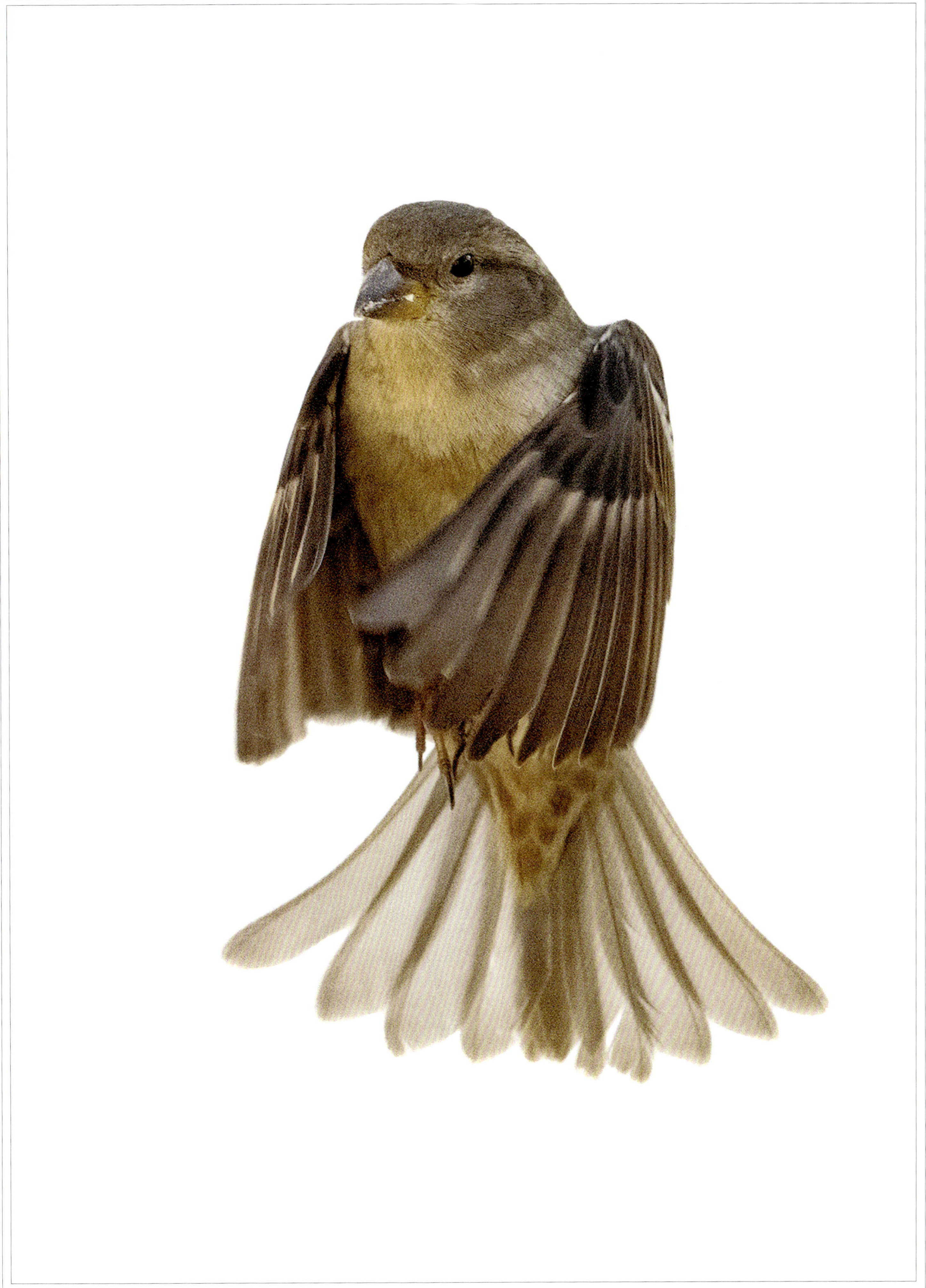

P233: Credit & Commentary

Title: Access to Otherness | Client: Gallerie Japonesque

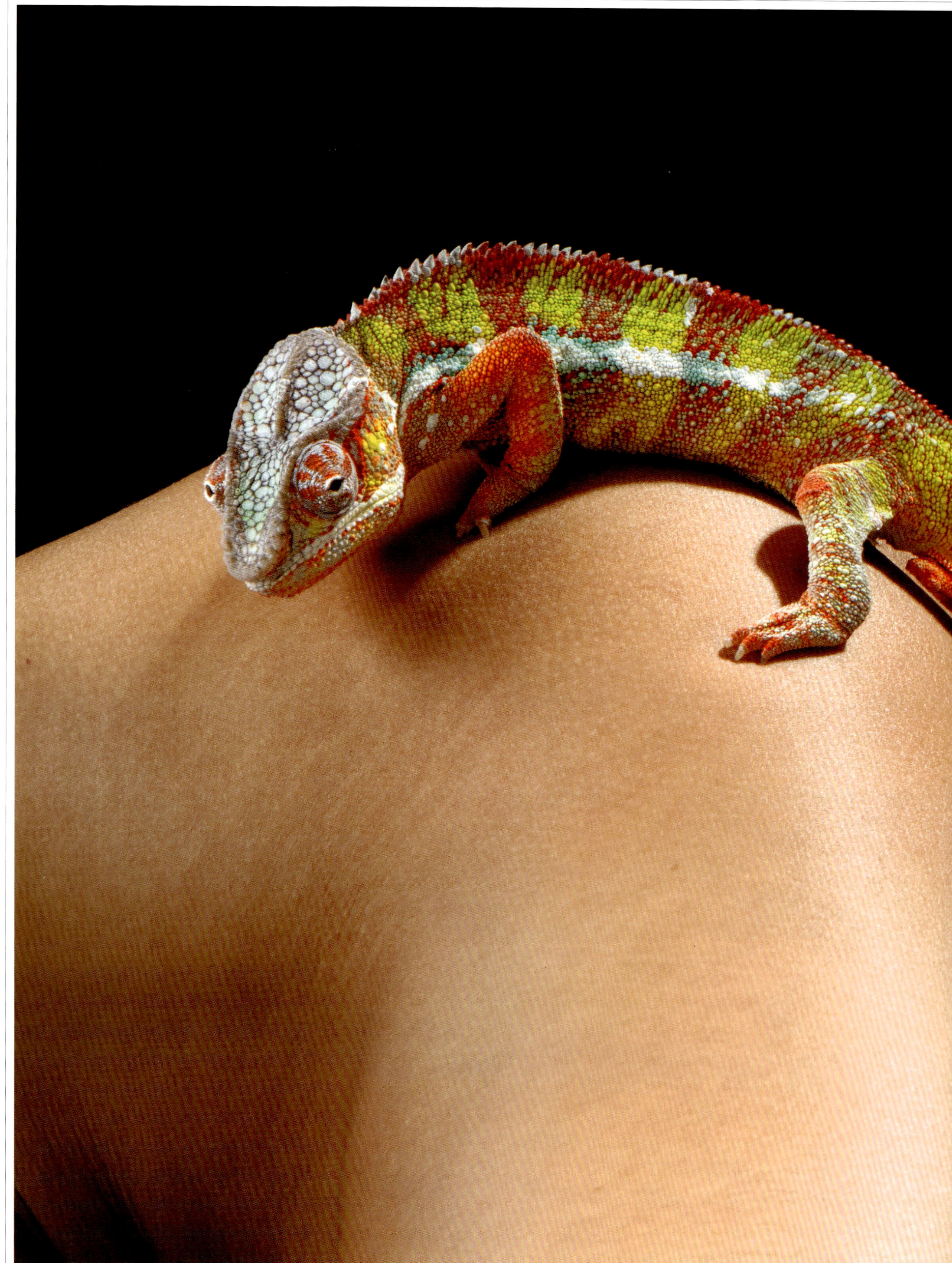

P233: Credit & Commentary

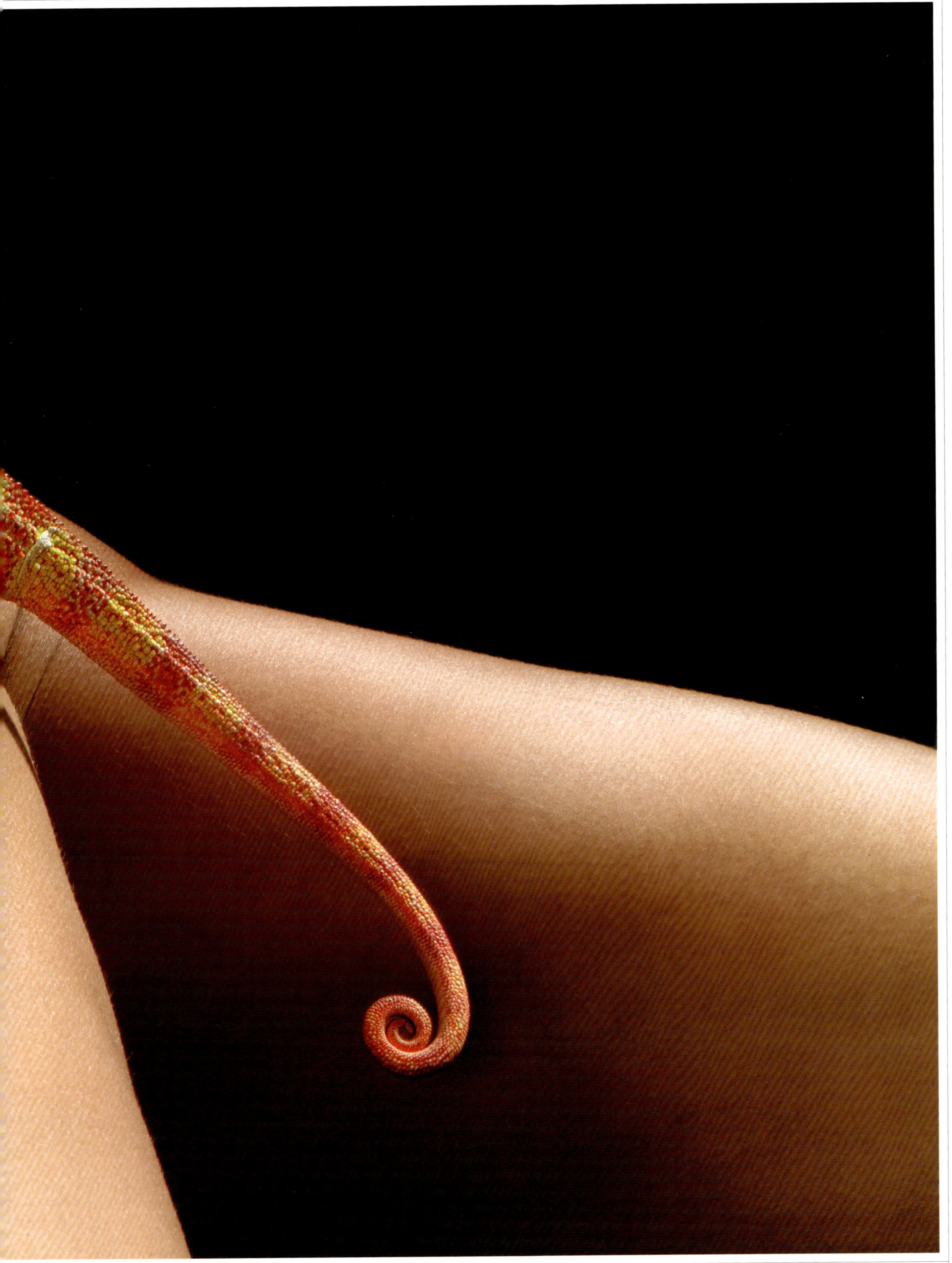

Title: Chameleon Bodyscape | **Client:** Self-initiated

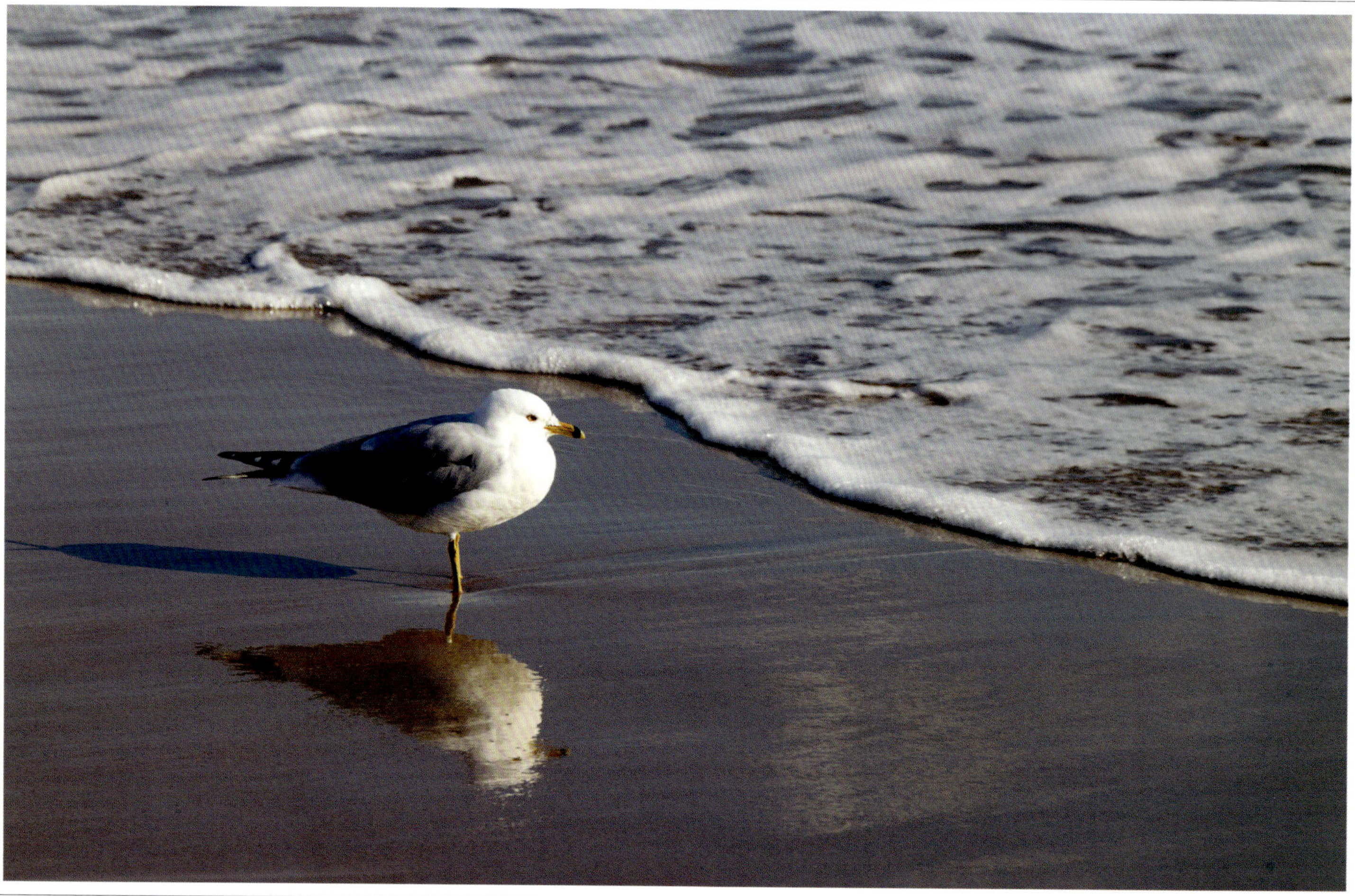

P233: Credit & Commentary **Title:** There is No Way But to Think of This and That | **Client:** Self-initiated

DARNELL MCCOWN GOLD ANIMALS/WILDLIFE

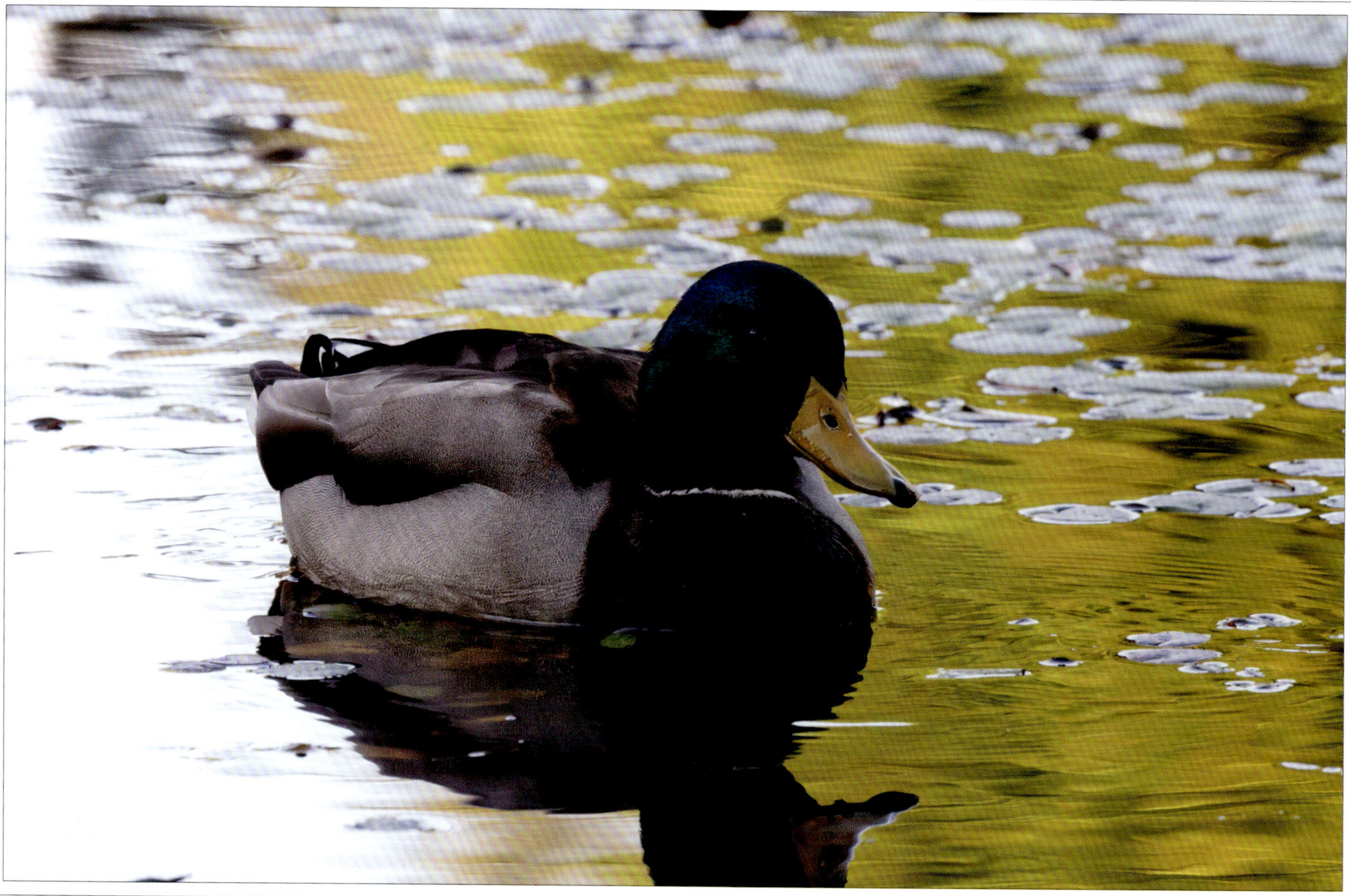

P233: Credit & Commentary **Title:** Mallard | **Client:** Self-initiated

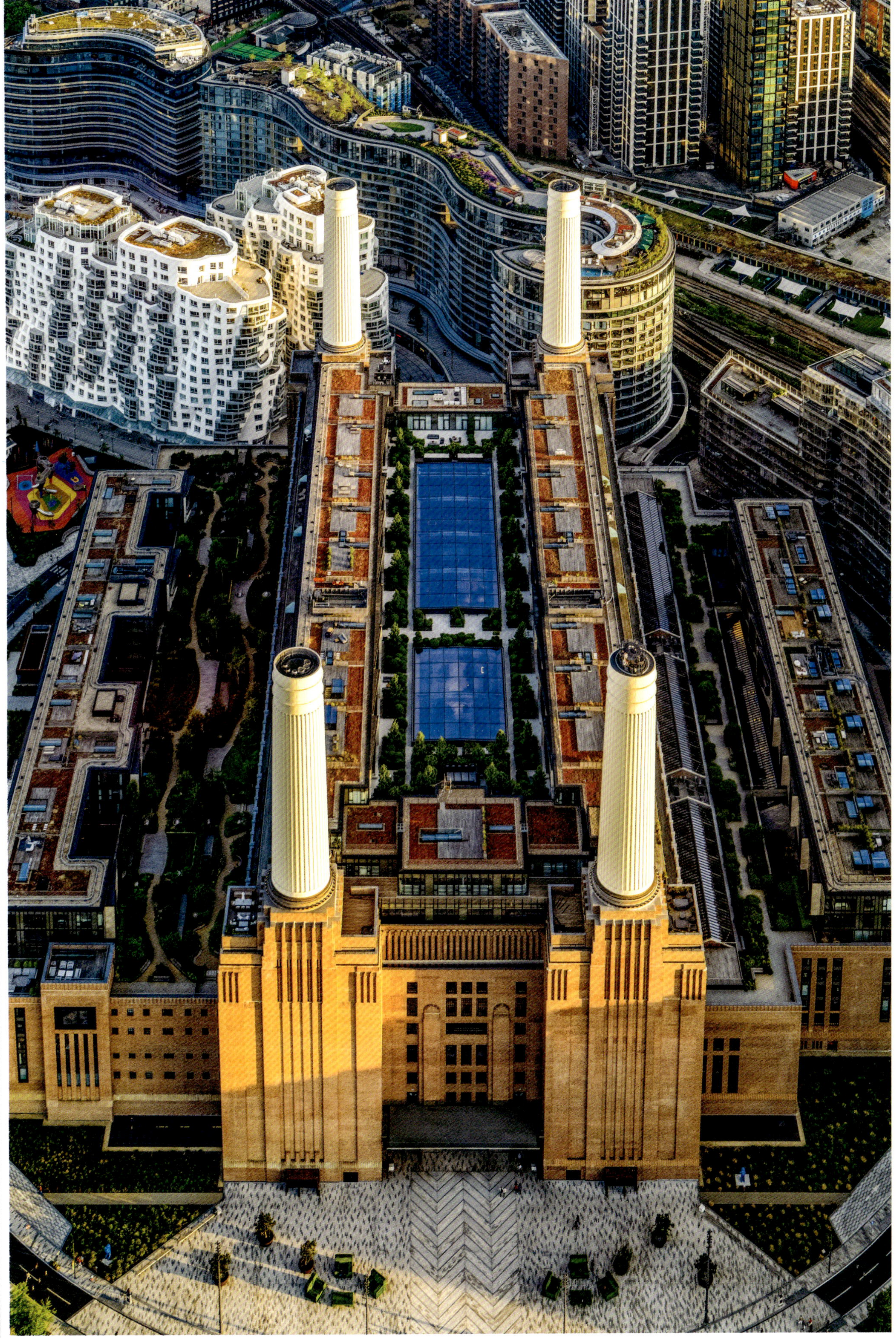

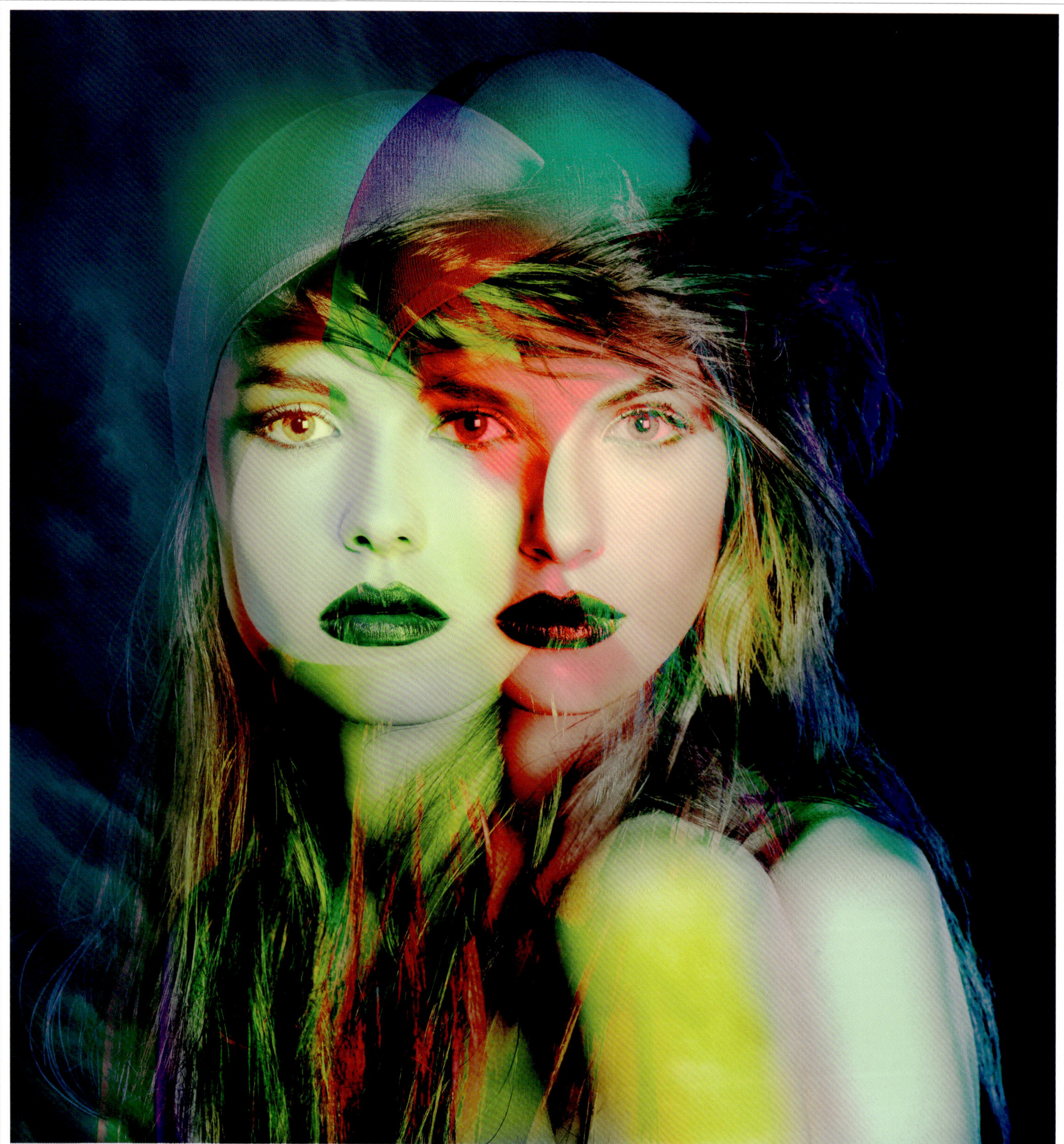

P223: Credit & Commentary

Title: Beauty Study #1516: Model Isabelle Sauer | **Client:** Self-initiated

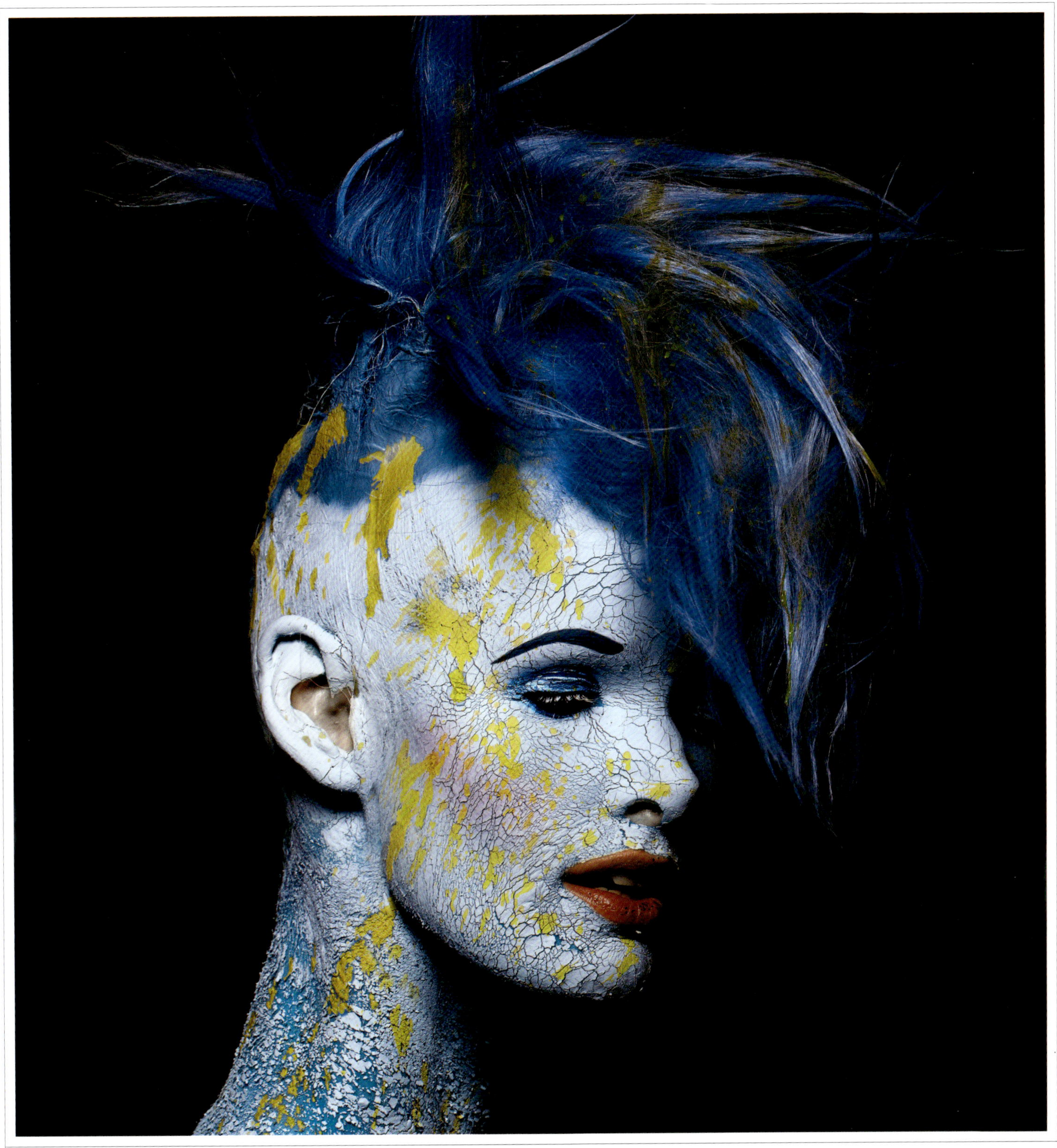

P223: Credit & Commentary

Title: Beauty Study #1126: Model Emilie Adams | **Client:** Self-initiated

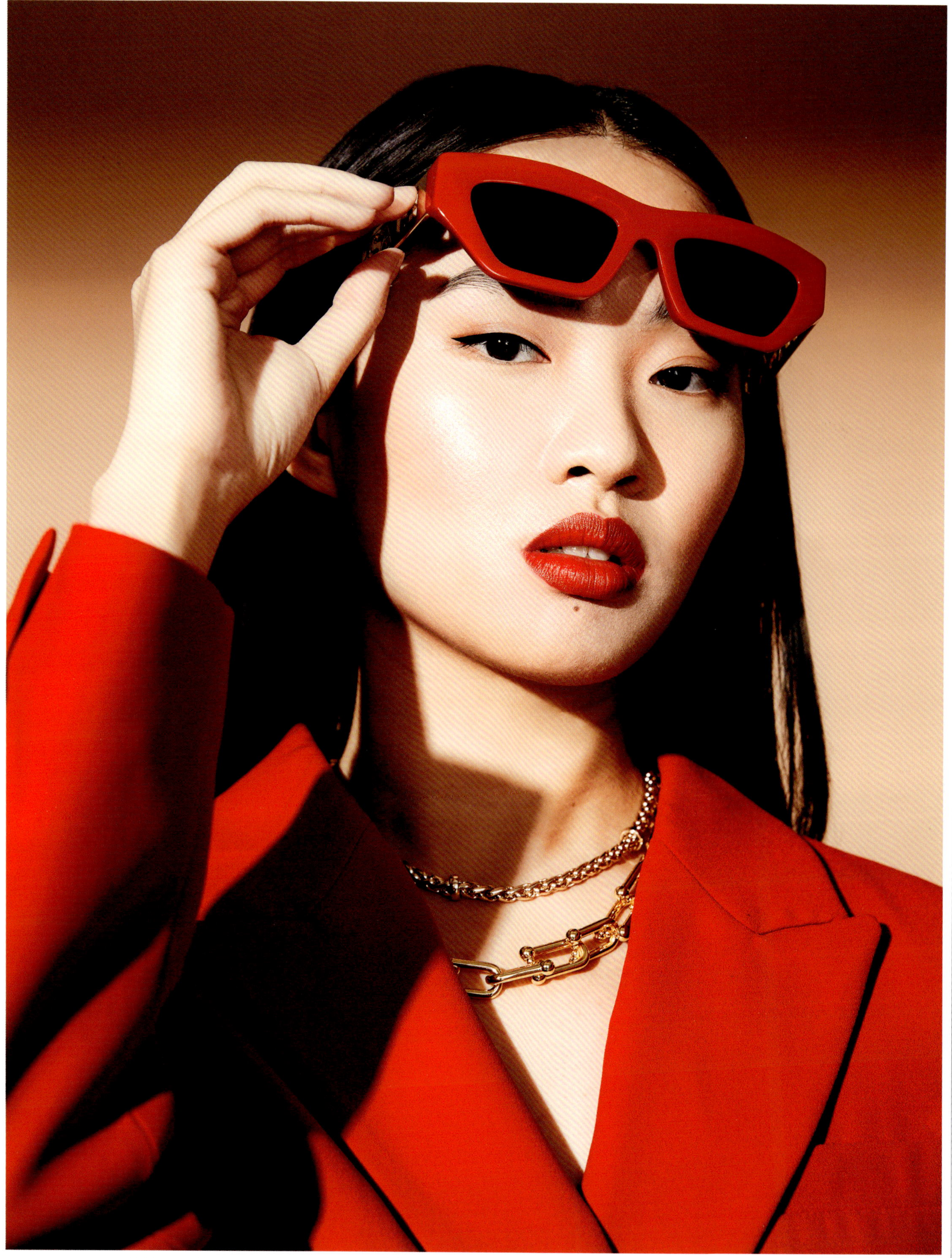

P233: Credit & Commentary

Title: Regal Lips | **Client:** Self-initiated

Image 1 of 2

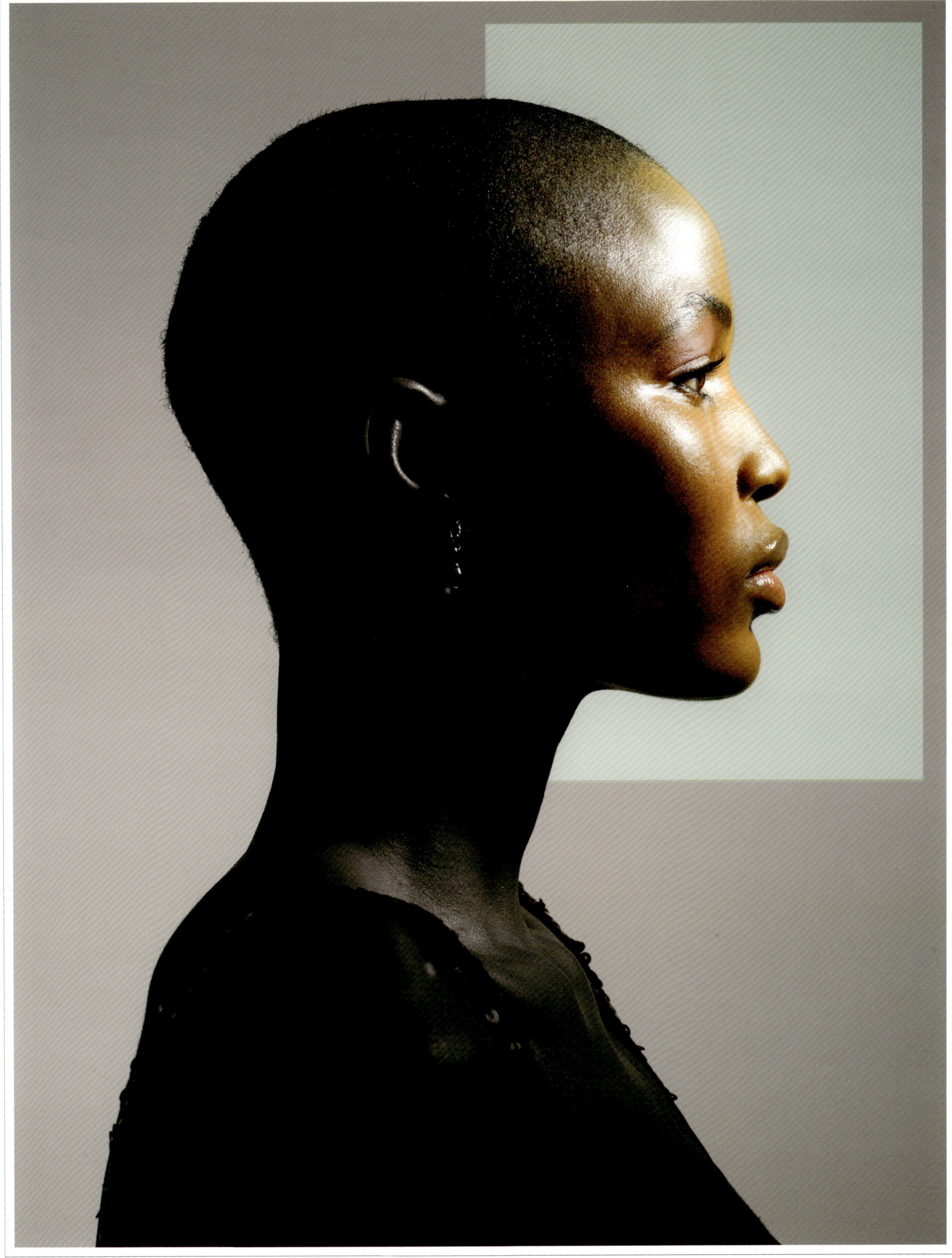

P233: Credit & Commentary

Title: Geometric Beauty | Client: Getty Images Creative

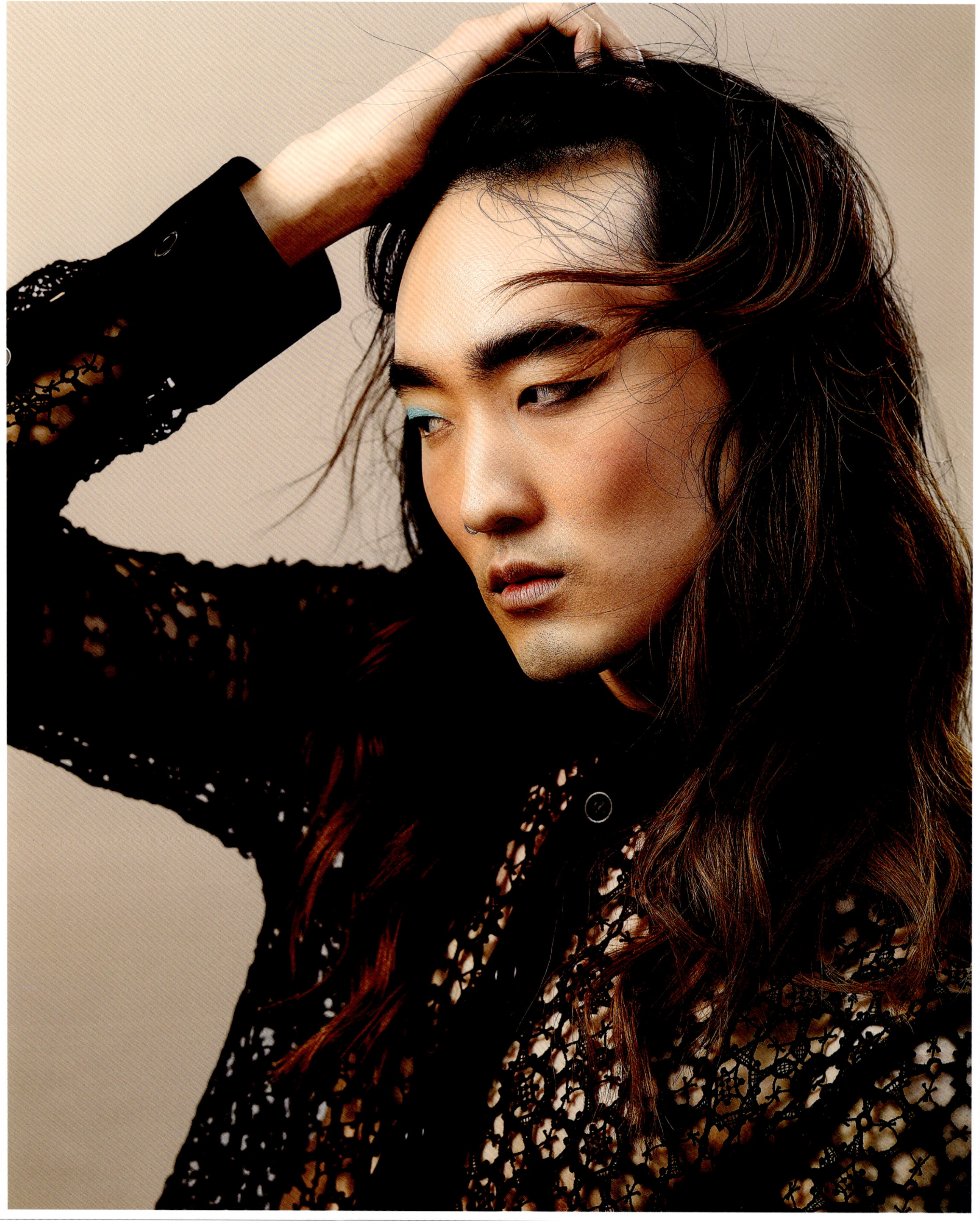

P233: Credit & Commentary Title: Beauty: Clean | Clients: House of Current, Self-initiated Image 1 of 4

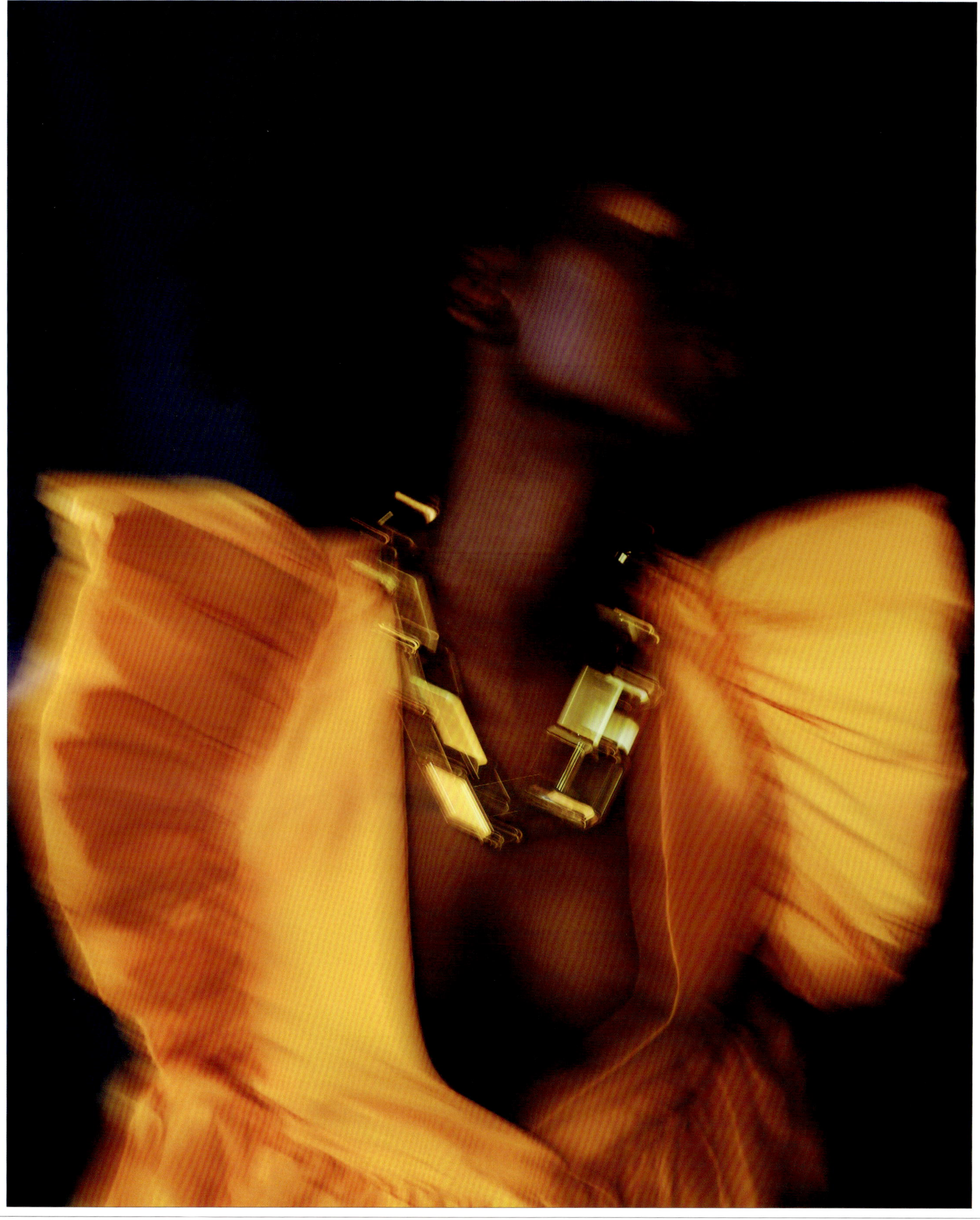

P233: Credit & Commentary

Title: Beauty: Motion | **Clients:** House of Current, Self-initiated

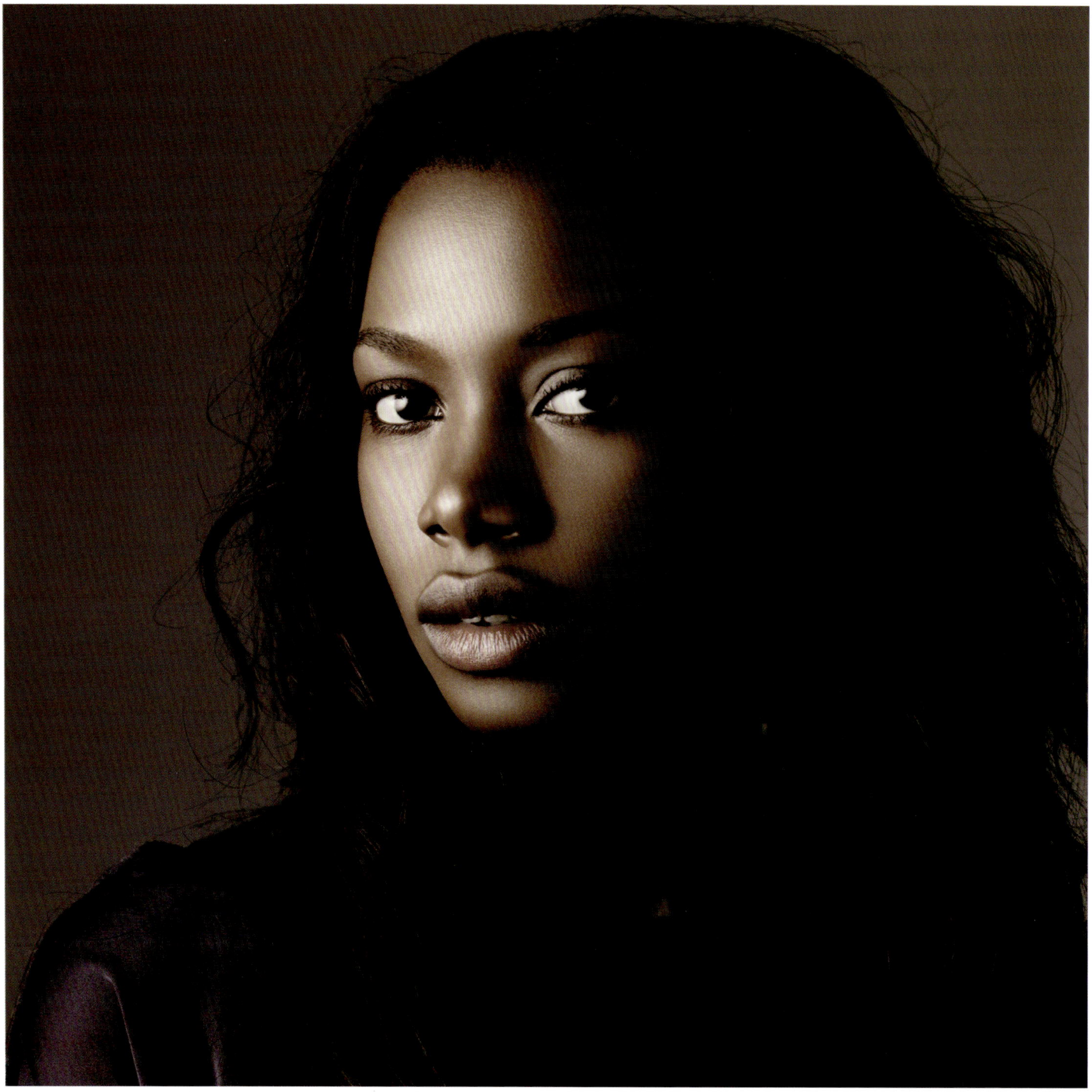

P234: Credit & Commentary

Title: Beauty Study #1386: Sigail Currie | **Client:** Self-initiated

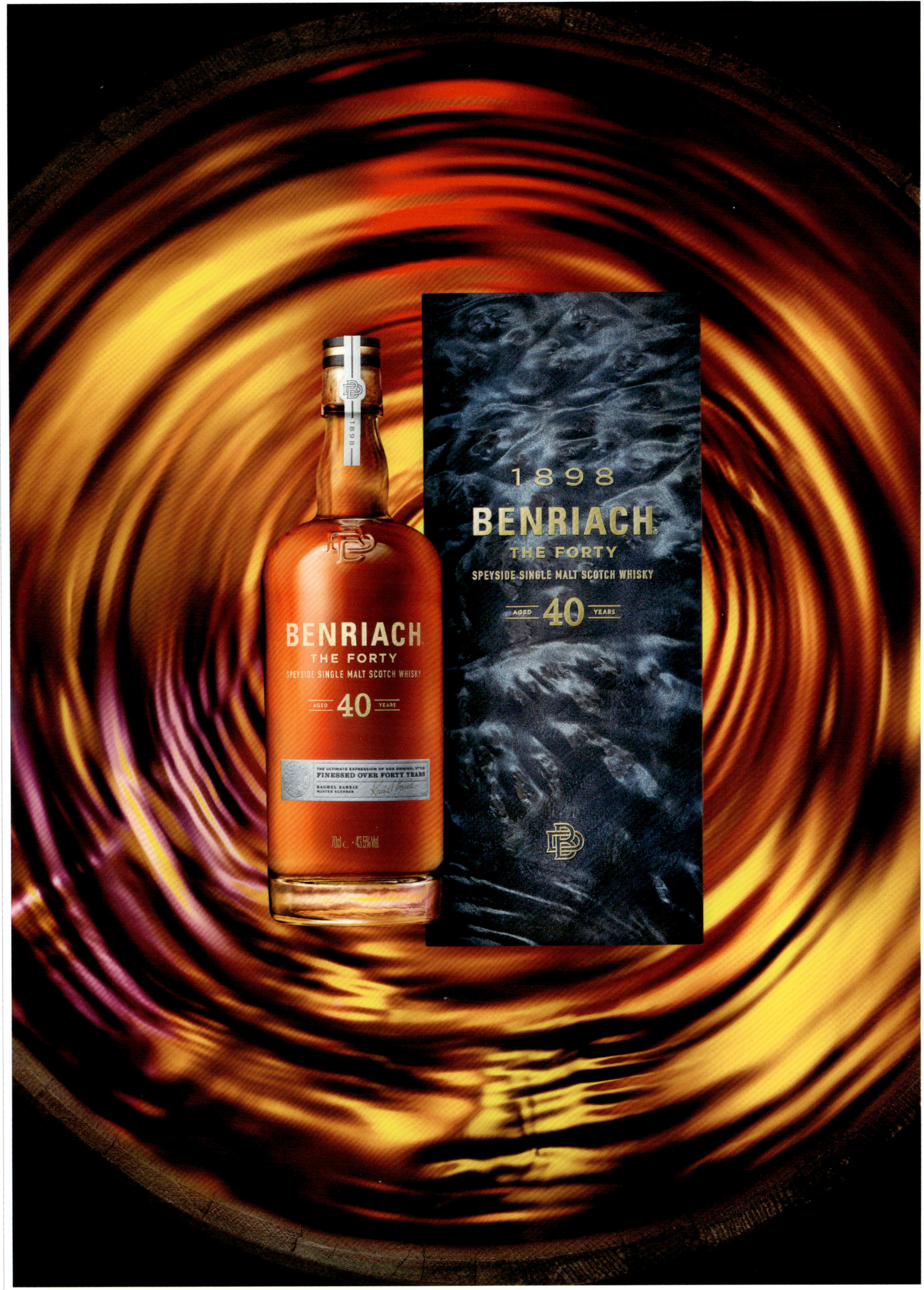

Title: Benriach: The Forty Year Old | **Client:** Benriach

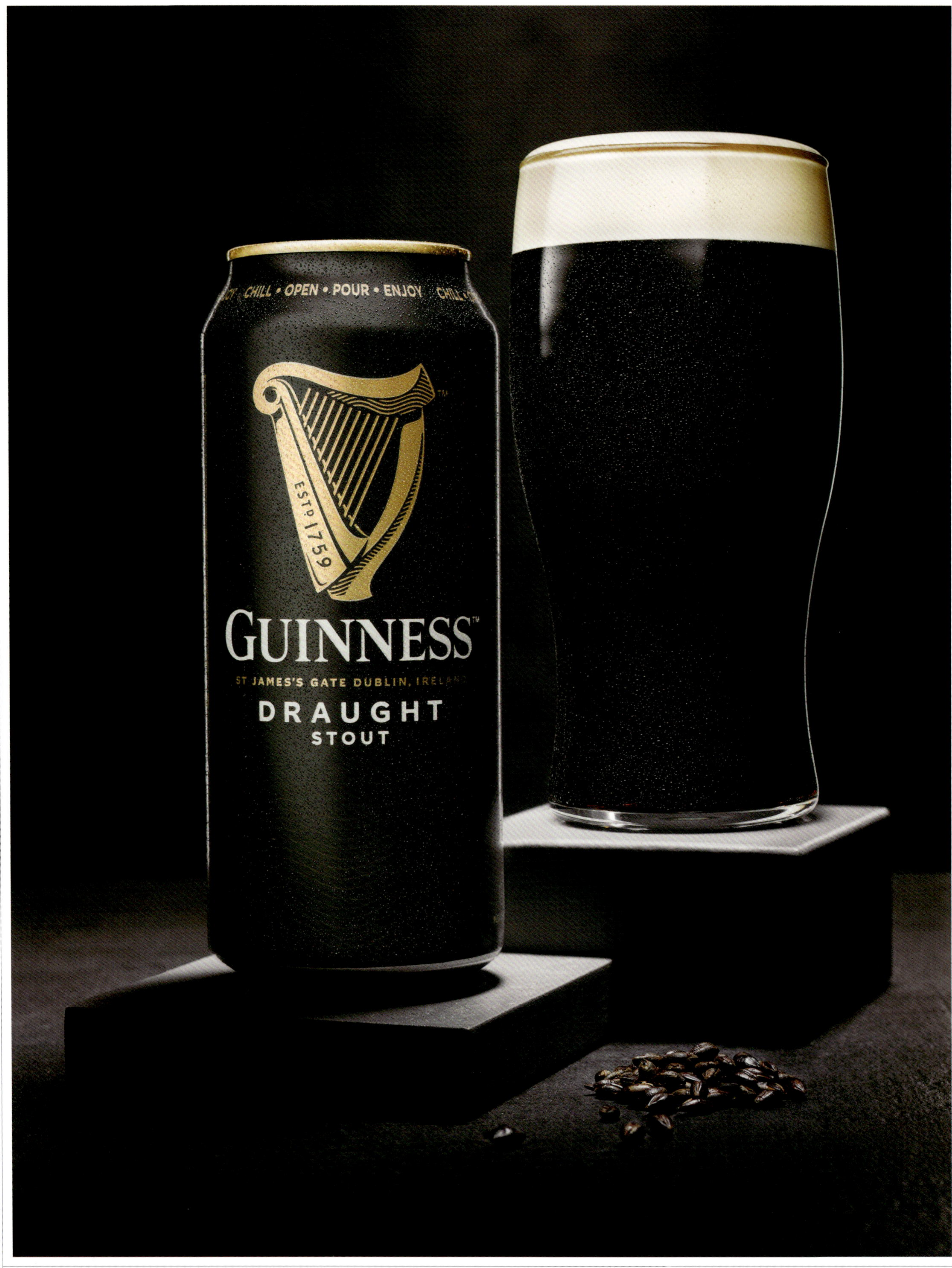

P234: Credit & Commentary Title: Madira Beer App | Client: Madira

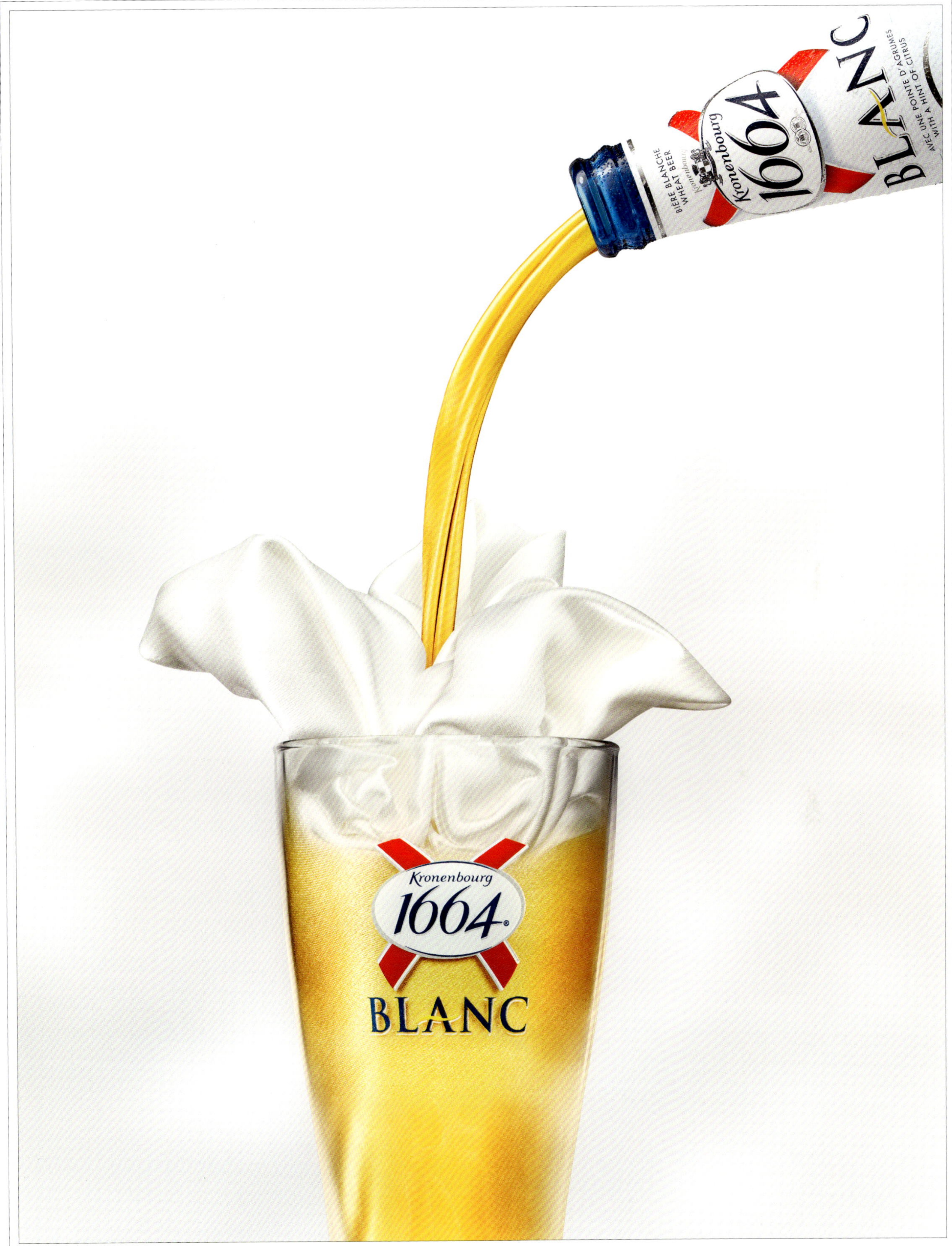

P234: Credit & Commentary

Title: Kronenbourg 1664 Blanc | Client: Carlsberg

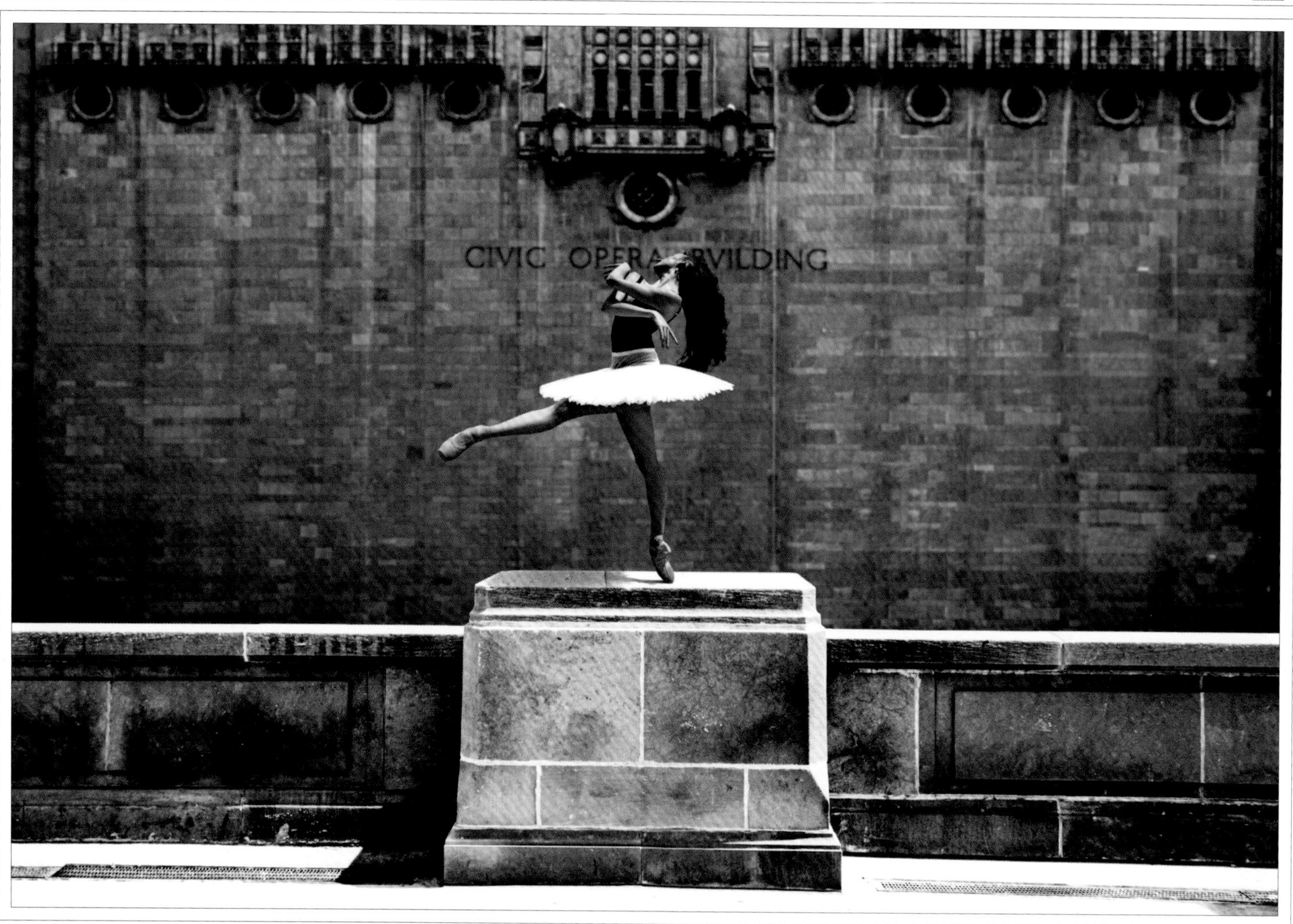

Title: Viola Bella at The Opera House in Chicago | Summer 2023
Client: Self-initiated | **P234:** Credit & Commentary

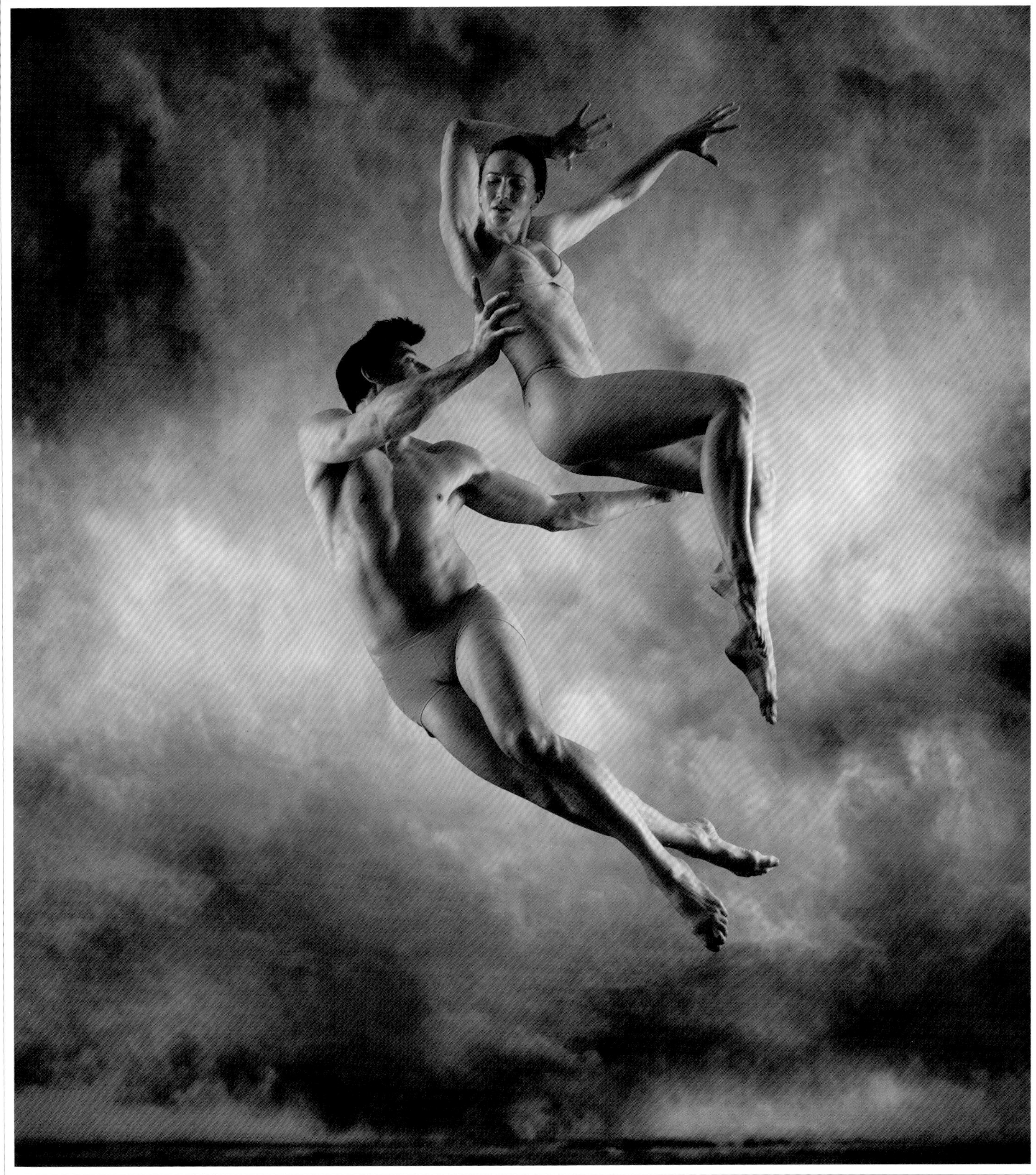

Title: Human Body Study, PAIRS #128: Dancers Casey Howes & Jake Warren
Client: Self-initiated | **P234:** Credit & Commentary

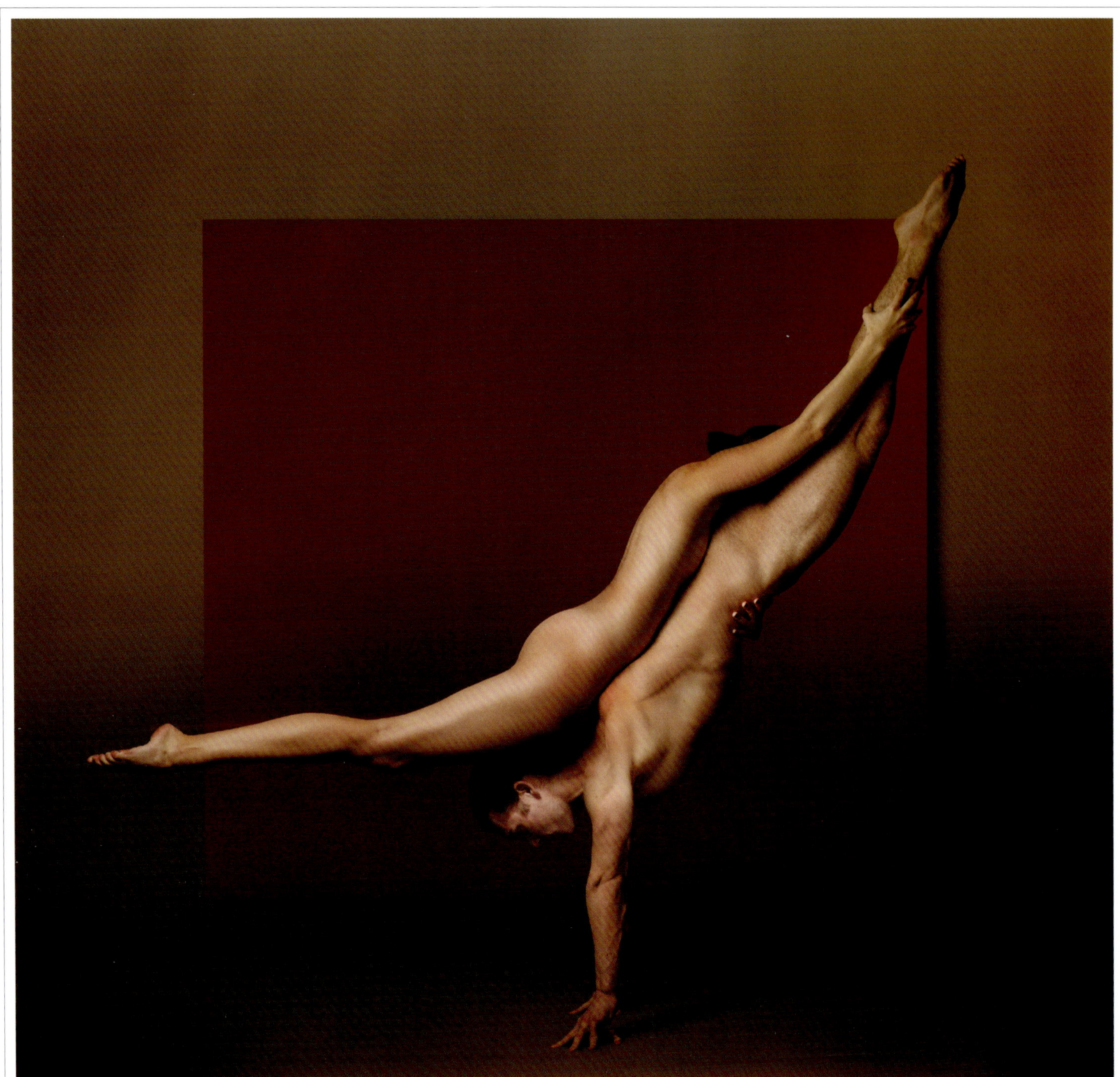

Title: Human Body Study, PAIRS #106: Dancers Elijah Dillehay & Holly Wilder
Client: Self-initiated | **P234:** Credit & Commentary

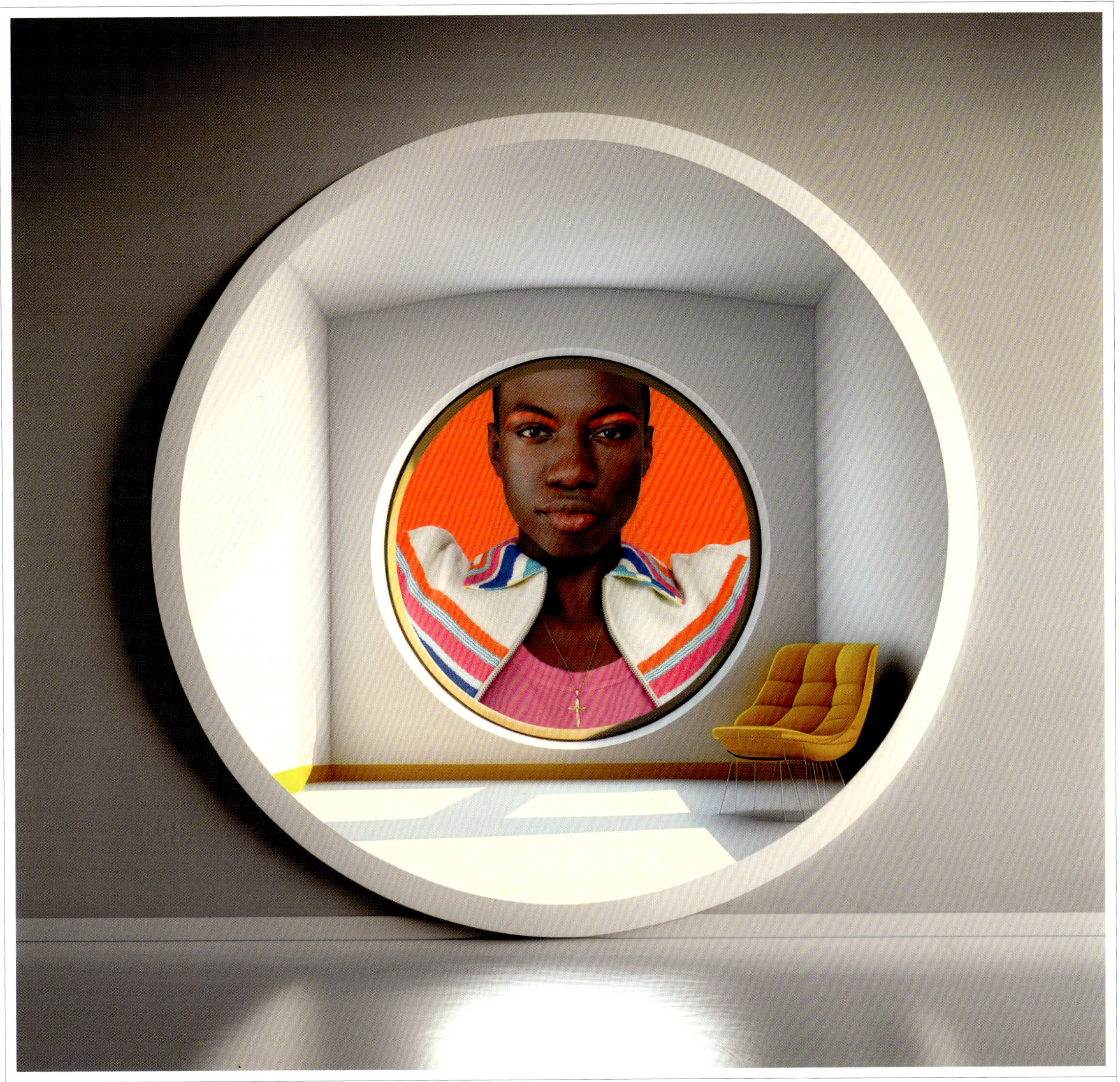

Title: Text to Dance | **Client:** San Francisco Ballet
P234: Credit & Commentary | Image 1 of 7

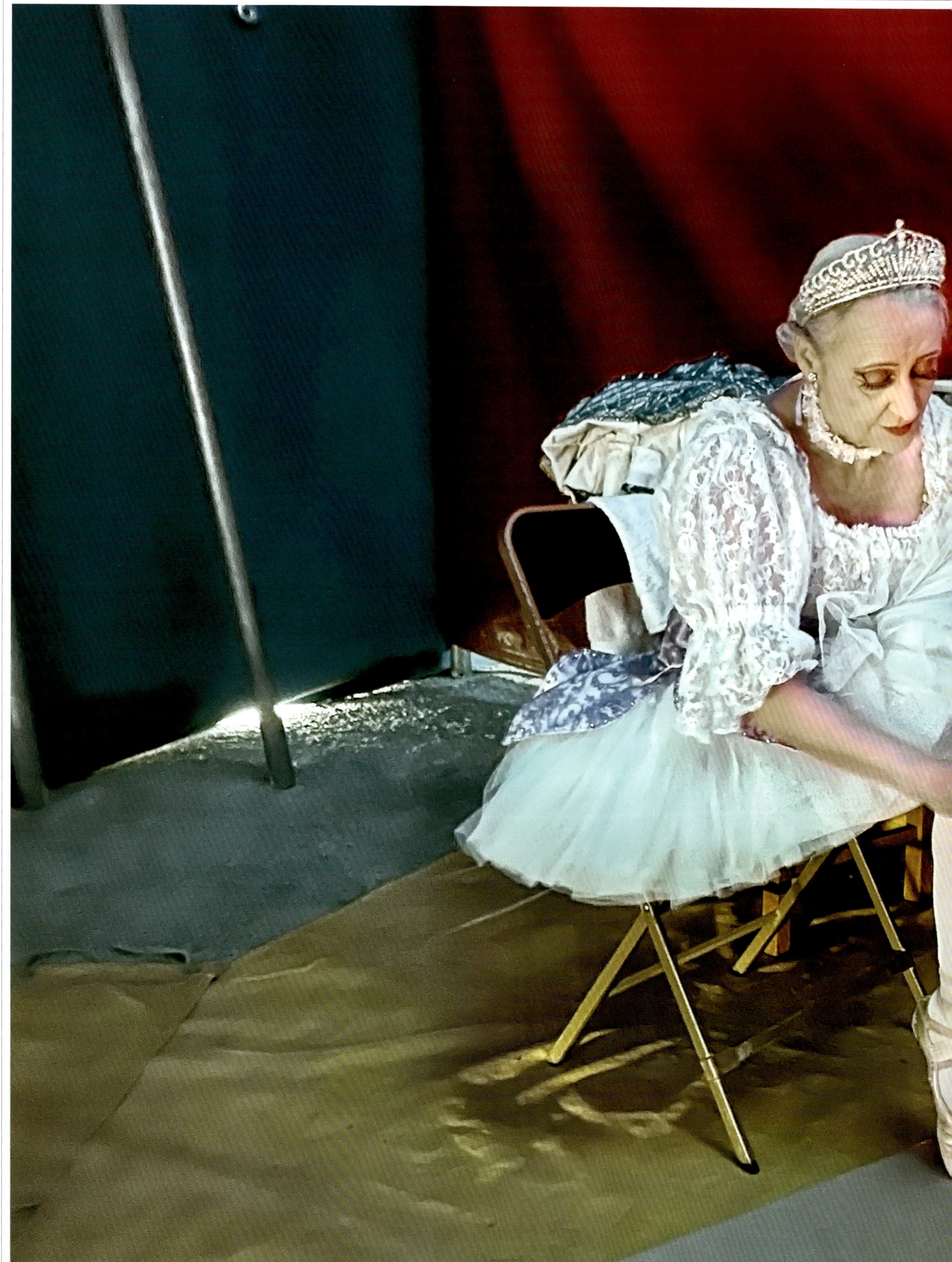

P234: Credit & Commentary

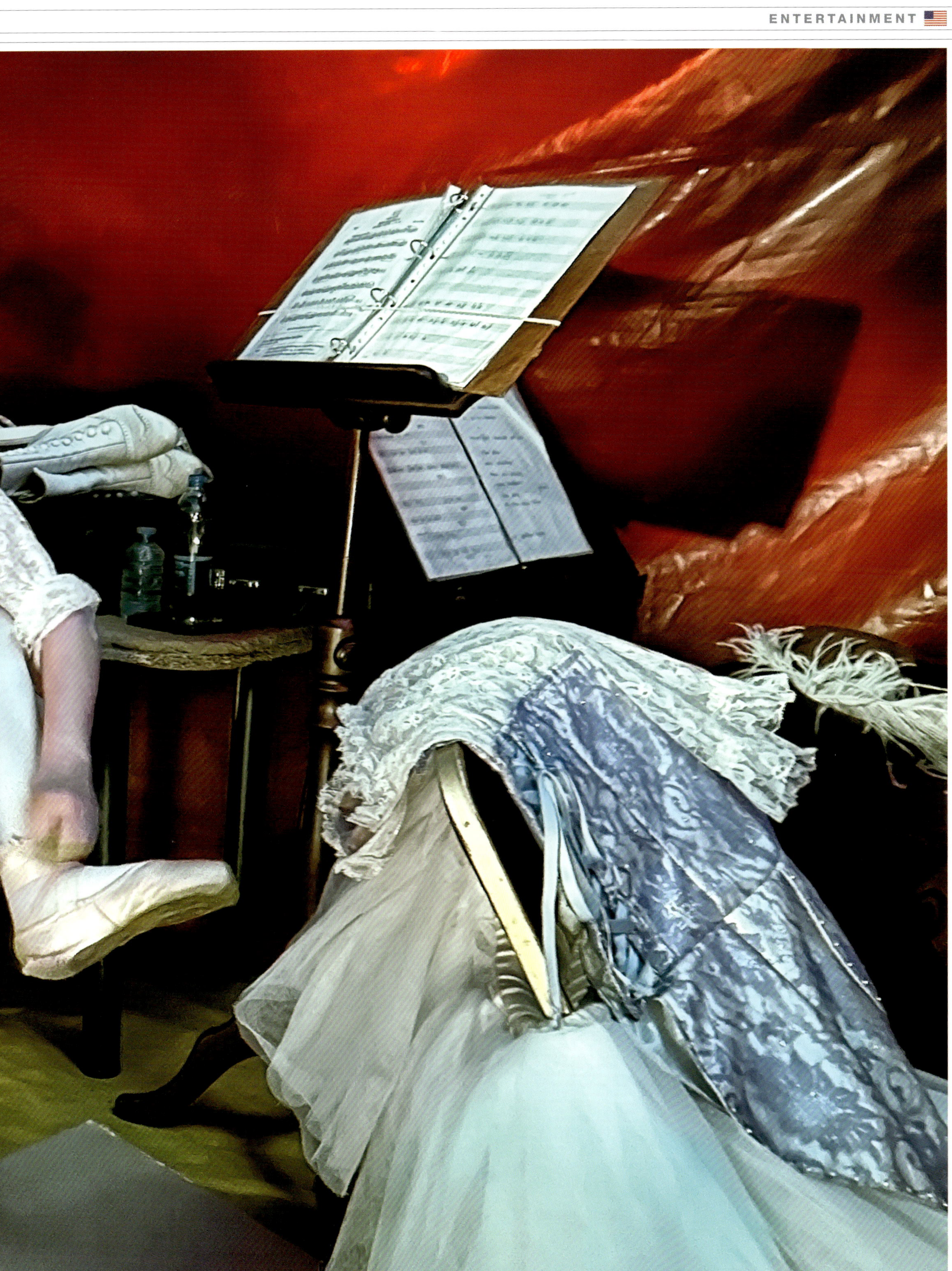

Title: Circus Tähti | **Client:** Self-initiated

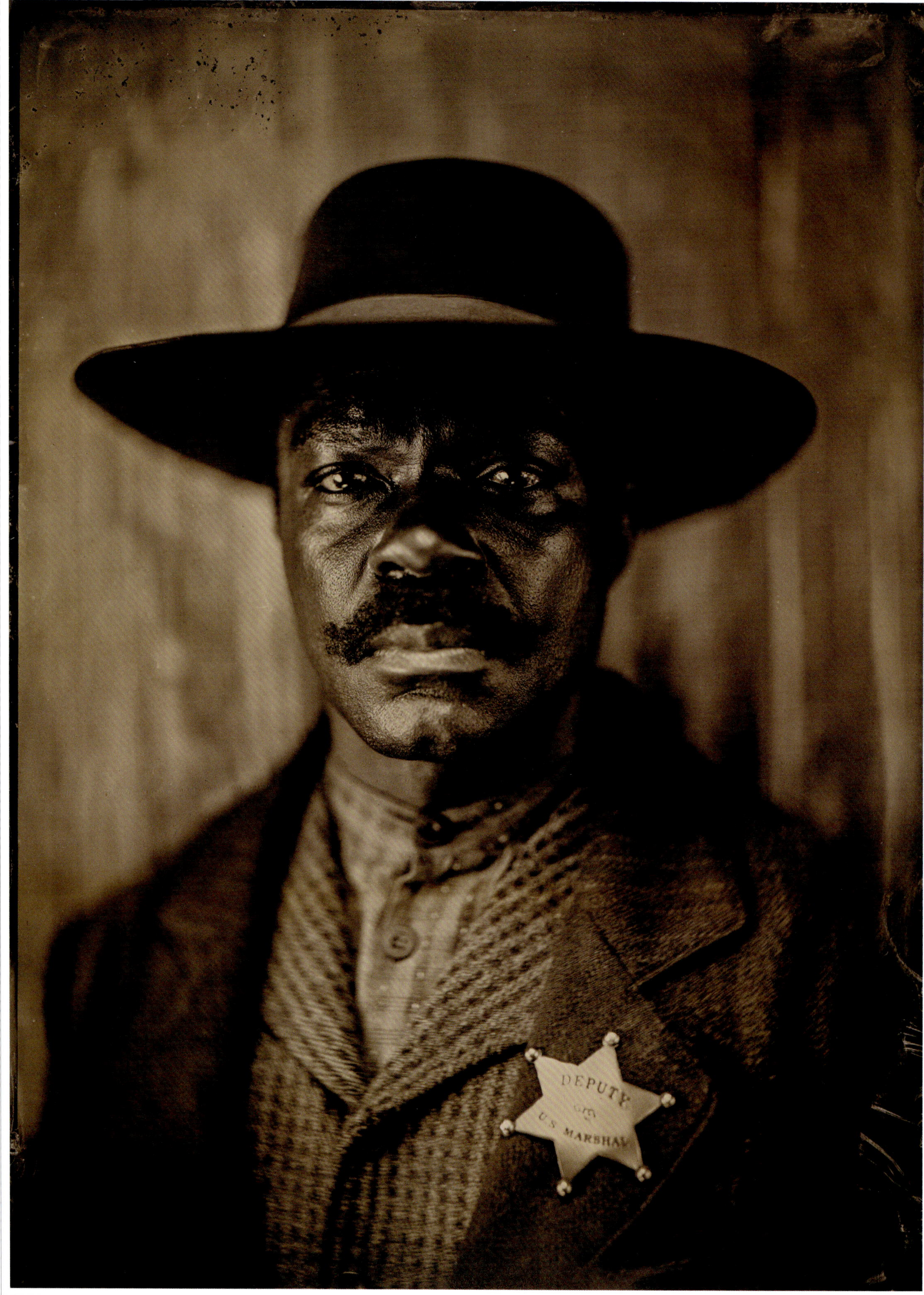

Title: Lawmen Bass Reeves Tin Types Portraits | **Client:** Paramount+

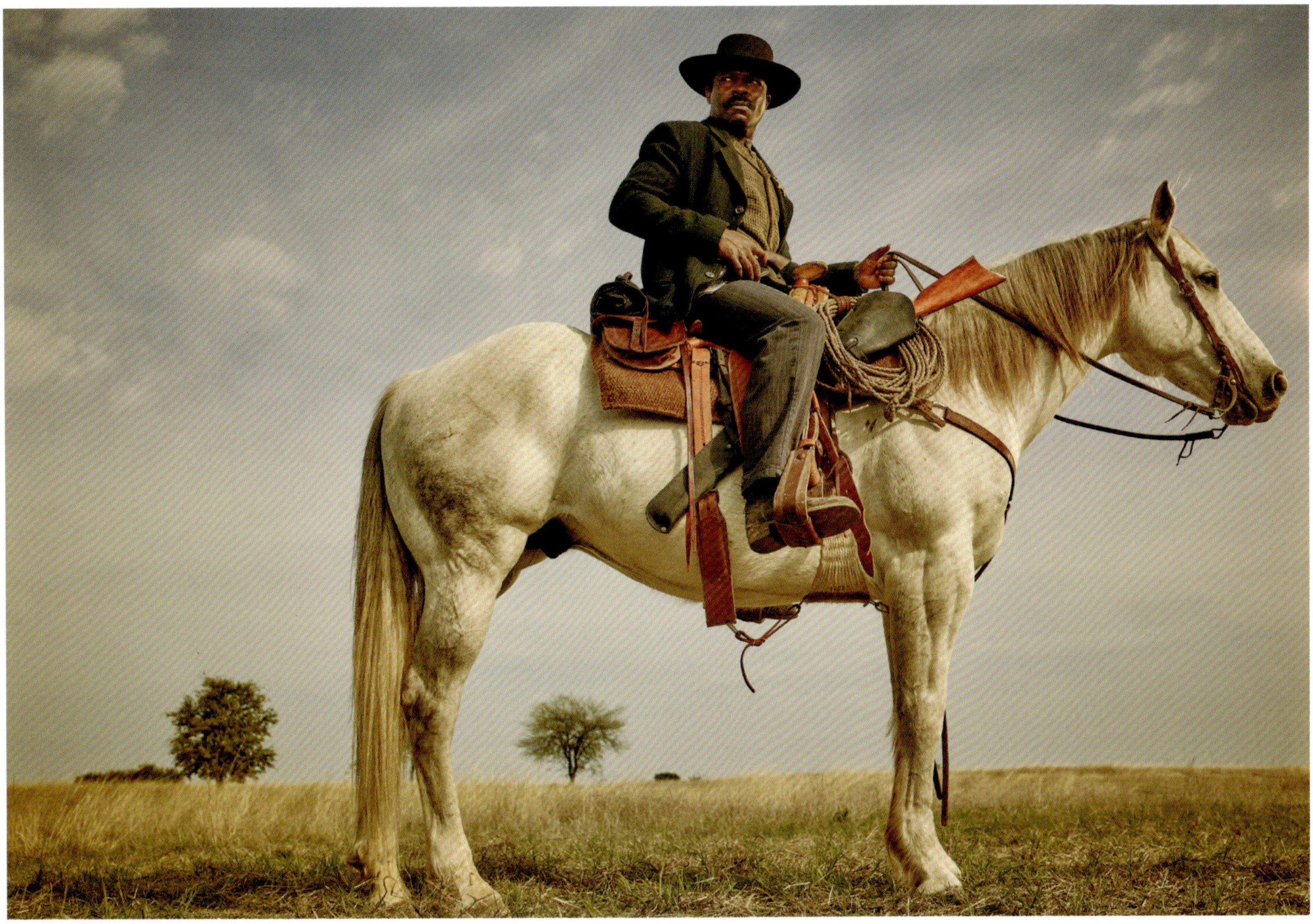

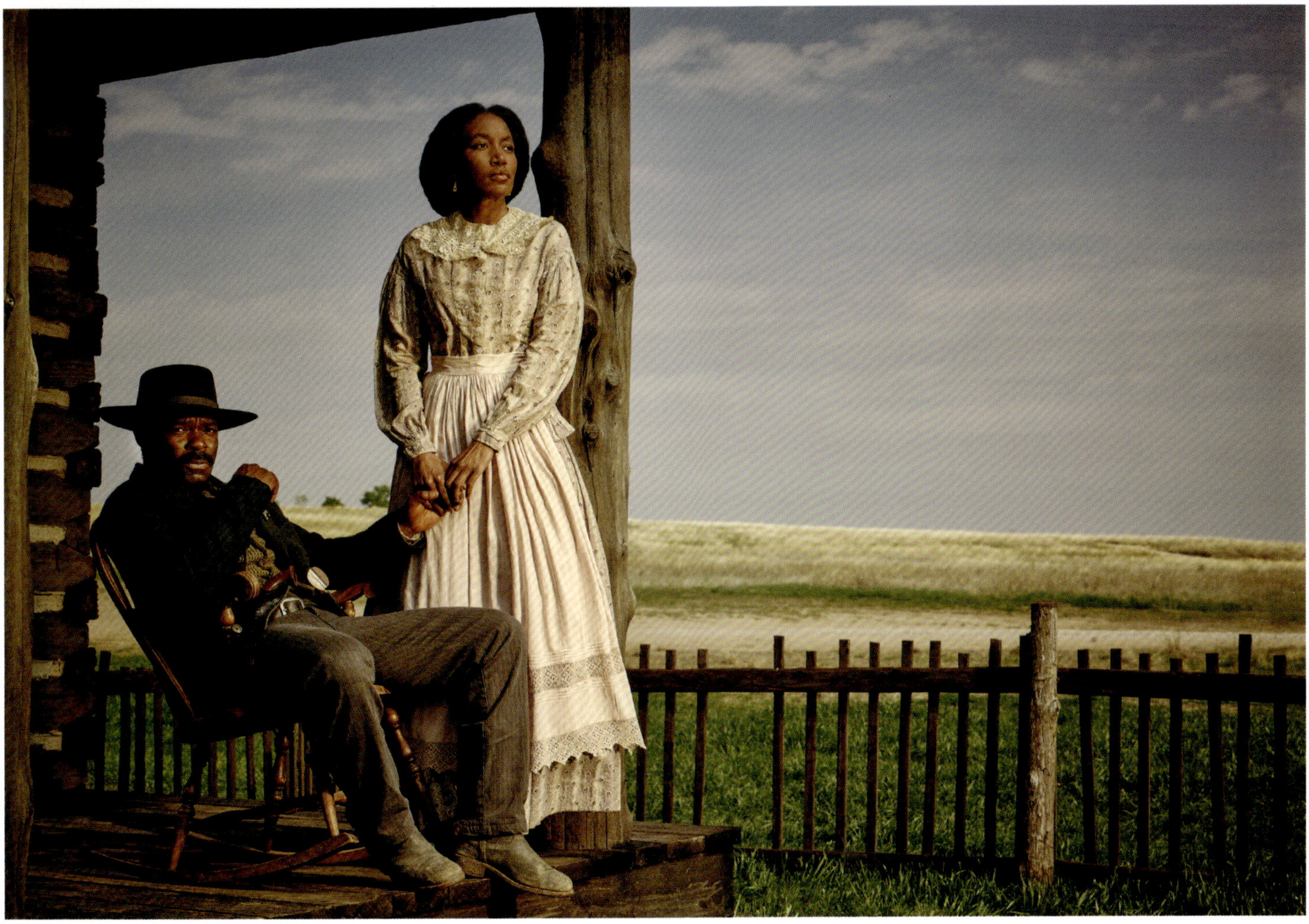

Title: Lawmen Bass Reeves Environmental Portraits | Client: Paramount+

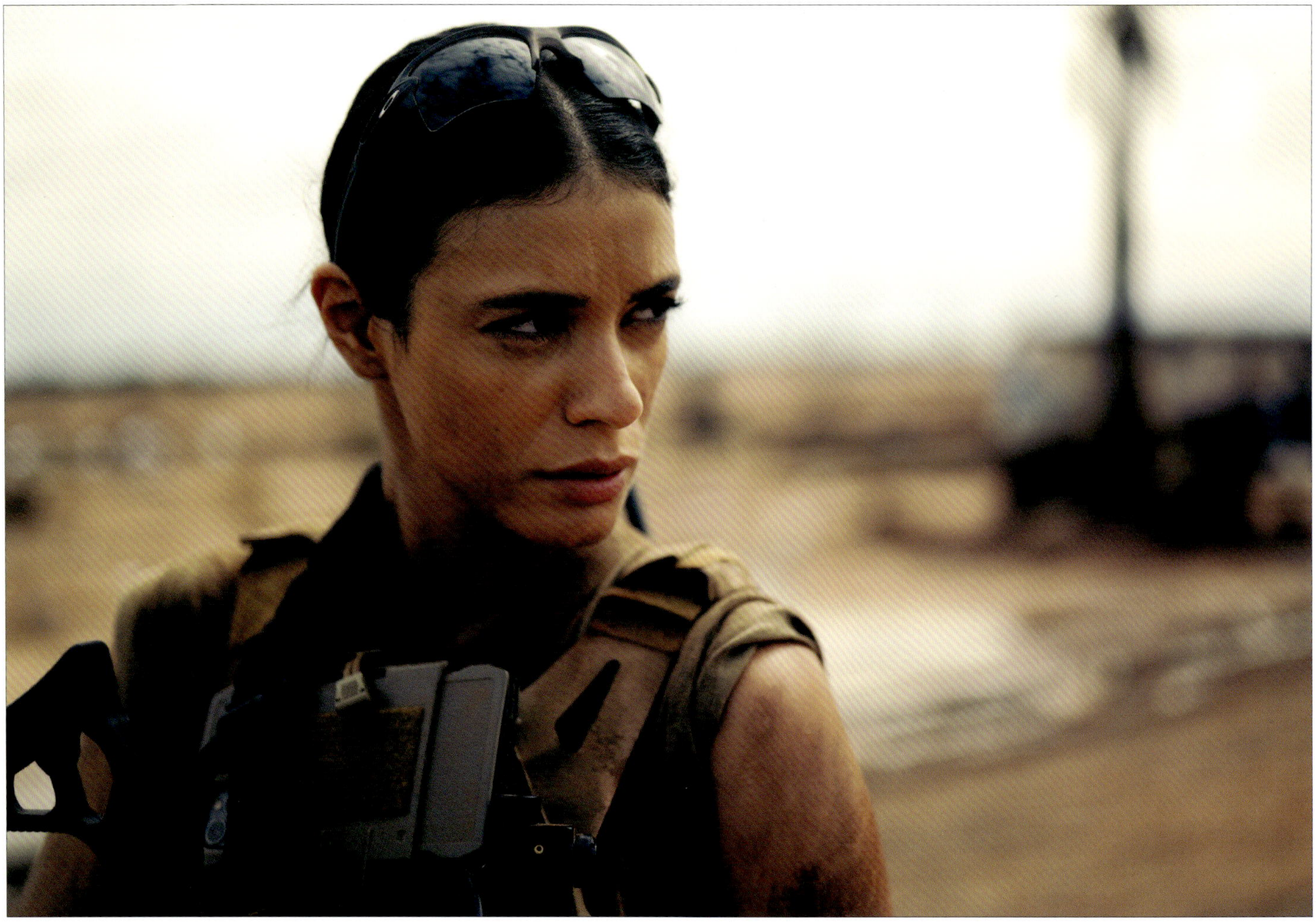

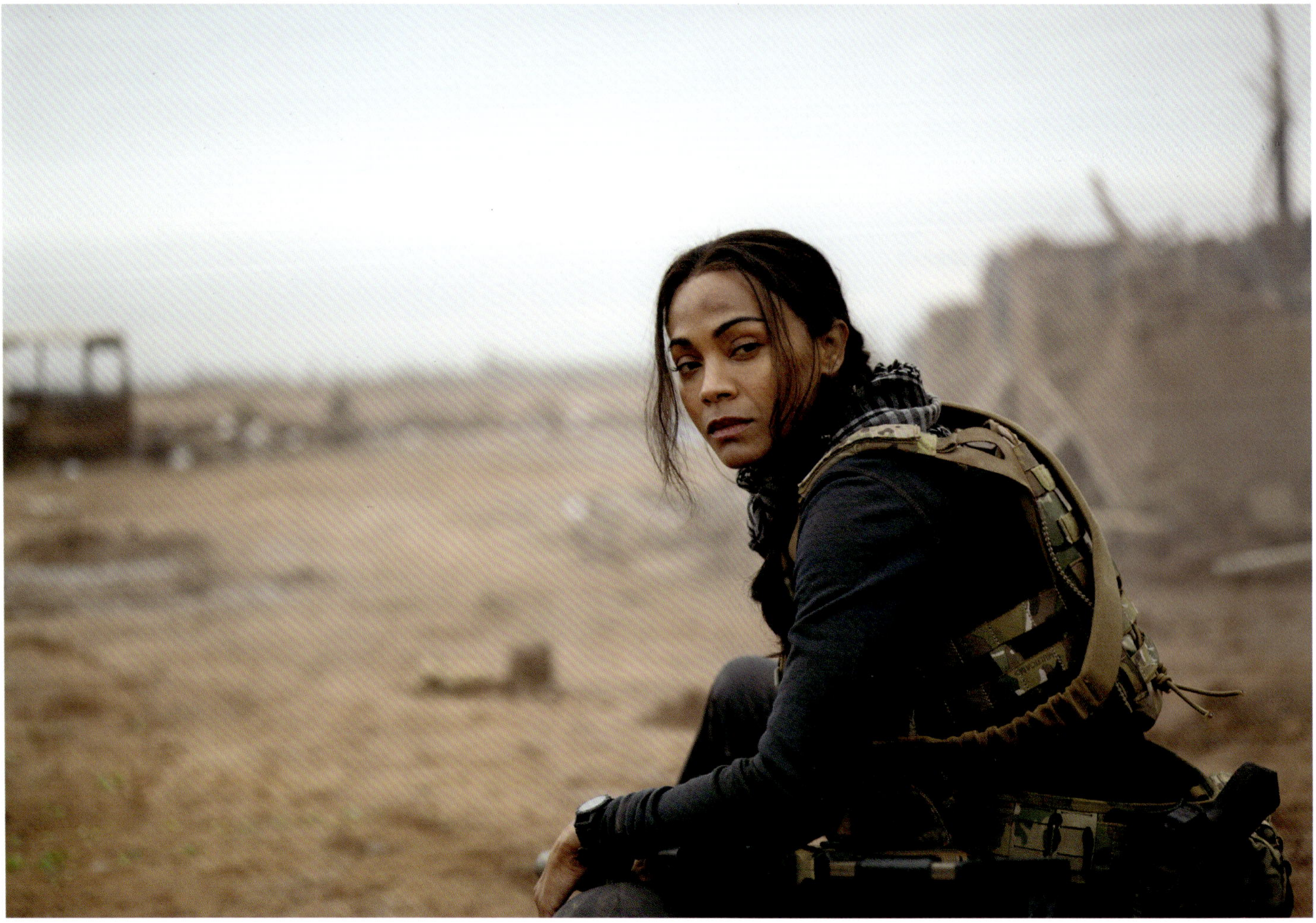

Title: Special Ops: Lioness Environmental Portraits | **Client:** Paramount+

Images 1, 2 of 5

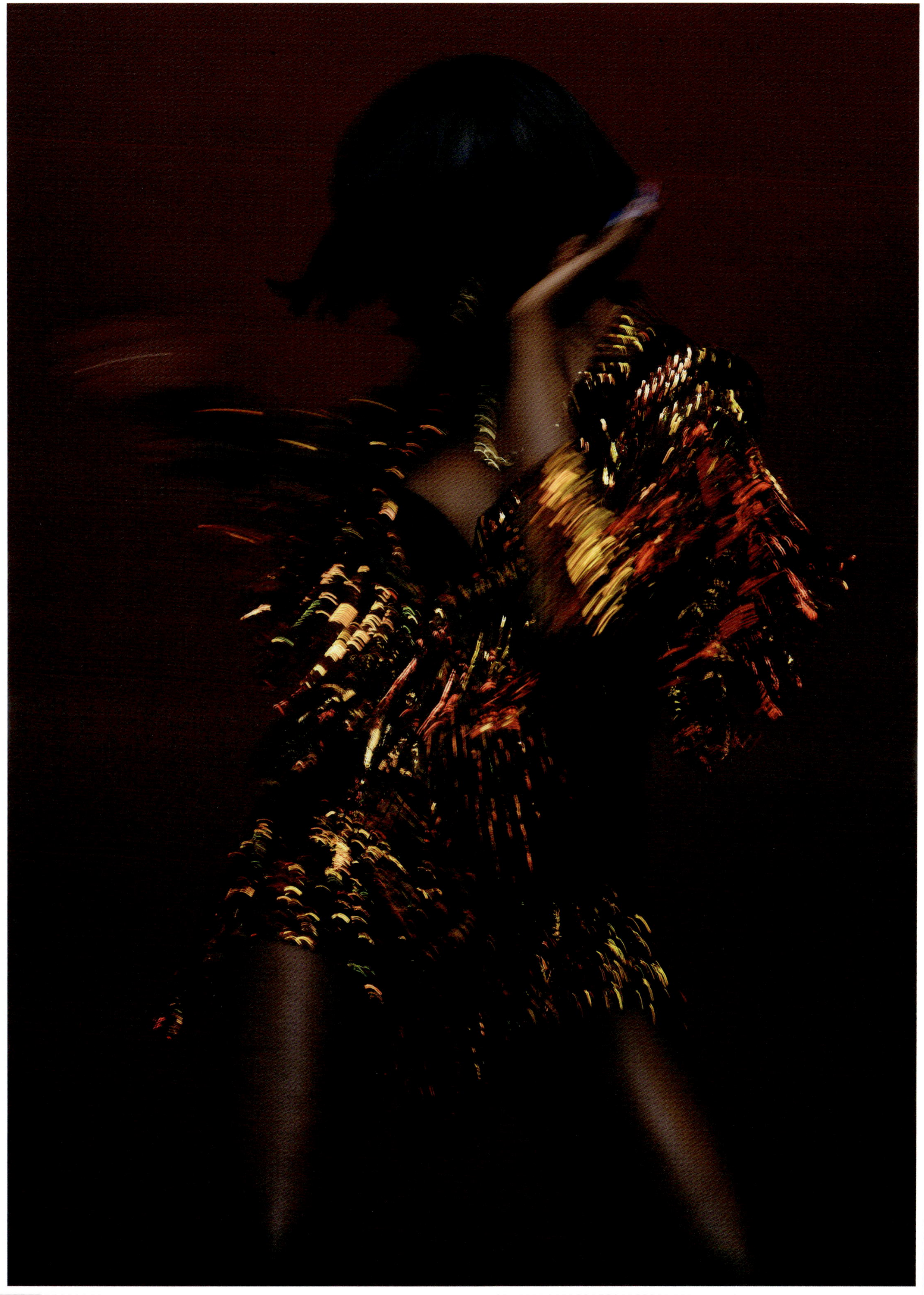

Title: AKOSIA | Client: Self-initiated

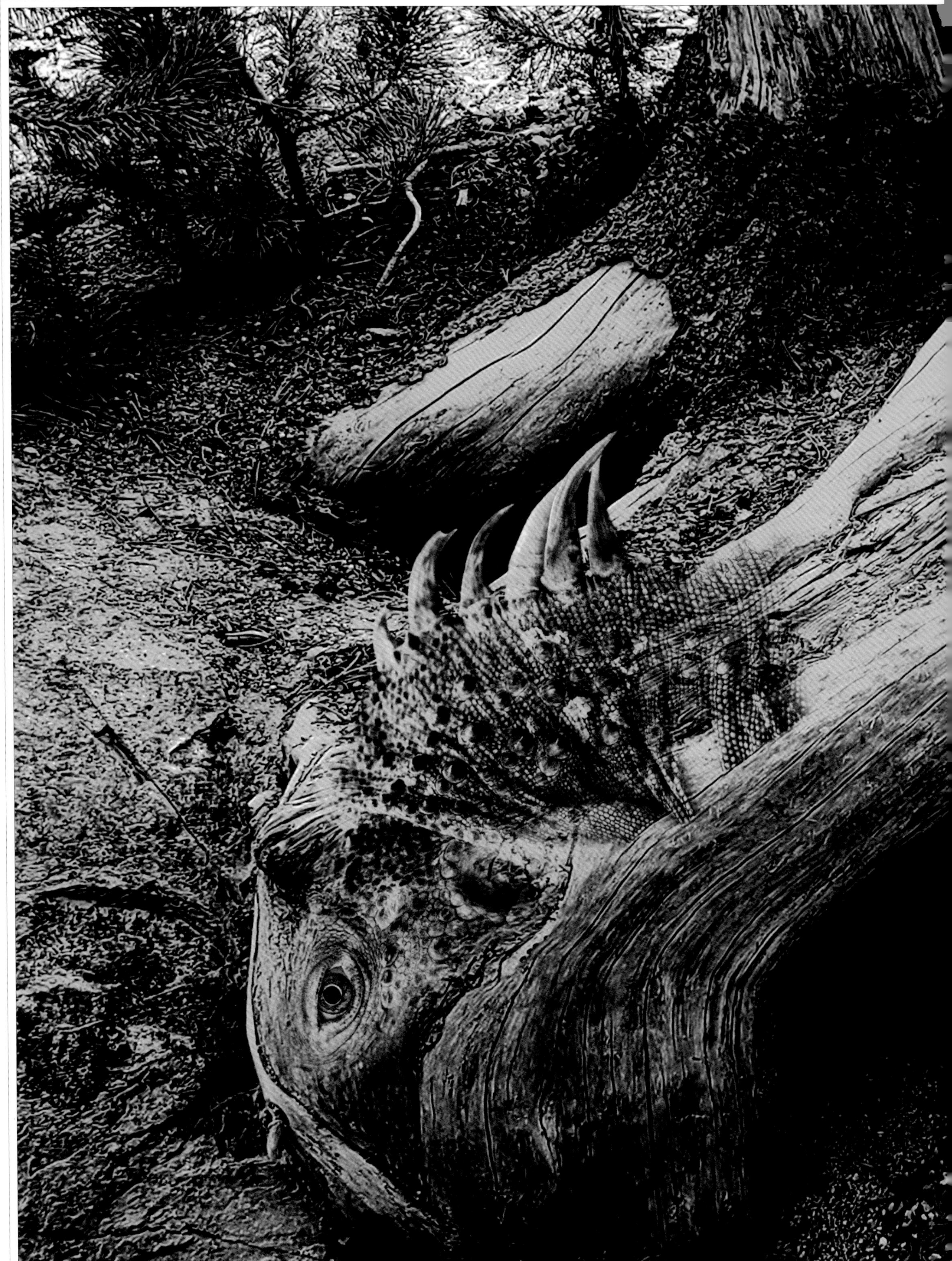

P234: Credit & Commentary

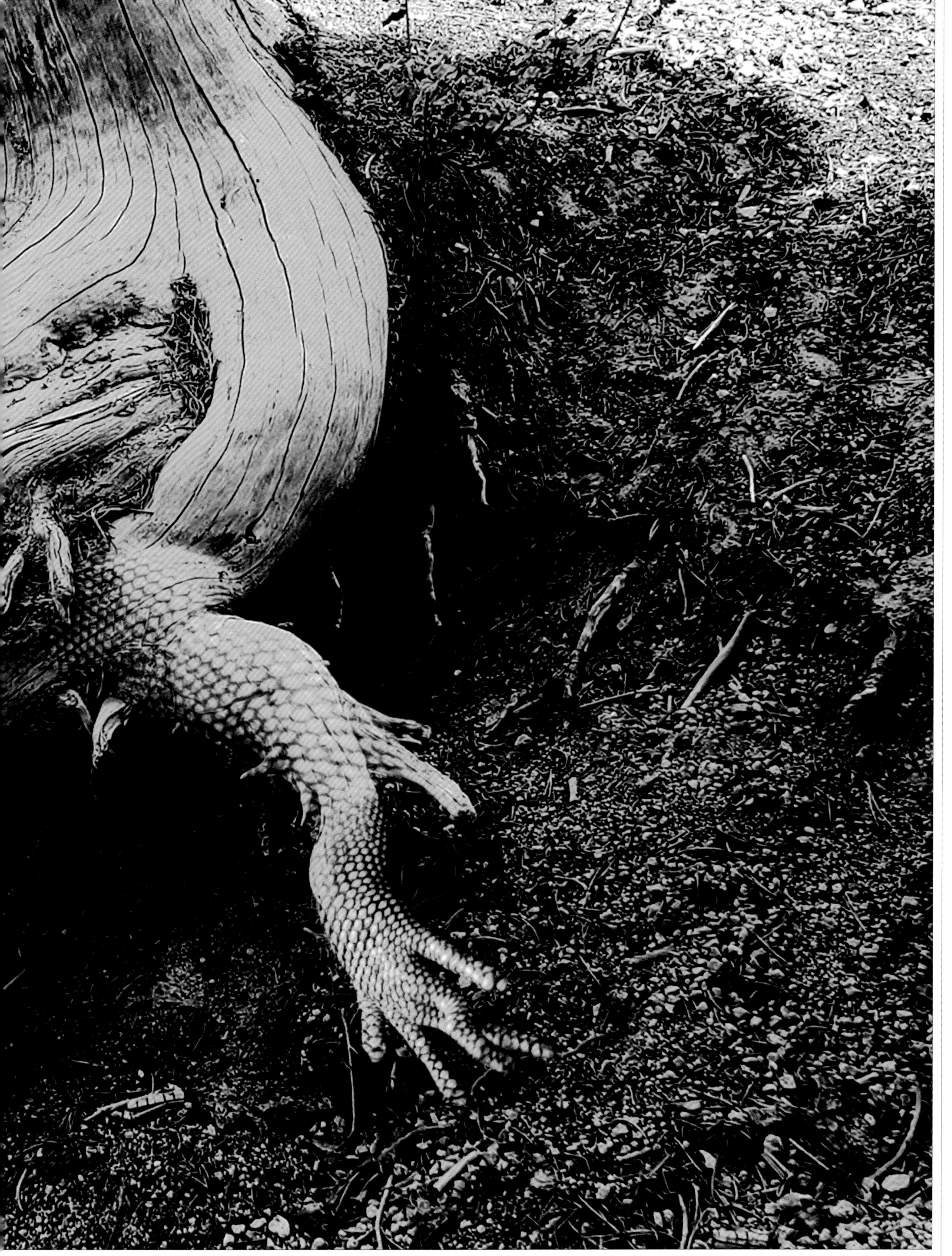

Title: Disappearing Roots | Client: ZEVEN Magazine

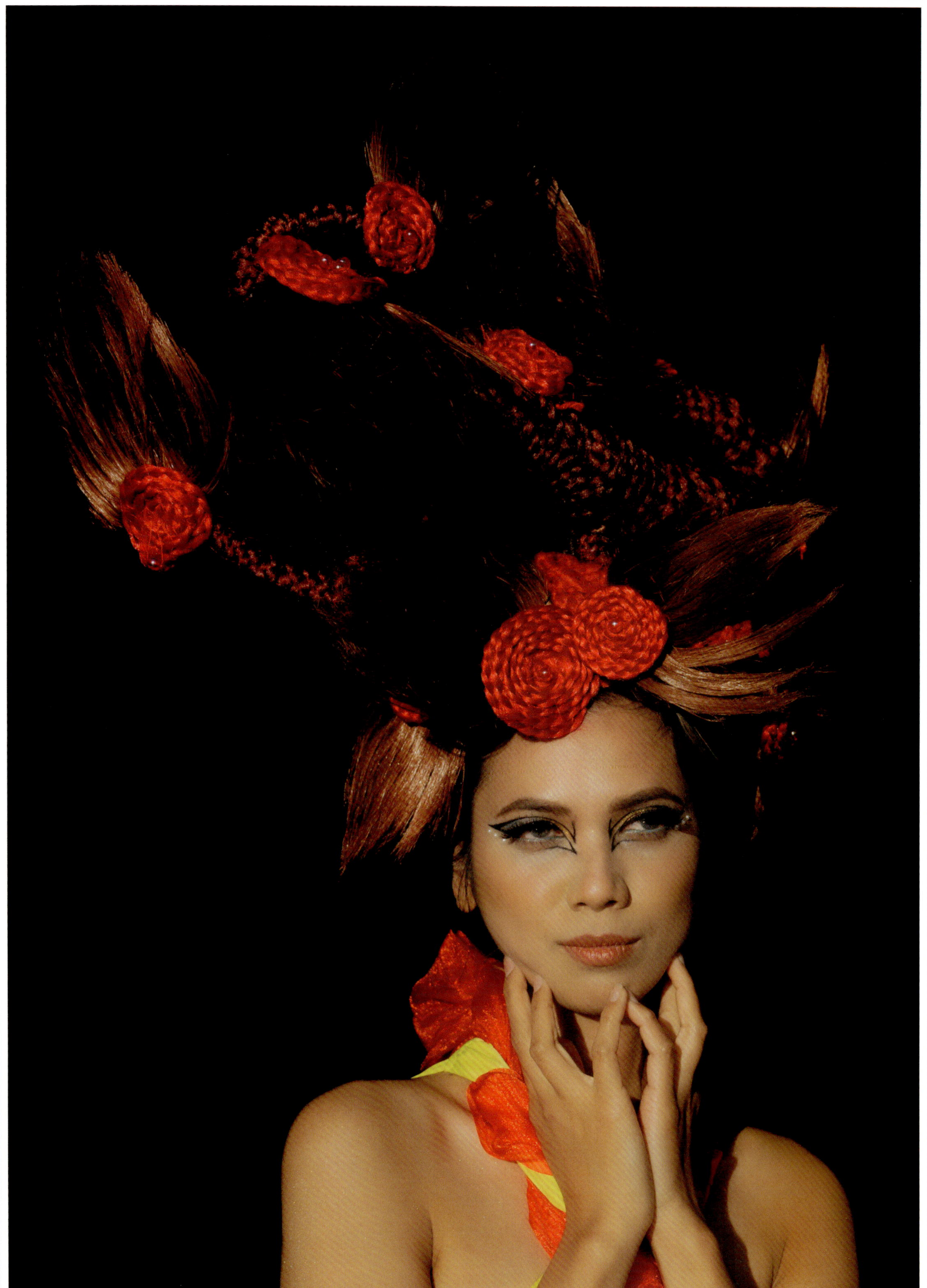

Title: A Thread of Hair | **Client:** AhKim Art of Hair

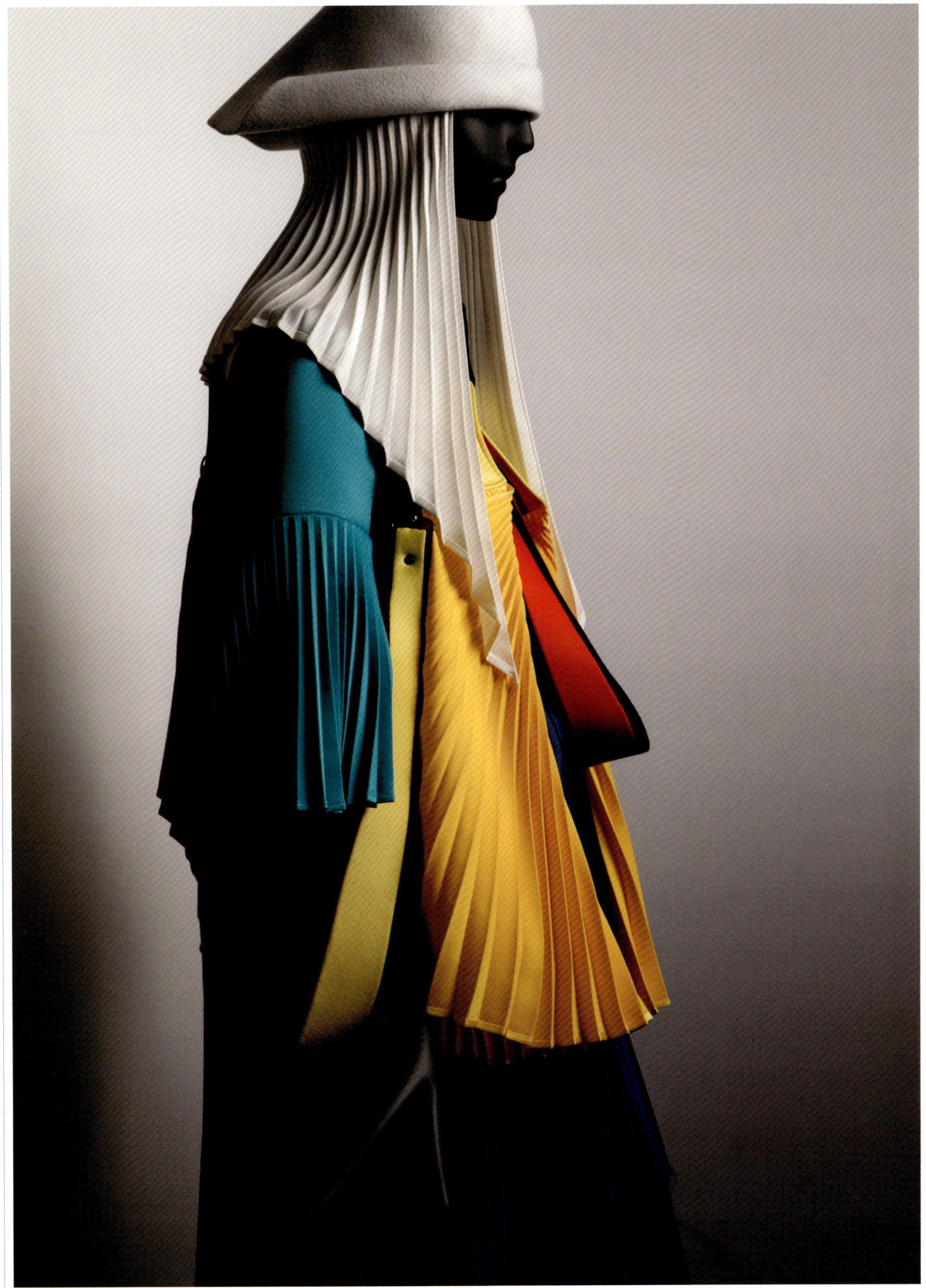

P235: Credit & Commentary **Title:** Robert Wun - "Between Reality & Fantasy" | **Client:** Savannah College of Art & Design

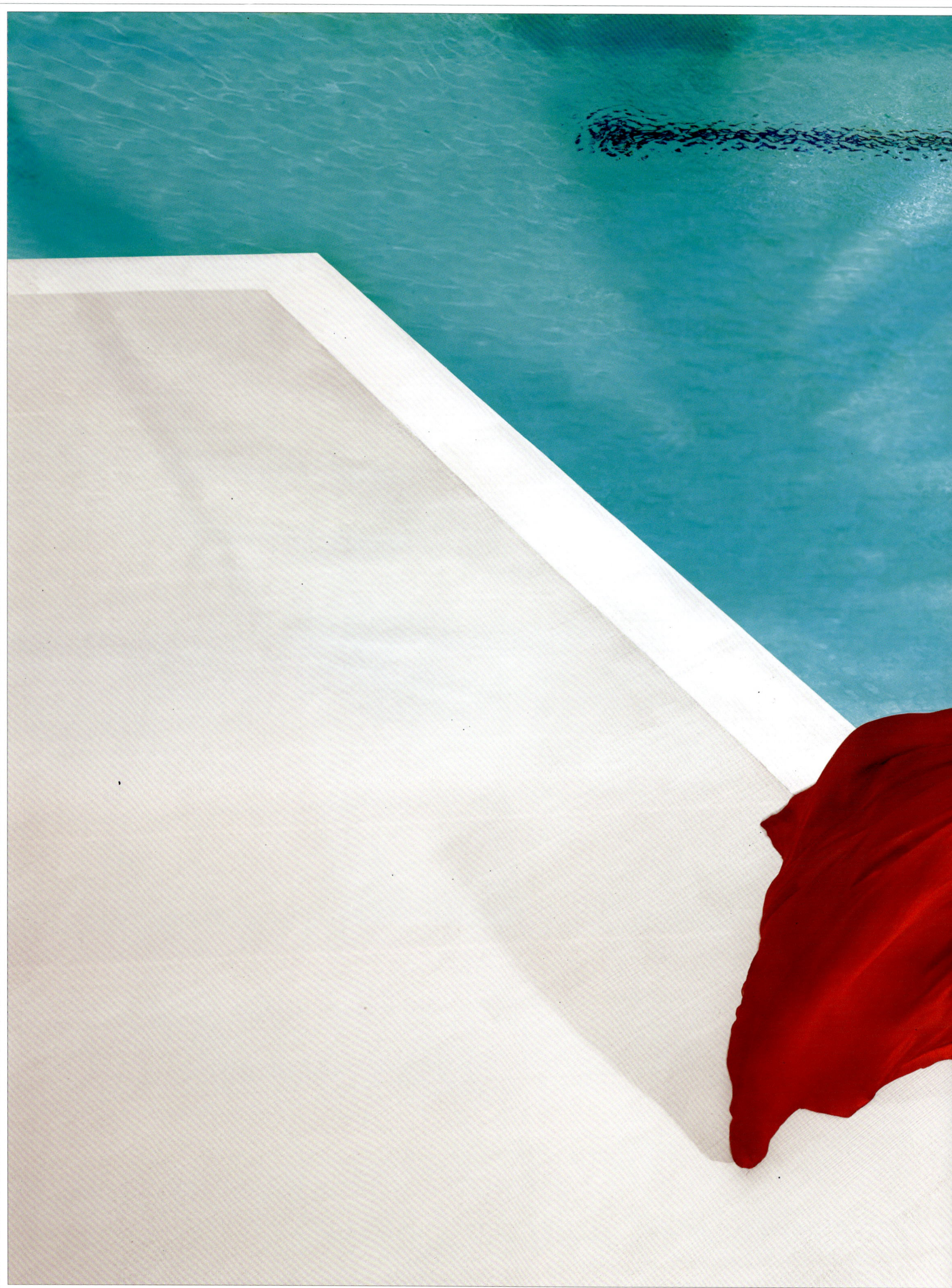

P234: Credit & Commentary

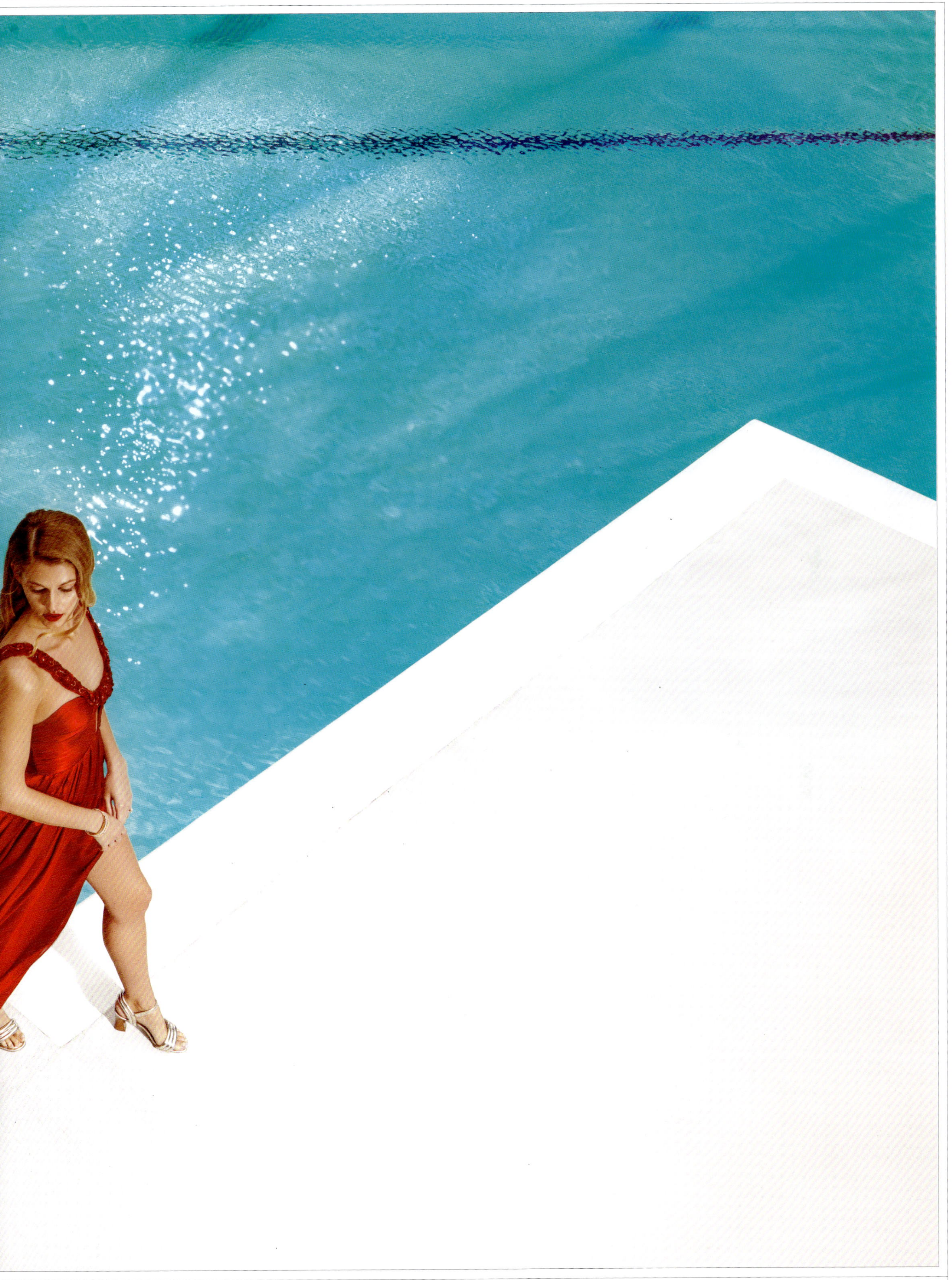

Title: Caribbean Dreaming | Client: Hour Media

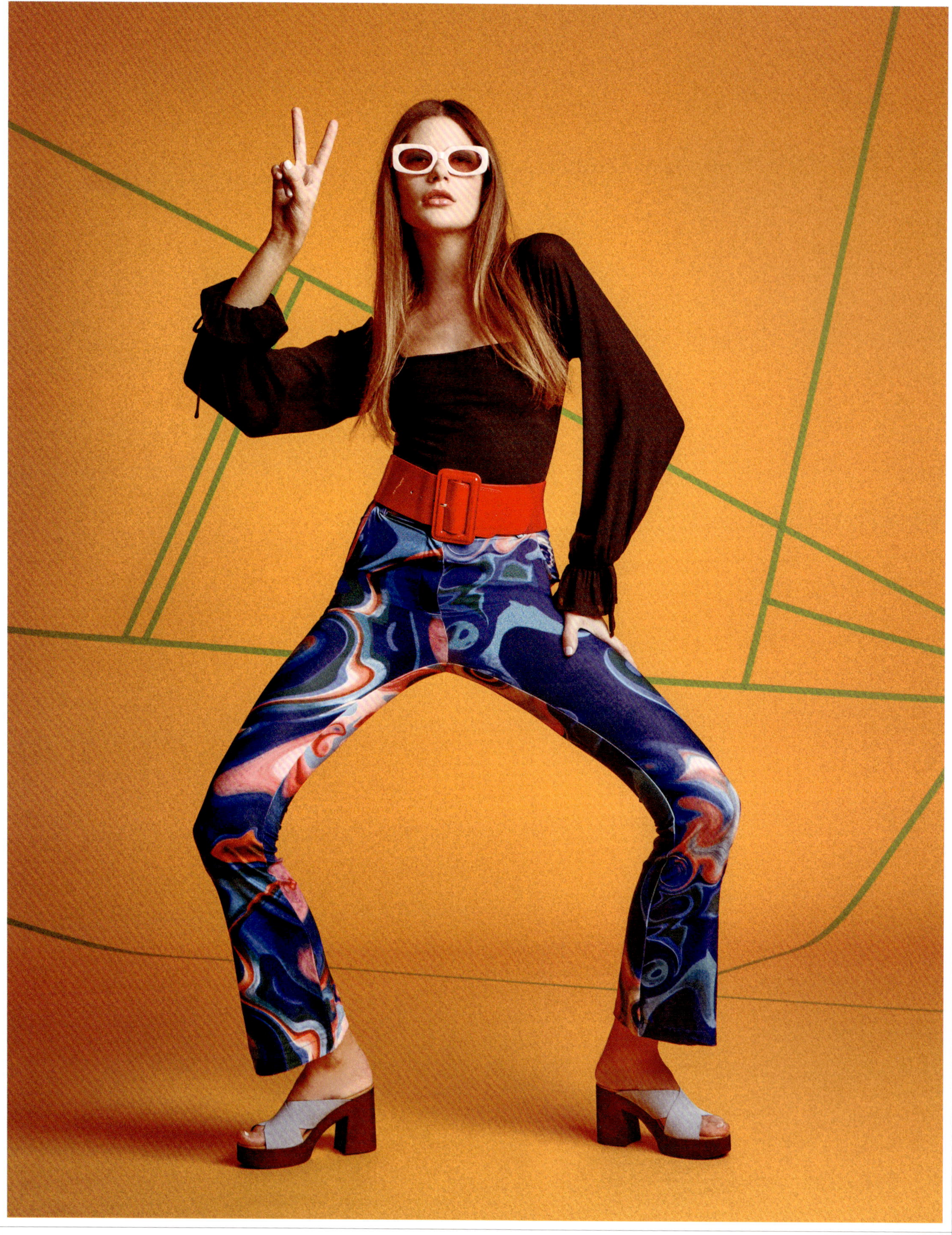

P235: Credit & Commentary

Title: The 70s Shoe | **Client:** Footwear Plus Magazine

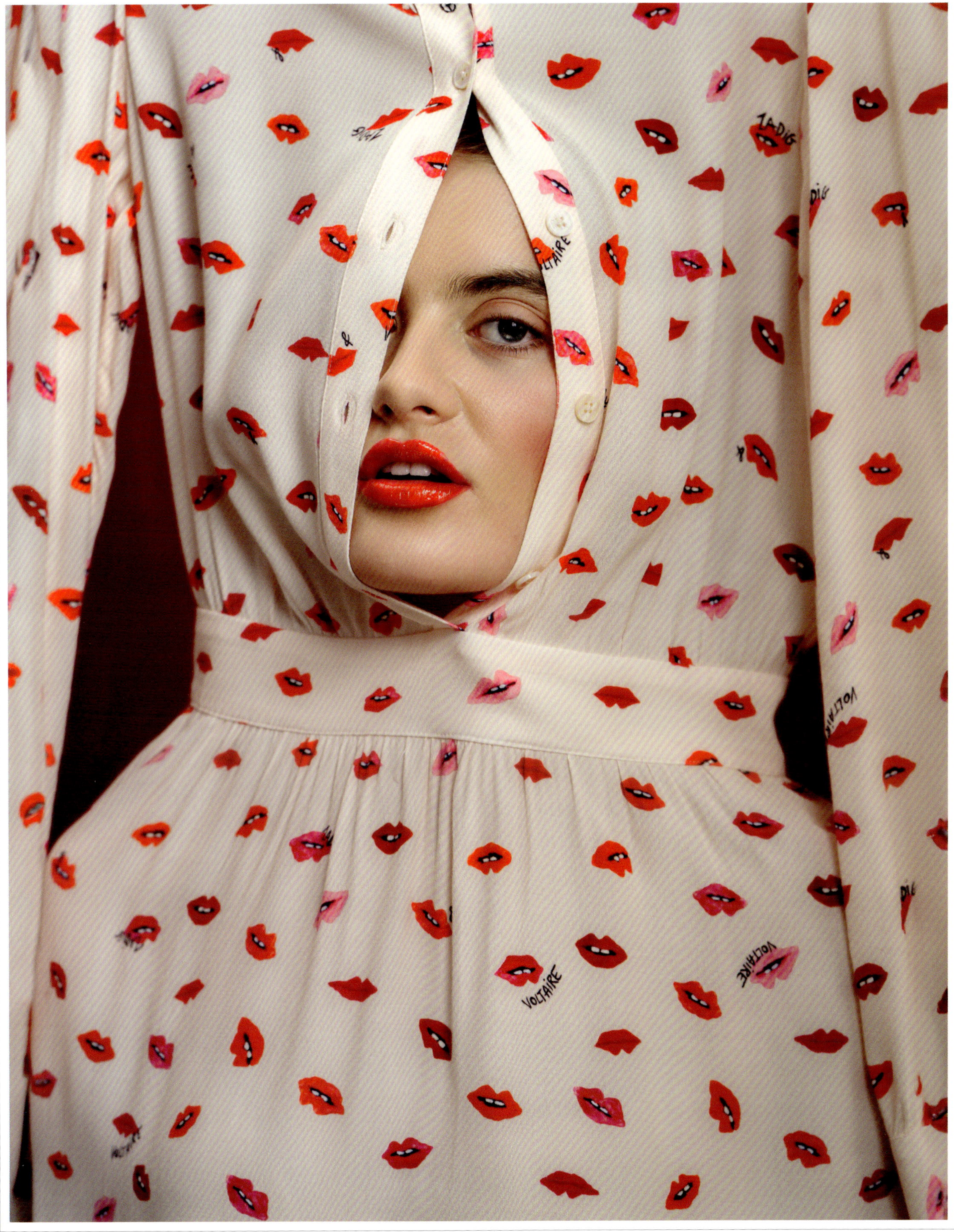

P235: Credit & Commentary

Title: Lips - Zadig and Voltaire | **Client:** Self-initiated

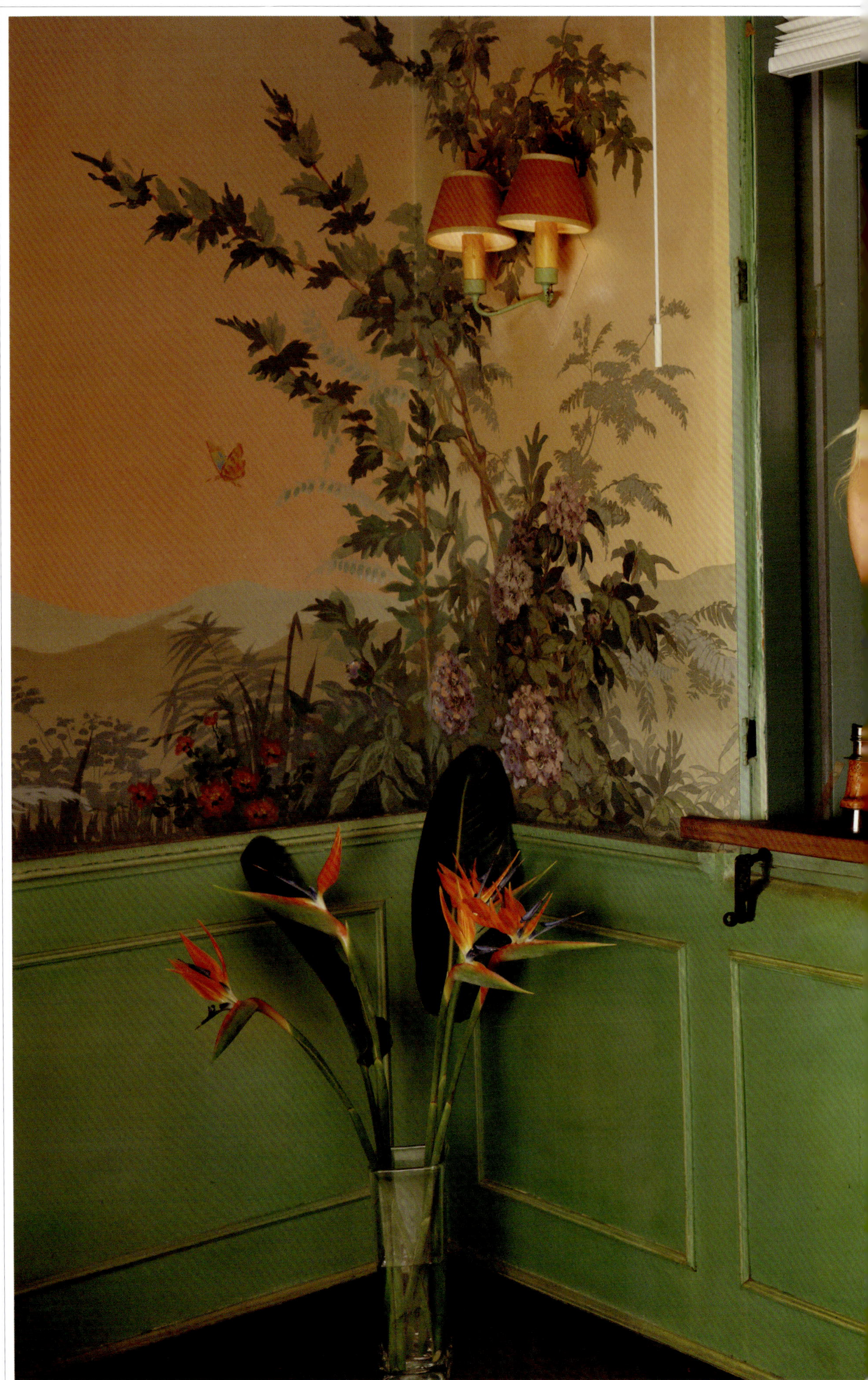

P235: Credit & Commentary

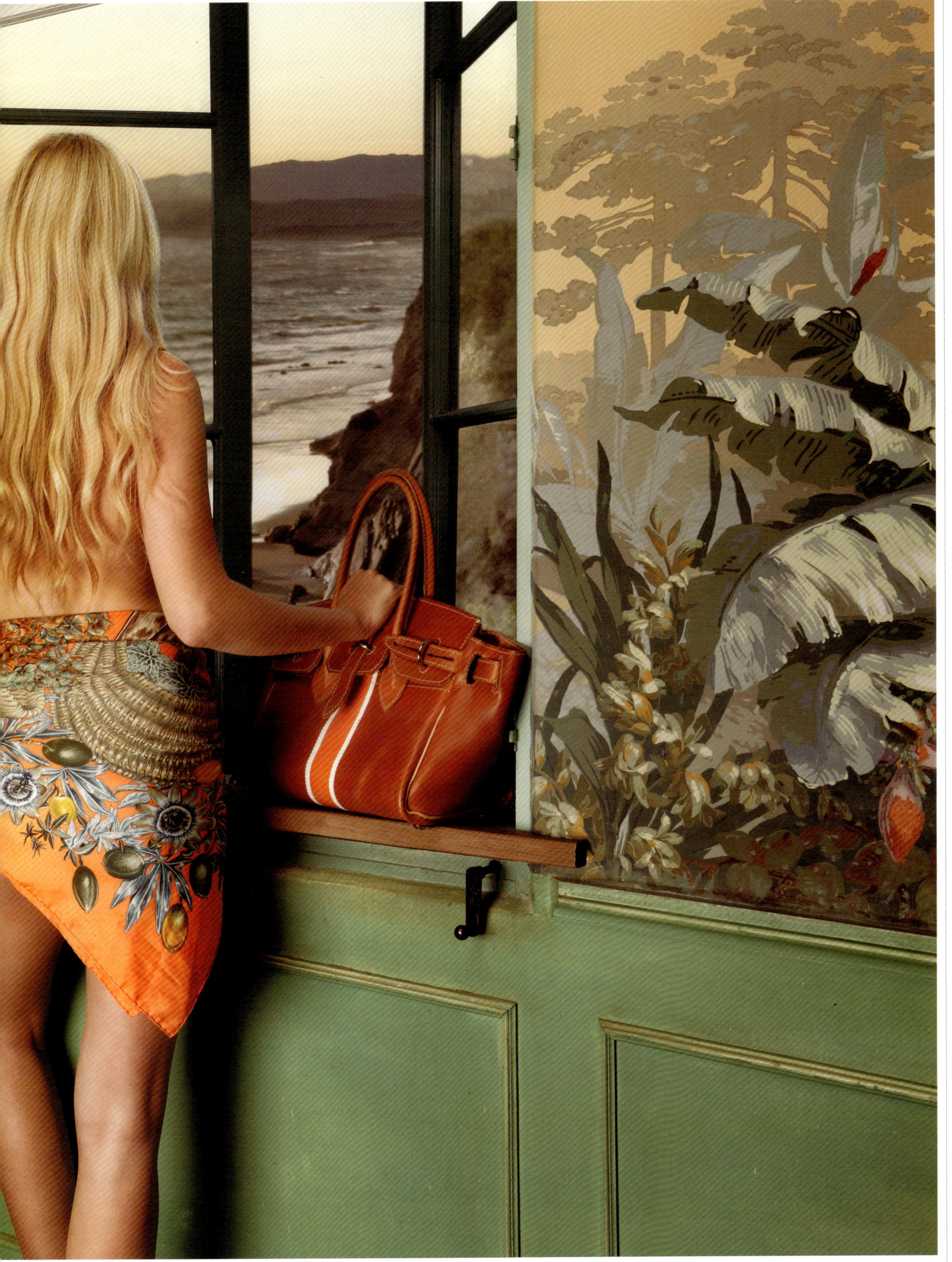

Title: Homer Campaign | Client: Terry R. Pillow

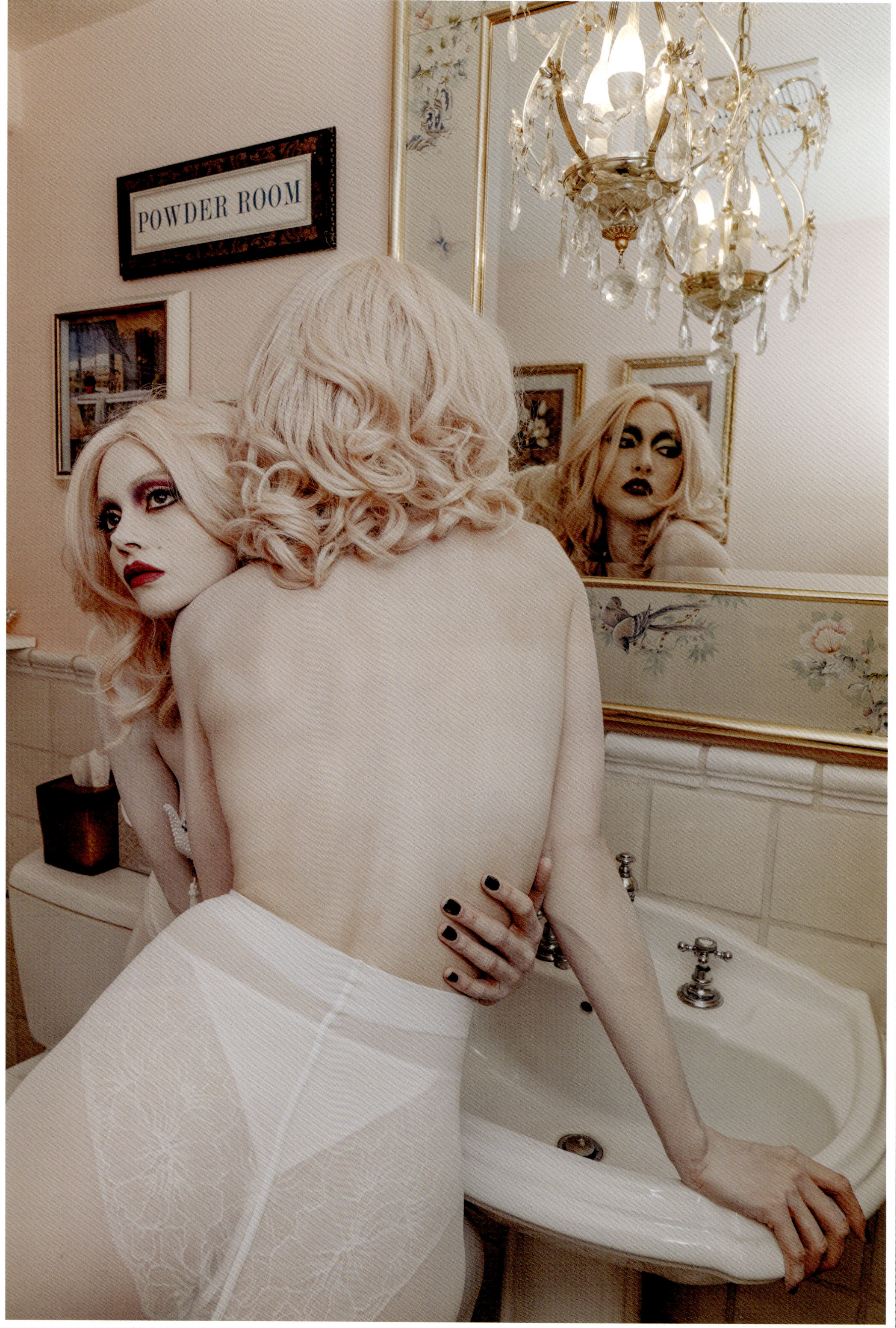

P235: Credit & Commentary

Title: Ghost Girls | **Client:** Self-initiated

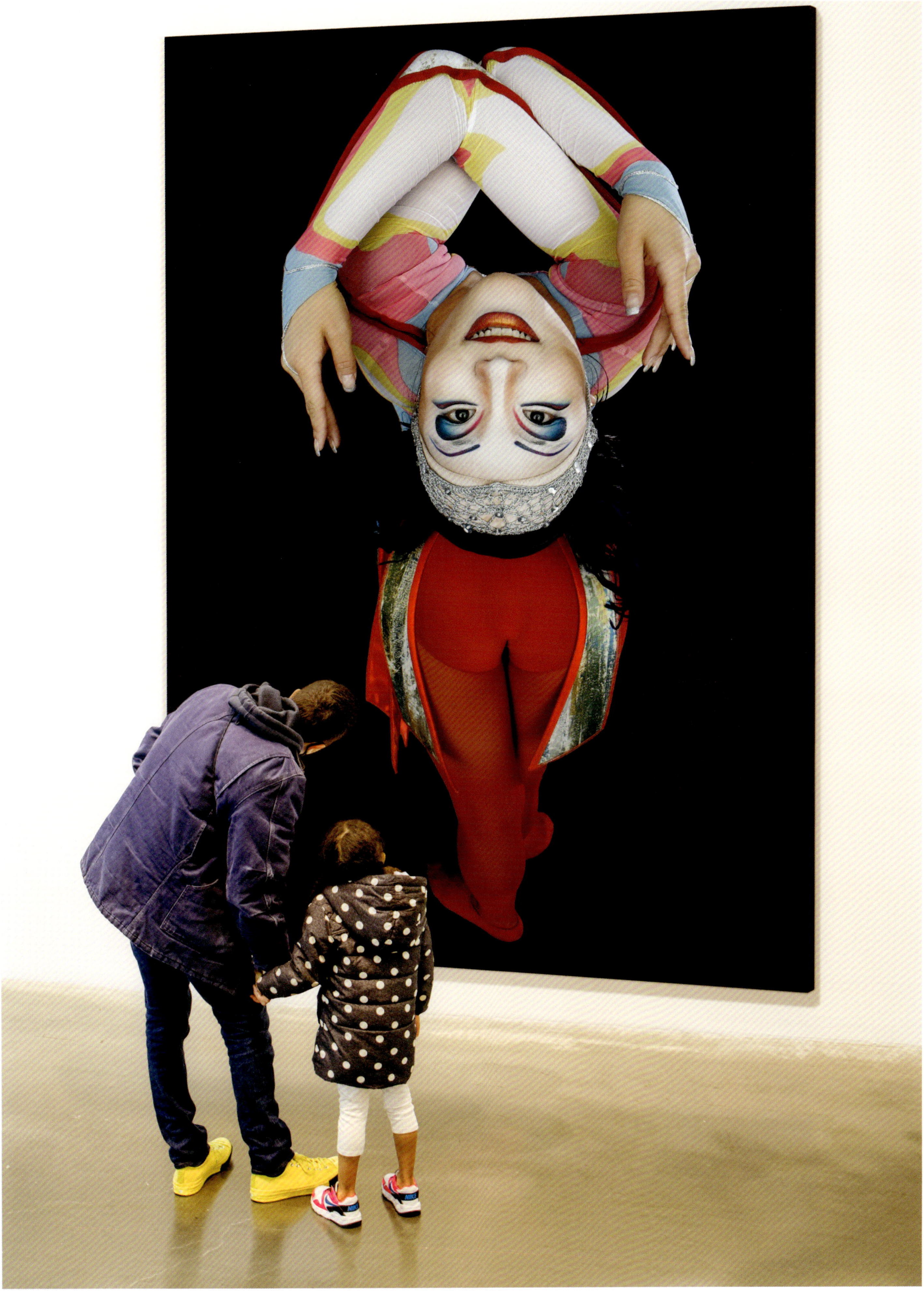

Title: Installation #248: Museum of Fine Arts, Boston + Cirque du Soleil O #83
Client: Self-initiated | **P235:** Credit & Commentary

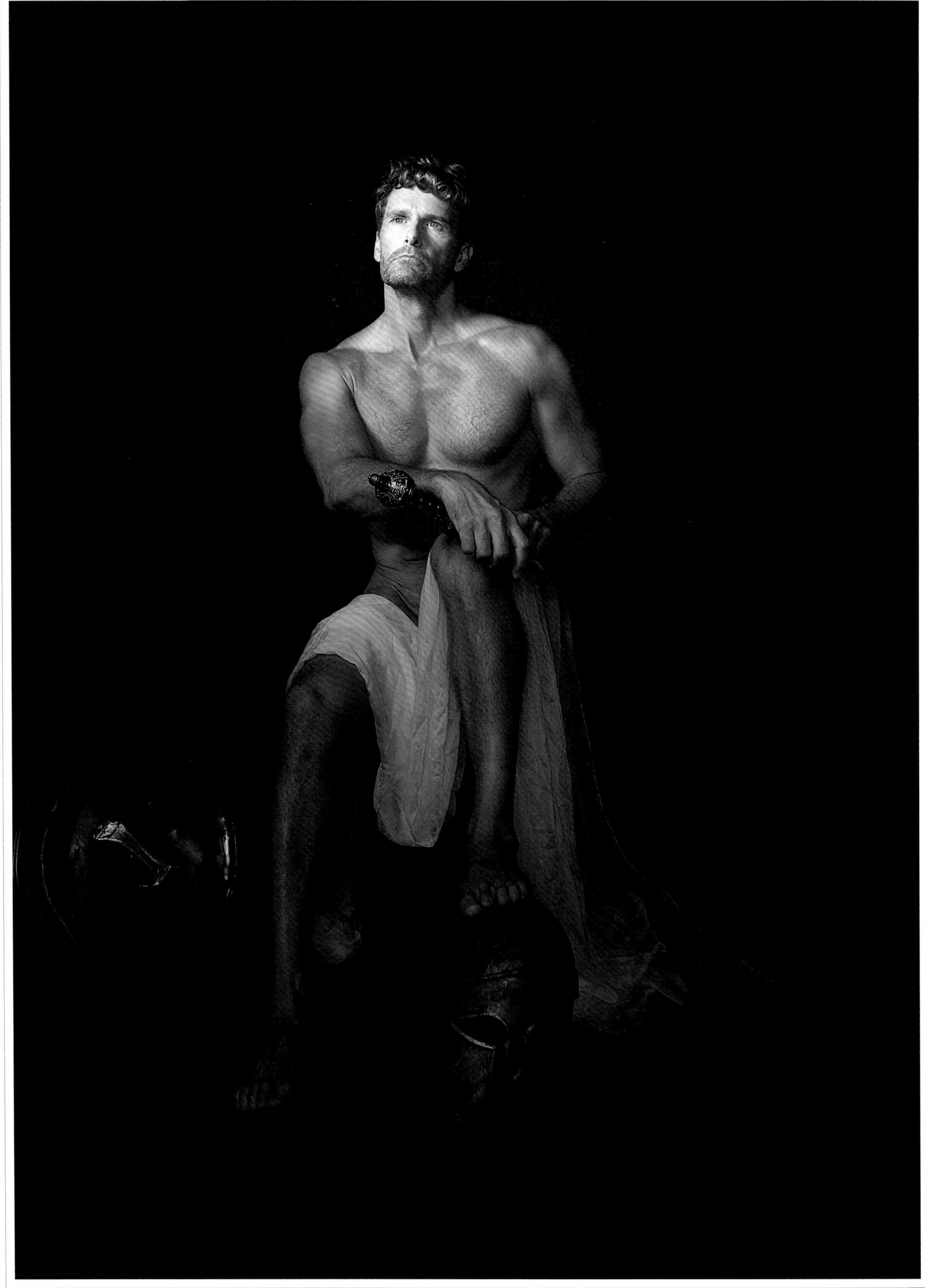

P235: Credit & Commentary

Title: Ares Contemplates the Cost of Courage | **Client:** God

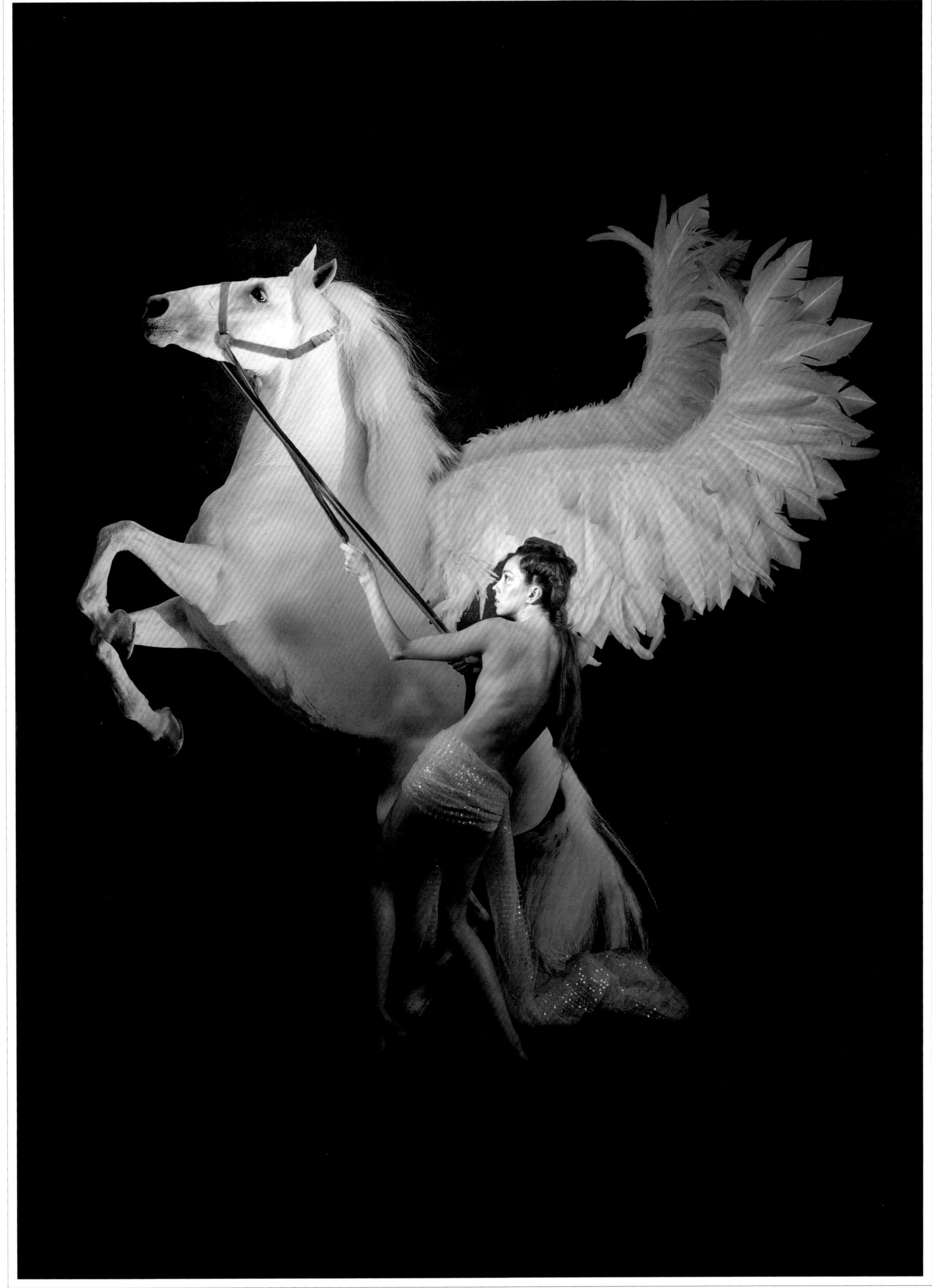

P235: Credit & Commentary

Title: Andromeda Rears Pegasus | Client: God

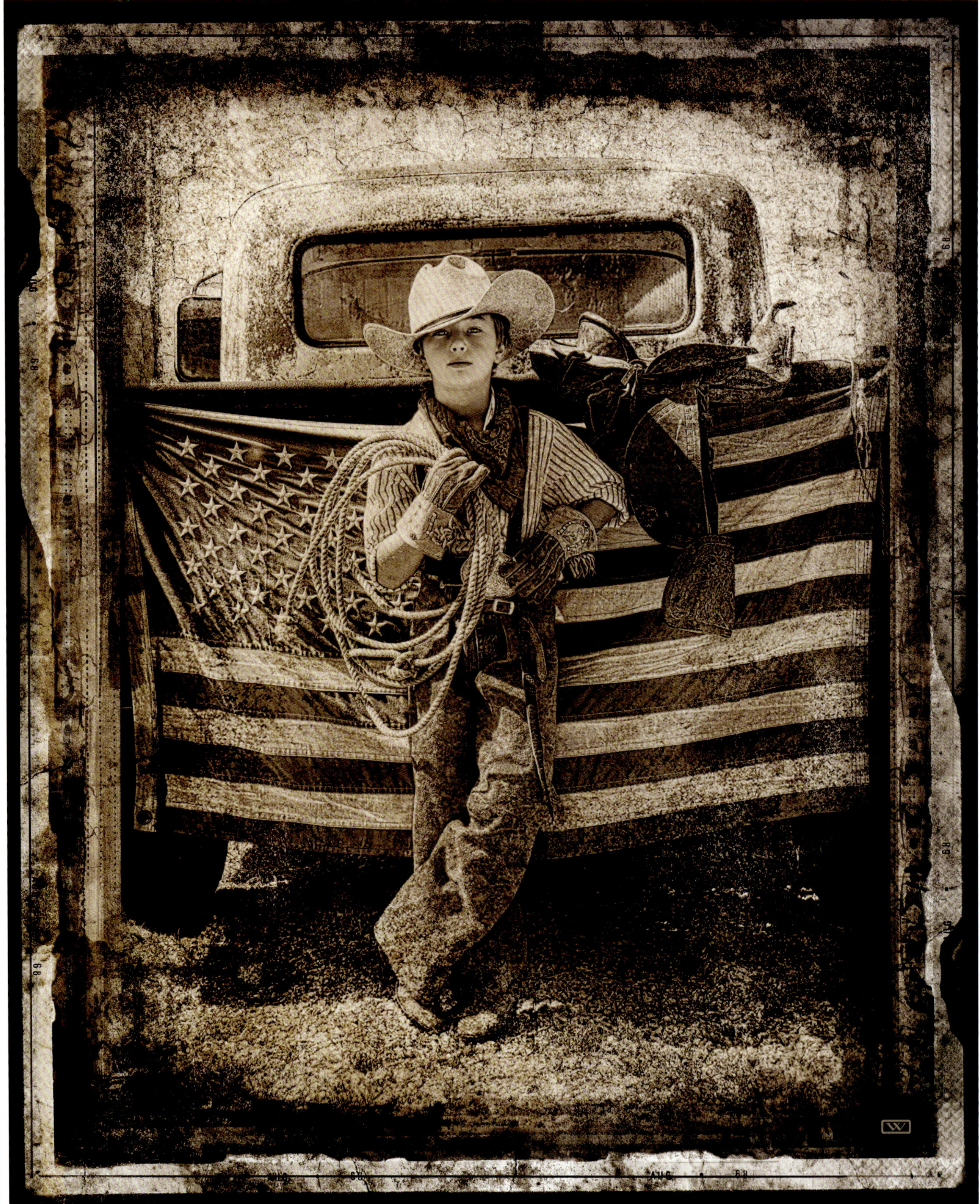

P235: Credit & Commentary Title: All-American Cowboys | Client: Self-initiated Image 1 of 3

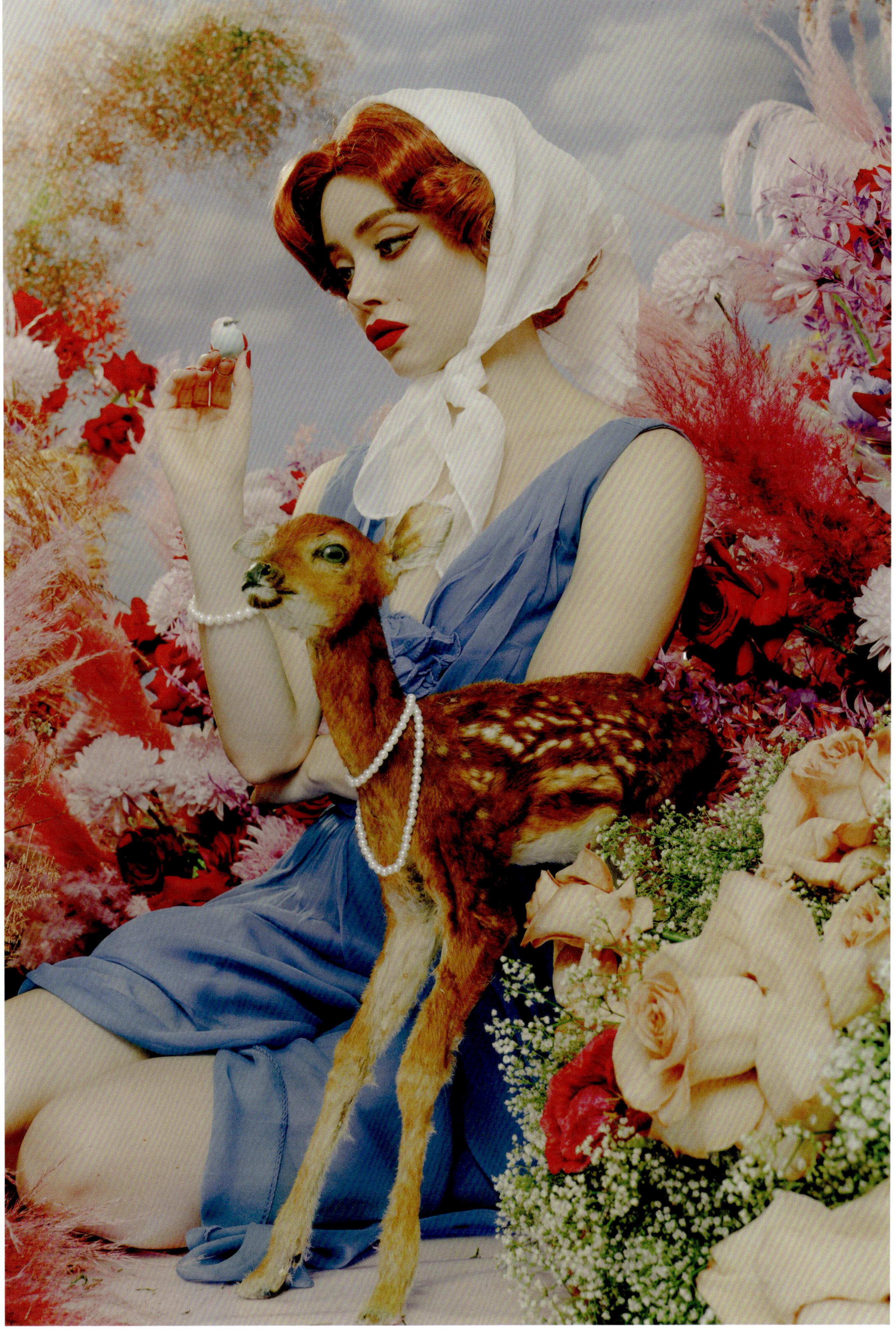

P235: Credit & Commentary Title: Scarlette 1960 | Client: Self-initiated

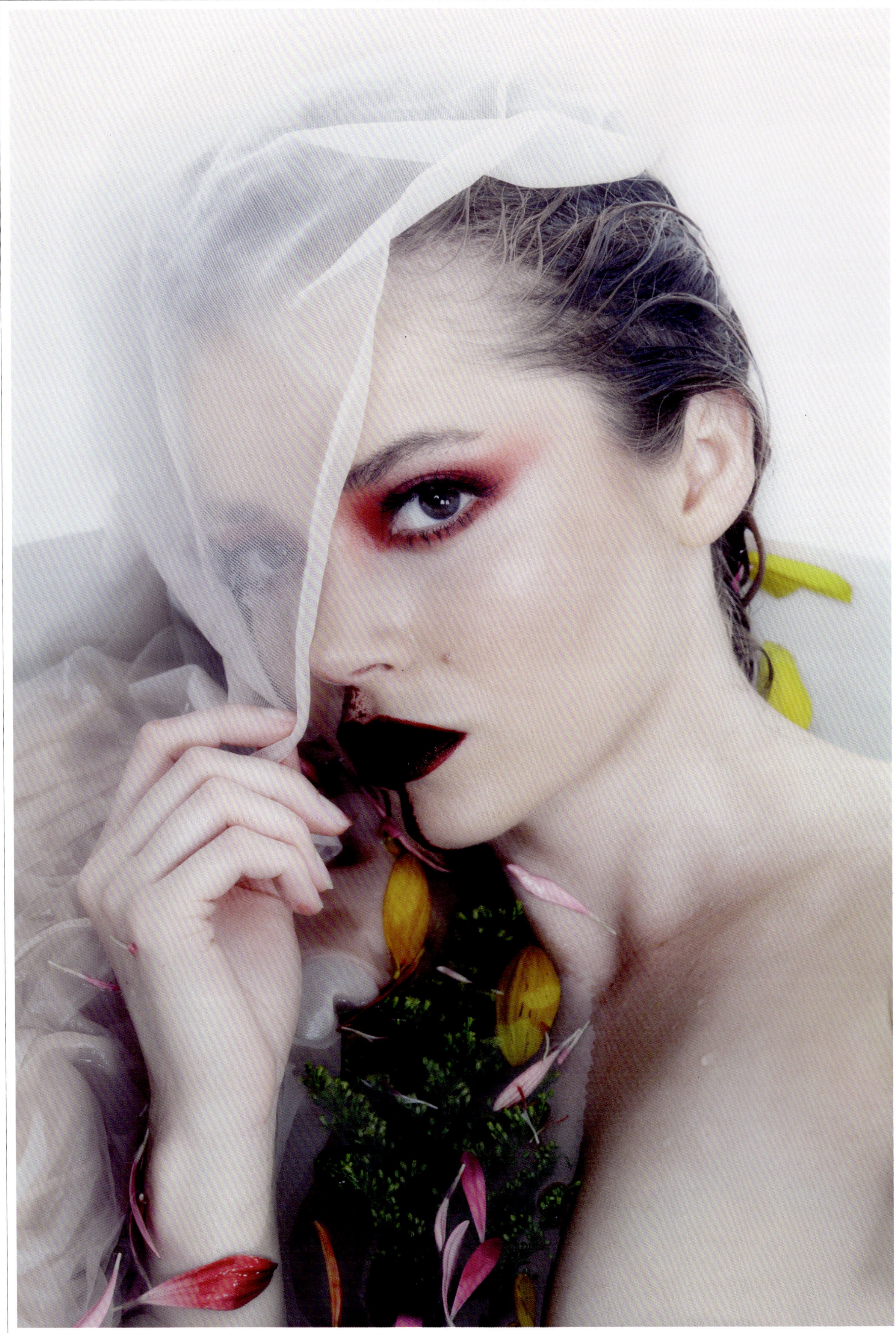

P235: Credit & Commentary

Title: Someday | Client: Self-initiated

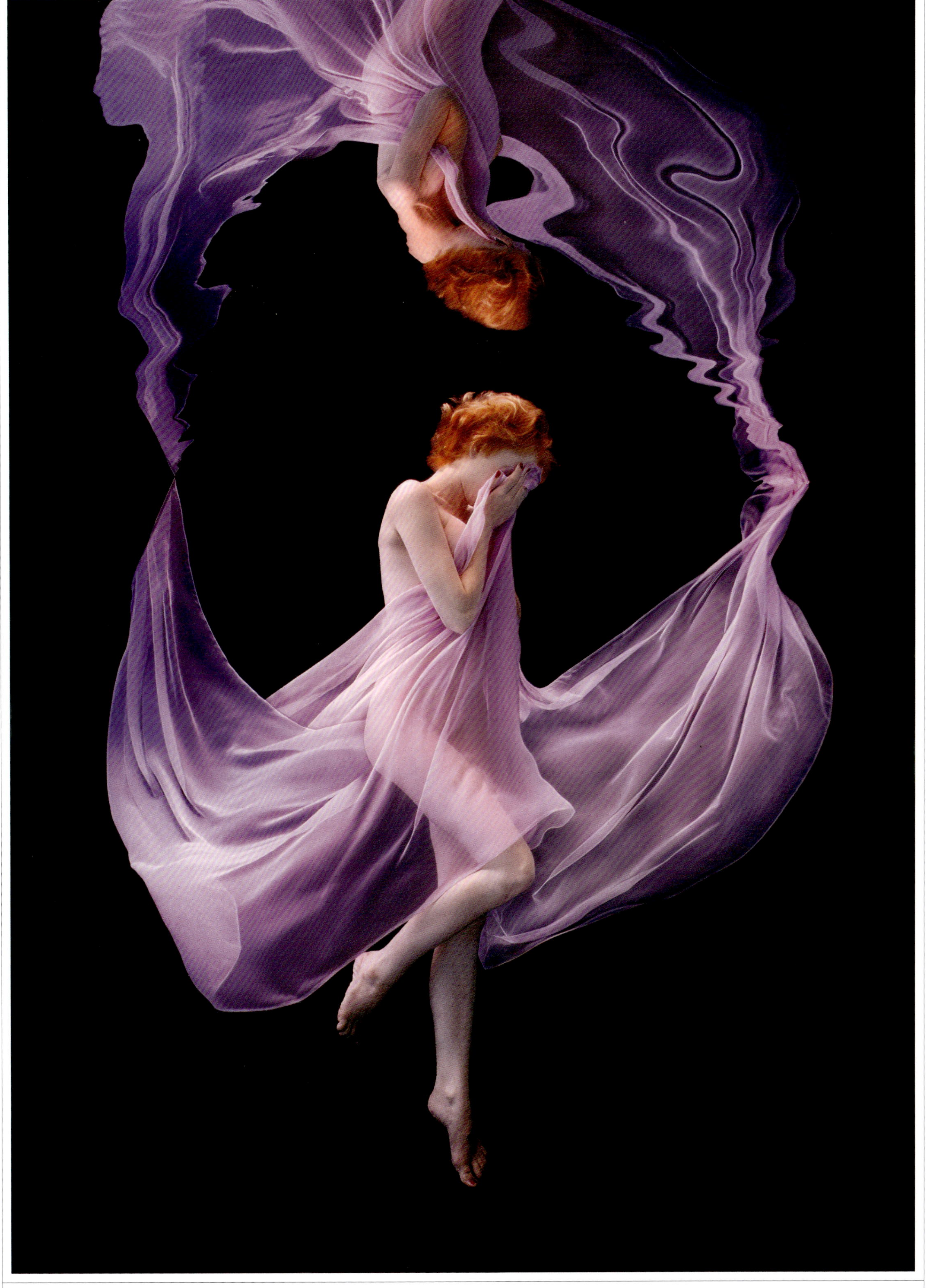

P236: Credit & Commentary **Title:** Underwater Study #980: Model Shawnee Free Jones | **Client:** Self-initiated

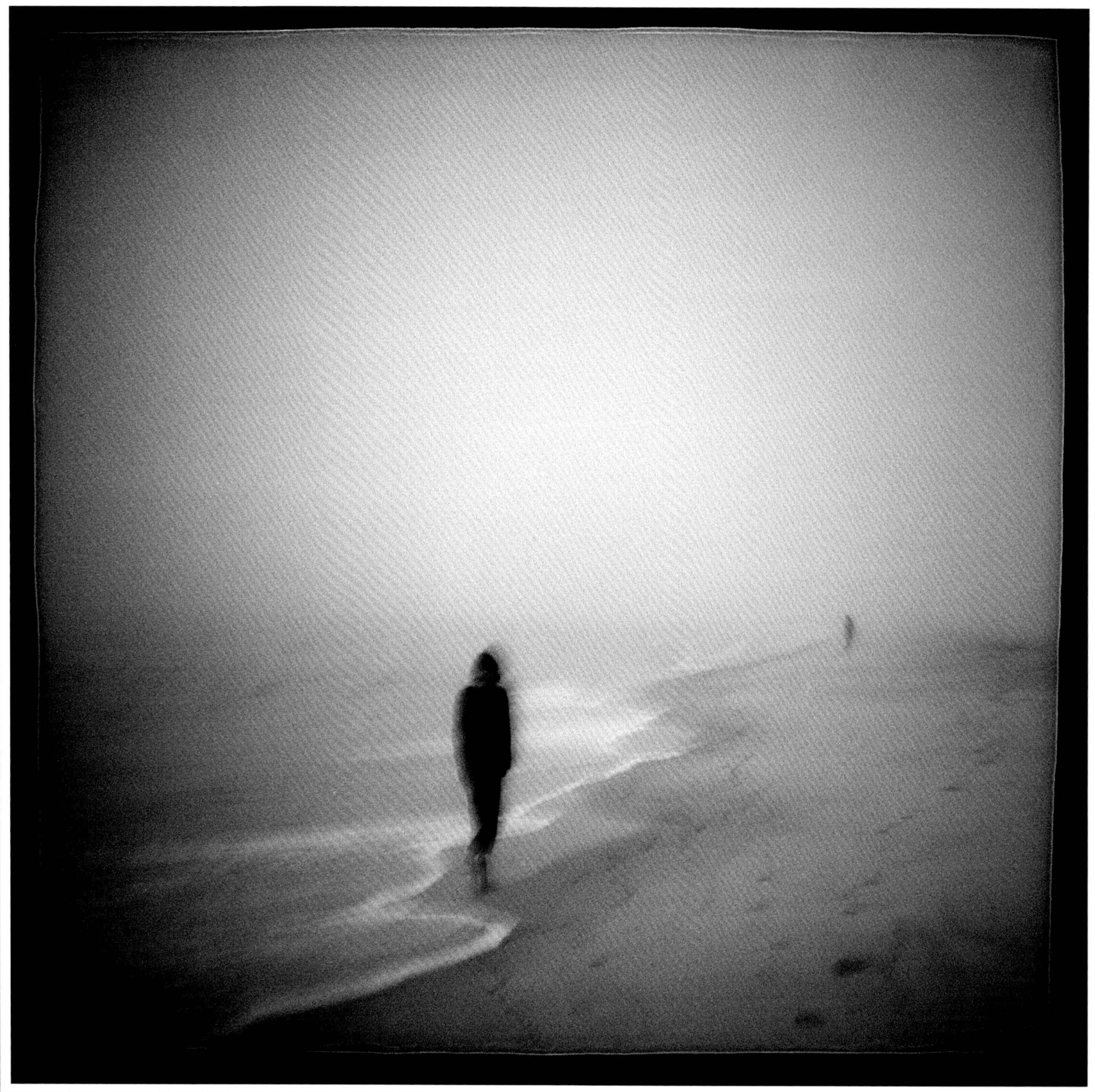

P236: Credit & Commentary

Title: So Far Away | **Client:** Self-initiated

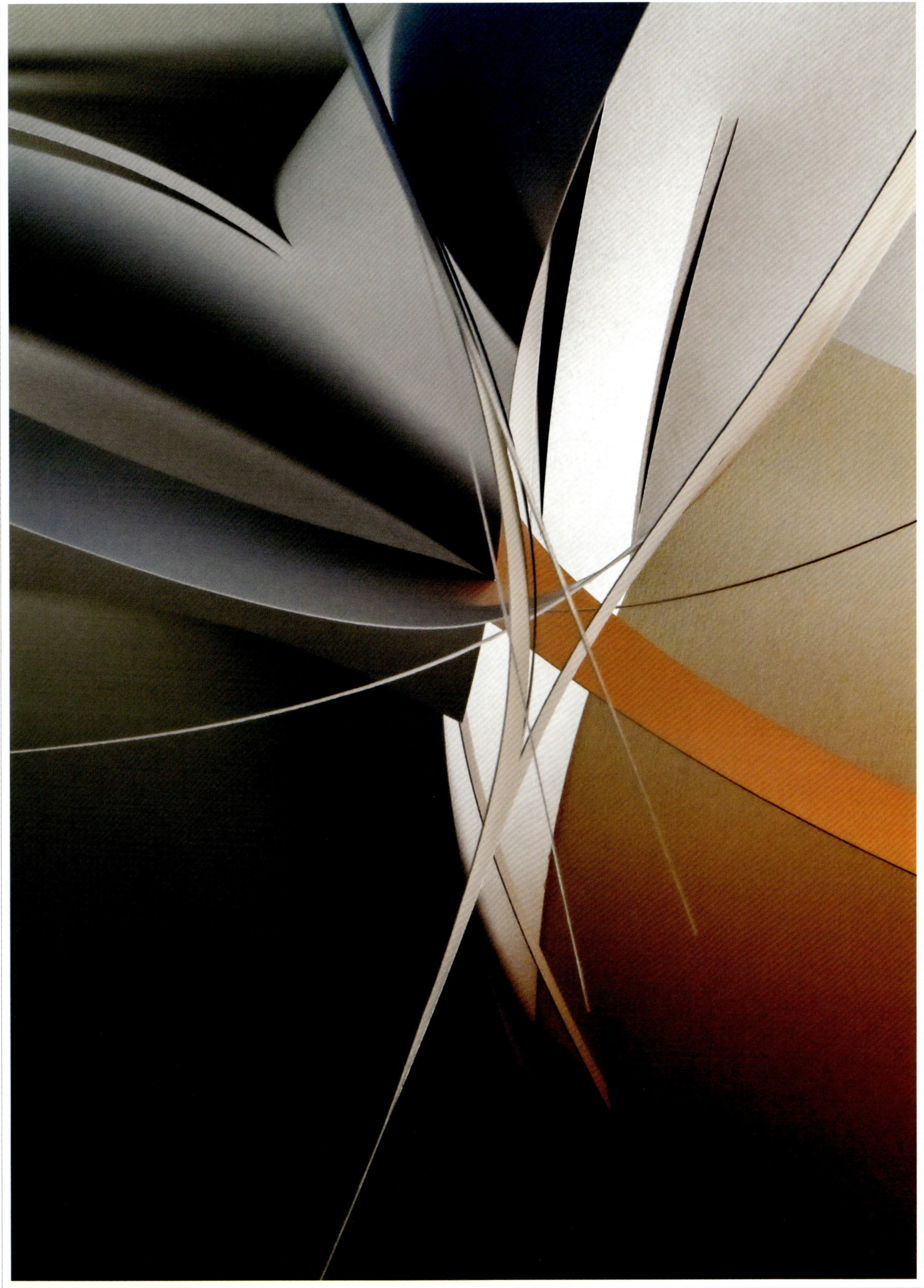

Title: Silent Dialogue | Client: Self-initiated

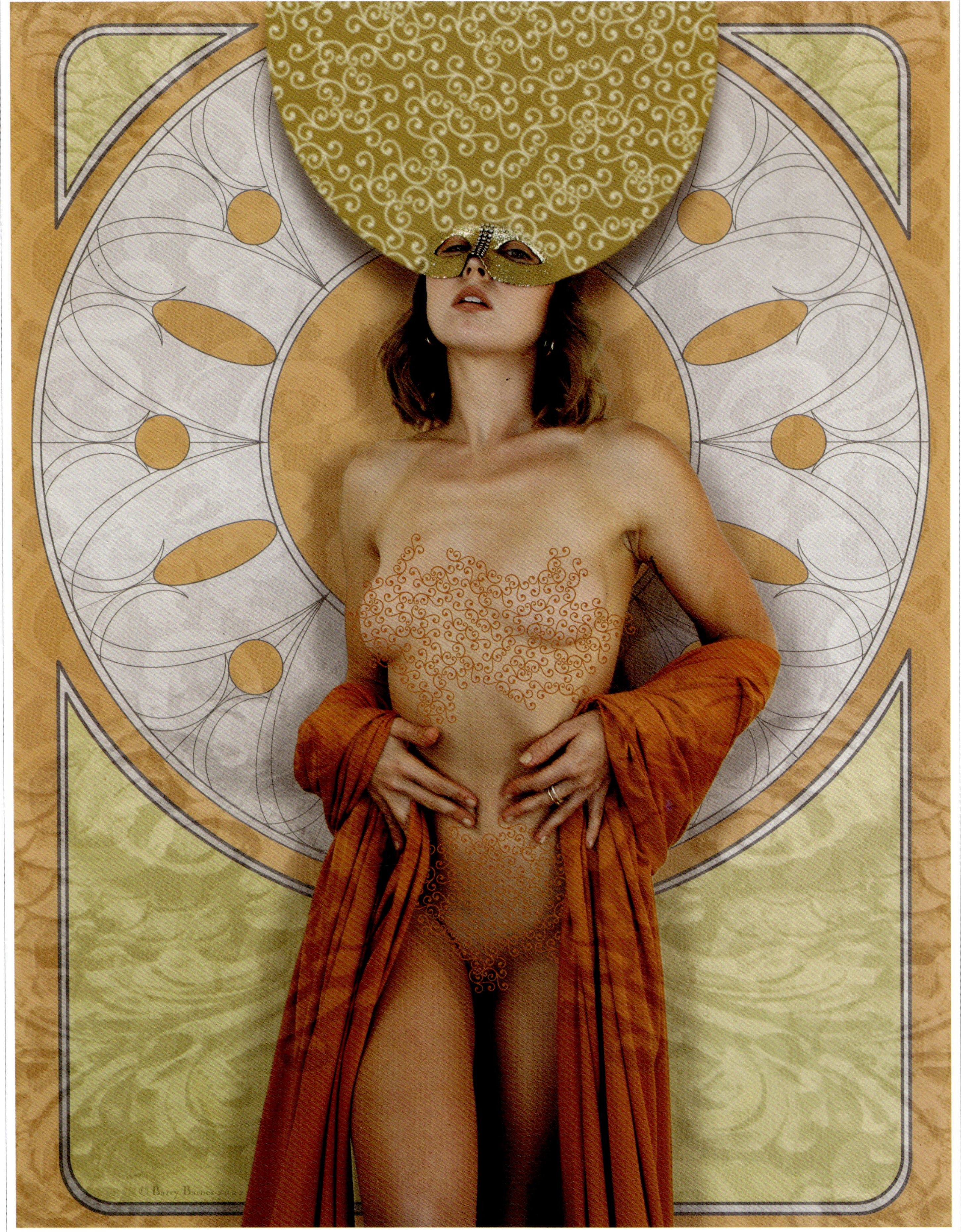

P236: Credit & Commentary

Title: de Sade Portfolio 2 | Client: Self-initiated

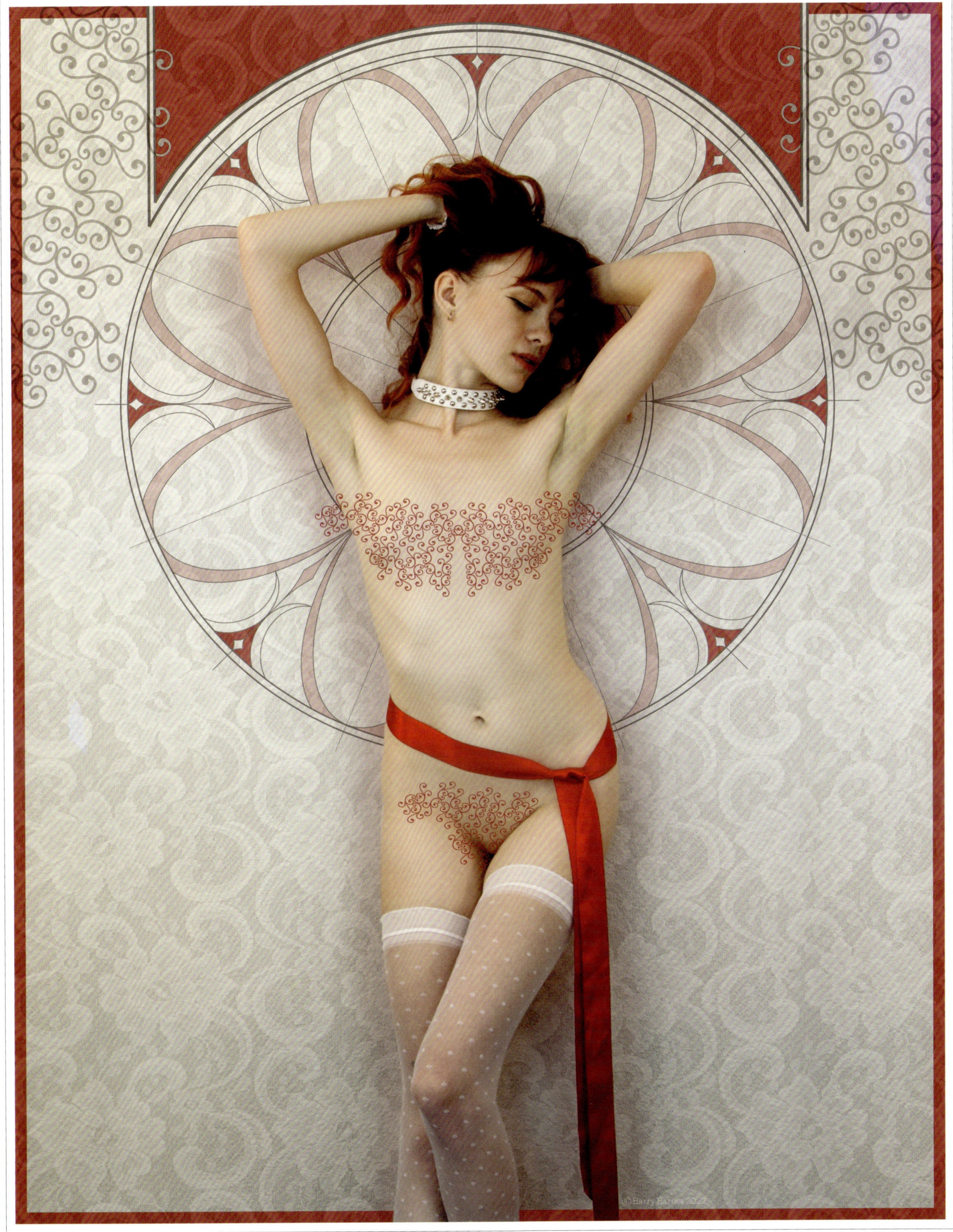

P236: Credit & Commentary

Title: de Sade Portfolio 1 | **Client:** Self-initiated

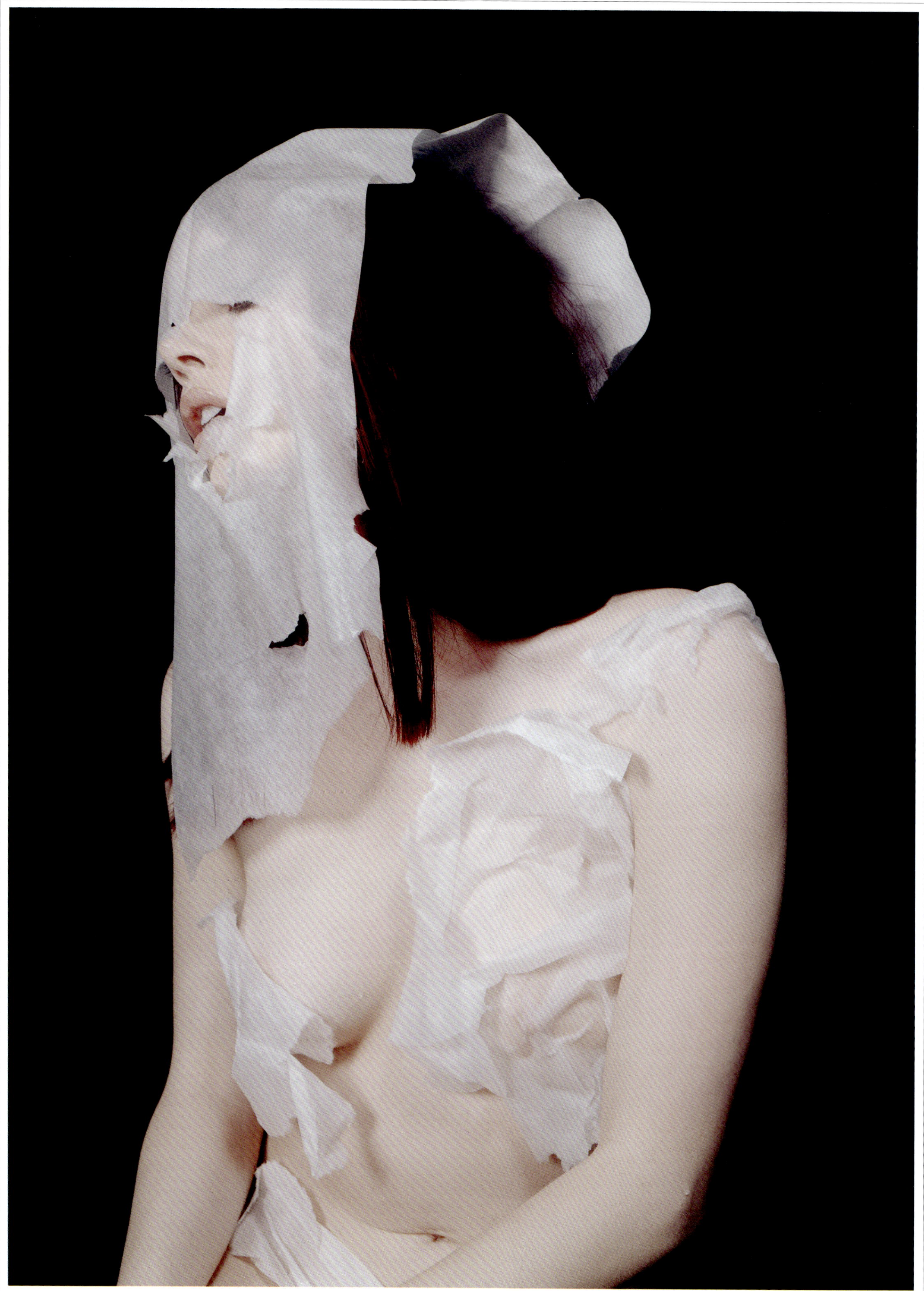

P236: Credit & Commentary

Title: Paper Thin | Client: Self-initiated

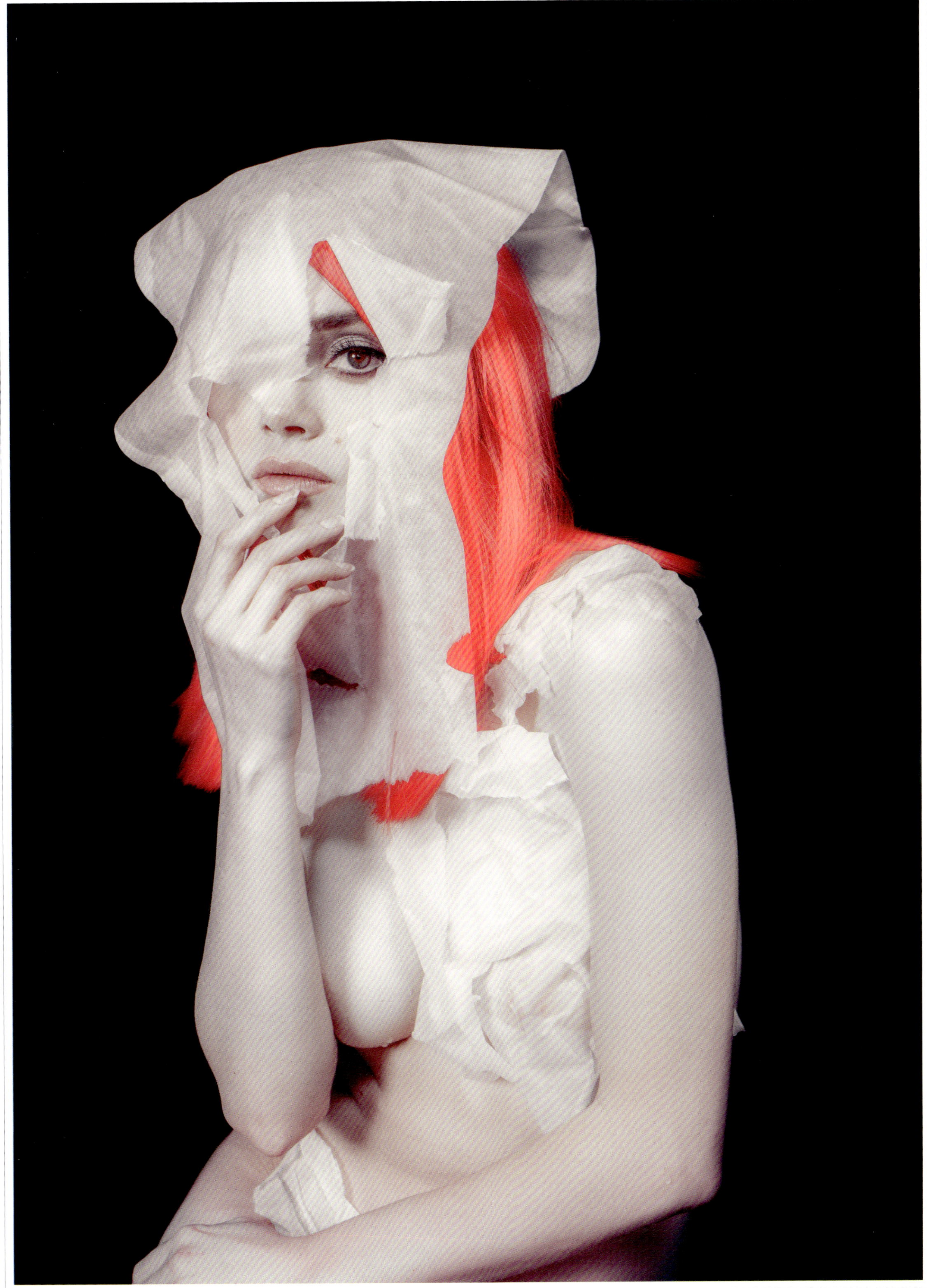

P236: Credit & Commentary

Title: Paper Thin | **Client:** Self-initiated

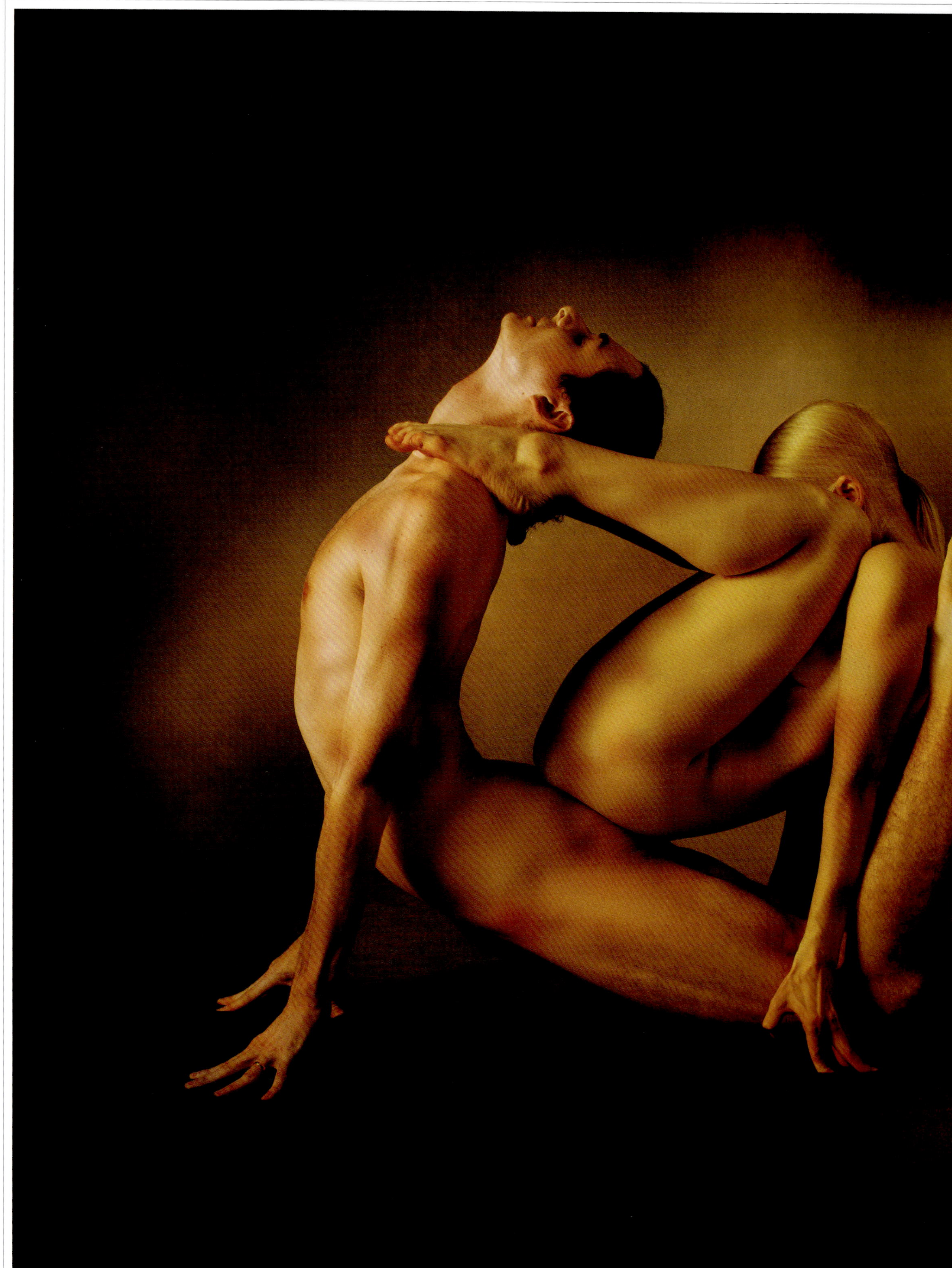

P236: Credit & Commentary

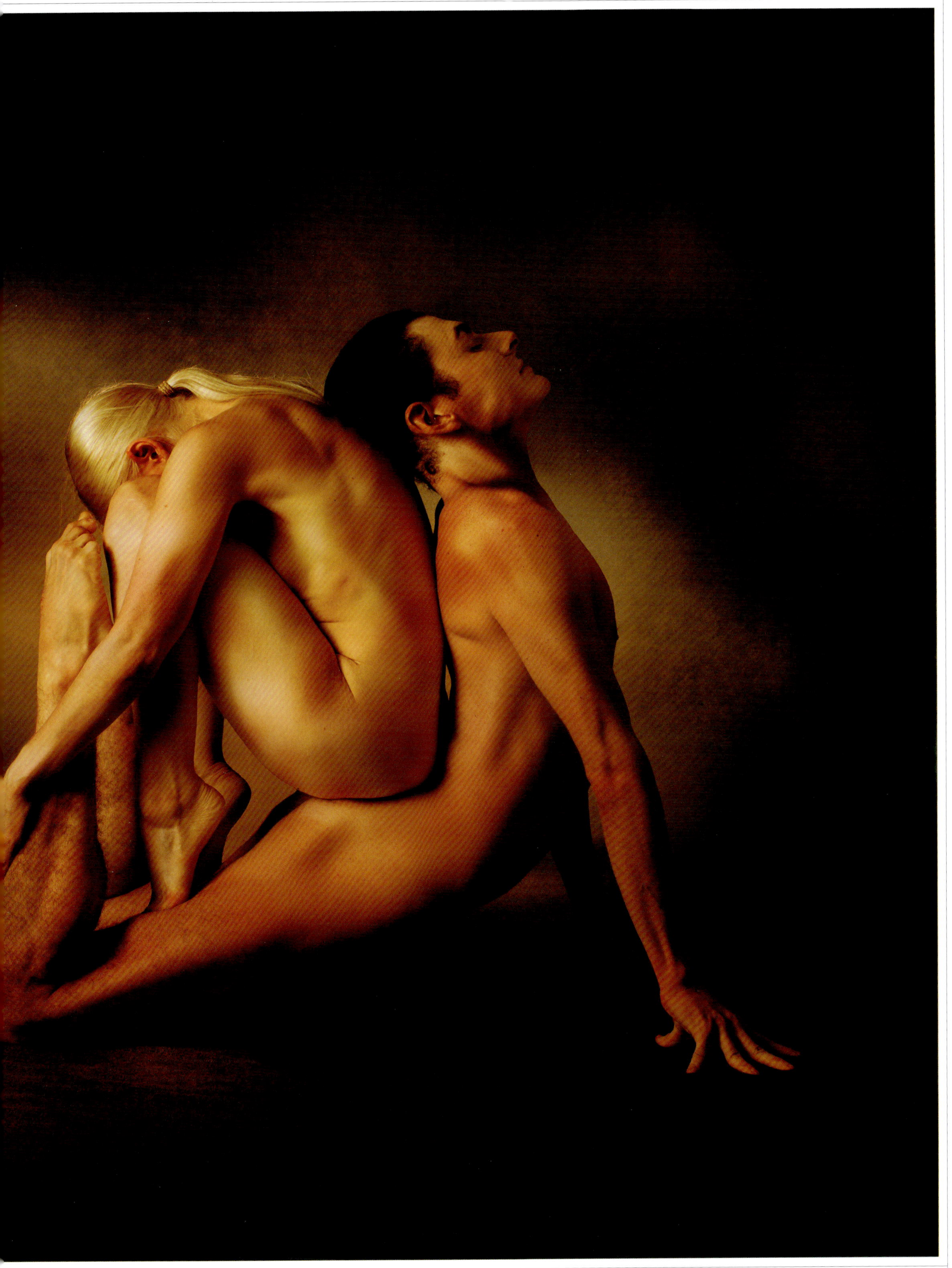

Title: Human Body Study, PAIRS #117: Dancers Emily Arden Jones & Joshua Leon Eguia | **Client:** Self-initiated

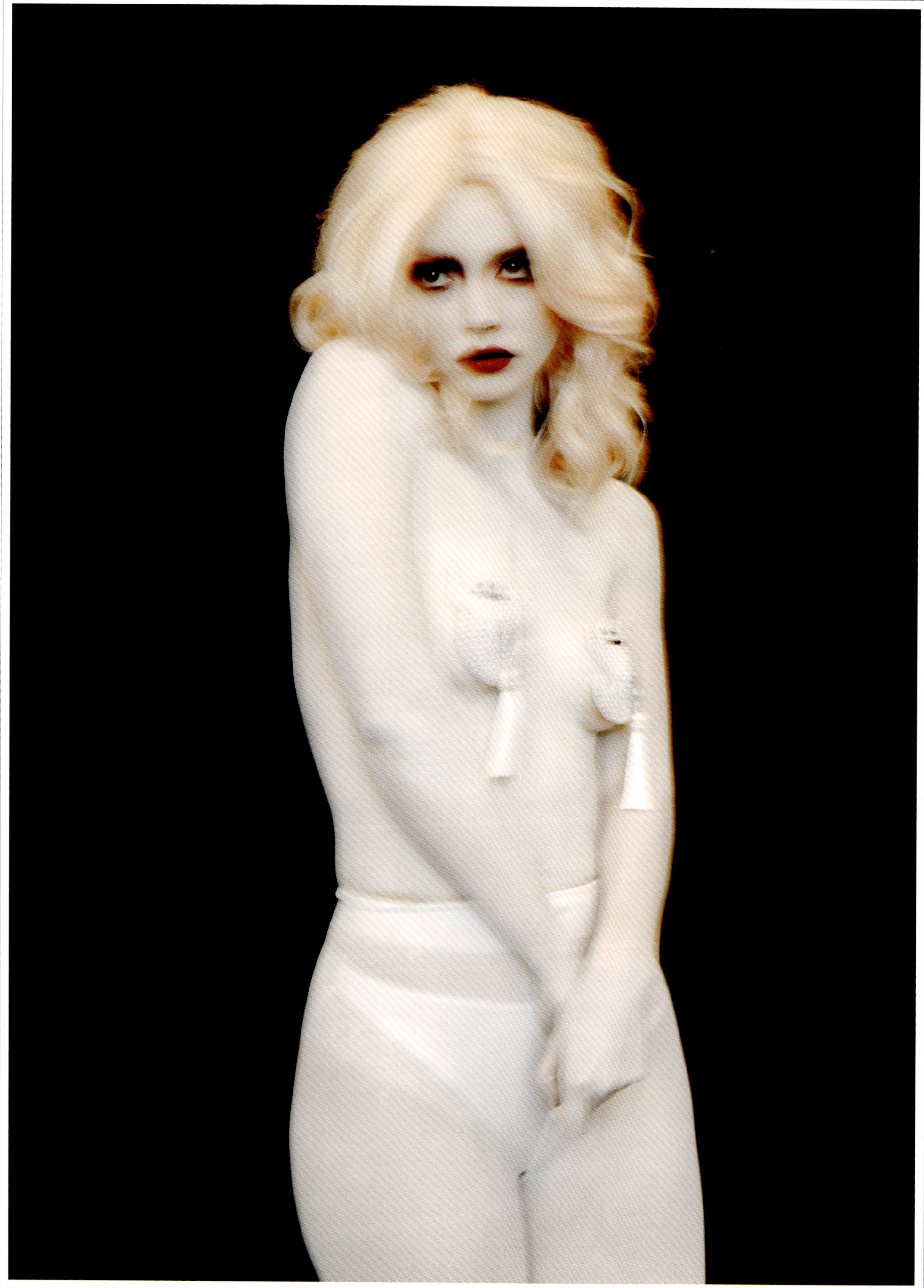

P236: Credit & Commentary

Title: Ghost Girl ~ Alina | **Client:** Self-initiated

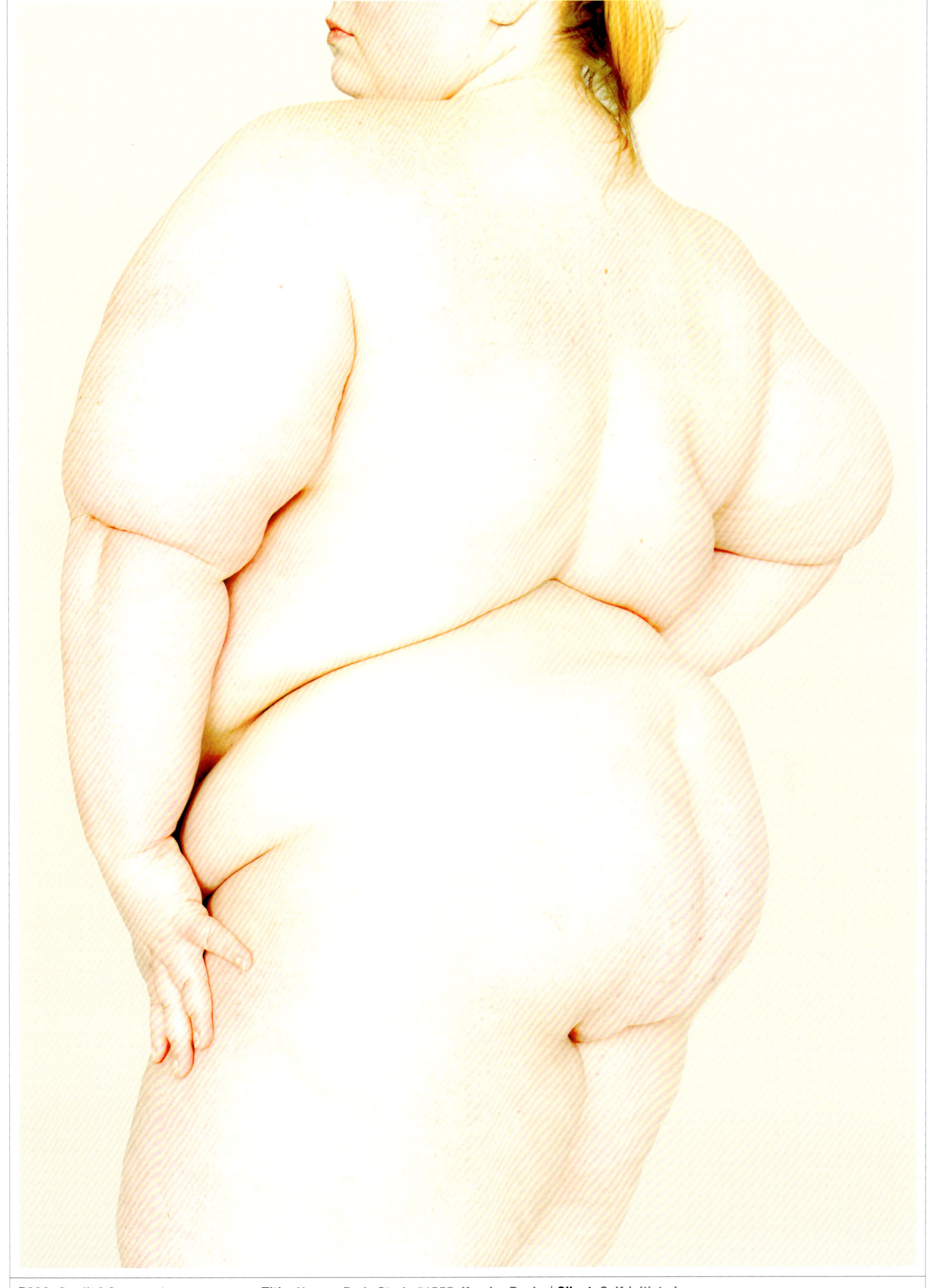

P236: Credit & Commentary

Title: Human Body Study #1555: Kendra Repko | **Client:** Self-initiated

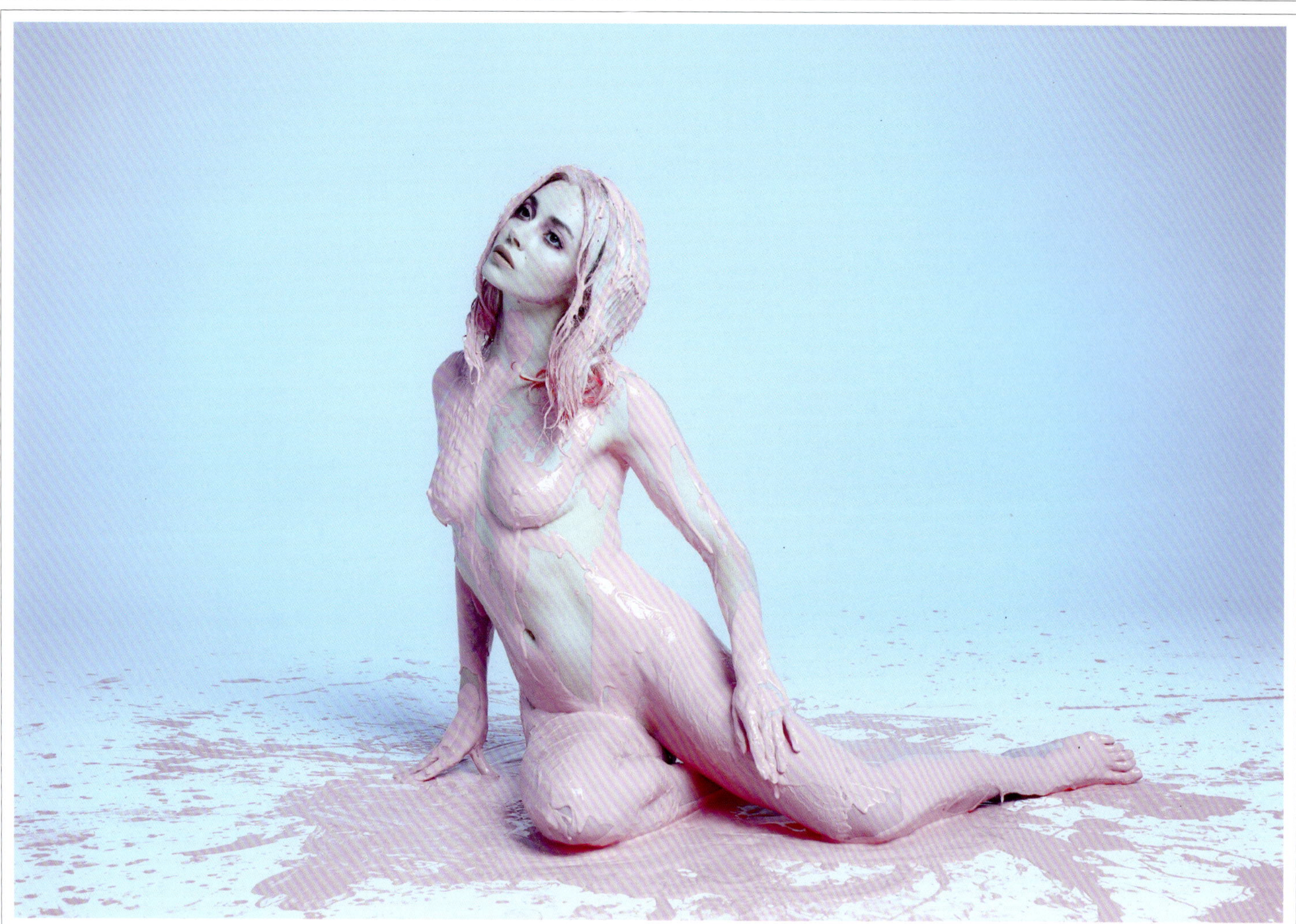

P236: Credit & Commentary

Title: Pigment of My Imagination | **Client:** Self-initiated

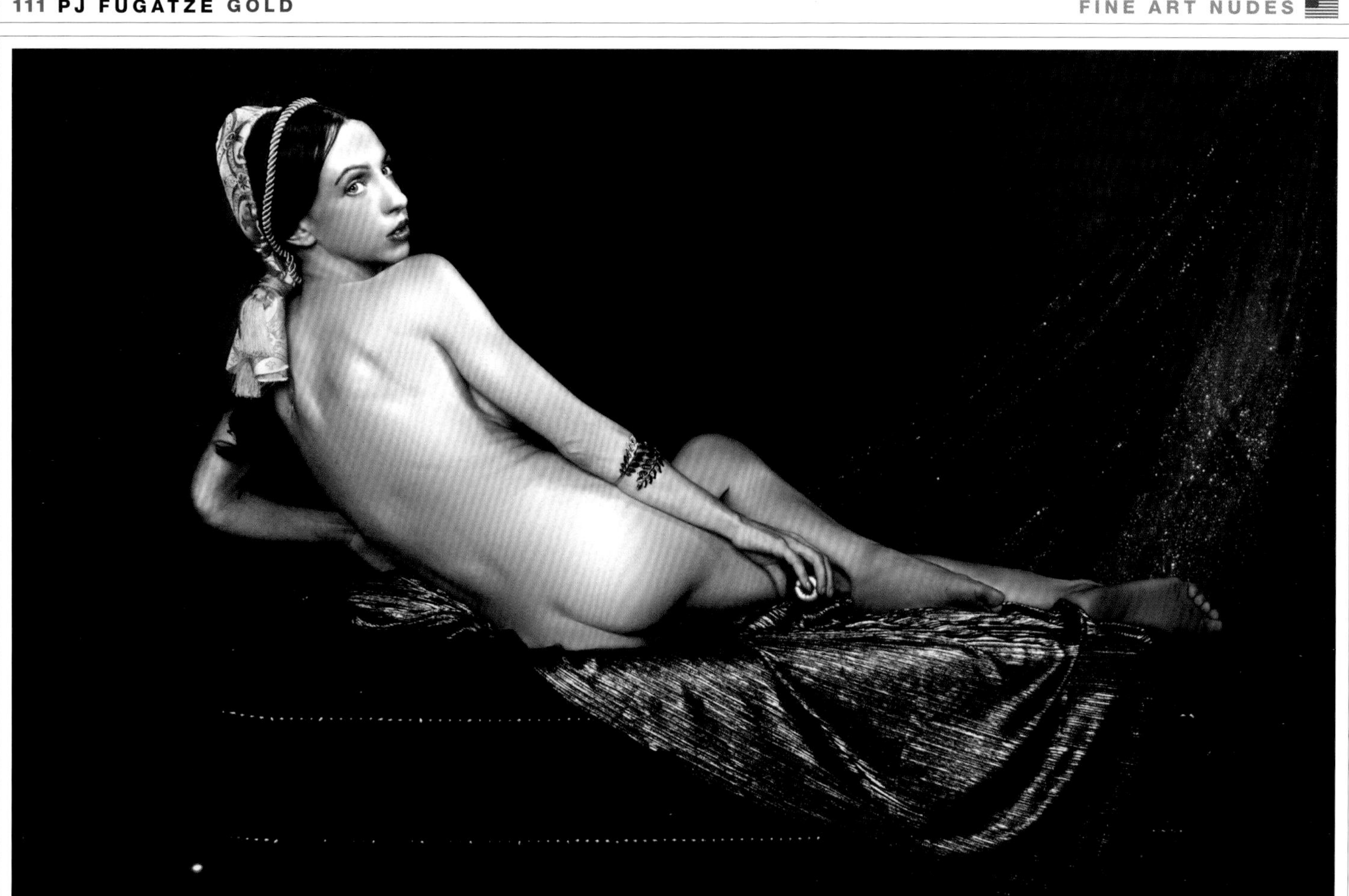

P236: Credit & Commentary **Title:** Odalisque | **Client:** Self-initiated

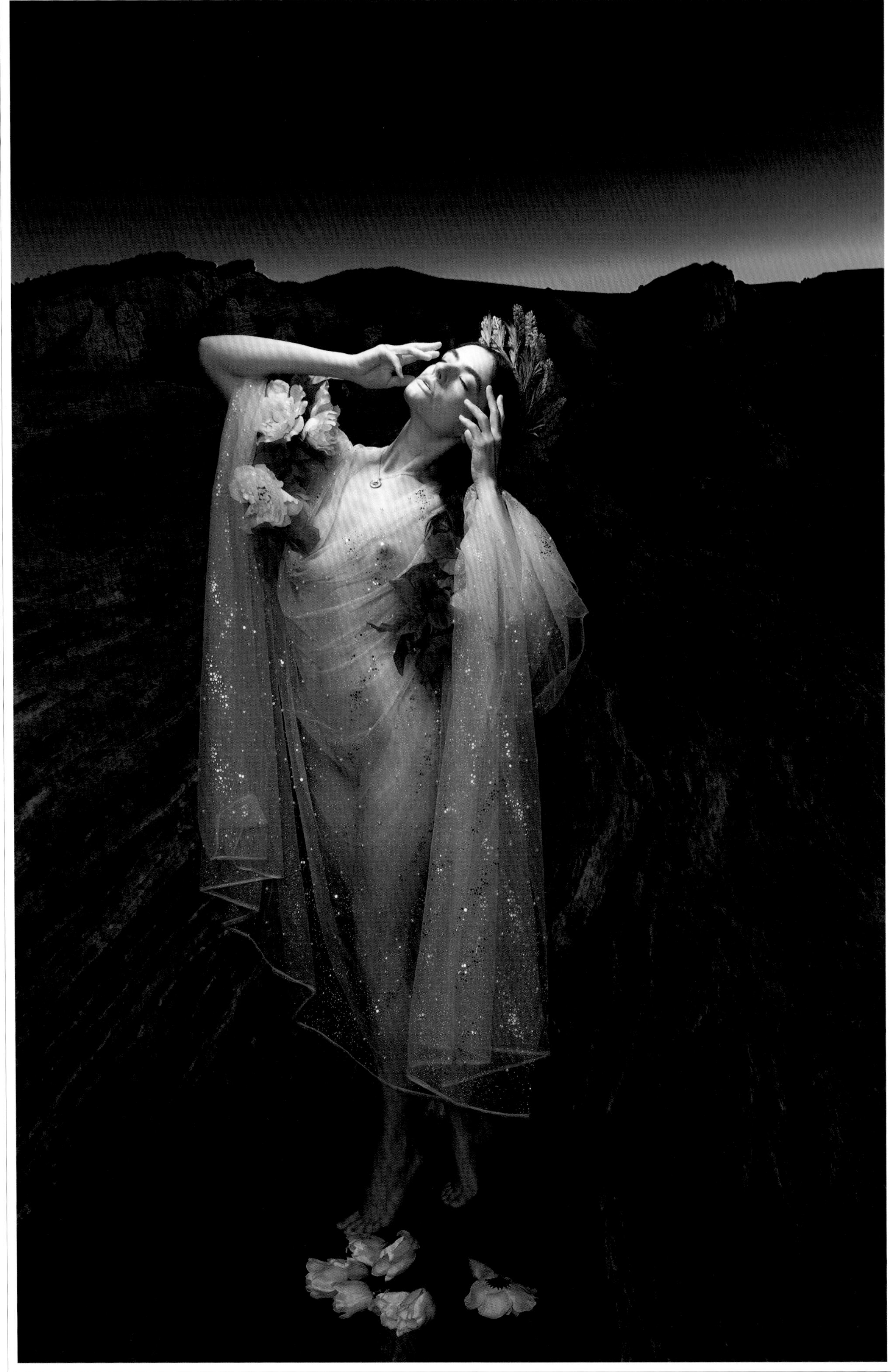

P236: Credit & Commentary **Title:** Persephone in Winter | **Client:** God

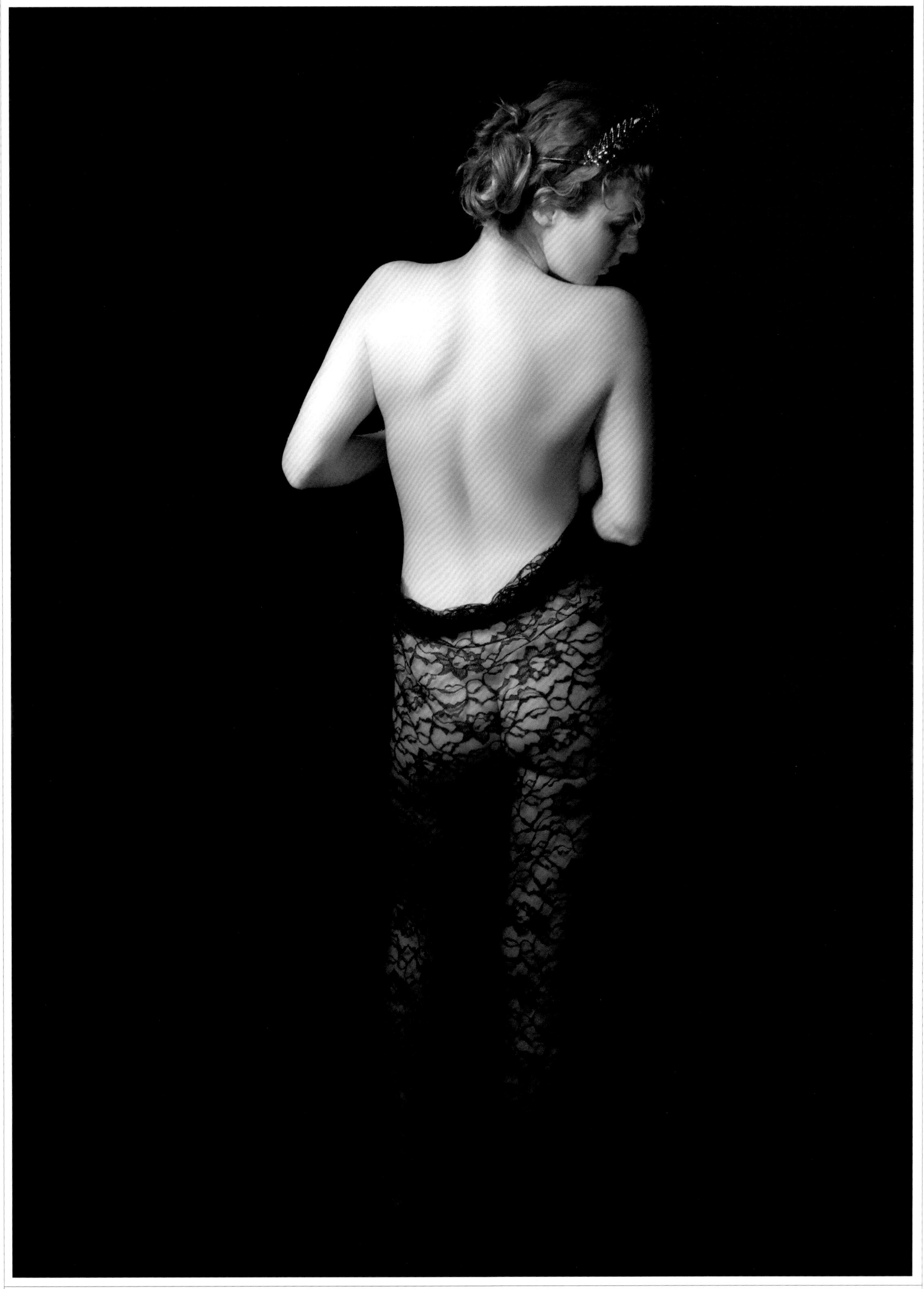

P236: Credit & Commentary

Title: Valpinçon Bather | **Client:** Self-initiated

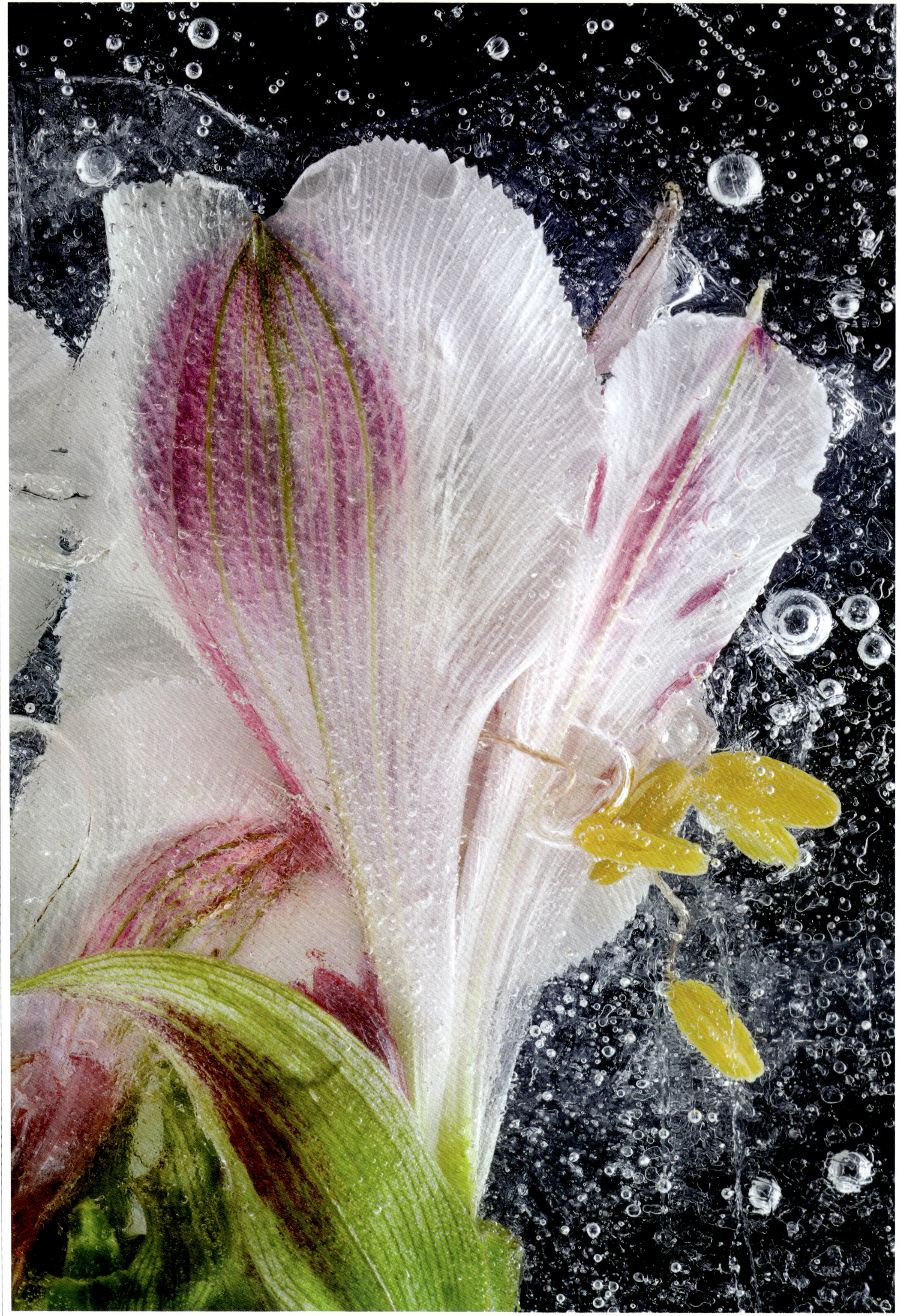

P236: Credit & Commentary Title: Fly by Night | Client: Self-initiated

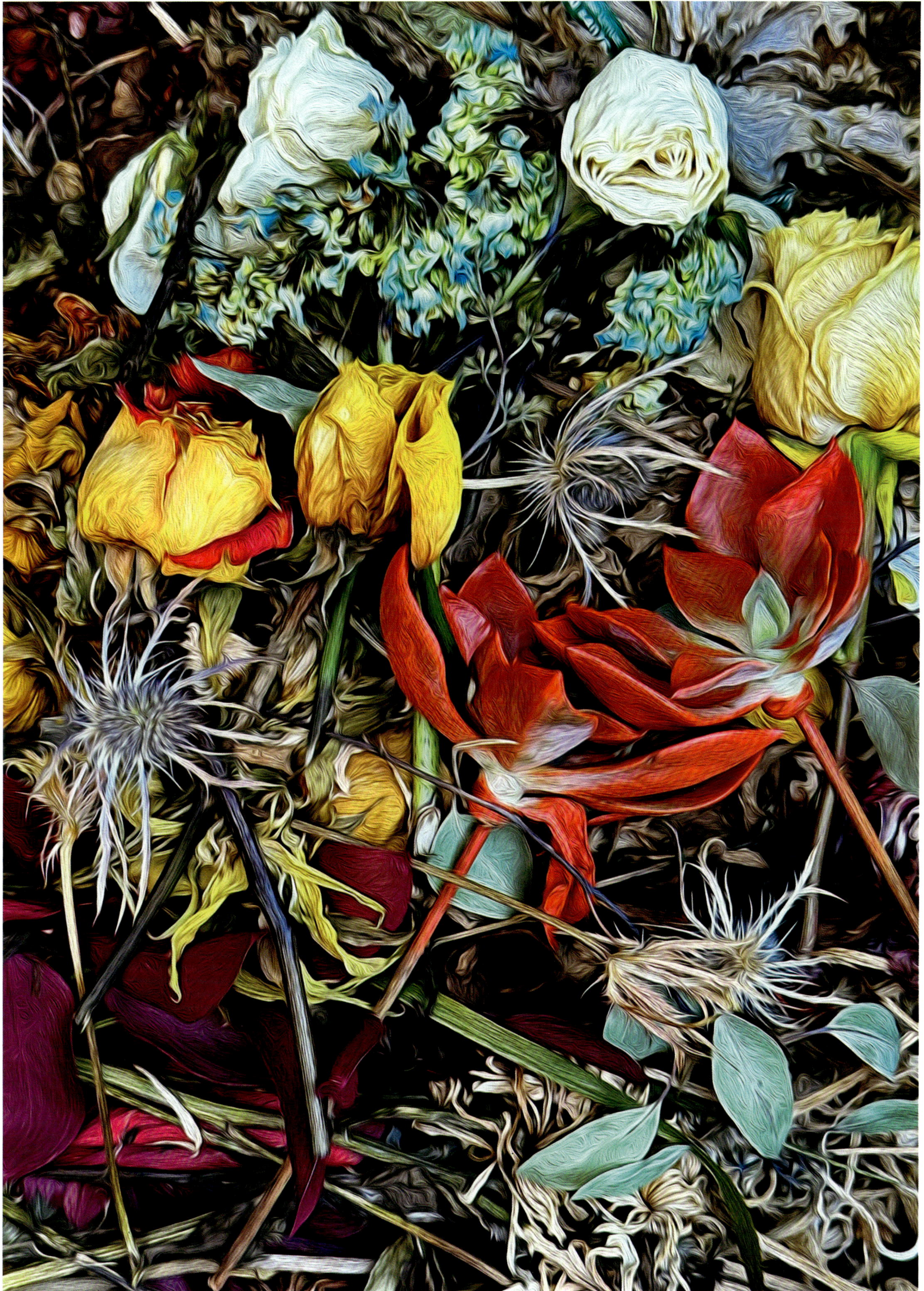

 Title: Last Bloom | Client: Self-initiated

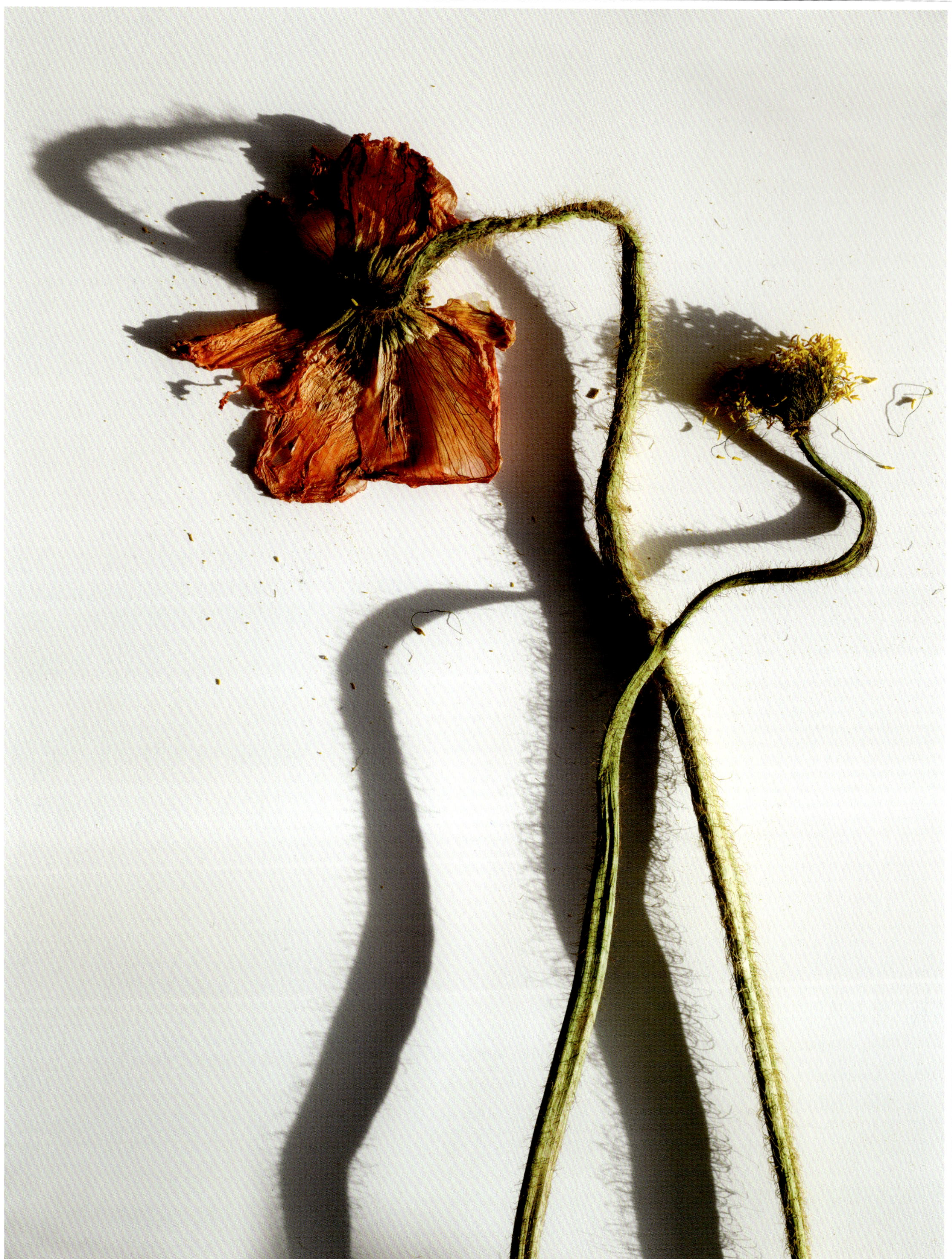

Title: Botanicals: Light and Shadow | Client: Self-initiated

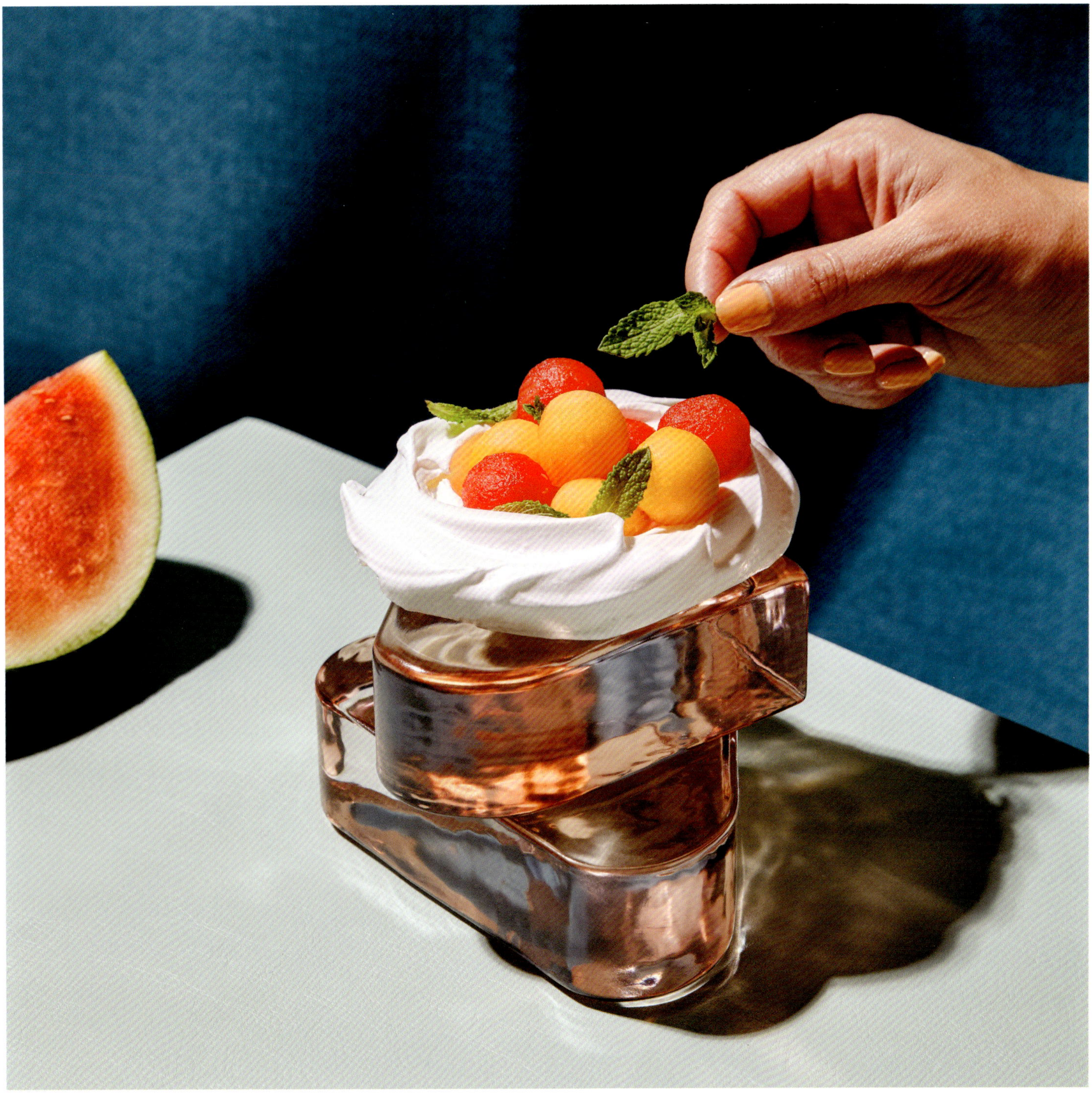

P236: Credit & Commentary

Title: Drink, Dessert, and Deconstruct | **Client:** Self-initiated

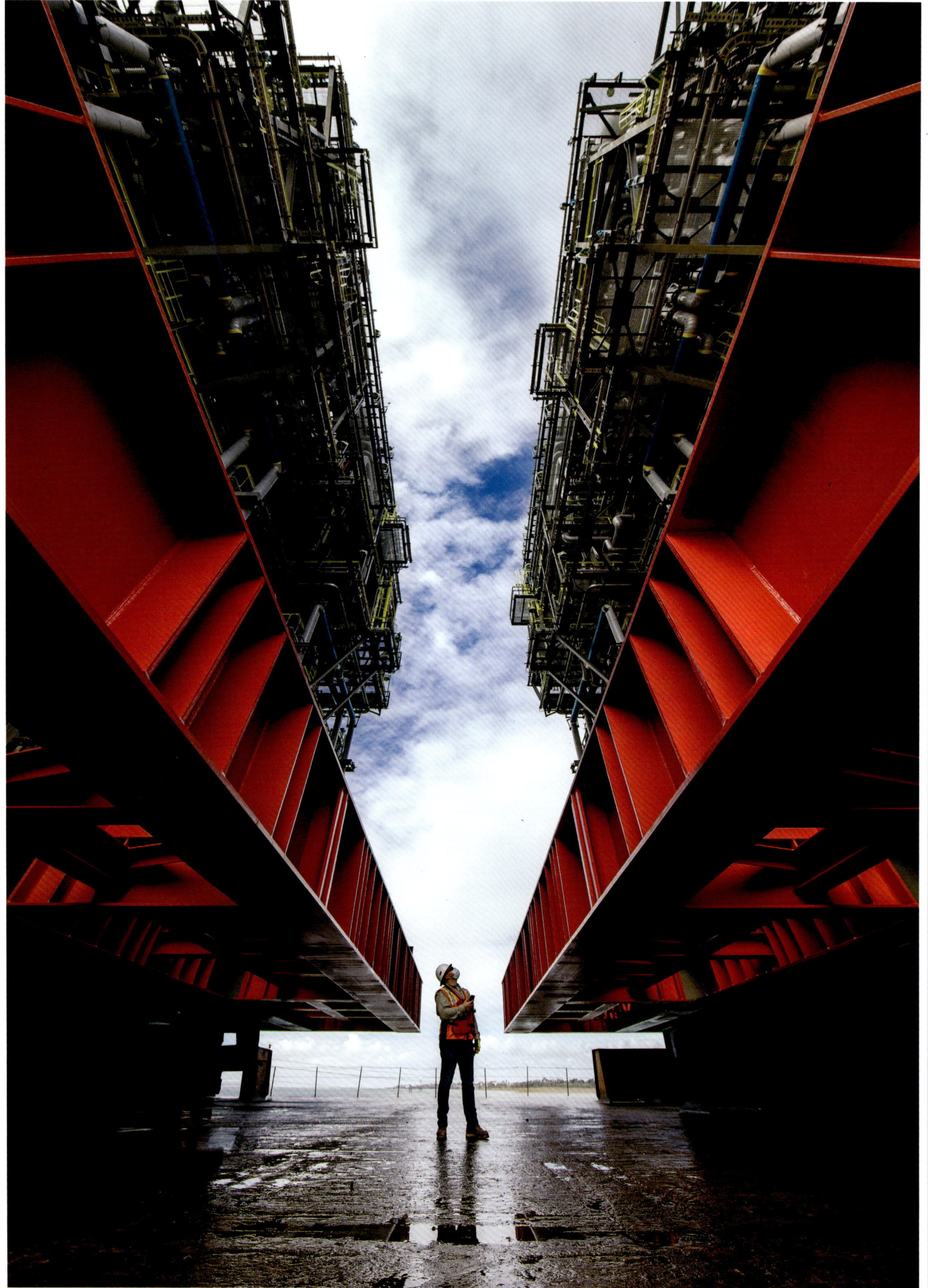

P237: Credit & Commentary

Title: Modules Movement and Assembly at GCGV | **Client:** ExxonMobil

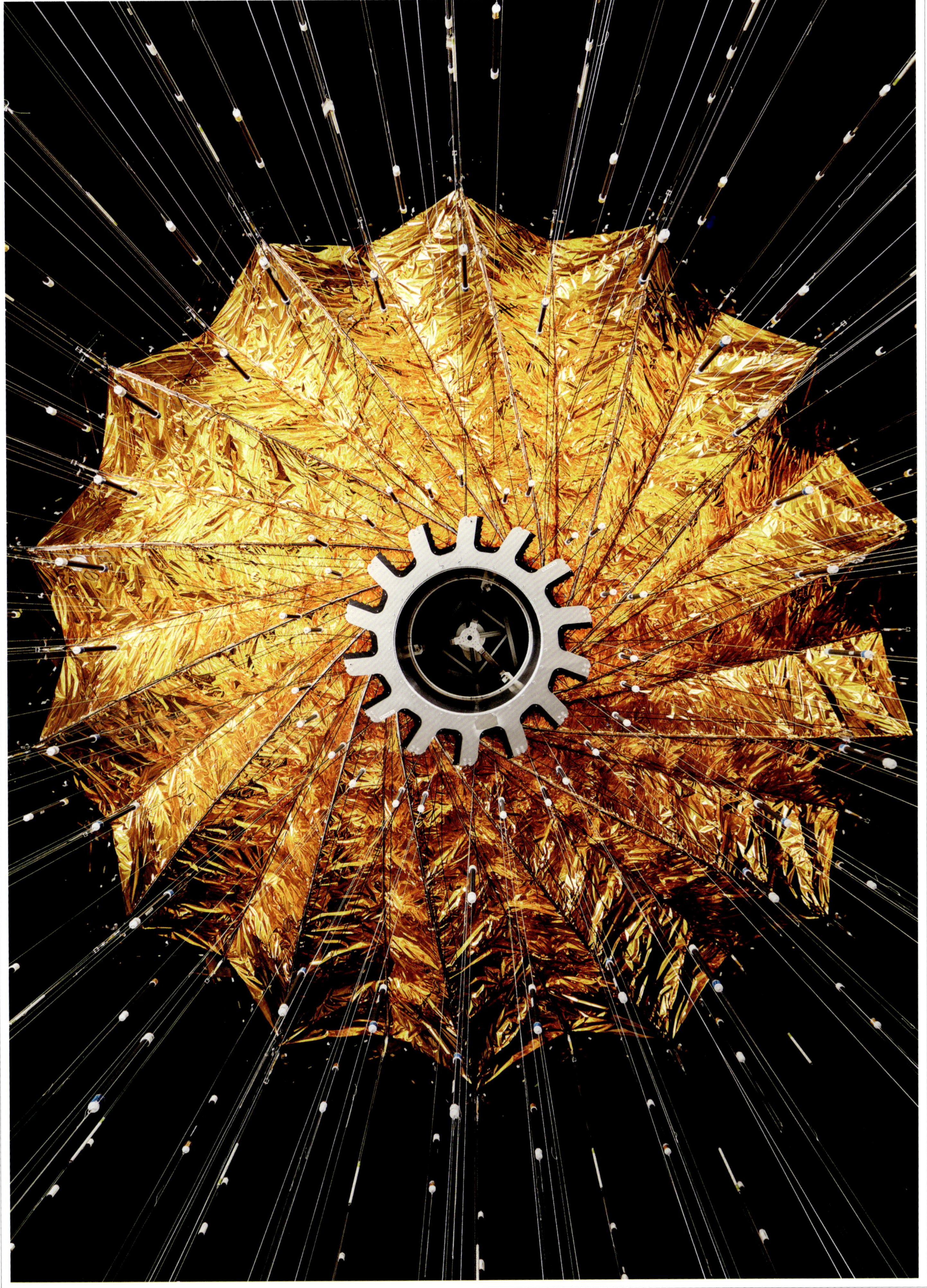

Title: NASA Starshade | Client: National Geographic Magazine

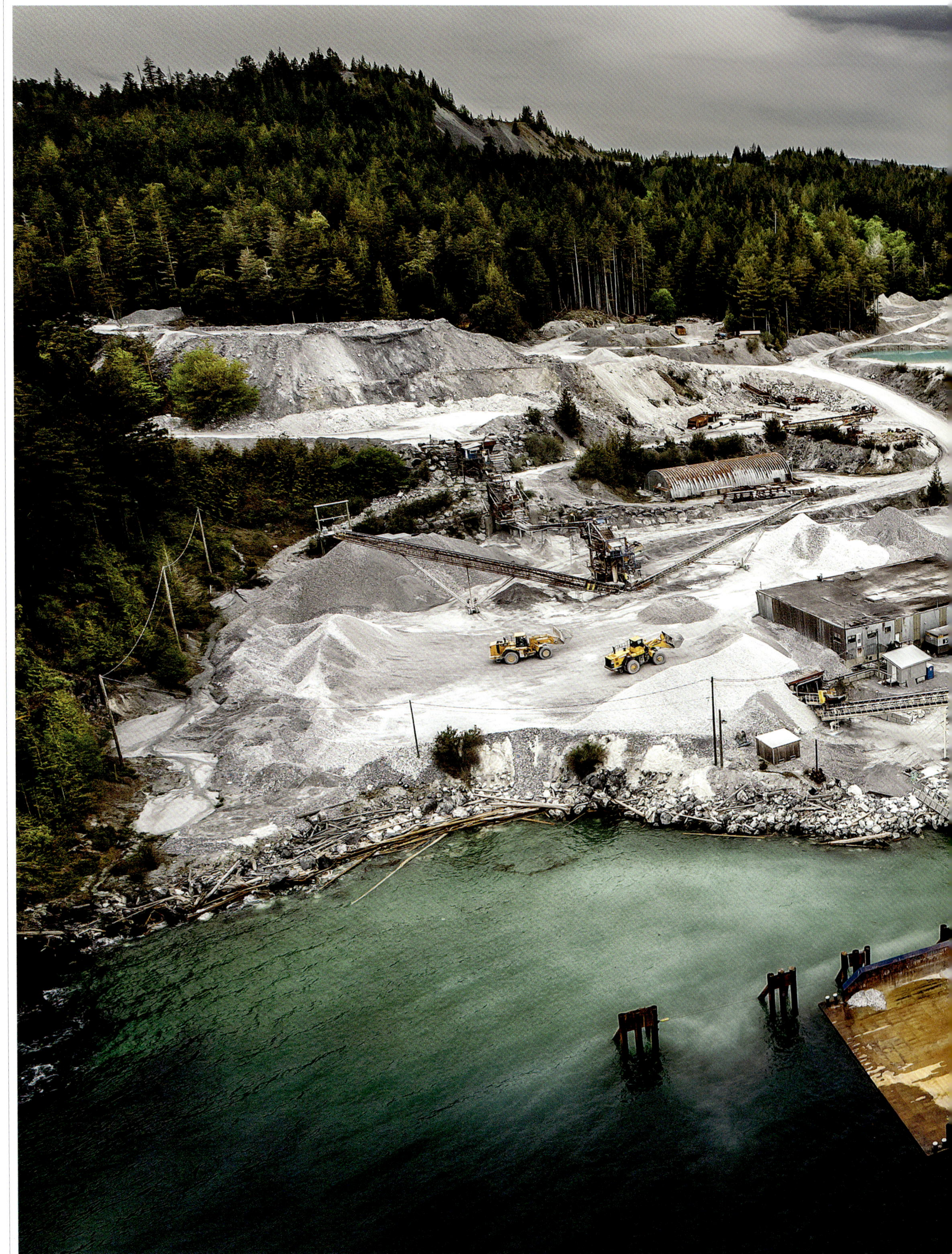

P237: Credit & Commentary

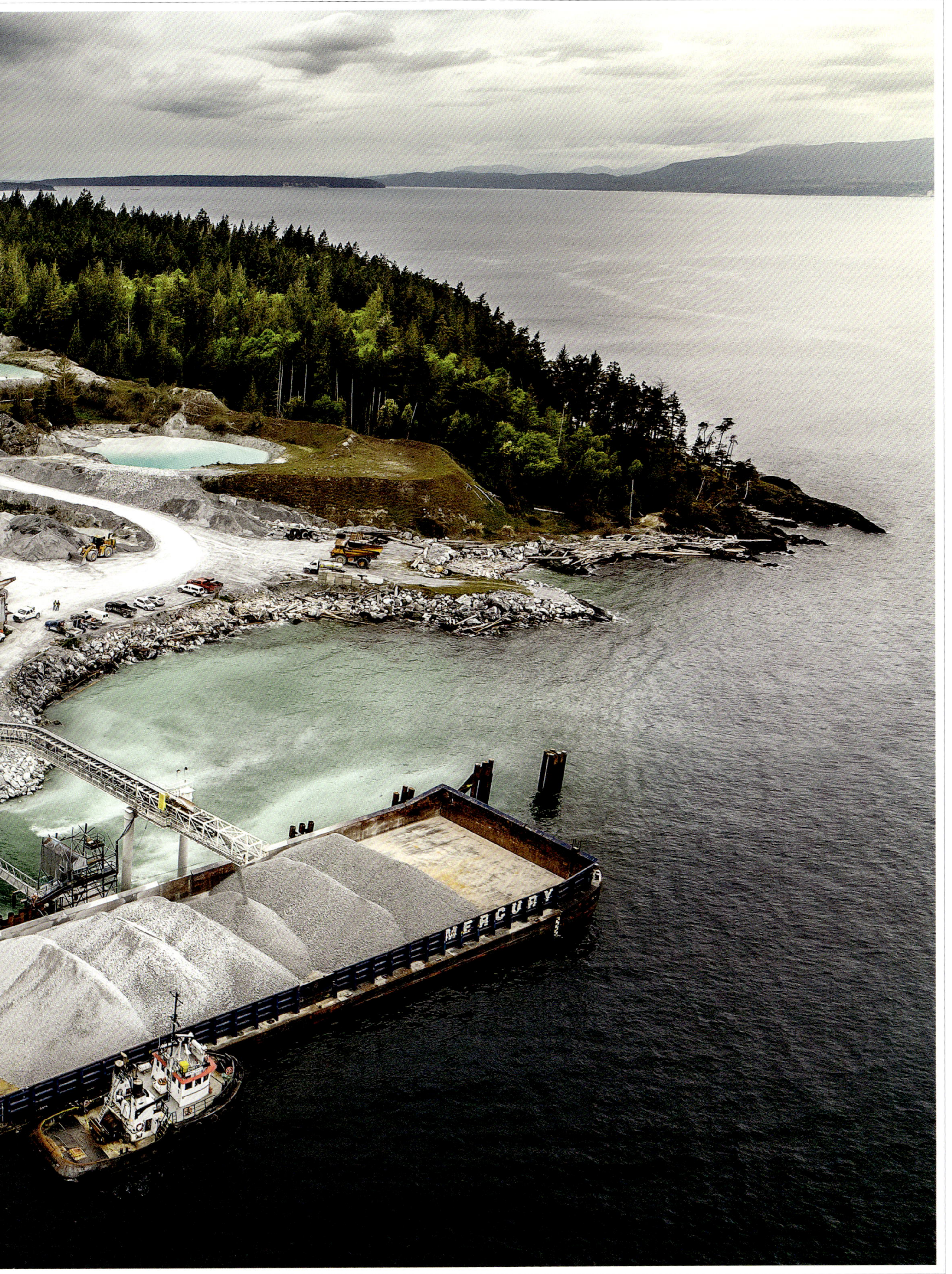

Title: Arcosa - Limestone Quarry in British Columbia, Canada | **Client:** Arcosa Specialty Materials

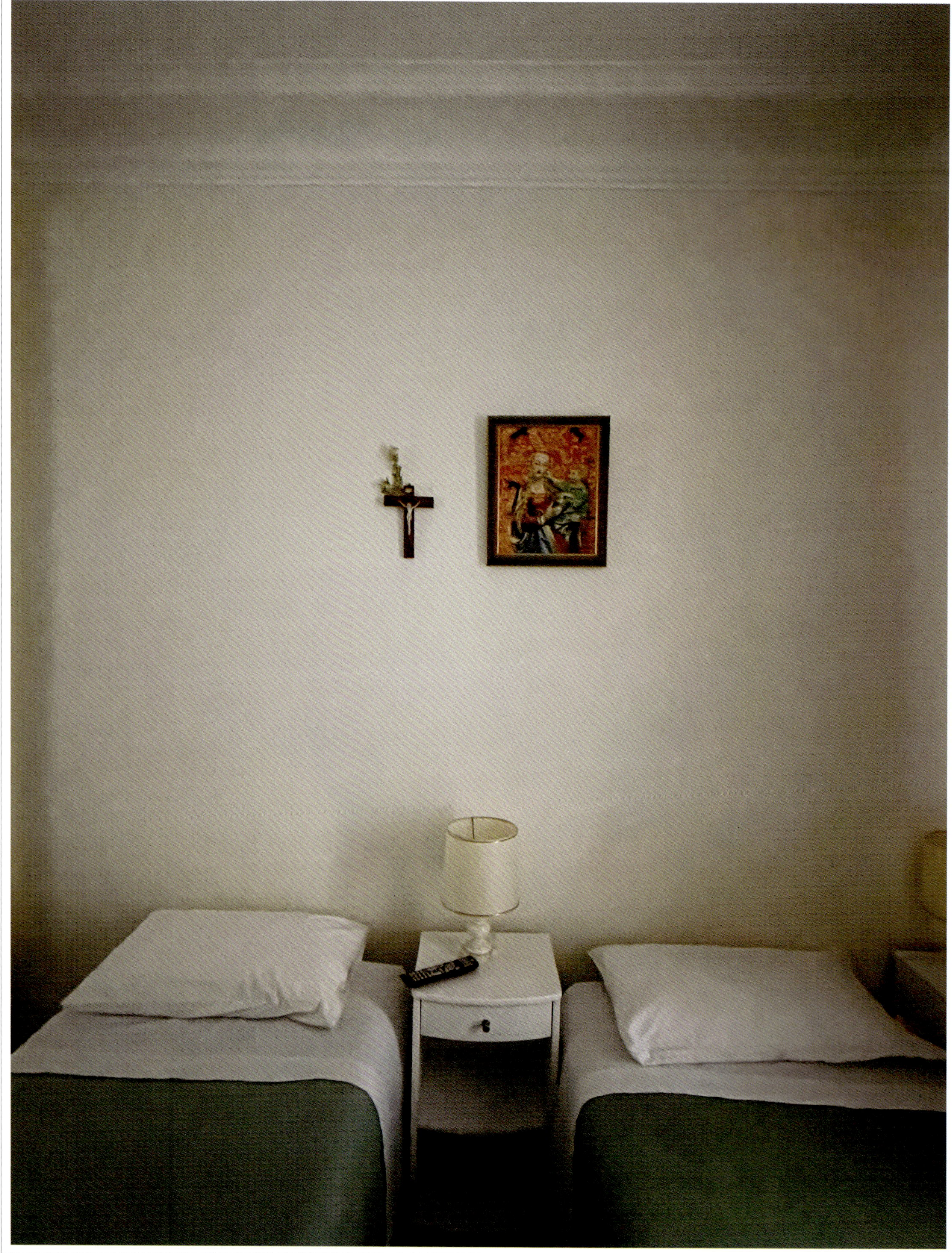

P237: Credit & Commentary

Title: Parisian Twins | Client: Self-initiated

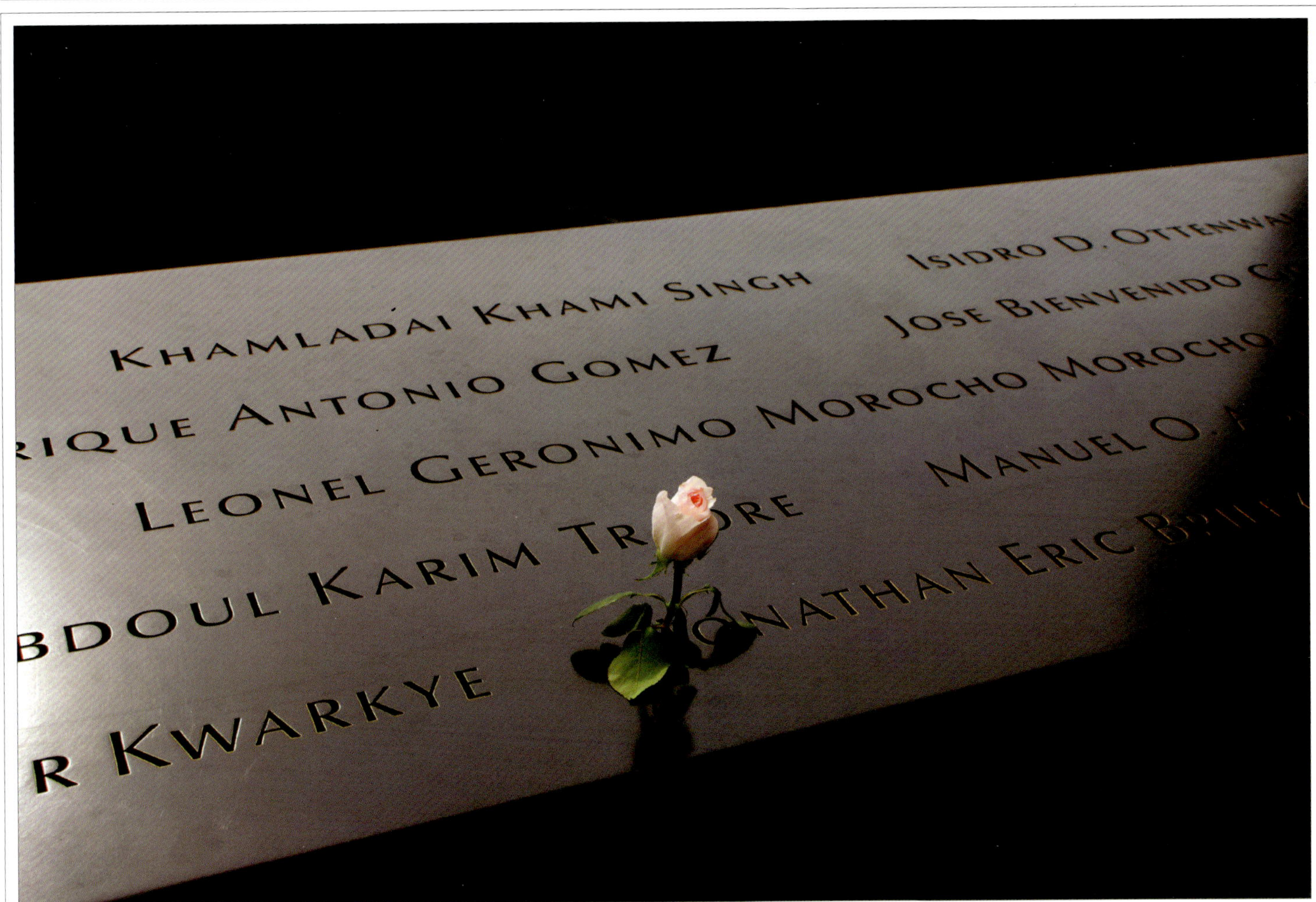

This photo was shot at the 9/11 Memorial in lower Manhattan in New York City, where, according to the 9/11 Memorial & Museum, the names of the 2,983 people who were killed in the terrorist attacks of both 1993 and 2001 are inscribed on bronze parapets edging the memorial pools.

For years, I traveled to Manhattan and often enjoyed dinner with a client at the Windows on the World restaurant at the top of the World Trade Center's North Tower. The 9/11 attacks broke my heart. While in New York in 2022, I visited both the One World Trade Center and the memorial. When I left the building that late afternoon and approached the fountain, I saw a pink rosebud rising up from one of the names. To me, it represented something beautiful manifesting from the pain we all went through that day. That beauty was freedom.

To shoot this photo, I used a Nikon D3X camera with a macro lens. I was lucky with the lighting; I captured the moment during the end of the day with blue light, so in the shot, everything was dark but the flower, which was bright and created a natural focal point that sparked my emotions. The photo is just how I shot it, without editing or cropping.

P237: Credit & Commentary **Title:** Liberty Flourishing | **Client:** ZEVEN Magazine

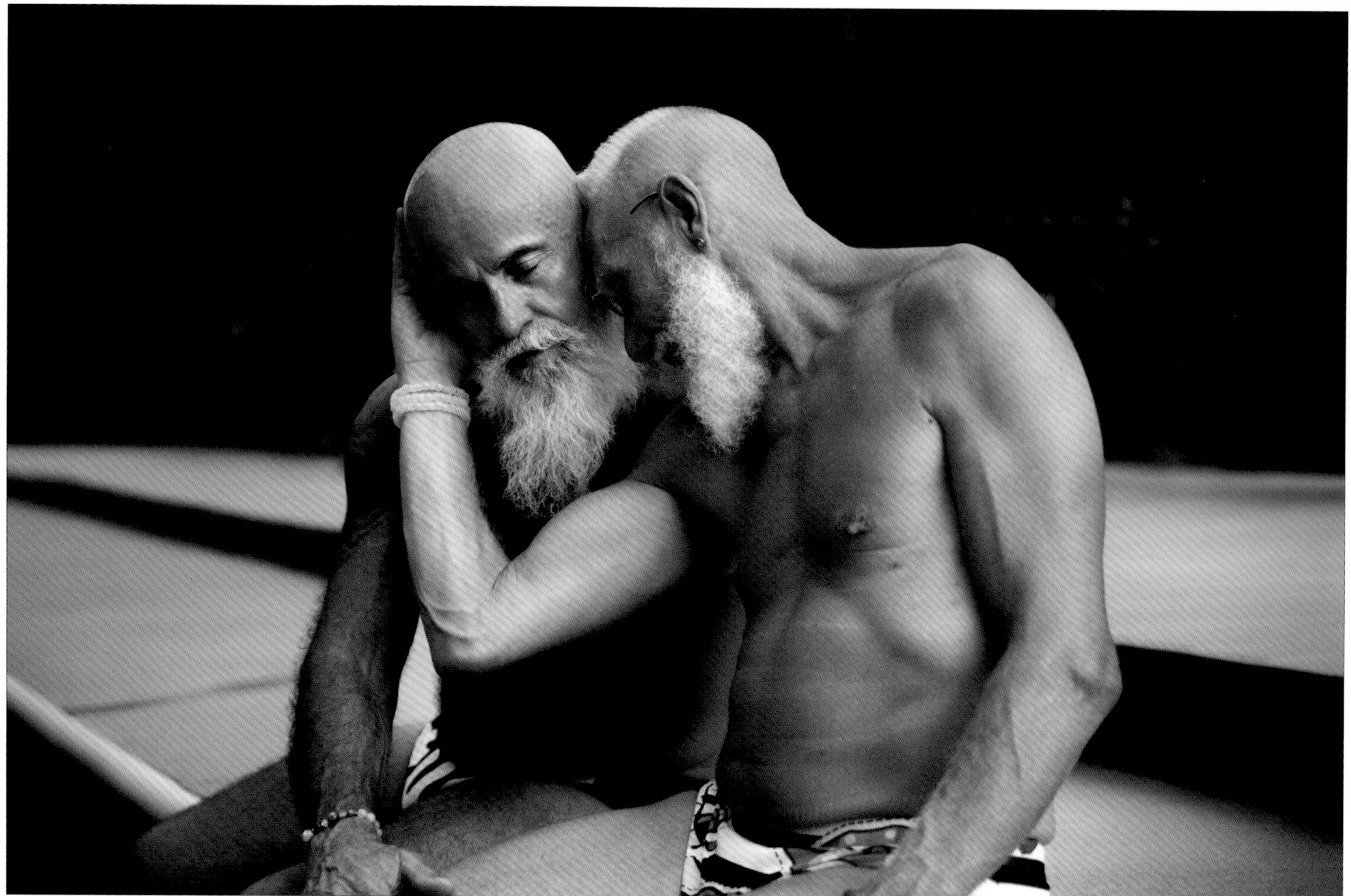

I've been working on a documentary, *Gay Home Movie,* chronicling gay history for the past five years. Along the way, I have met some amazing people who agreed to be interviewed and photographed for the film.
I was immediately drawn to David and Patric, who I met by chance at a campground on a weekend getaway. There was something of a Socratic air about them.
Before taking out my camera, I approached them, and we talked for about an hour. I didn't ask many questions, allowing them to gradually open up on their terms. I then shared my own life experiences as a fellow member of the LGBTQ community. During the shoot, I gave them some direction but mostly allowed them to just be themselves.
At one point, I asked Patric to cradle David's head in his arm. The gesture felt natural yet sculpted, like classical Greek figures. What emerges in the final image is something solid and timeless, like the life they've built together.
Historical art is often an influence in my work. It's never something that is planned. Instead, it is revealed to me in the process. As photographers, I think it's important to remain open to our muses, wherever they may take us.

P237: Credit & Commentary

Title: David and Patric | **Client:** Self-initiated

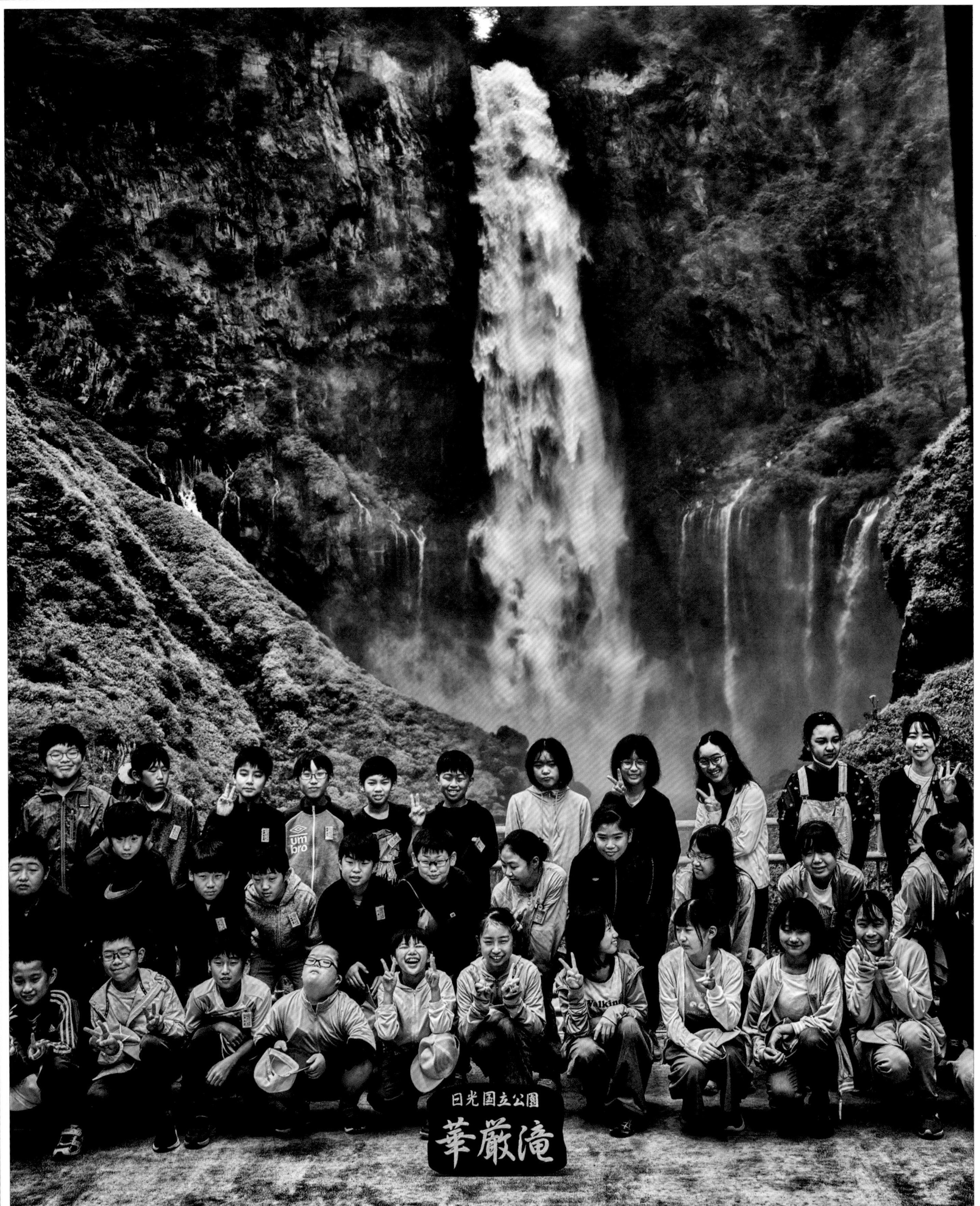

The image "Children with Waterfall" came about while visiting the great waterfalls in Nikko National Park. Based in the Kantō region, on the main island of Honshū in Japan, the park was established in 1934. It's very popular with tourists, and multiple school trips were visiting the falls that day. The teacher was setting up a final group portrait of the class in front of the falls and allowed me to take this picture. The children were wonderful, polite, and very happy to be there. The camera used was a Leica M10 Monochrom with a 35mm lens.

P237: Credit & Commentary **Title:** Children with Waterfall | **Client:** Self-initiated

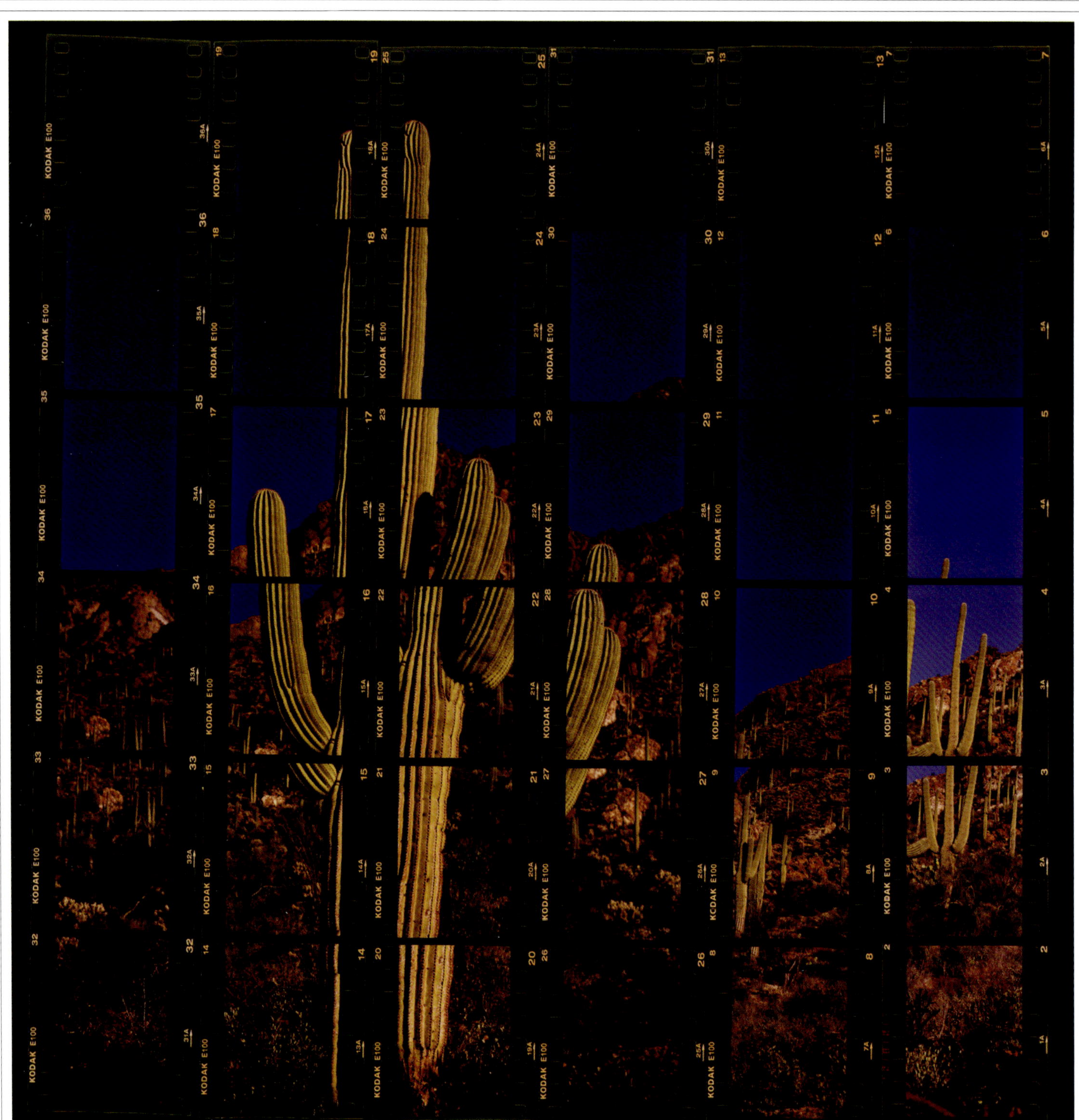

P237: Credit & Commentary **Title:** The King of the Desert | **Client:** Self-initiated Image 1 of 5

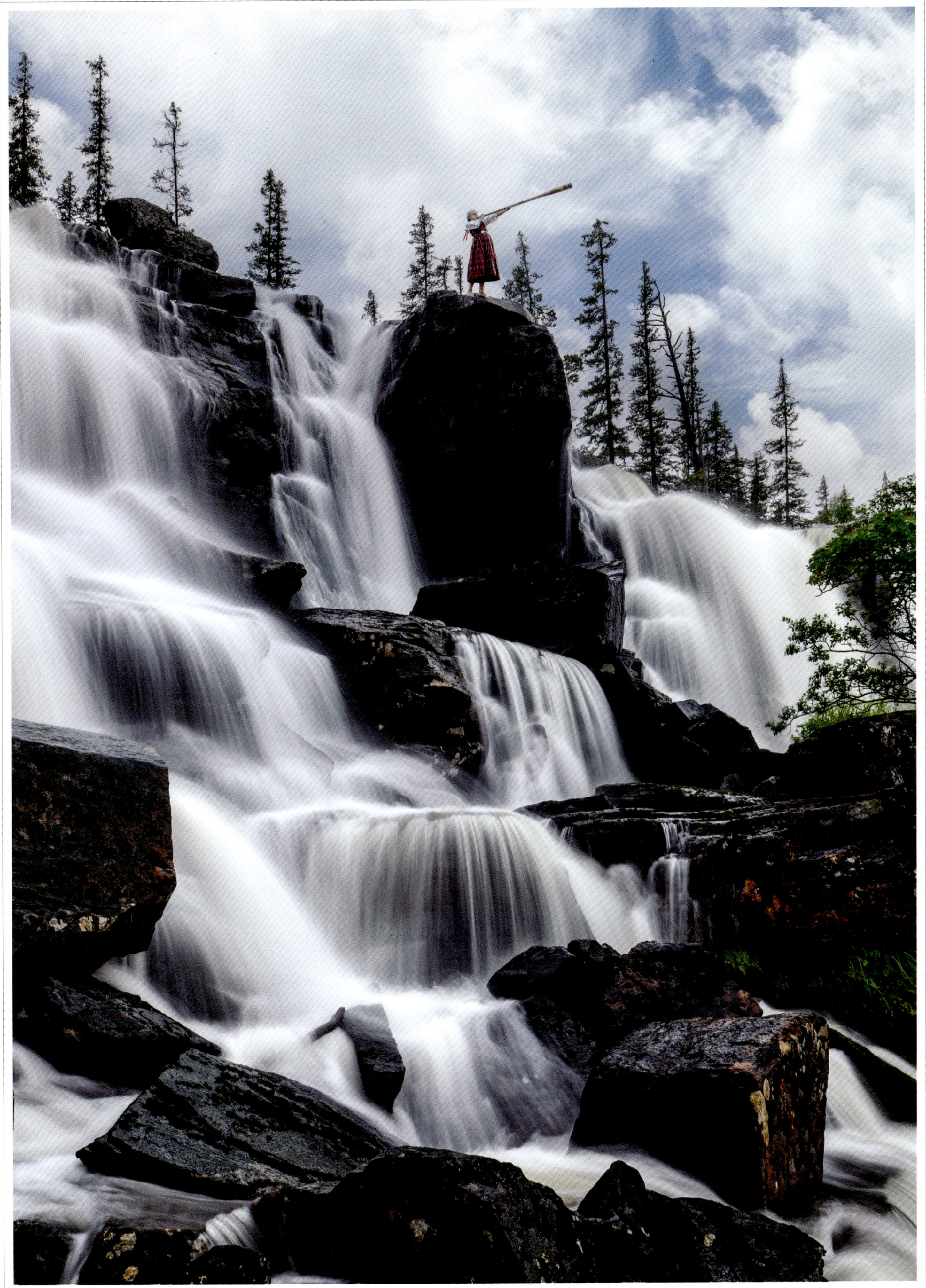

P237: Credit & Commentary

Title: The Girl in the Waterfall | Client: Self-initiated

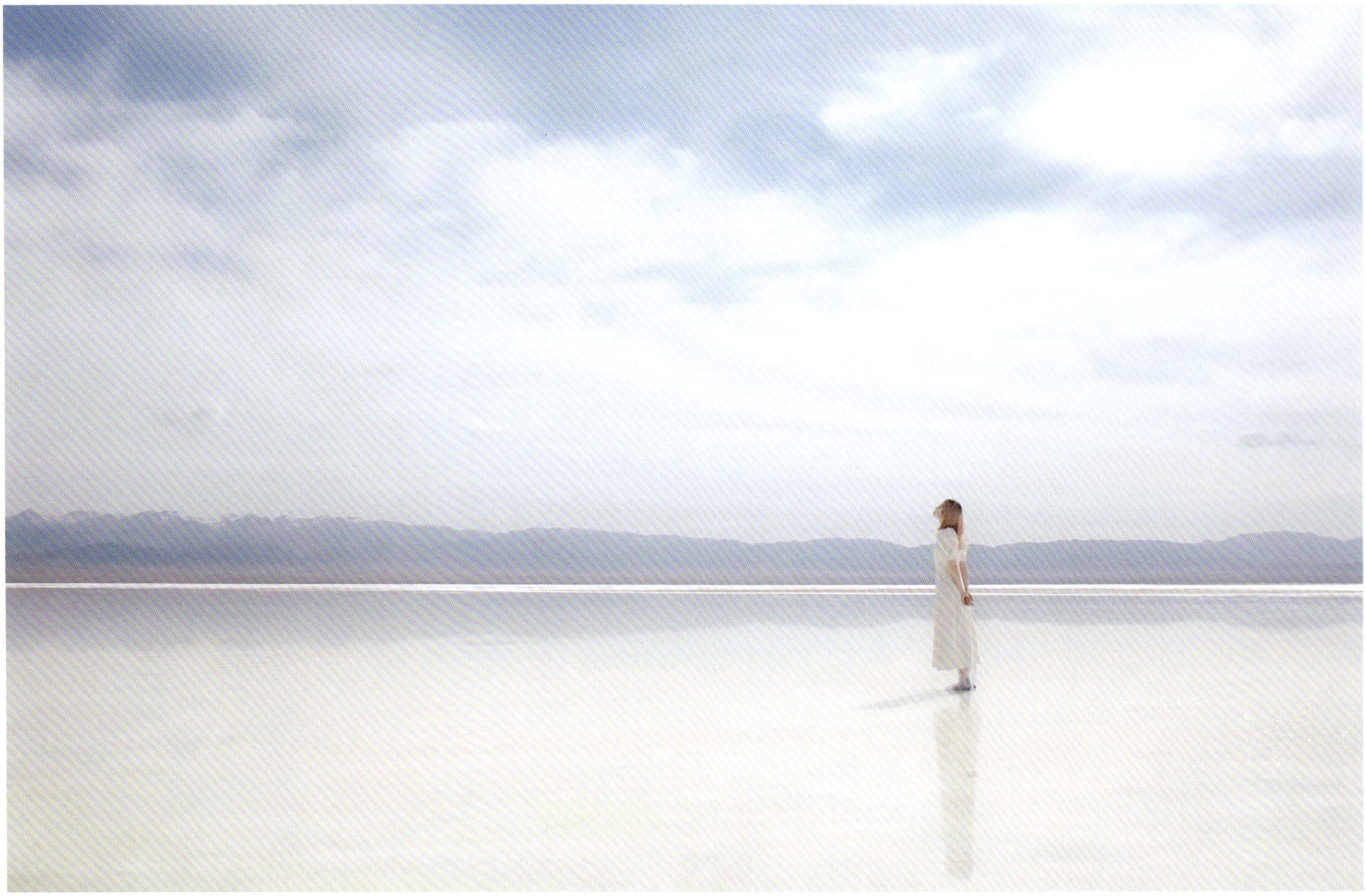

YICHEN WANG GOLD

LANDSCAPE

P237: Credit & Commentary

Title: A Breath | **Client:** Self-initiated

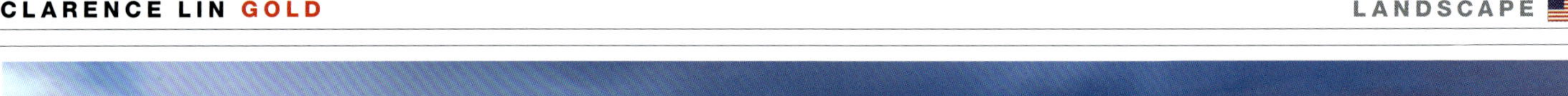

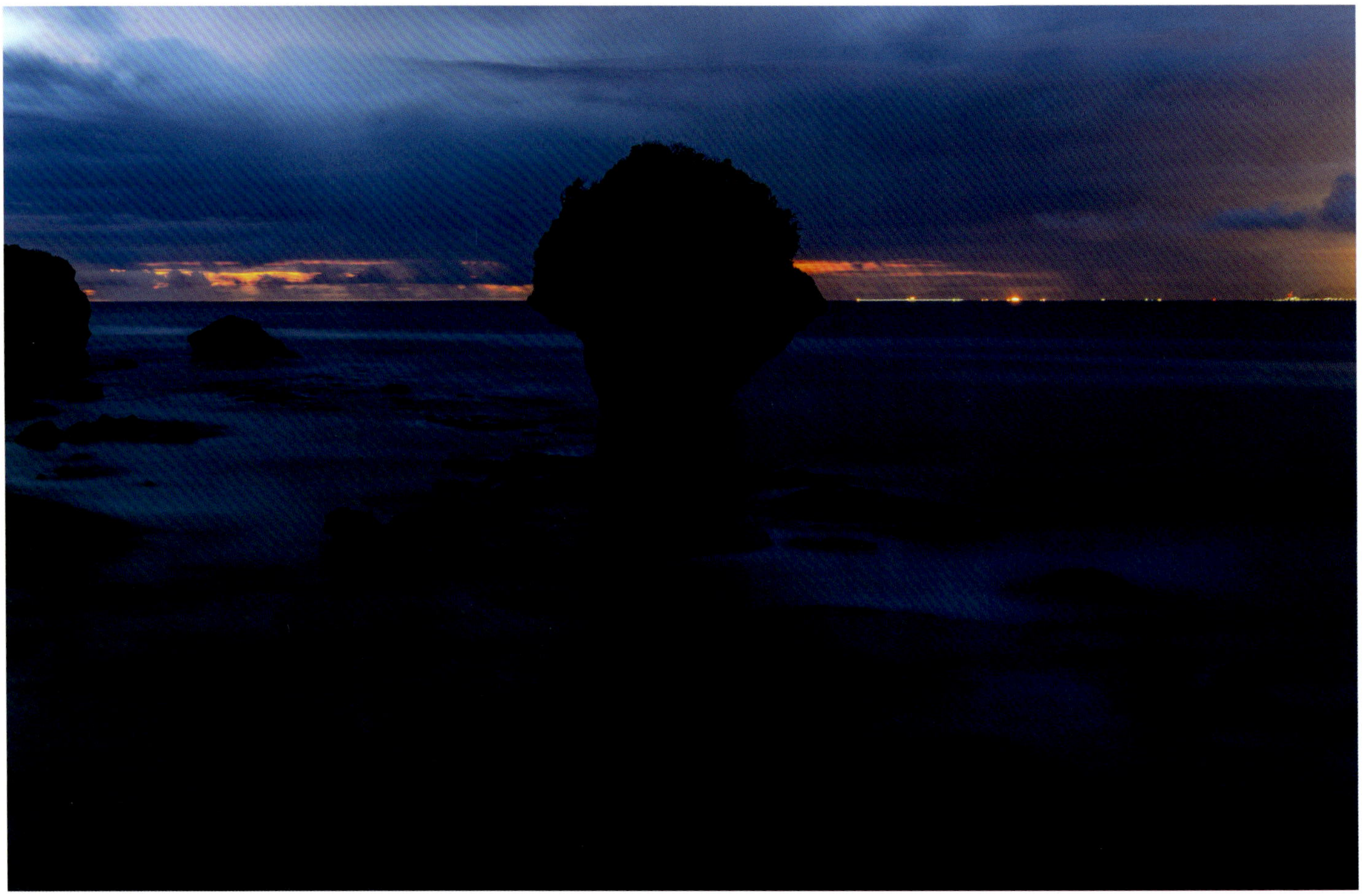

CLARENCE LIN GOLD

LANDSCAPE

P237: Credit & Commentary

Title: Vase Rock | **Client:** Self-initiated

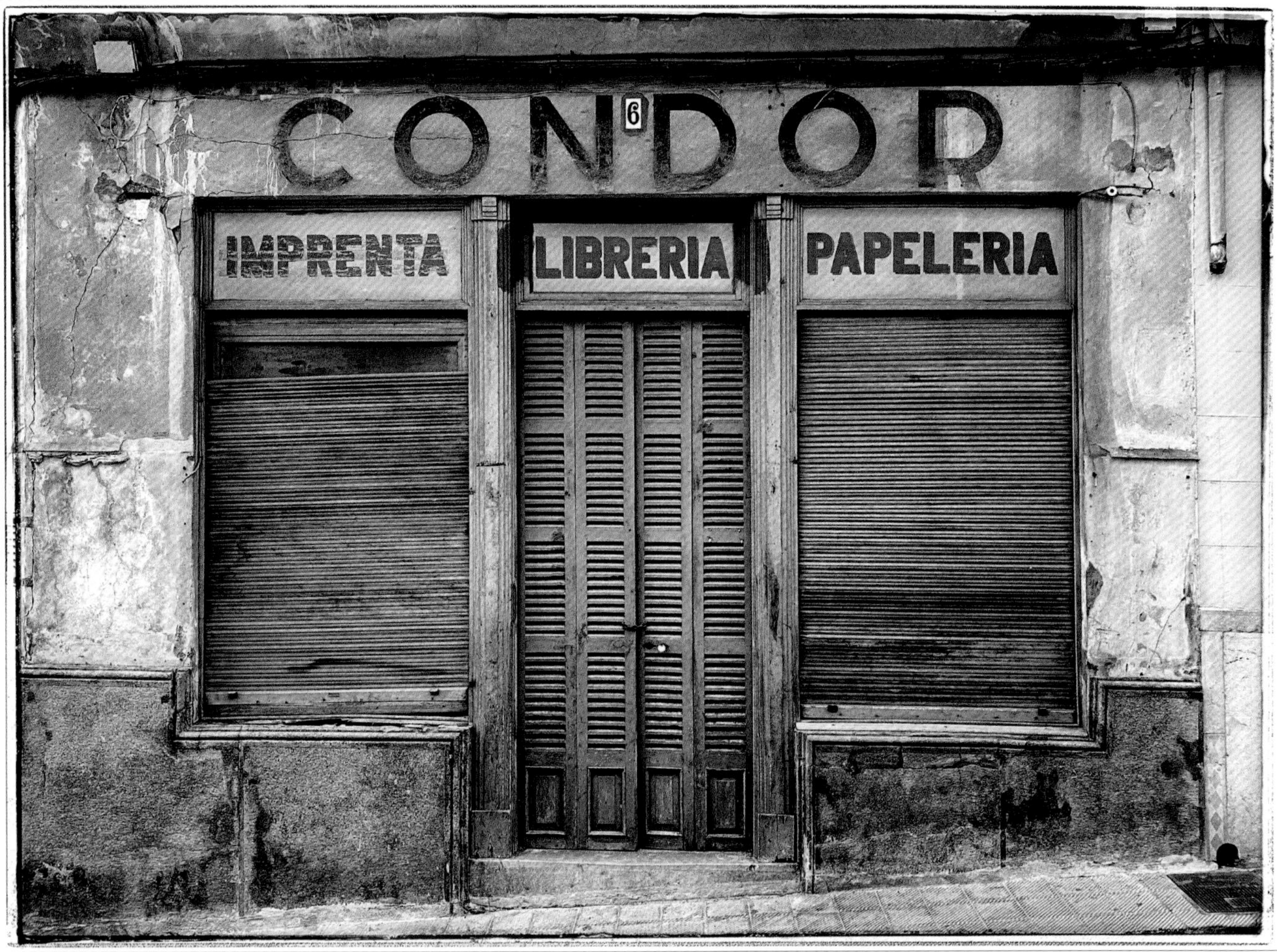

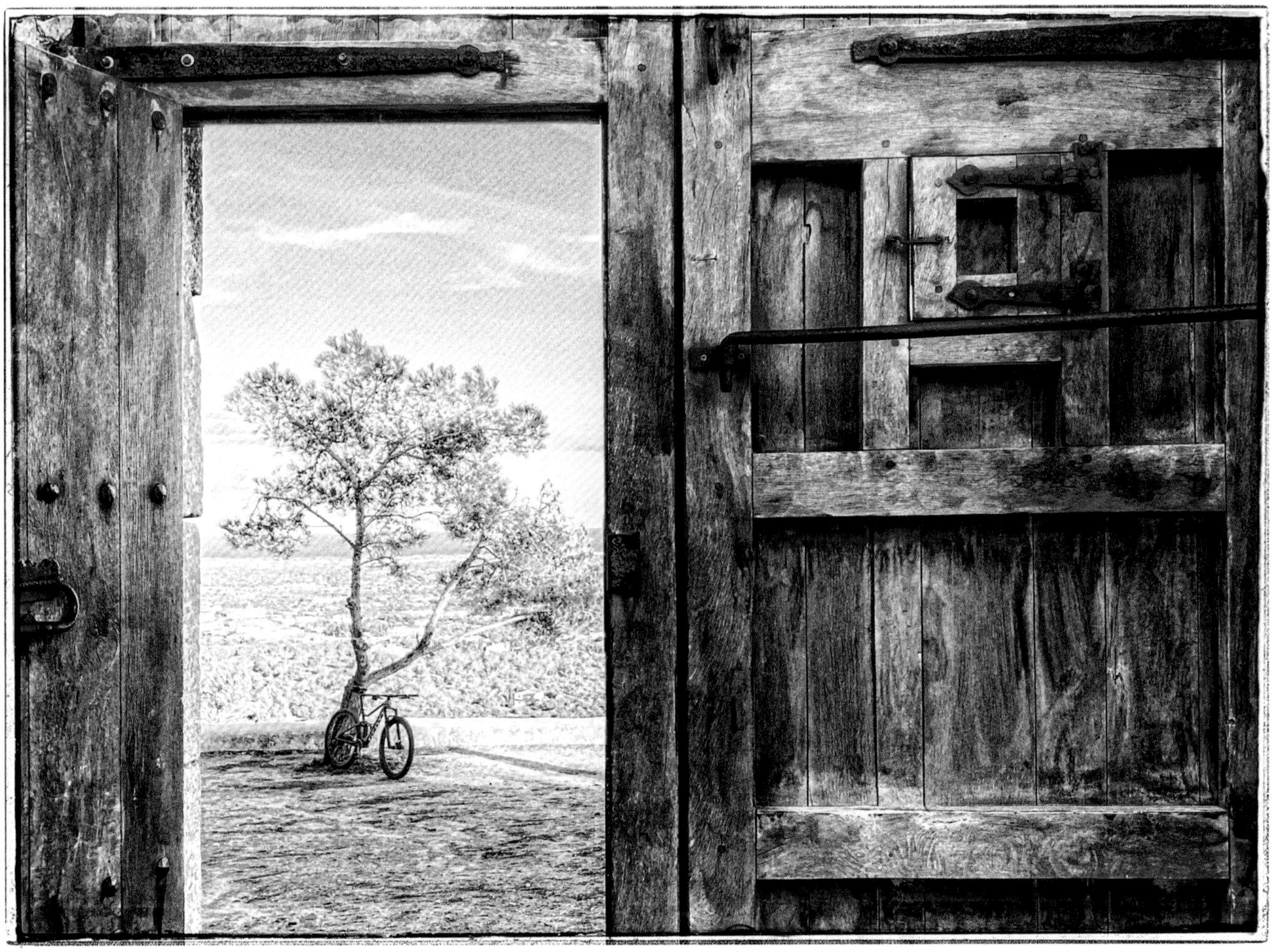

P237: Credit & Commentary

Title: Journey of Discovery | **Client:** Self-initiated

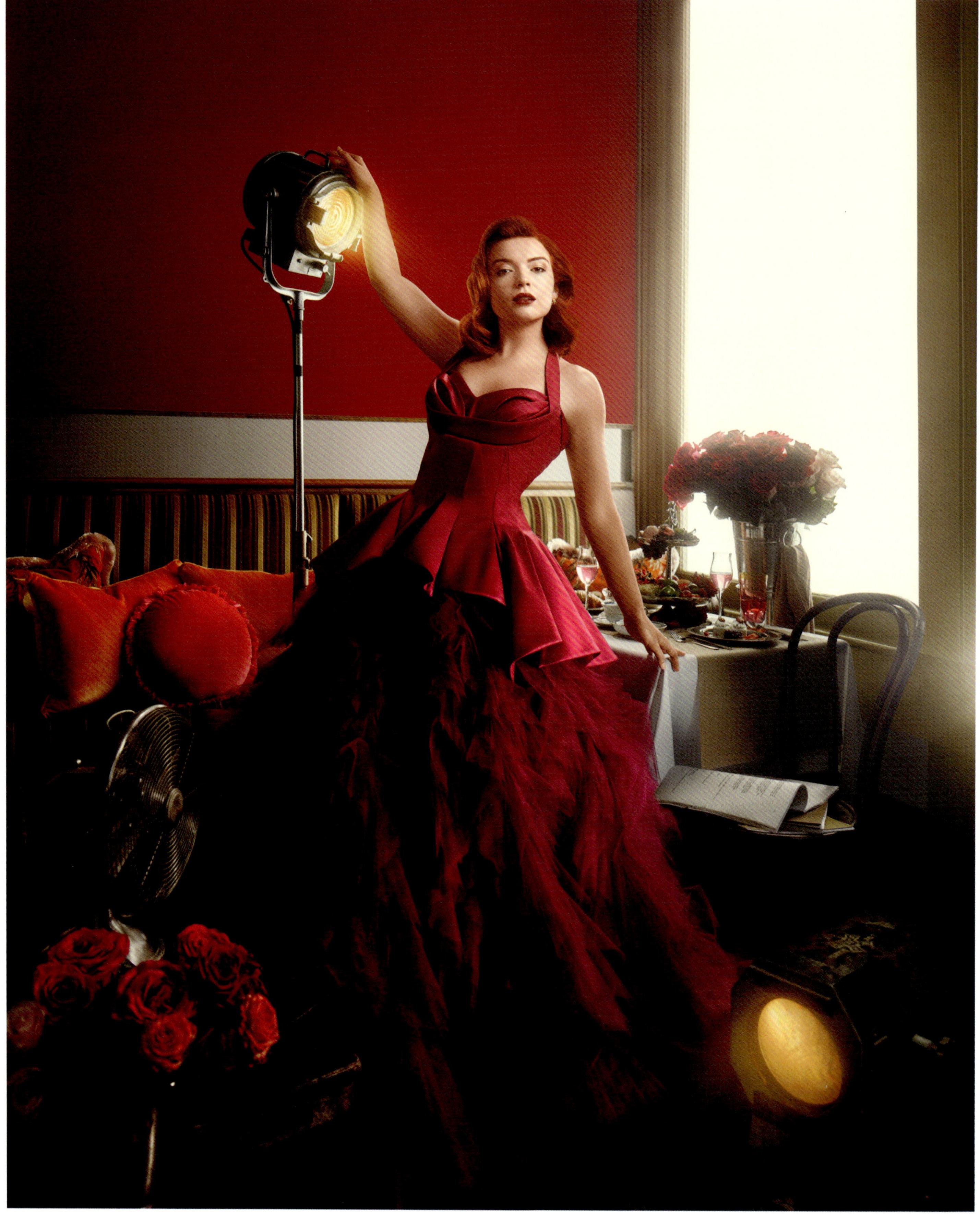

P237: Credit & Commentary

Title: SCAD Film Festival 25th Anniversary | Client: Savannah College of Art & Design

Image 1 of 5

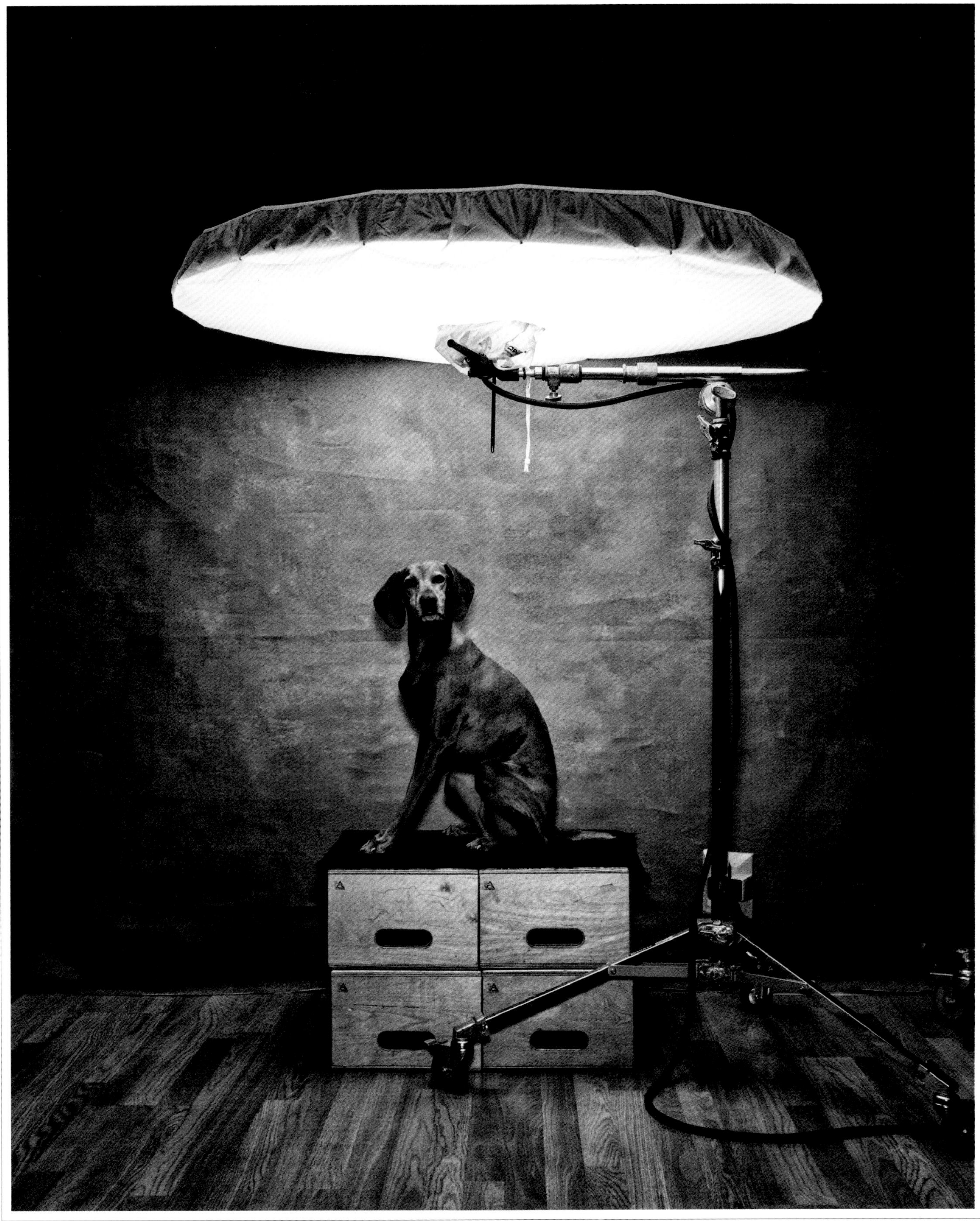

P237: Credit & Commentary

Title: Jo 2 | **Client:** Self-initiated

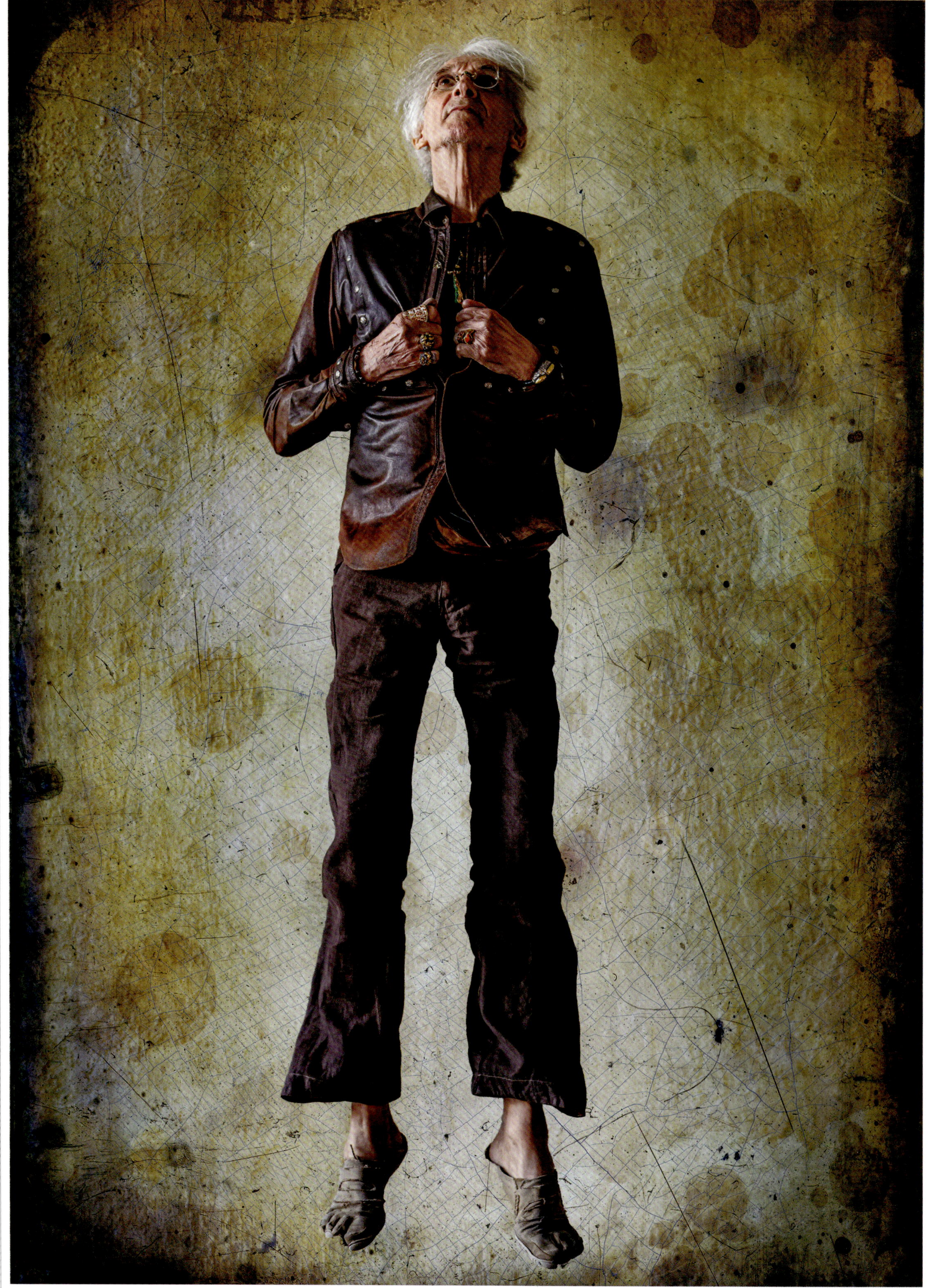

P237: Credit & Commentary

Title: Leathercrafting, Tucson AZ | Client: Self-initiated

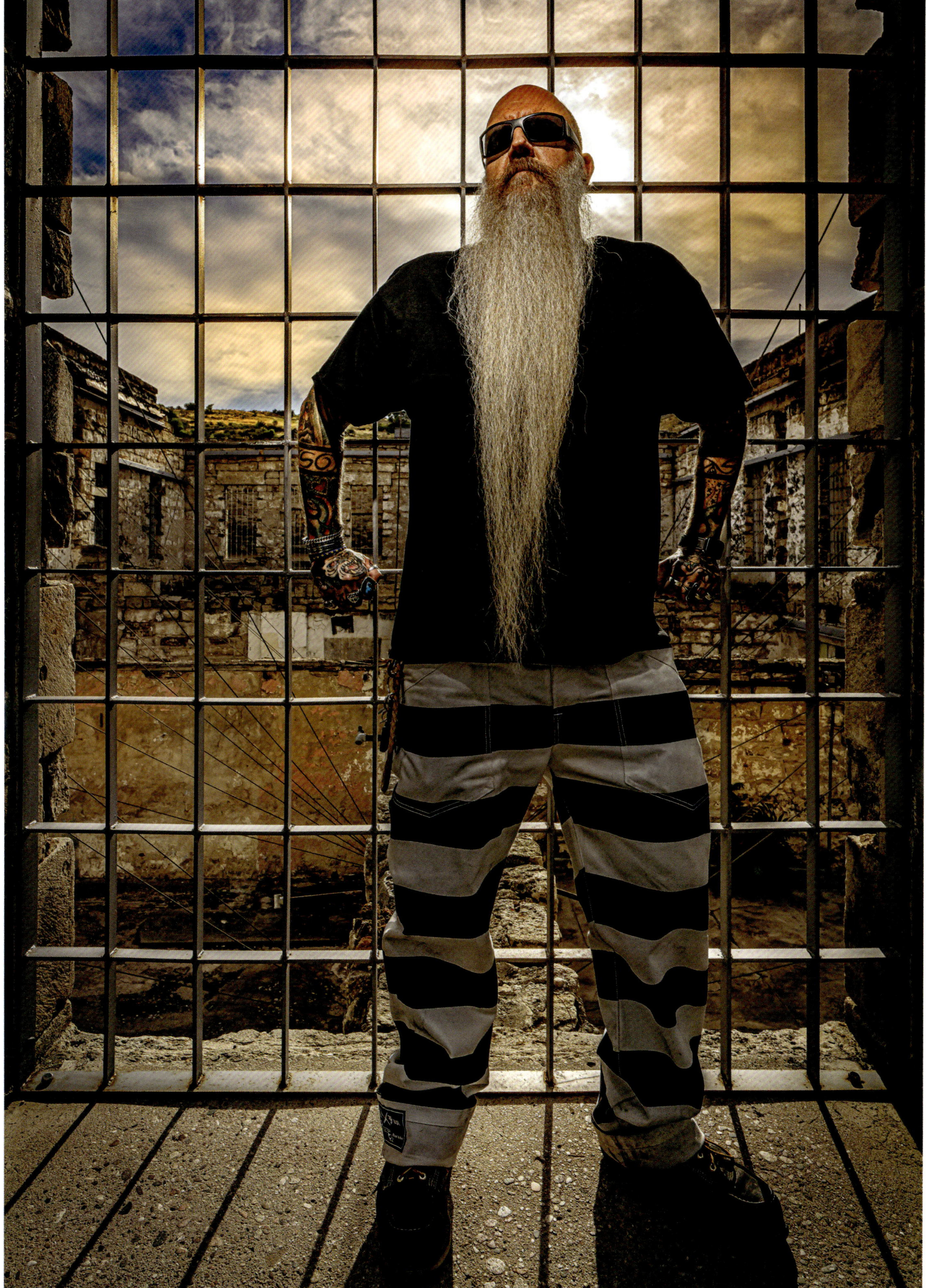

P238: Credit & Commentary

Title: Bars and Stripes | **Client:** Self-initiated

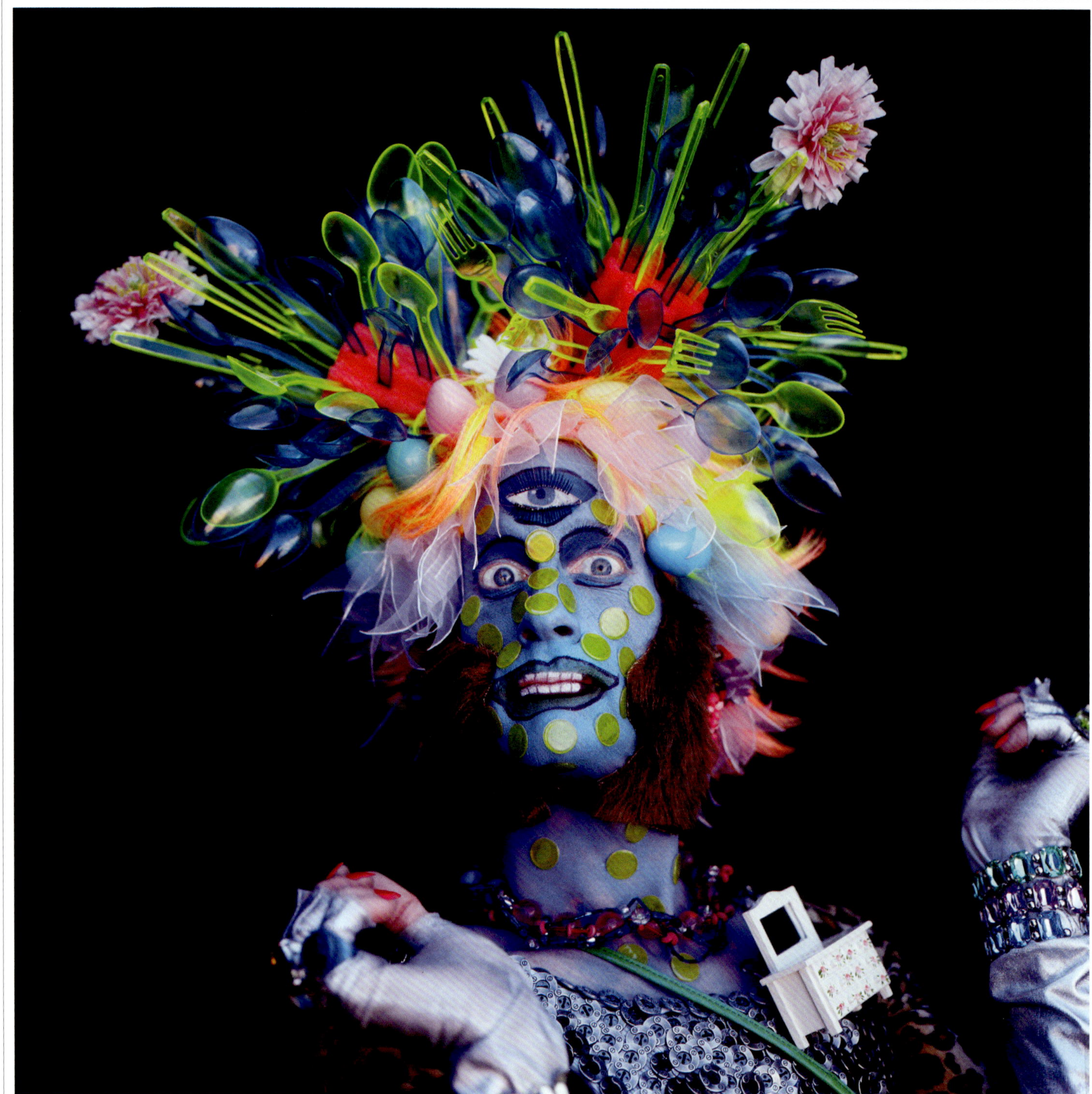

P238: Credit & Commentary

Title: David Faulk, Folsom Street Fair | **Client:** Self-initiated

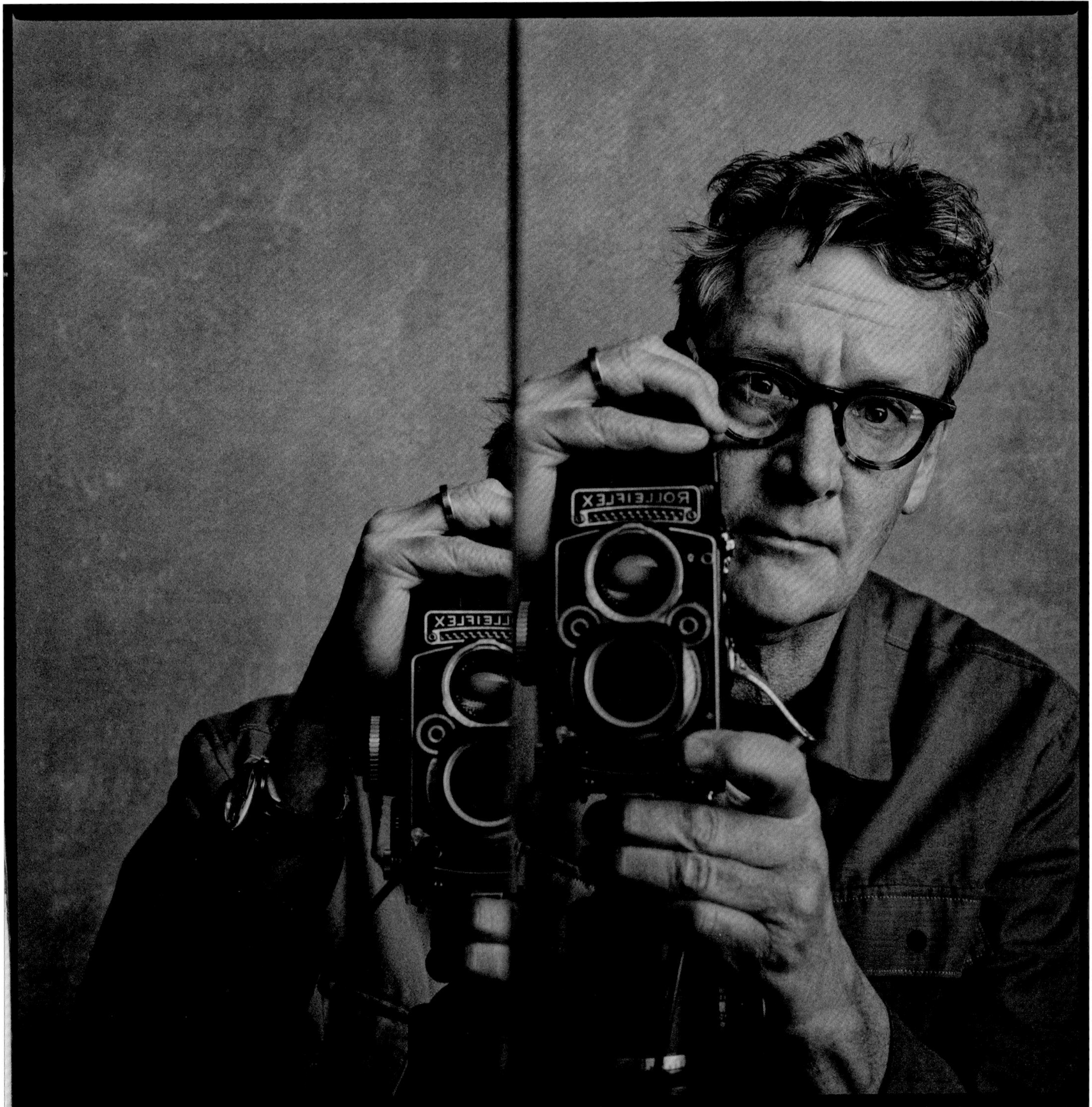

P238: Credit & Commentary **Title:** Self Portrait | **Client:** Self-initiated

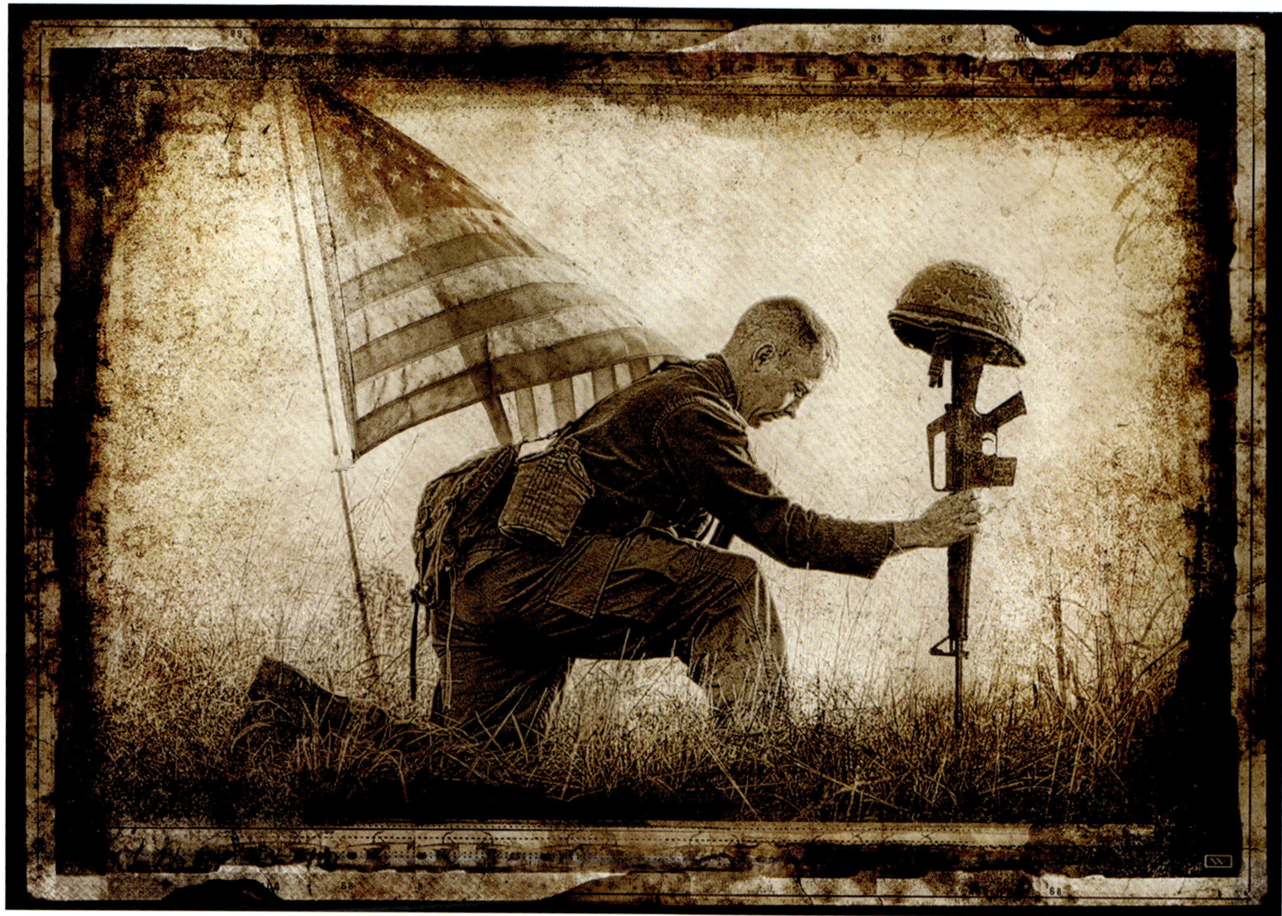

Title: Never Forgotten - In Honor of Our American Veterans
Client: JCVT (Jefferson County Veterans Tribute) | **P238:** Credit & Commentary

LAURIE FRANKEL GOLD

PORTRAITS

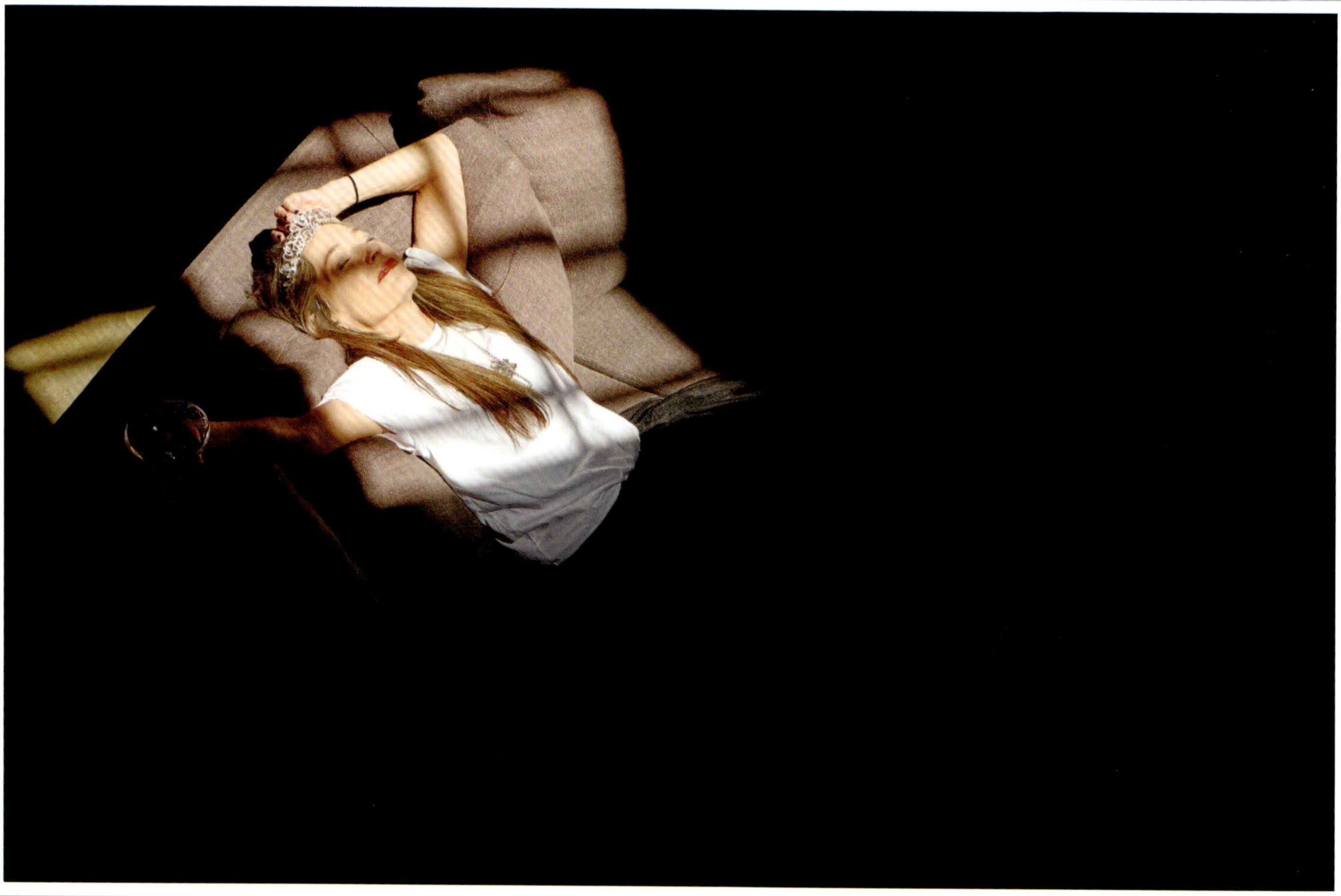

P238: Credit & Commentary

Title: Fashion is Exhausting | **Client:** Self-initiated

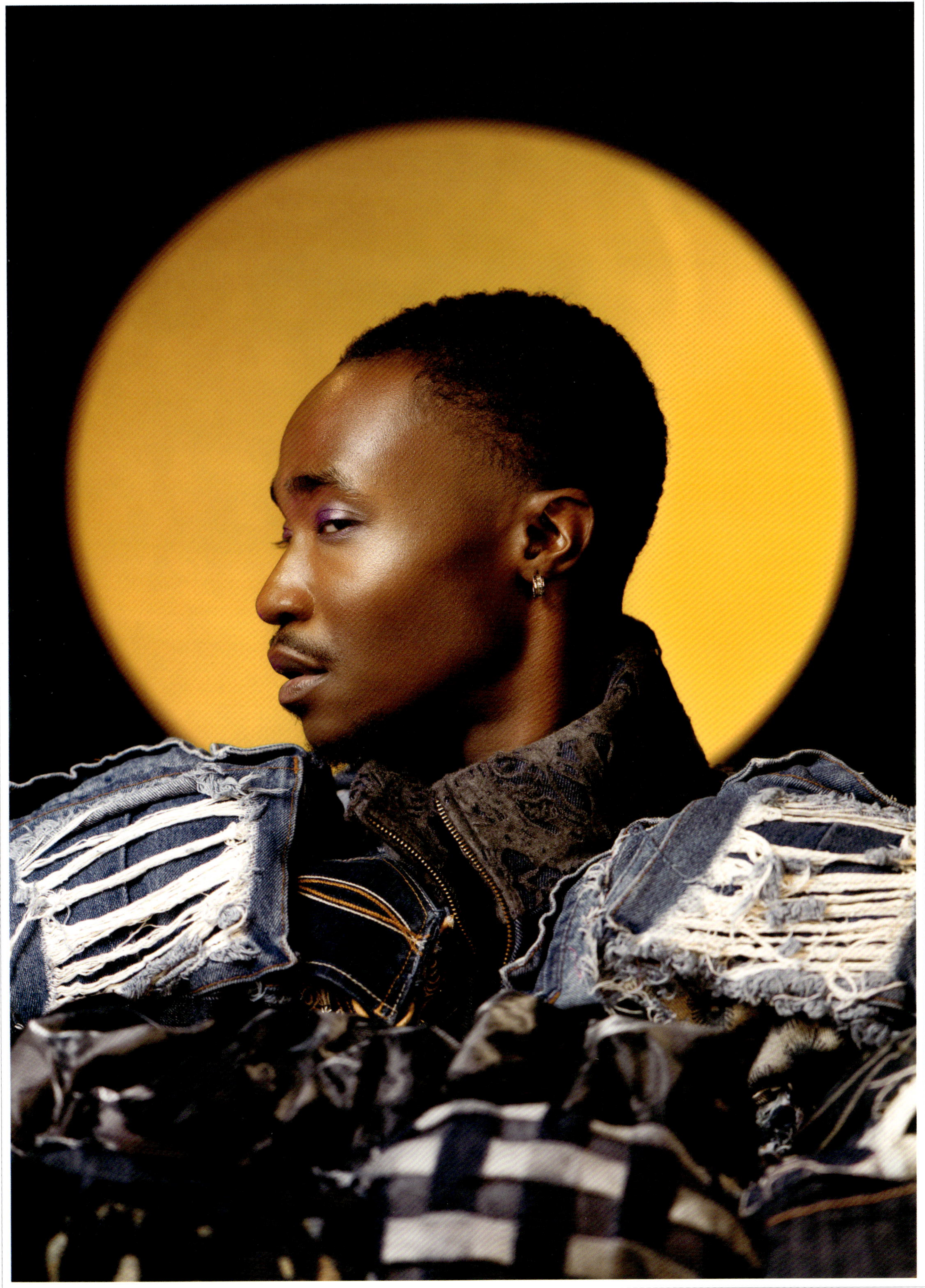

P238: Credit & Commentary

Title: Golden Boy | **Client:** Savannah College of Art & Design

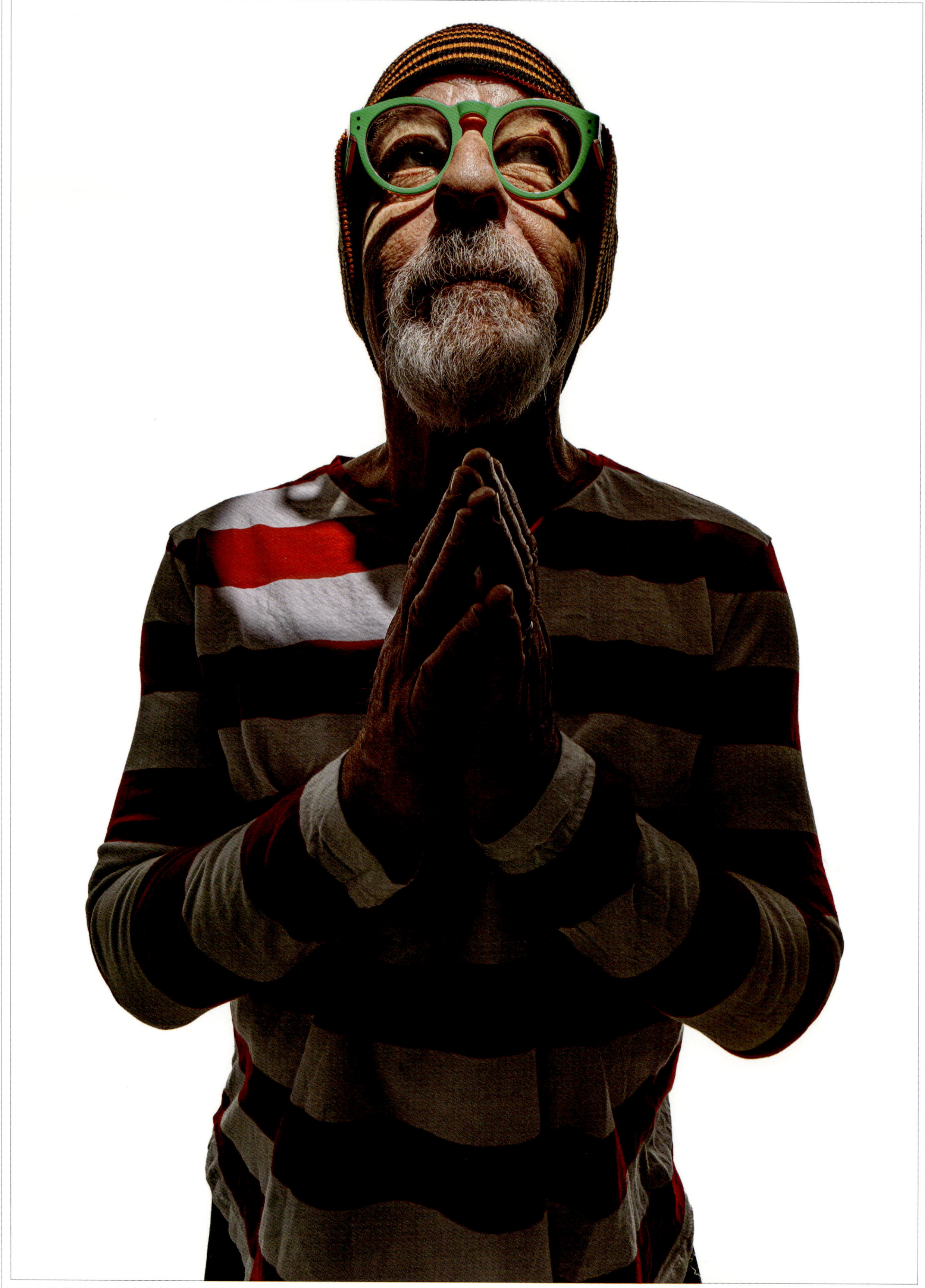

P238: Credit & Commentary

Title: Where's Jerry Joseph | **Client:** Artist Commission

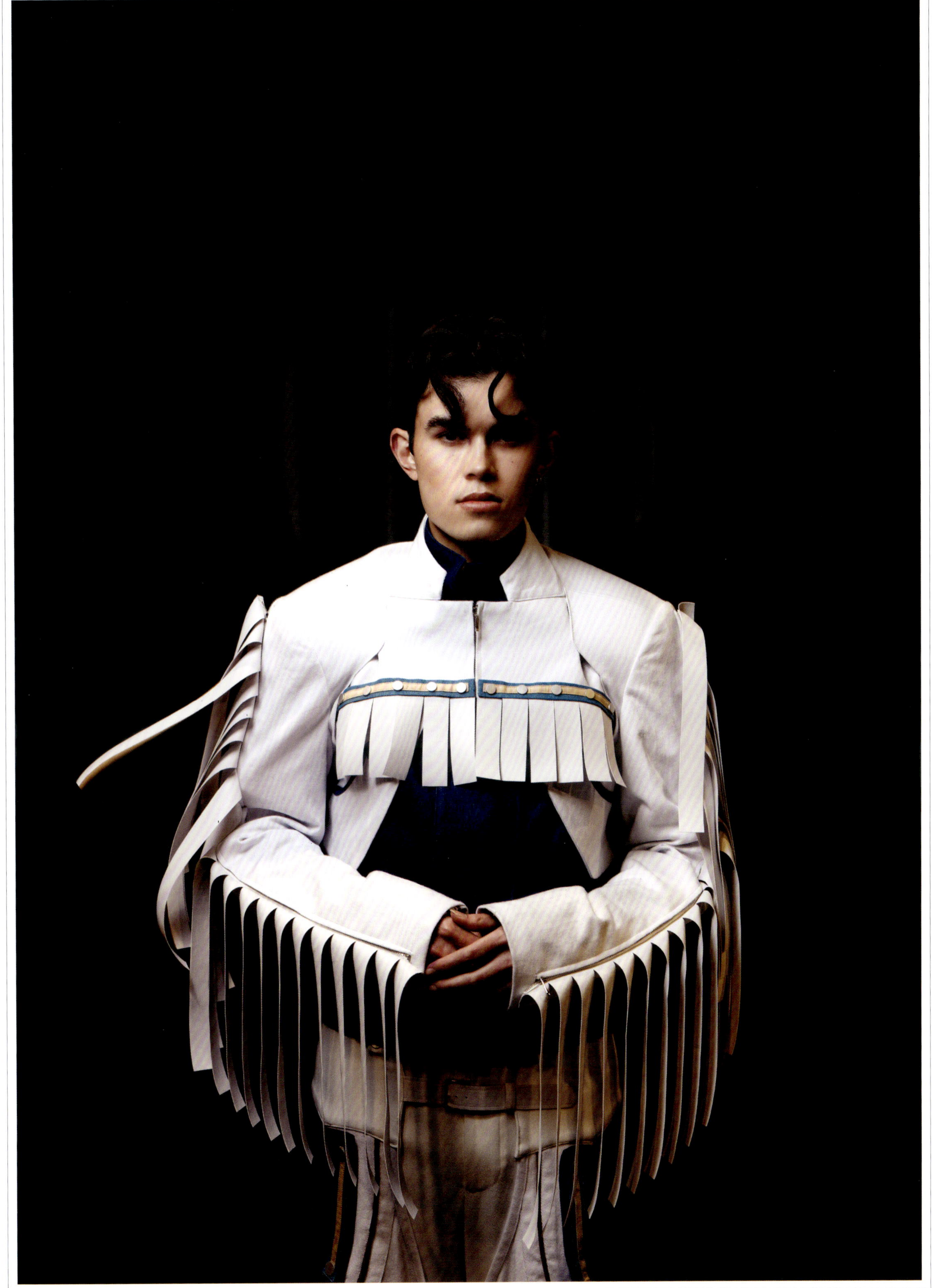

P238: Credit & Commentary

Title: Asymmetry | Client: Savannah College of Art & Design

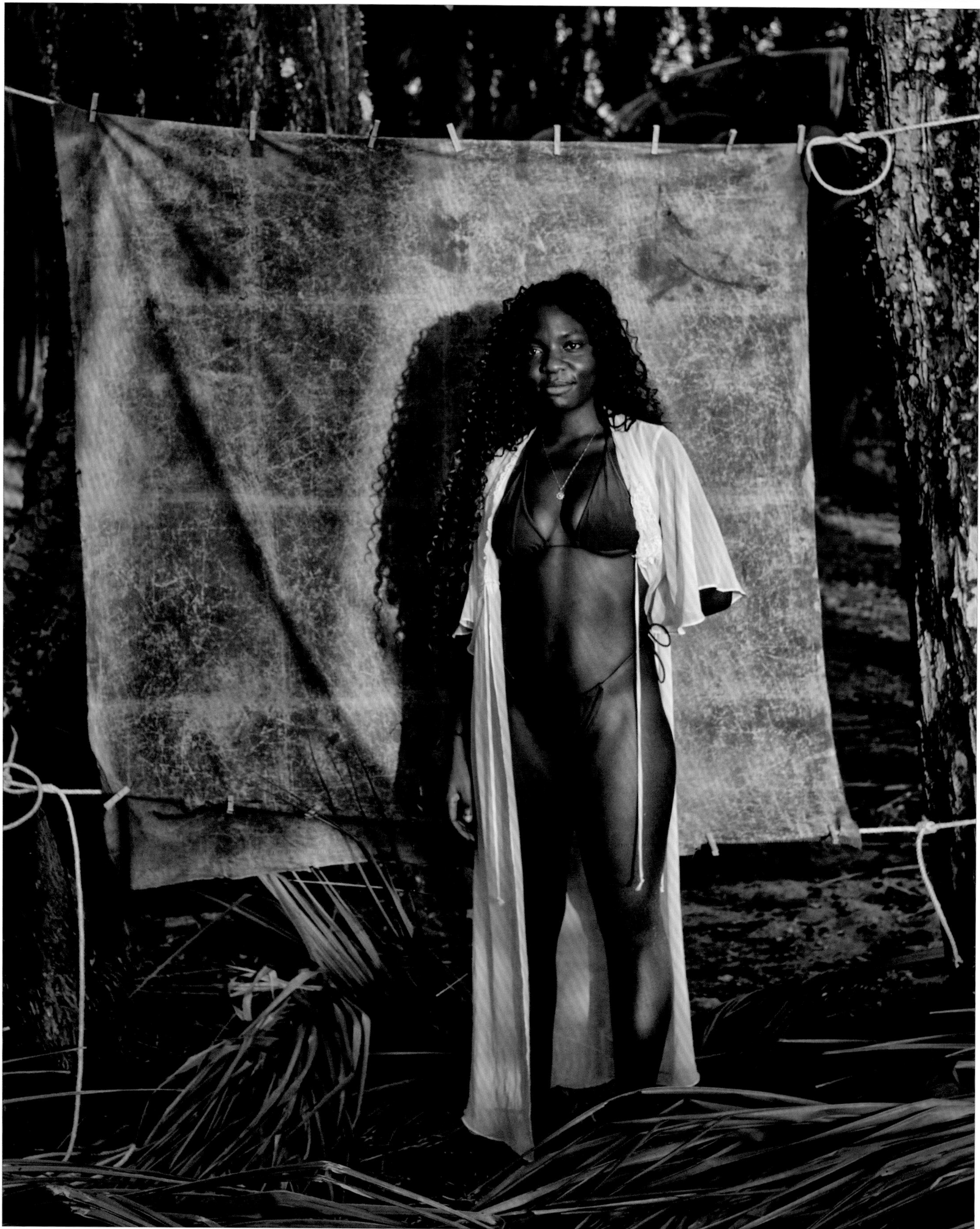

P238: Credit & Commentary

Title: Portraits in Costa Rica | **Client:** Self-initiated

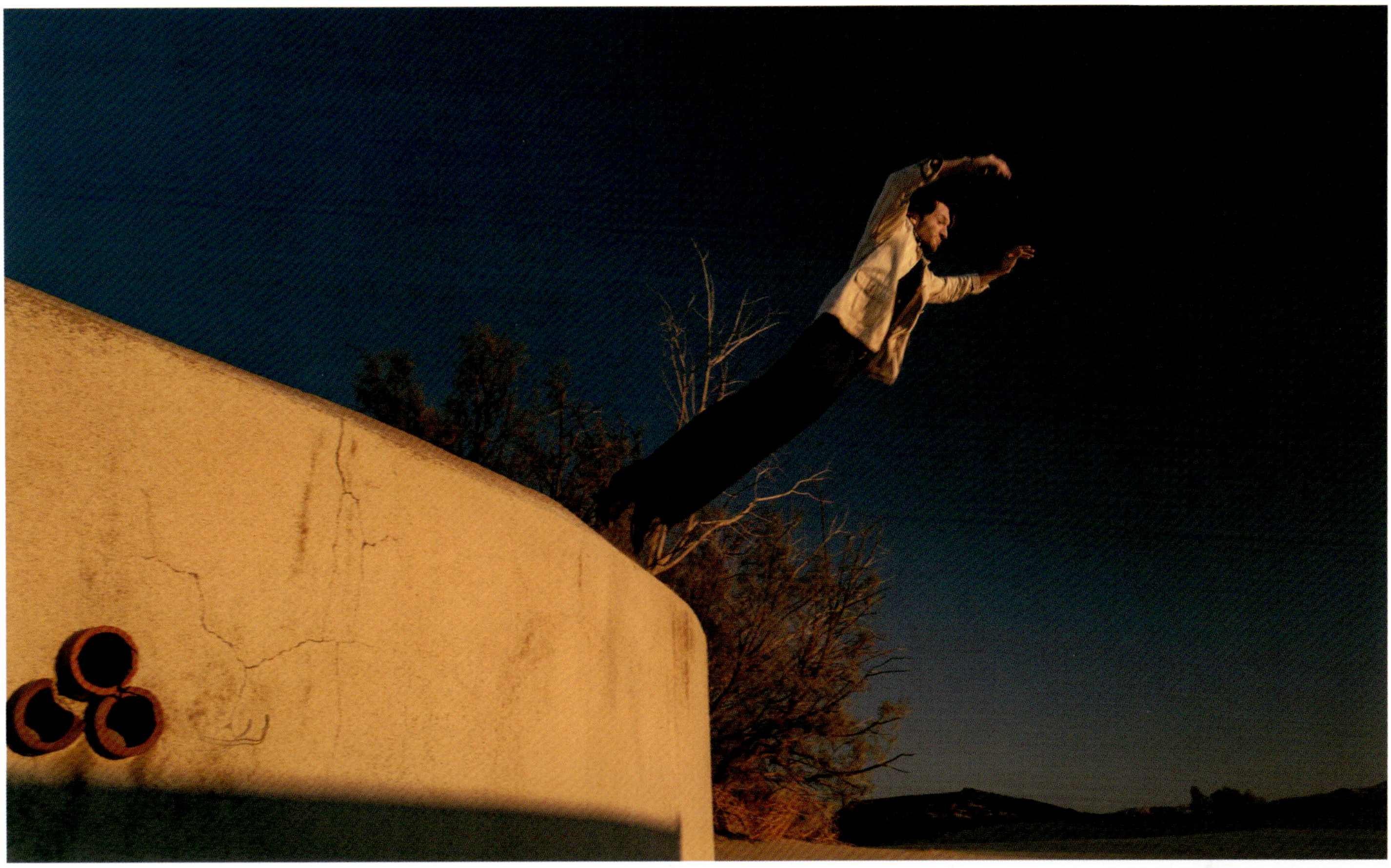

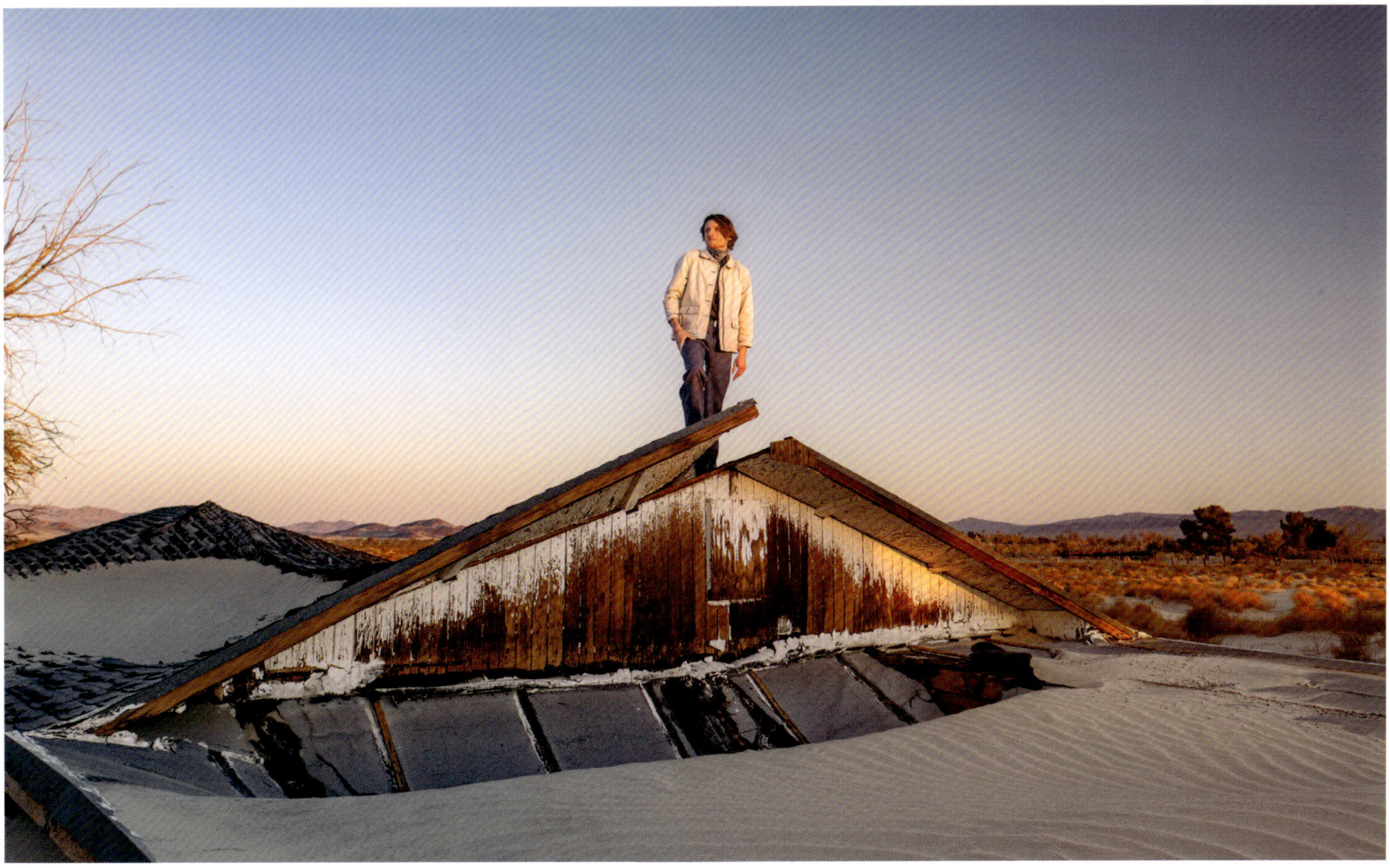

Title: About You | Clients: About You, Max Poscente

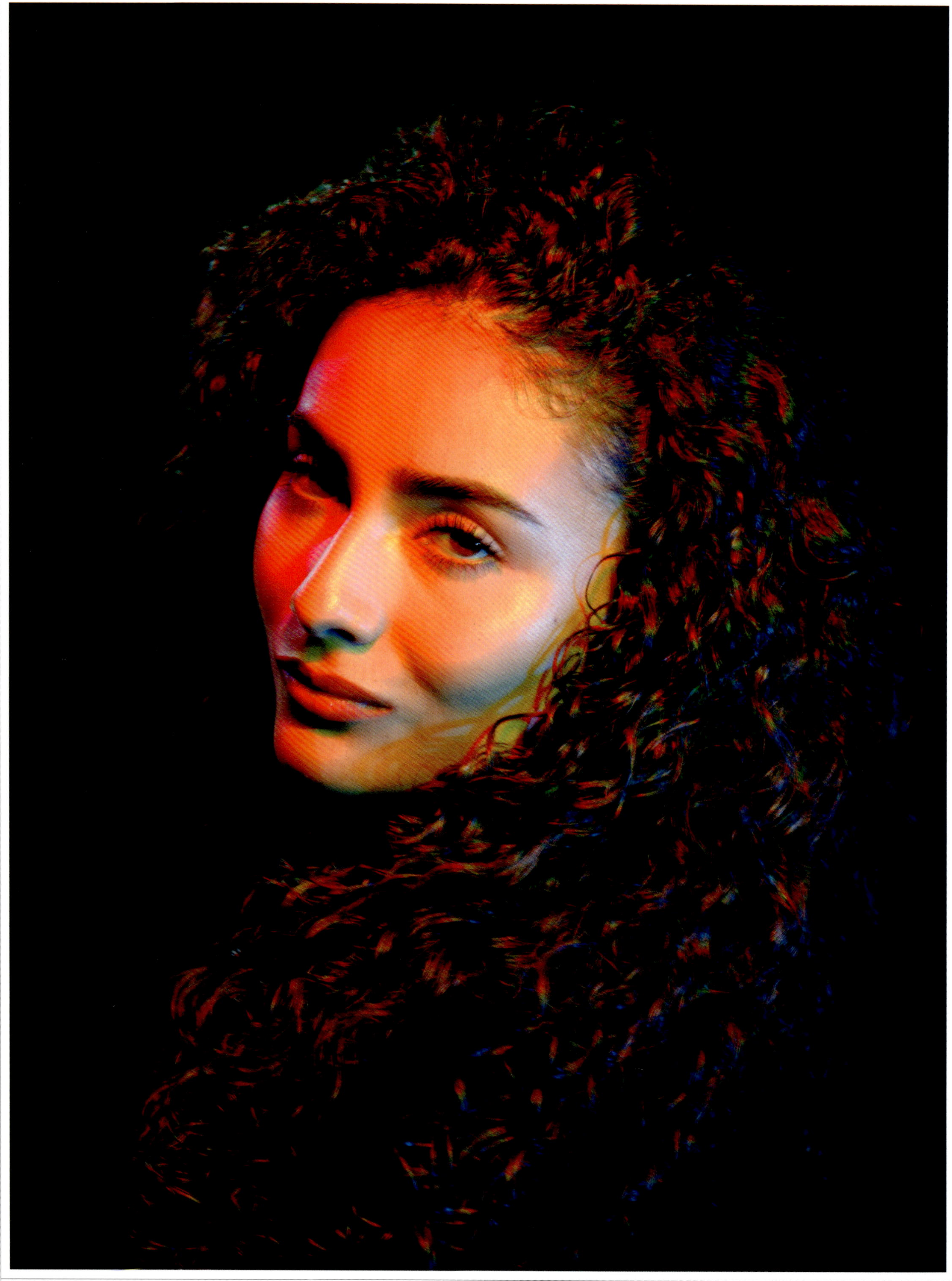

P238: Credit & Commentary **Title:** Portrait of Jennell Juarez | **Clients:** Book Project, Self-initiated

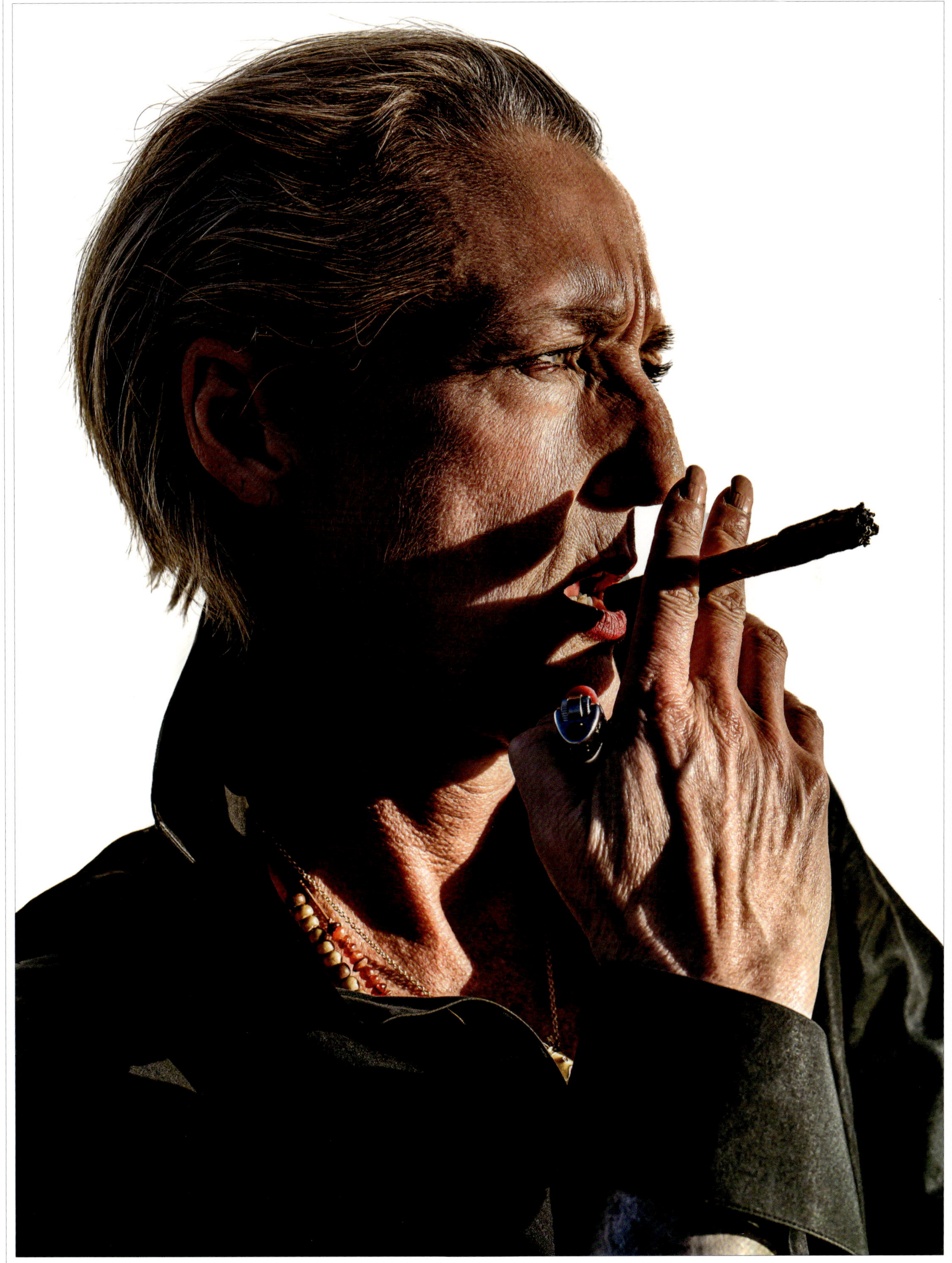

P238: Credit & Commentary

Title: Kati Brunini | **Client:** Self-initiated

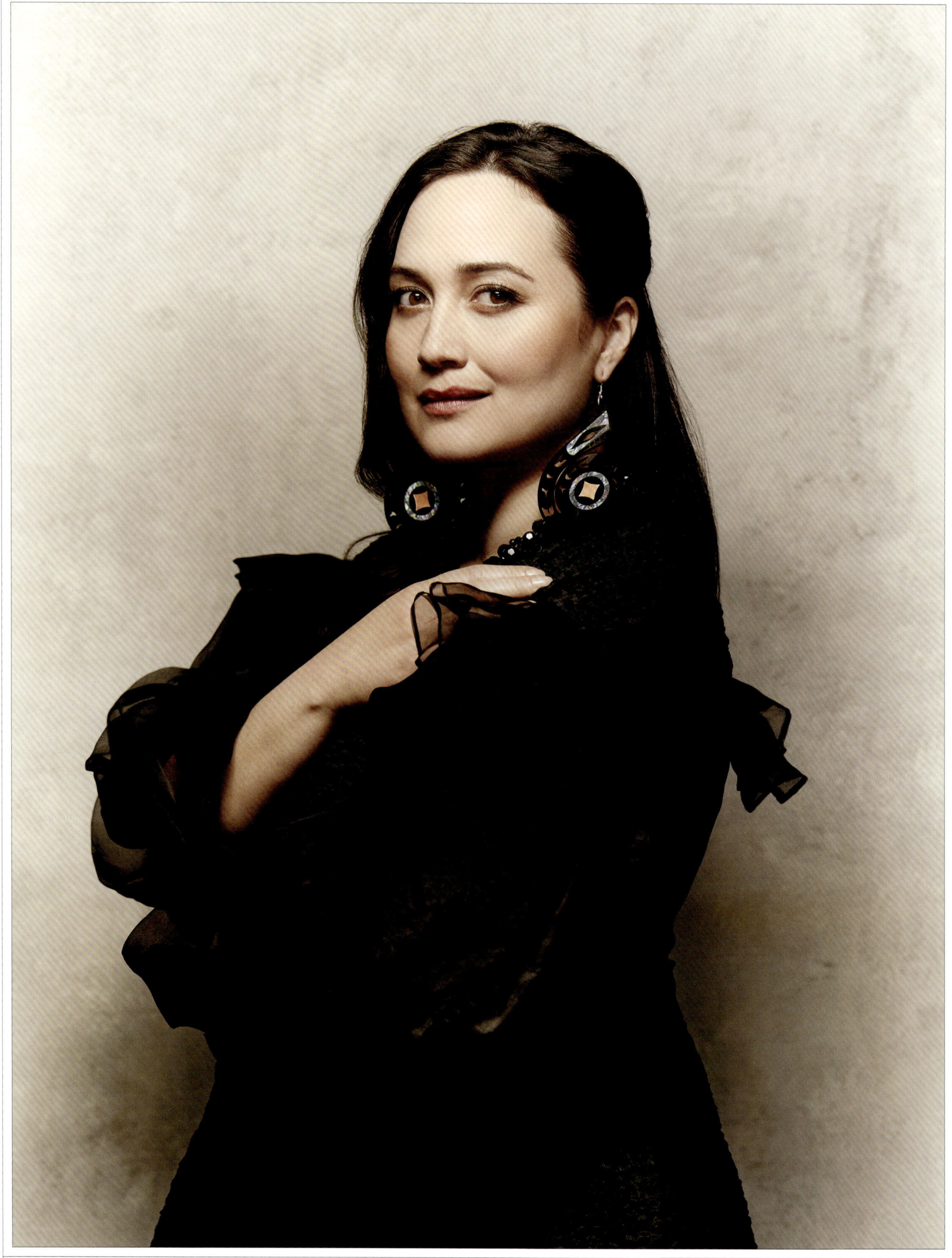

P238: Credit & Commentary

Title: Lily Gladstone, 2023 | **Client:** The Hollywood Reporter

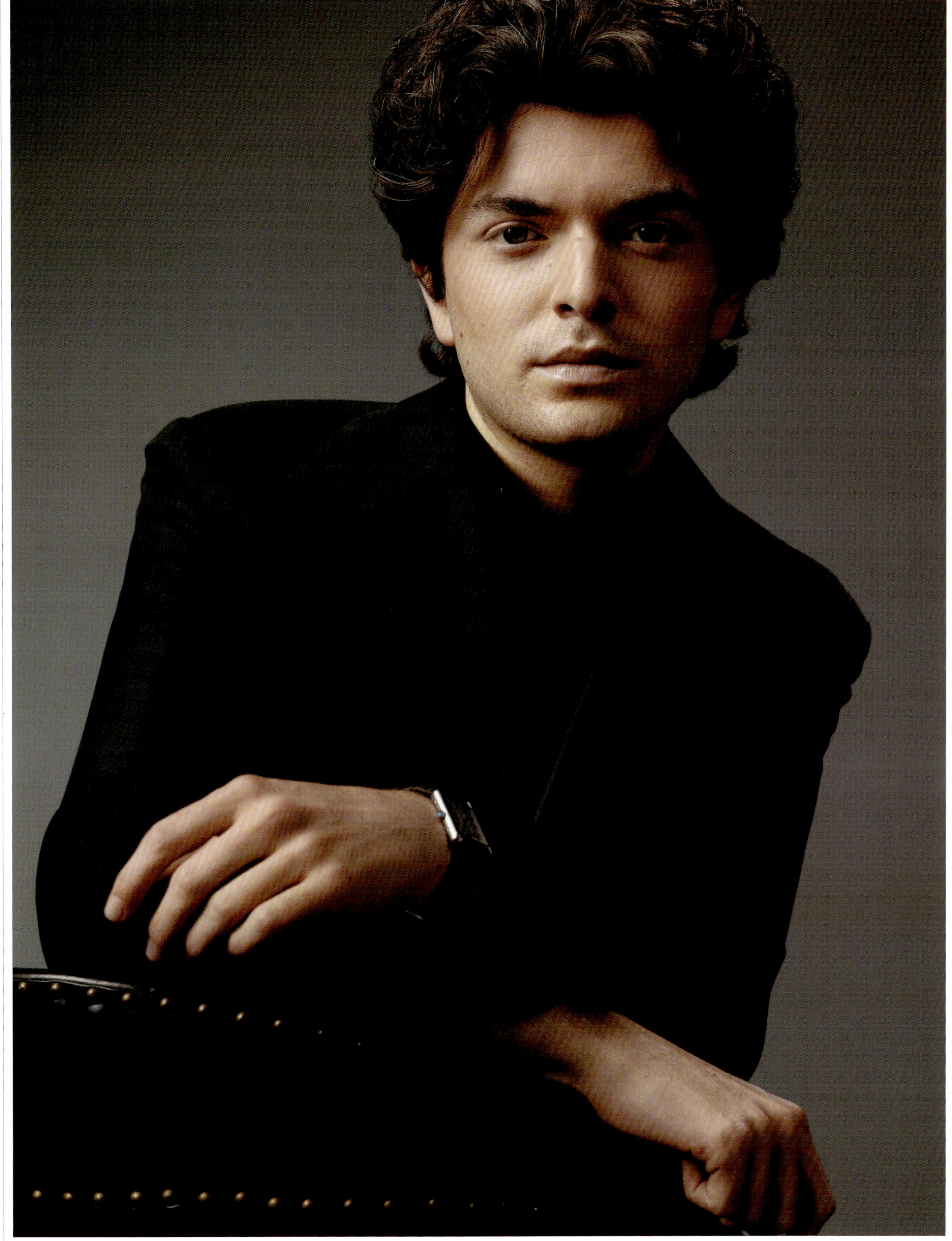

P238: Credit & Commentary

Title: Showcase | Client: Savannah College of Art & Design

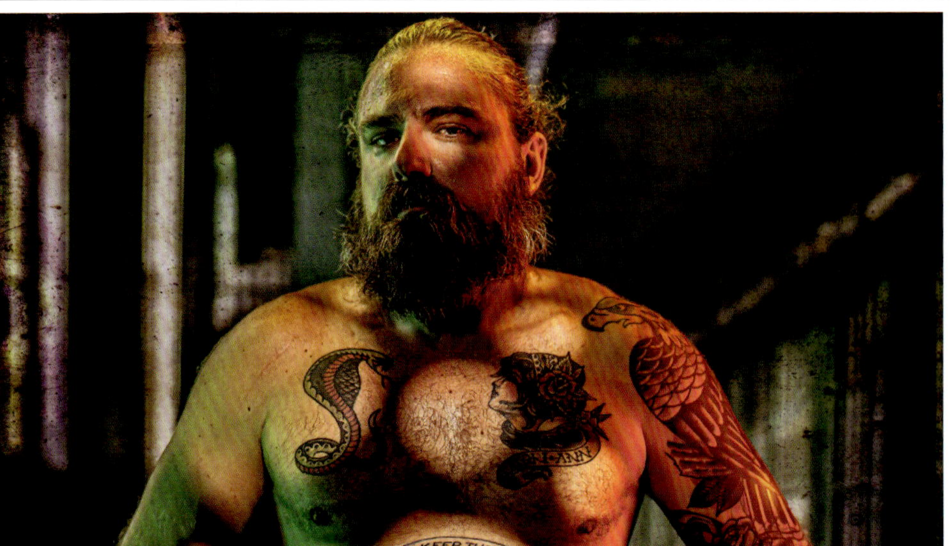

Title: Tattoos at the Prison 2, Boise ID
Client: Self-initiated | **P238:** Credit & Commentary

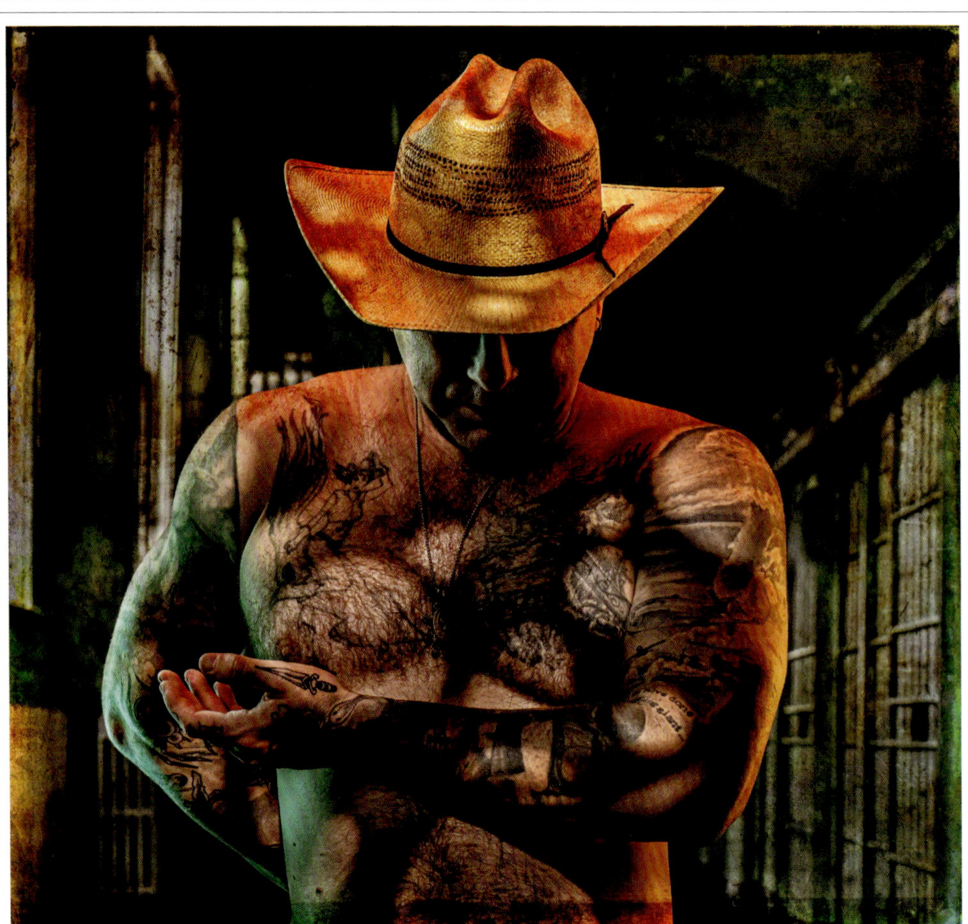

Title: Tattoos at the Prison 3, Boise ID
Client: Self-initiated | **P238:** Credit & Commentary

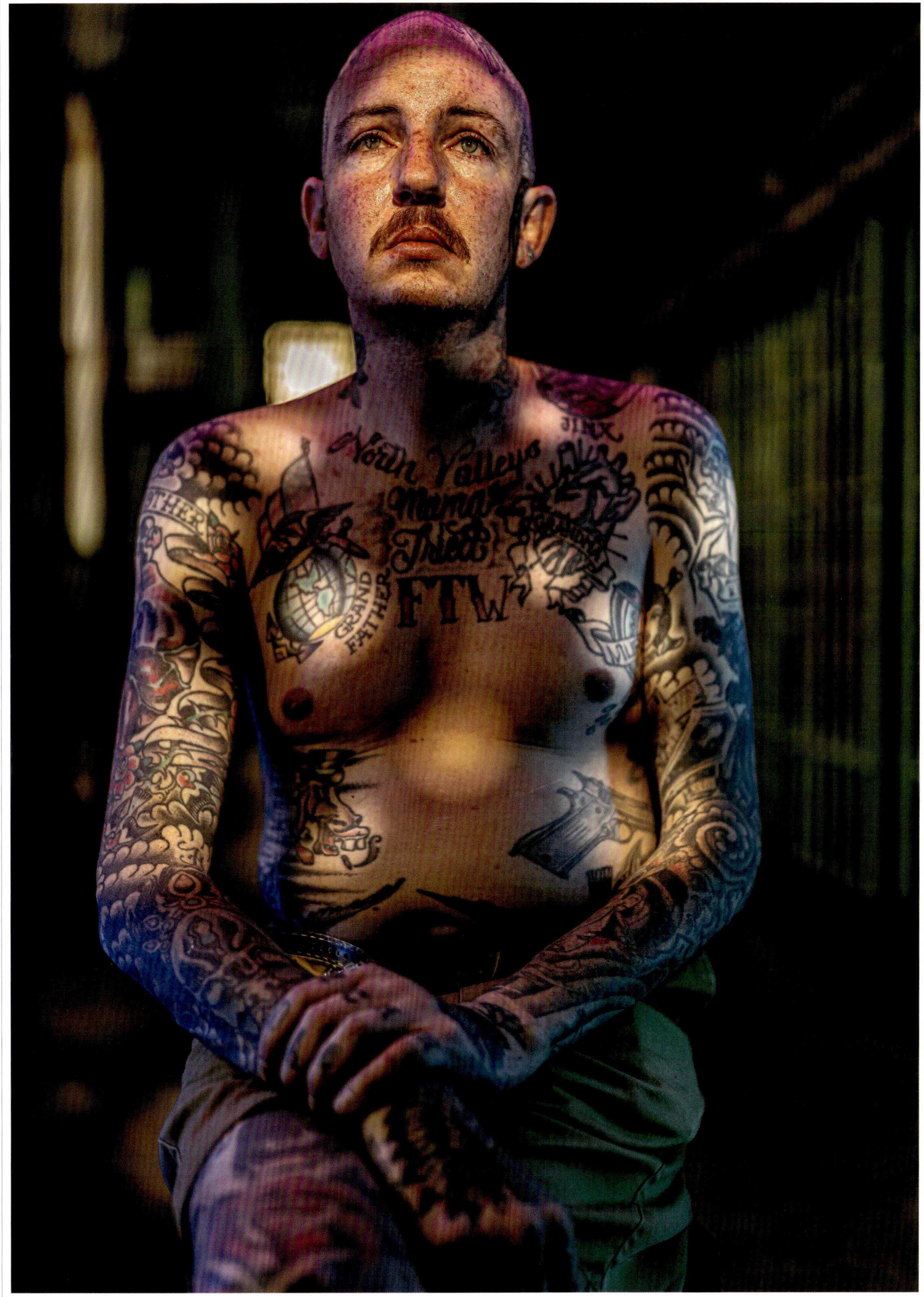

P238: Credit & Commentary

Title: Tattoos at the Prison 1, Boise ID | **Client:** Self-initiated

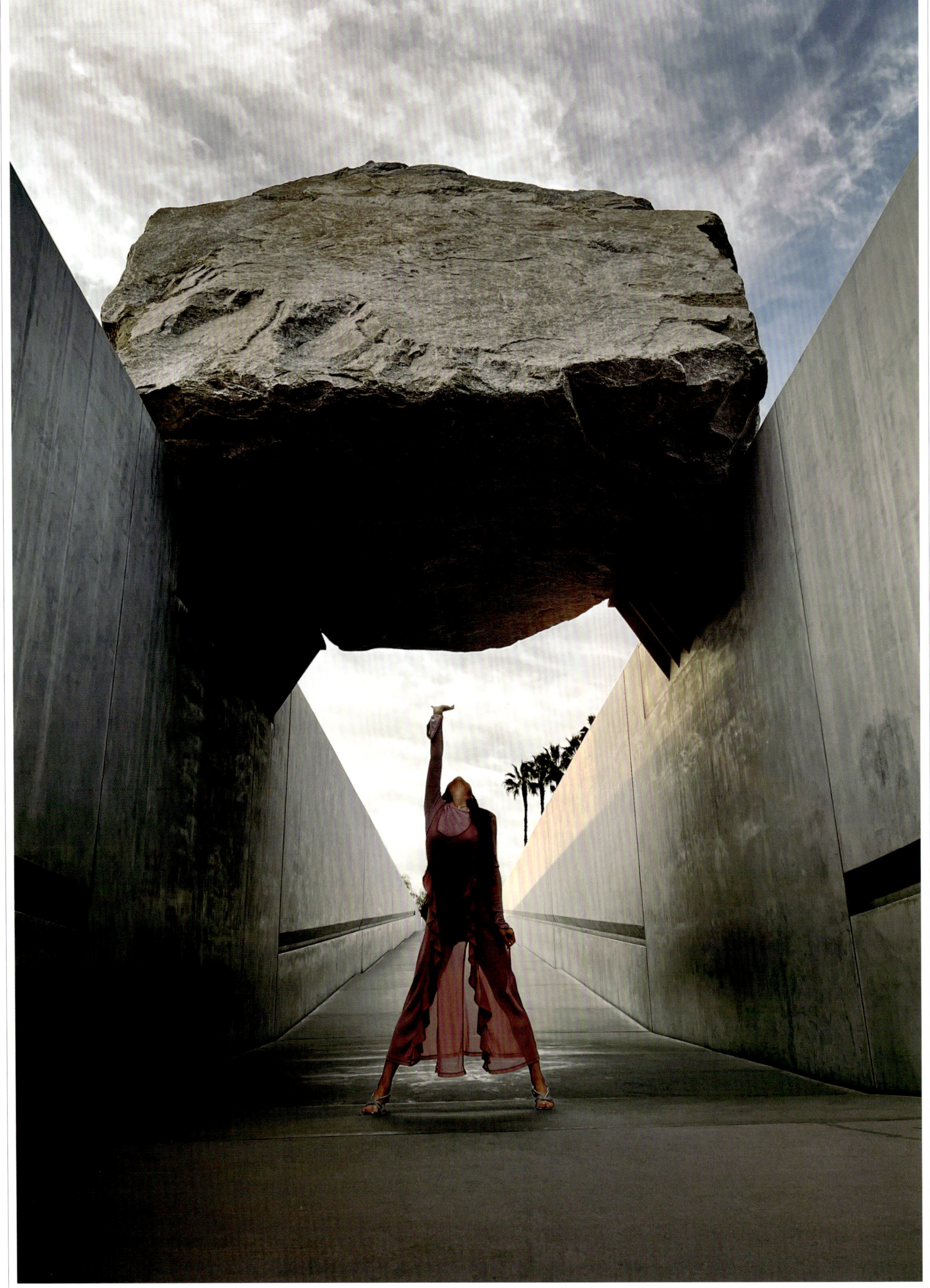

P238: Credit & Commentary

Title: UPRiGHT | **Client:** Fong Captain

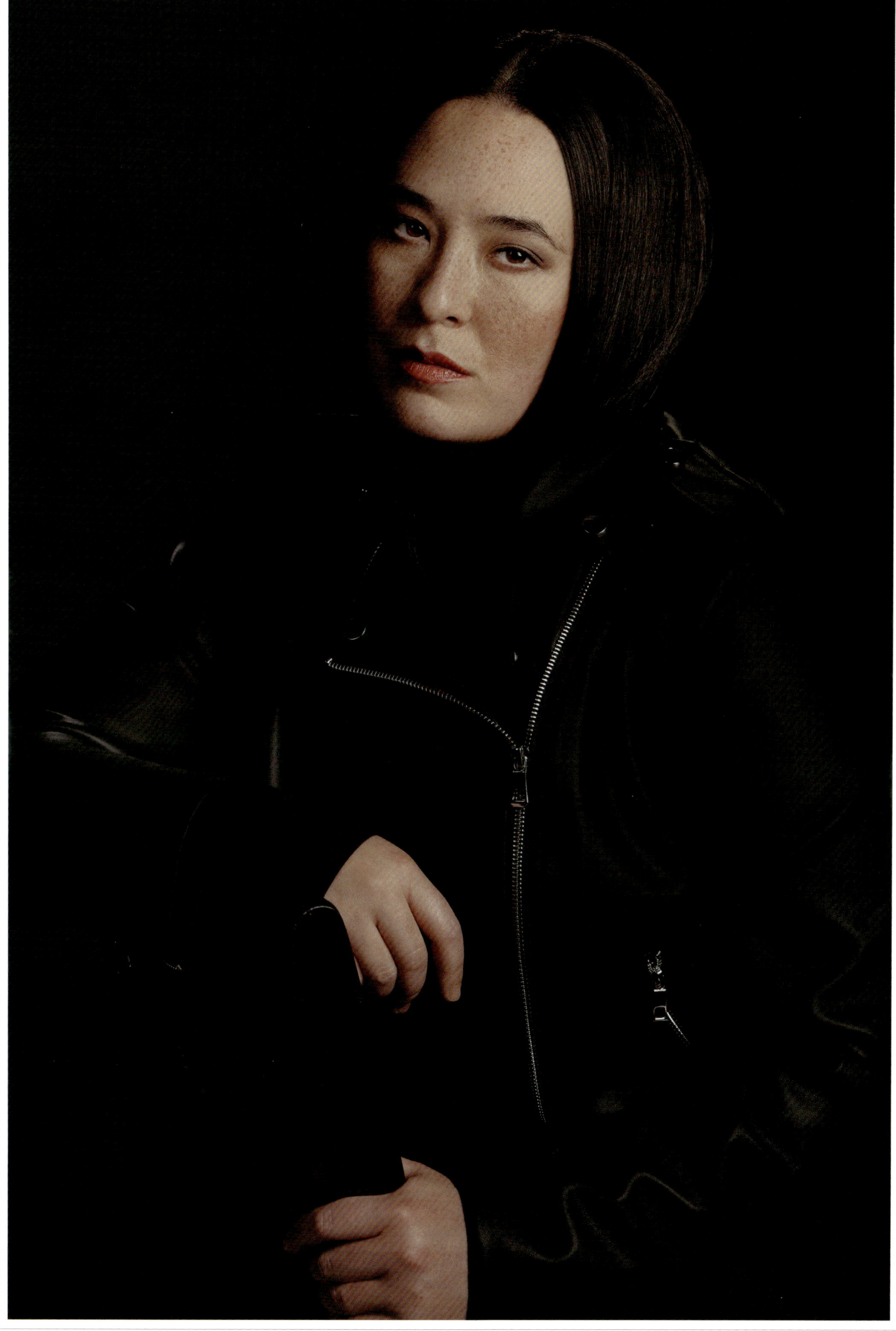

P238: Credit & Commentary

Title: Rising Stars | **Client:** Savannah College of Art & Design

Image 1 of 4

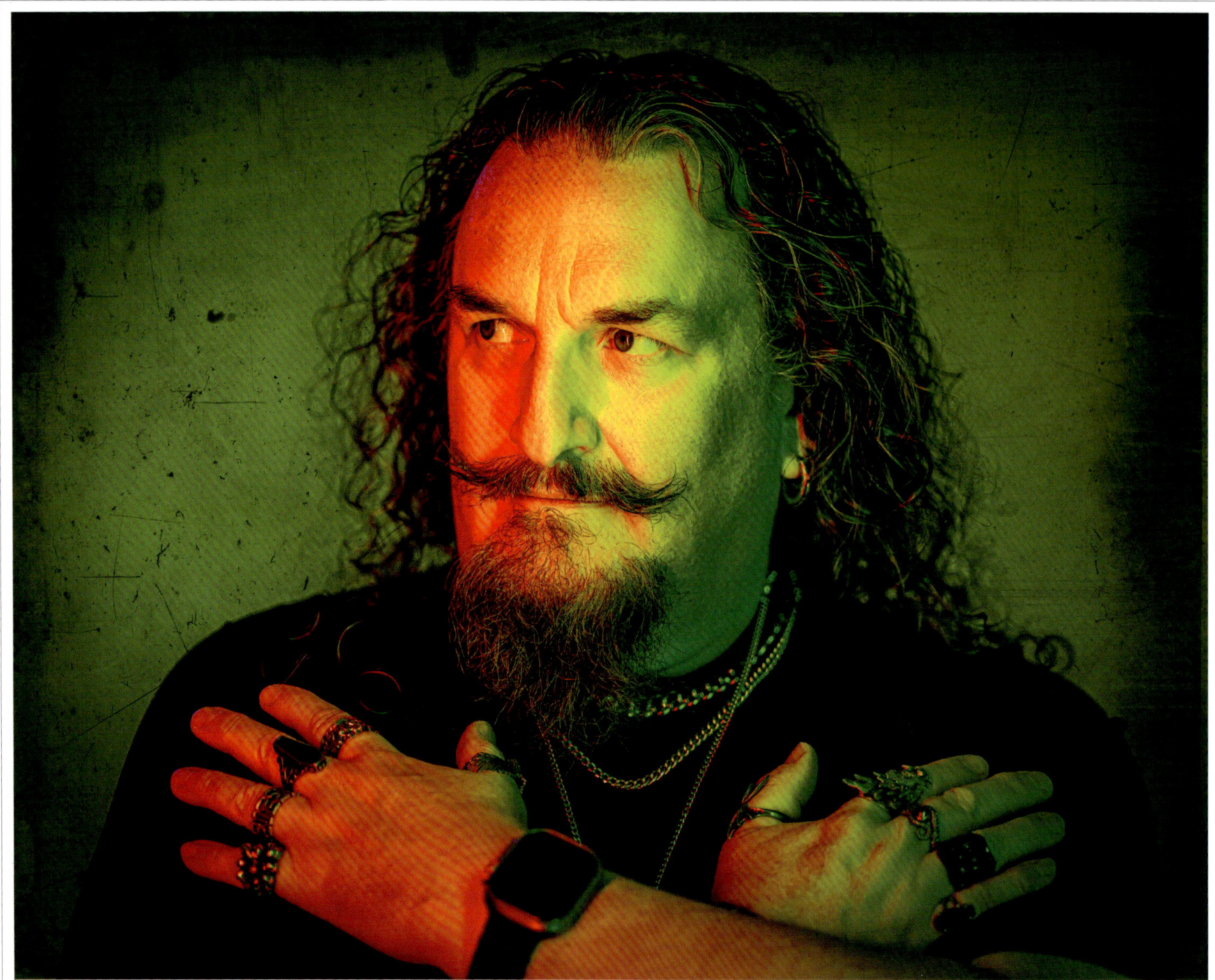

P238: Credit & Commentary

Title: Matthew Hepworth | **Client:** Self-initiated

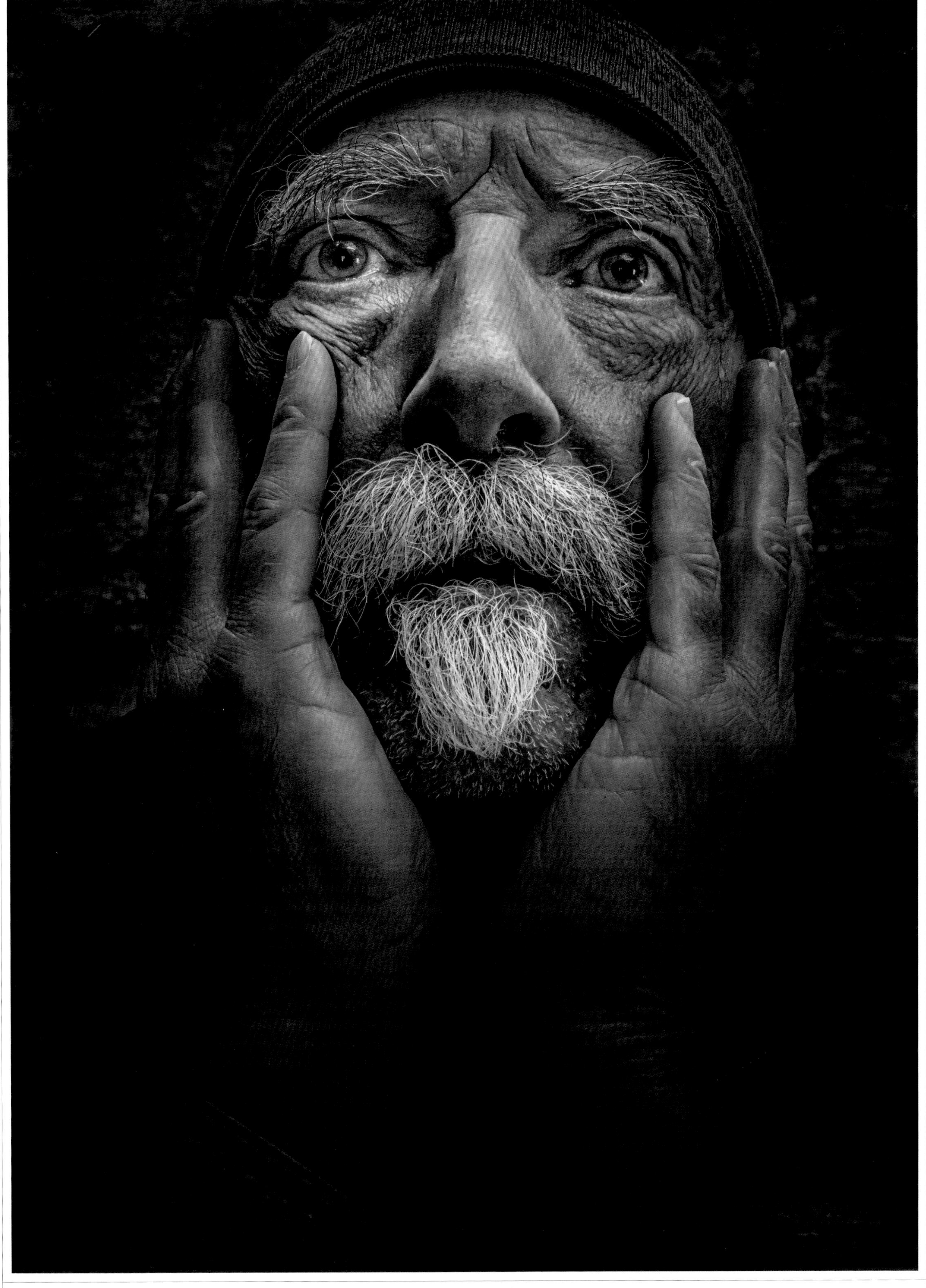

P238: Credit & Commentary

Title: San Miguel Cafe, Dan Bullard | **Client:** Self-initiated

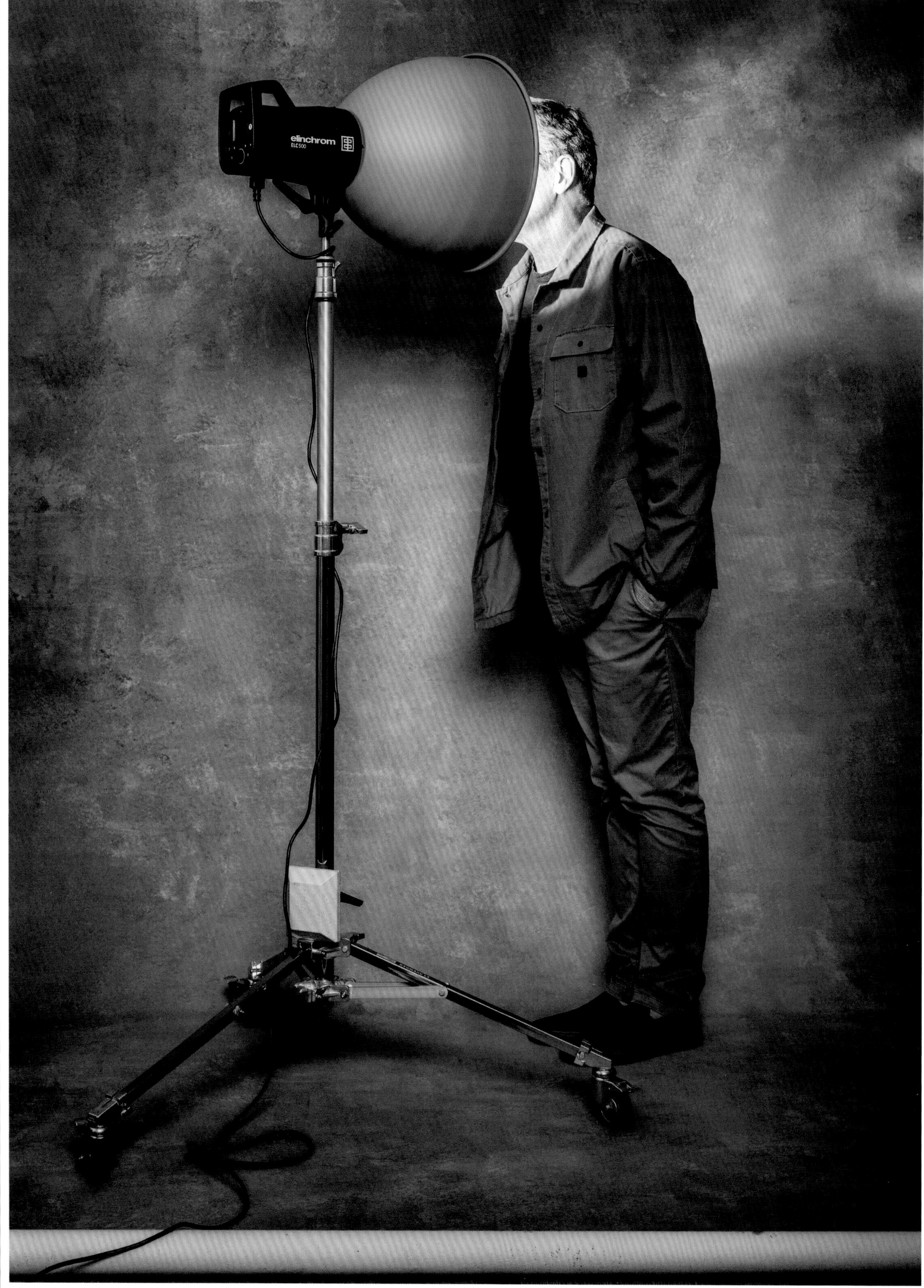

P238: Credit & Commentary

Title: Obstructed Portraits | Client: Self-initiated

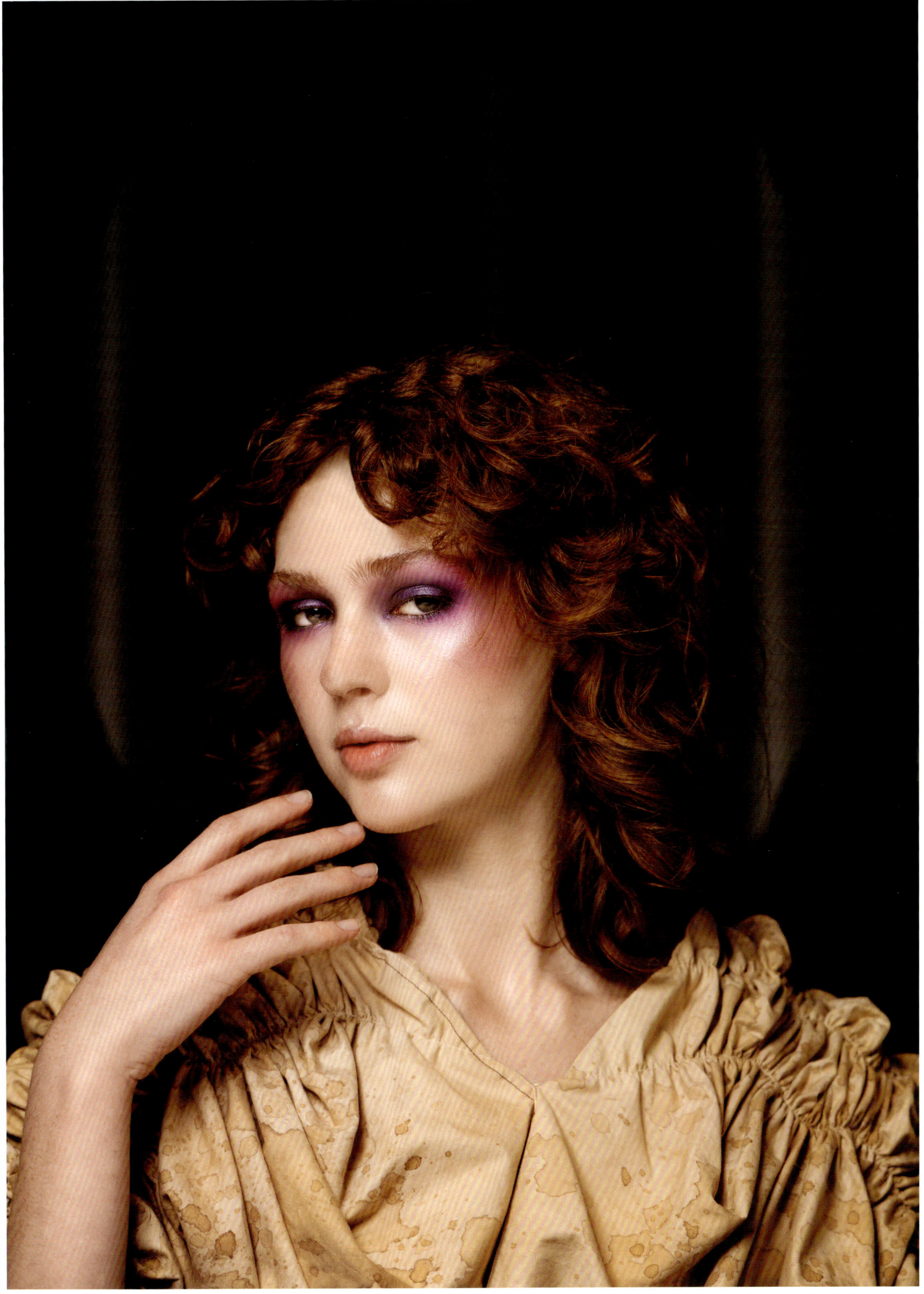

P238: Credit & Commentary

Title: Si Las Miradas Mataran | Client: Savannah College of Art & Design

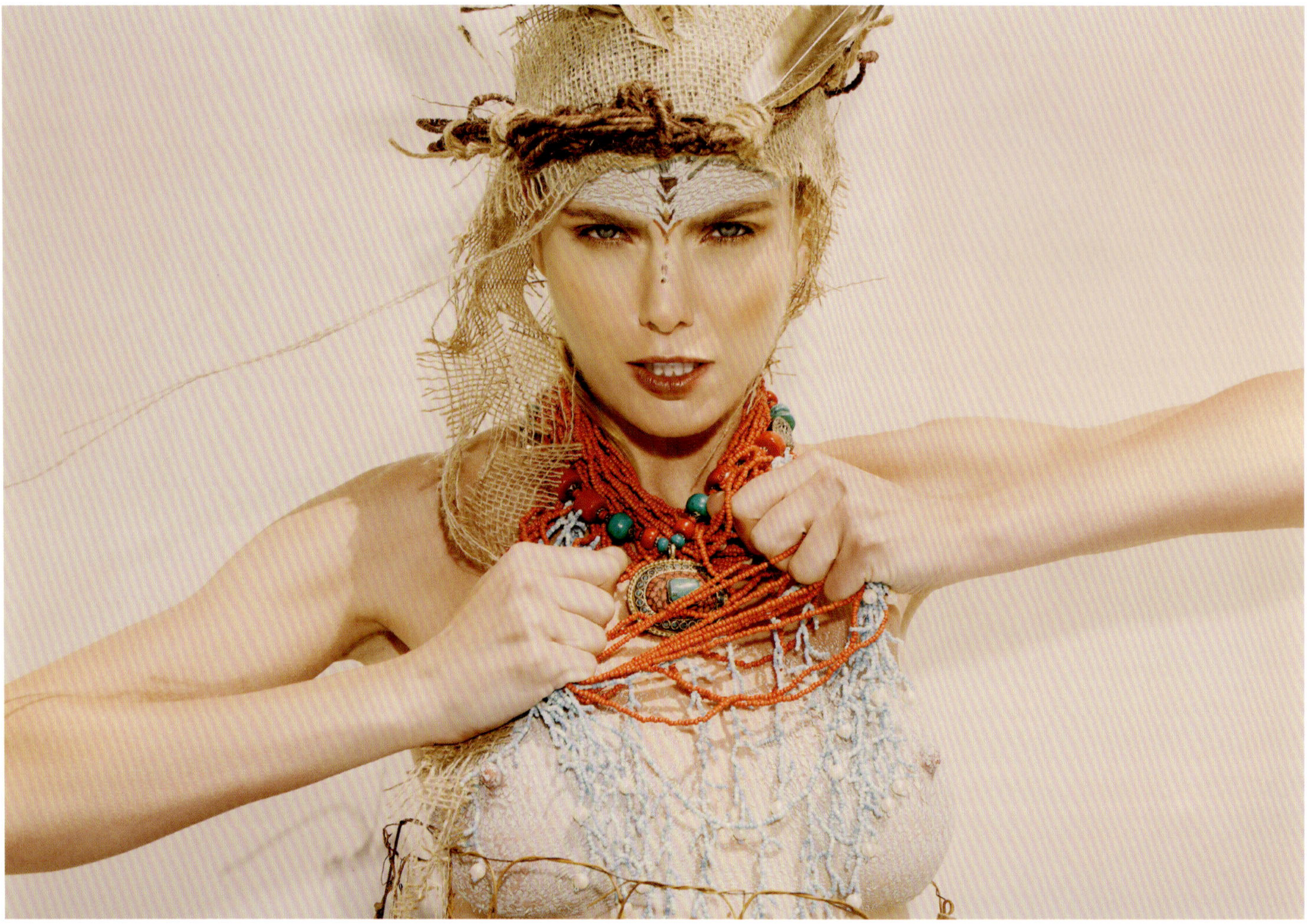

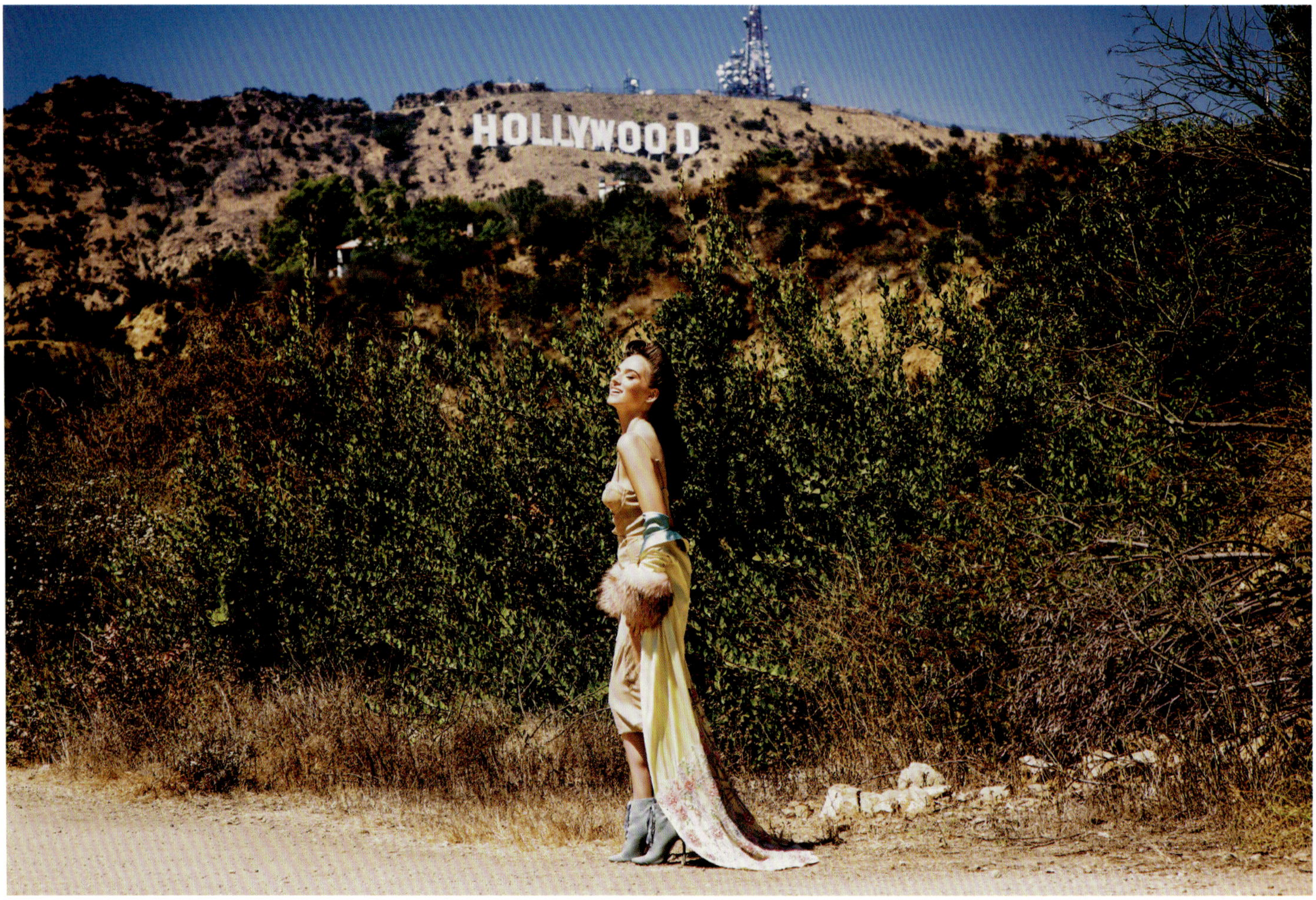

Title: Celebrities + Super Talent Prestige International Magazine | **Clients:** Prestige International Magazine, Self-initiated
P238: Credit & Commentary | Images 1, 2 of 7

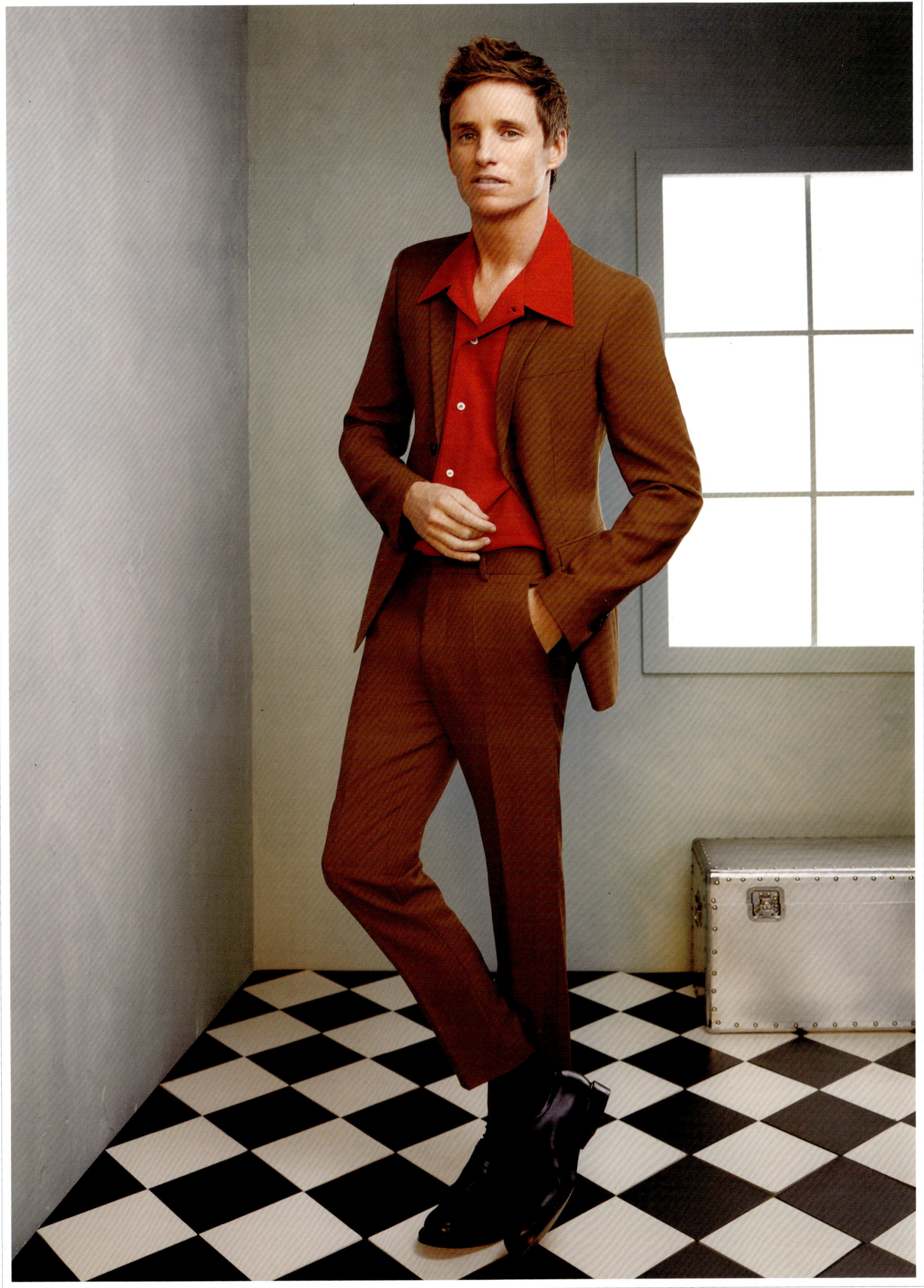

P239: Credit & Commentary

Title: Redmayne | **Client:** Savannah College of Art & Design

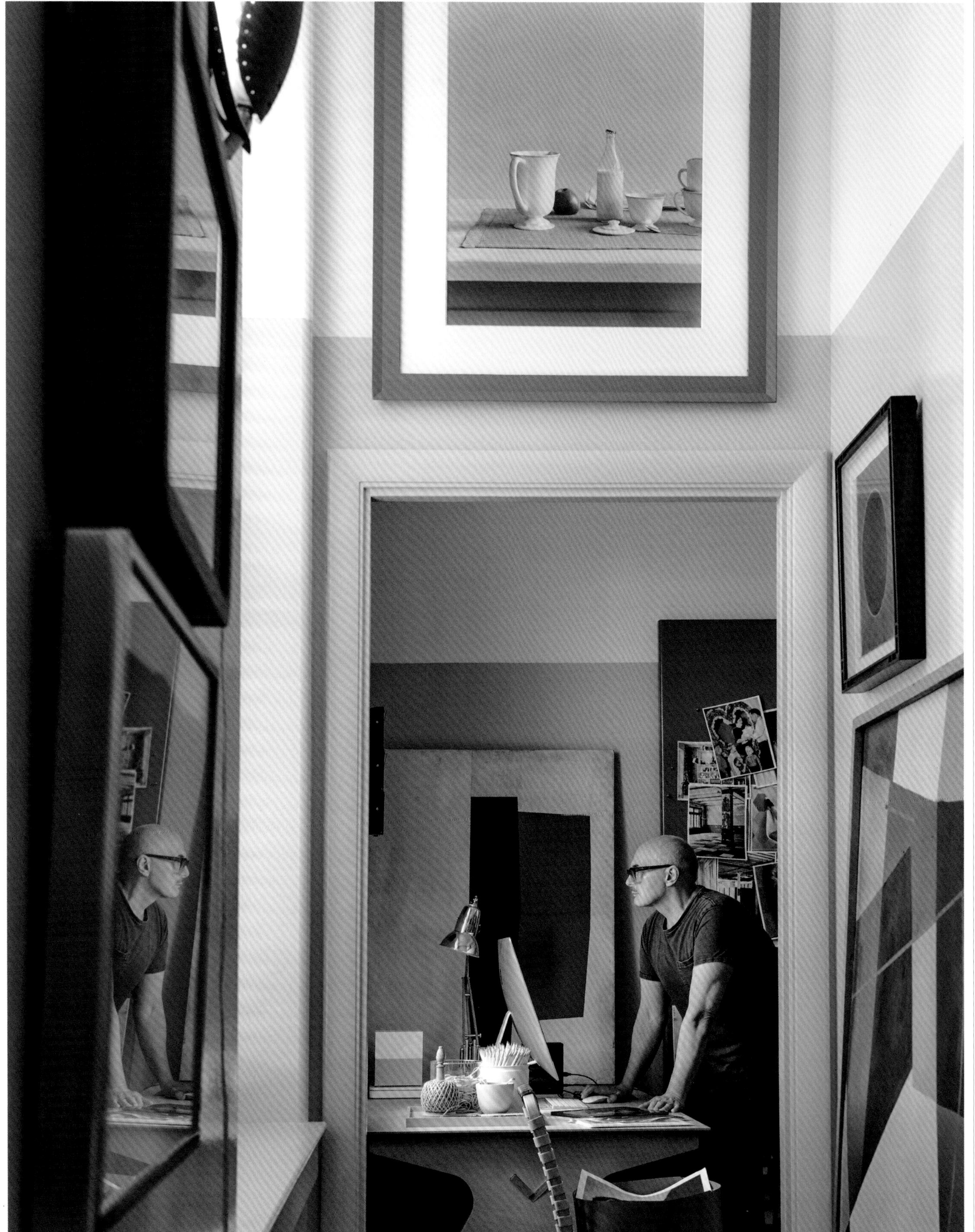

P239: Credit & Commentary

Title: Standing Desk | **Client:** Robert Valentine

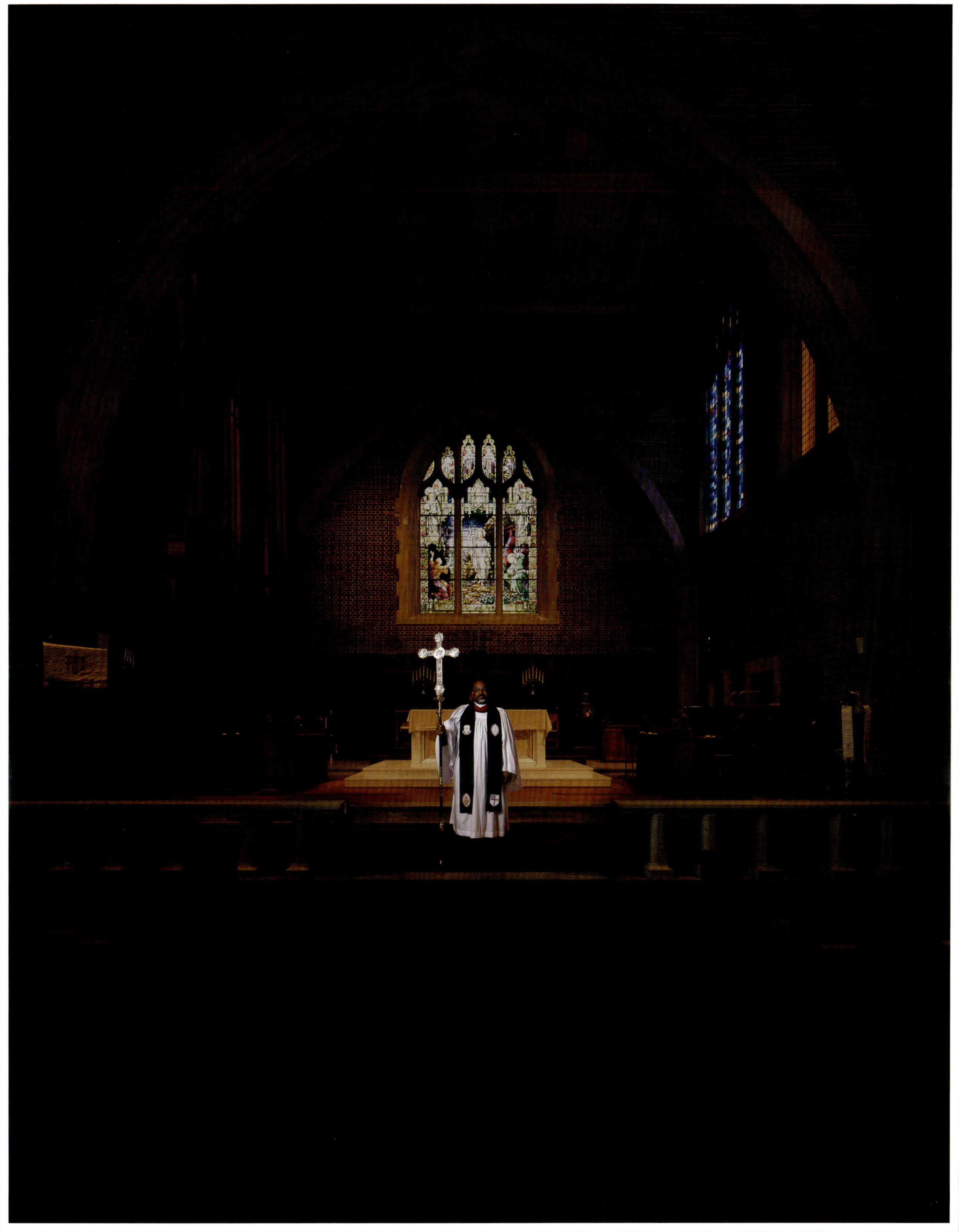

P239: Credit & Commentary

Title: Sacred Paradox | **Client:** Self-initiated

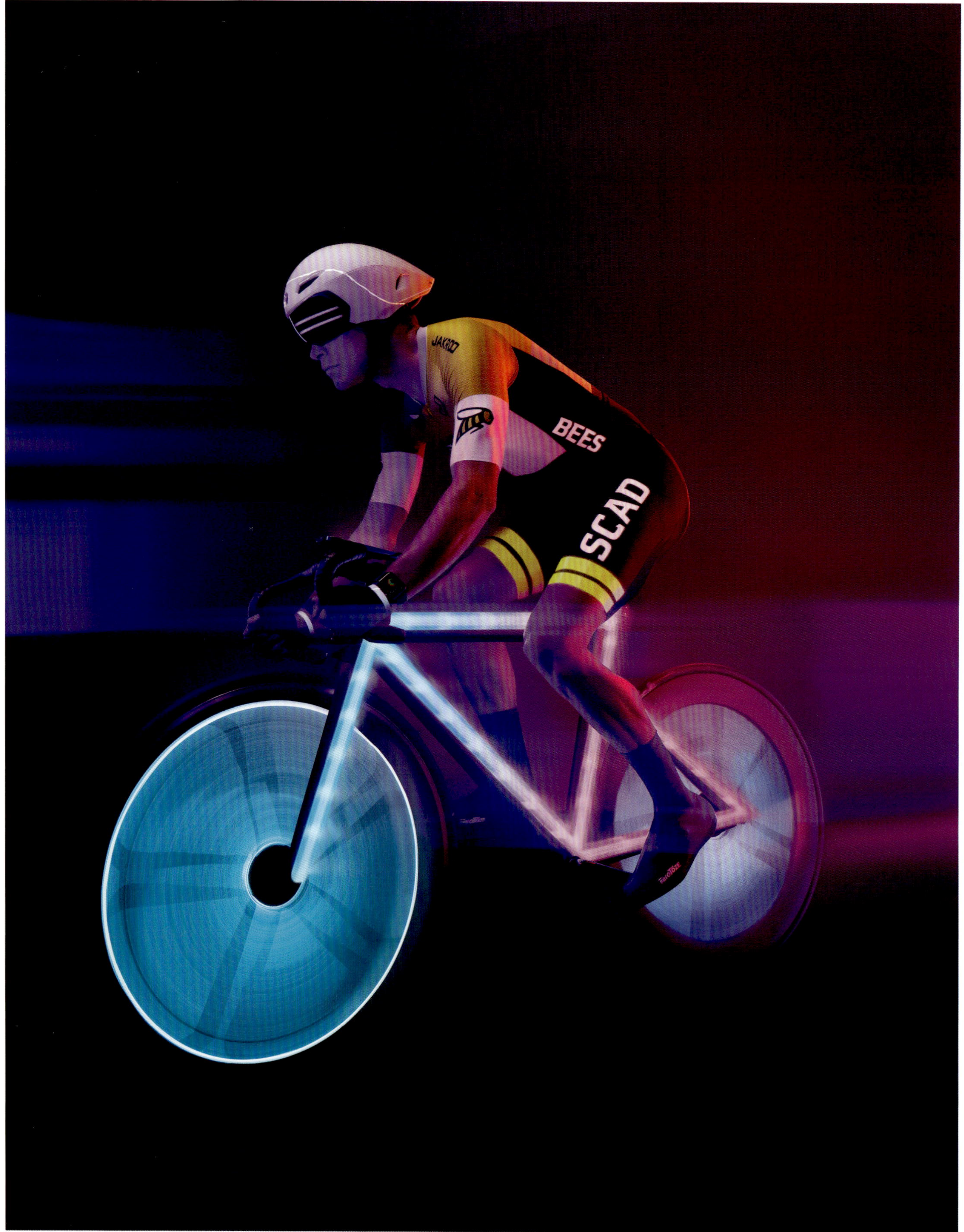

P239: Credit & Commentary

Title: Speed | **Client:** Savannah College of Art & Design

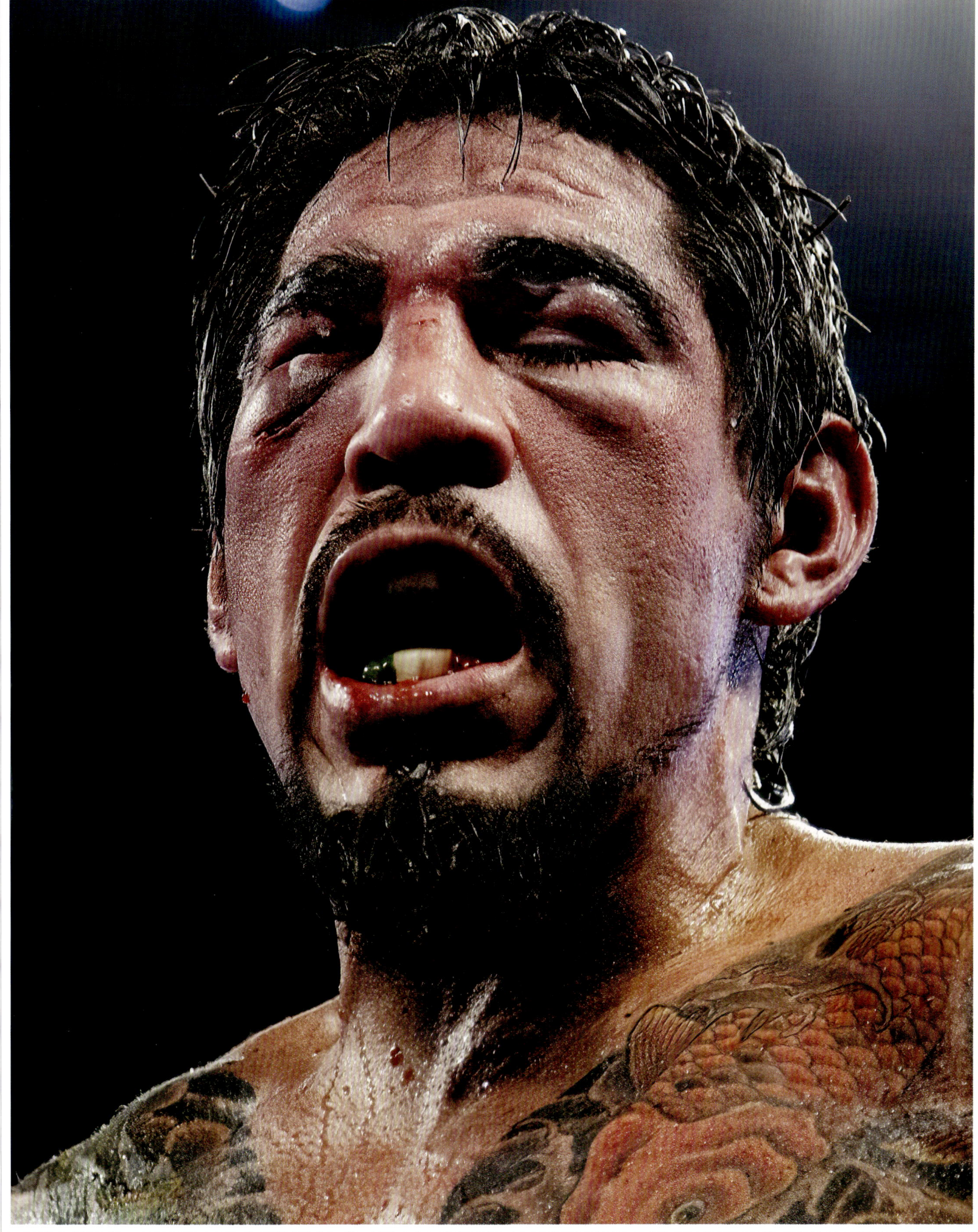

Title: Boxer Antonio Margarito After the Fight, Cowboys Stadium, Texas
Client: Self-initiated | **P239:** Credit & Commentary

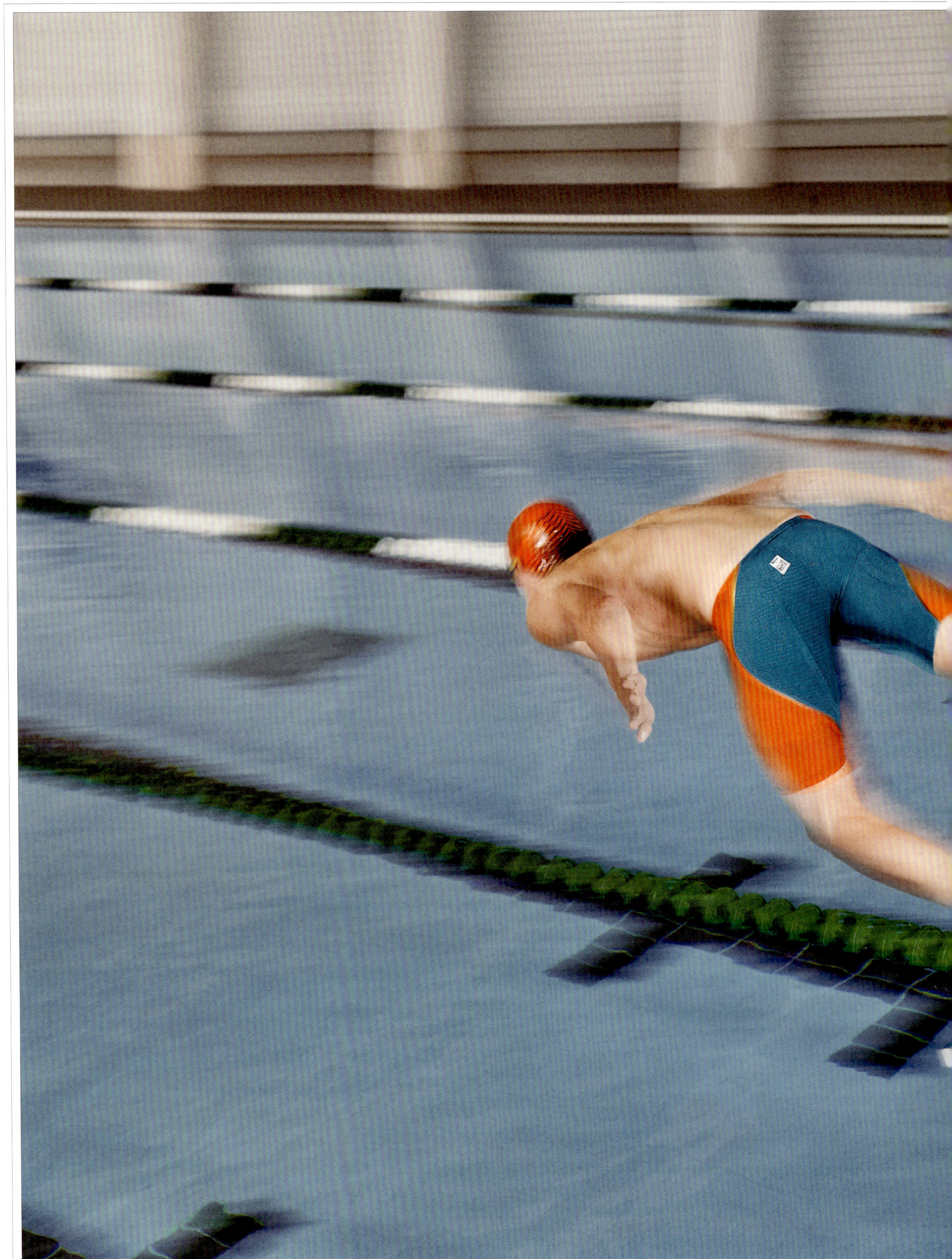

P239: Credit & Commentary

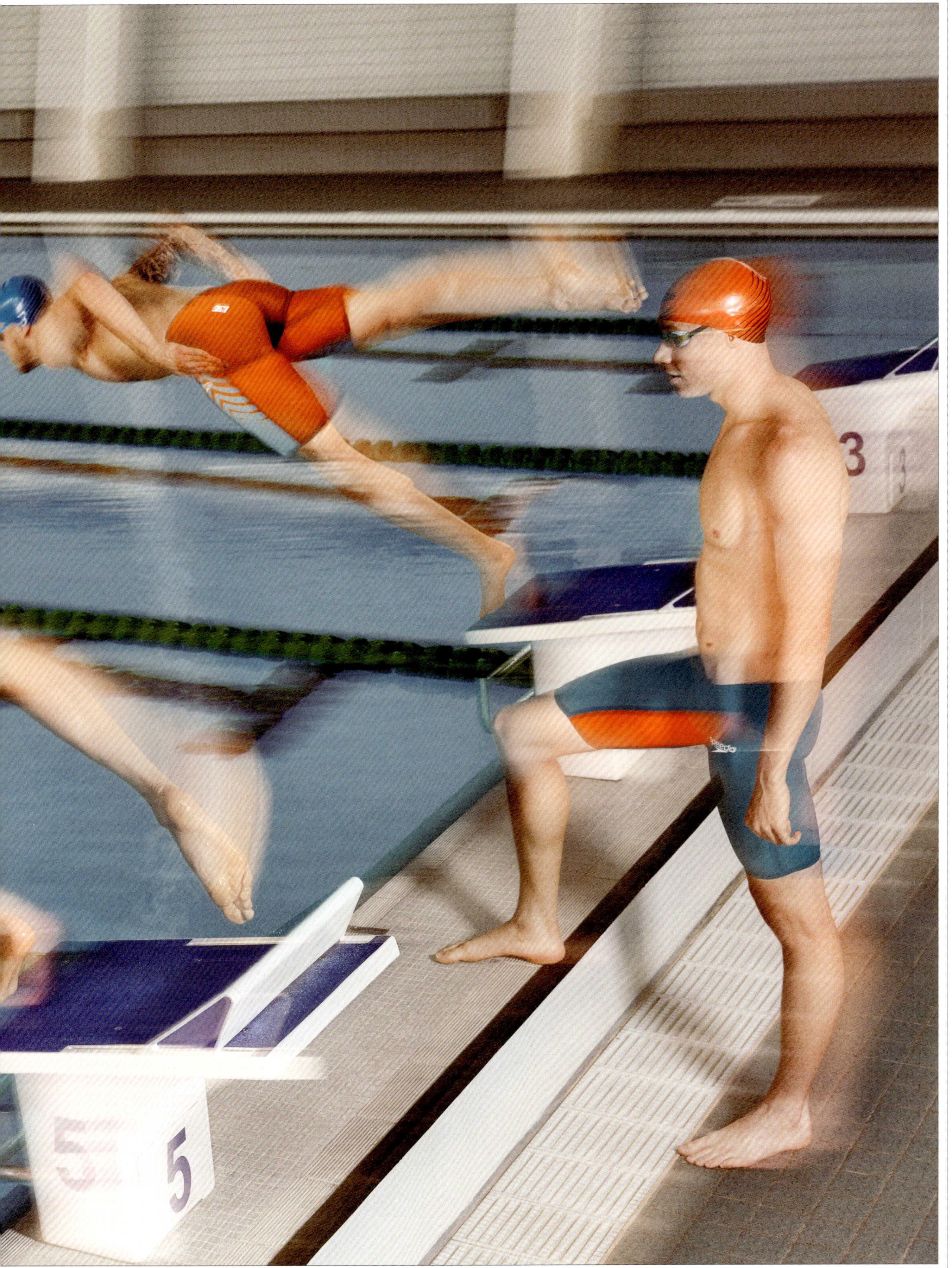

Title: Speedo Fastskin Campaign | **Client:** Speedo

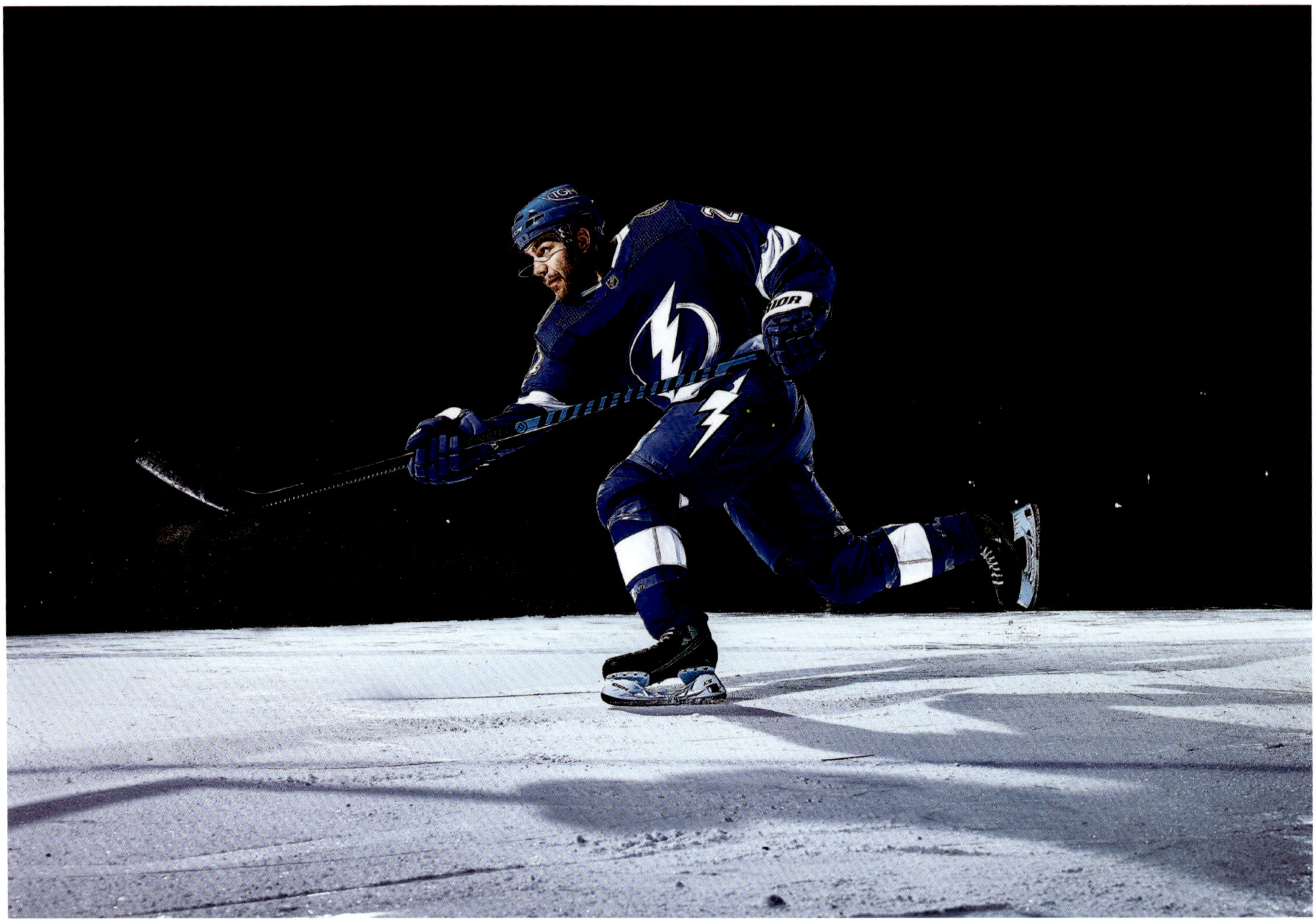

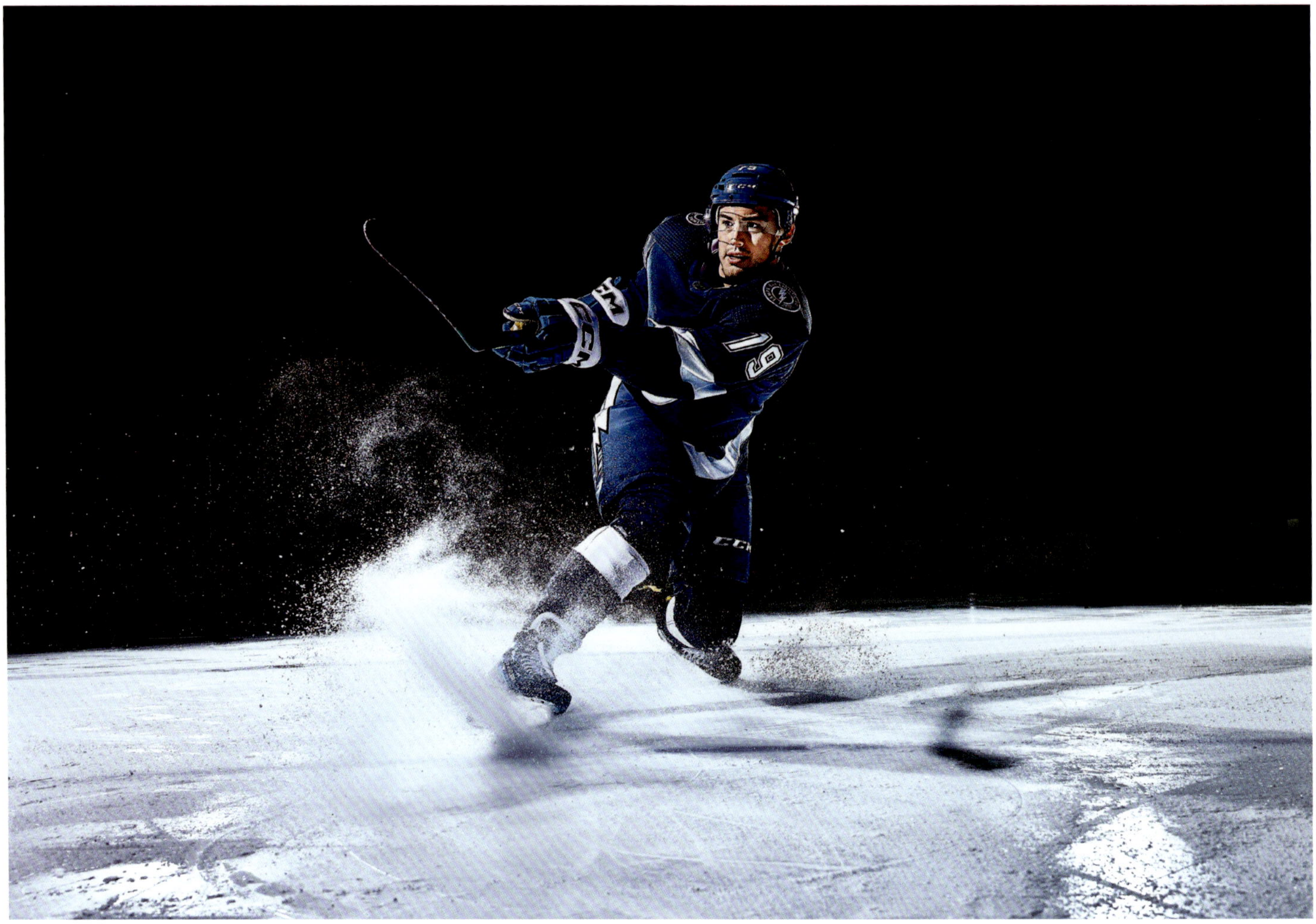

P239: Credit & Commentary **Title:** 23/24 Season Stills | **Client:** Tampa Bay Lightning Images 1, 2 of 7

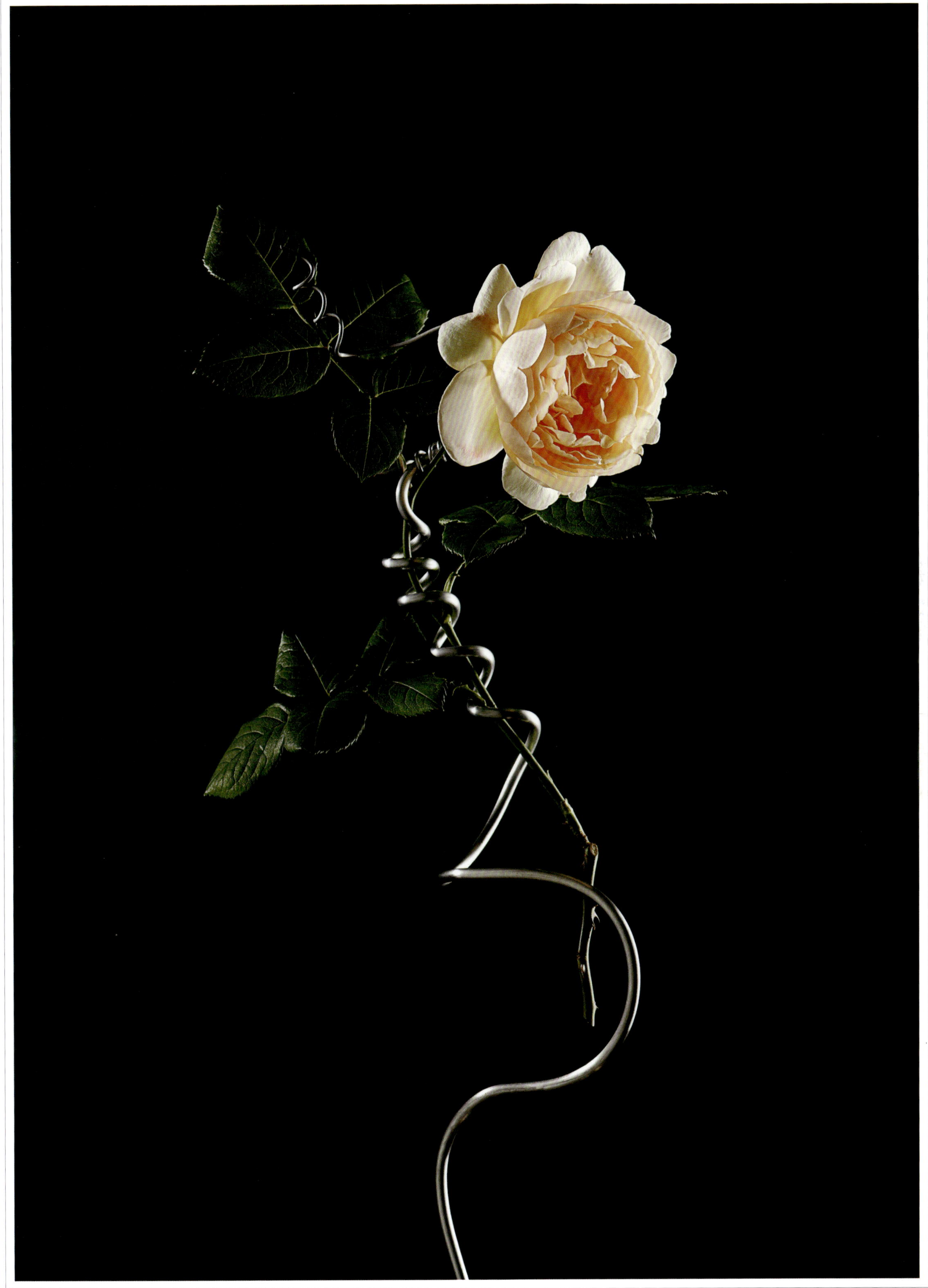

P239: Credit & Commentary

Title: Wired Flowers | Client: Self-initiated

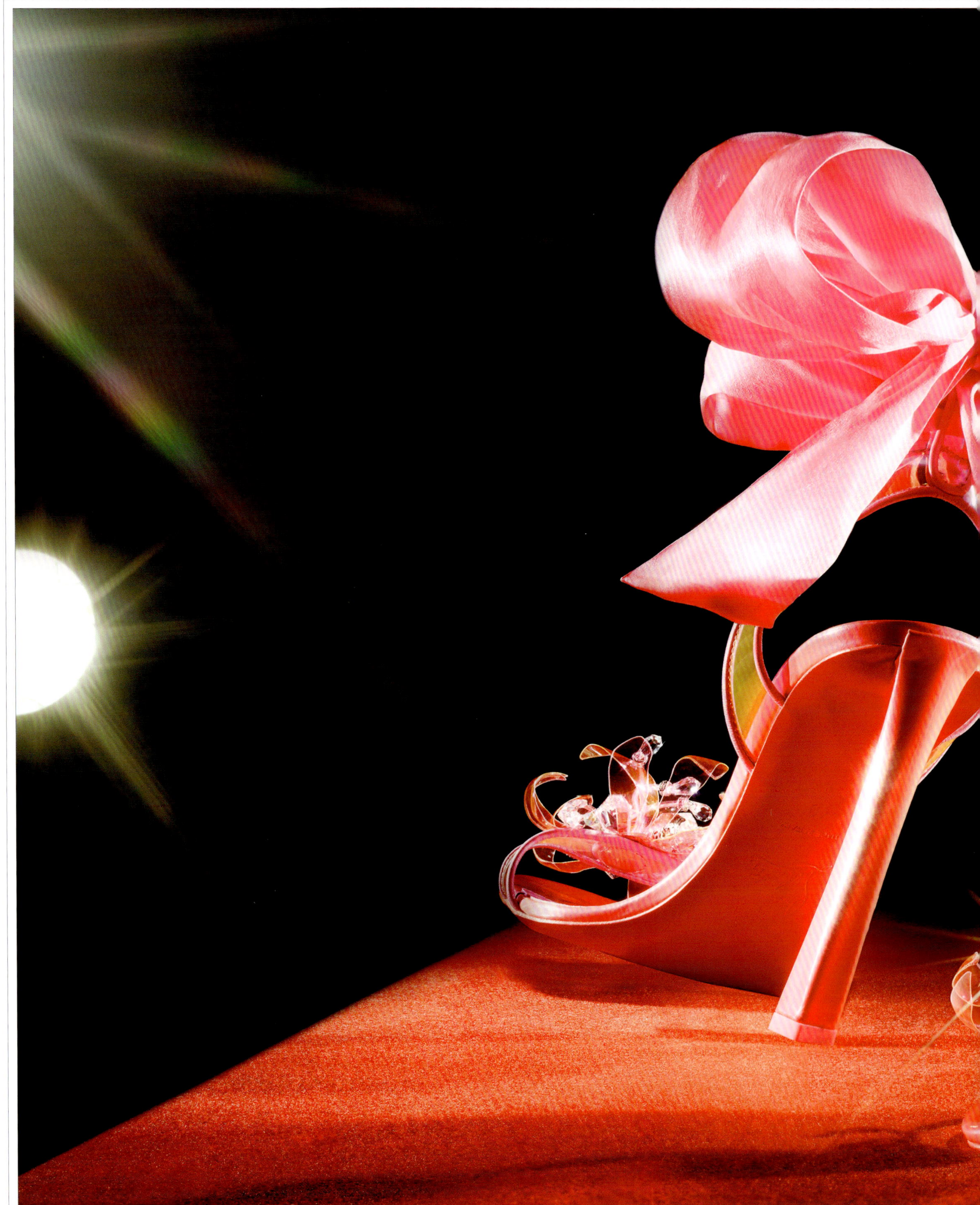

P239: Credit & Commentary

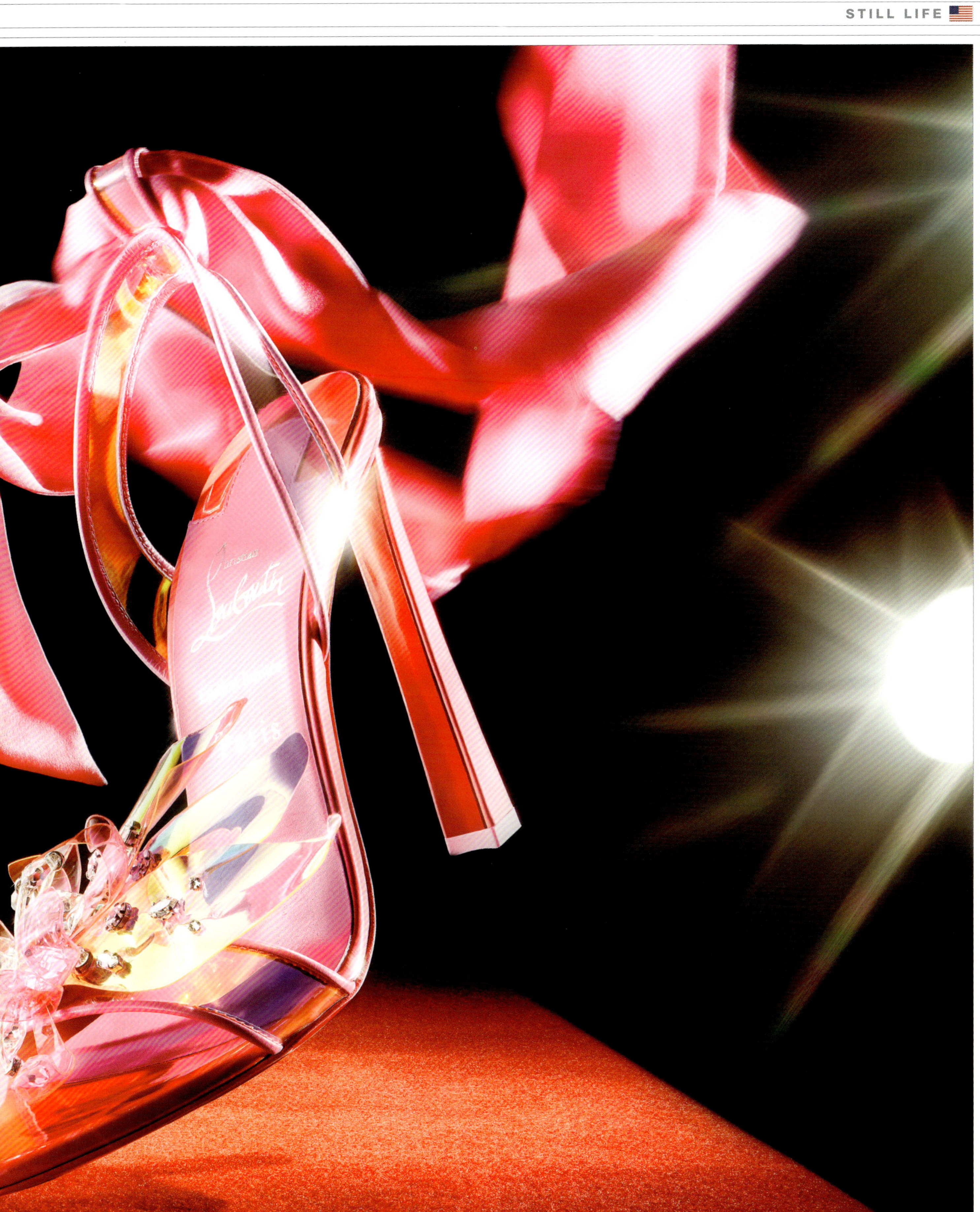

Title: Sole Stoppers | Client: Genlux Magazine

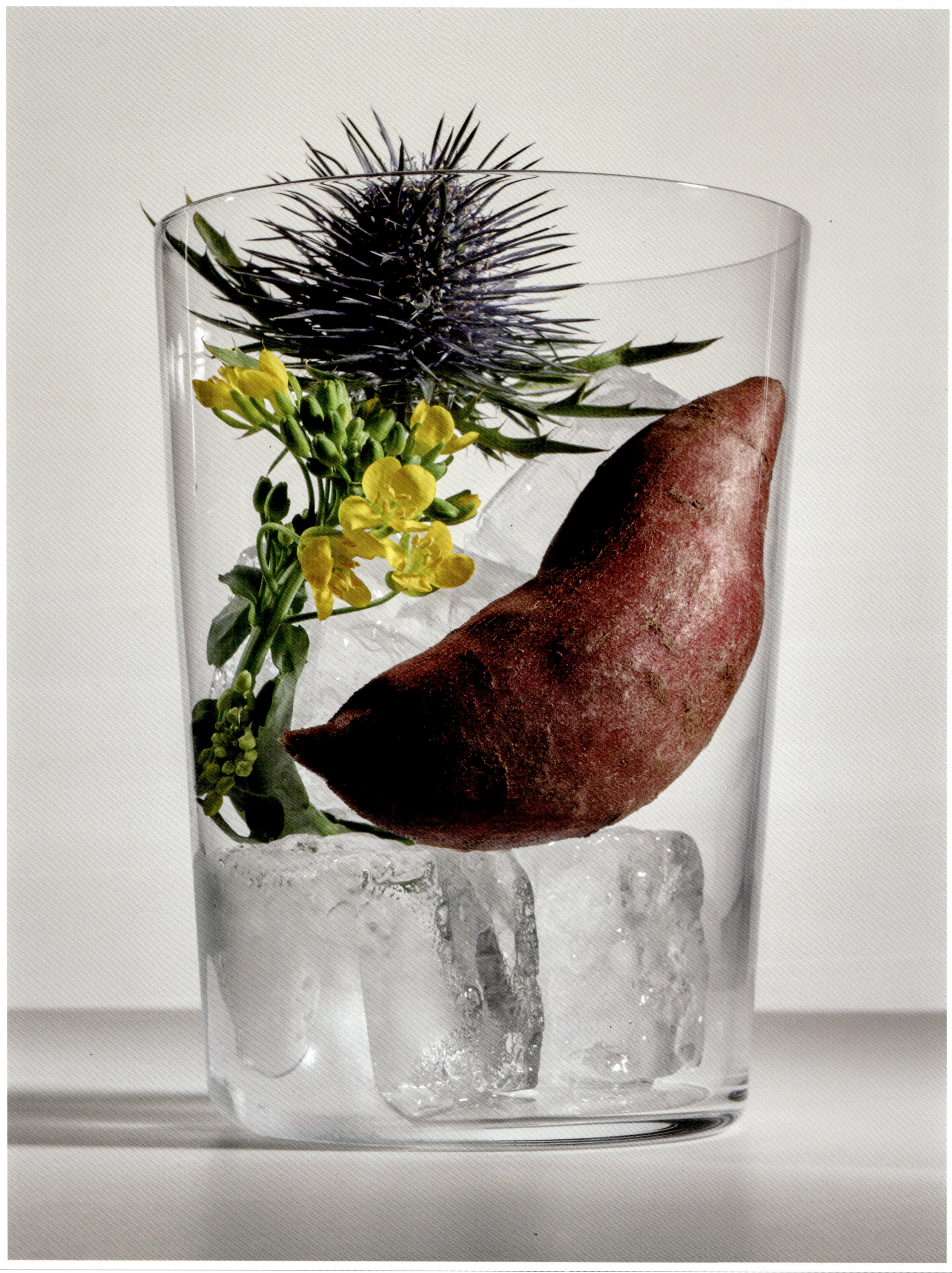

P239: Credit & Commentary

Title: Glass Still Life | **Client:** Self-initiated

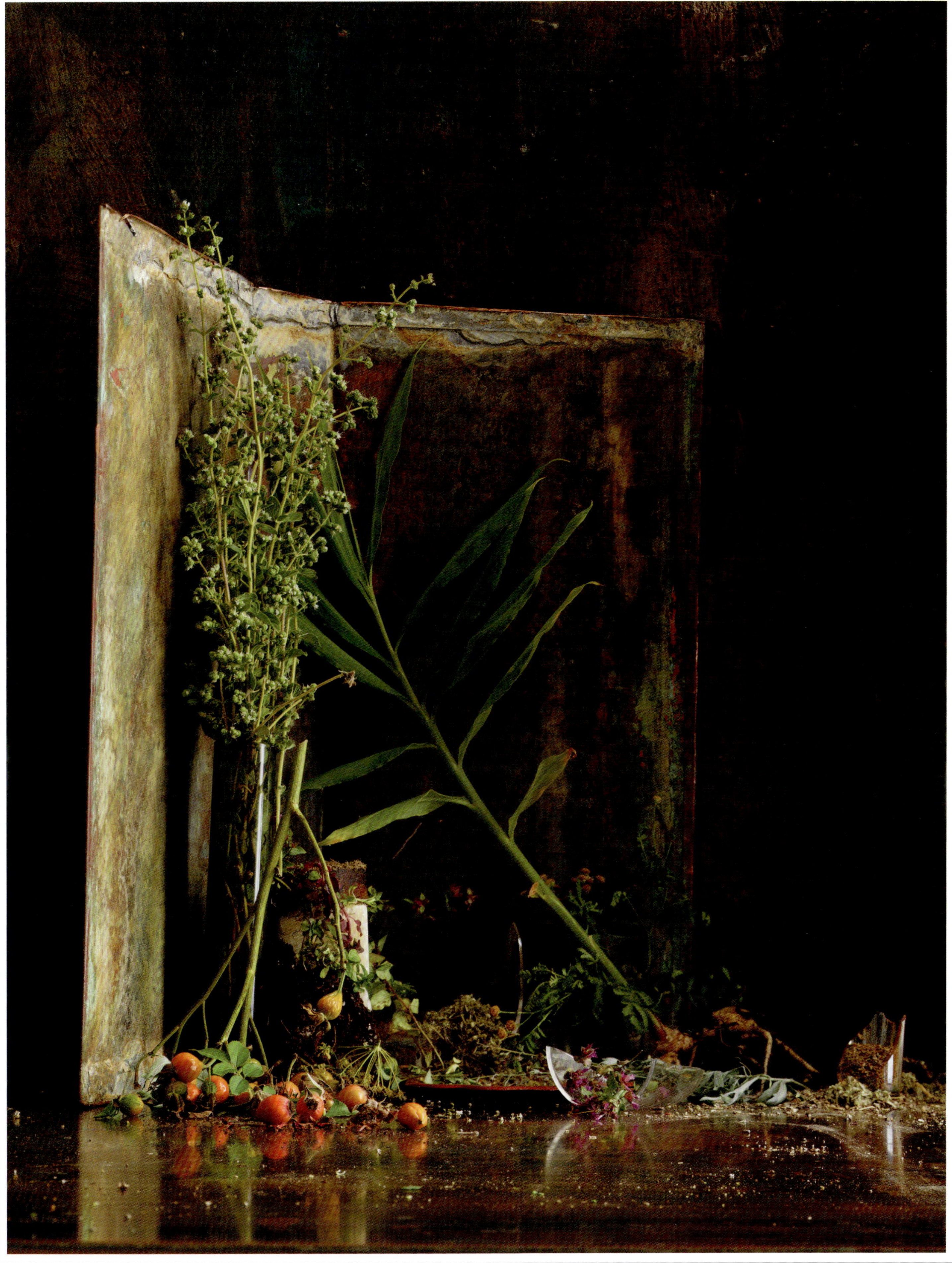

P239: Credit & Commentary

Title: Aftermath: The Overturning of Roe vs. Wade | **Client:** Washington Post

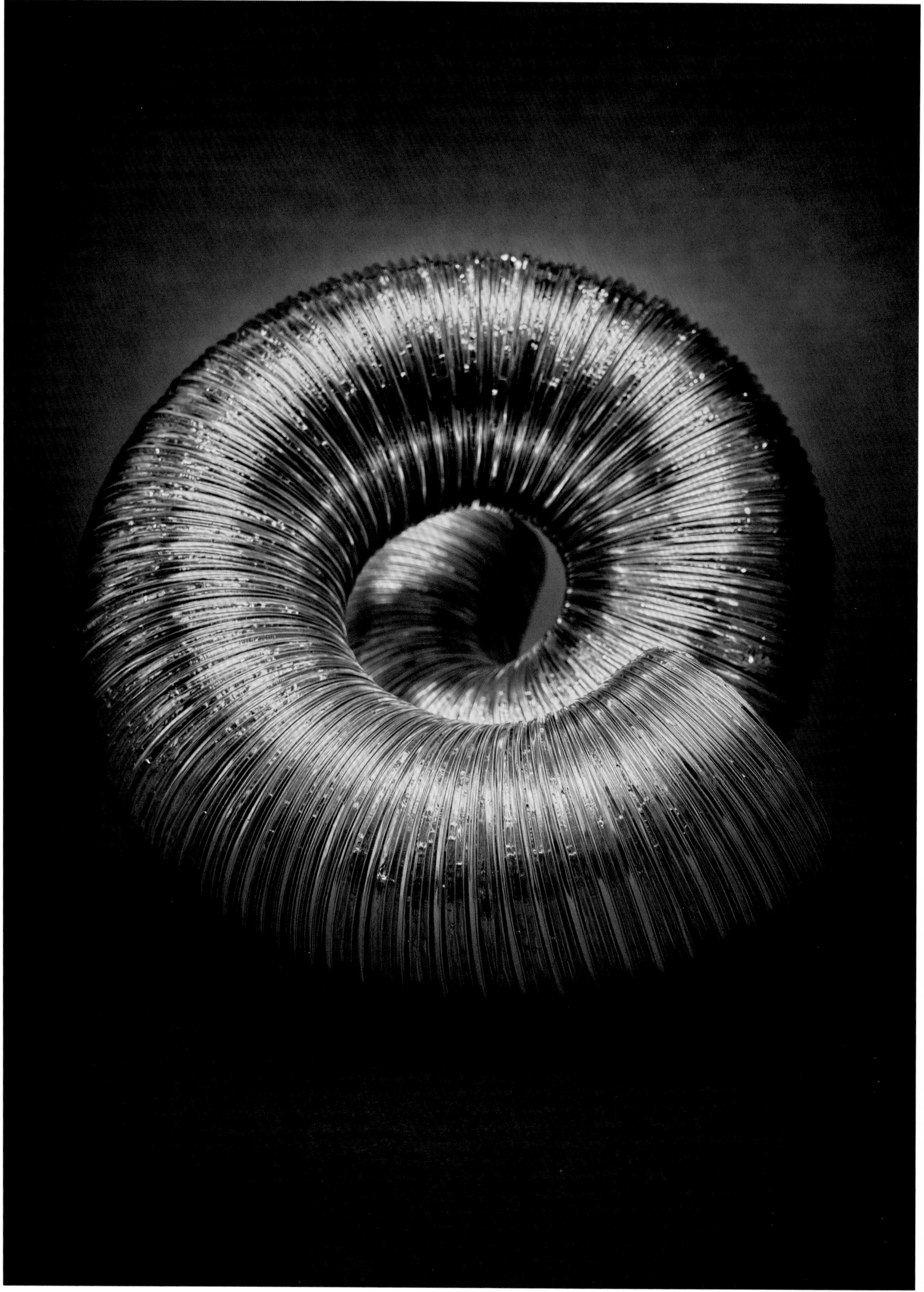

P240: Credit & Commentary

Title: Air Duct | Client: Self-initiated

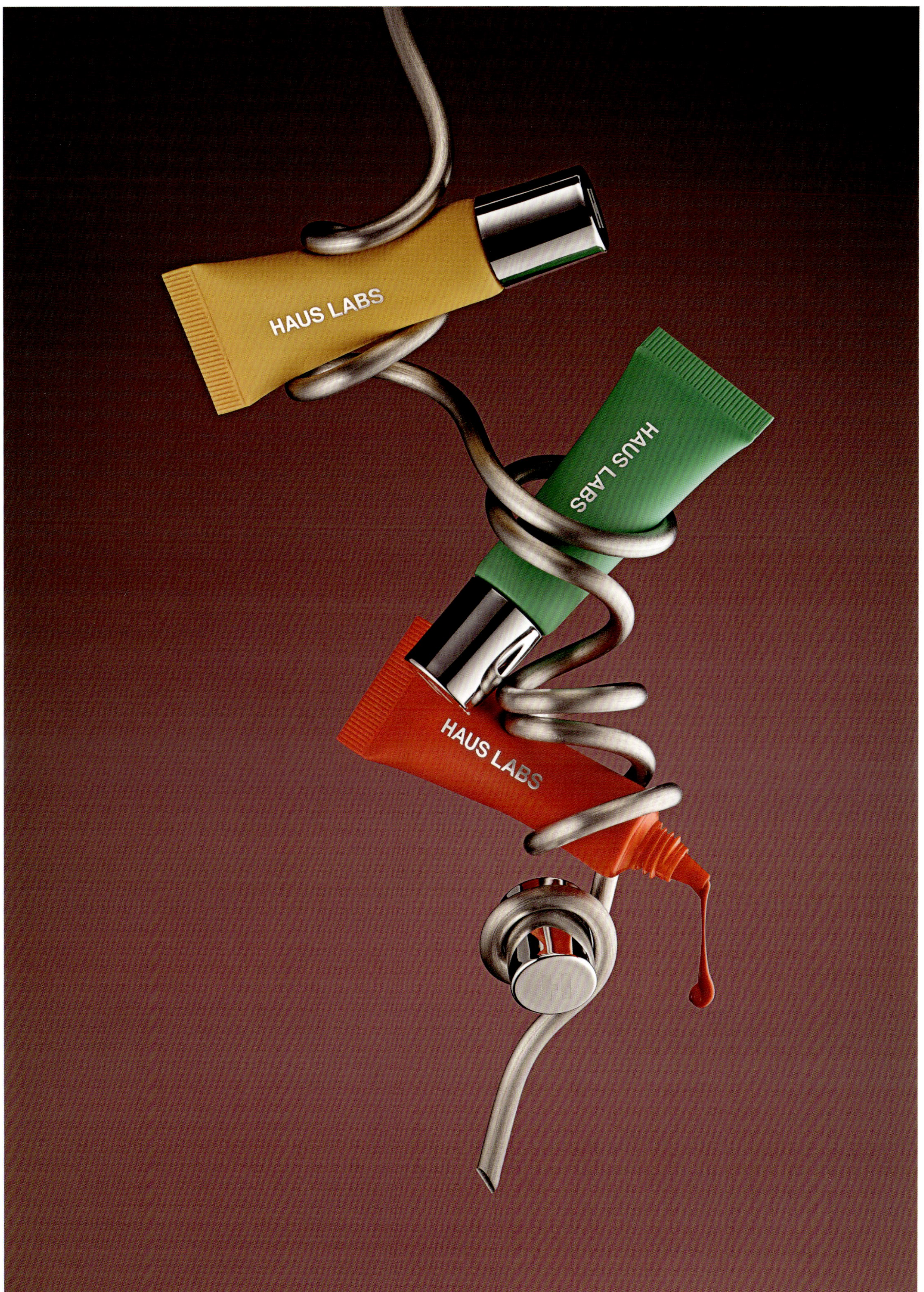

Title: Wired Cosmetics | Client: Self-initiated

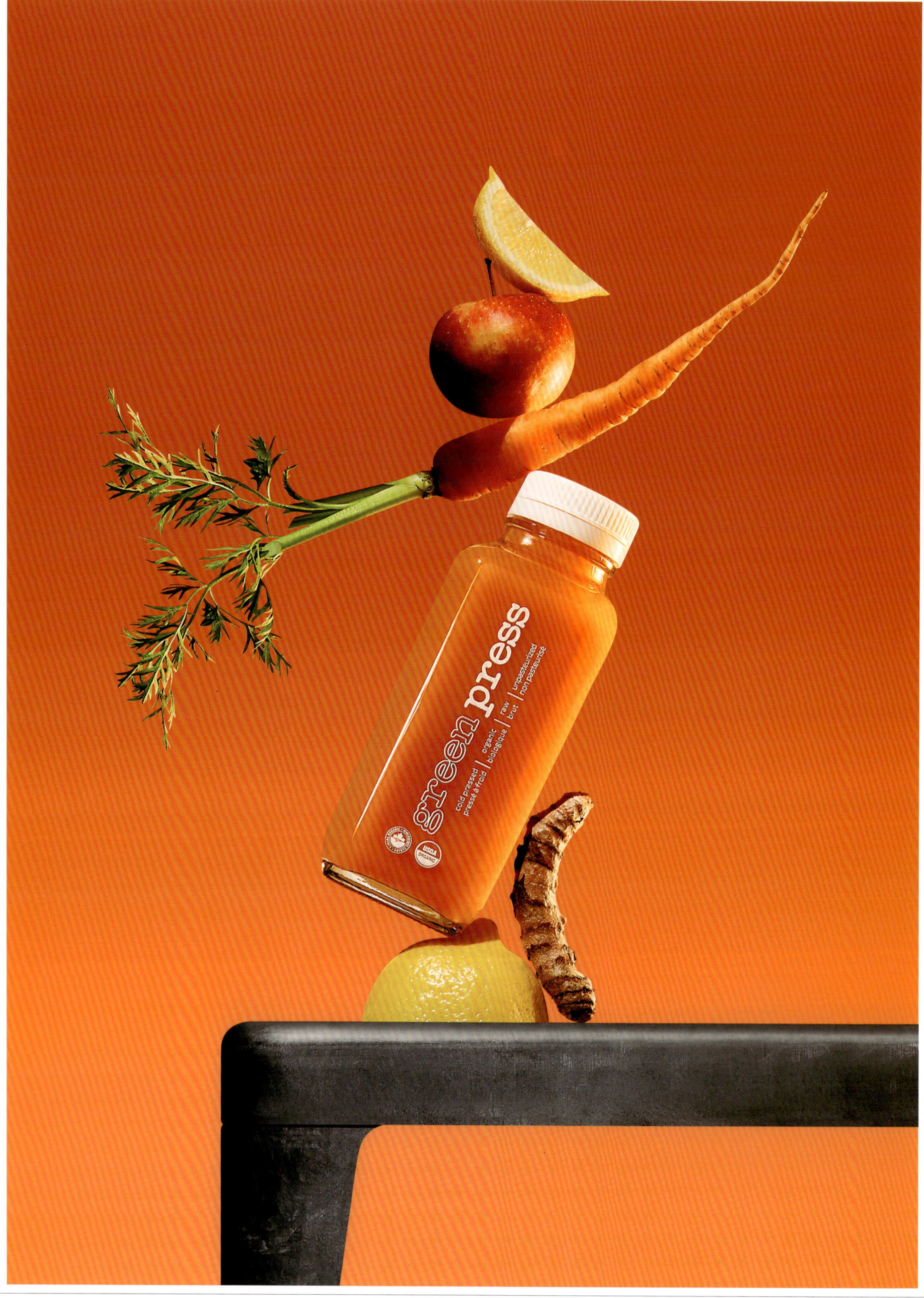

P240: Credit & Commentary

Title: Green Press Juice | **Client:** JSW Green Press Juice

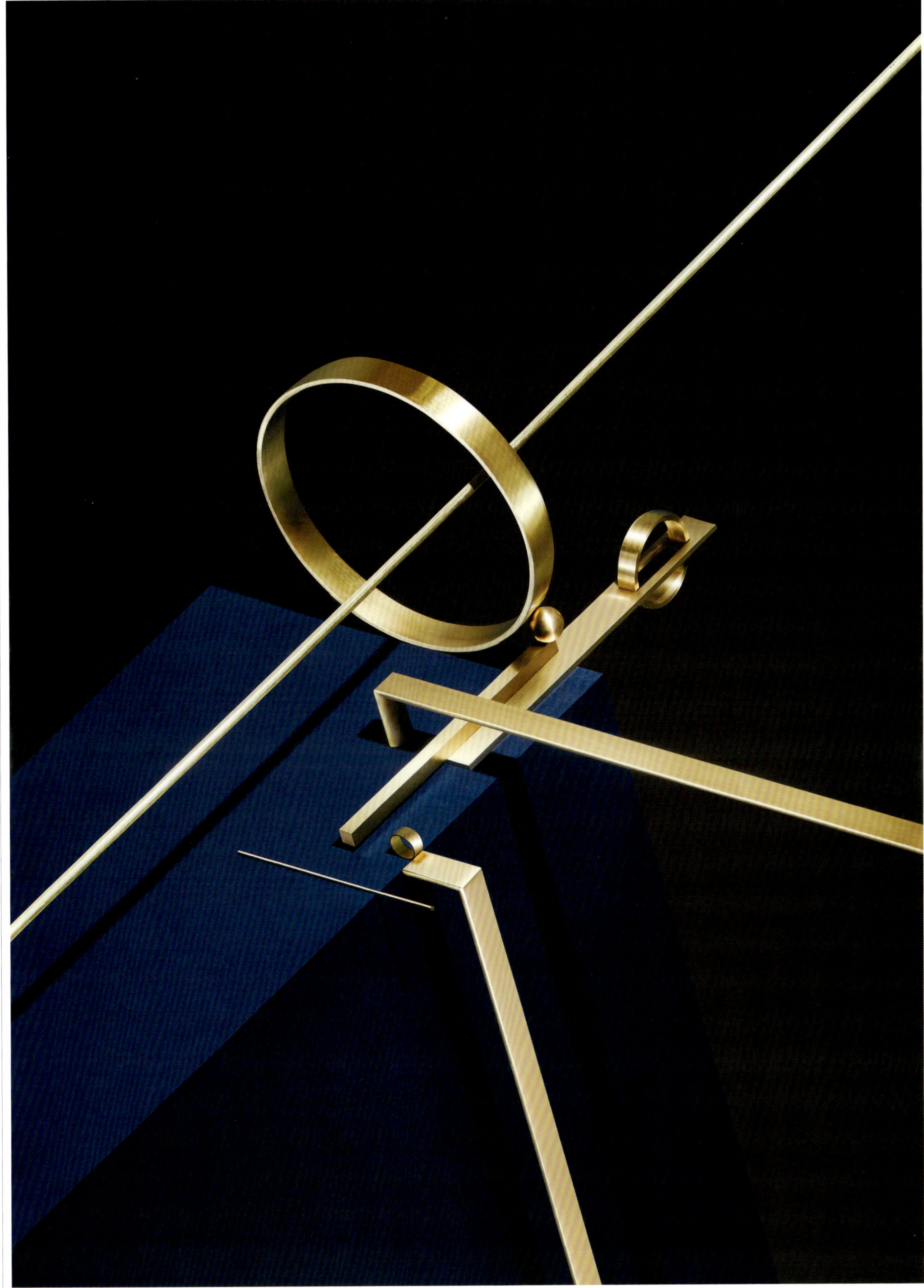

P240: Credit & Commentary

Title: Heavy Metals: Brass | **Client:** JSW

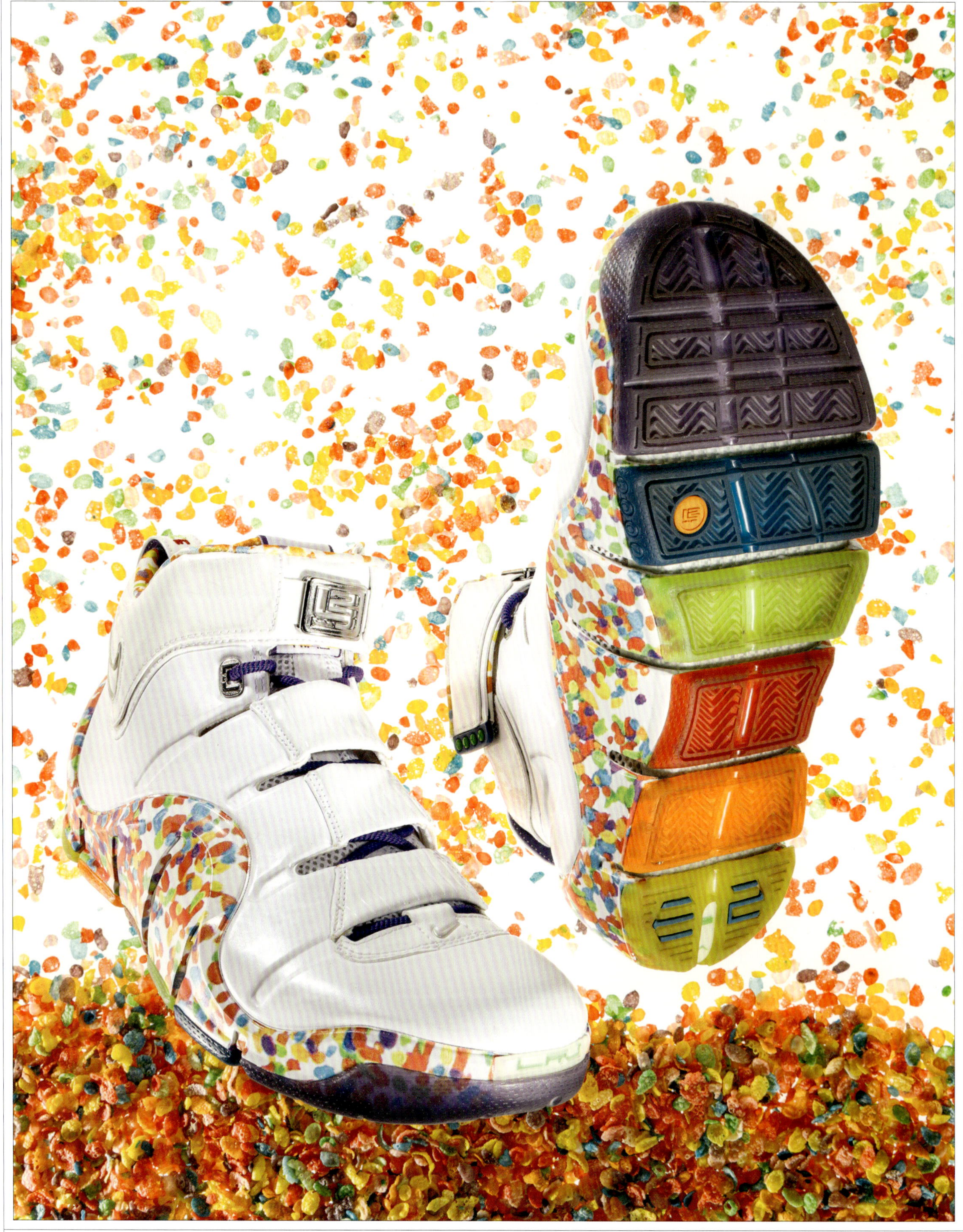

P240: Credit & Commentary

Title: Lebron's Fruity Pebbles | **Clients:** Arman Salemi, Heritage Auction

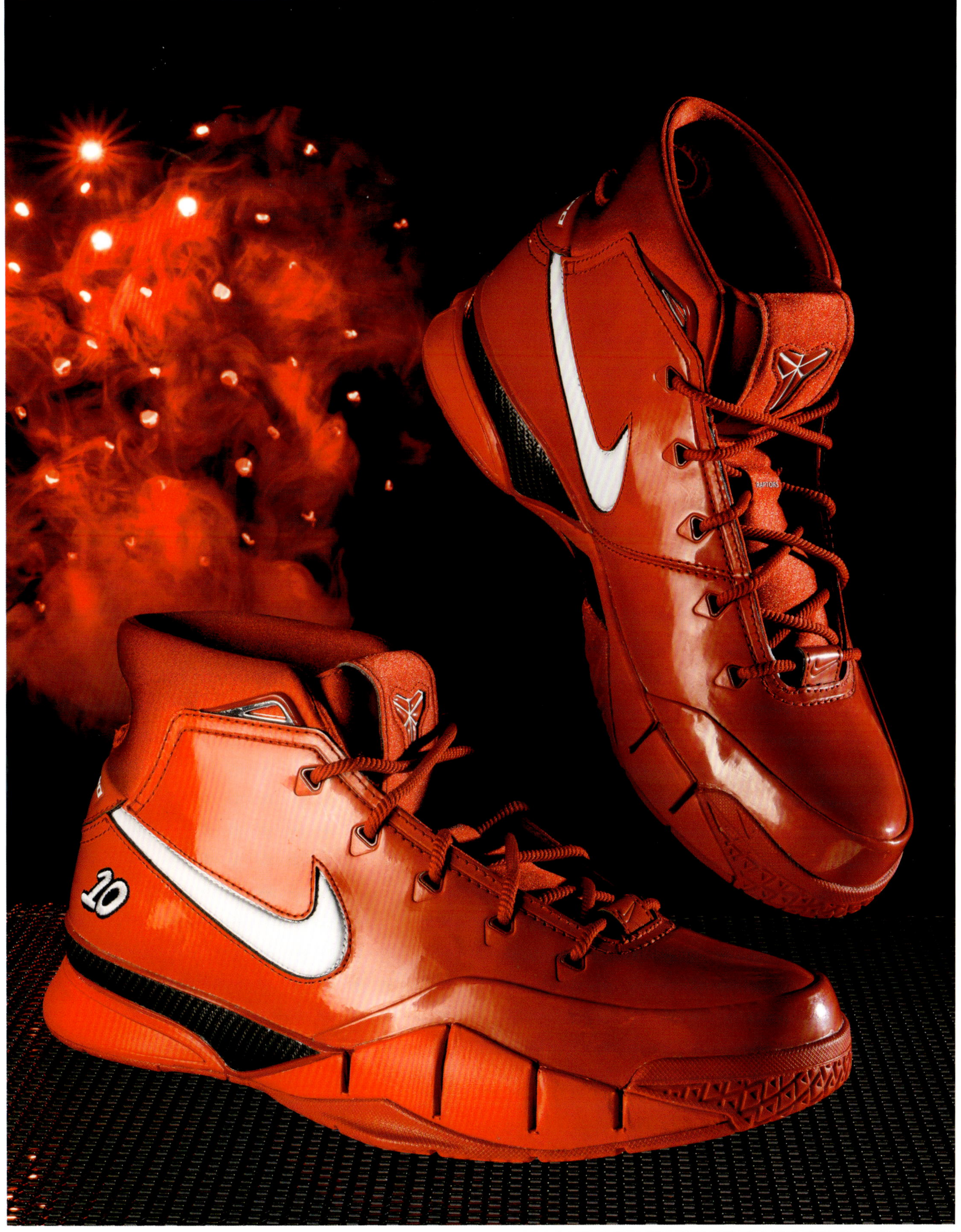

P240: Credit & Commentary

Title: Trifecta Sneakers | Client: Arman Salemi

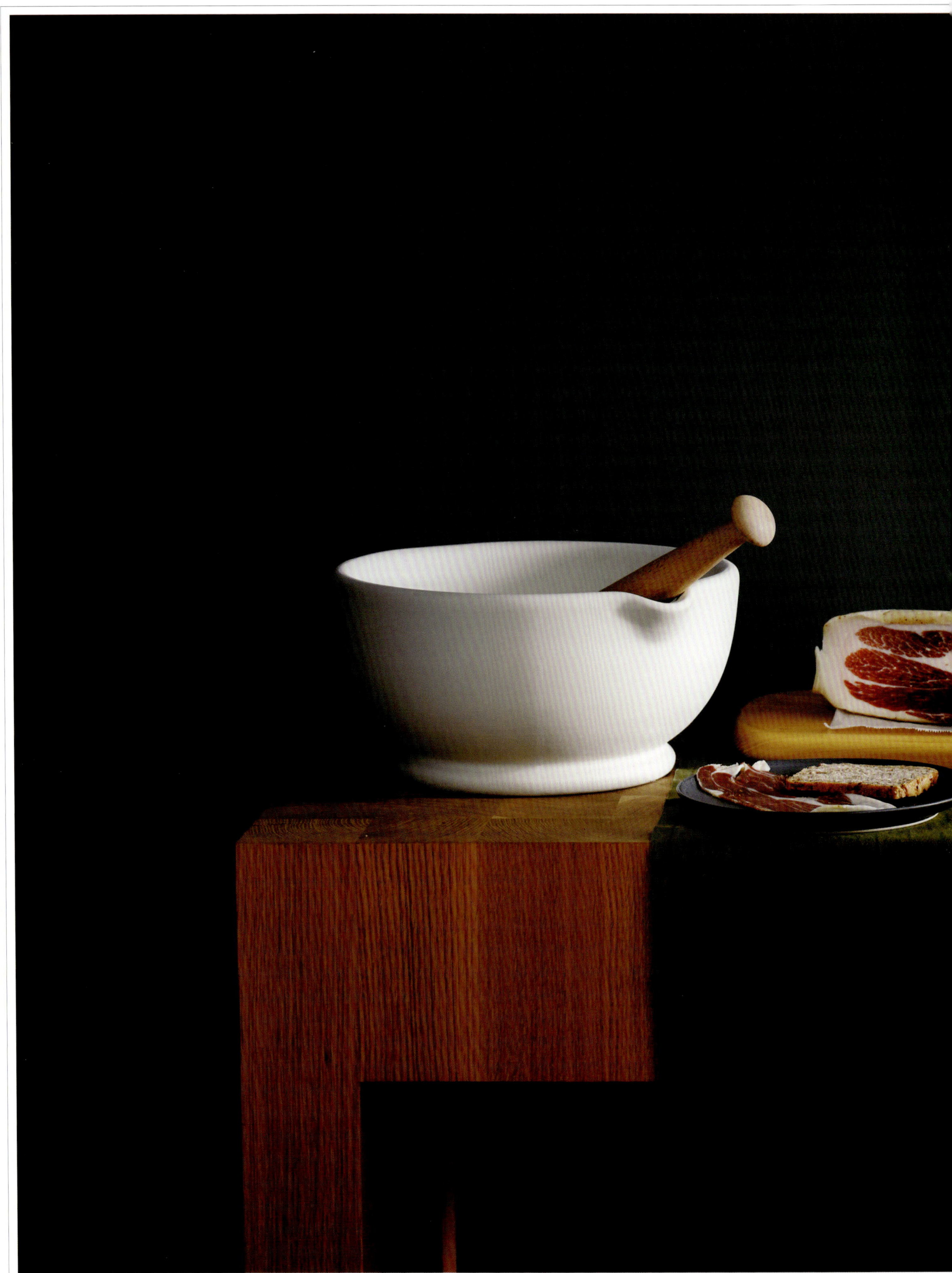

P240: Credit & Commentary

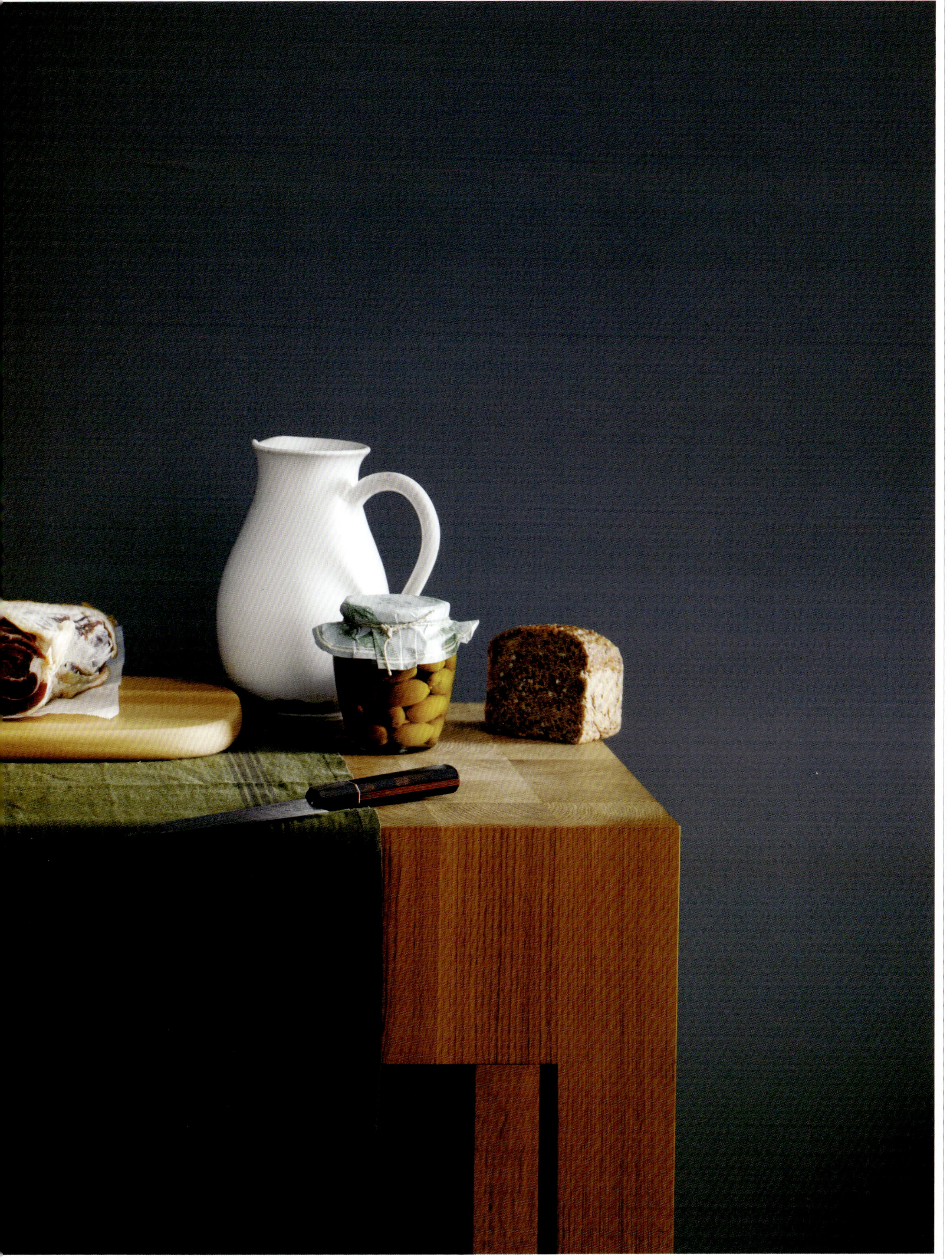

Title: Pitcher and Prosciutto | **Client:** March

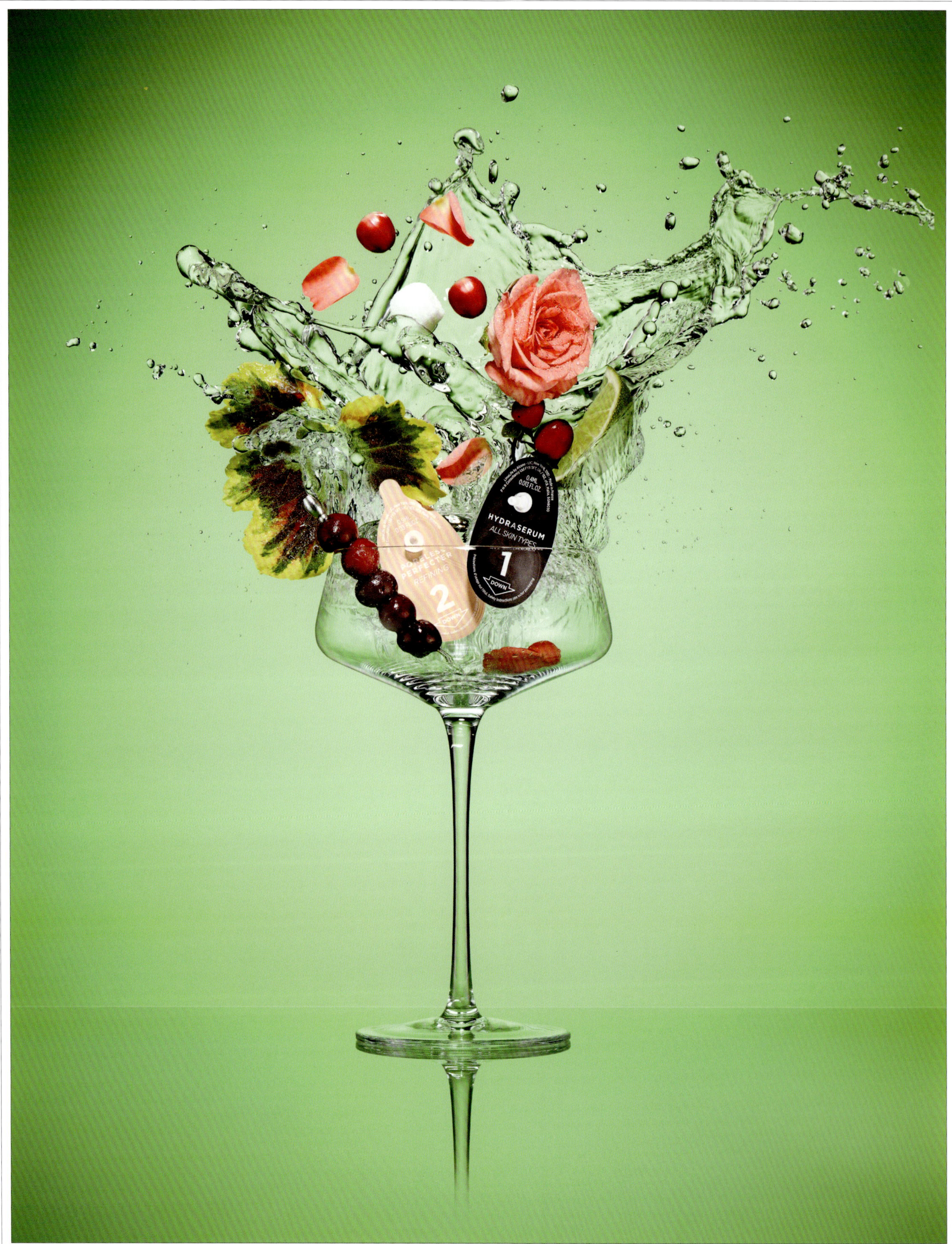

P240: Credit & Commentary

Title: LimeLife Skincare Series | **Client:** LimeLife by Alcone

Image 1 of 6

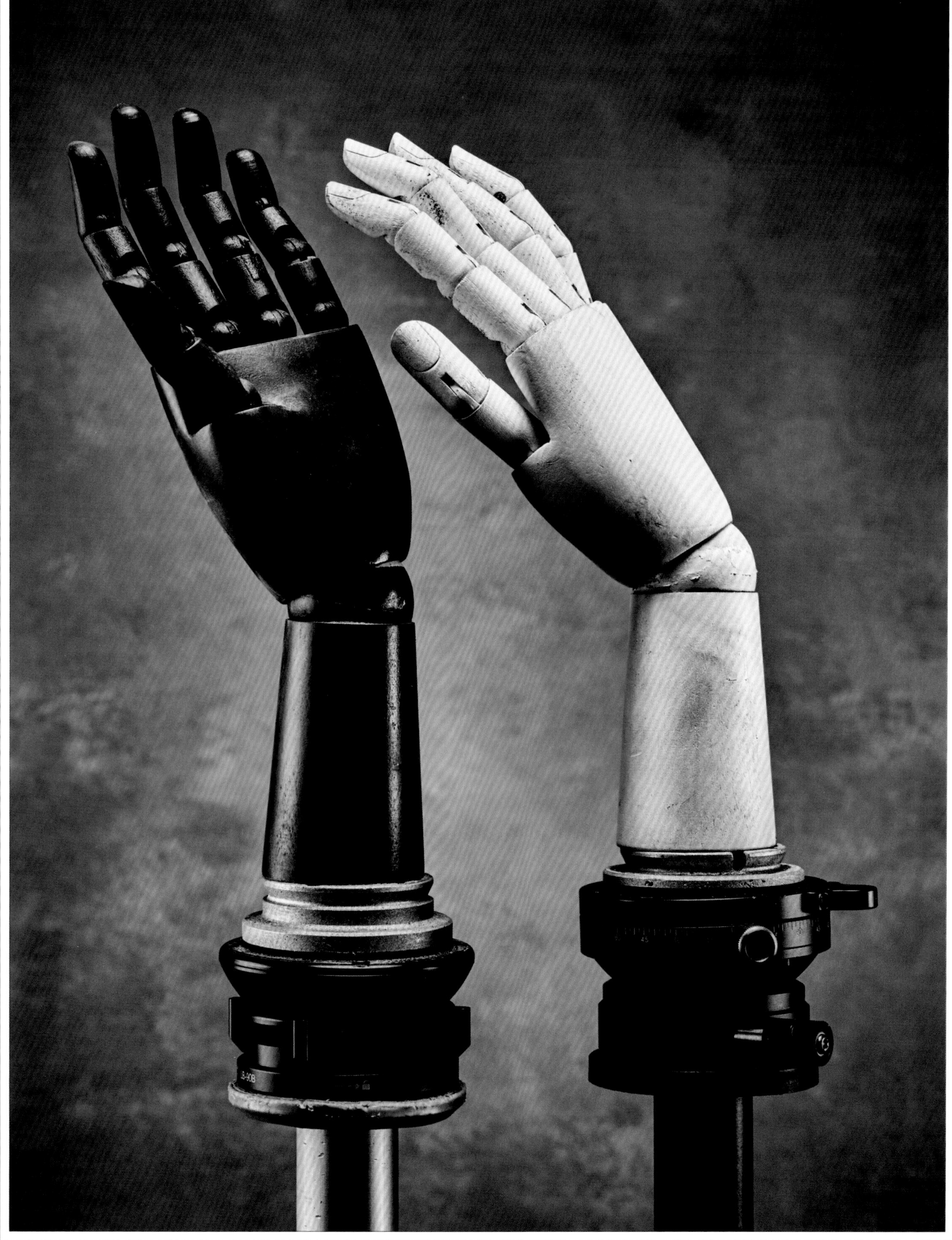

P240: Credit & Commentary

Title: Race Study | **Client:** Self-initiated

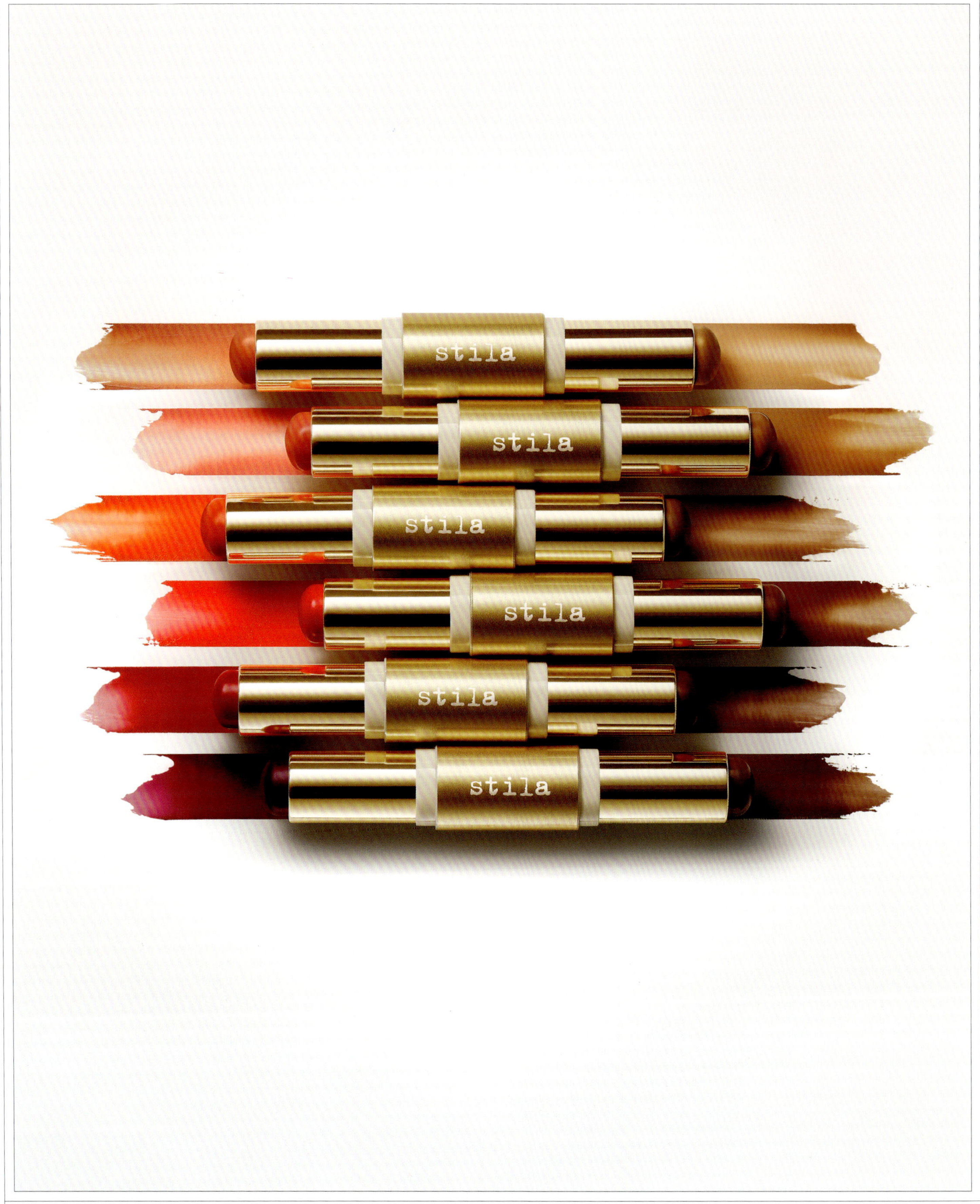

P240: Credit & Commentary

Title: Stila Duo Sticks | **Client:** Stila Cosmetics

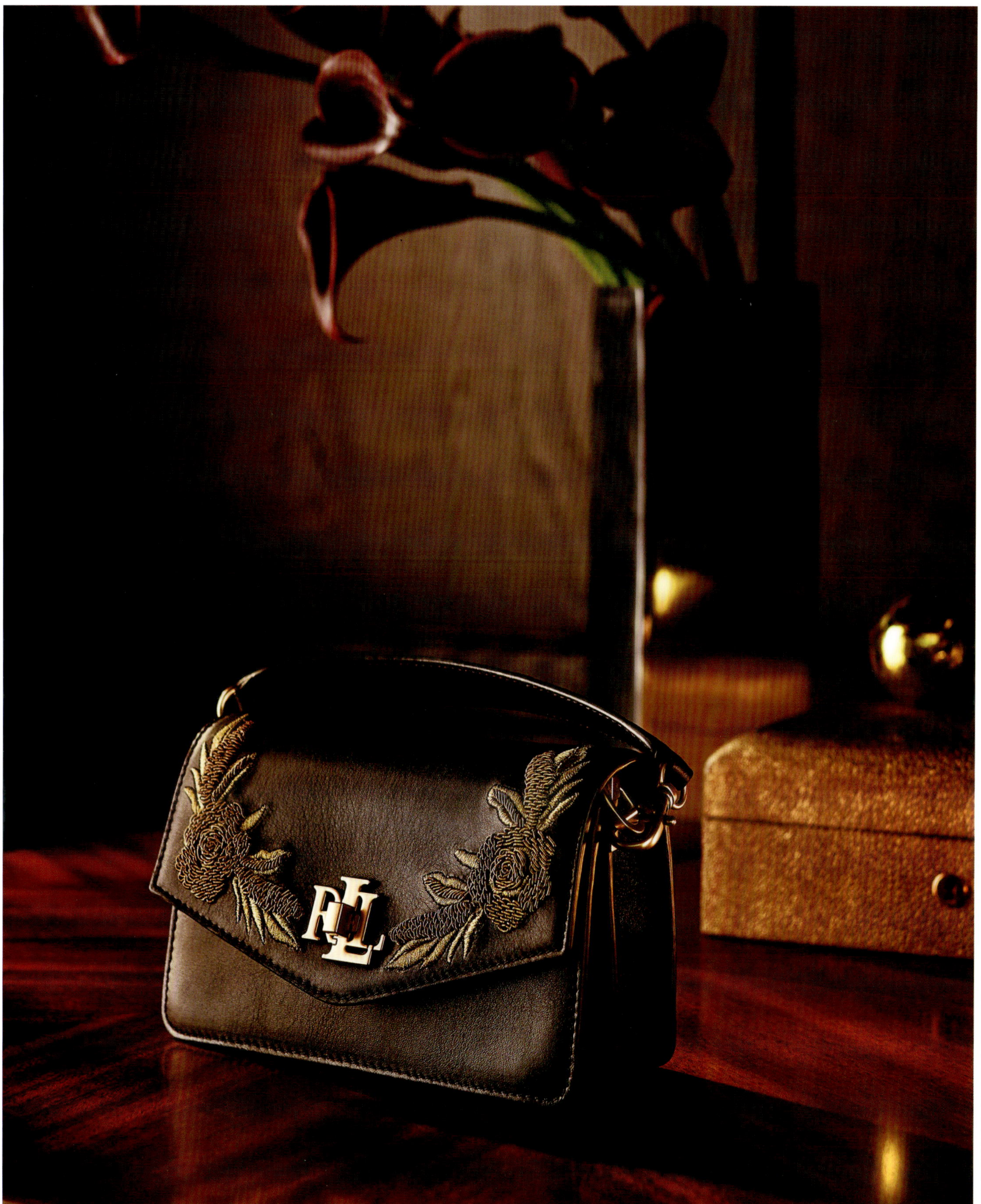

P240: Credit & Commentary

Title: Lauren Holiday 02 | **Client:** Ralph Lauren

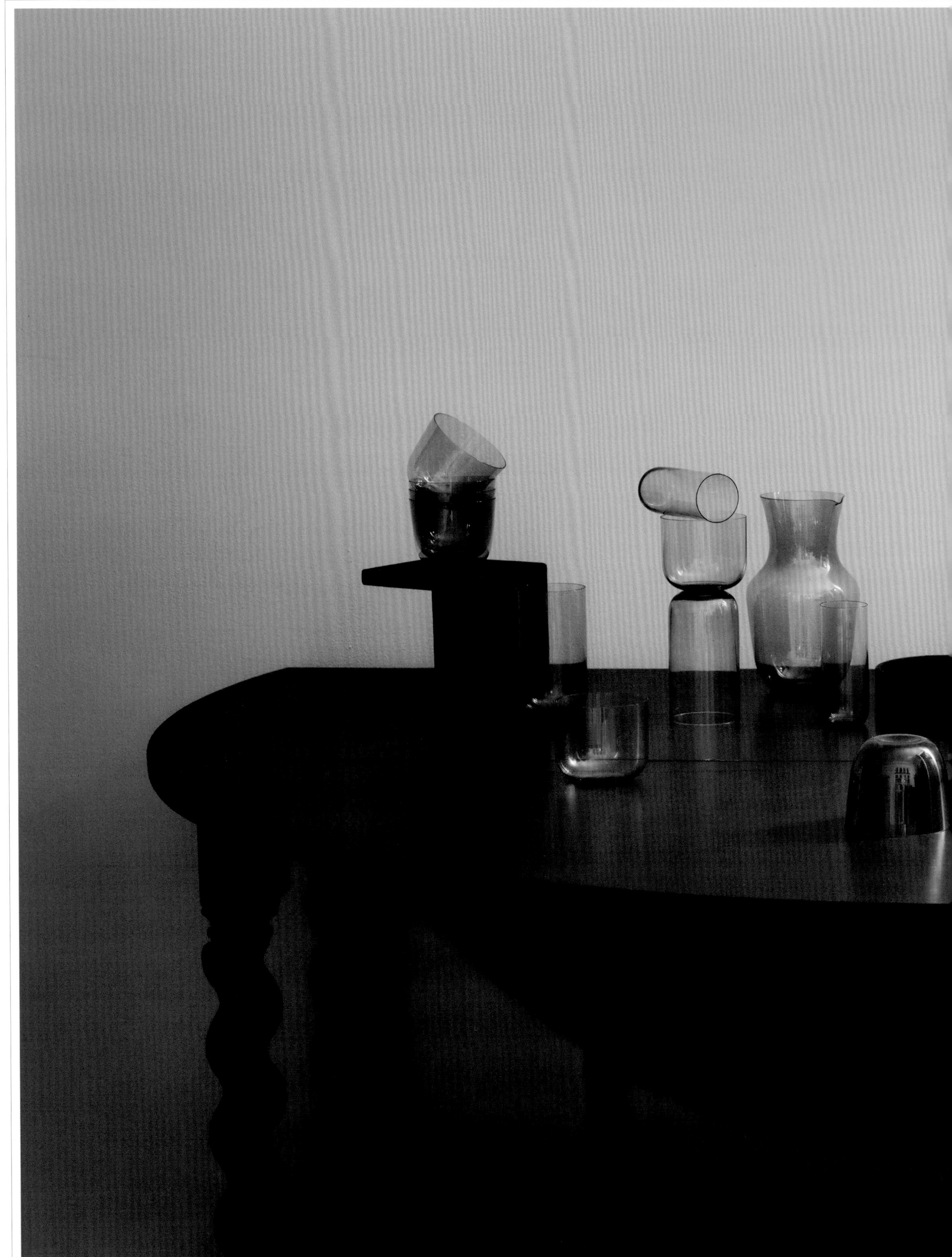

P240: Credit & Commentary

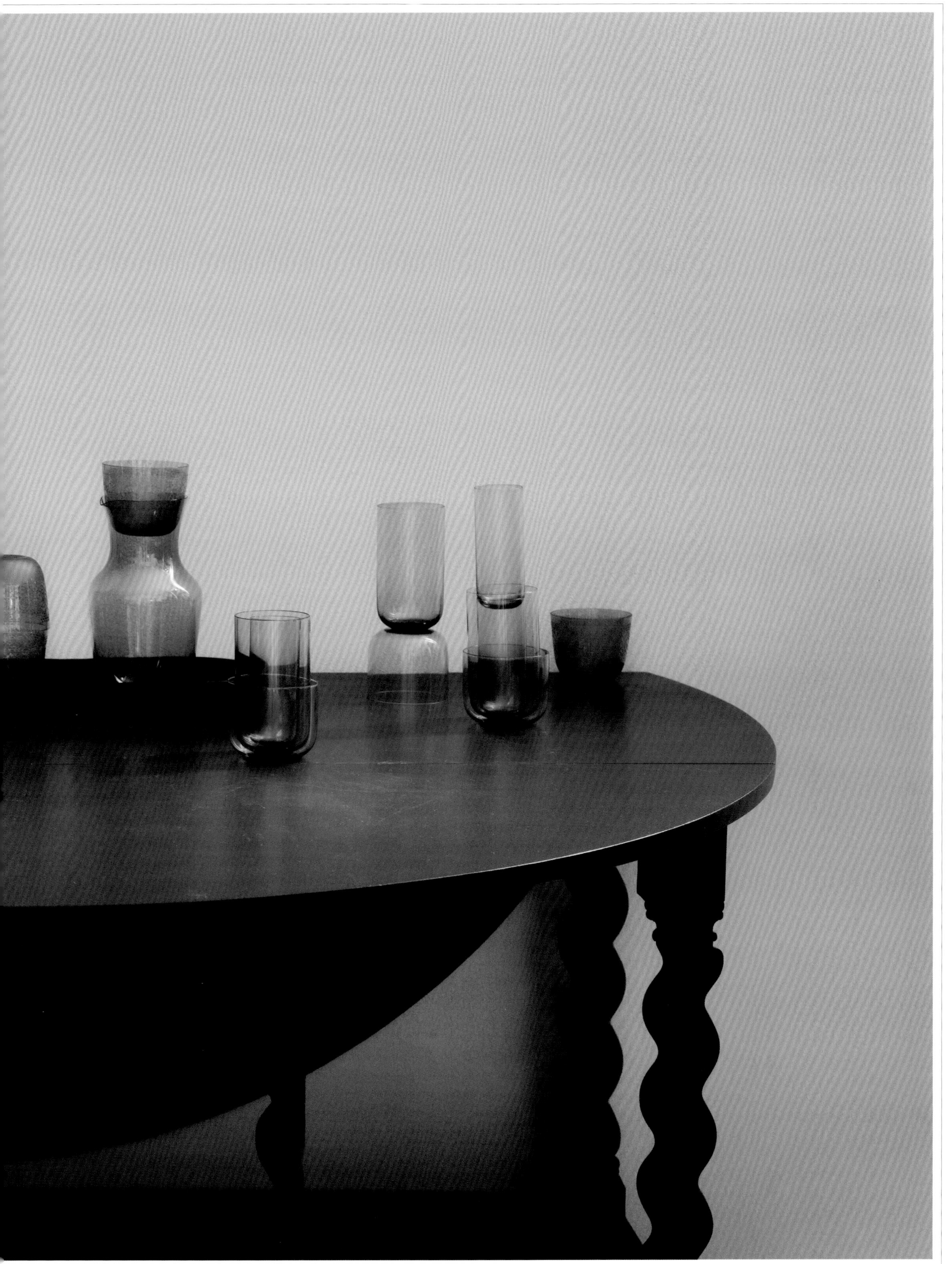

Title: Grey Glassware | **Client:** March

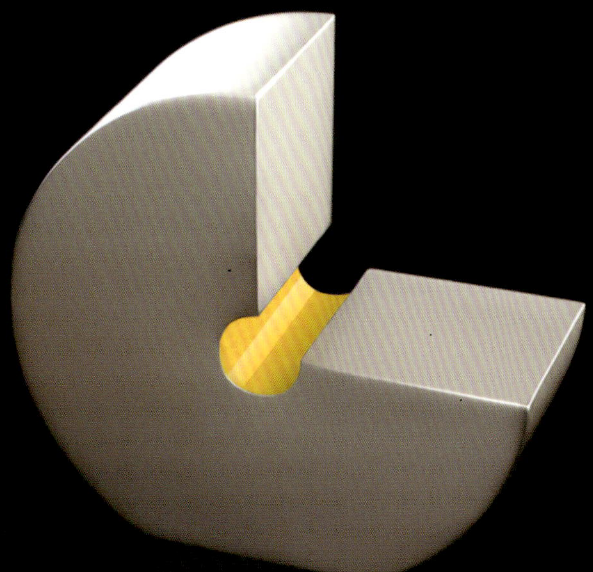

FLORIN GABOR

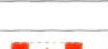

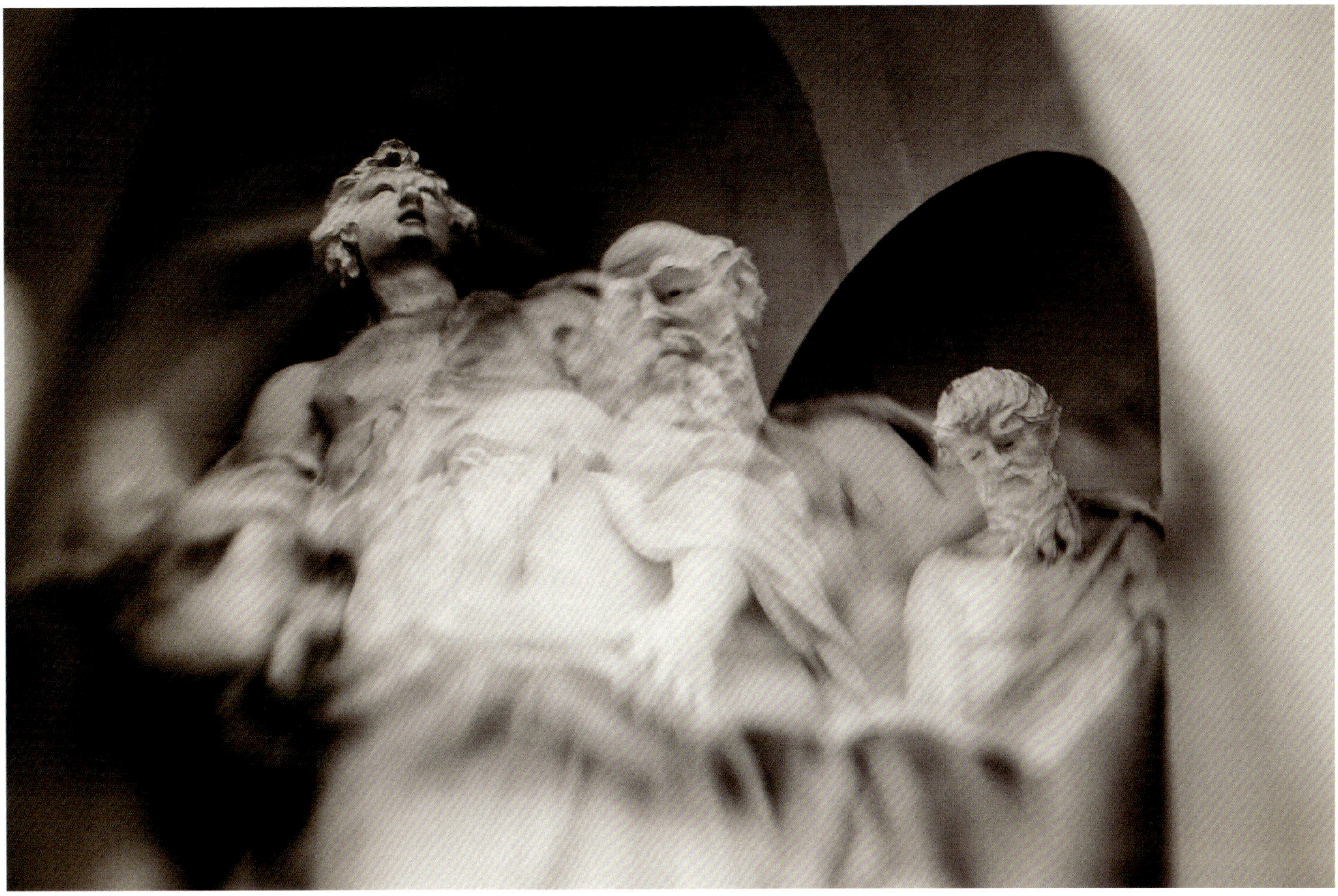

Title: InMuse | **Client:** Lithuanian Academy of Music & Theatre

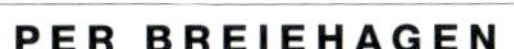

PER BREIEHAGEN

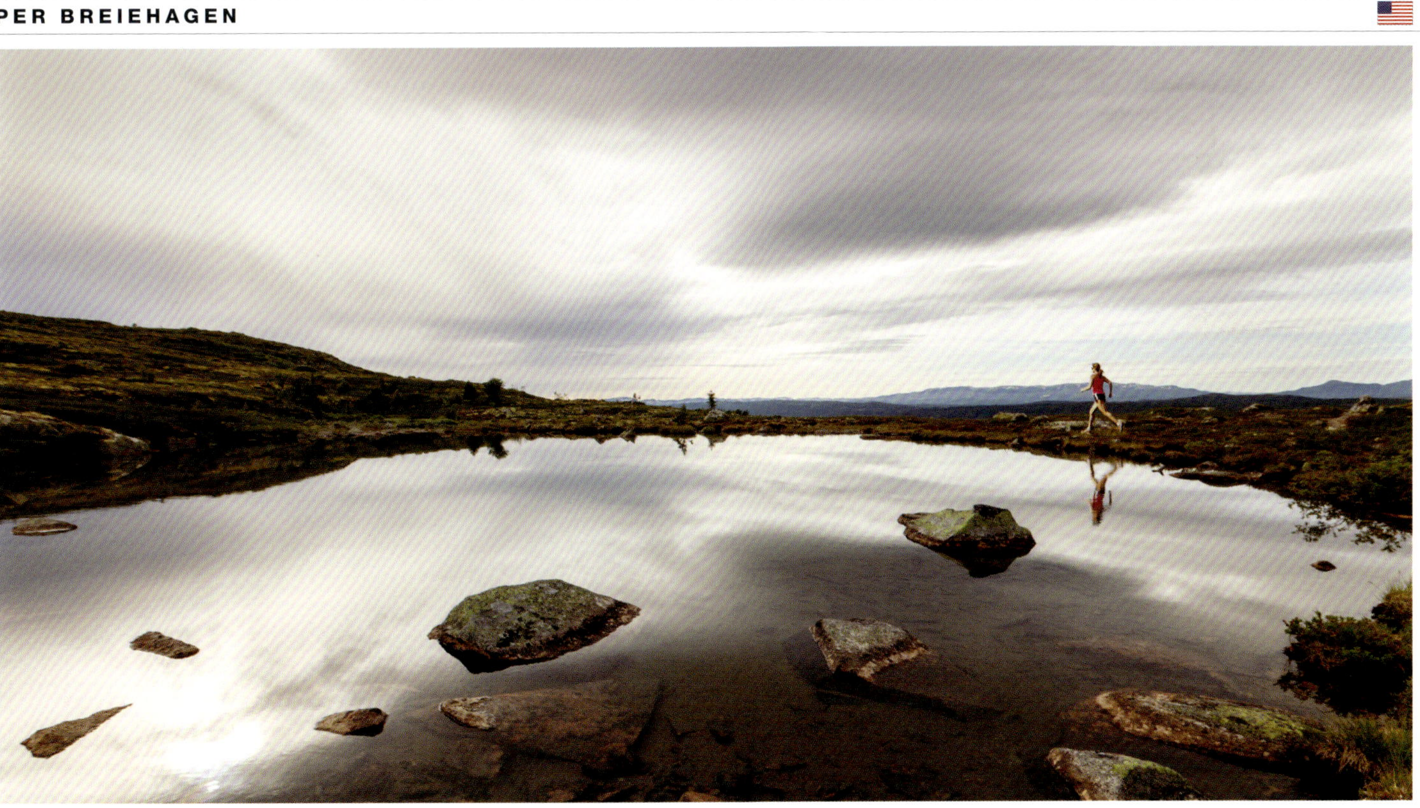

Title: Mountain Mirror | **Client:** Self-initiated

PATRICK MOLNAR

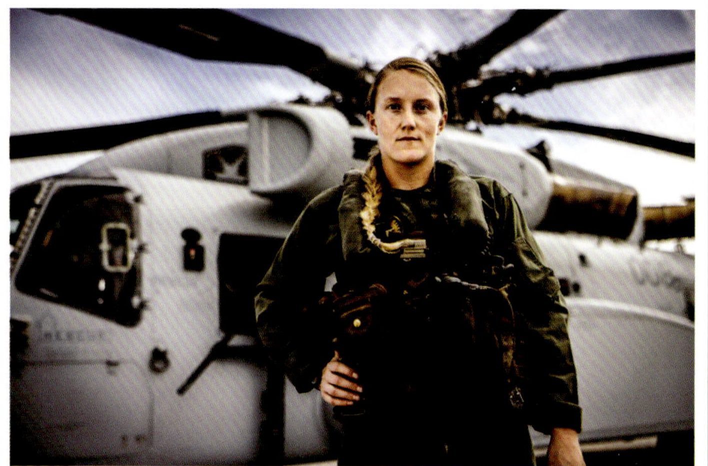

Title: USMC #1 | Client: Marines

PATRICK MOLNAR

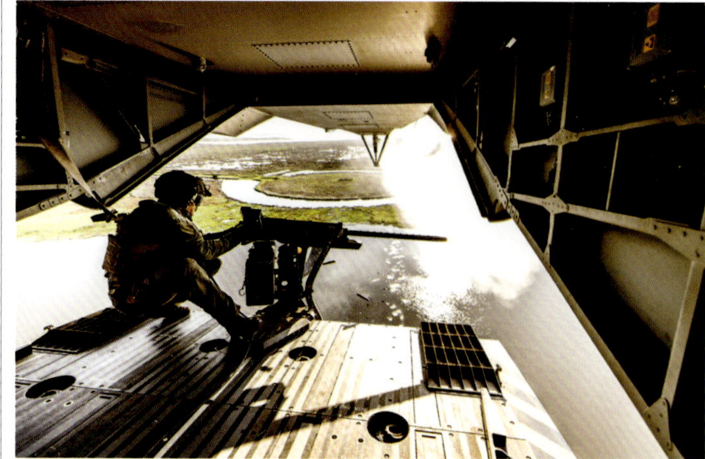

Title: USMC #2 | Client: Marines

PATRICK MOLNAR

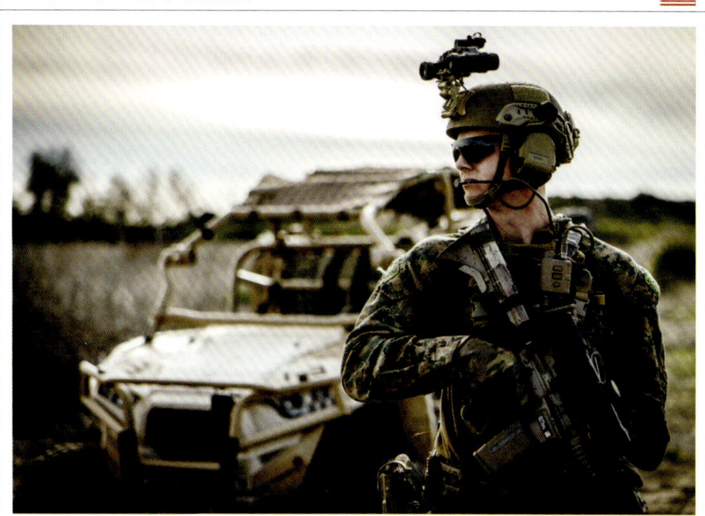

Title: USMC #7 | Client: Marines

PATRICK MOLNAR

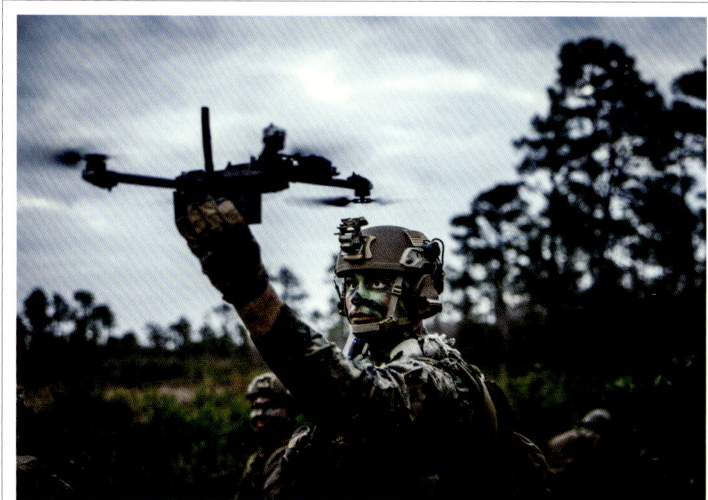

Title: USMC #5 | Client: Marines

PATRICK MOLNAR

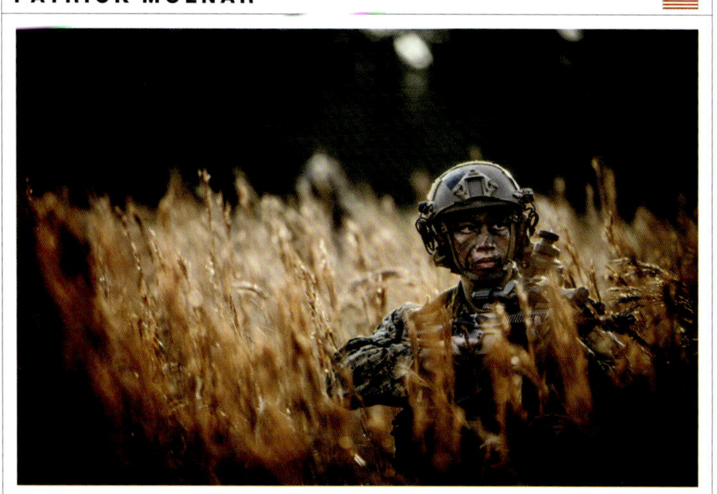

Title: USMC #8 | Client: Marines

PATRICK MOLNAR

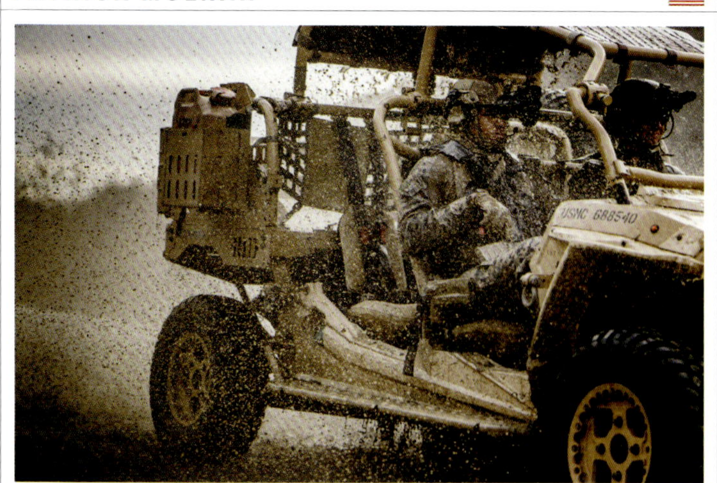

Title: USMC #4 | Client: Marines

JAN KALISH

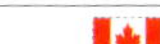

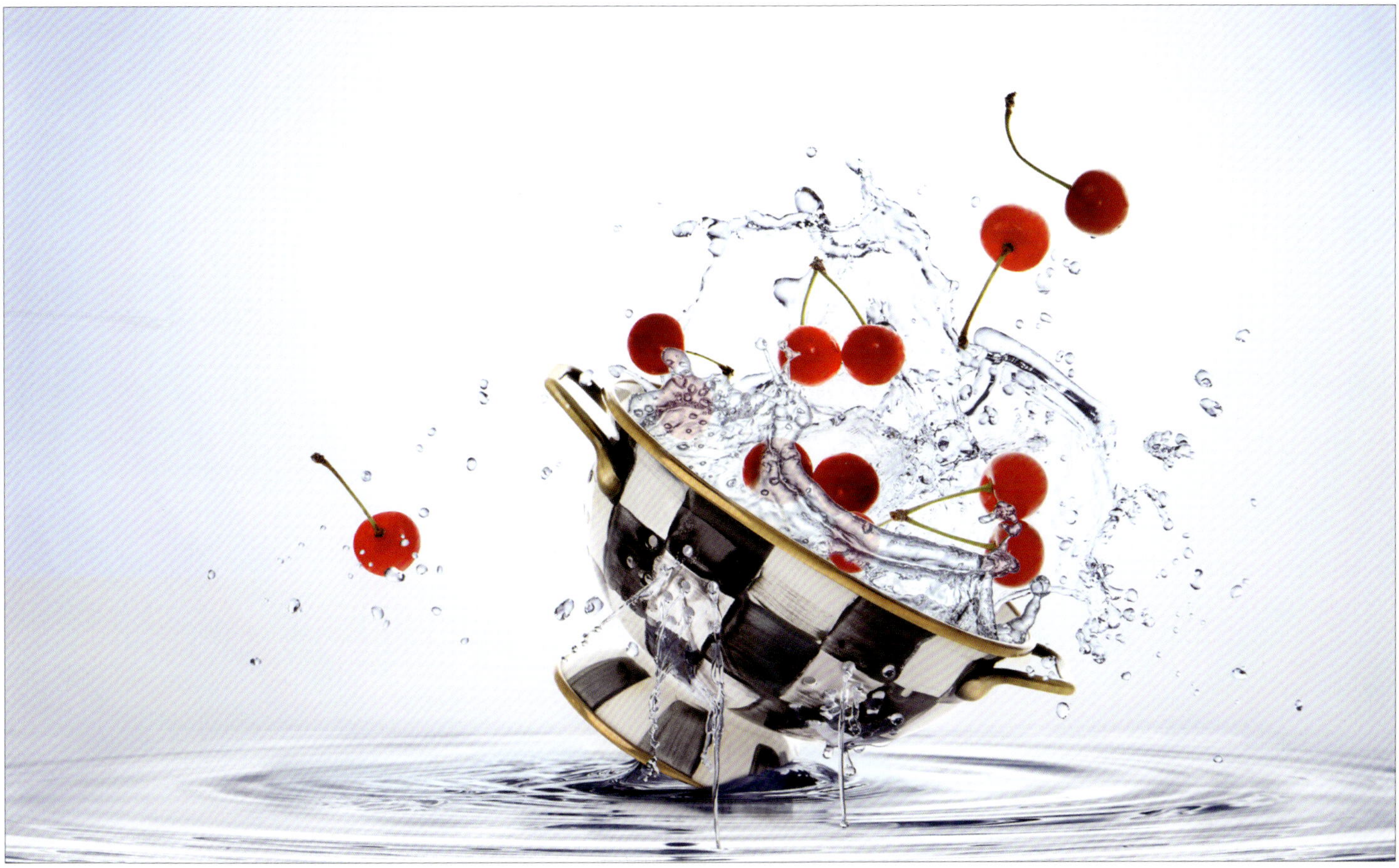

Title: Summer Cherry Drop | **Client:** Self-initiated

DARNELL MCCOWN

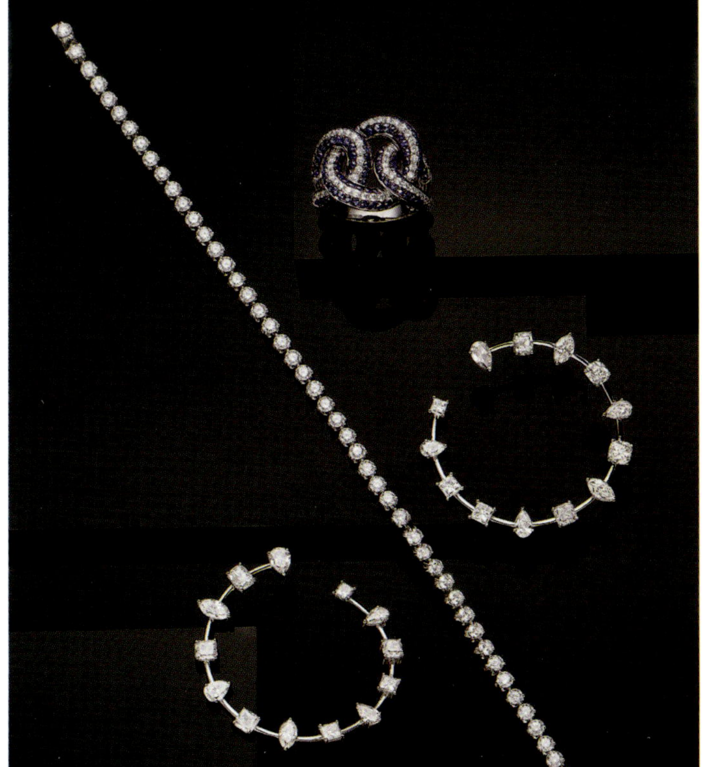

Title: 23193 August Luxe Jewels Showcase Postcard
Clients: Jill Burgum, Heritage Auctions

DARNELL MCCOWN

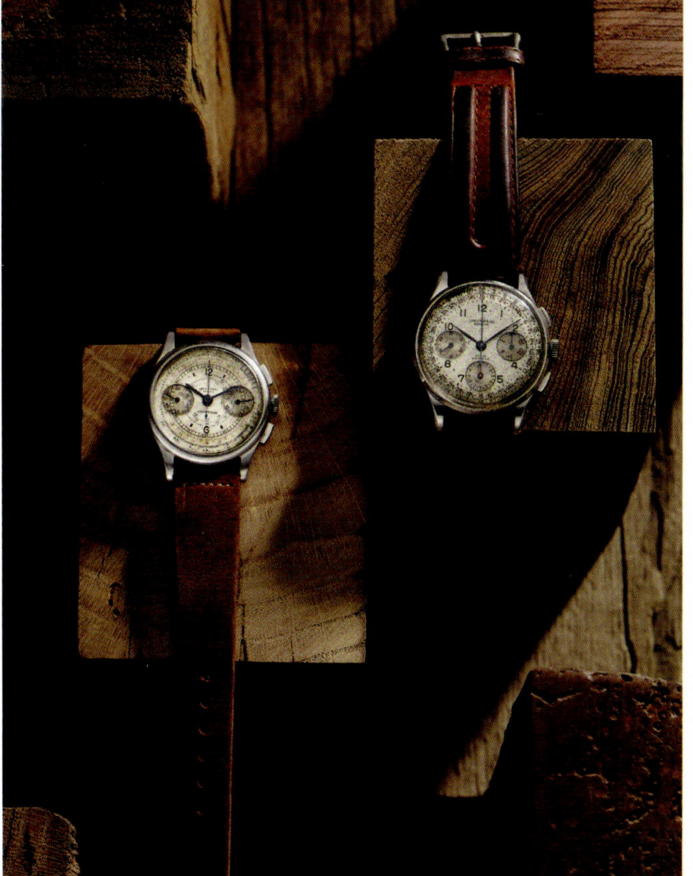

Title: Feature Images from Watches & Fine Timepieces #5550
Clients: Jim Wolf, Heritage Auctions

PATRICK MOLNAR

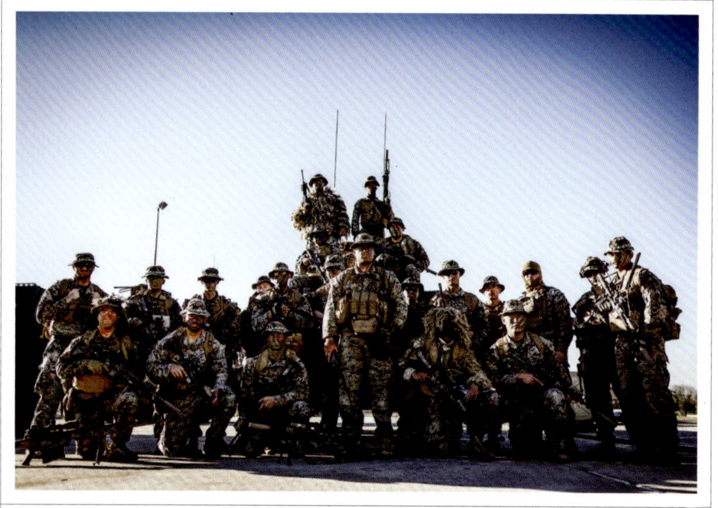

Title: USMC #3 | **Client:** Marines

PATRICK MOLNAR

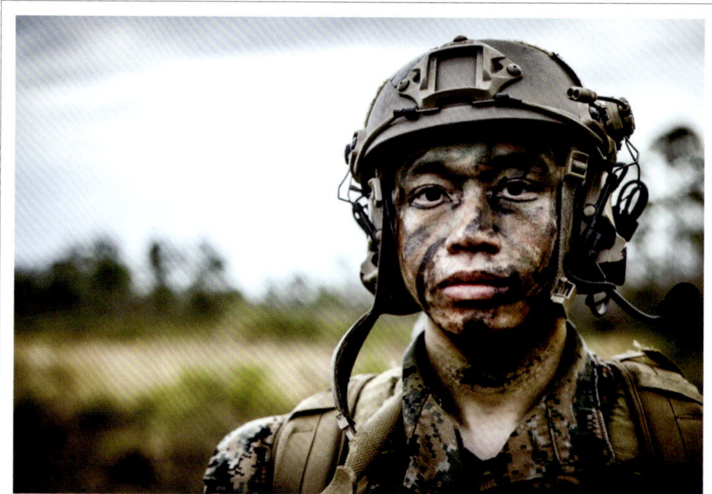

Title: USMC #6 | **Client:** Marines

TATSURO NISHIMURA

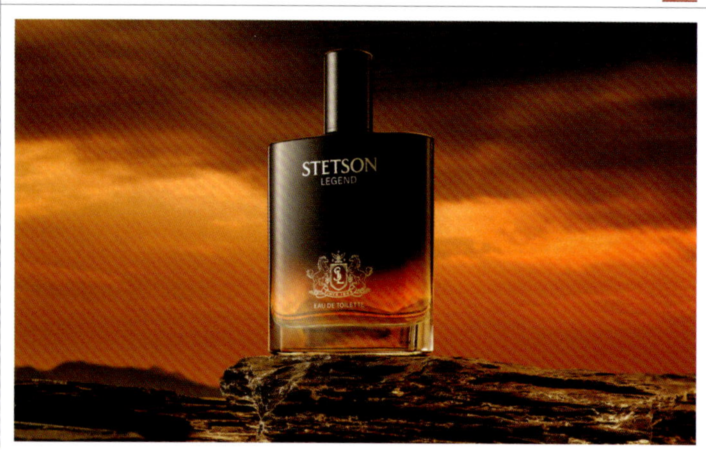

Title: Stetson Legend | **Client:** Stetson USA

JAN KALISH

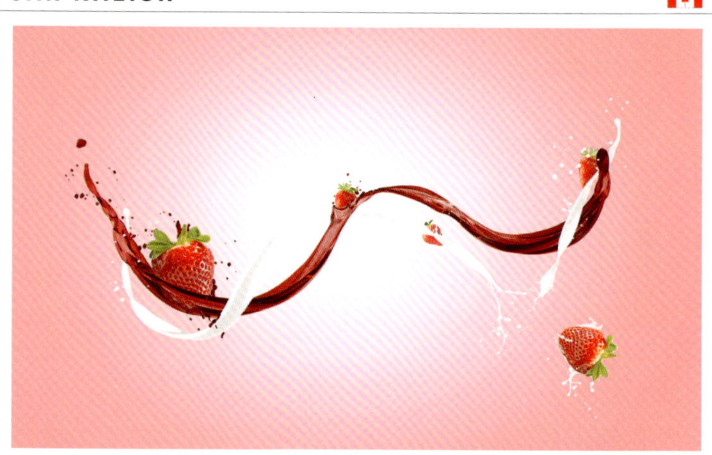

Title: Simply Strawberries and Cream | **Client:** Self-initiated

HOUSE OF CURRENT

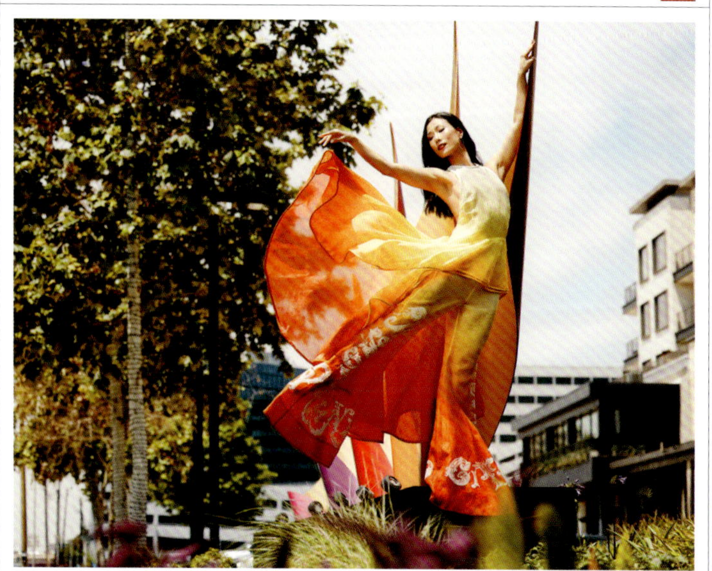

Title: River Oaks District | **Client:** River Oaks District

LUCY SCHOENFELD

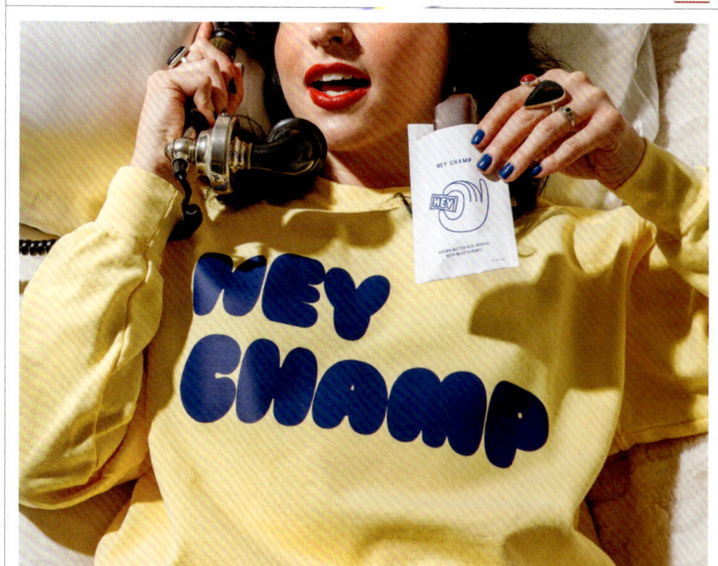

Title: Hey Champ Launch | **Client:** Hey Champ

HOUSE OF CURRENT

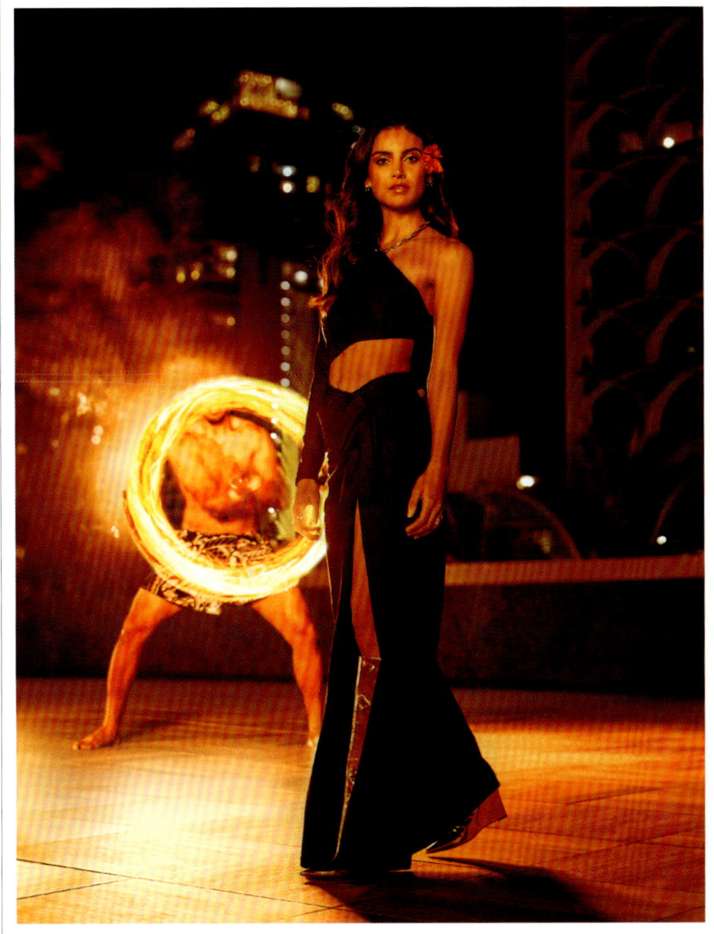

Title: Royal Hawaiian Center | **Client:** Royal Hawaiian Center

AARON LEE

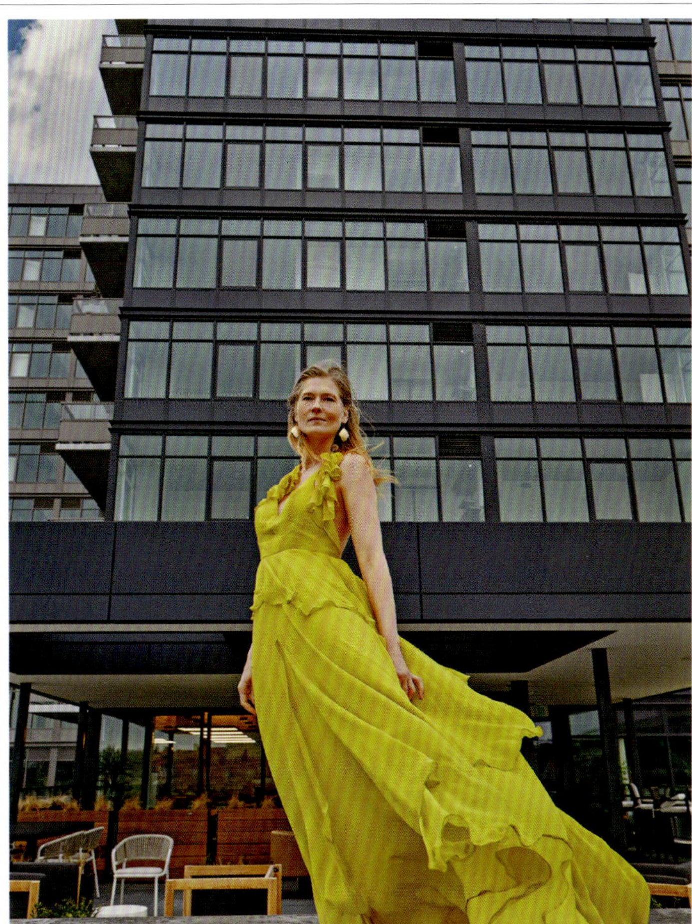

Title: The Sutton | **Client:** Lincoln Property Company

HOUSE OF CURRENT

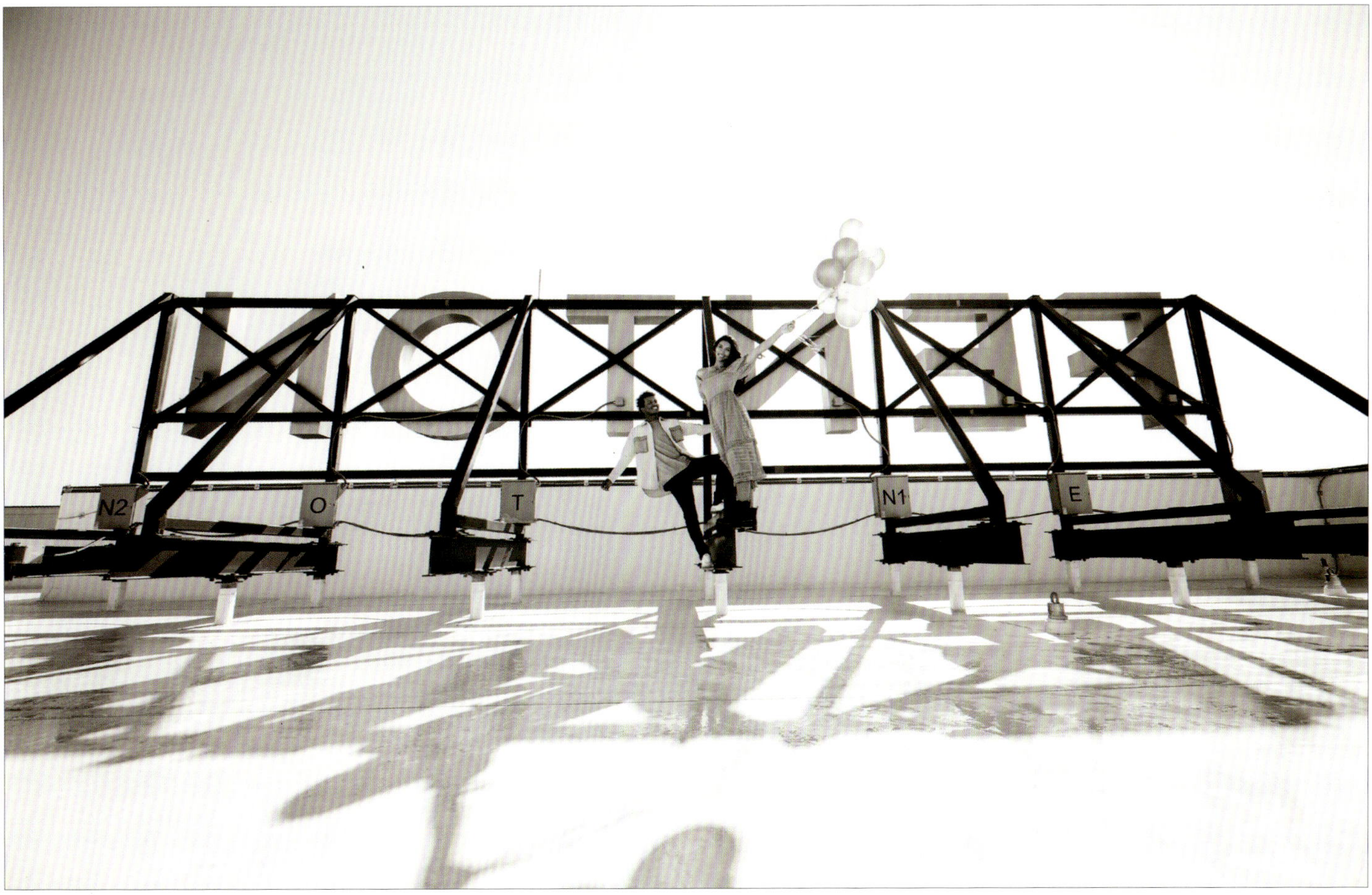

Title: This is the Life | **Client:** Fenton

LENNETTE NEWELL

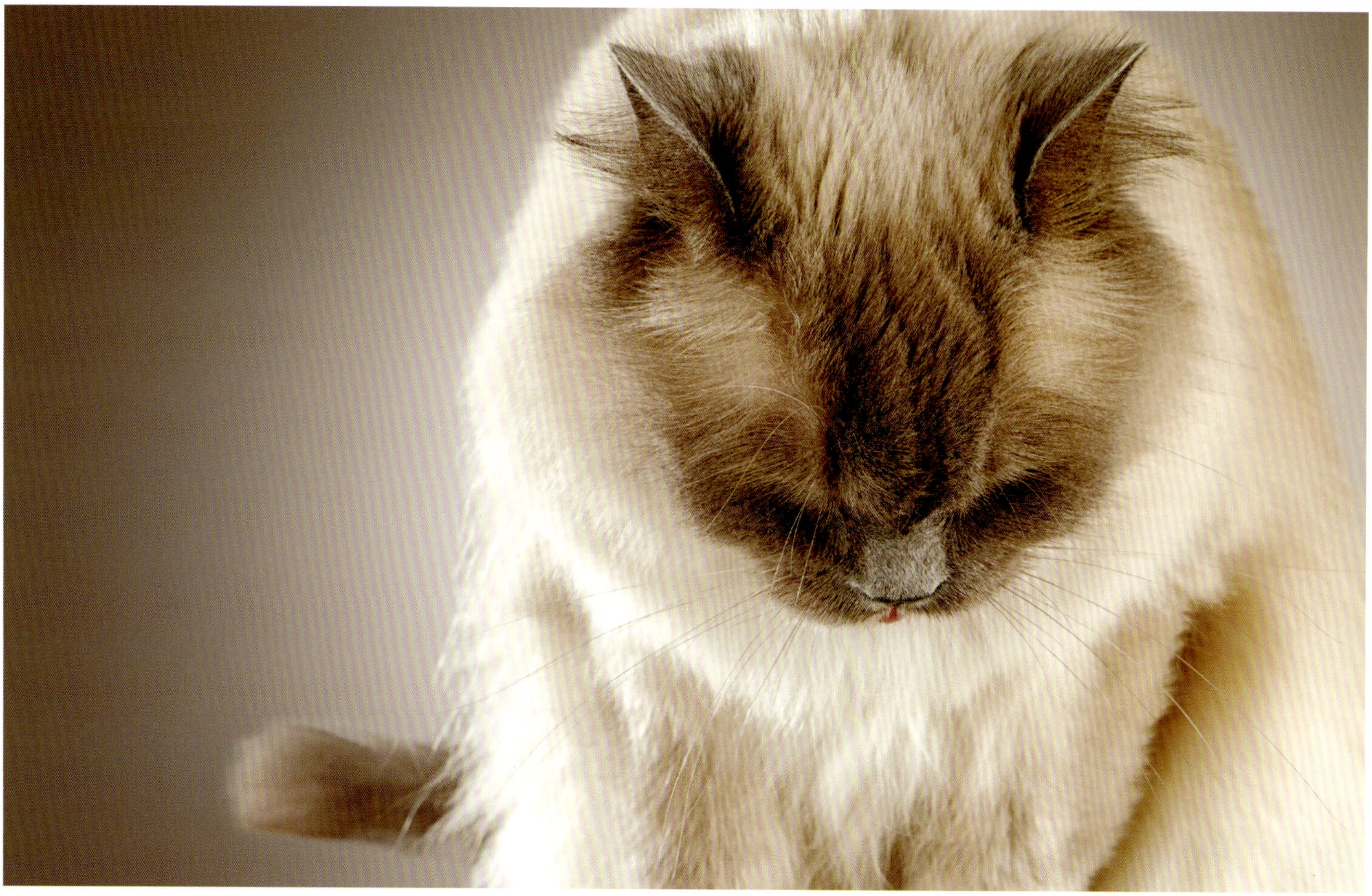

Title: Mysterious | **Clients:** Nutro Pet Food, MARS Pet Care

JANG WON LEE

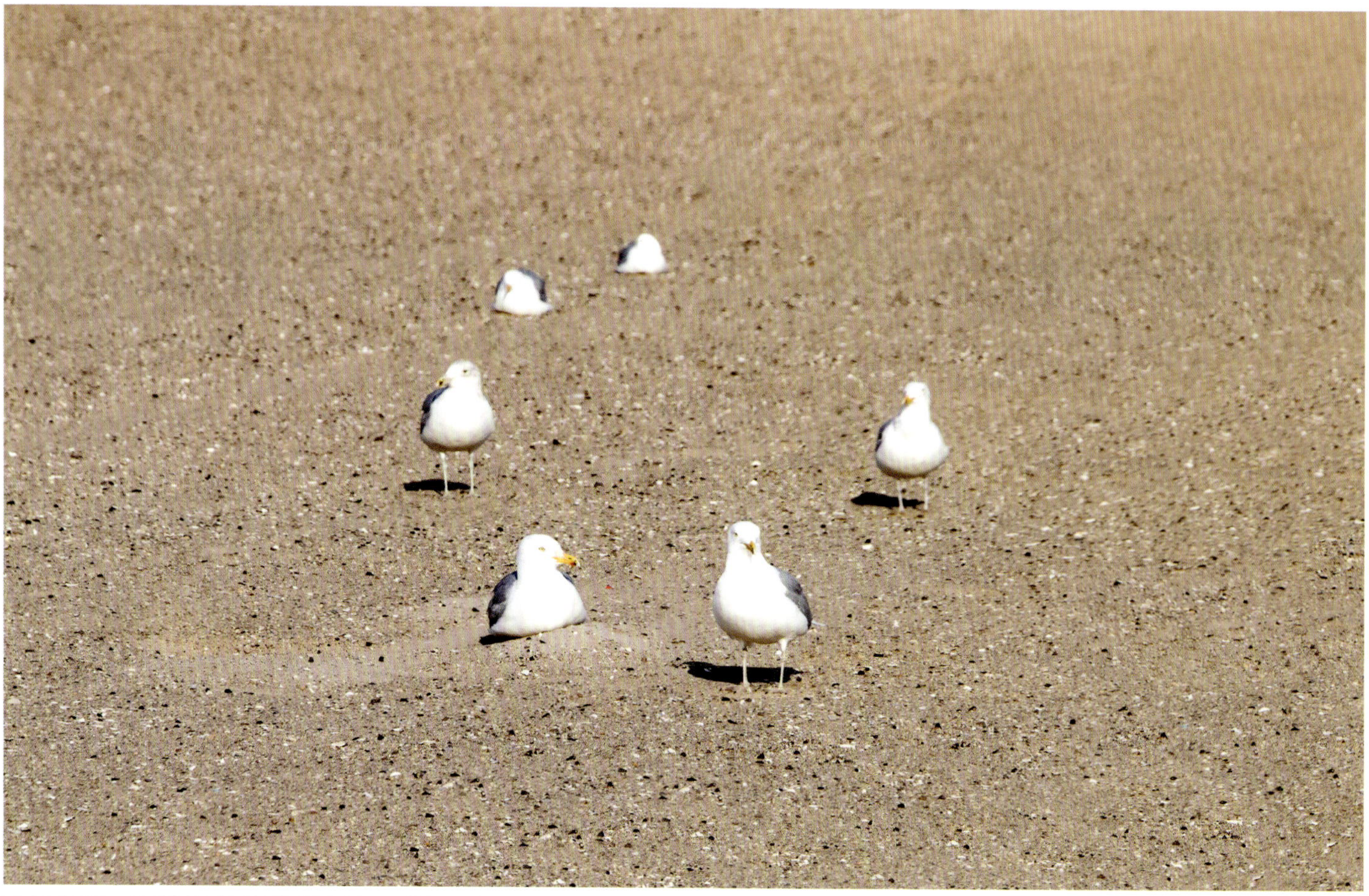

Title: A Cozy Yet Elegant Day Out | **Client:** Self-initiated

JAMES HAEFNER

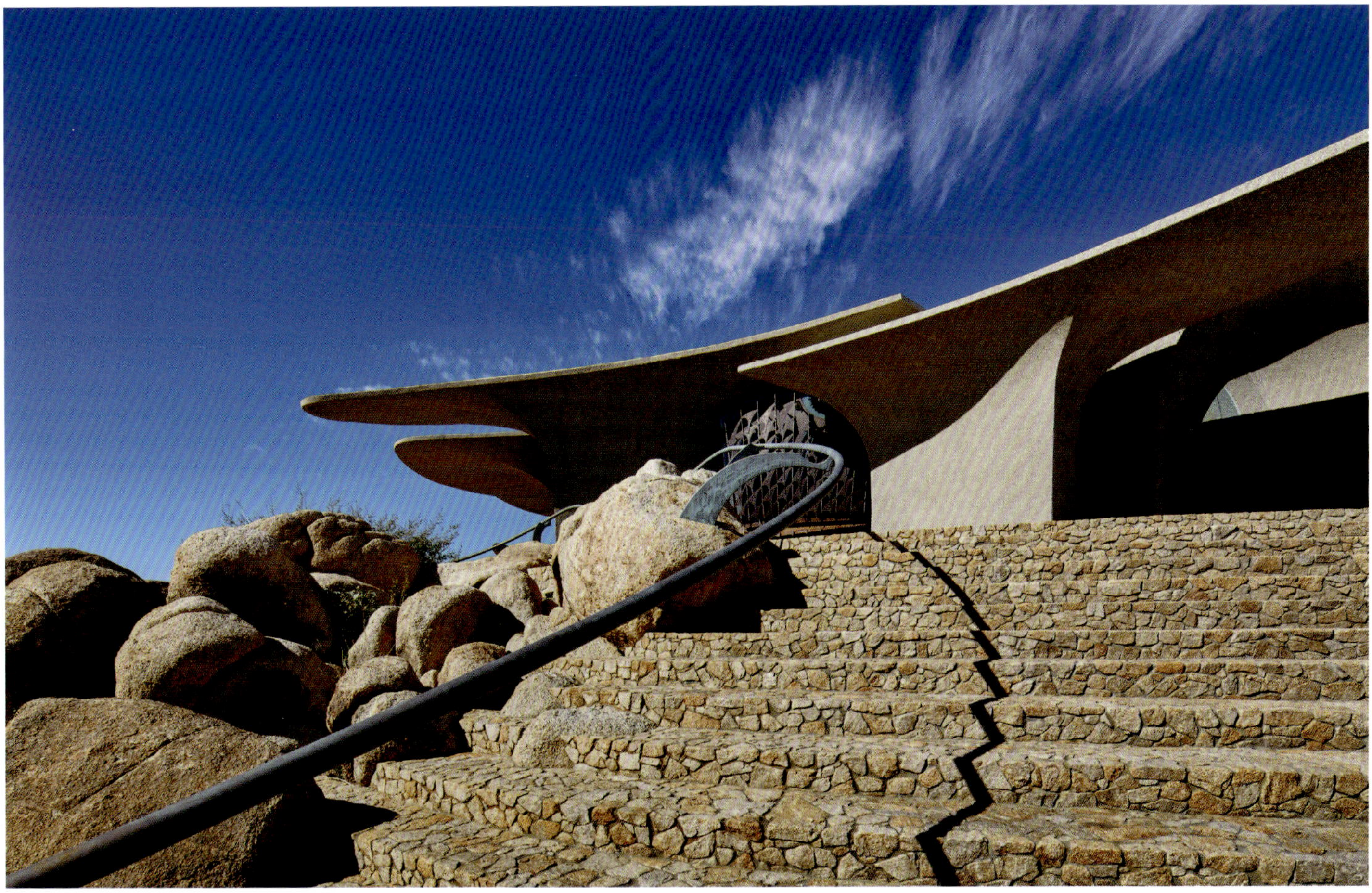

Title: Kellogg-Doolittle House | **Client:** Kellogg-Doolittle House

VICTOR ROMERO

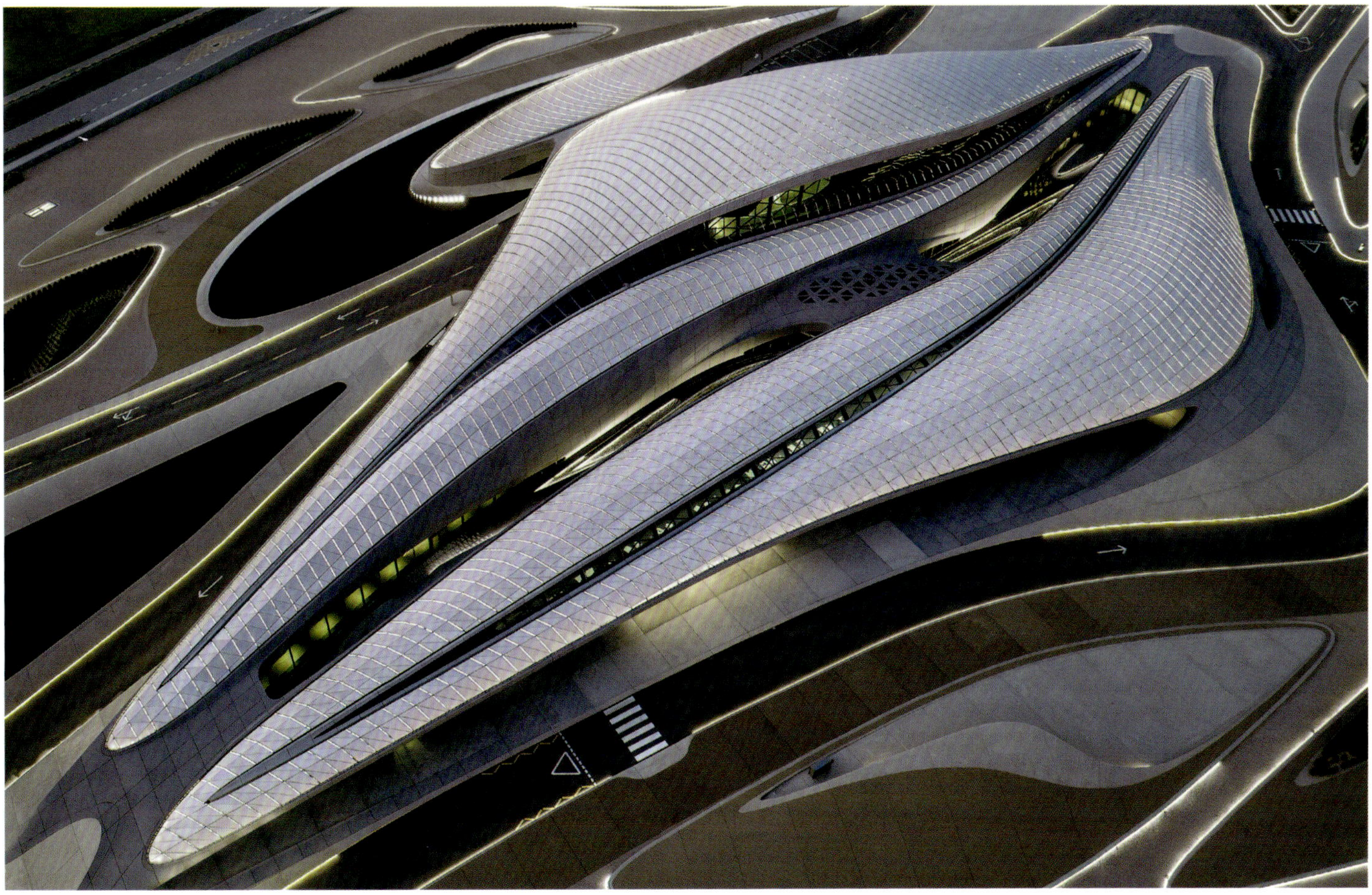

Title: BEEAH Headquarters, Zaha Hadid Architects, Sharjah, UAE | **Client:** Shawati Magazine

ARIEL FREANER

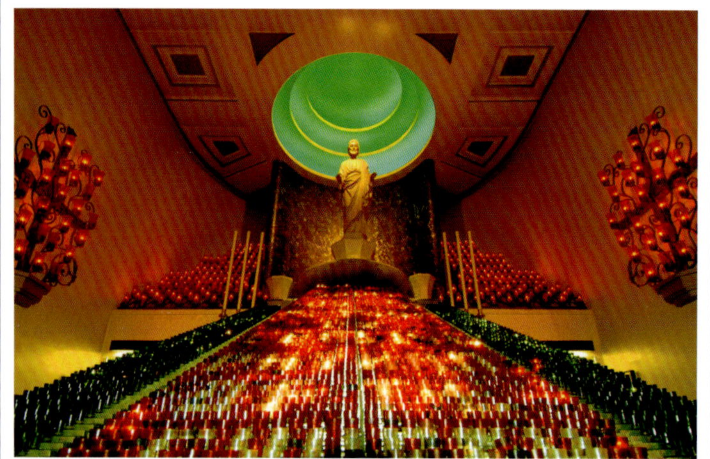

Title: Montreal Church Altar | **Client:** ZEVEN Magazine

ARIEL FREANER

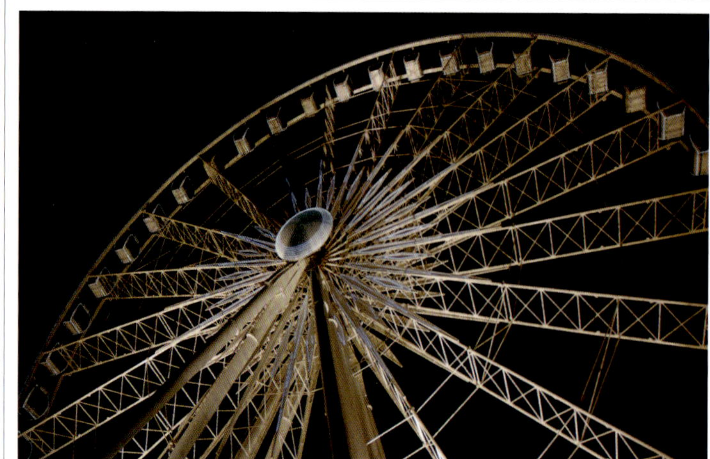

Title: Niagara Falls Wheel | **Client:** ZEVEN Magazine

CAMERON DAVIDSON

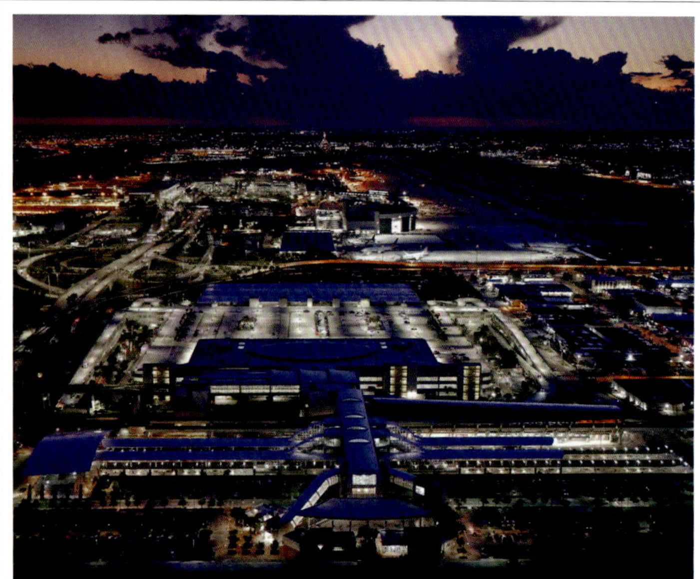

Title: Miami International Airport | **Client:** Prologis

ARIEL FREANER

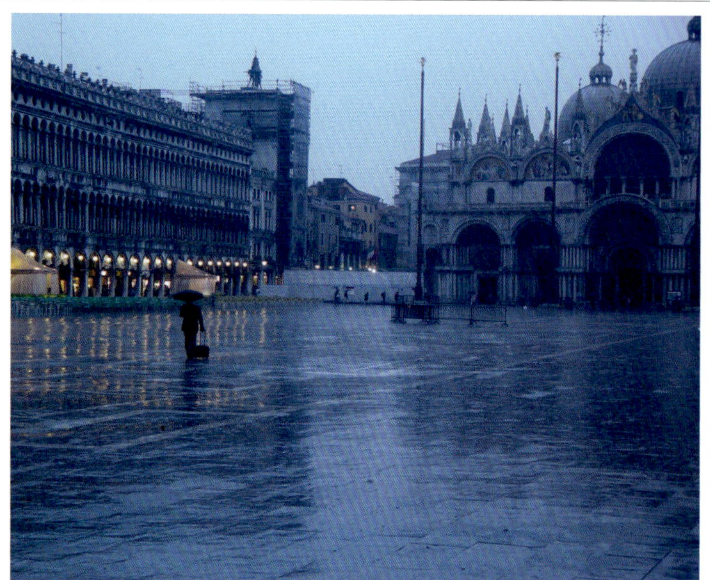

Title: Venice Evening Late Arrival | **Client:** ZEVEN Magazine

ARIEL FREANER

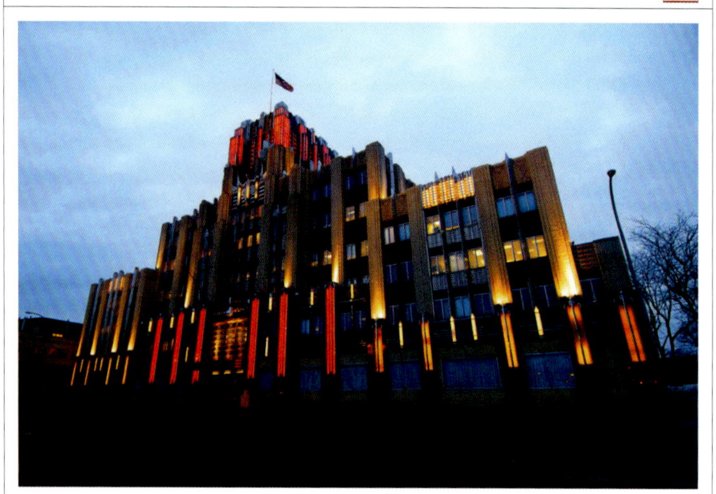

Title: Art Deco Nights | **Client:** ZEVEN Magazine

NATHAN BERGFELT

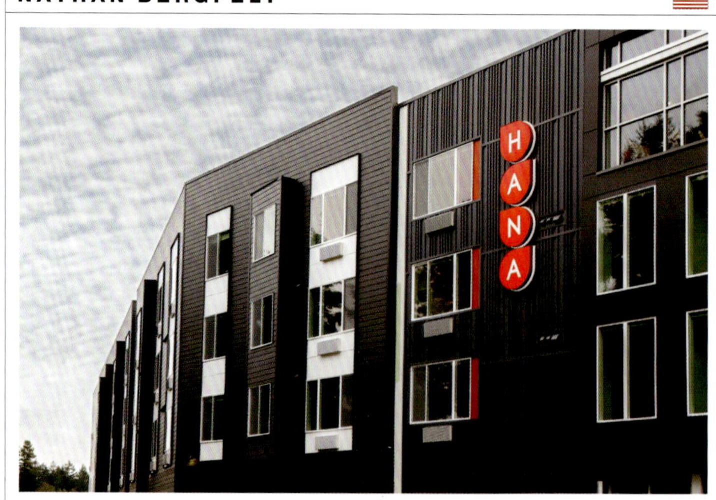

Title: Hana Apartments: Architectural Photoshoot | **Client:** Fore Property

DAVID BROWN

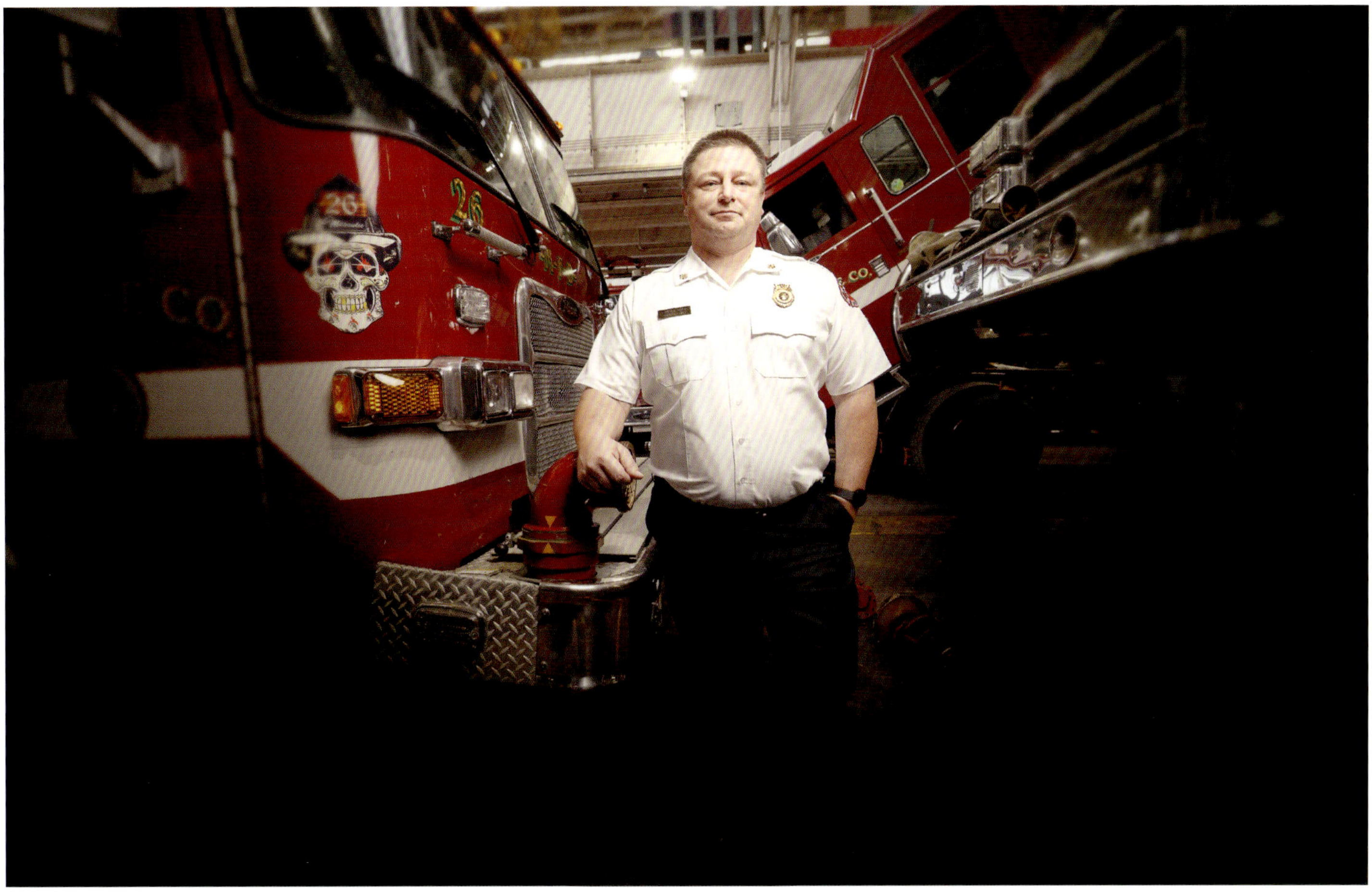

Title: MFD Repair Shop | **Client:** Snap-on Tools

MIKE BASSE

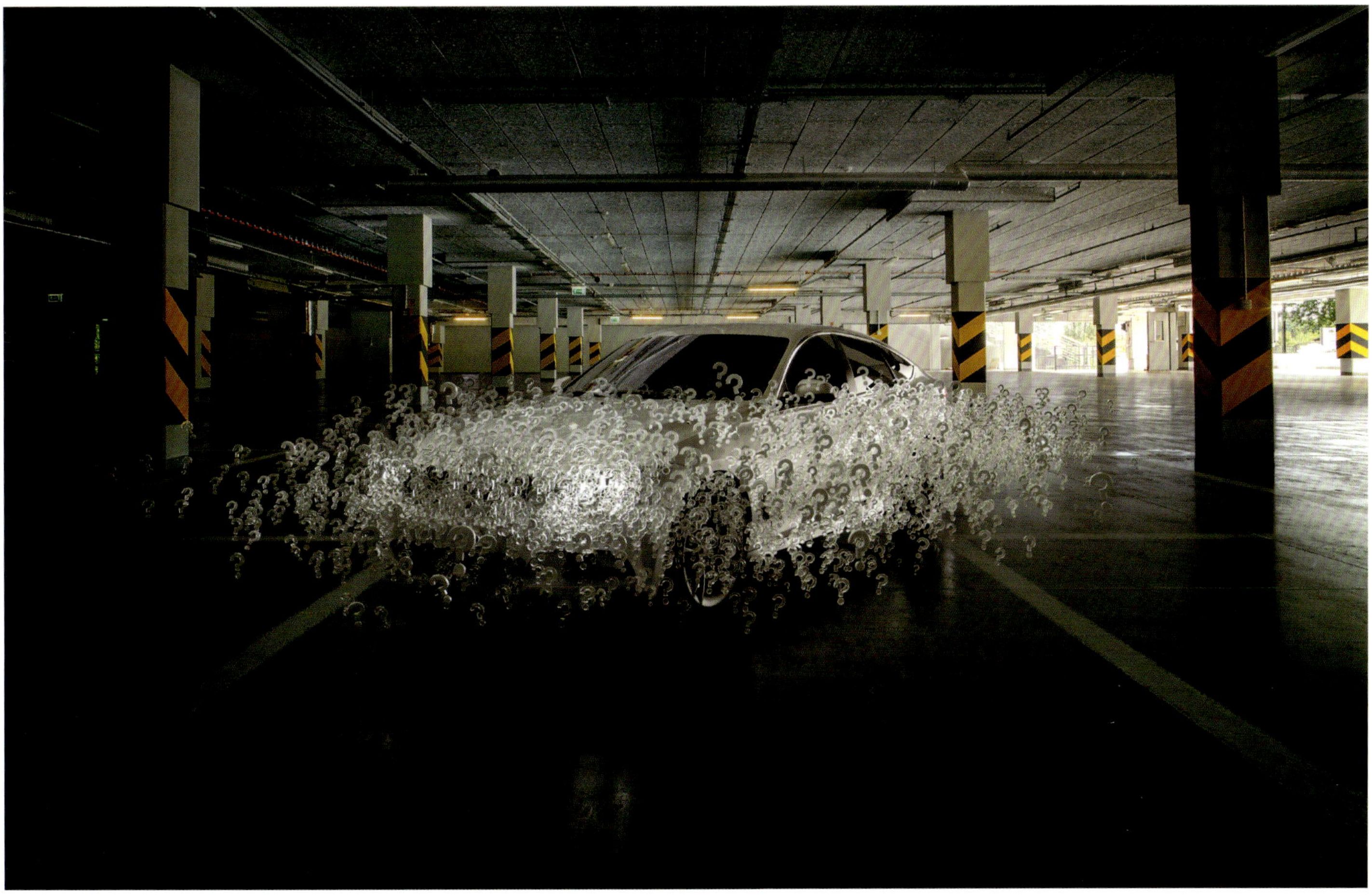

Title: Questions Conquered | **Client:** Snap-on Diagnostics

JONATHAN KNOWLES

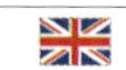

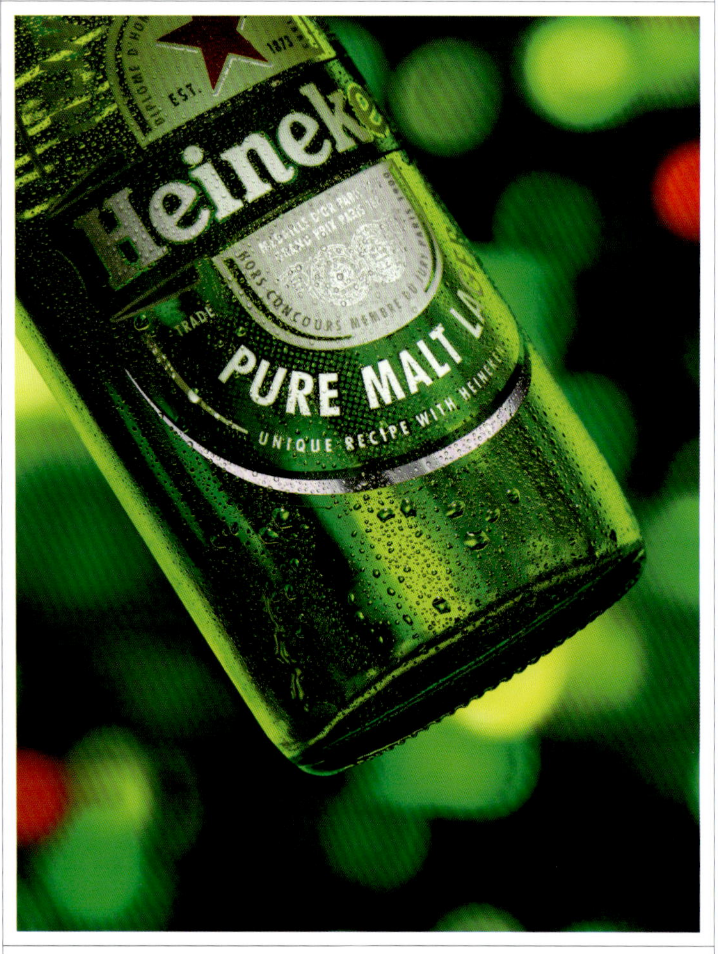

Title: Heineken Pure Malt | **Client:** Heineken

JONATHAN KNOWLES

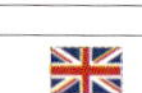

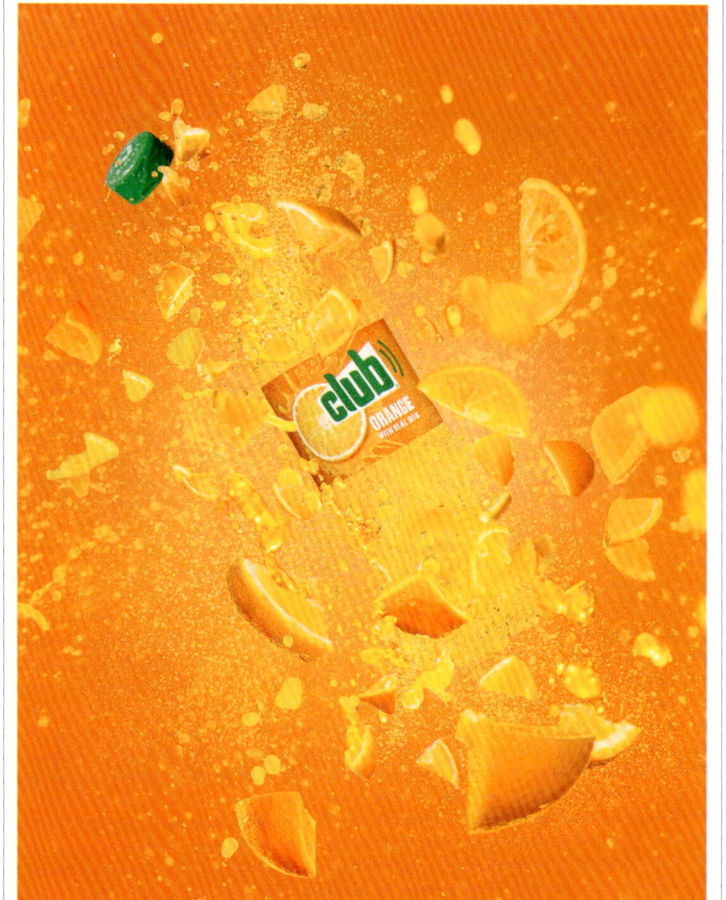

Title: Club Orange | **Client:** Britvic

SCOTT LOWDEN

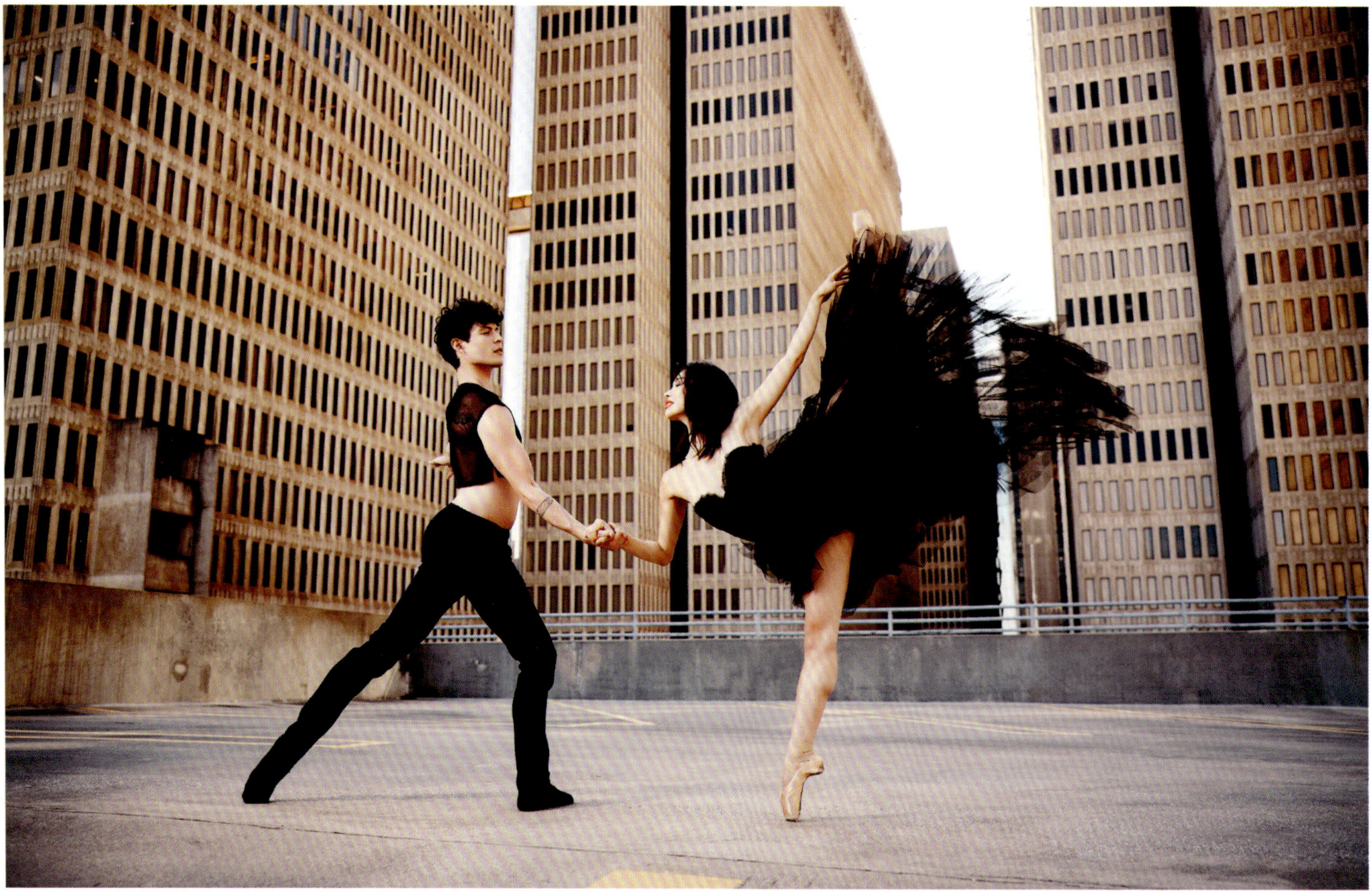

Title: Urban Dance | **Clients:** House of Current, Self-initiated

JÉRÔME BRUNET

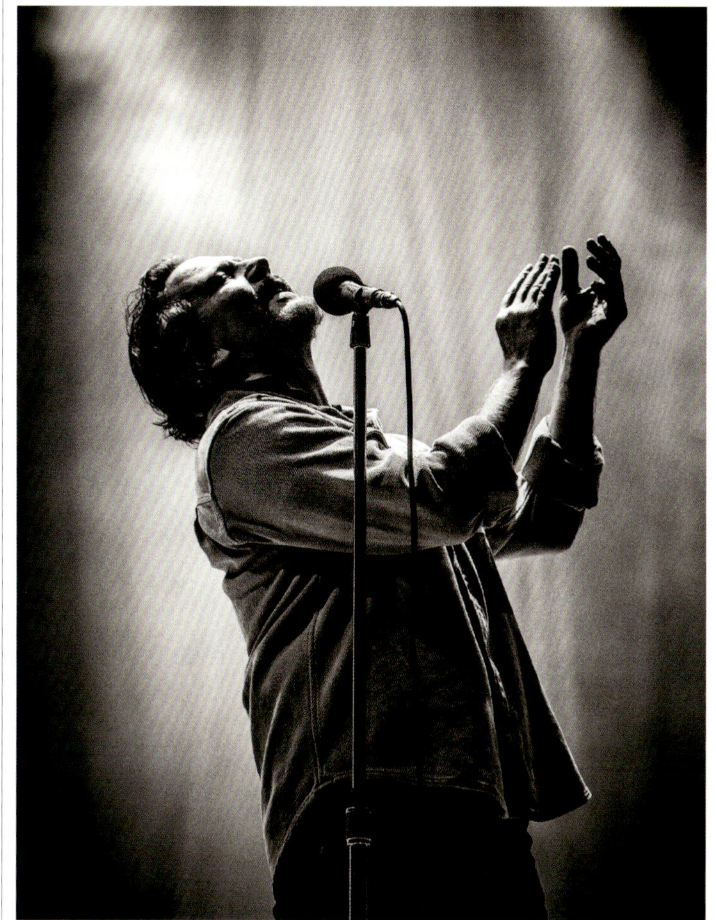

Title: Eddie Vedder | **Client:** Rock Cellar Magazine

CRAIG CUTLER

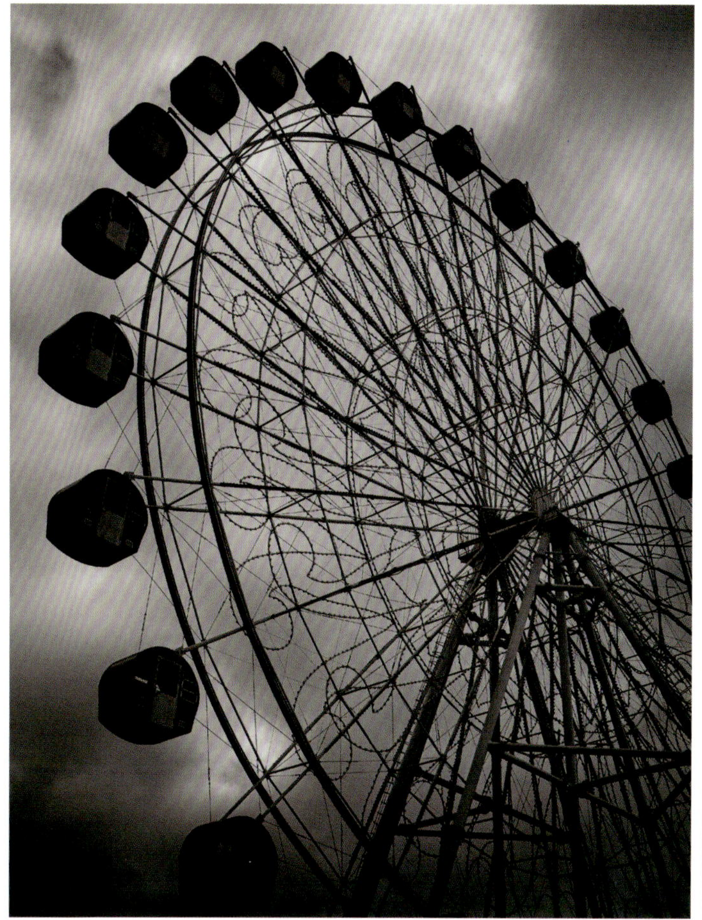

Title: Ferris Wheel, Tokyo | **Client:** Self-initiated

CAMERON DAVIDSON

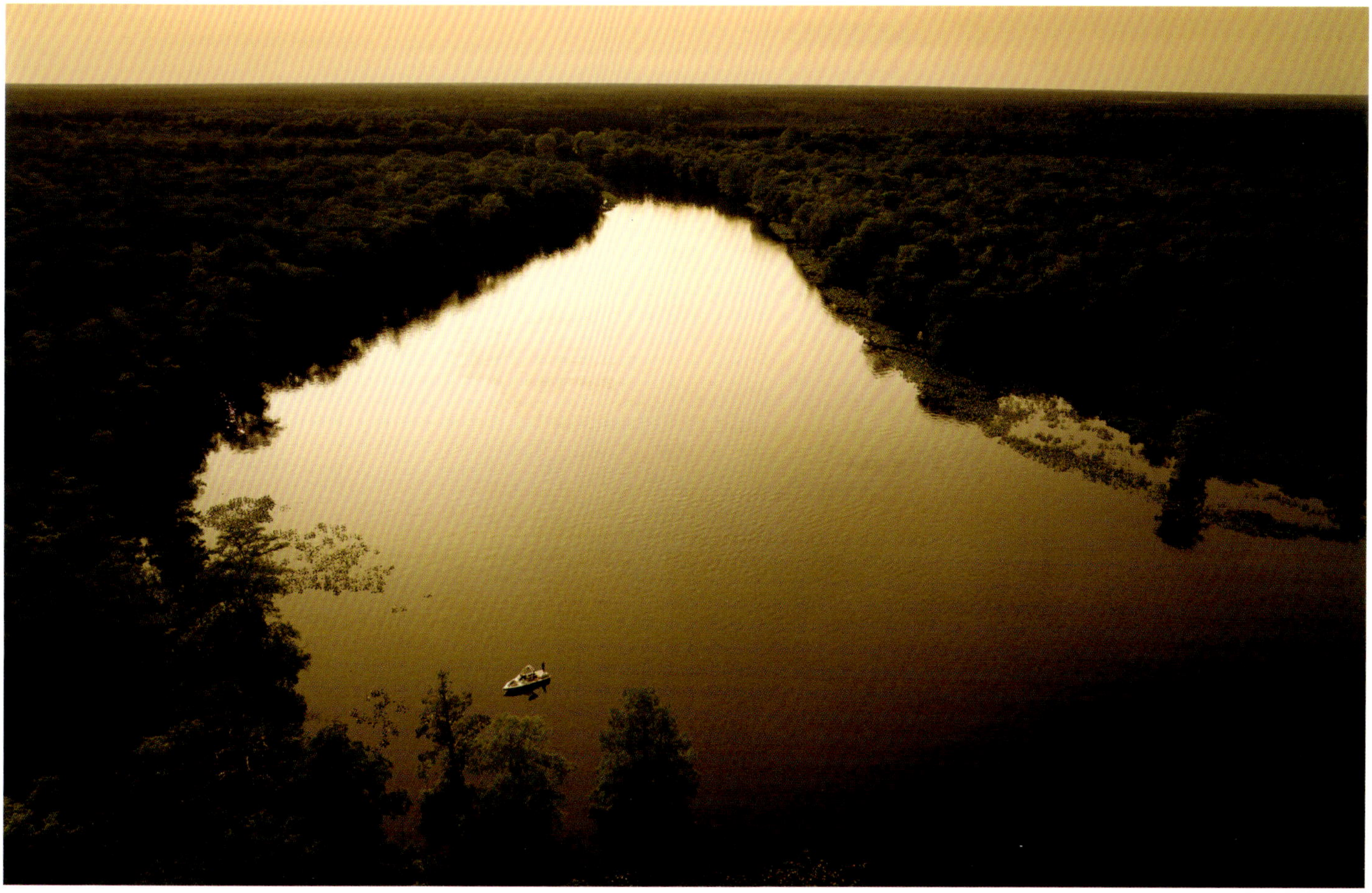

Title: Nature Conservancy | Pokomoke River of Maryland | **Client:** The Nature Conservancy

CRAIG CUTLER

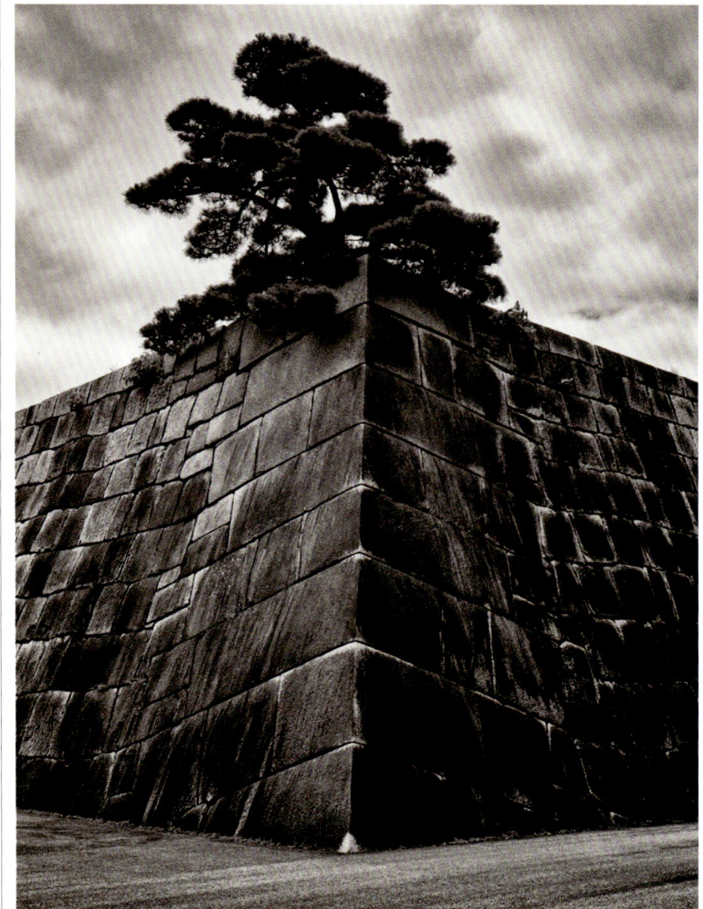

Title: Imperial Palace Tokyo | **Client:** Self-initiated

FANGQIU HUANG

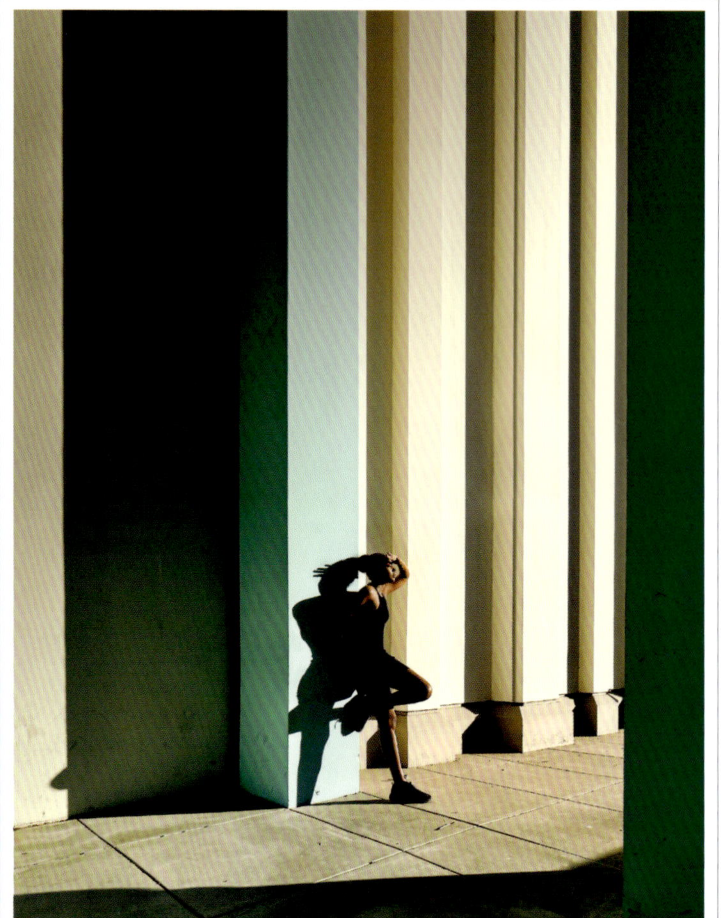

Title: Beyond | **Client:** Fong Captain

SCOTT LOWDEN

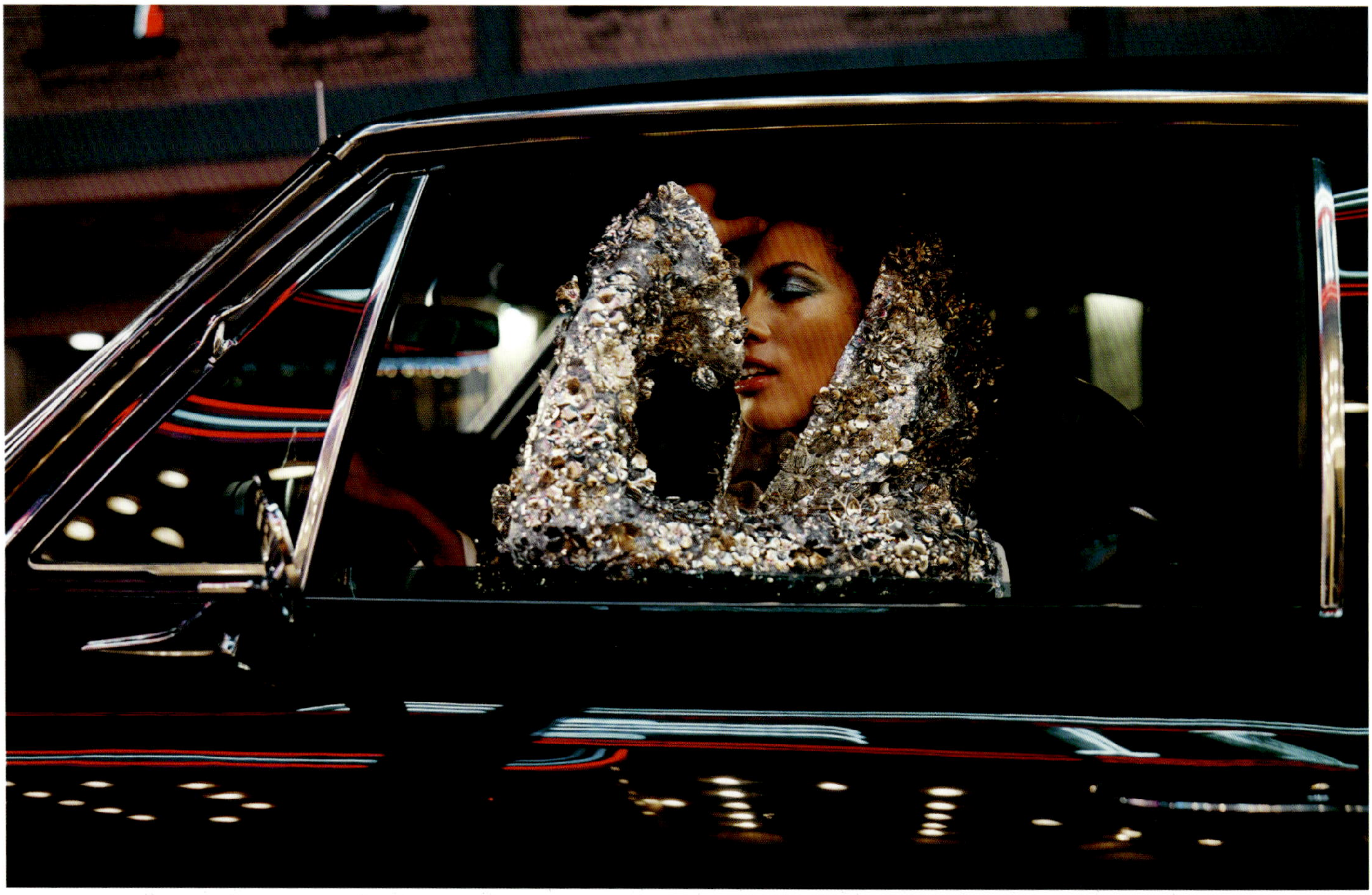

Title: Hawaii Theater | **Clients:** House of Current, Self-initiated

ZOE ADLERSBERG

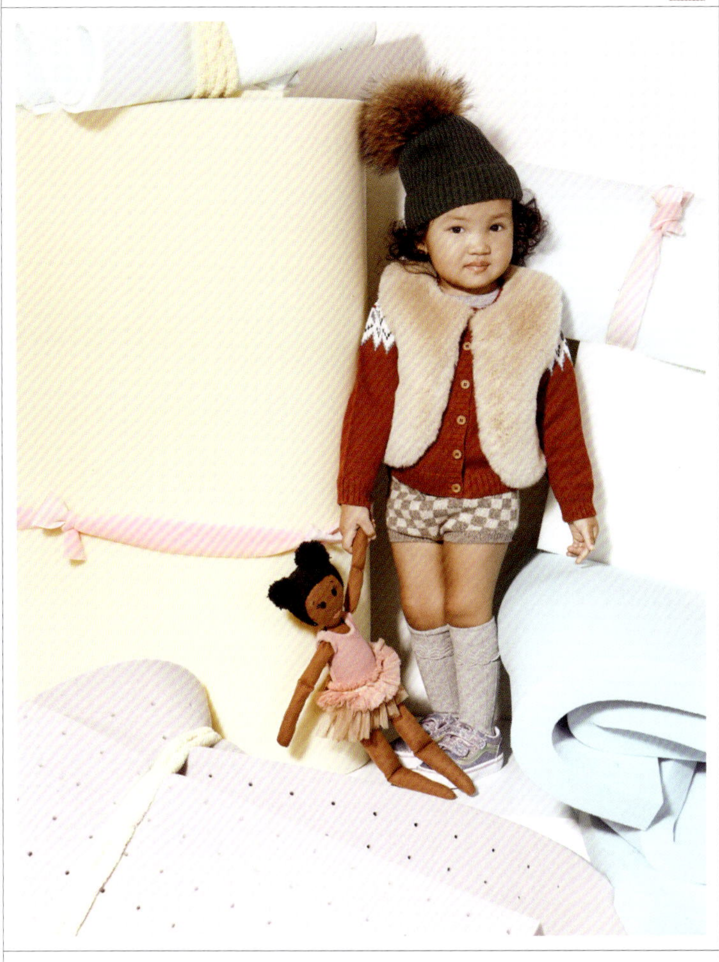

Title: Squish | **Client:** Earnshaw's Magazine

SAVANNAH COLLEGE OF ART & DESIGN

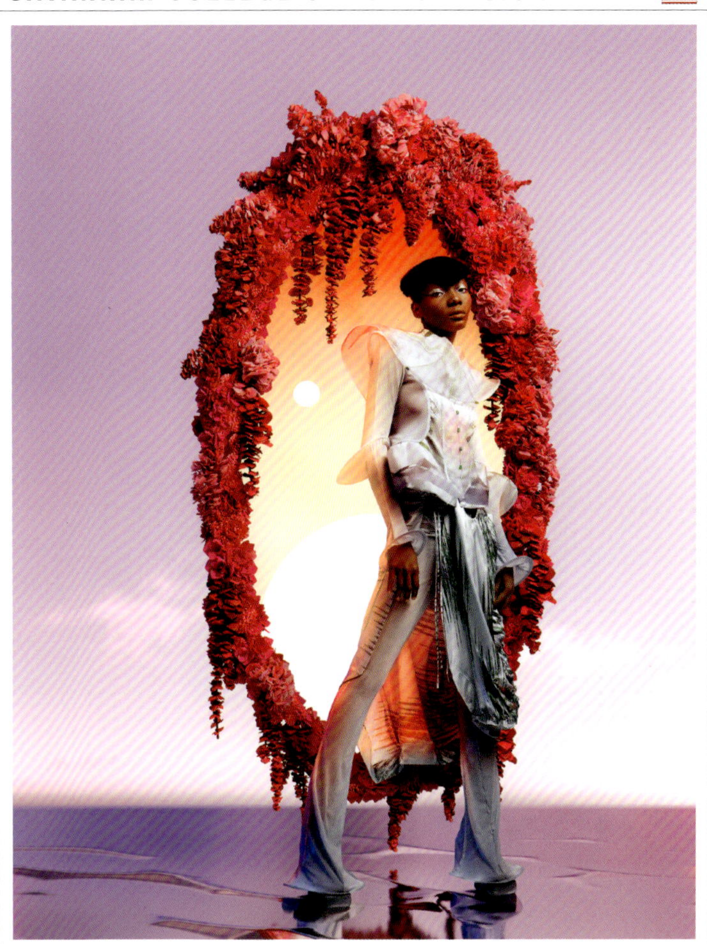

Title: Lei Zhang | **Client:** Savannah College of Art & Design

SAVANNAH COLLEGE OF ART & DESIGN

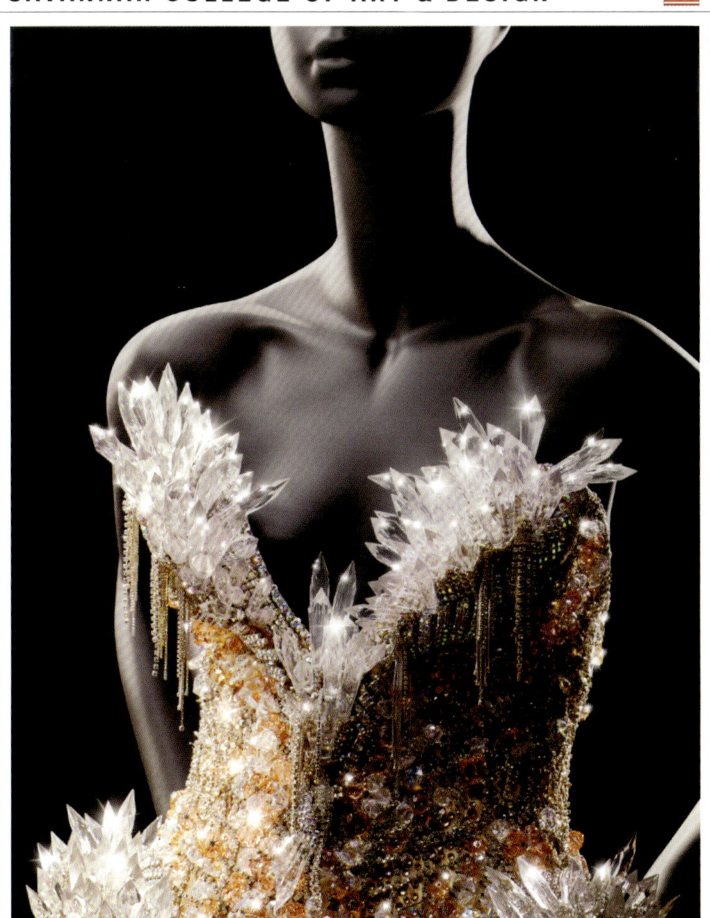

Title: The Blonds "Glamour, Fashion, Fantasy"
Client: Savannah College of Art & Design

SAVANNAH COLLEGE OF ART & DESIGN

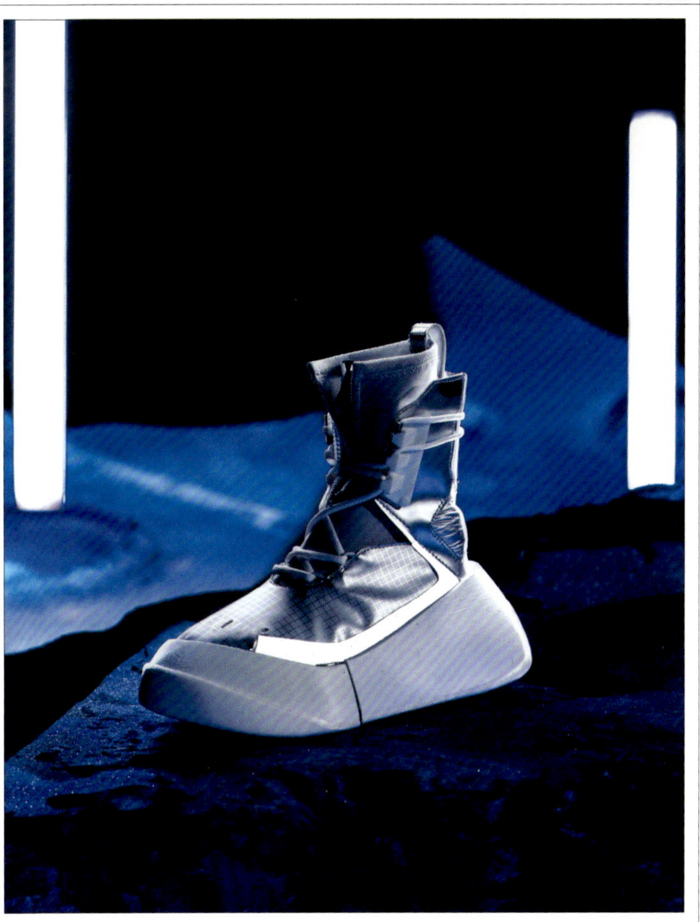

Title: Frozen Hiking Boots
Client: Savannah College of Art & Design

CRAIG BROMLEY

Title: Always You | Client: Self-initiated

PATRICK TREGENZA

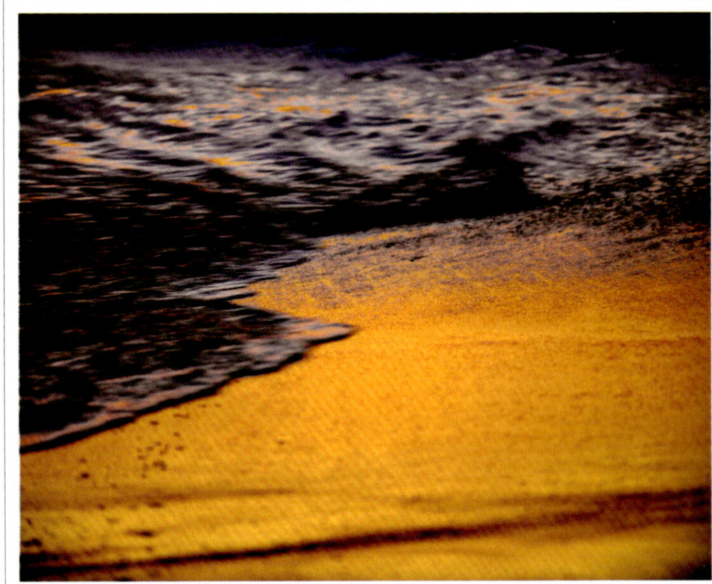

Title: Patrick Tregenza | Client: Self-initiated

SCOTT LOWDEN

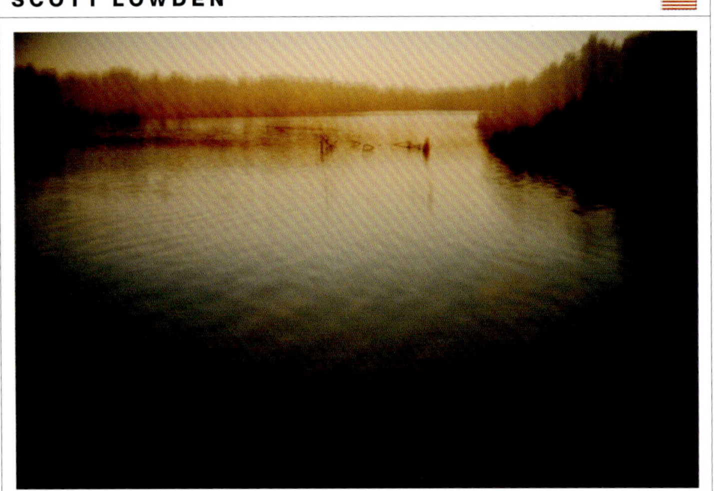

Title: Terra Nostra | Client: Self-initiated

CLARENCE LIN

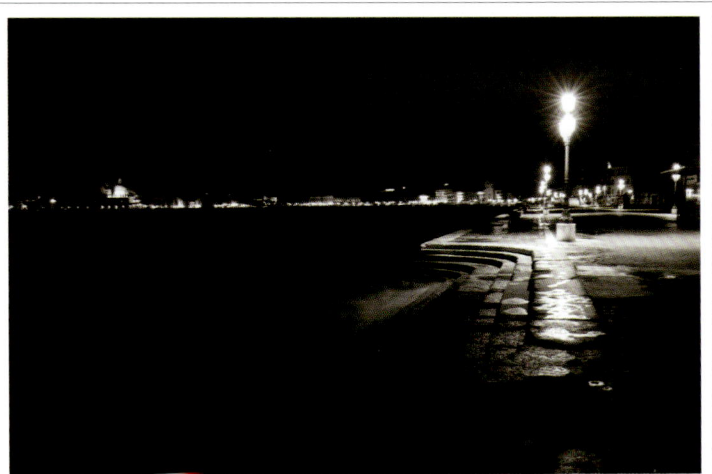

Title: Venice | Client: Self-initiated

HARRY RIFKIN

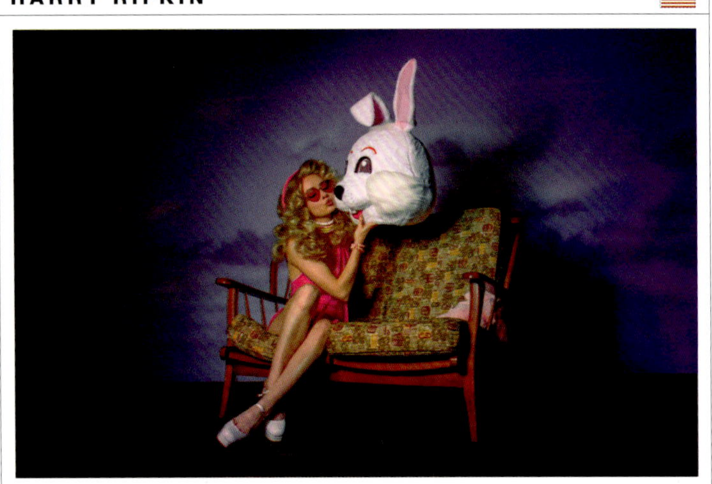

Title: Hippety-Hop | Client: Self-initiated

ARIEL FREANER

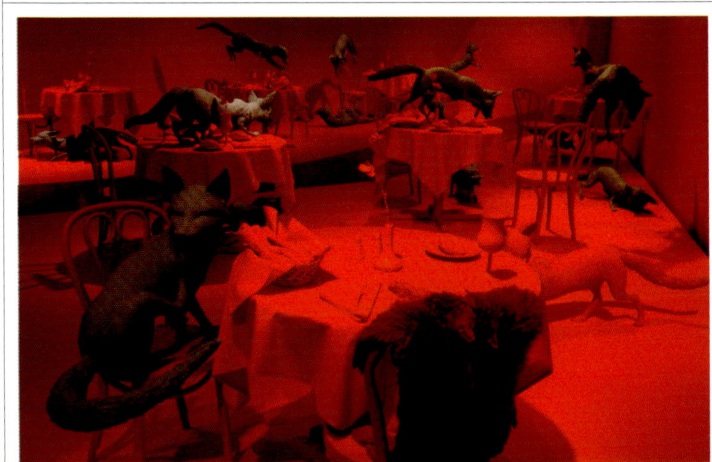

Title: Denver Museum Foxes | Client: ZEVEN Magazine

HARRY RIFKIN

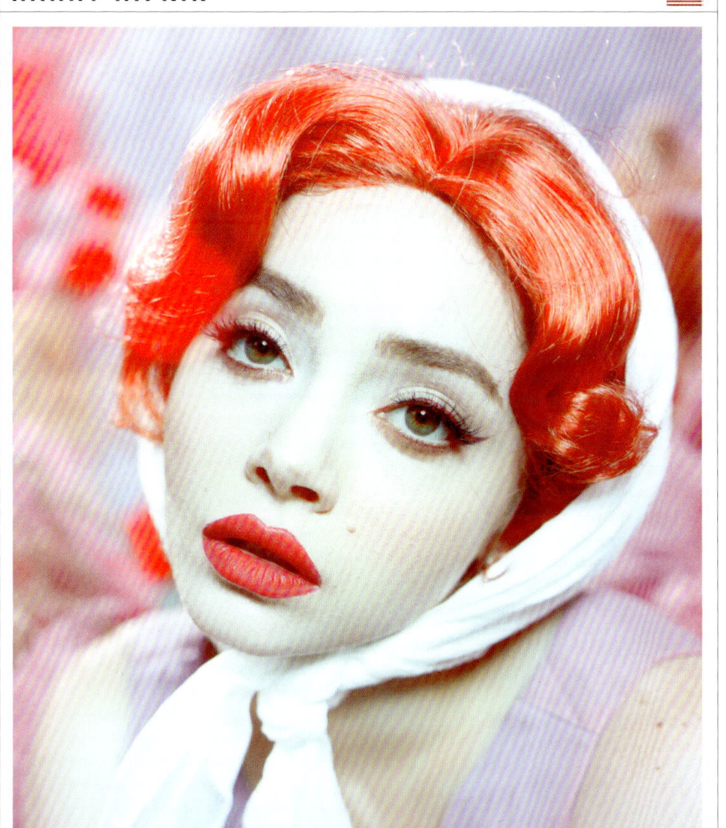

Title: Scarlette 1960 | **Client:** Self-initiated

HARRY RIFKIN

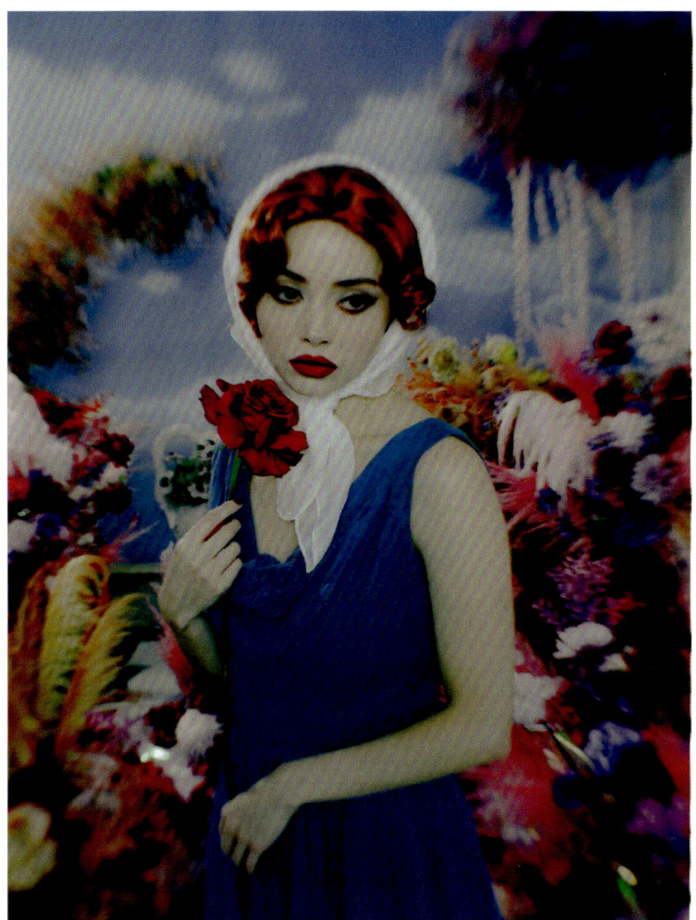

Title: Scarlette 1960 | **Client:** Self-initiated

HARRY RIFKIN

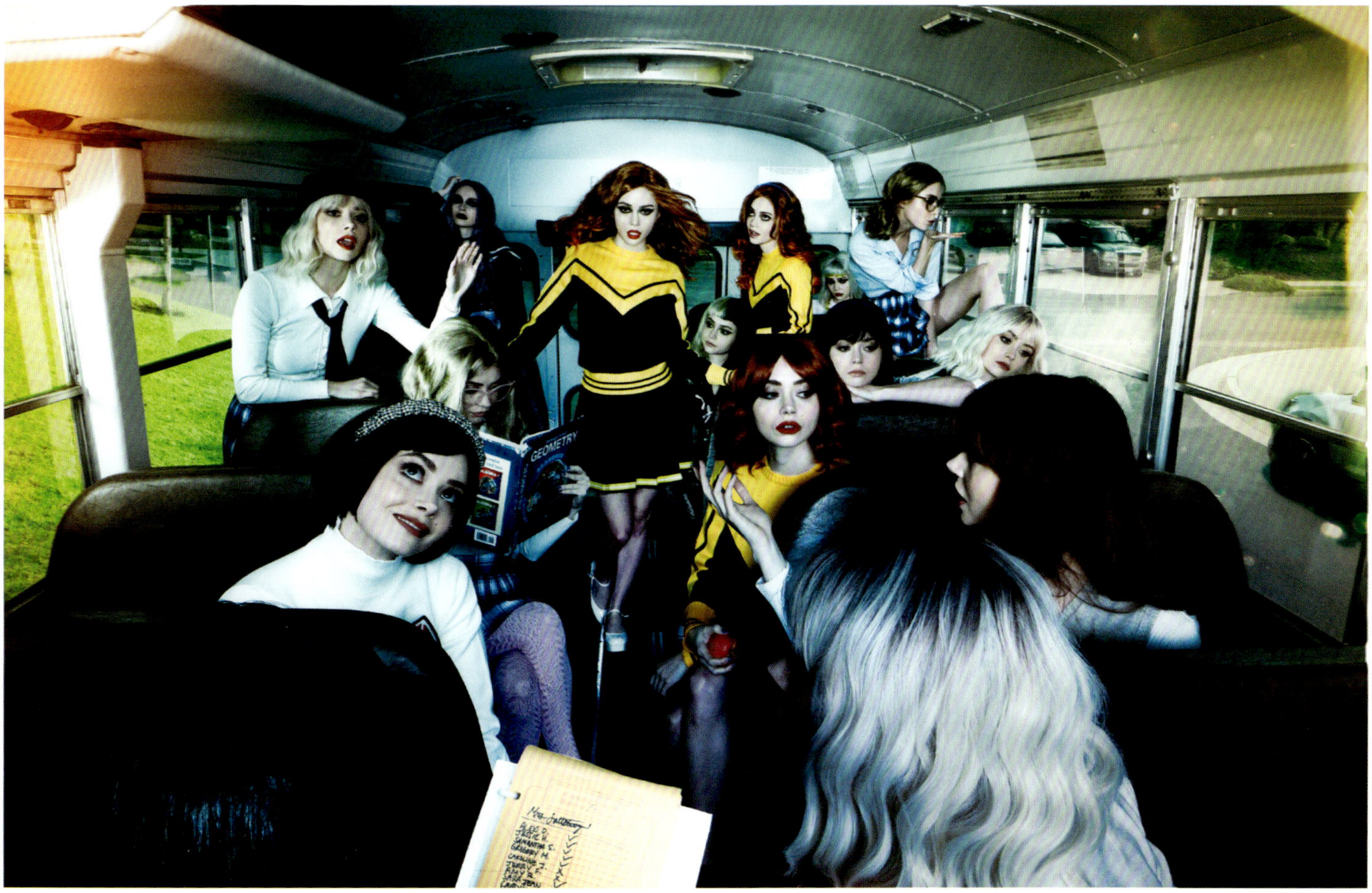

Title: The Girls of Saint Mary Elizabeth Preparatory School | **Client:** Self-initiated

HARRY RIFKIN

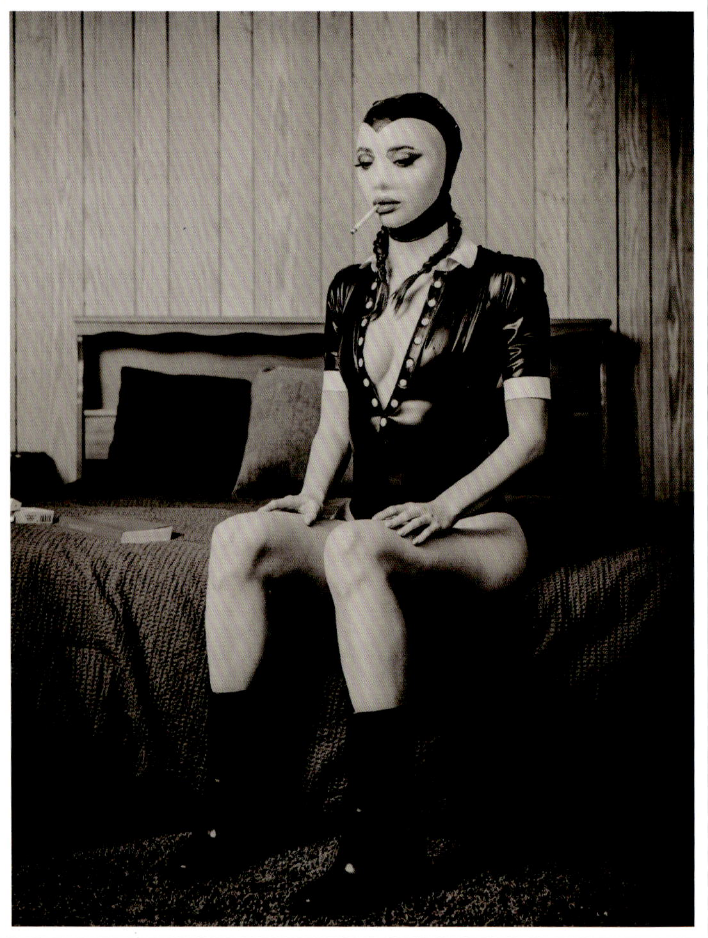

Title: The Notion of Confusion | **Client:** Self-initiated

HARRY RIFKIN

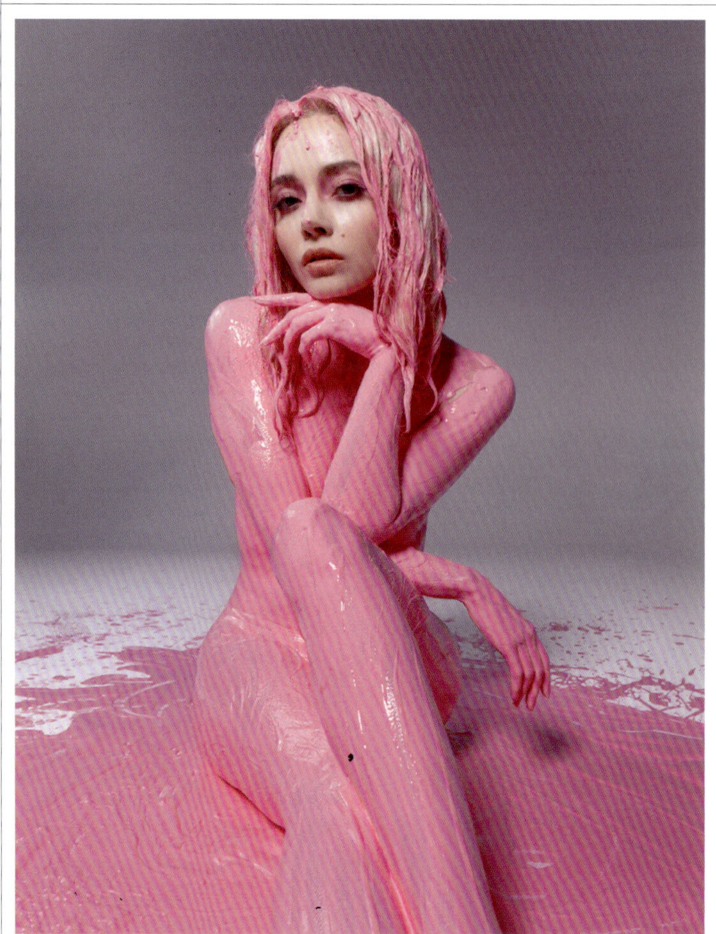

Title: Pigment of My Imagination | **Client:** Self-initiated

HARRY RIFKIN

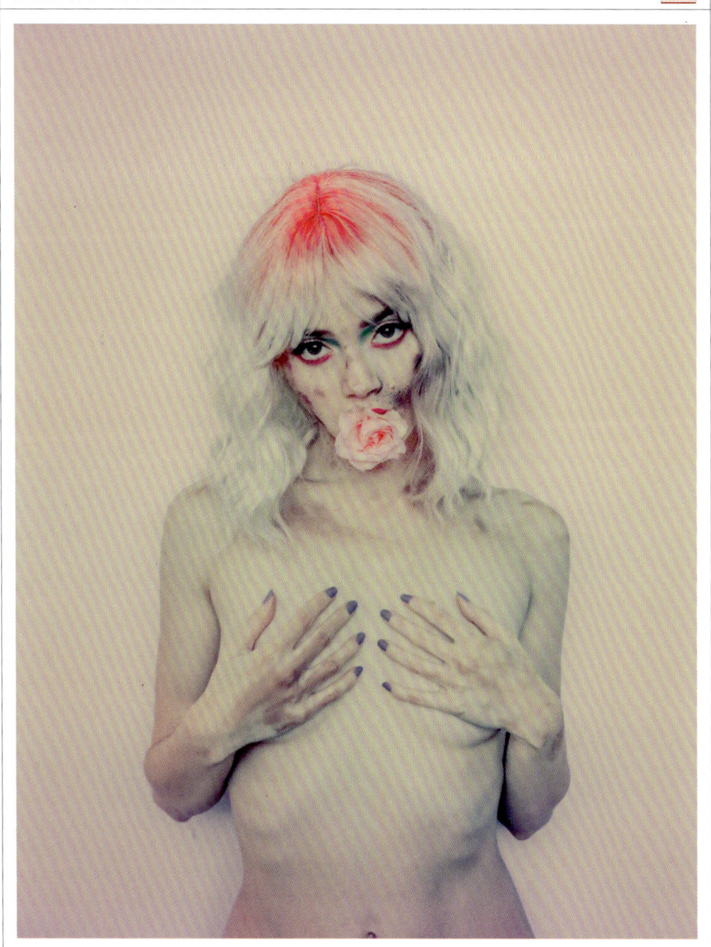

Title: Blossom | **Client:** Self-initiated

HARRY RIFKIN

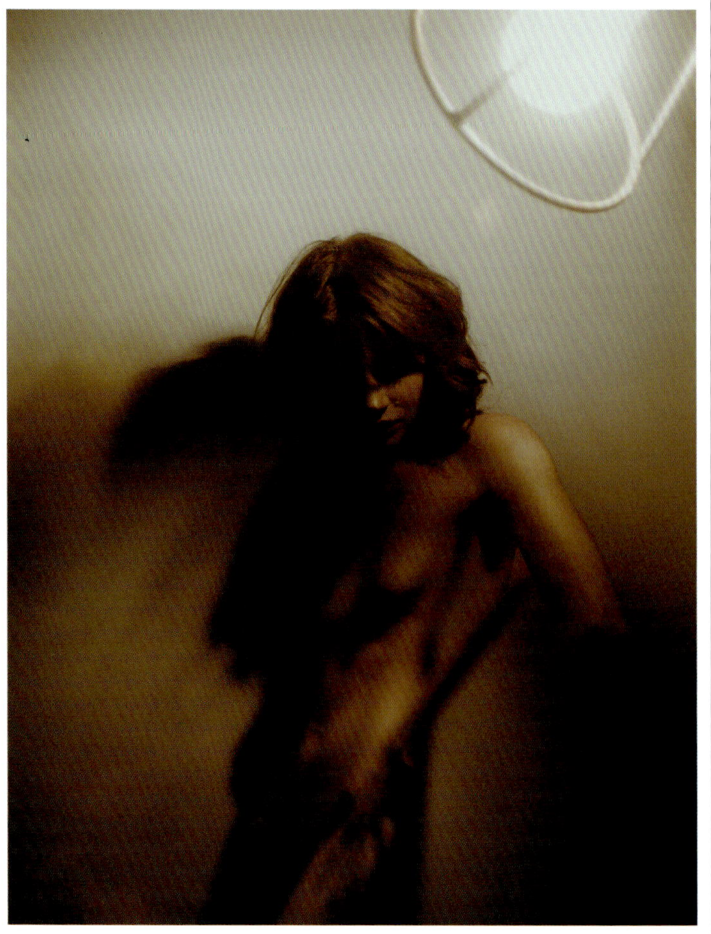

Title: The Bare Bulb Project | **Client:** Self-initiated

HARRY RIFKIN

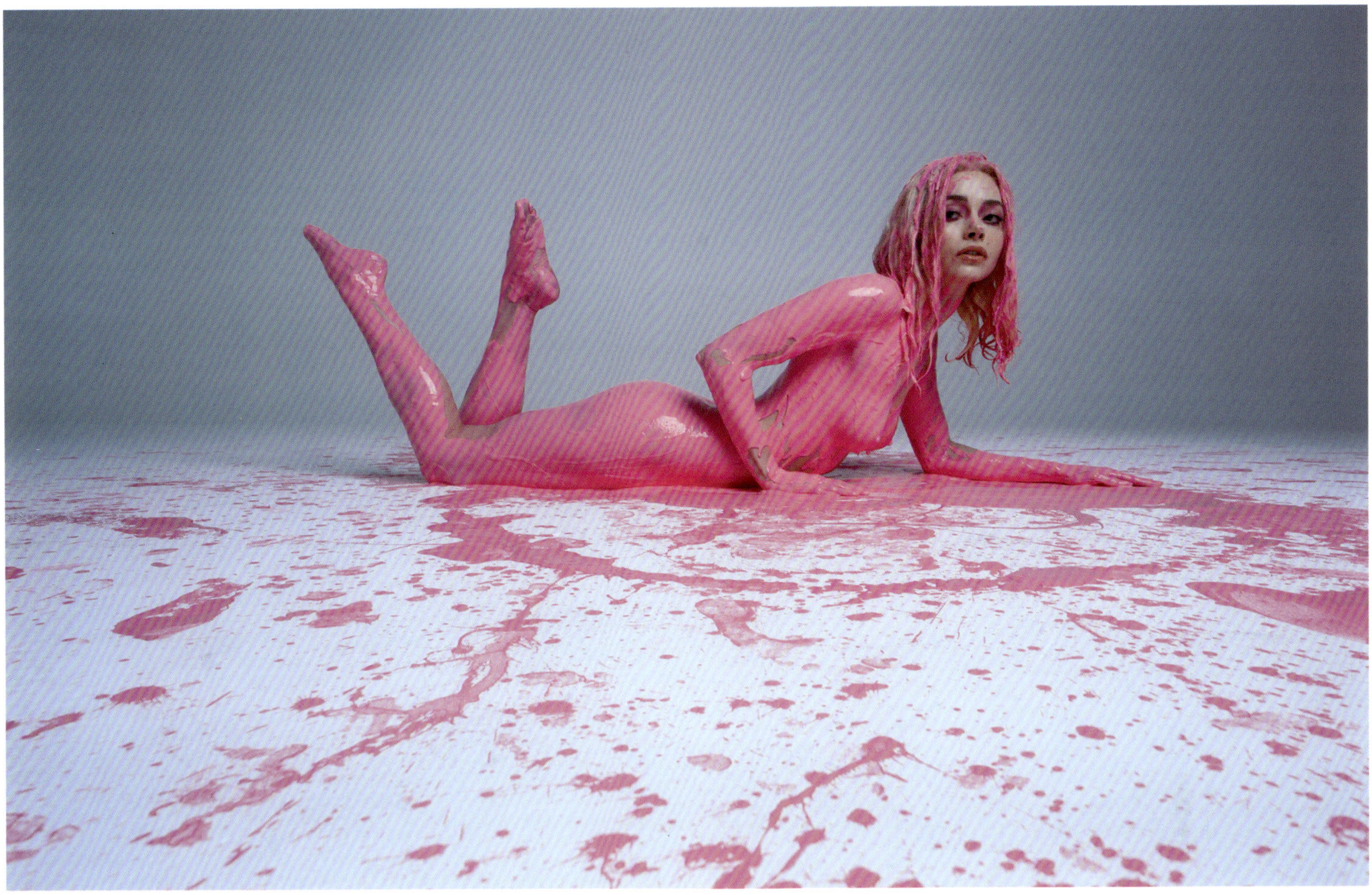

Title: Pigment of My Imagination | Client: Self-initiated

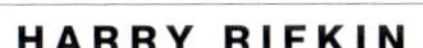

HARRY RIFKIN

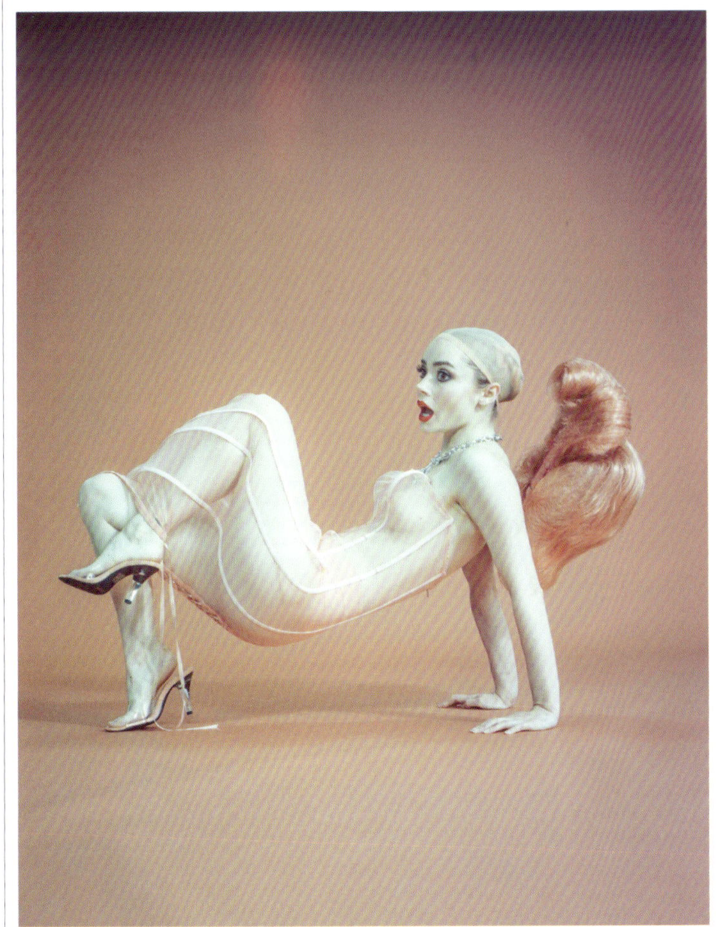

Title: Visions in My Head | Client: Self-initiated

HARRY RIFKIN

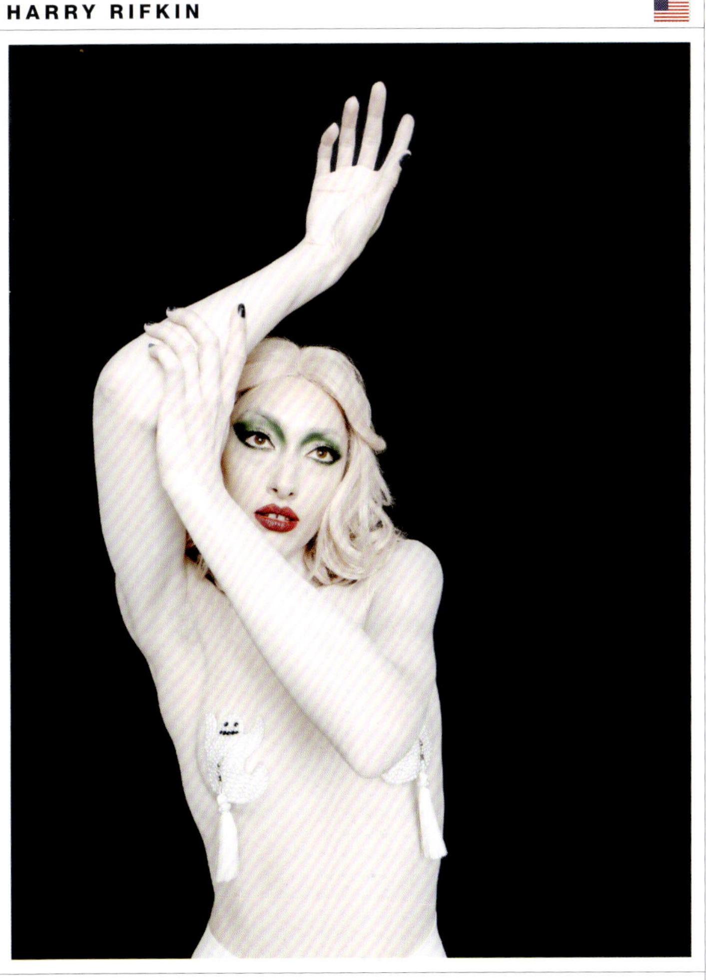

Title: Ghost Girl ~ Abby | Client: Self-initiated

LAURIE FRANKEL

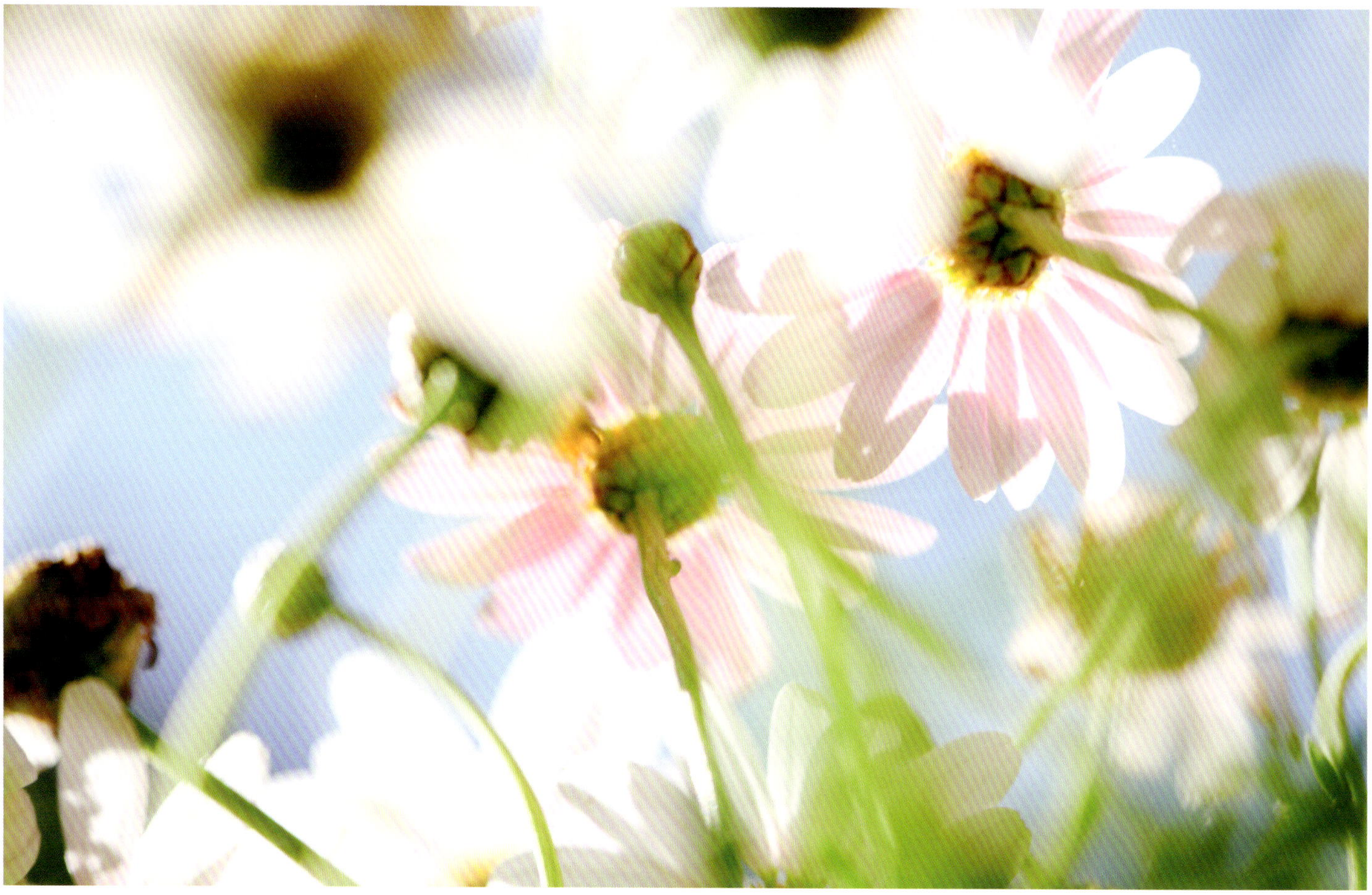

Title: Daisies from Below | **Client:** Eat Your Flowers

LAURIE FRANKEL

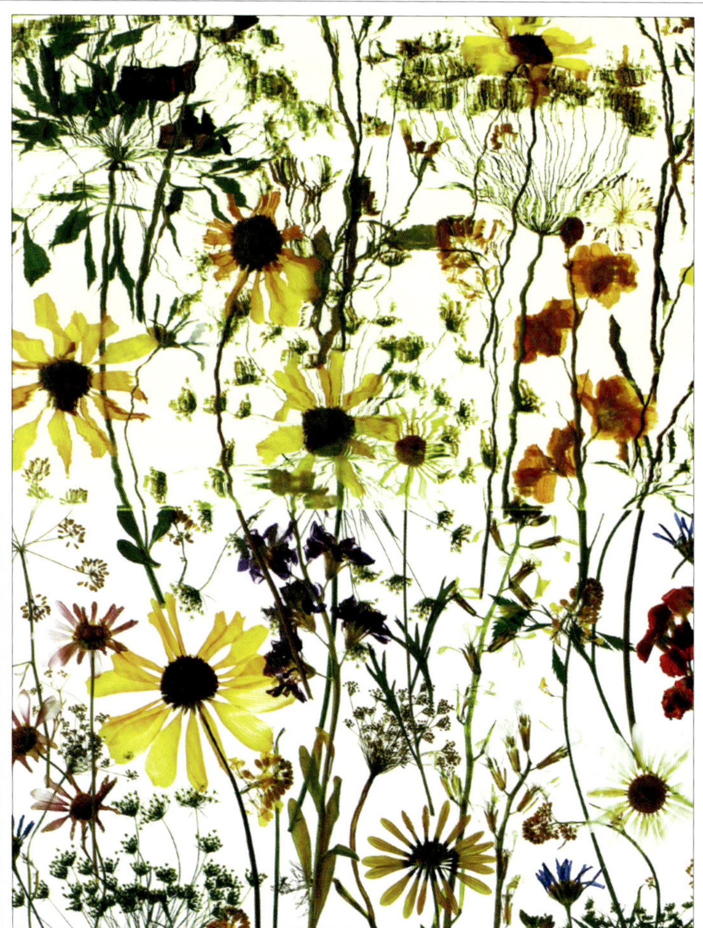

Title: Floral Patterns | **Client:** Eat Your Flowers

CRAIG CUTLER

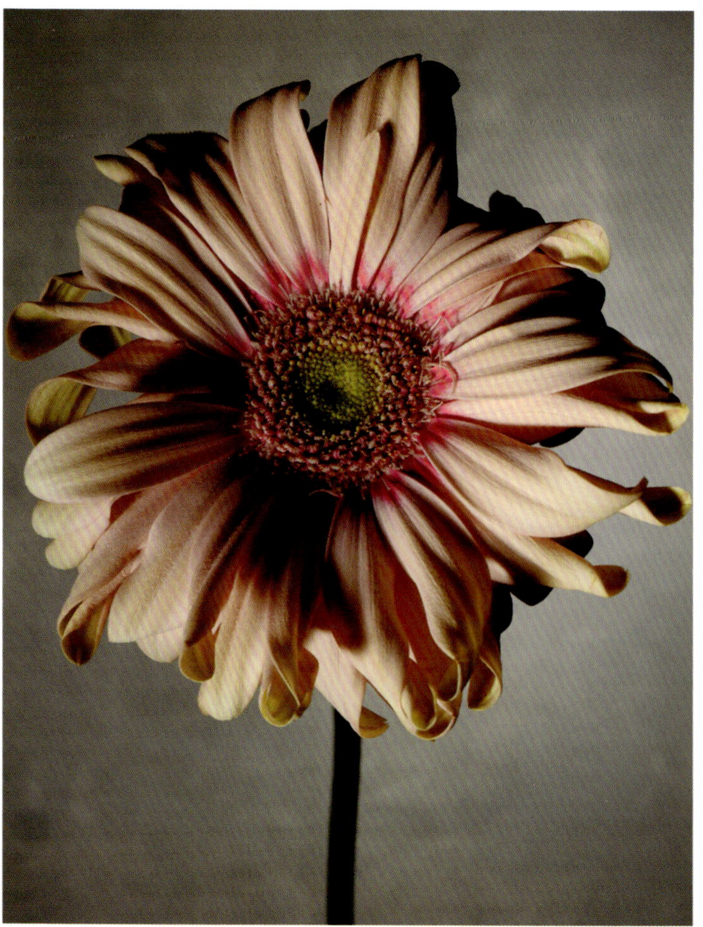

Title: Flower 1 | **Client:** Self-initiated

CRAIG CUTLER

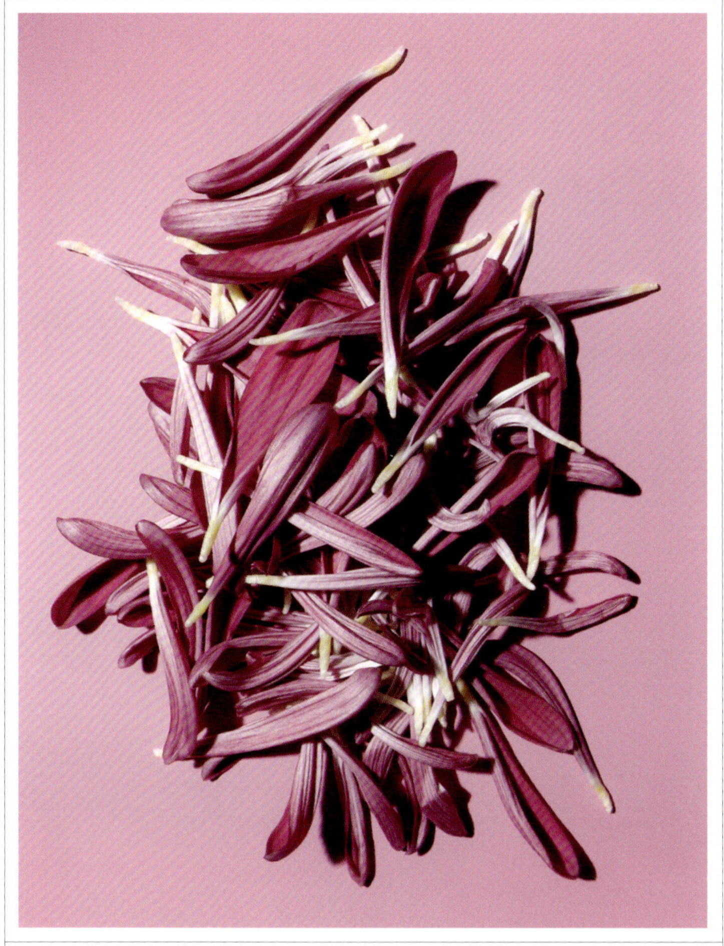

Title: Petals on Color Series | **Client:** Self-initiated

LAURIE FRANKEL

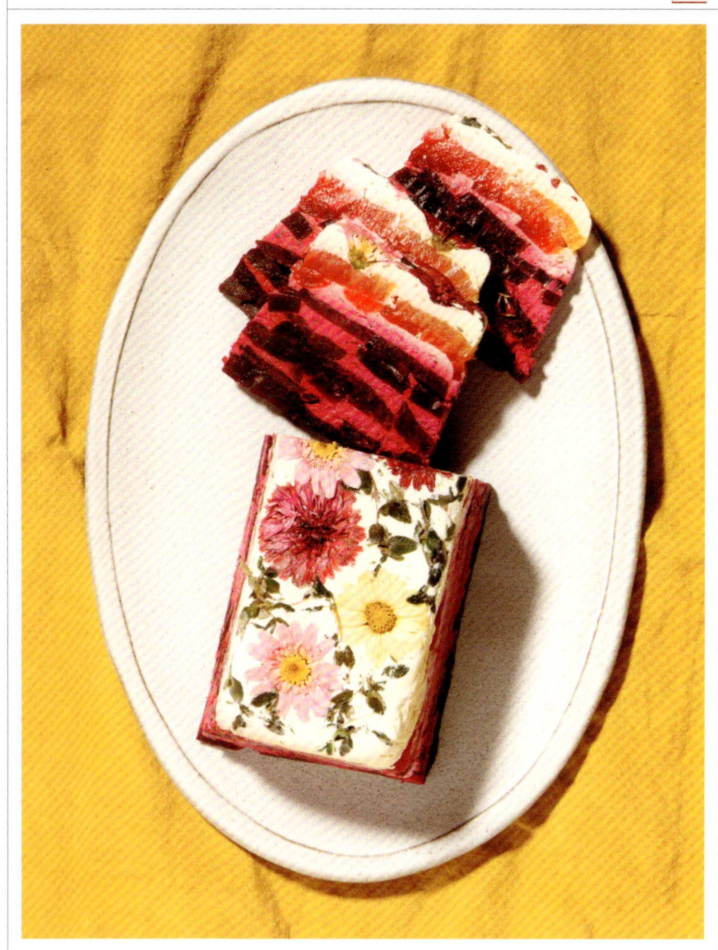

Title: Floral Beets | **Client:** Eat Your Flowers

DYLAN SWART

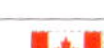

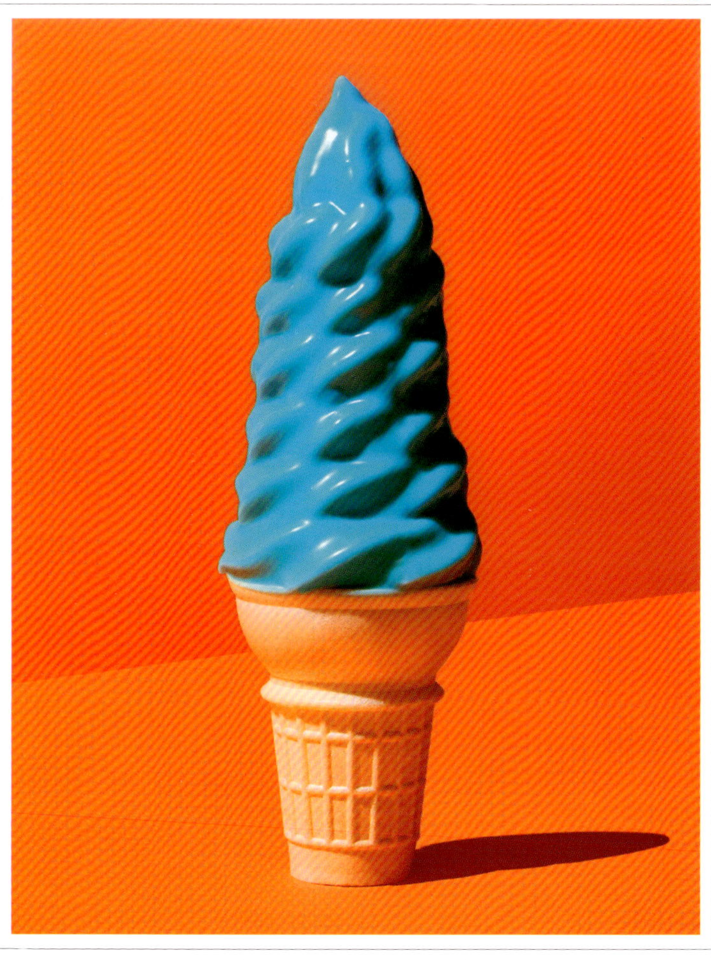

Title: Summer Vibes | **Client:** Drizzle

CRAIG CUTLER

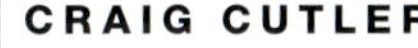

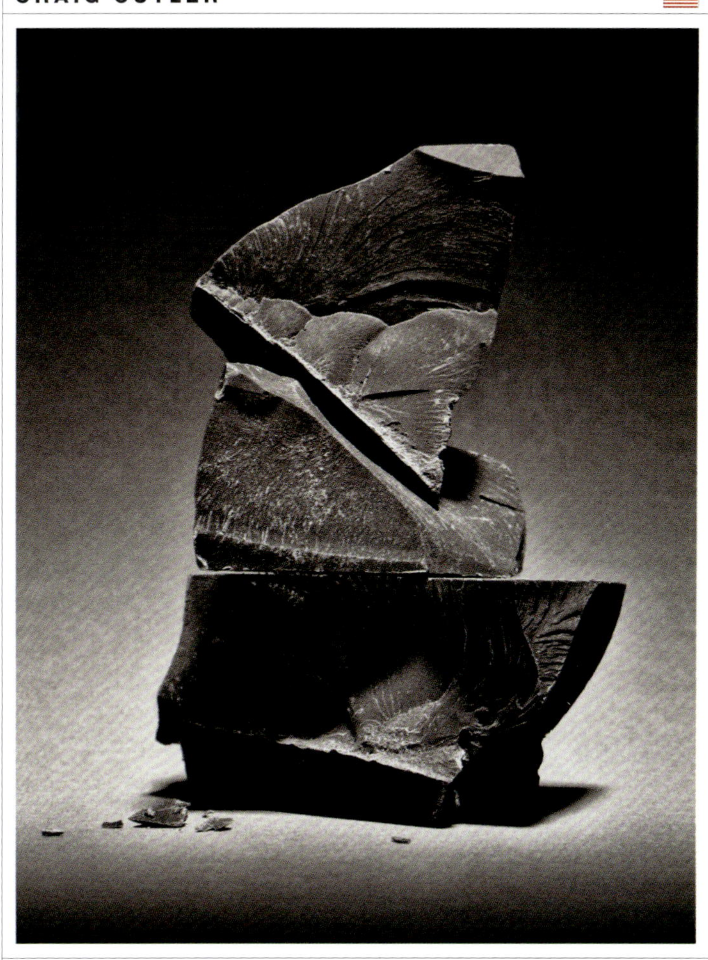

Title: Chocolate Sculptures | **Client:** Self-initiated

EVI ABELER

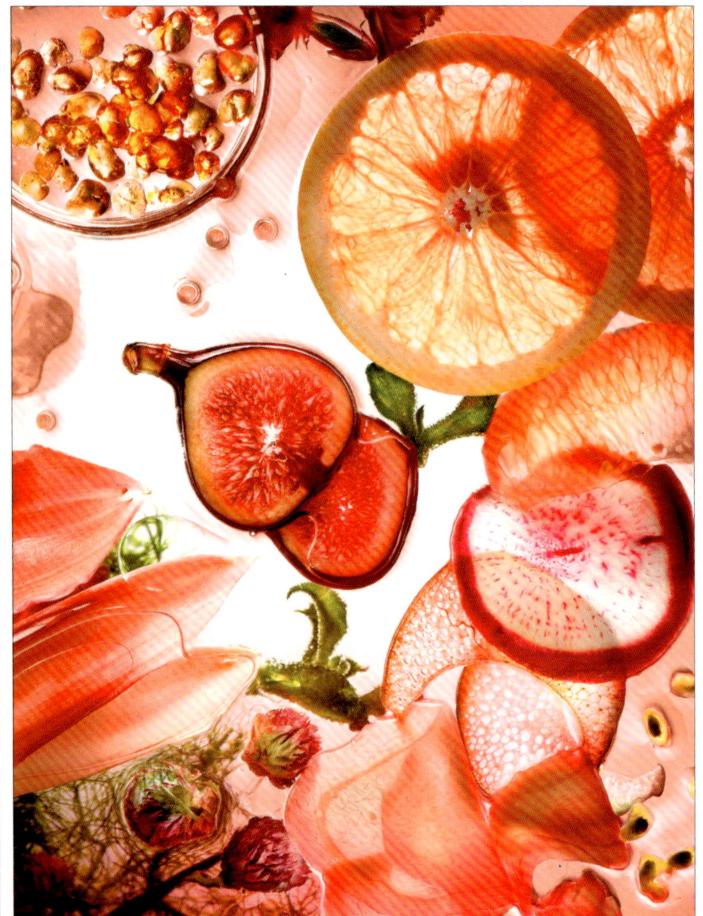

Title: Feast Your Senses | **Client:** Marina Bay Sands

JAN KALISH

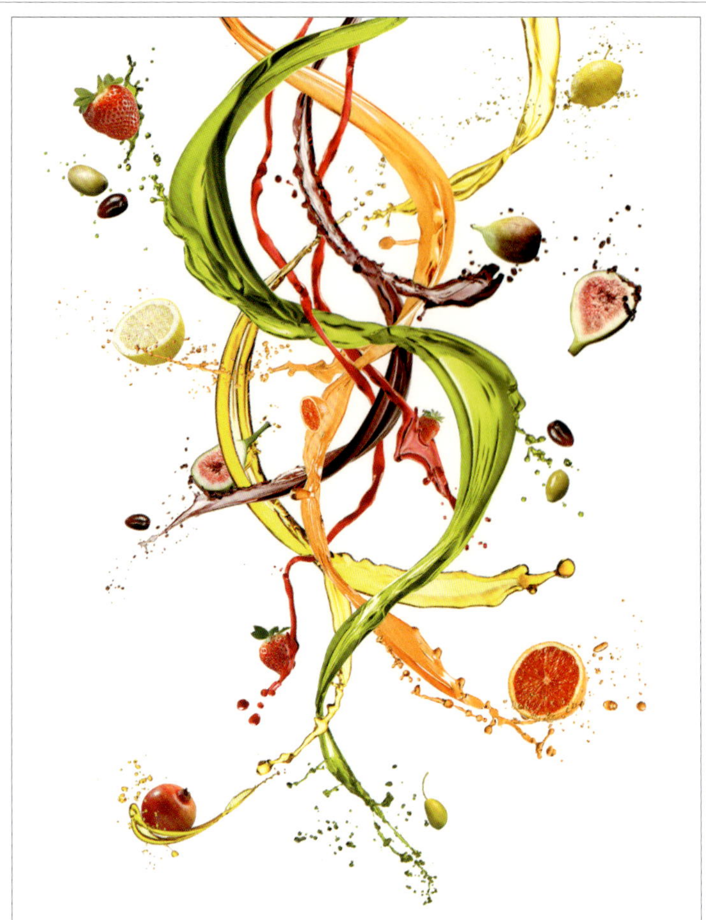

Title: Balsamic Acid Parties | **Client:** Global Gardens

ARIEL FREANER

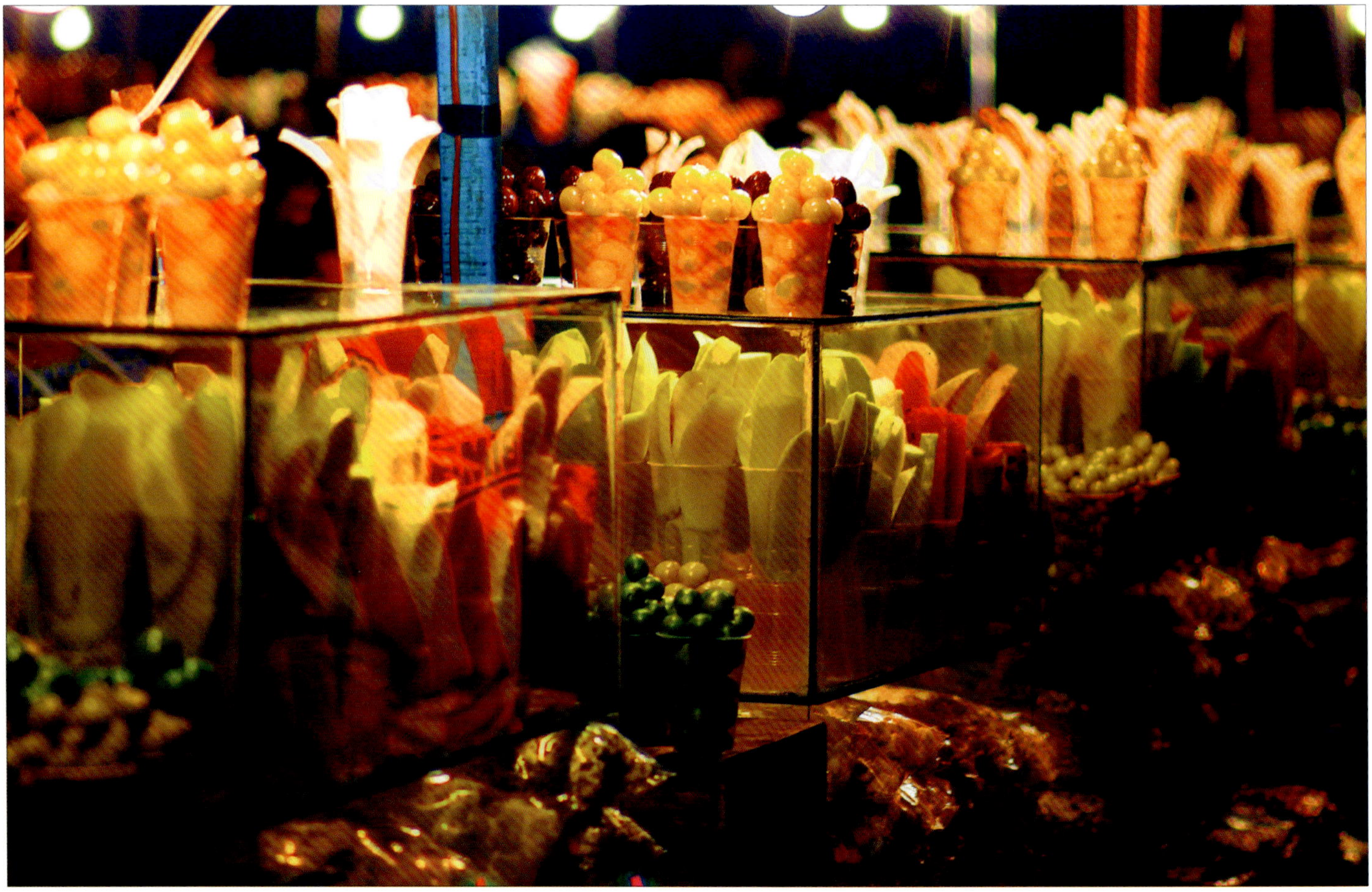

Title: Tijuana Evening Delight | **Client:** ZEVEN Magazine

LAURIE FRANKEL

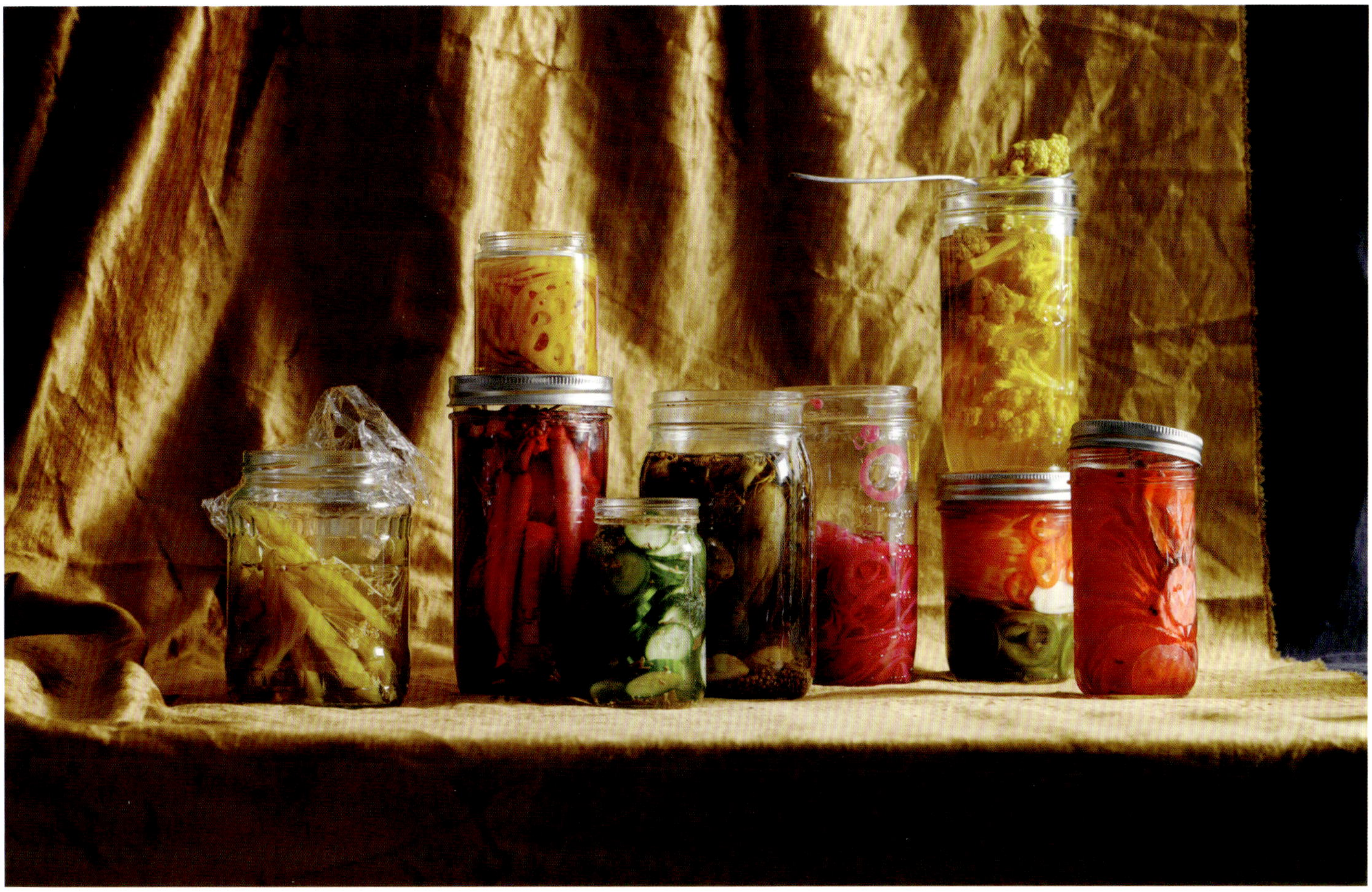

Title: Colorfully Pickling | **Client:** Eat Your Flowers

ARIEL FREANER

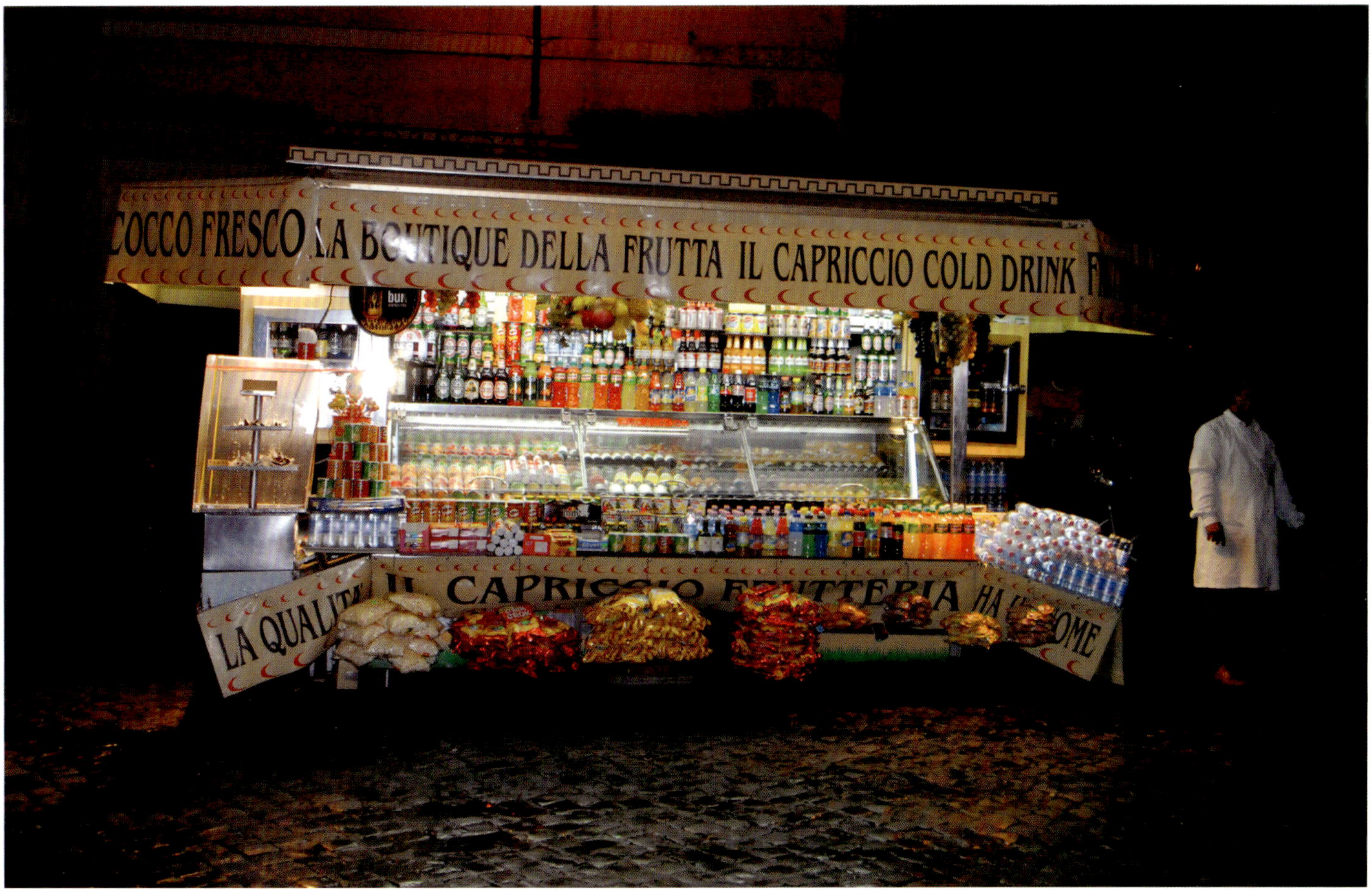

Title: Italy - Rome Midnight Snack Delight | **Client:** ZEVEN Magazine

TADD MYERS

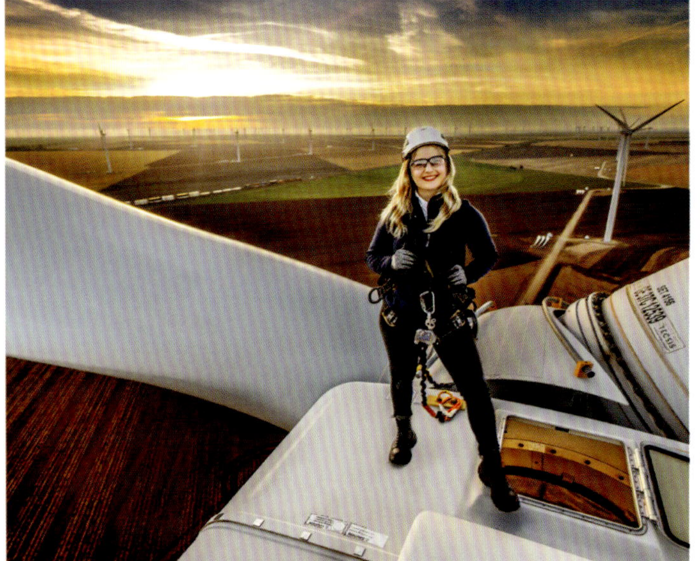

Title: Engineer Portrait Standing on Windmill Tower | **Client:** RWE

ROBERT SEALE

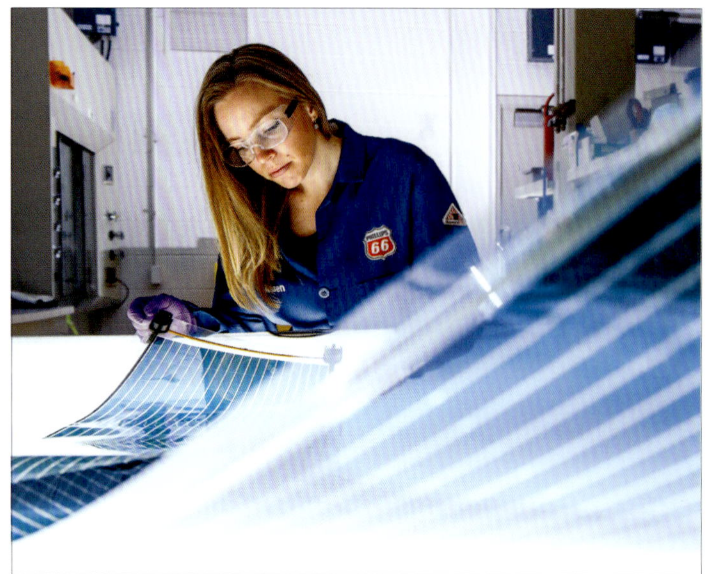

Title: Alternative Energy Research Lab Series | **Client:** Phillips 66

TADD MYERS

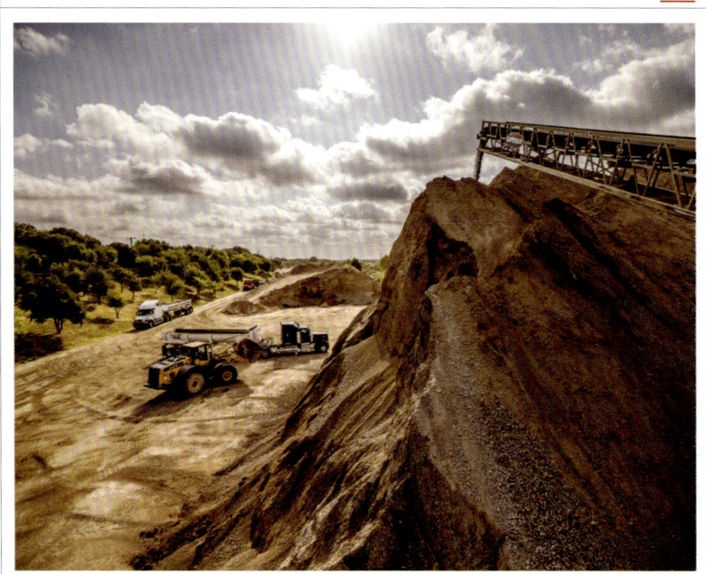

Title: Arcosa - Concrete Recycling Facility
Client: Arcosa Specialty Materials

ROGER MASTROIANNI

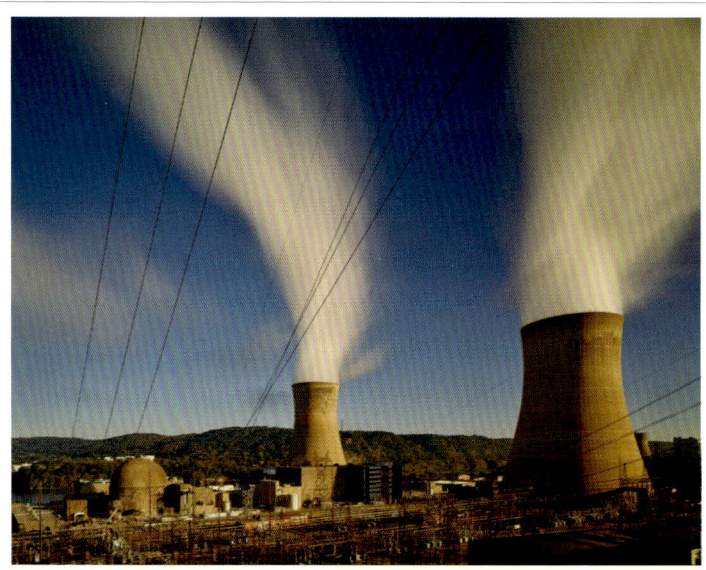

Title: Nuclear Landscape Photography Reimagined
Client: Energy Harbor

ARIEL FREANER

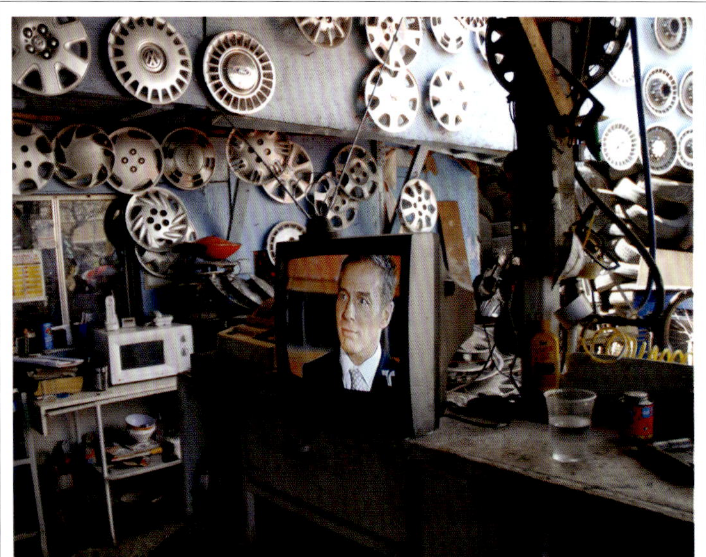

Title: Tijuana Afternoon at Work
Client: ZEVEN Magazine

ROBERT SEALE

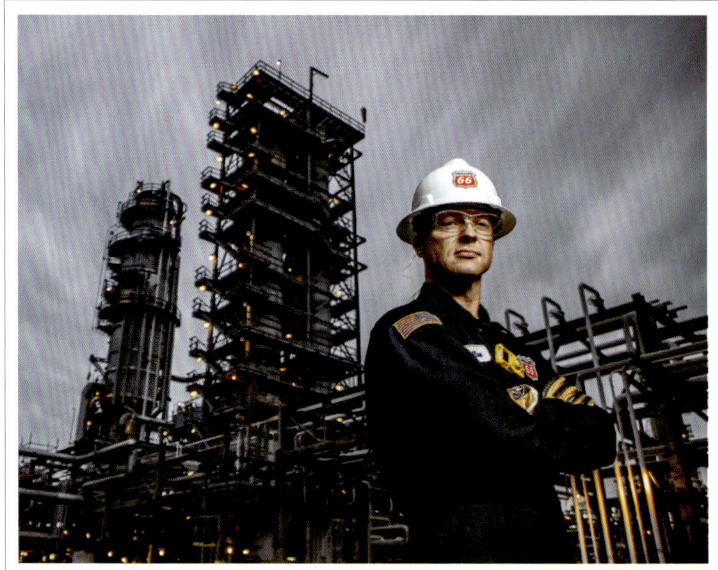

Title: Industrial Facilities Around the US for Annual Report
Client: Phillips 66

TADD MYERS

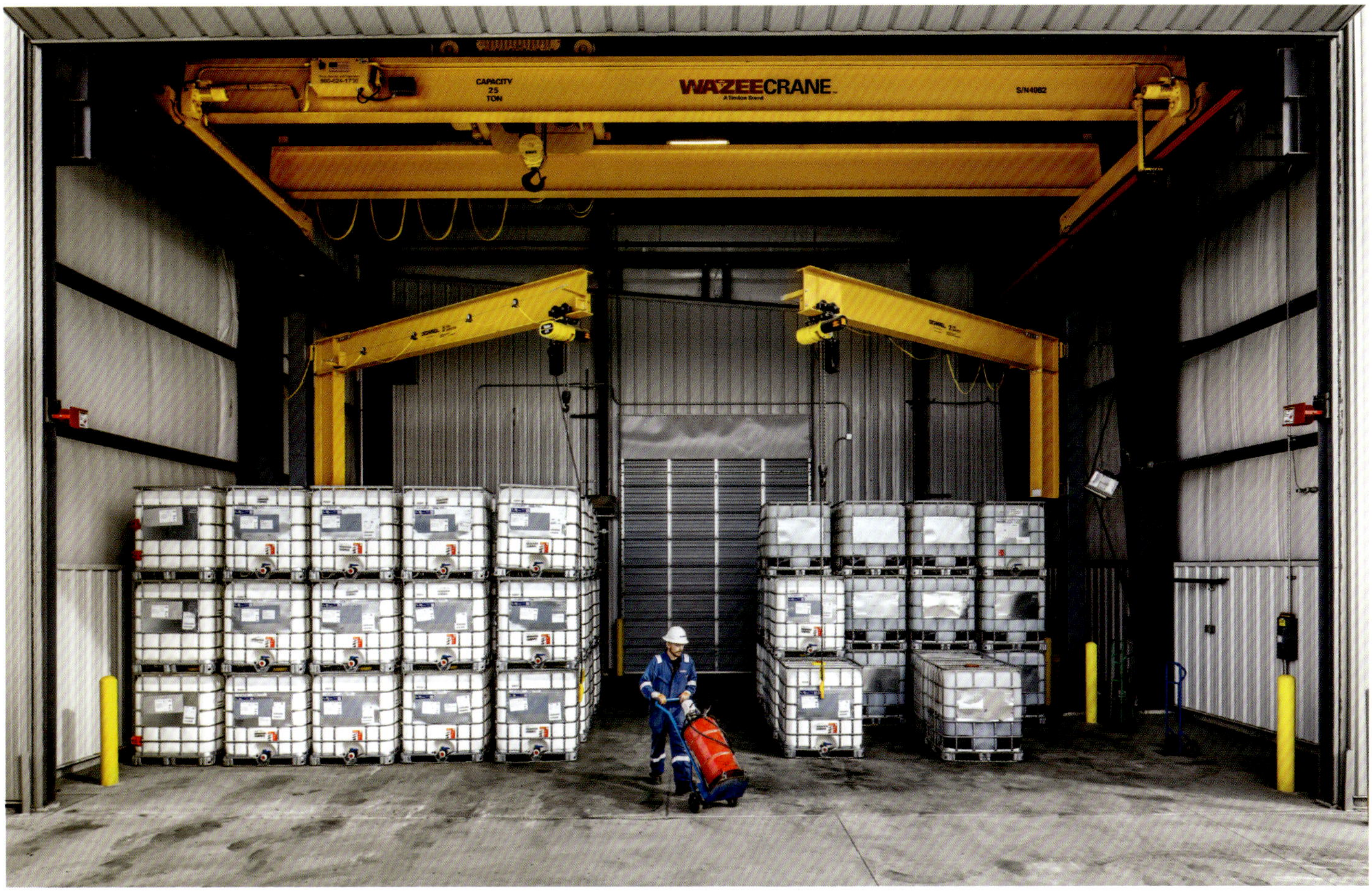

Title: SLB Energy Series | Client: SLB Energy

TADD MYERS

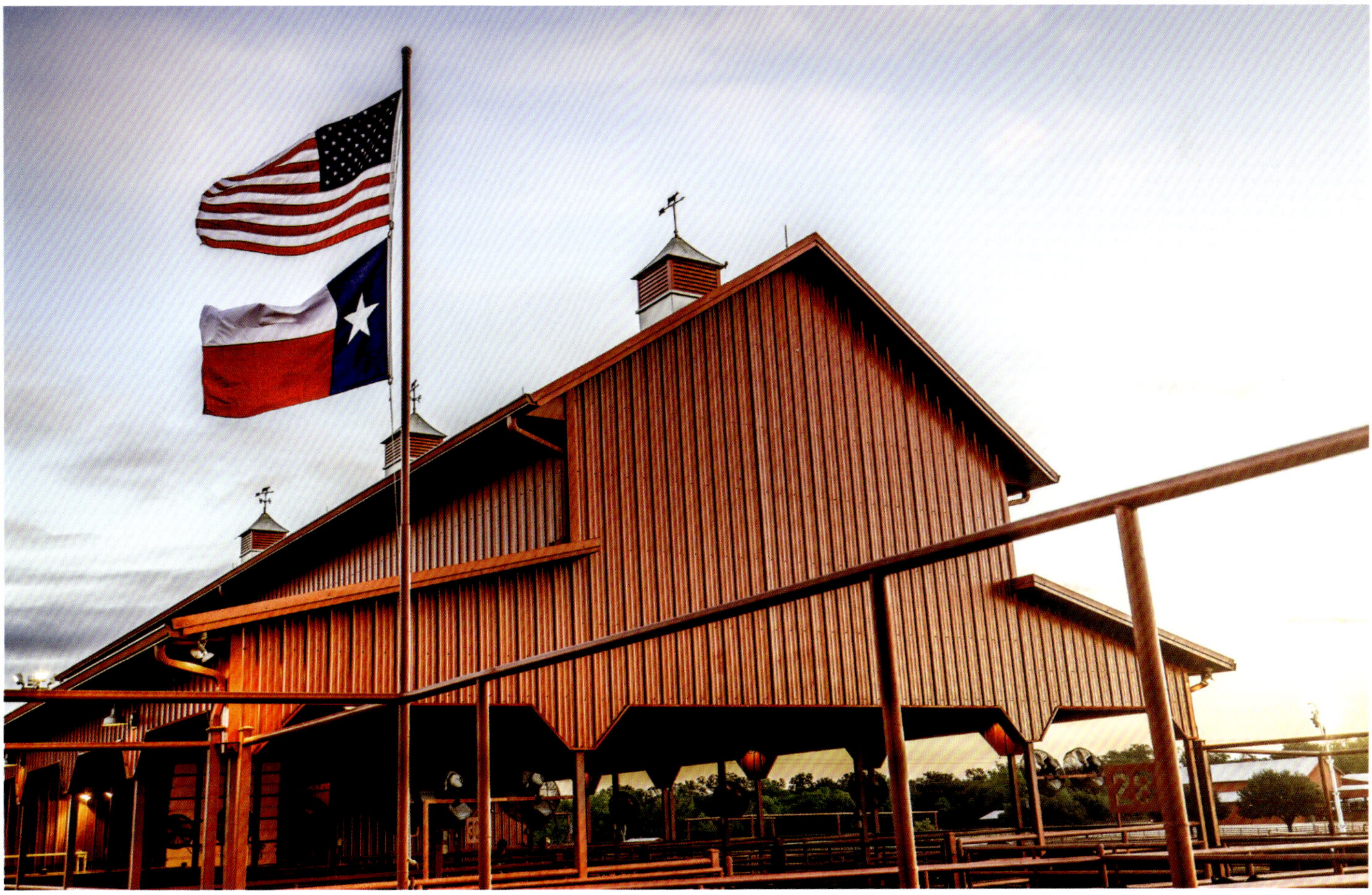

Title: 44 Farms - Sale Day | Client: 44 Farms

TADD MYERS

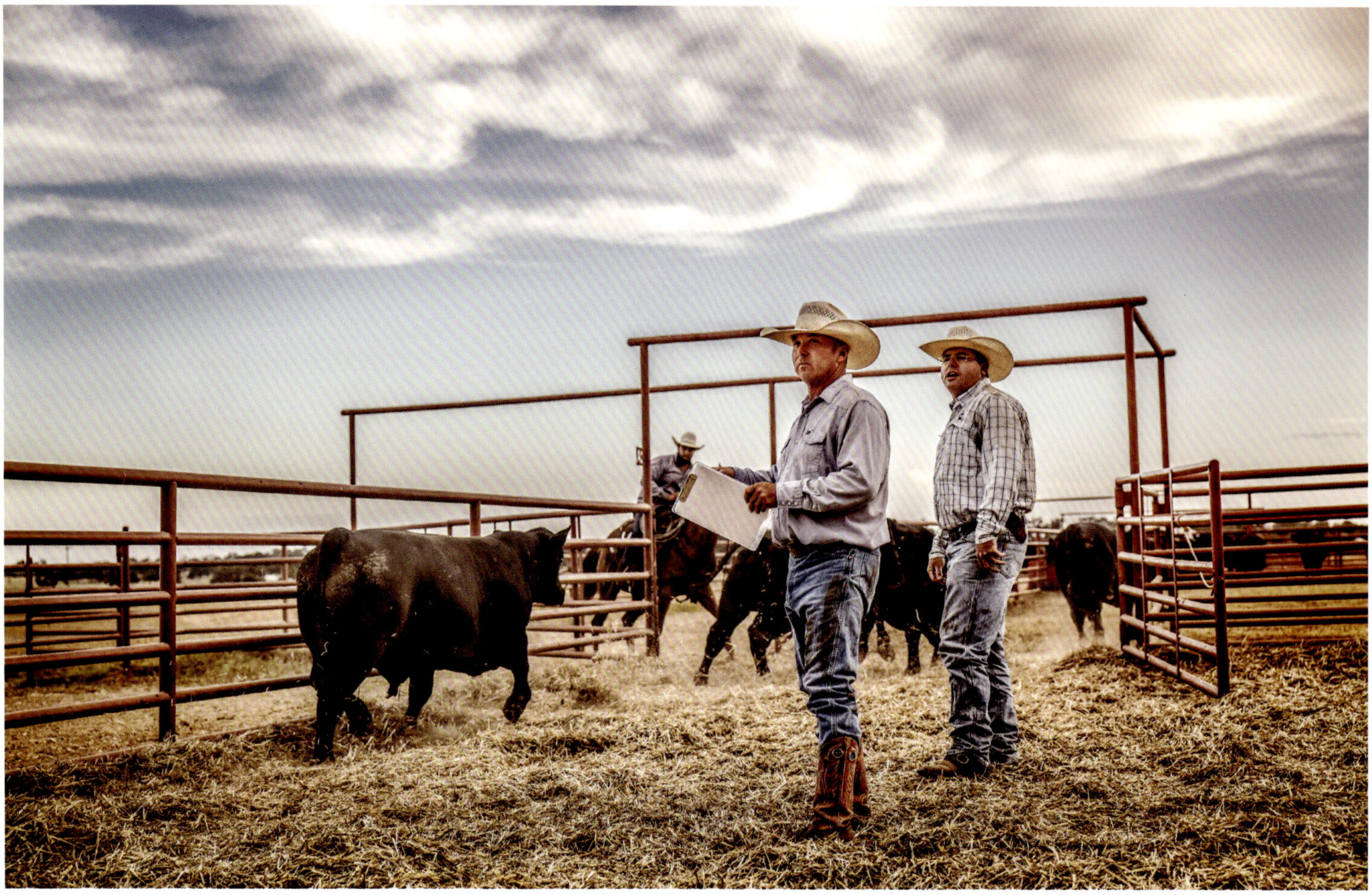

Title: 44 Farms - Sorting Cattle | **Client:** 44 Farms

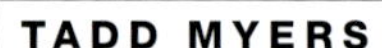

TADD MYERS

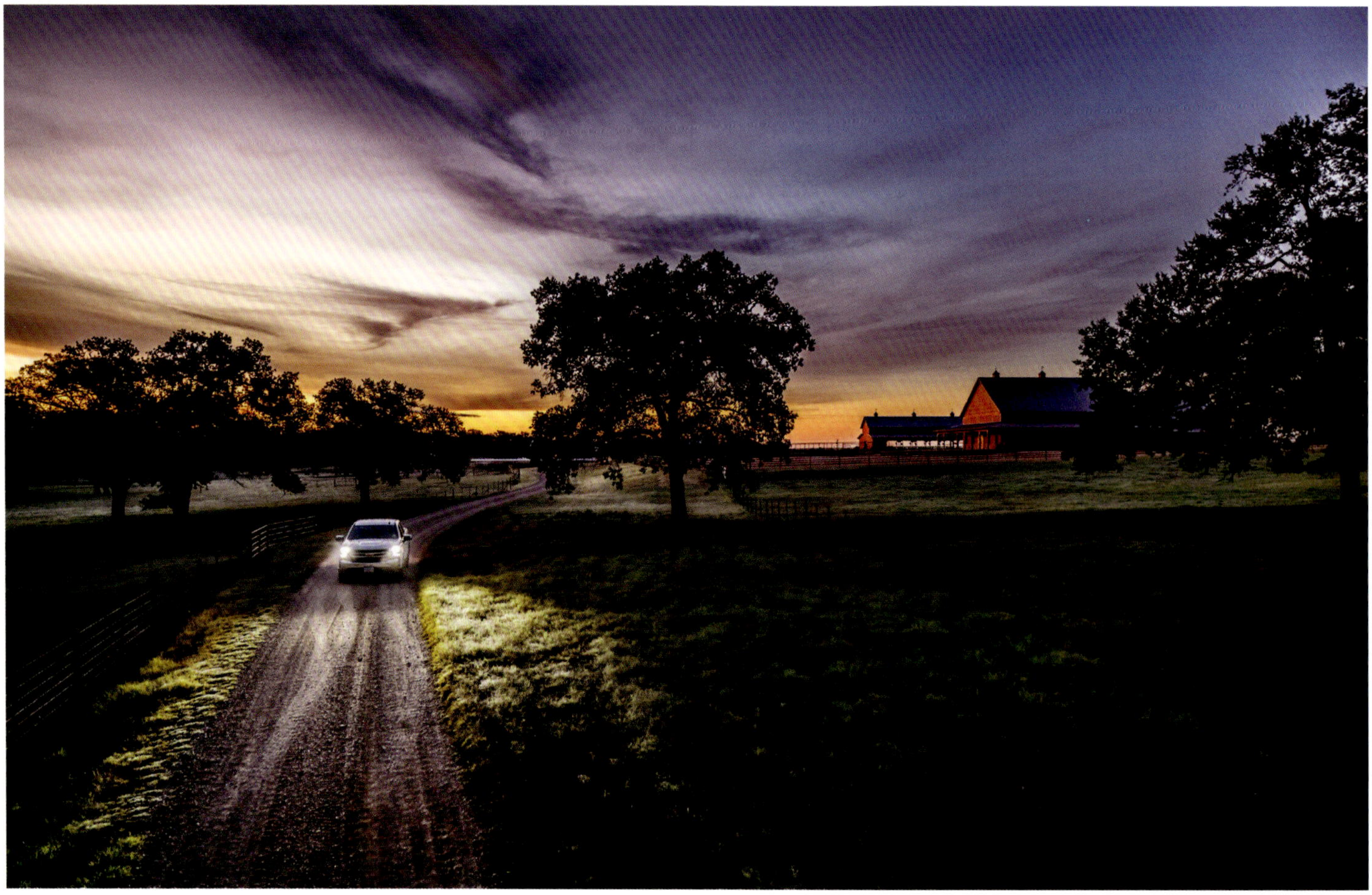

Title: 44 Farms - Life on the Farm | **Client:** 44 Farms

LINDSAY SIU

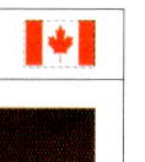

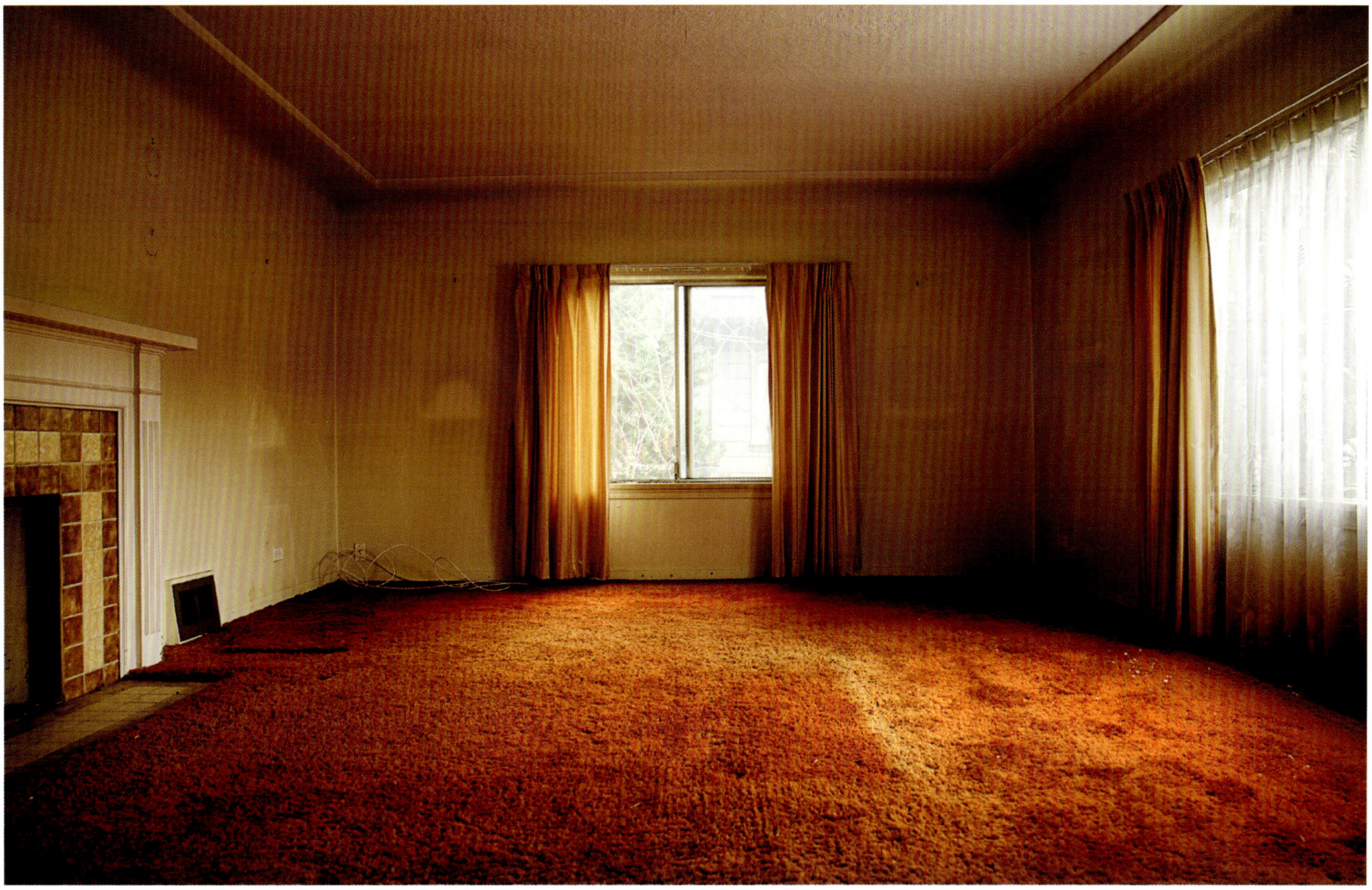

Title: Dream House | **Client:** Self-initiated

LAURIE FRANKEL

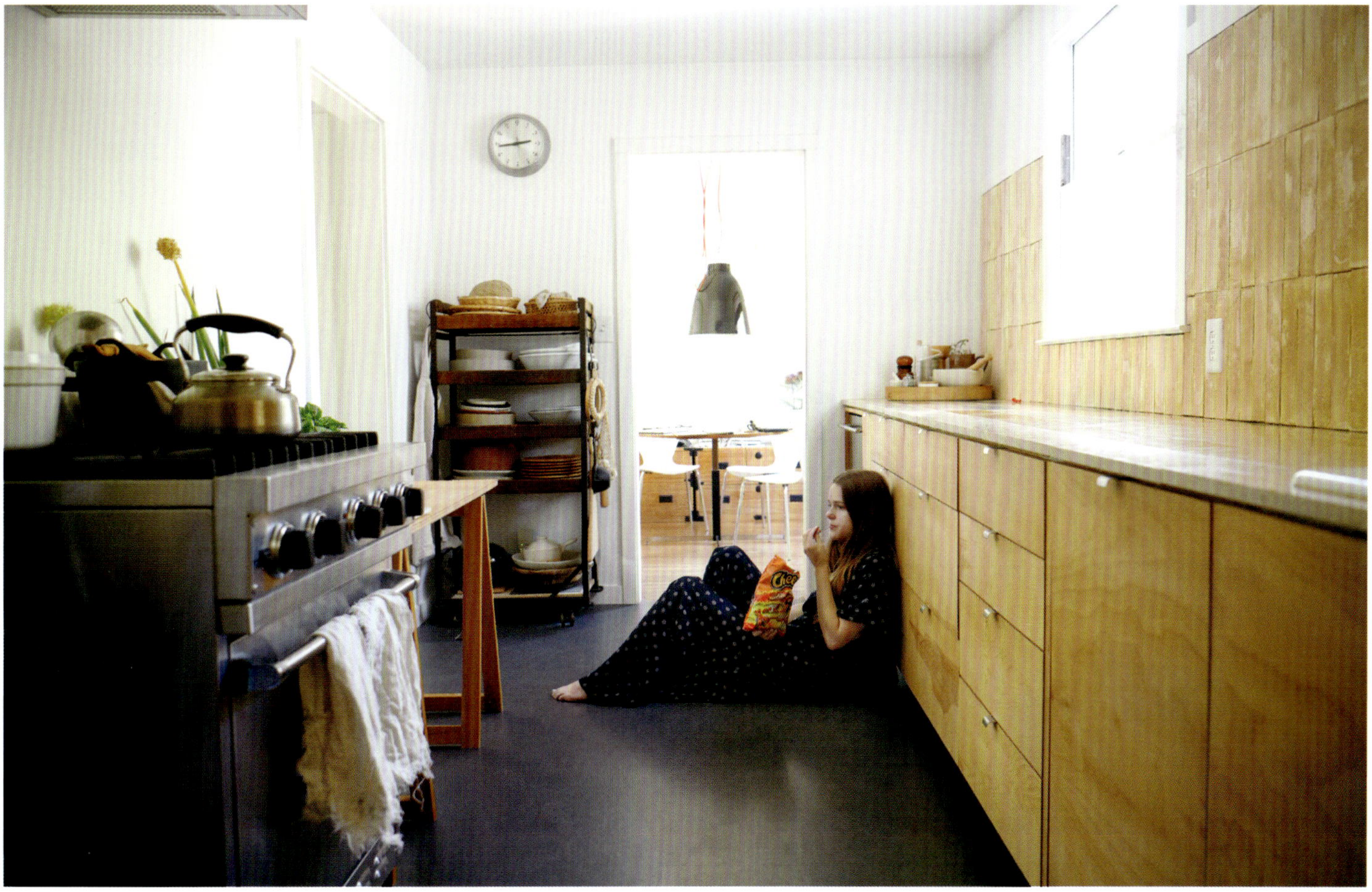

Title: Peace and Cheetos | **Client:** Self-initiated

ARTEM NAZAROV

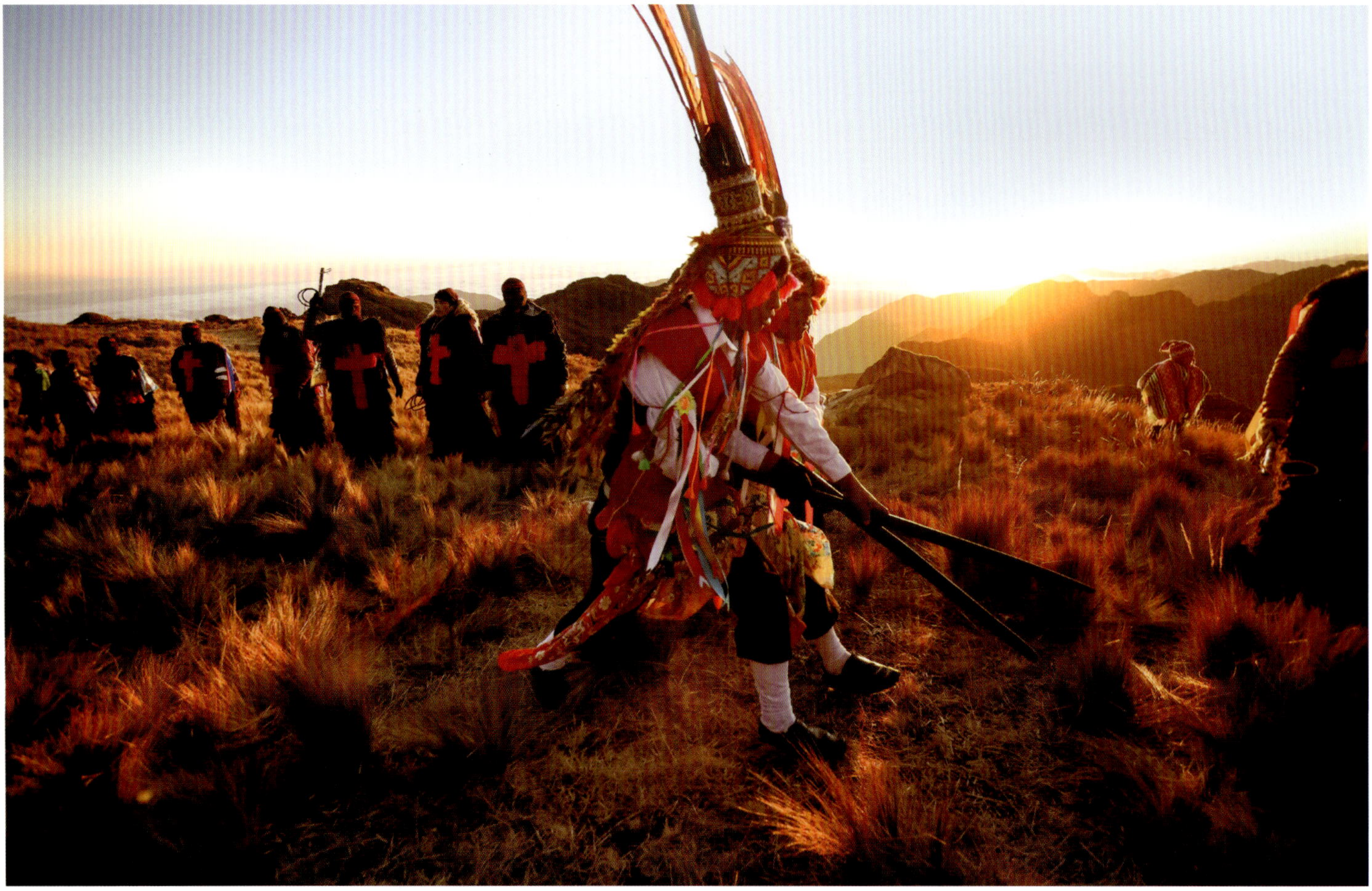

Title: Inti: The Sun God | **Client:** Self-initiated

CRAIG CUTLER

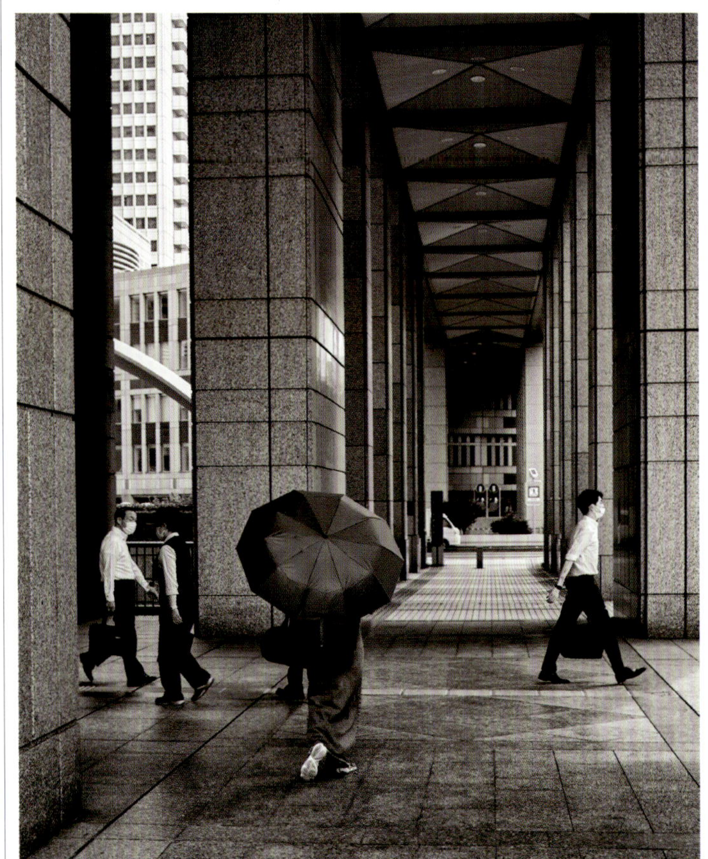

Title: Parasol in Tokyo | **Client:** Self-initiated

CRAIG CUTLER

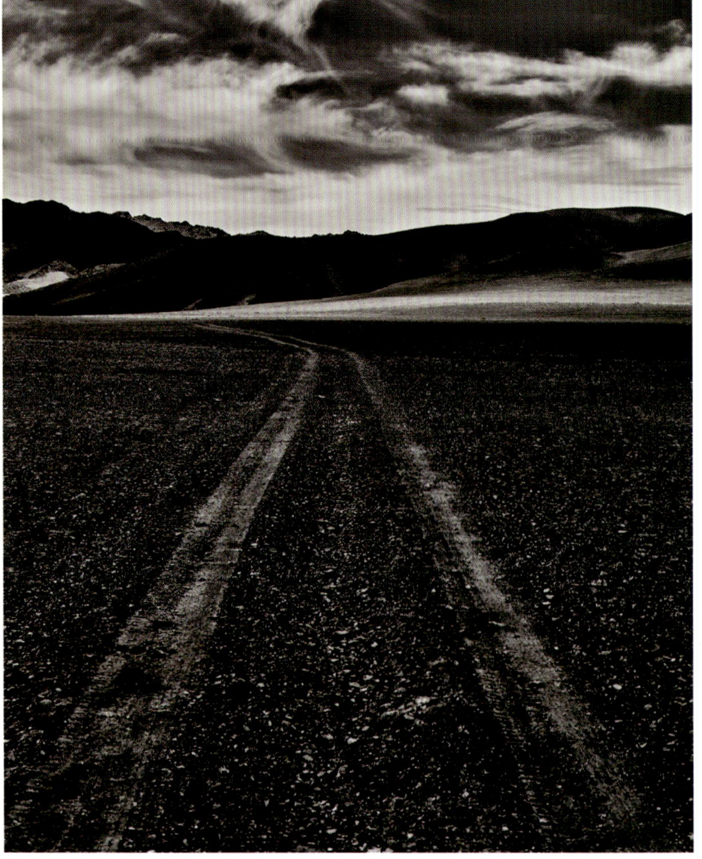

Title: Mongolian Desert | **Client:** Self-initiated

JARED LEEDS

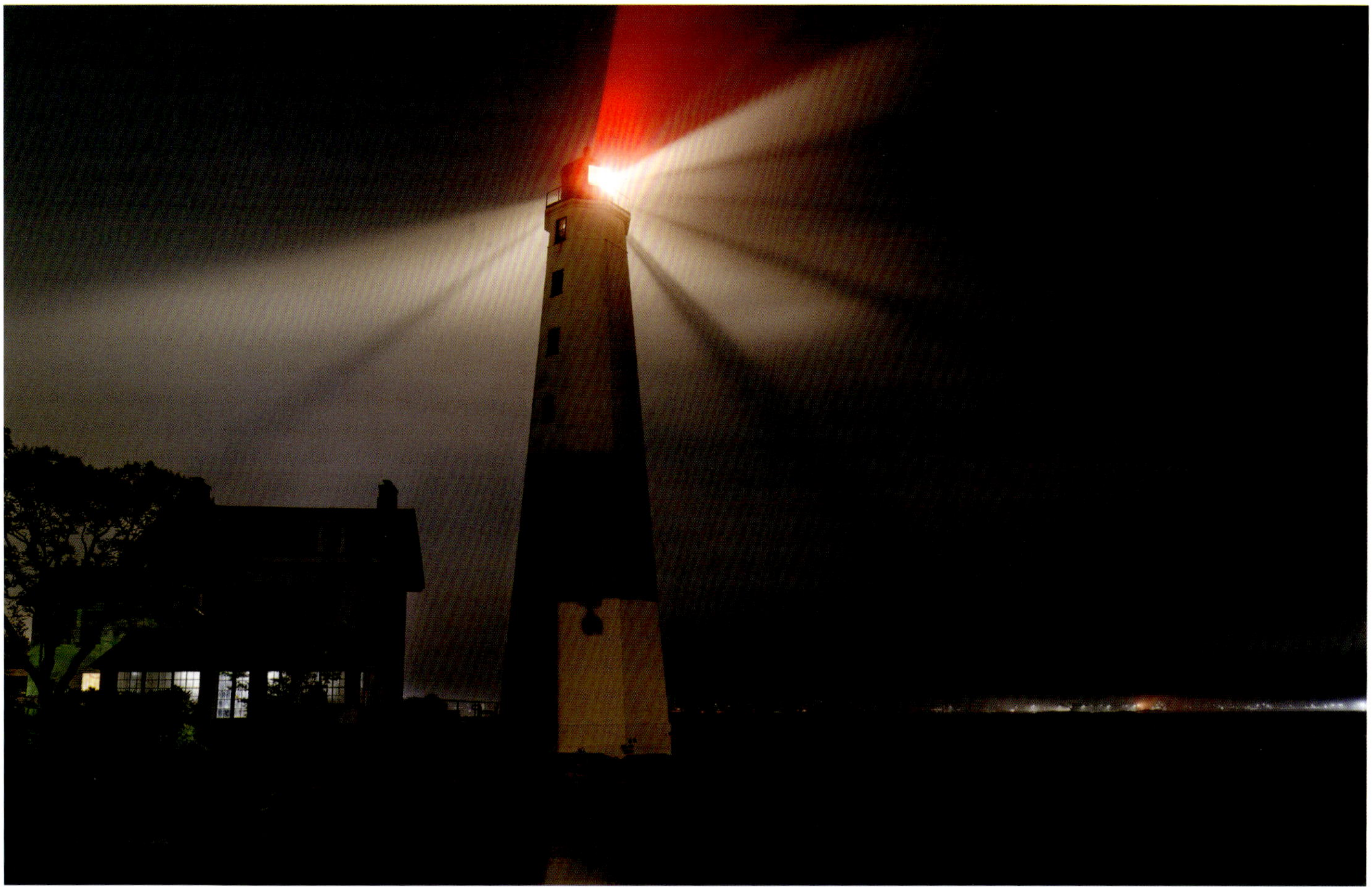

Title: New London Ledge Lighthouse | **Client:** Self-initiated

DAVID WESTPHAL

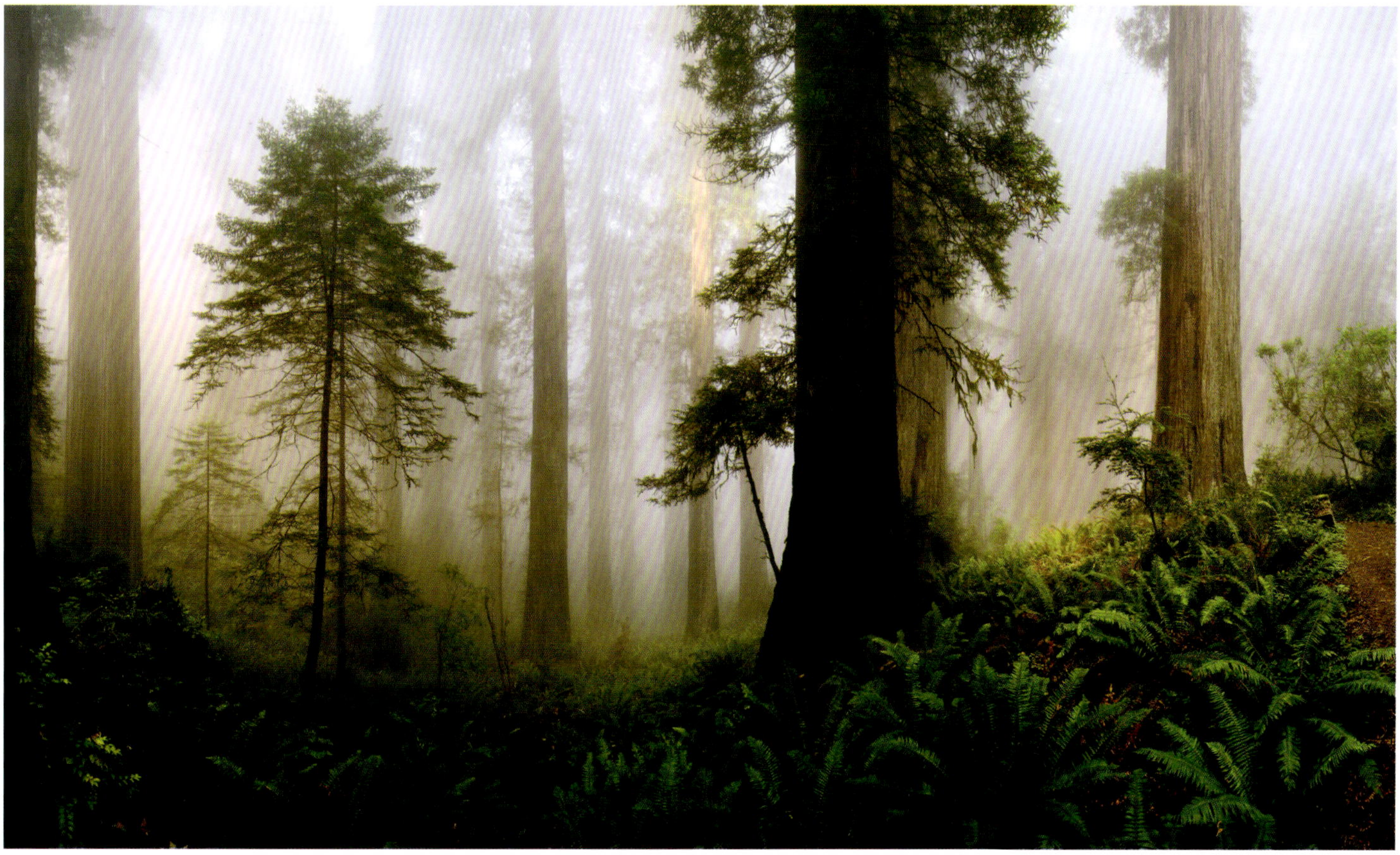

Title: Redwoods: Atmosphere | **Client:** Self-initiated

JIM BRENNAN

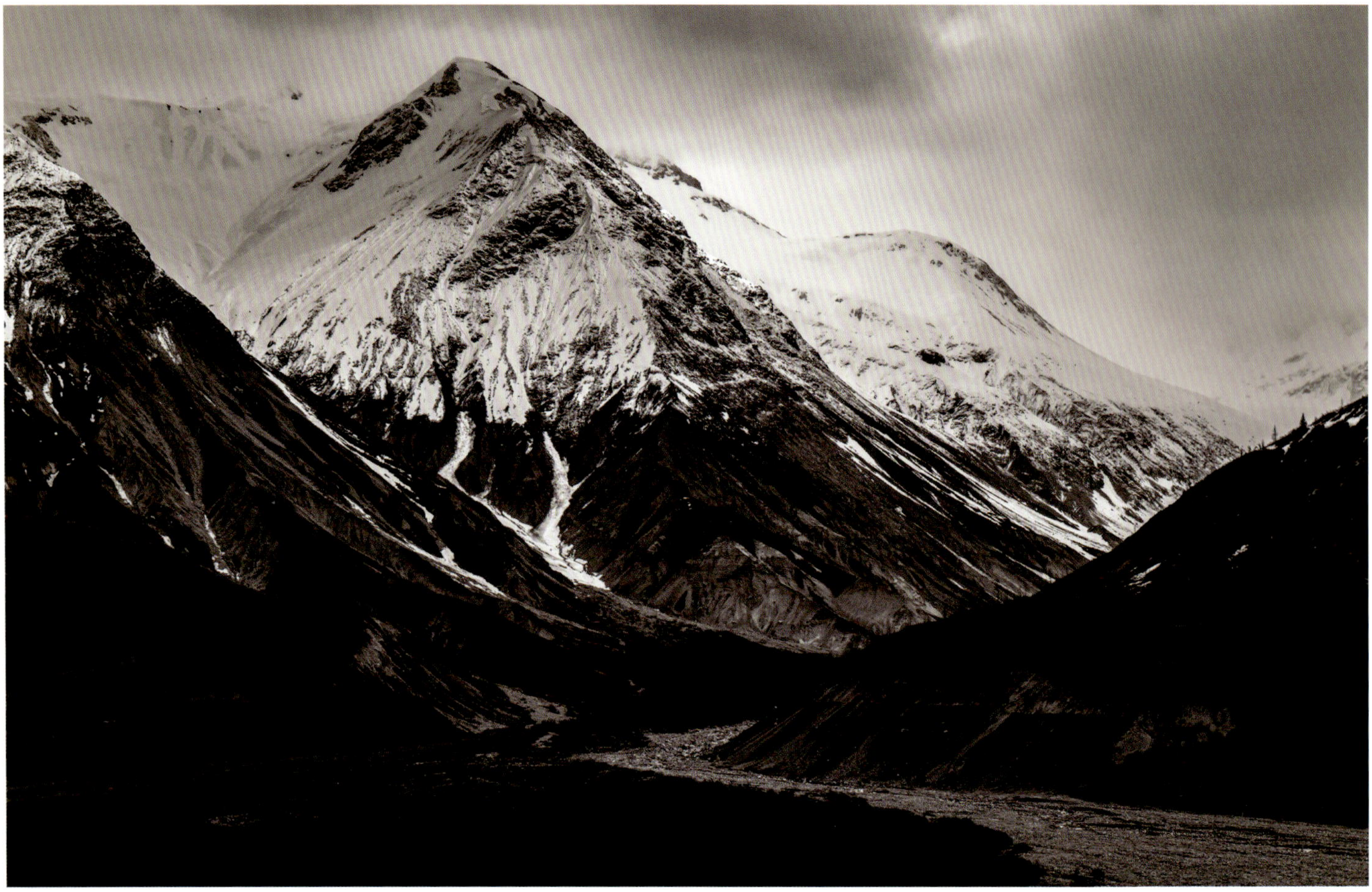

Title: Alaska Climate ChangED | **Client:** Self-initiated

MIKE BASSE

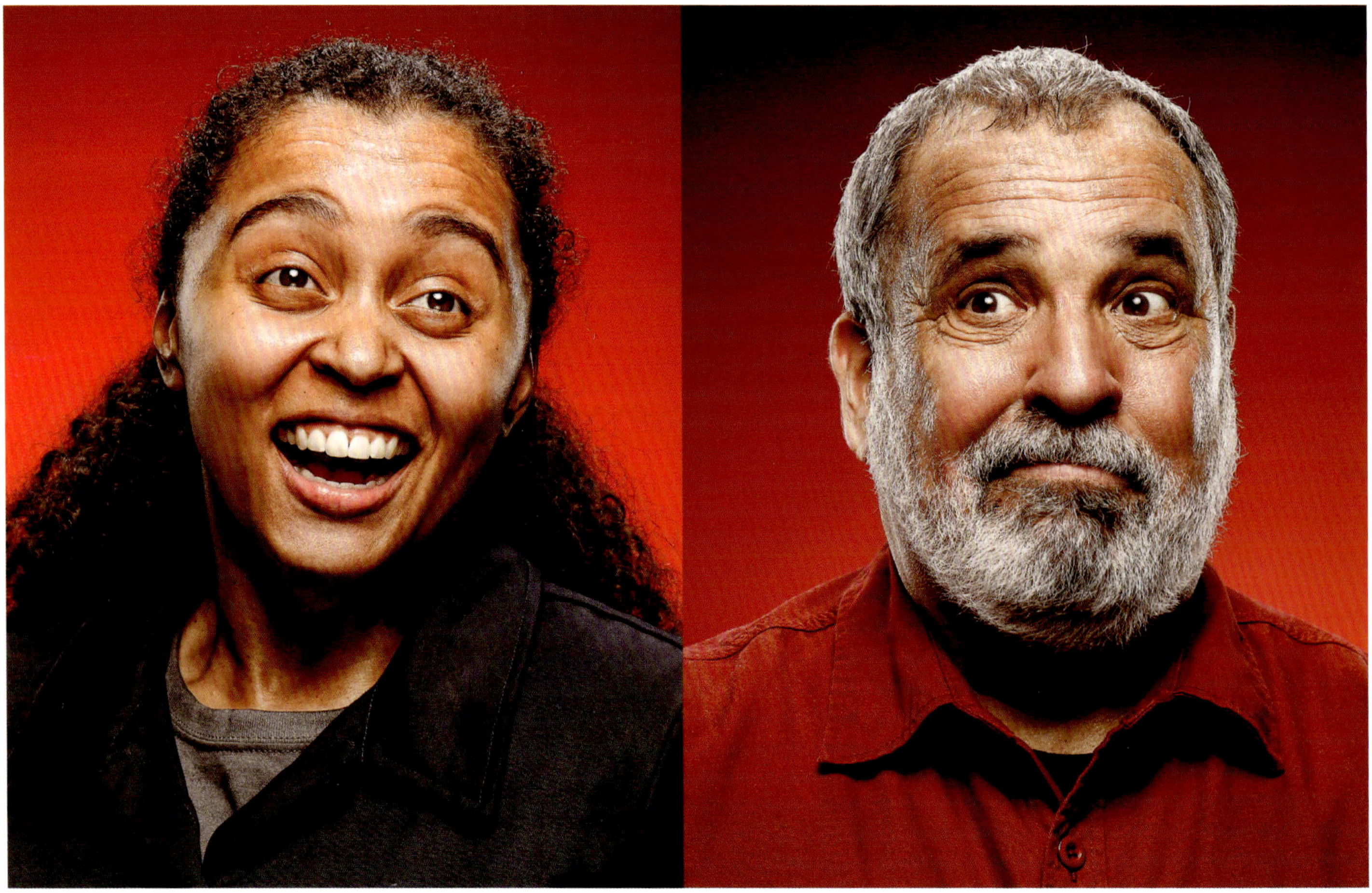

Title: Joy of Techs | **Client:** Snap-on Diagnostics

YICHEN WANG

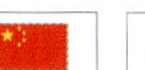

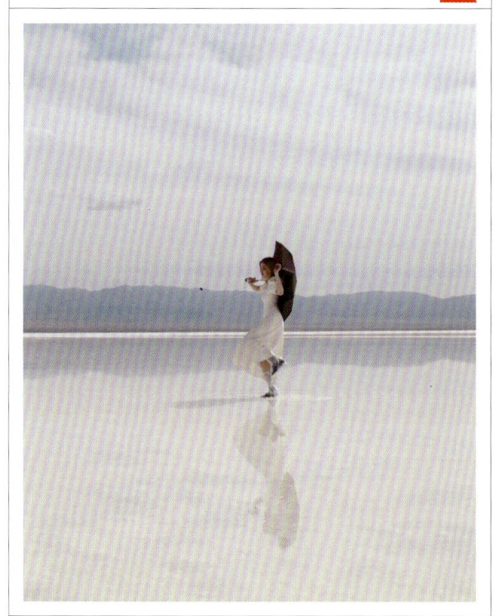

Title: Dance | **Client:** Self-initiated

MICHAEL WINOKUR

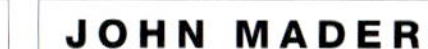

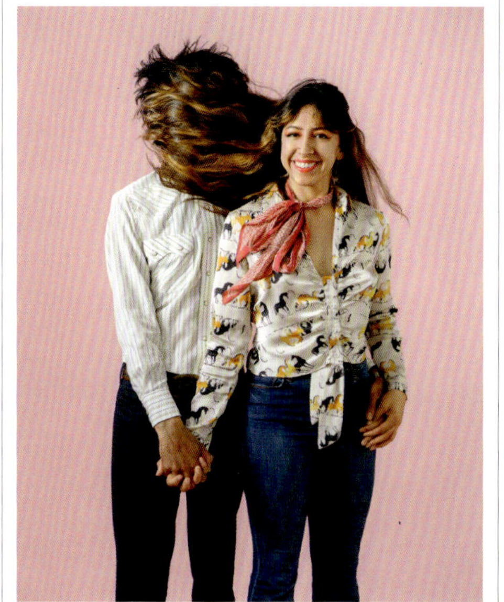

Title: Good Hair Day | **Client:** Self-initiated

JOHN MADERE

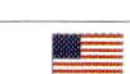

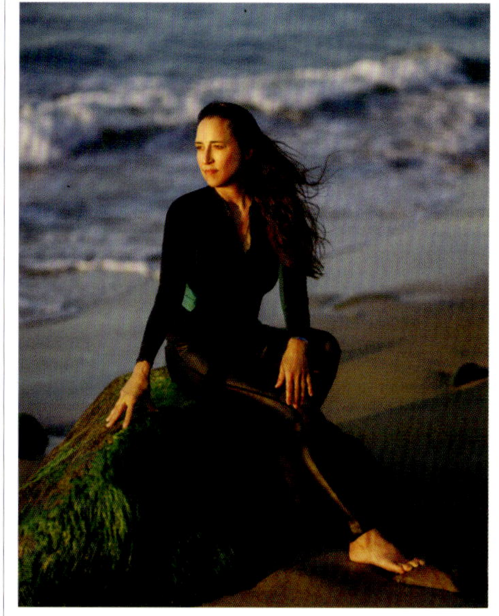

Title: Katherine | **Client:** Self-initiated

CRAIG BROMLEY

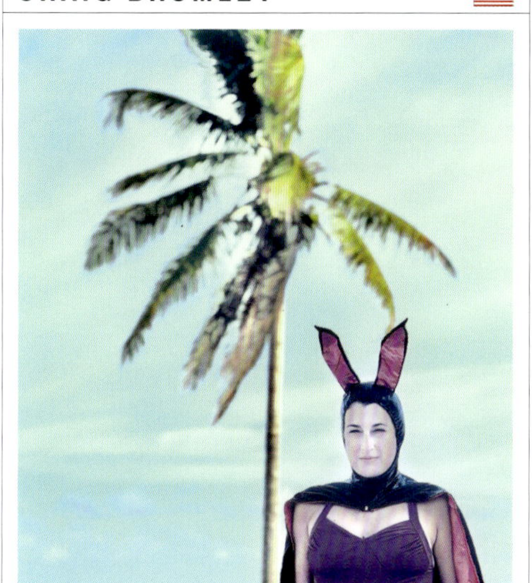

Title: Bunny Ward
Client: Bunny Ward

ARIEL FREANER

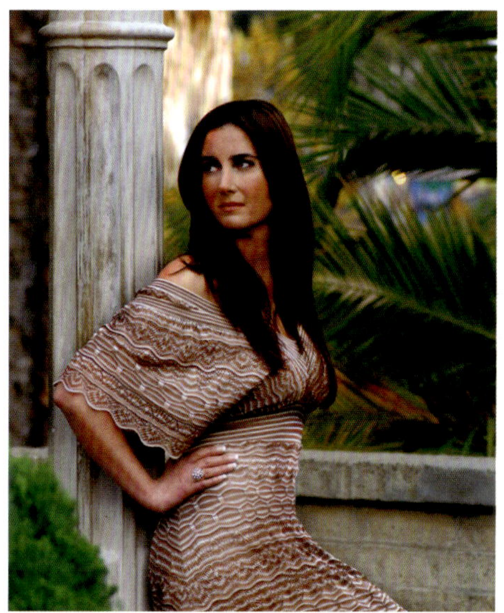

Title: Espy in Balboa Park
Clients: ESPY, Esperanza Jimenez

SAVANNAH COLL. OF ART & DESIGN

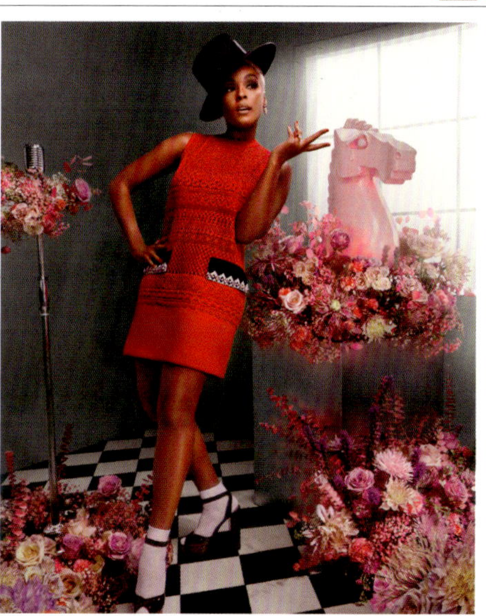

Title: Janelle Monae
Client: Savannah College of Art & Design

CRAIG BROMLEY

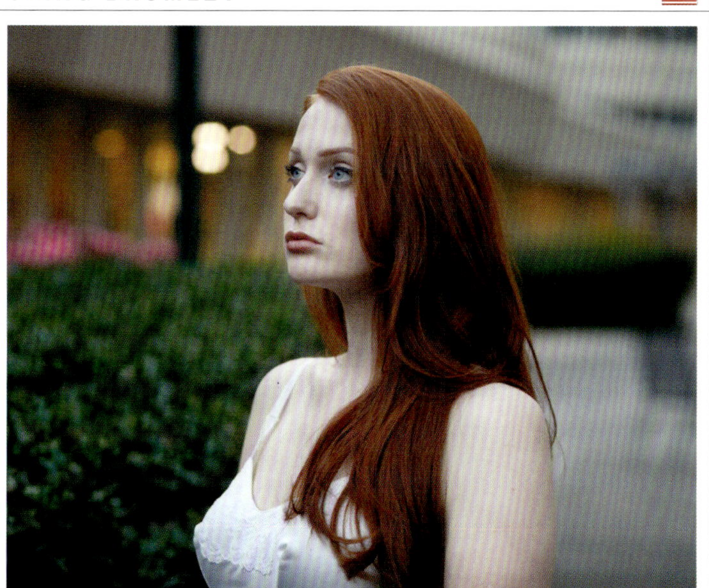

Title: Those Blue Eyes | **Client:** Actor

LAURIE FRANKEL

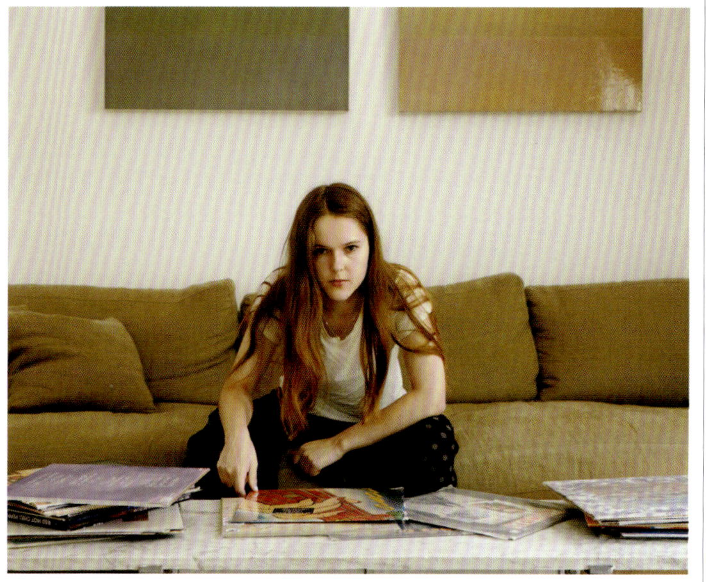

Title: Don't Mess with My Vinyl | **Client:** Self-initiated

SAVANNAH COLL. OF ART & DESIGN

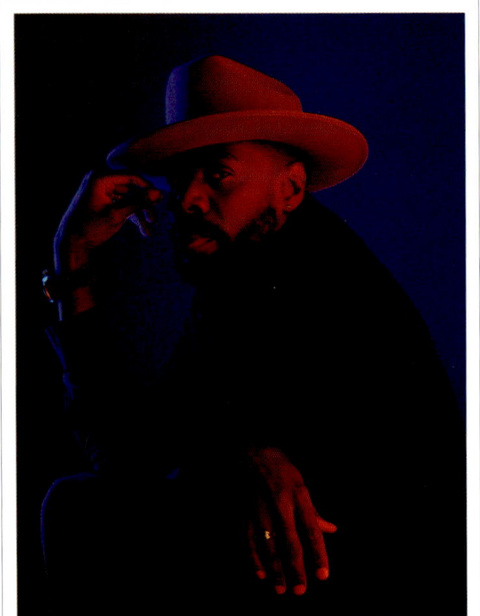

Title: Coleman Domingo
Client: Savannah College of Art & Design

MICHAEL SCHOENFELD

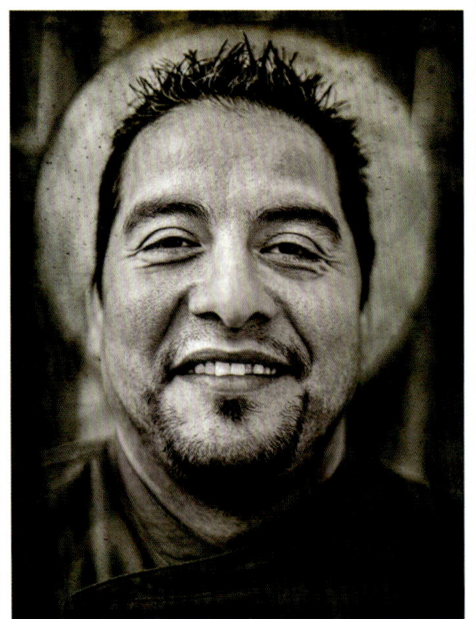

Title: Rodrigo, Vintage Restaurant
Client: Self-initiated

ROBERT SEALE

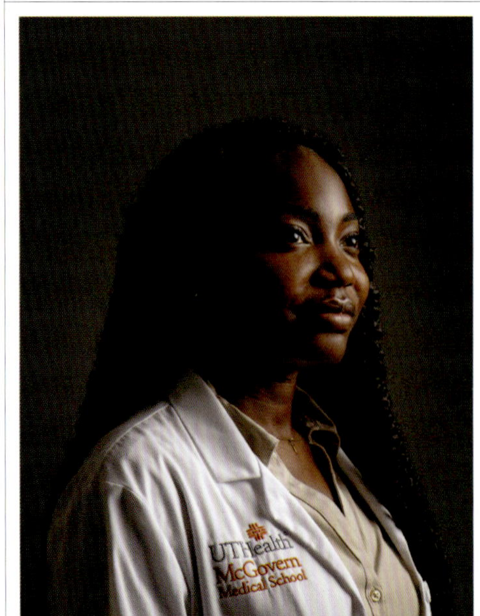

Title: Healthcare/Medical Industry Photography for Development Fundraising
Client: UTHealth Houston

ROGER MASTROIANNI

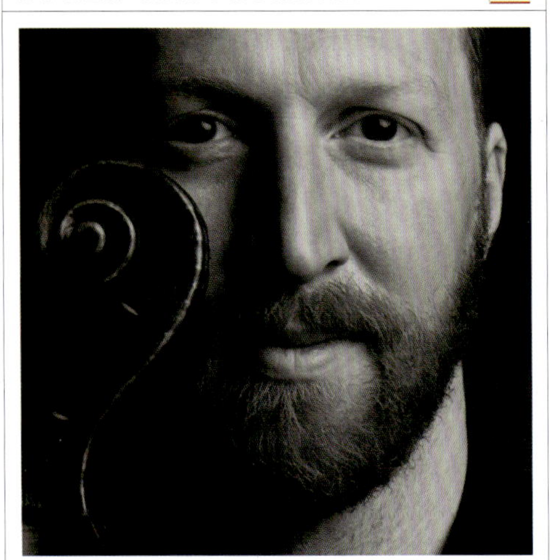

Title: Capturing Excellence: Intimate Portraits of the Cleveland Orchestra's Finest Musicians
Client: The Cleveland Orchestra

LINDSAY SIU

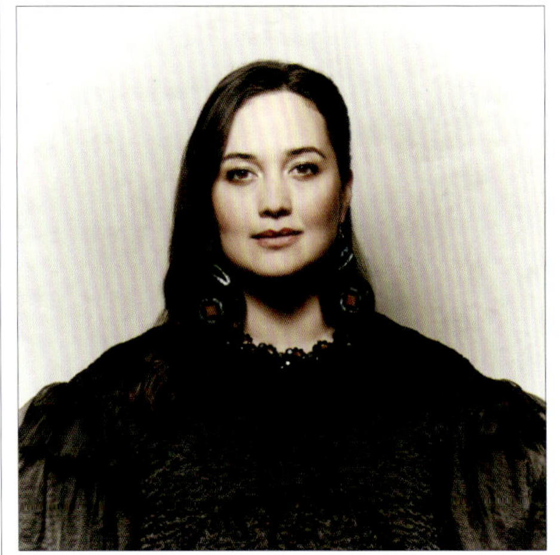

Title: Lily Gladstone Series
Client: The Hollywood Reporter

MICHAEL SCHOENFELD

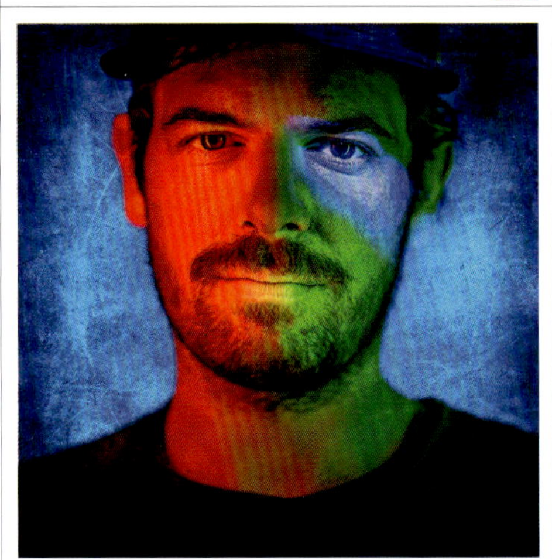

Title: Nathaniel
Client: Self-initiated

MICHAEL SCHOENFELD

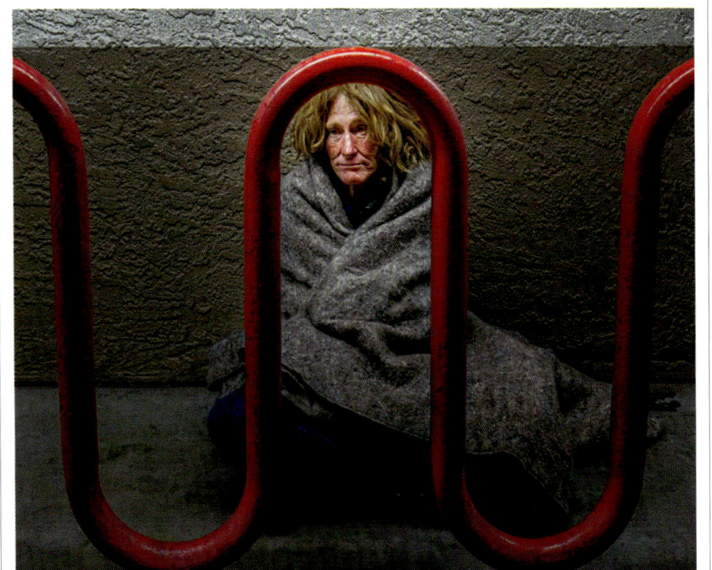

Title: Convenience Store, Tucson AZ | **Client:** Self-initiated

ARIEL FREANER

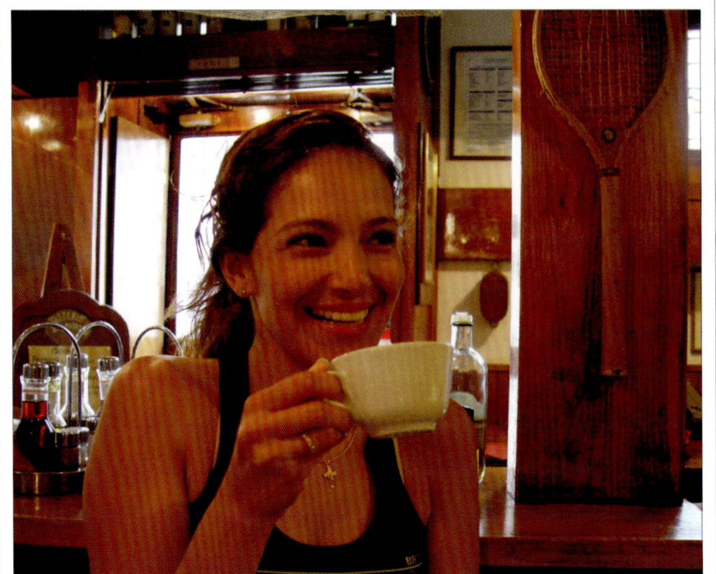

Title: Yolanda | **Client:** ZEVEN Magazine

ELLIS VENER

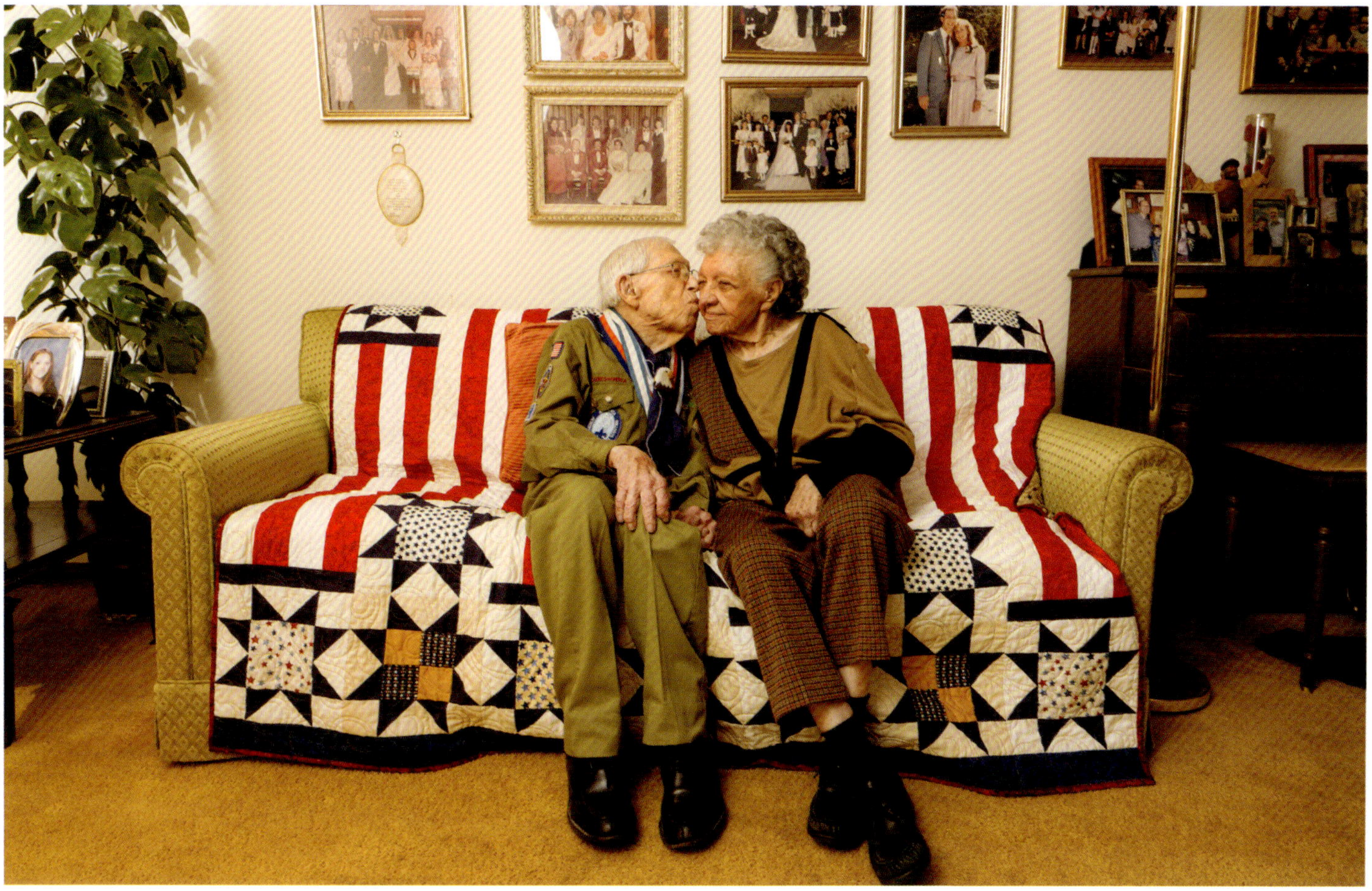

Title: Josiah and His Wife Birdie Benator at Their Home on the Occasion of His 100th Birthday, January 7, 2022, Atlanta, Georgia | **Client:** Private Commission

CRAIG CUTLER

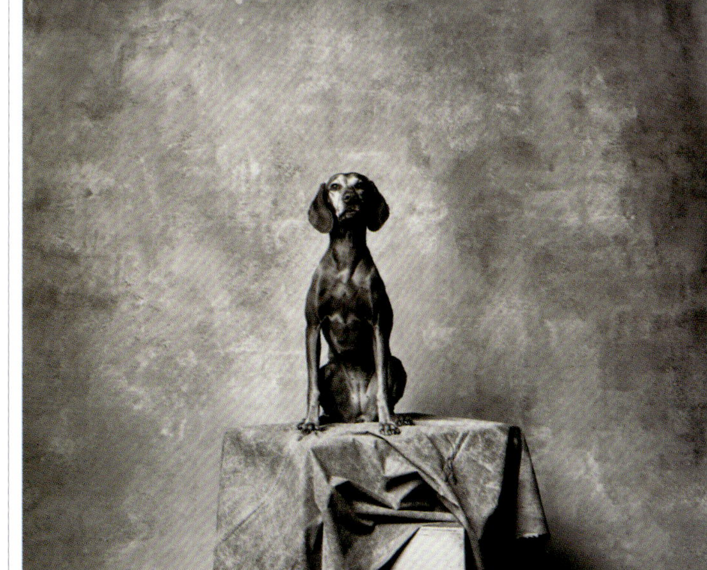

Title: Jo 1 | **Client:** Self-initiated

SAVANNAH COLLEGE OF ART & DESIGN

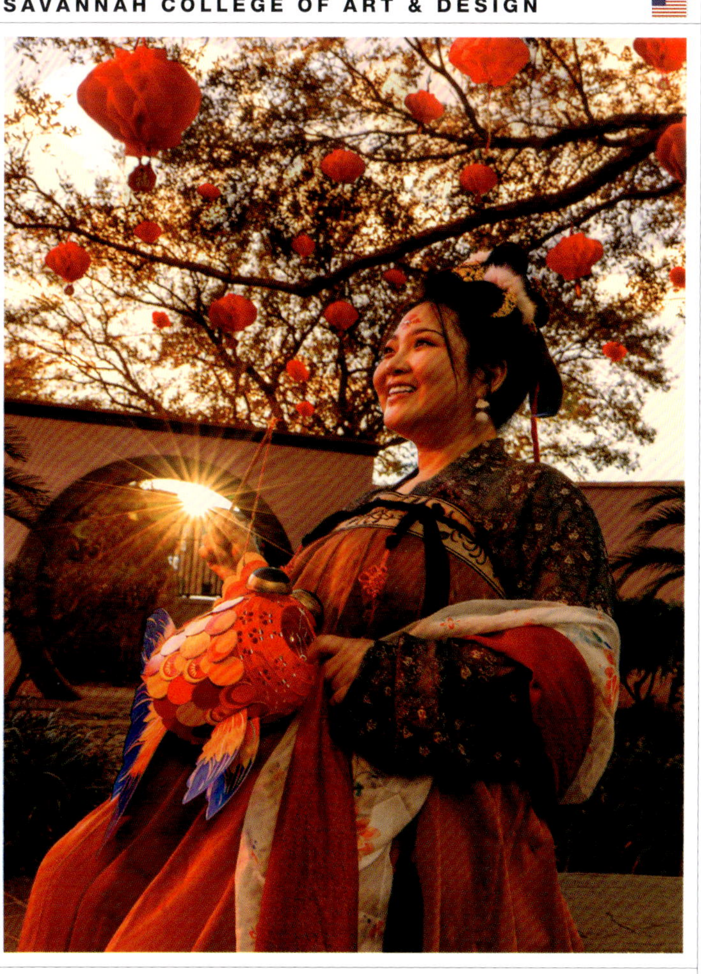

Title: Chinese New Year | **Client:** Savannah College of Art & Design

LINDSAY SIU

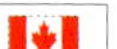

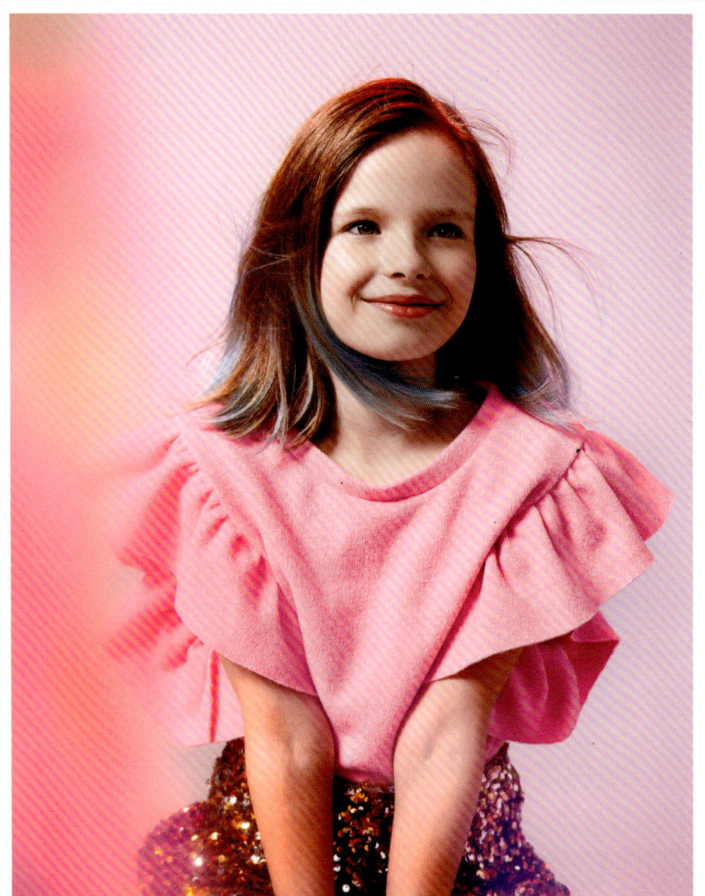

Title: The Future is Female | **Client:** Self-initiated

LAURIE FRANKEL

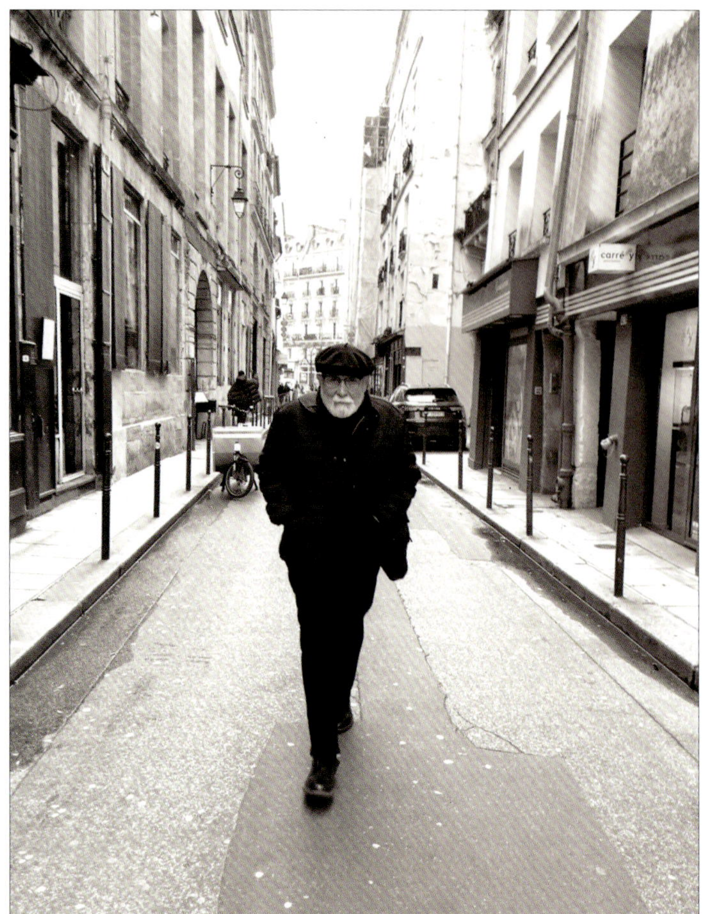

Title: Street Professor | **Client:** Self-initiated

SAVANNAH COLLEGE OF ART & DESIGN

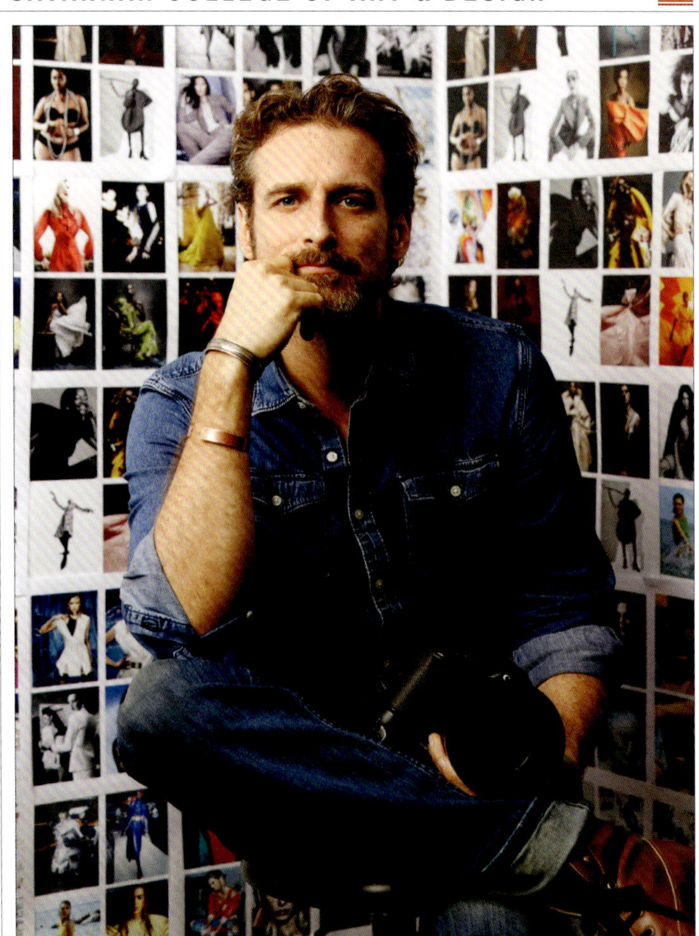

Title: Alexi Lubomirski | **Client:** Savannah College of Art & Design

SAVANNAH COLLEGE OF ART & DESIGN

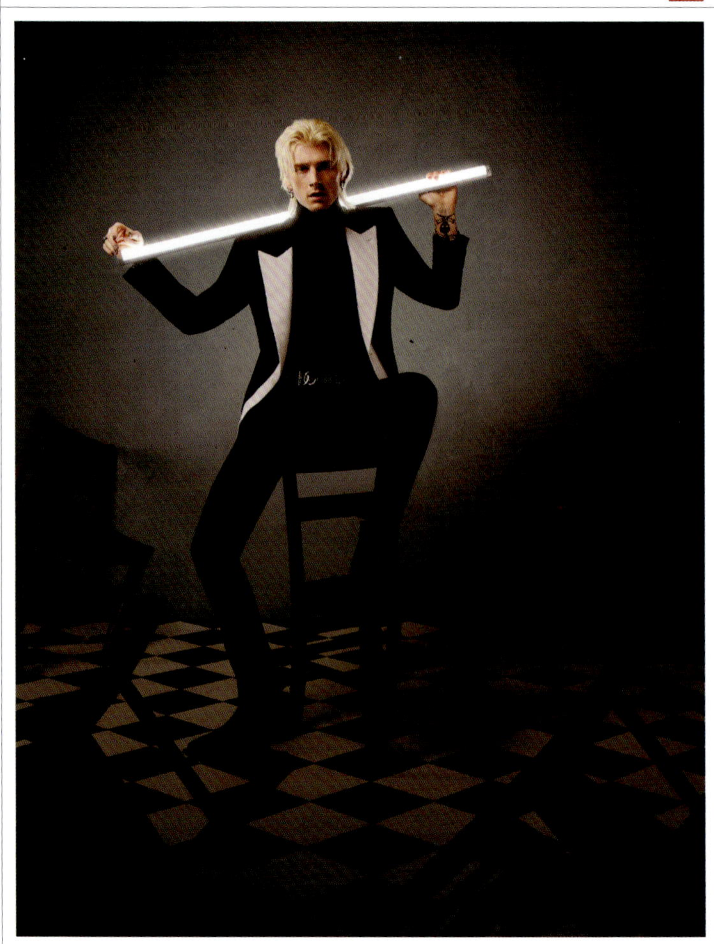

Title: Colson Baker | **Client:** Savannah College of Art & Design

TADD MYERS

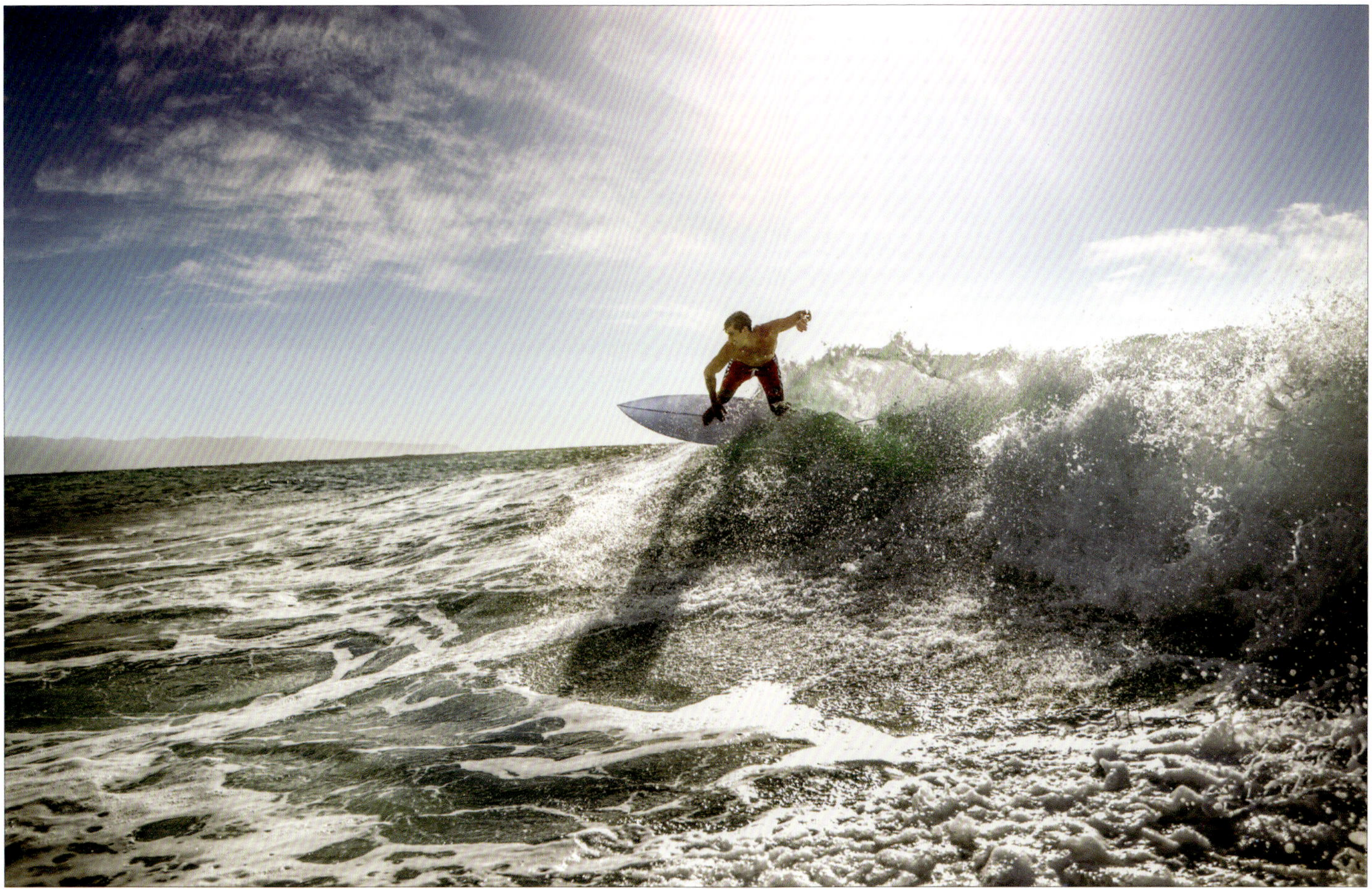

Title: Orthofix - Patient Profile - Surfer | Client: Orthofix Medical Devices

ERIC MELZER

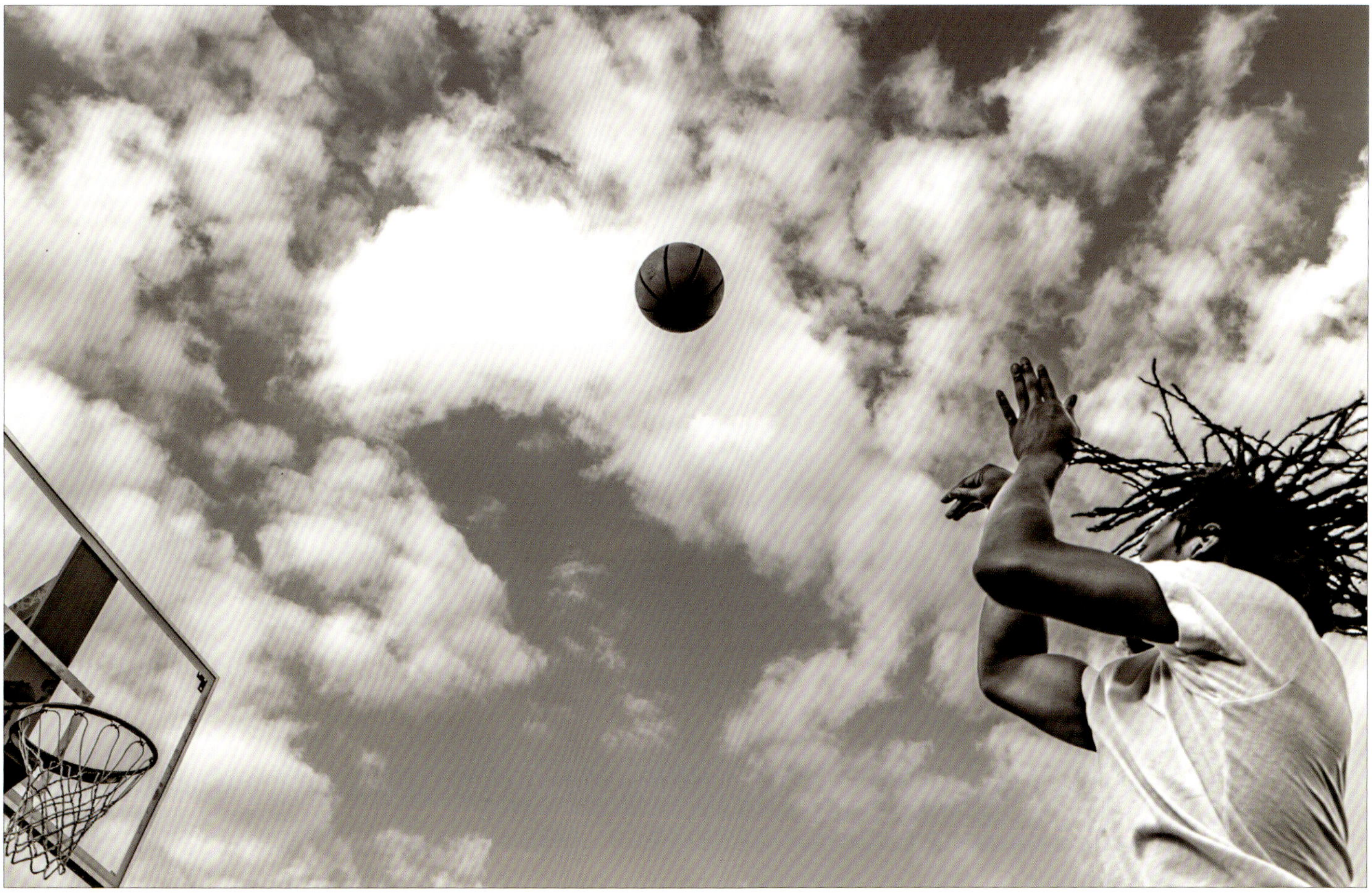

Title: Hoopin' | Client: The Play Project

PATRICK MOLNAR

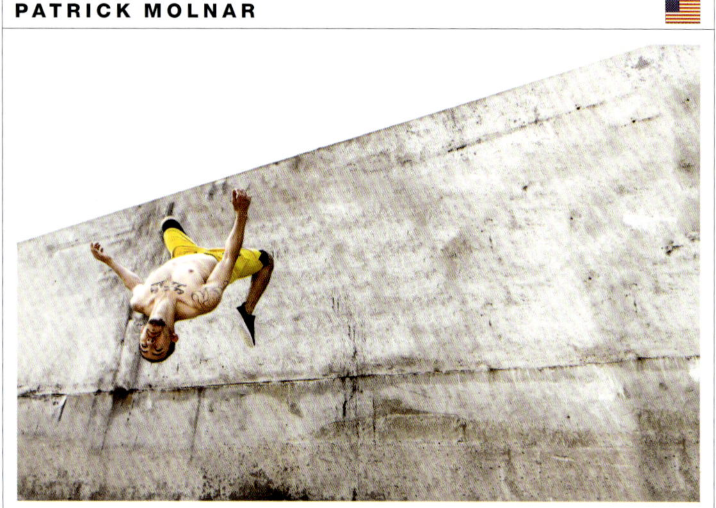

Title: Stunt #1 | **Client:** Self-initiated

PATRICK MOLNAR

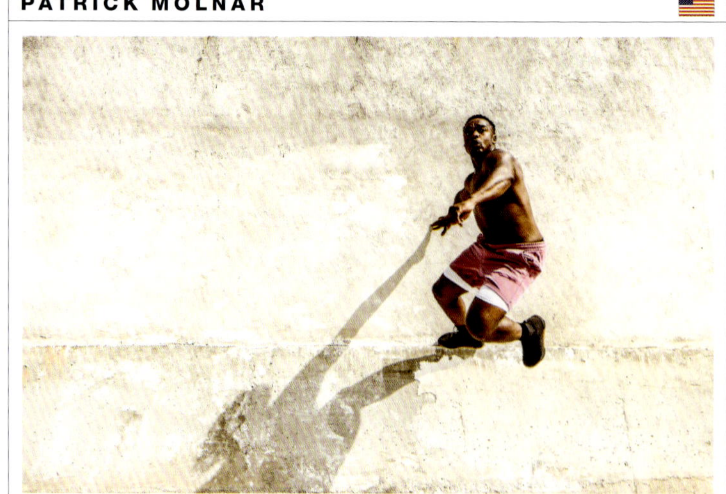

Title: Stunt #3 | **Client:** Self-initiated

PATRICK MOLNAR

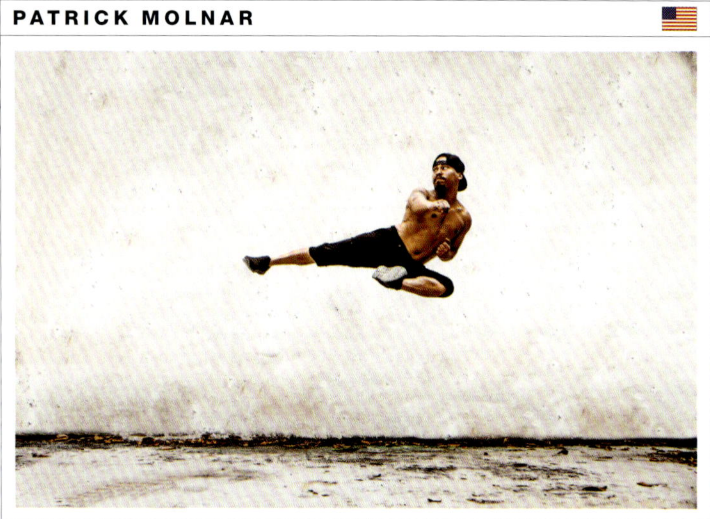

Title: Stunt #5 | **Client:** Self-initiated

PATRICK MOLNAR

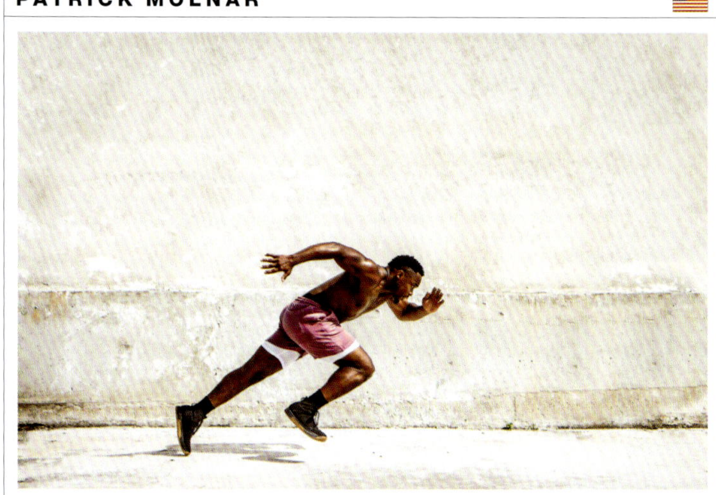

Title: Stunt #4 | **Client:** Self-initiated

JARED LEEDS

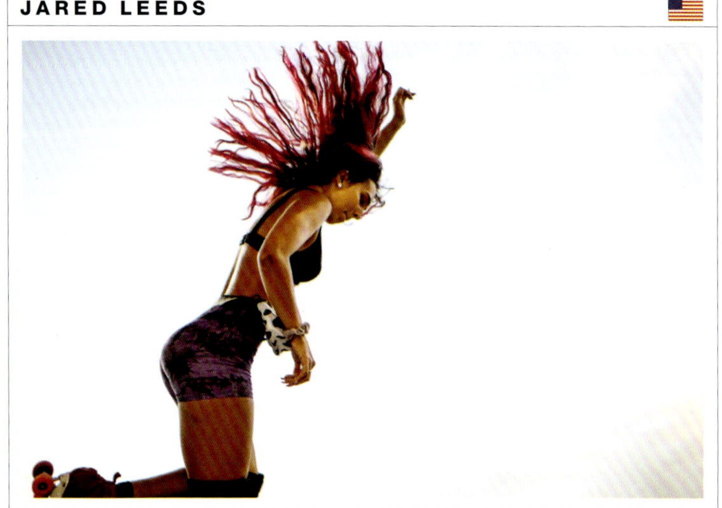

Title: Alexis and Enrique | **Client:** Self-initiated

ERIC MELZER

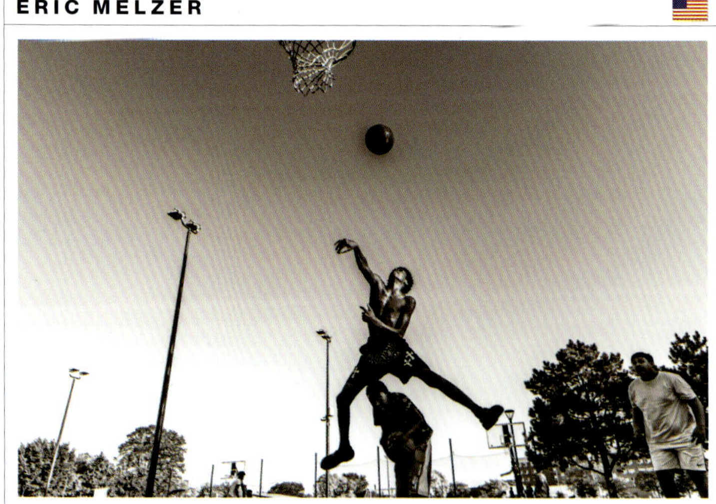

Title: Leap Frog | **Client:** The Play Project

BRANDON TUSHKOWSKI

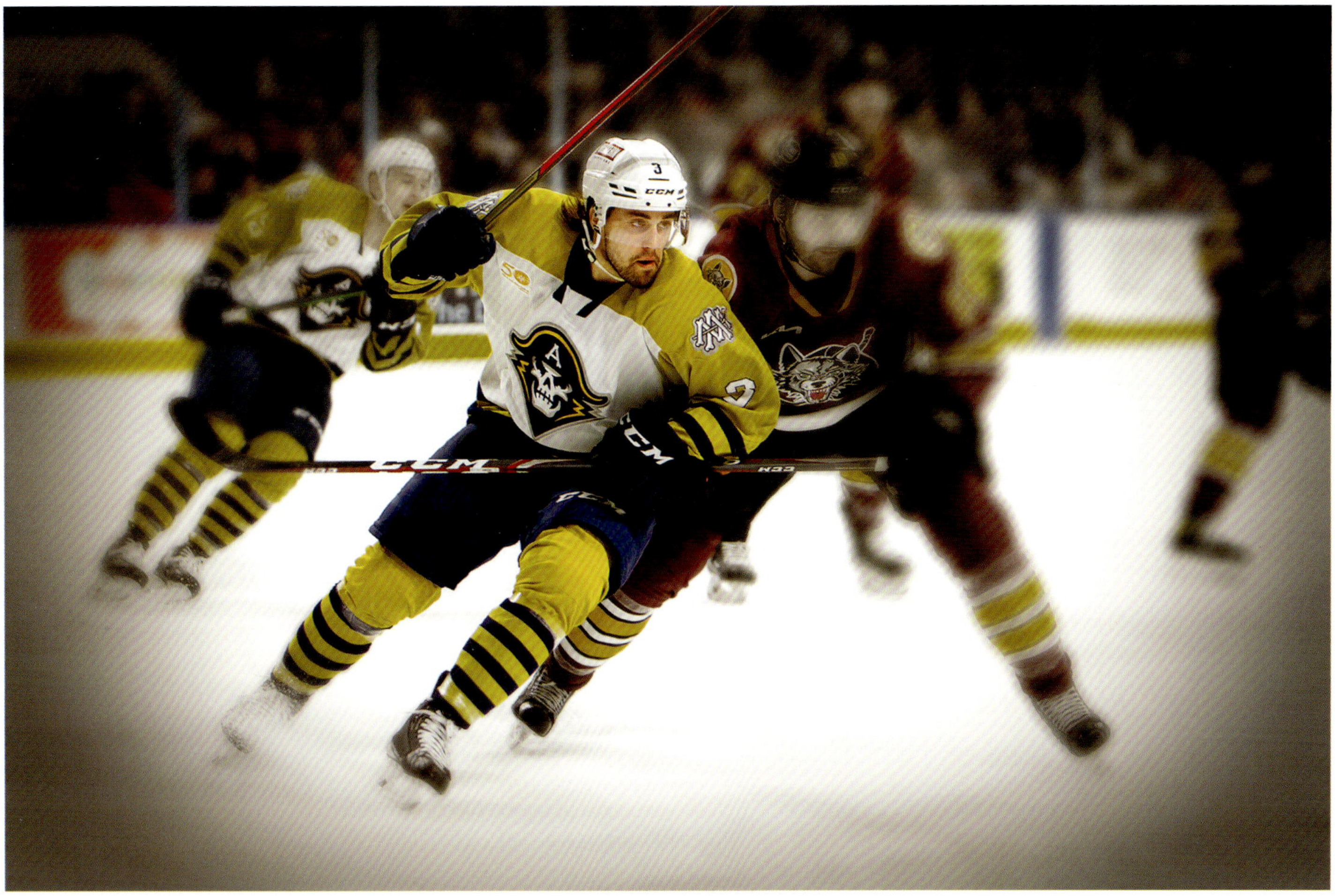

Title: Milwaukee Admirals/SOWI Program | **Client:** Milwaukee Admirals

GRANT GUNDERSON

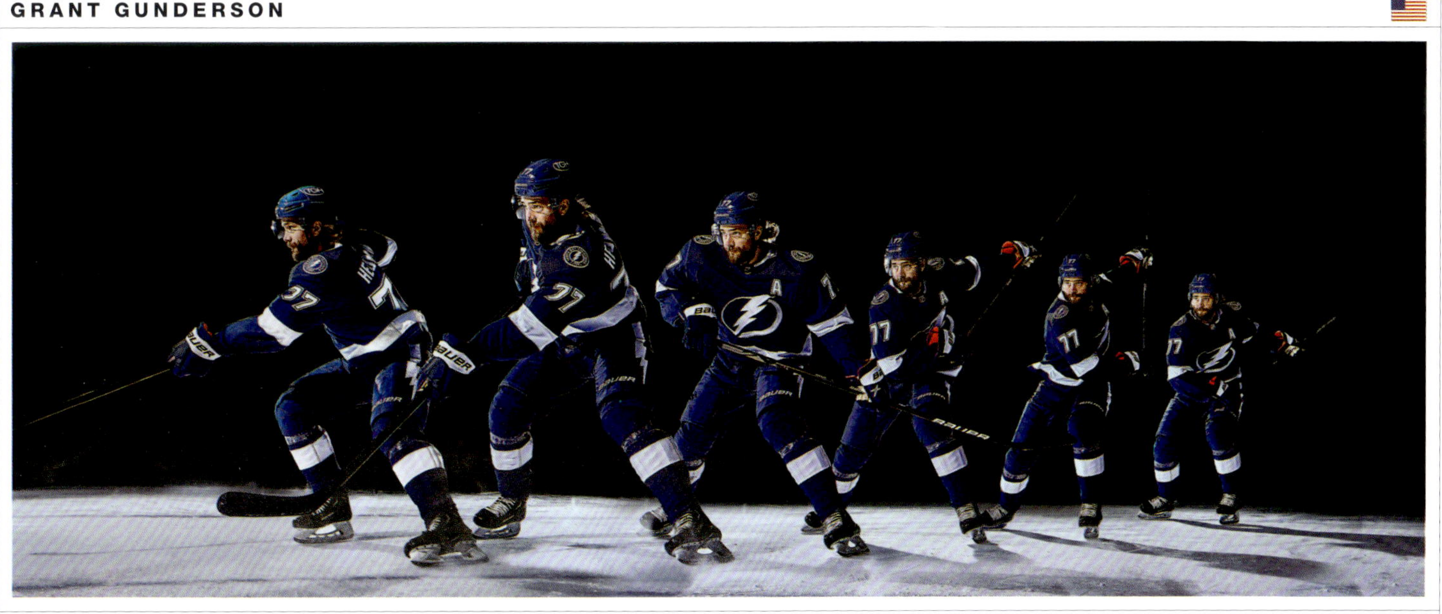

Title: 23/24 Season Motion | **Client:** Tampa Bay Lightning

ERIC MELZER

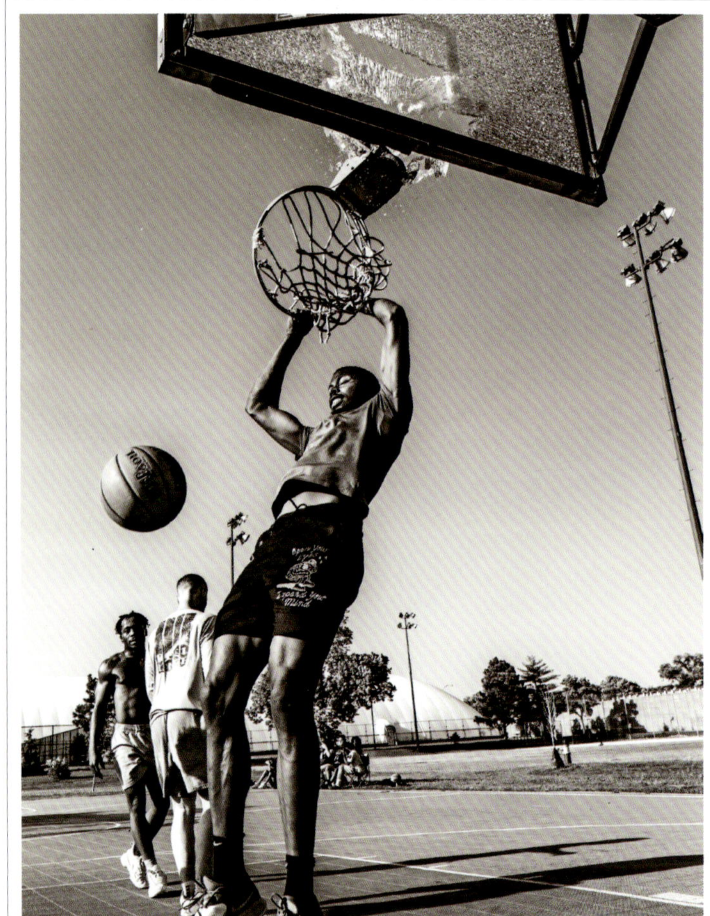

Title: Shattered | **Client:** The Play Project

CRAIG CUTLER

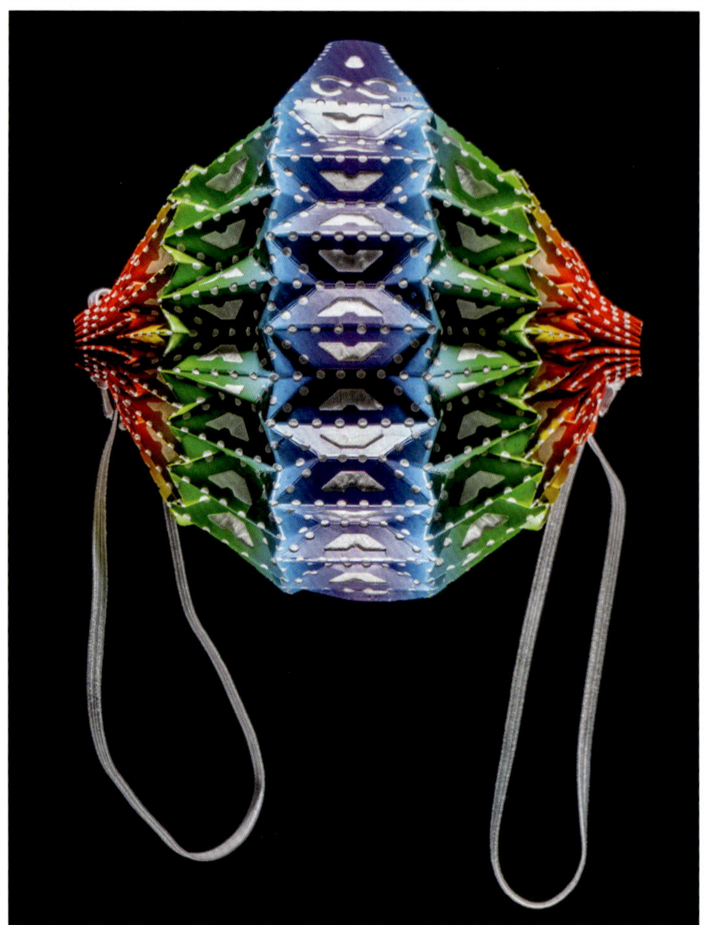

Title: Origami Masks | **Client:** National Geographic Magazine

TAKAHIRO IGARASHI

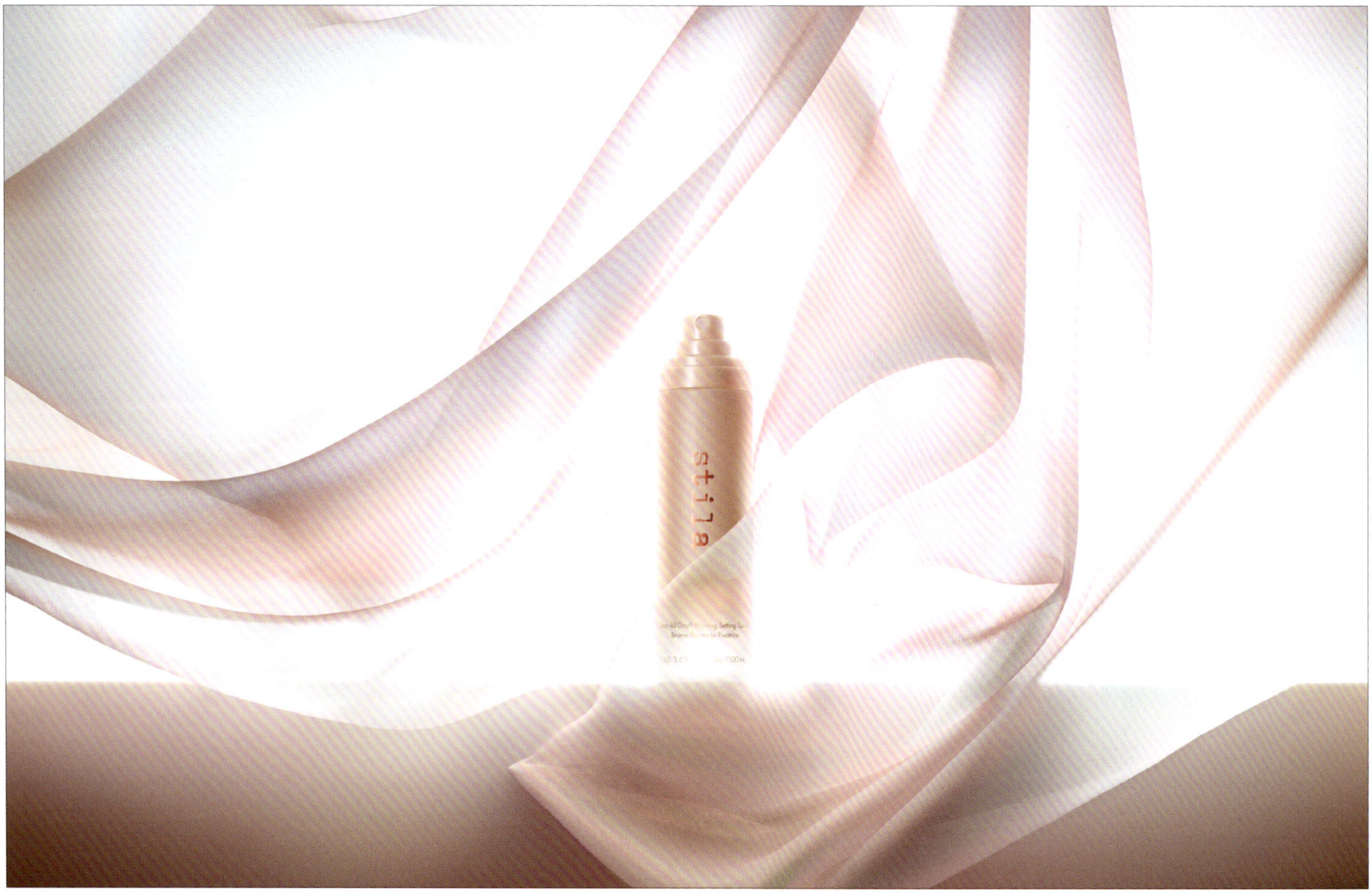

Title: Stila Sheer Radiance | **Client:** Stila Cosmetics

CRAIG CUTLER

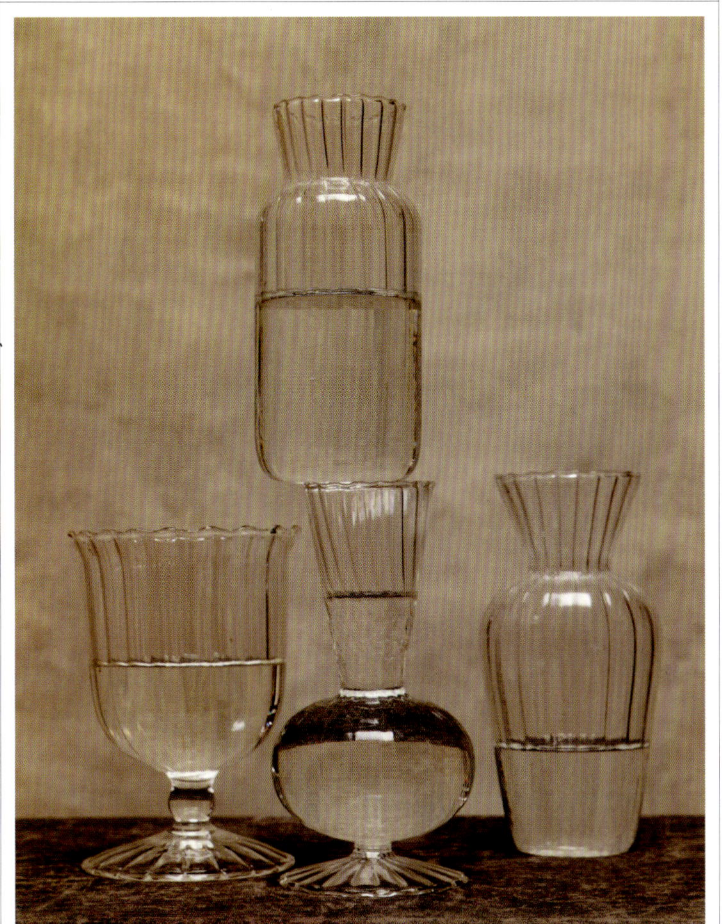

Title: Glass and Water | **Client:** Self-initiated

CRAIG CUTLER

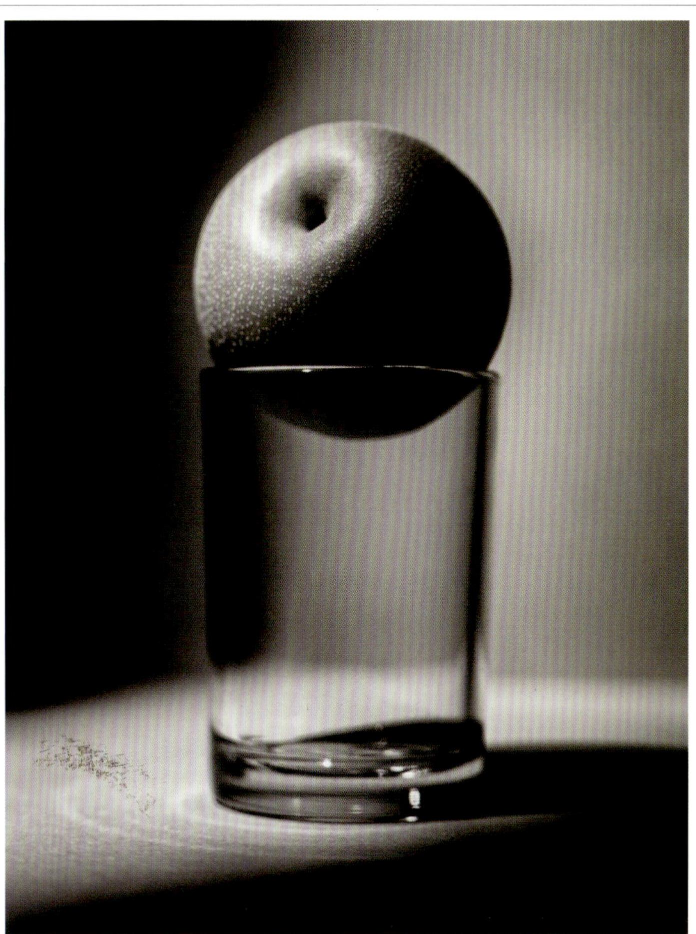

Title: Single Glass Series | **Client:** Self-initiated

LAURIE FRANKEL

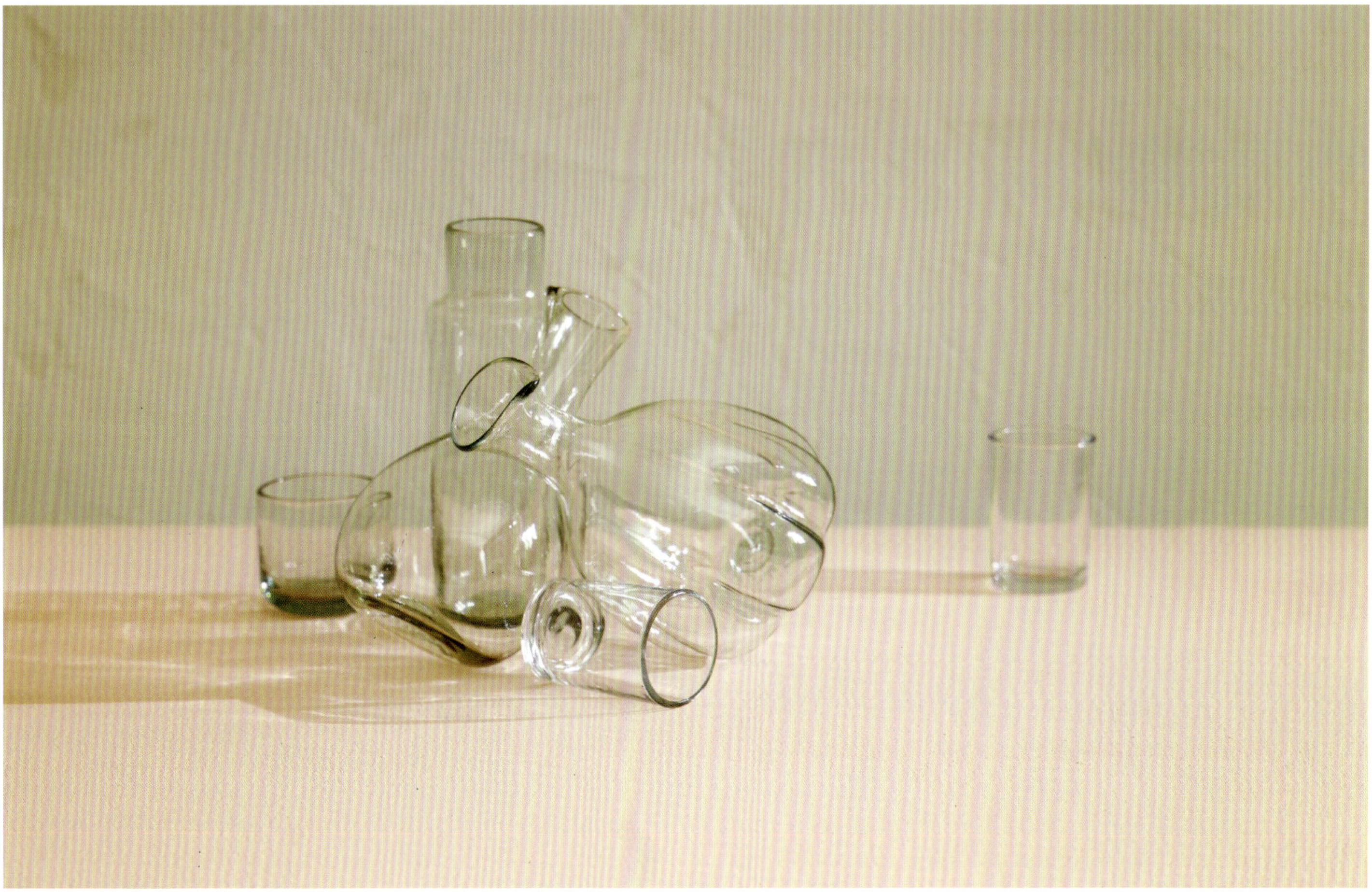

Title: Glassware at Ease | **Client:** March

NICHOLAS DUERS

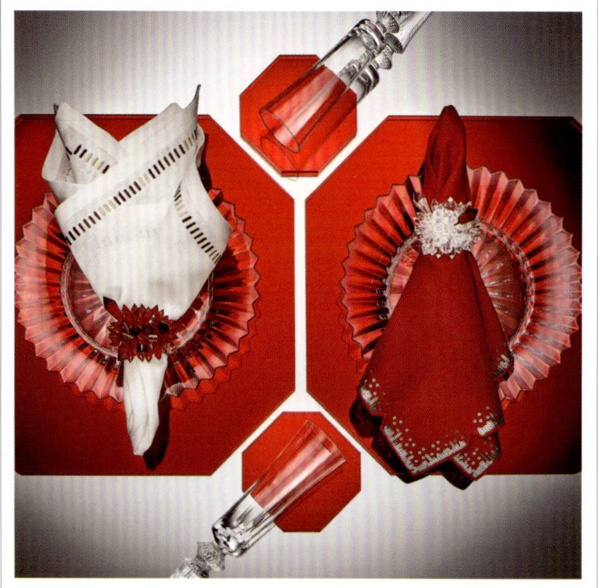

Title: Baccarat x Kim Seybert | **Clients:** Baccarat, Kim Seybert

NICHOLAS DUERS

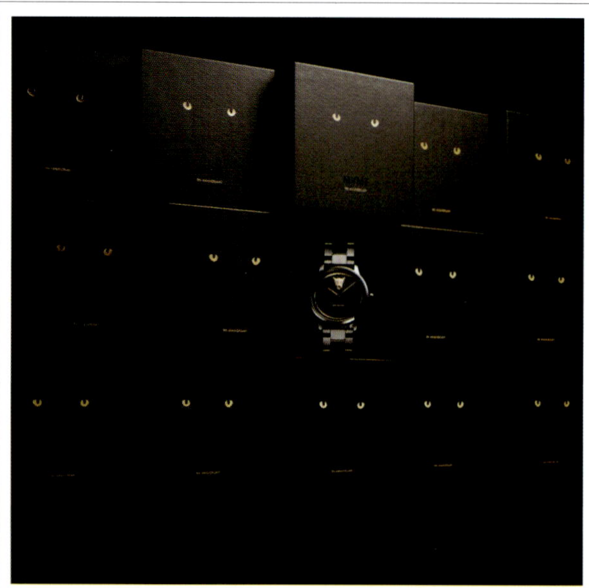

Title: MVMT 9Yr Anniversary | **Client:** MVMT

NICHOLAS DUERS

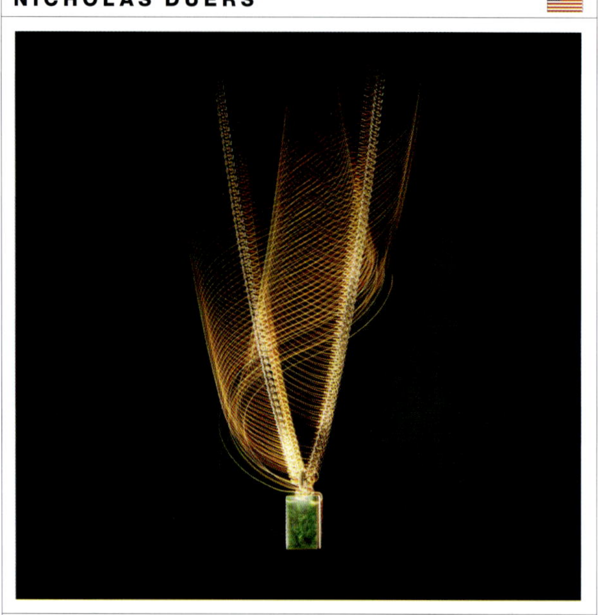

Title: MVMT x Kim Rose | **Client:** MVMT

NICHOLAS DUERS

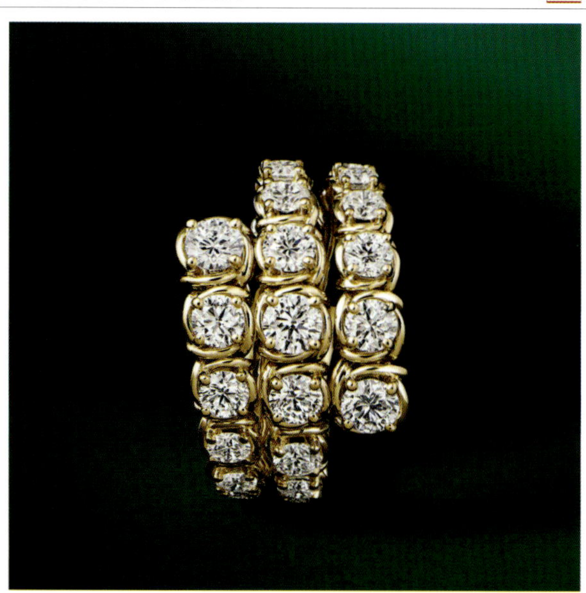

Title: ALink / 2023 Rebrand | **Client:** ALink Jewelry

NICHOLAS DUERS

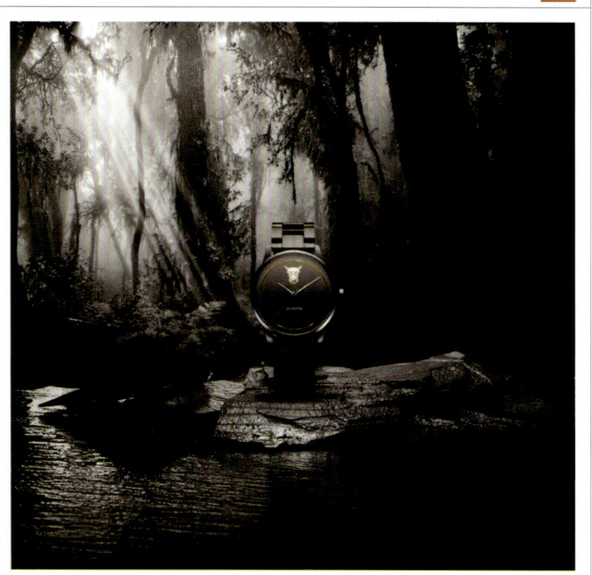

Title: MVMT 9Yr Anniversary 02
Client: MVMT

NICHOLAS DUERS

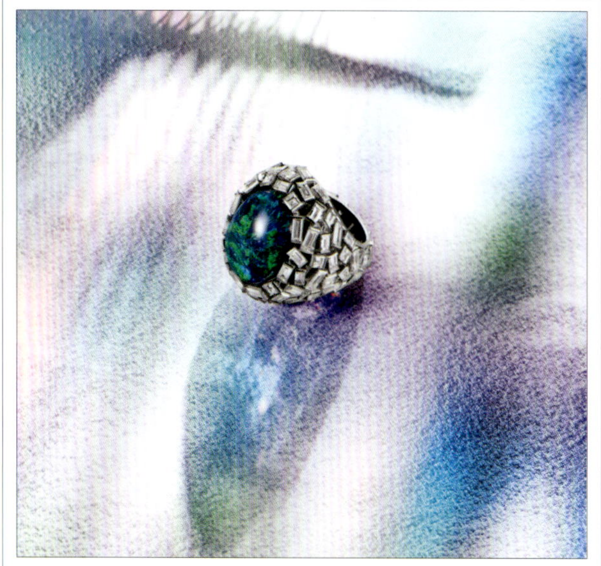

Title: Noblesse Mag x Tiffany / September 2023
Clients: Noblesse Magazine, Tiffany & Co.

ANDRIEN TRUJILLO

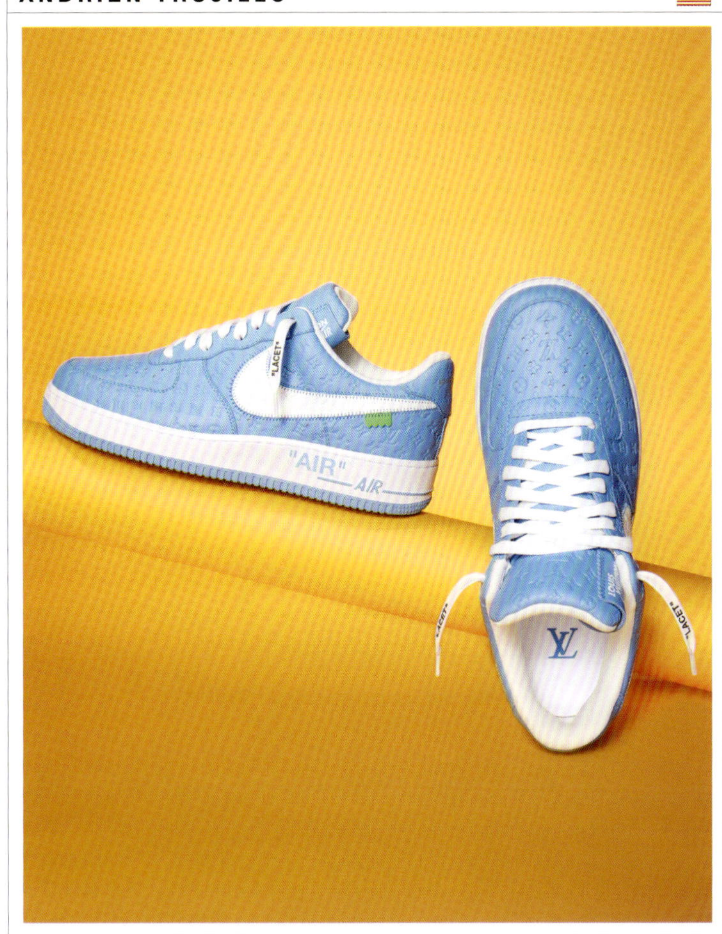

Title: Louis Vuitton x Nike Air Force 1 Low University Blue Friends and Family Virgil Abloom | **Client:** Arman Salemi

JOSEPH SARACENO

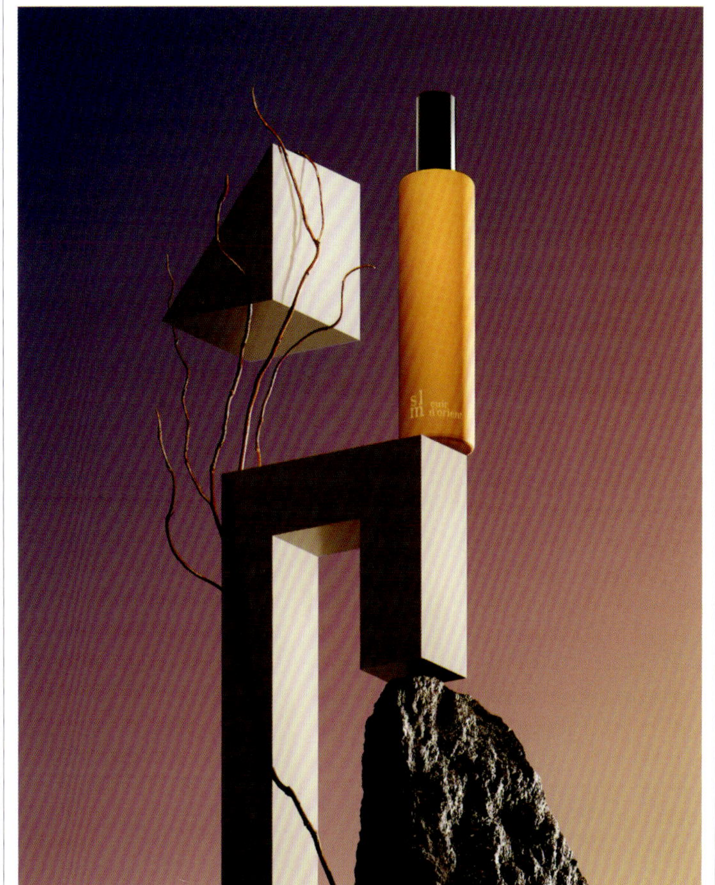

Title: Natural Balance
Client: Scentury Magazine

TAKAHIRO IGARASHI

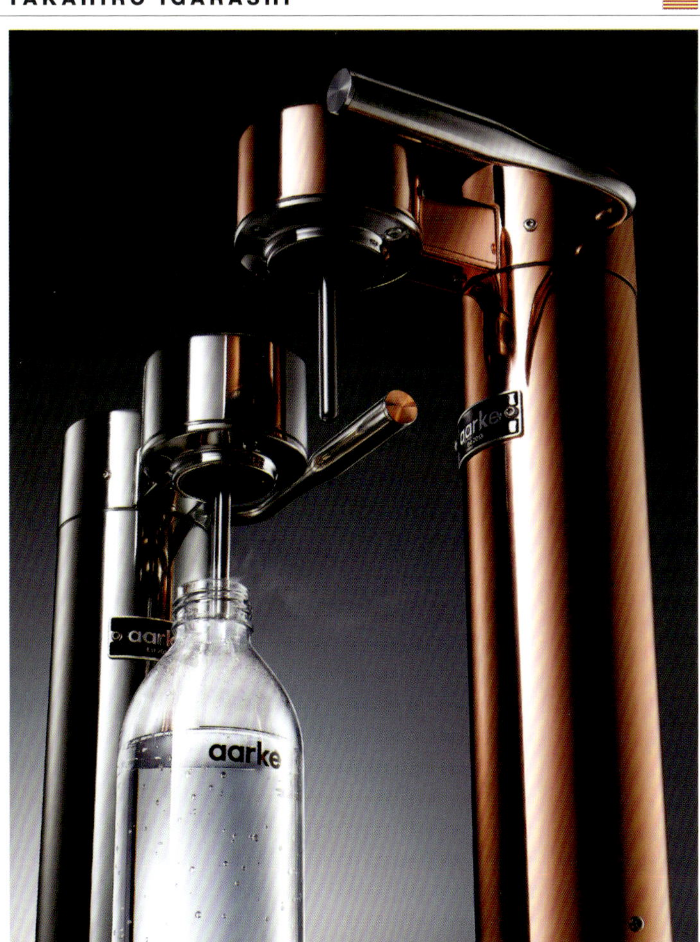

Title: Aarke Carbonator 3 Pair | **Client:** Aarke

TAKAHIRO IGARASHI

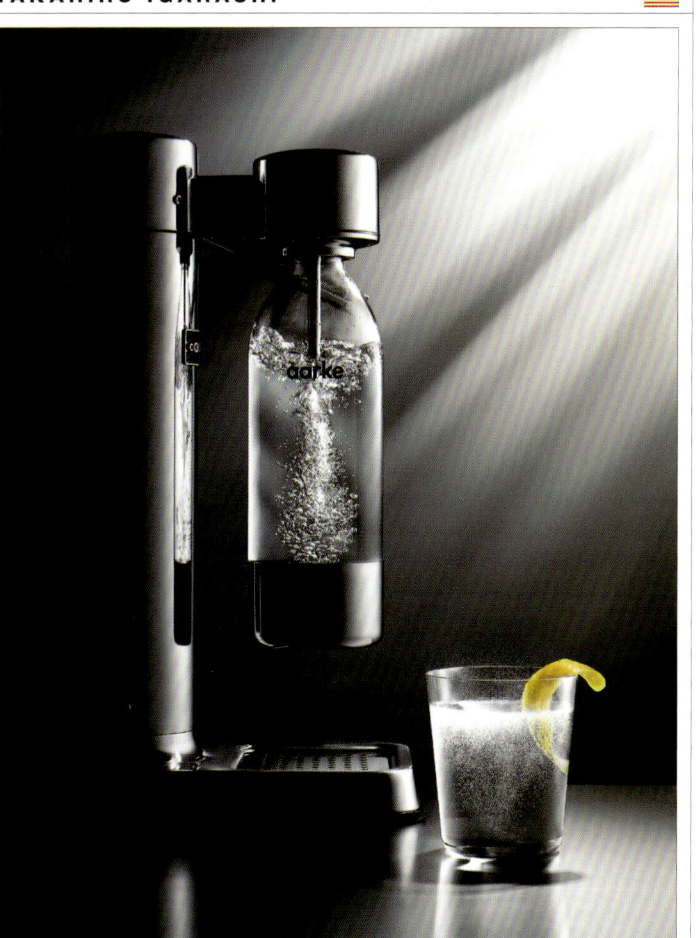

Title: Aarke Carbonator 3 Serve | **Client:** Aarke

LAURIE FRANKEL

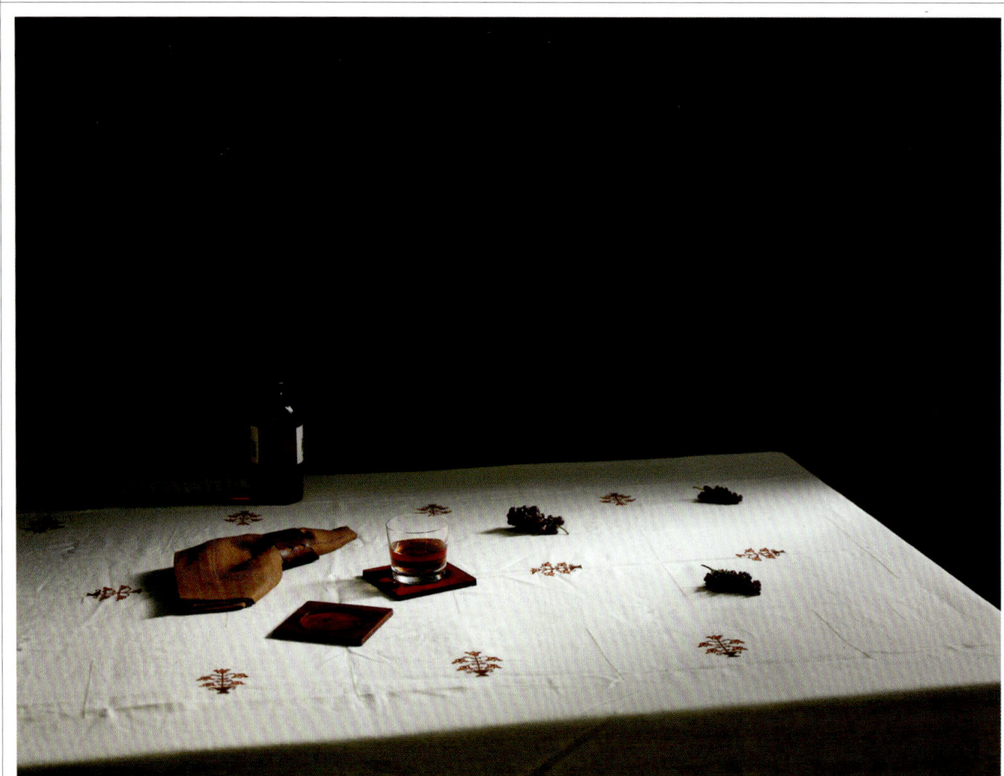

Title: Tablecloth | **Client:** March

NICHOLAS DUERS

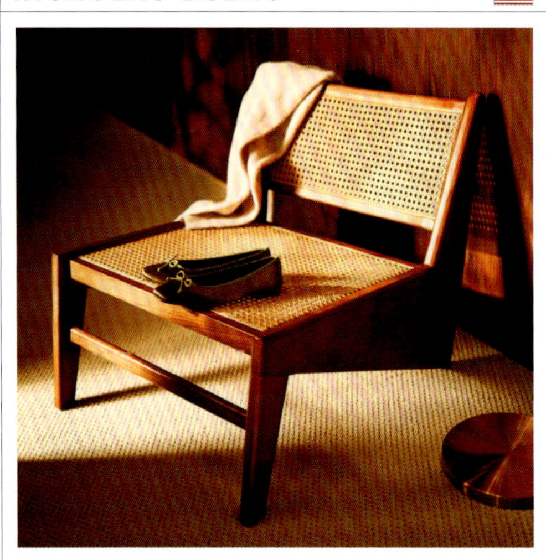

Title: Walmart / Fall23 Fashion | **Client:** Walmart

NICHOLAS DUERS

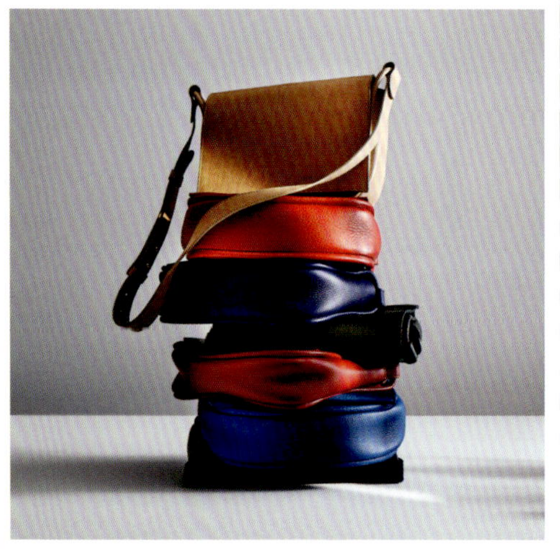

Title: NKA Workshop | **Client:** NKA Workshop

NICHOLAS DUERS

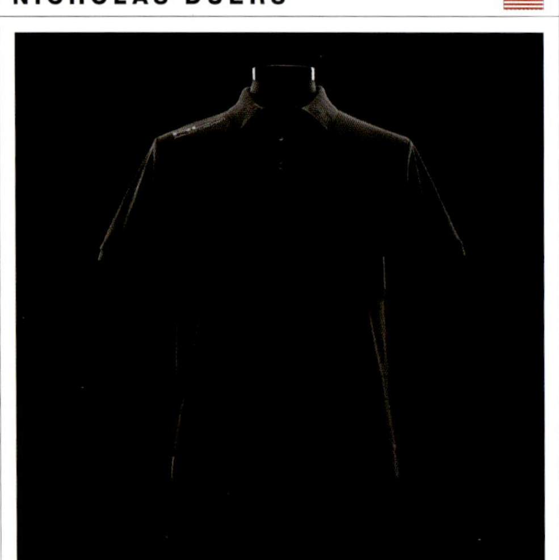

Title: RLX | **Client:** Ralph Lauren

NICHOLAS DUERS

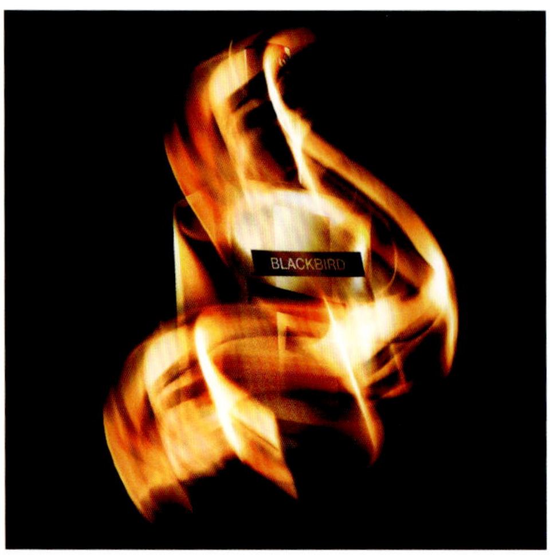

Title: Targa Fragrance | **Client:** Self-initiated

NICHOLAS DUERS

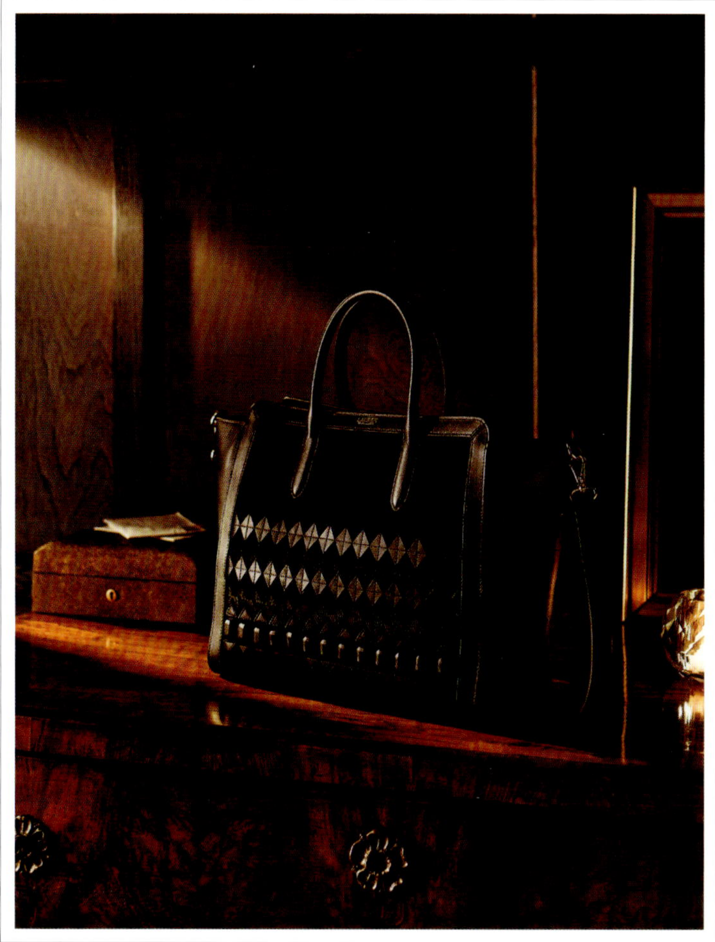

Title: Lauren Holiday 01 | **Client:** Ralph Lauren

NICHOLAS DUERS

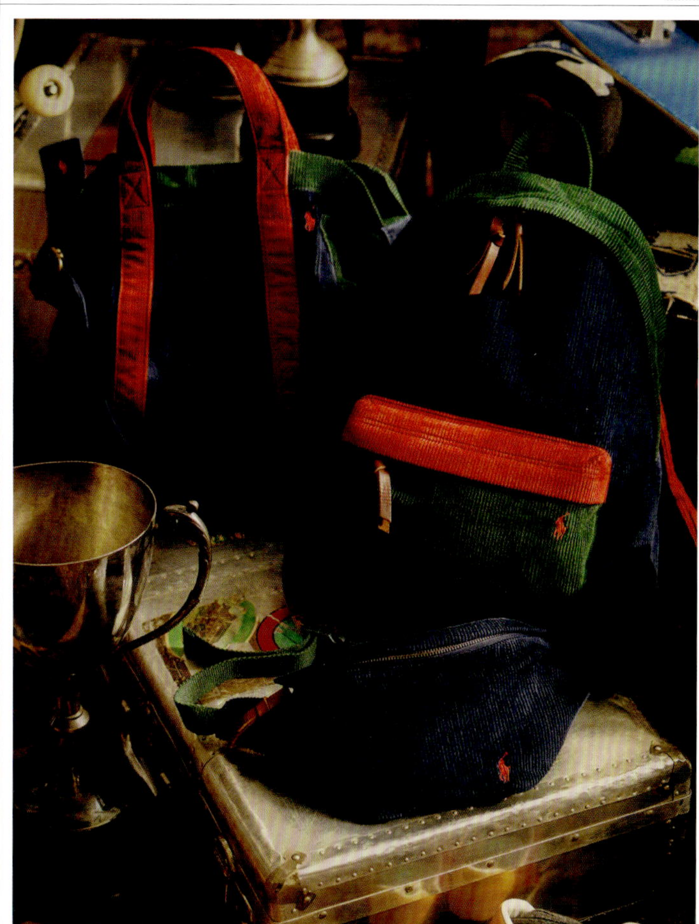

Title: RL X Active Club | **Client:** Ralph Lauren

NICHOLAS DUERS

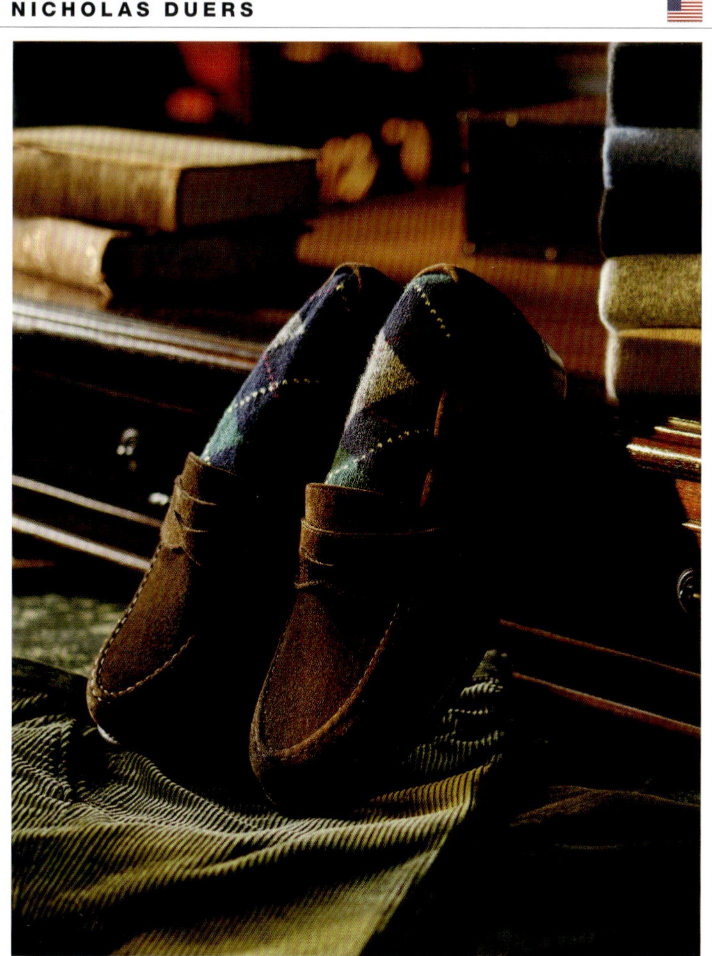

Title: Polo Bar | **Client:** Ralph Lauren

NICHOLAS DUERS

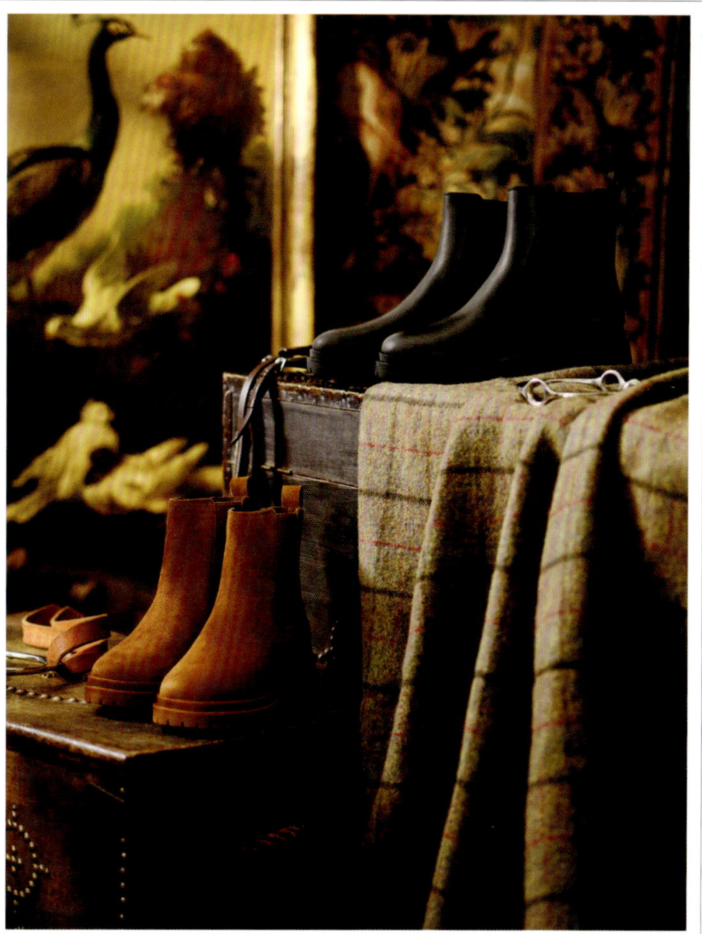

Title: RL Footwear | **Client:** Ralph Lauren

Graphis Film/Video

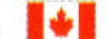

LINDSAY SIU, RETHINK

ADVERTISING

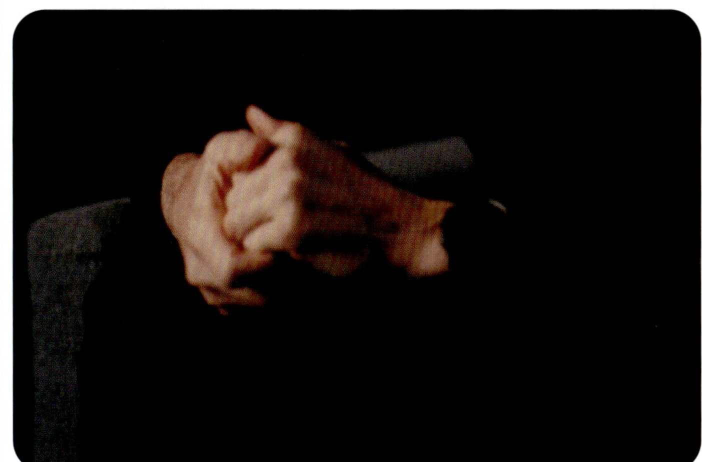

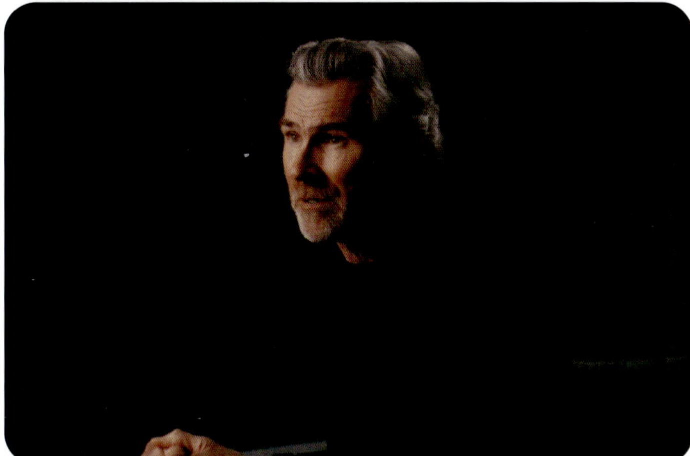

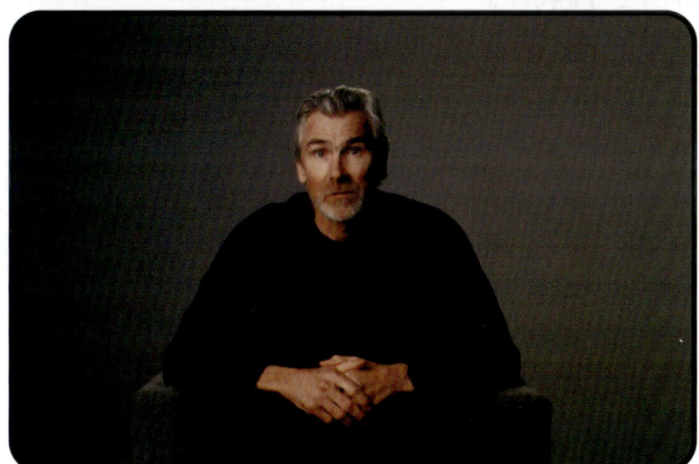

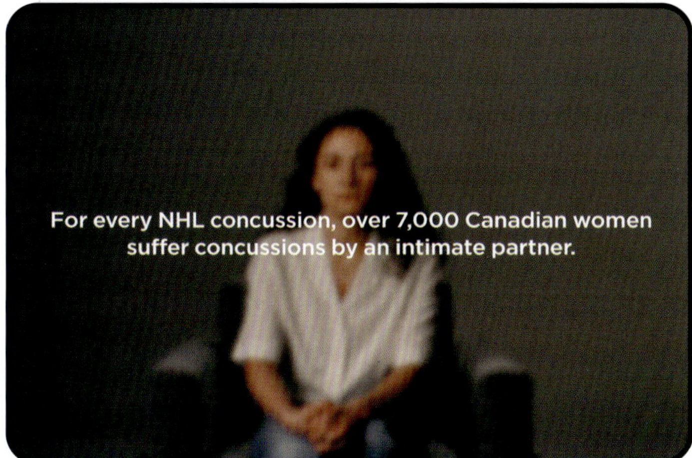

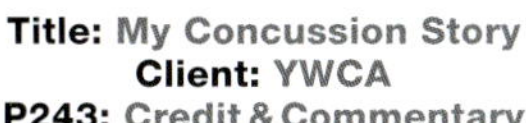

Title: My Concussion Story
Client: YWCA
P243: Credit & Commentary

NICHOLAS DUERS

STILL LIFE

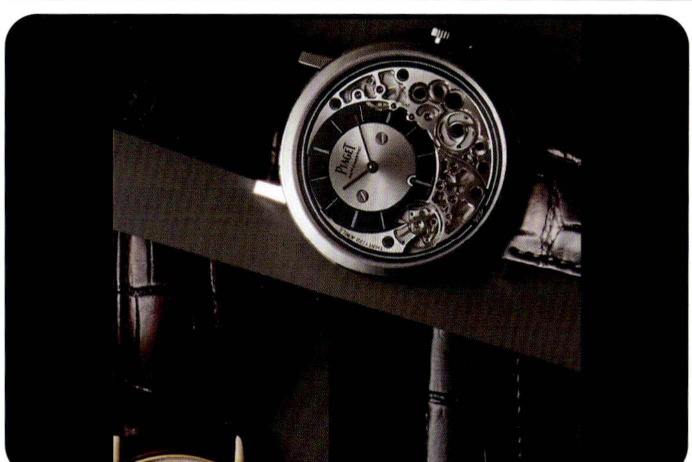

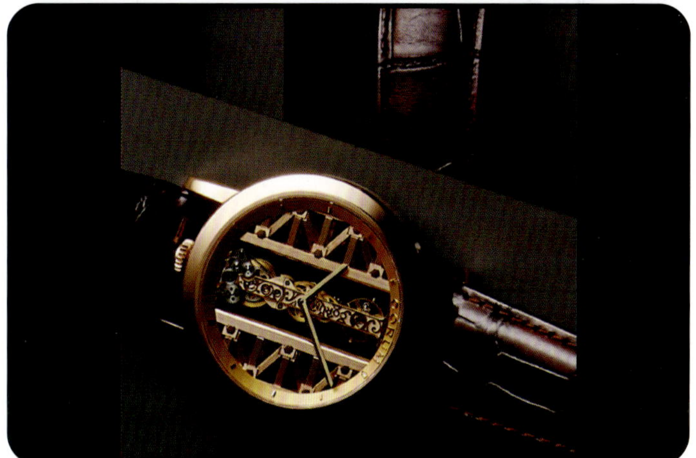

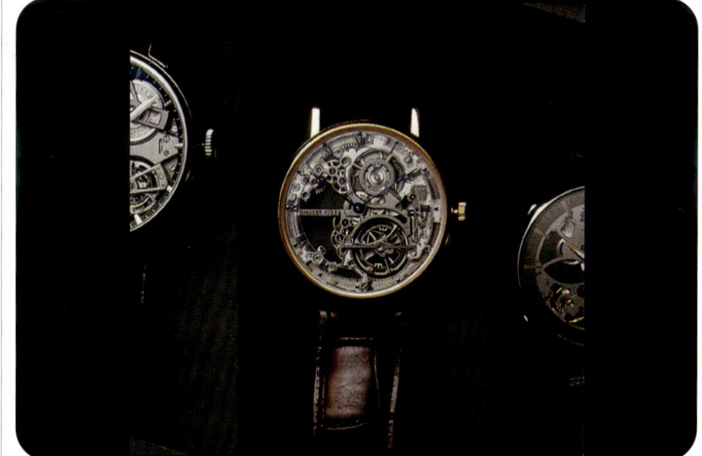

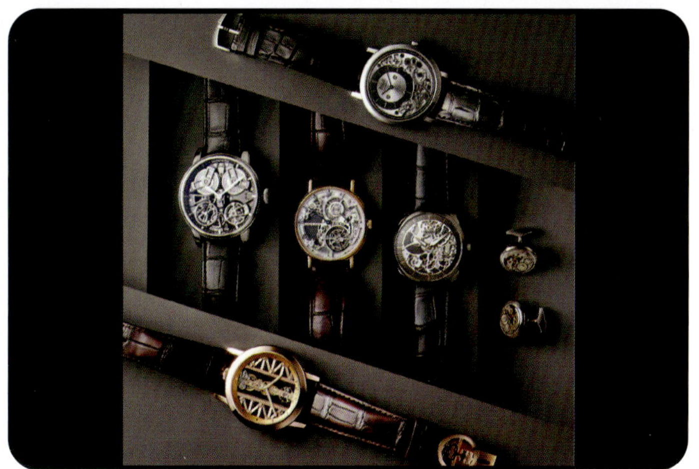

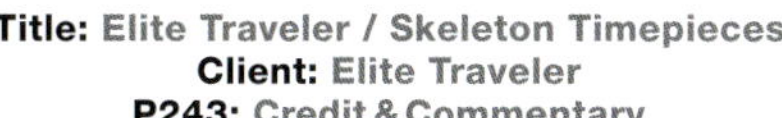

Title: Elite Traveler / Skeleton Timepieces
Client: Elite Traveler
P243: Credit & Commentary

CLARENCE LIN

FINE ART

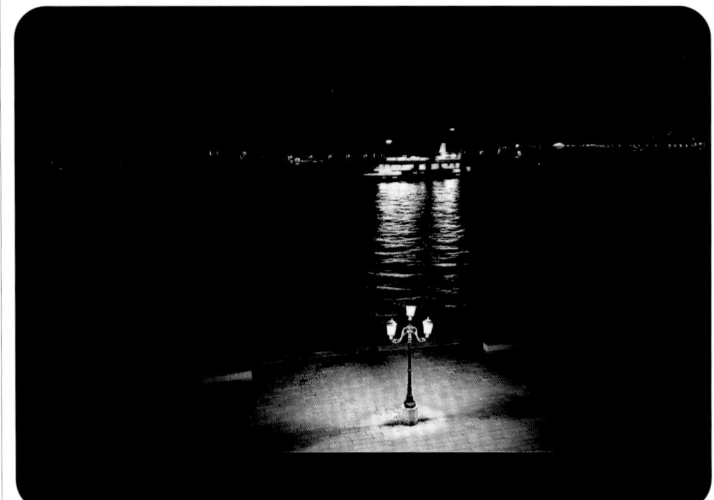

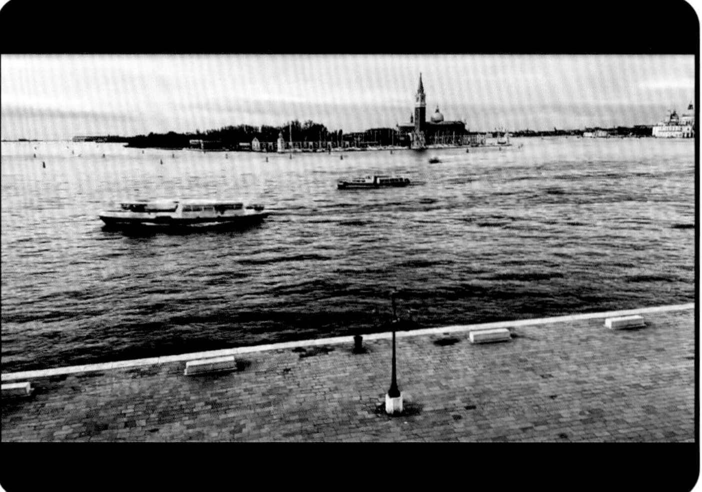

Title: Venice
Client: Self-initiated

CLARENCE LIN

FINE ART

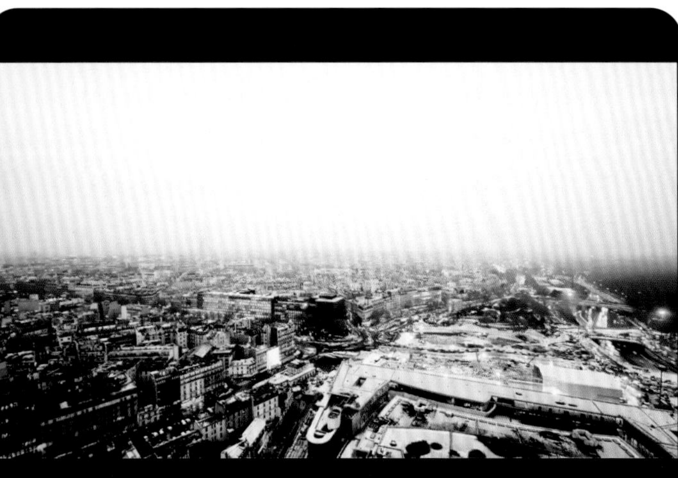

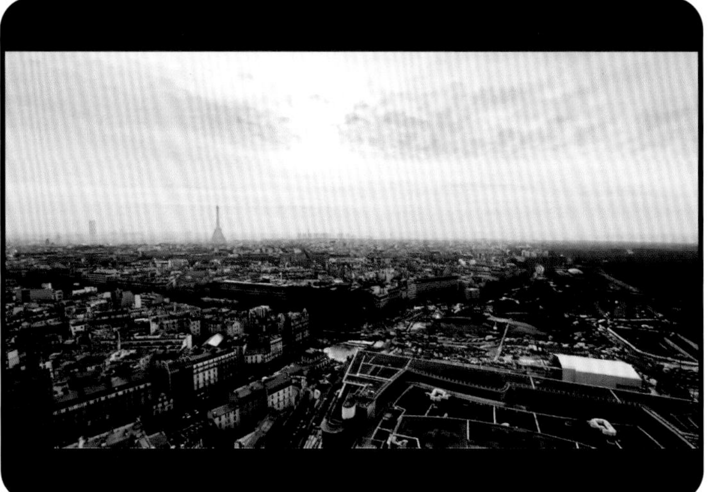

Title: Paris
Client: Self-initiated

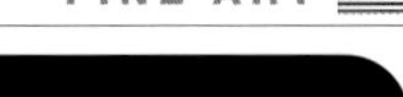

CLARENCE LIN

FINE ART

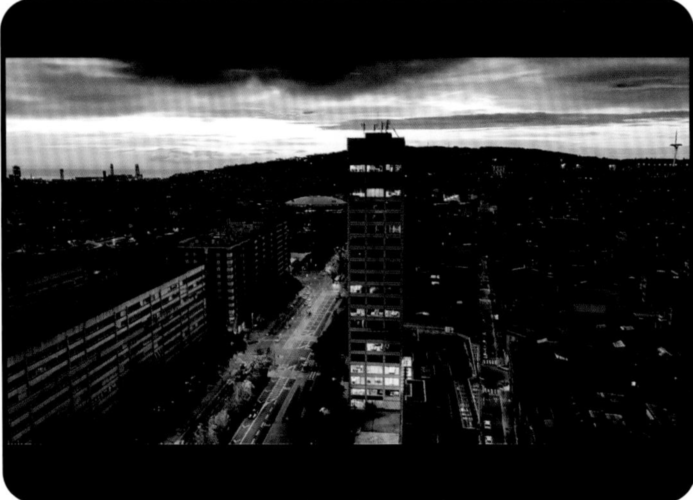

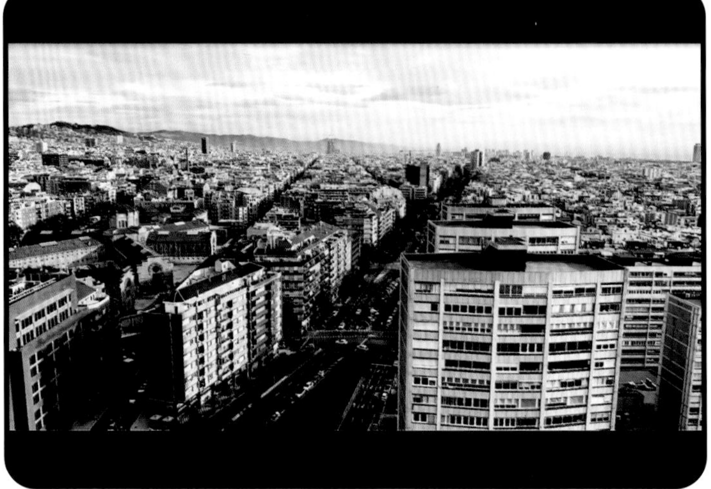

Title: Barcelona
Client: Self-initiated

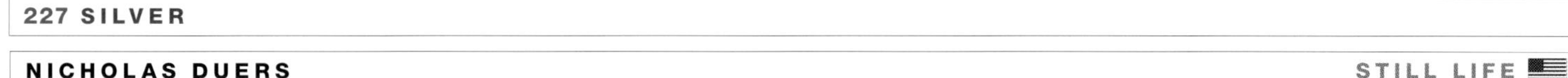

NICHOLAS DUERS STILL LIFE

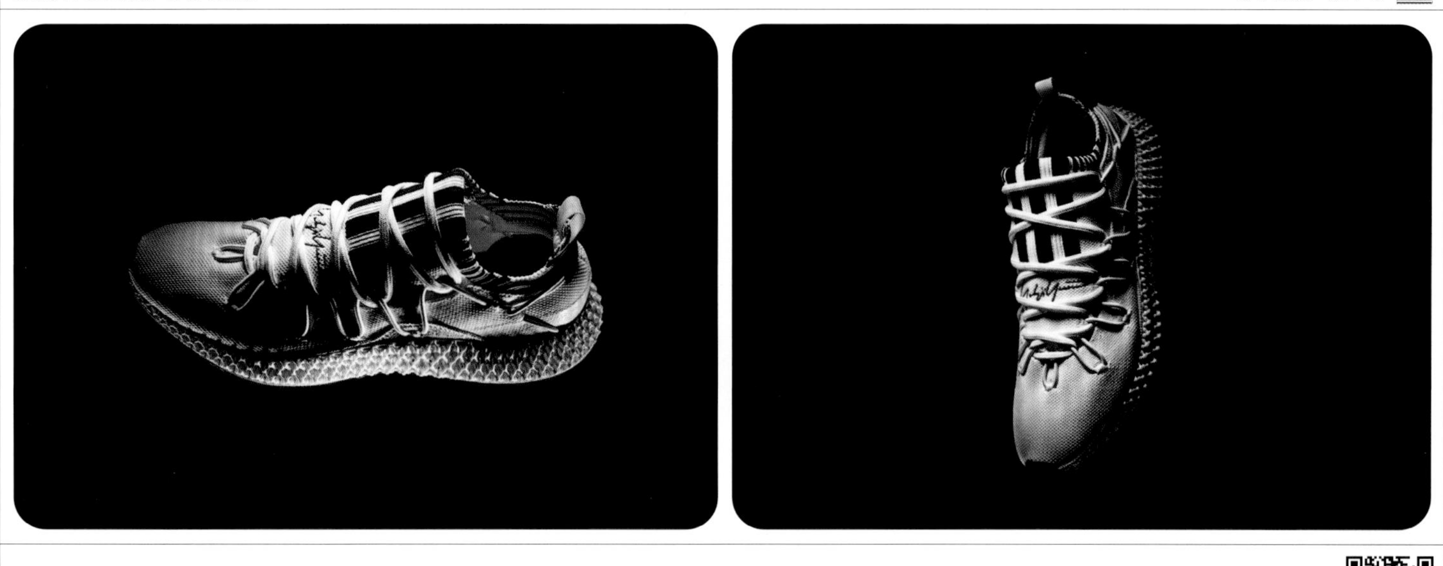

Title: Y3 / Adidas
Client: Y3 / Adidas

NICHOLAS DUERS STILL LIFE

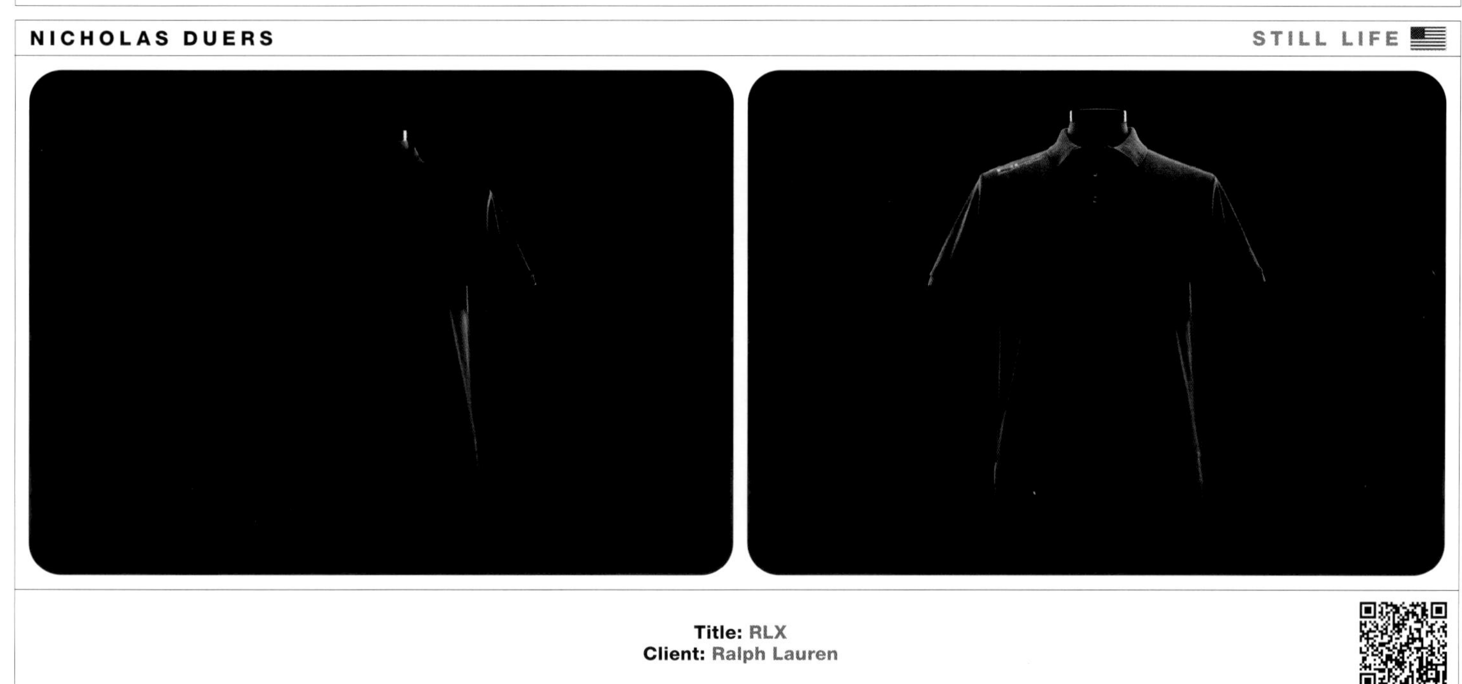

Title: RLX
Client: Ralph Lauren

Reflecting on my past experiences of showcasing work in the Graphis Photography Competition, I am grateful for the exposure and recognition it has afforded me.

The judging criteria has not only provided a fair evaluation of my submissions, but has also contributed to the photographic community's growth.

Hadley Stambaugh, *Photographer & Creative Director of Photography, Savannah College of Art & Design*

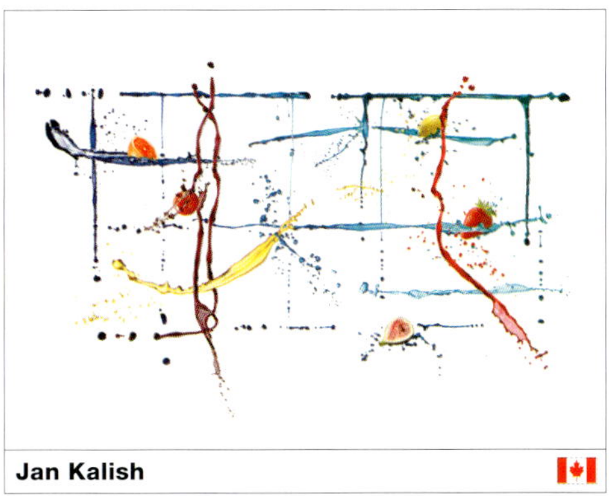
Jan Kalish

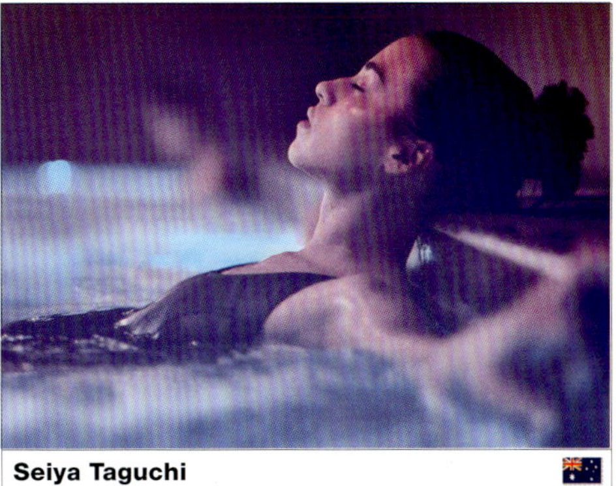
Seiya Taguchi

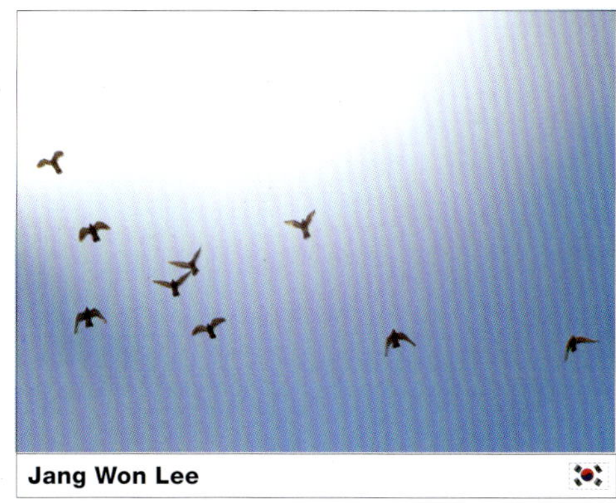
Jang Won Lee

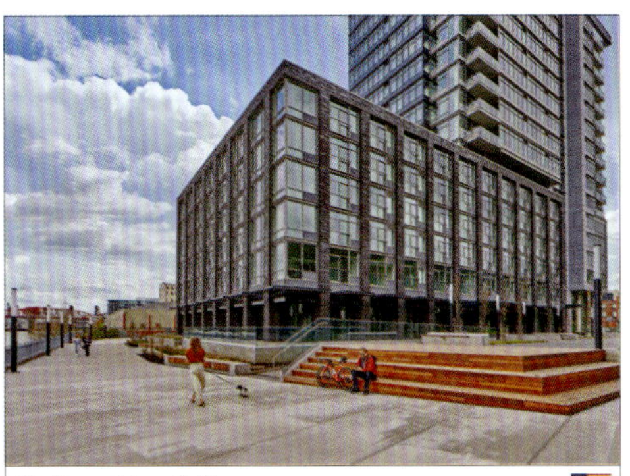
Nathan Bergfelt

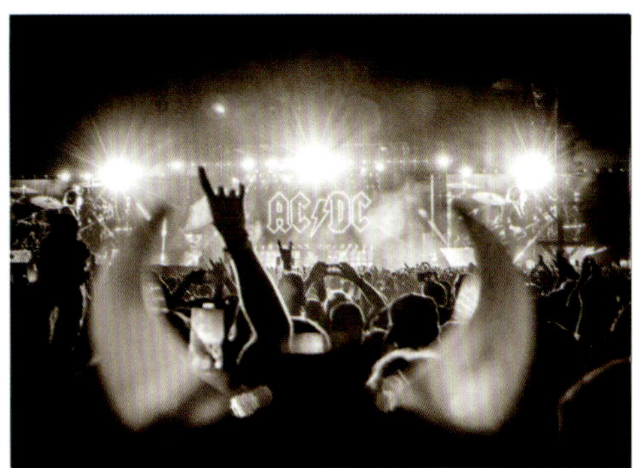

Jérôme Brunet

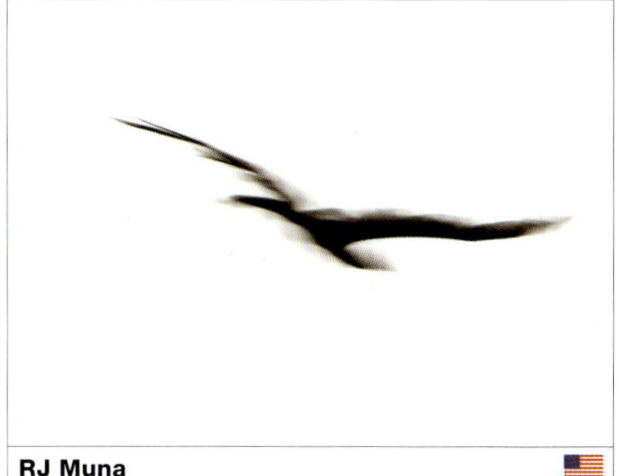
RJ Muna

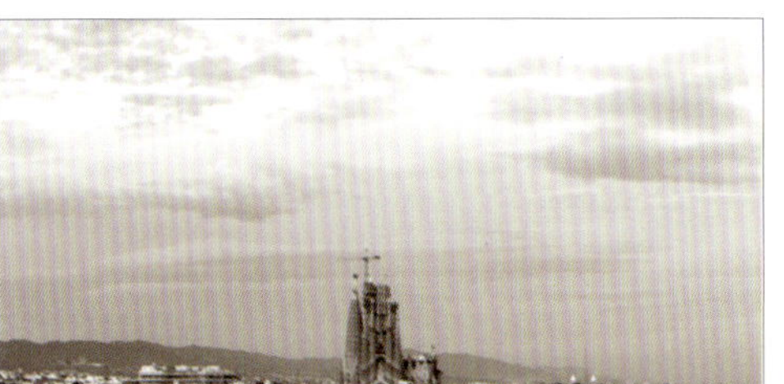
Clarence Lin

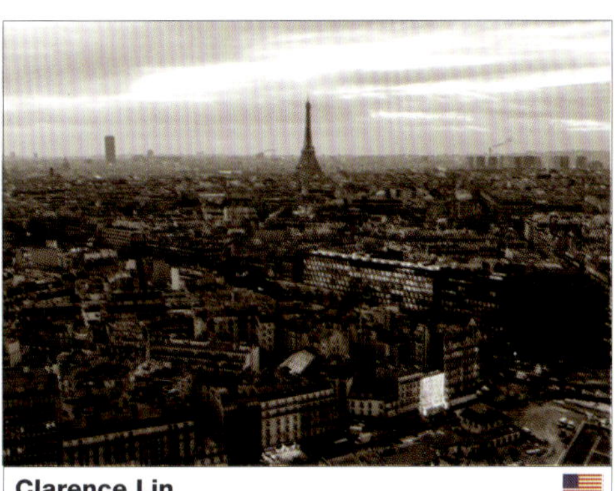
Clarence Lin

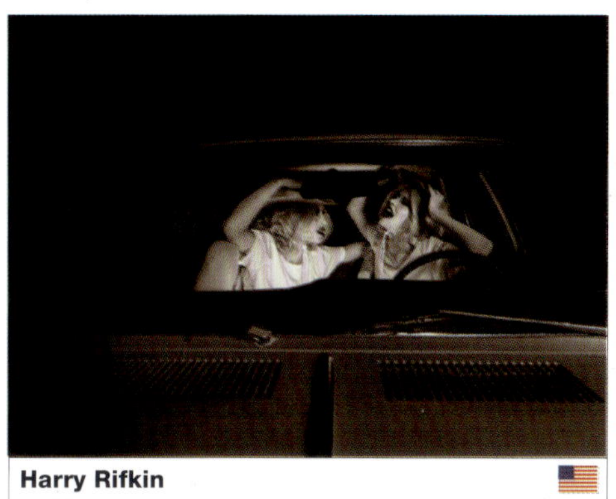
Harry Rifkin

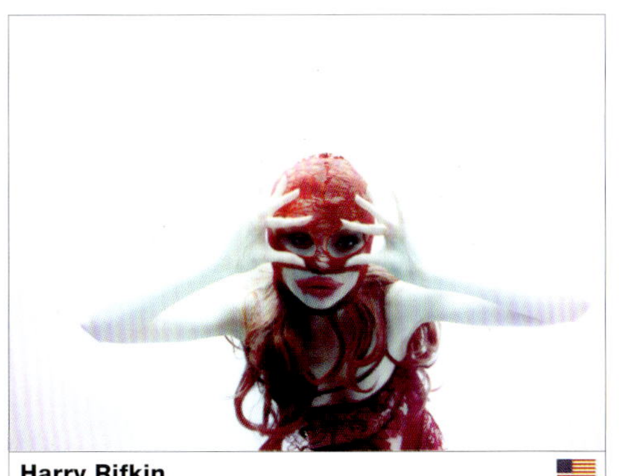
Harry Rifkin

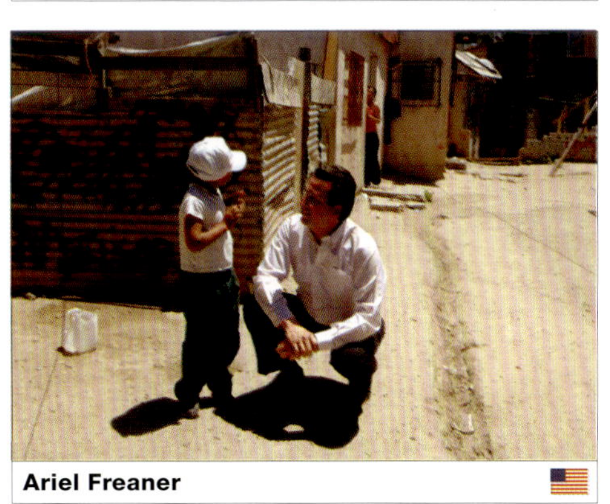
Ariel Freaner

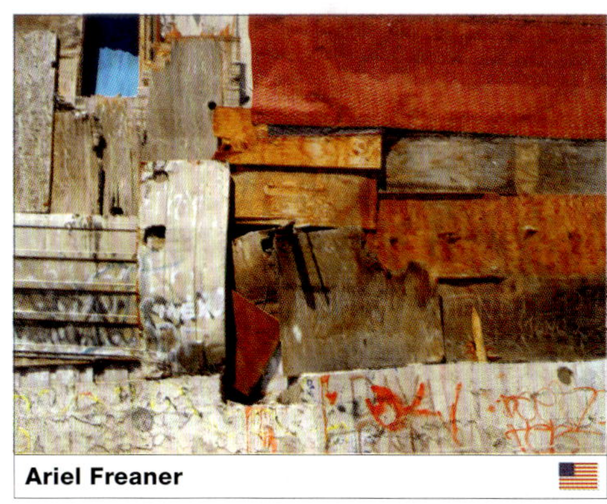
Ariel Freaner

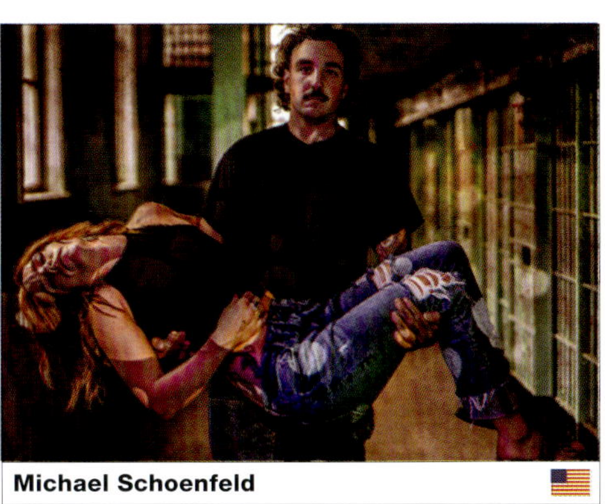
Michael Schoenfeld

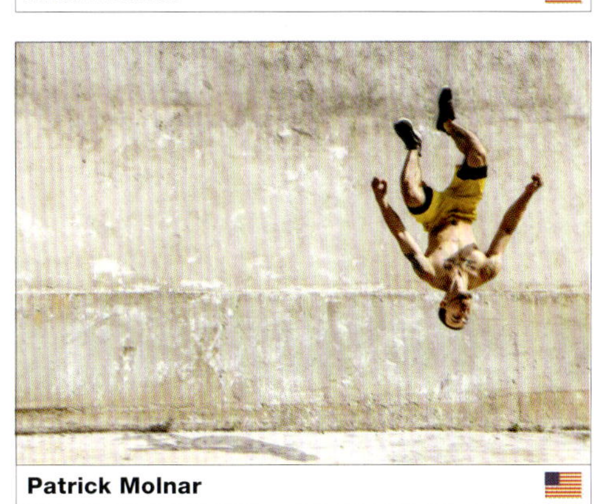
Patrick Molnar

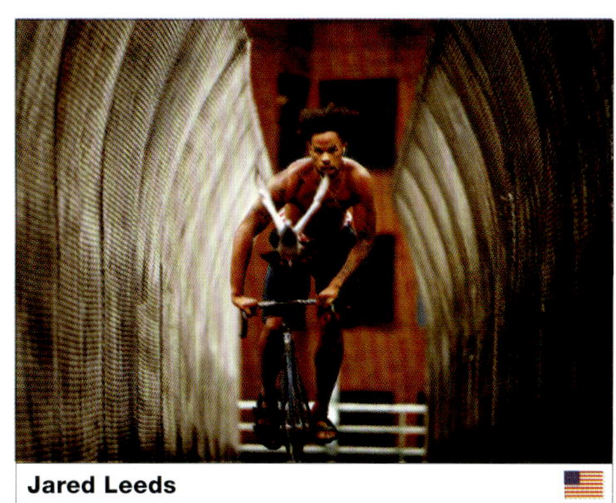
Jared Leeds

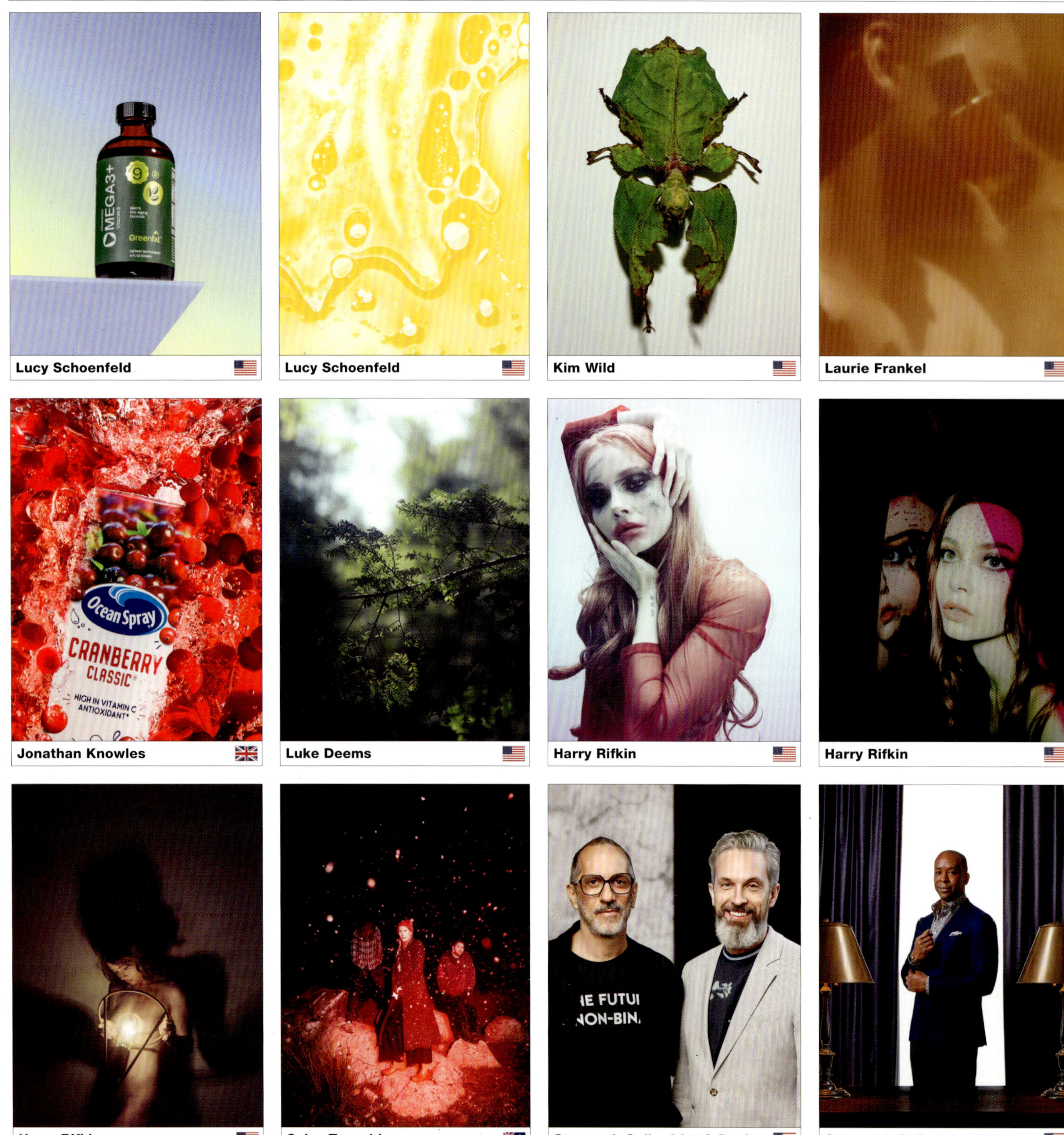

Lucy Schoenfeld
Lucy Schoenfeld
Kim Wild
Laurie Frankel
Jonathan Knowles
Luke Deems
Harry Rifkin
Harry Rifkin
Harry Rifkin
Seiya Taguchi
Savannah Coll. of Art & Design
Savannah Coll. of Art & Design

The range of themes and styles in the entries I reviewed for the Graphis Photography Competition was inspiring and refreshing.

It's exciting to know that so many artists are pushing themselves, their talent, and their craft to create compelling and meaningful work.

Nick Hall, *Photographer, Nick Hall Photography*

PLATINUM WINNERS:

32, 33 PHEASANTS AND PEAFOWL | Photographer: Peter Samuels
Client: Private Commission | Equipment: Sony A-1, Zeiss 55mm Lens, Sigma Art 85mm Lenses
Main Contributor: Peter Samuels

Assignment: When I was asked to photograph a private collection of pheasants and peacocks for a private commission, the project's scope quickly grew to a book project on this beautiful bird species.
Approach: The owner of these birds had them in various aviaries on his property and decided to use his garage as my studio, making bringing the birds to the set easier.
Results: Myself and my client are thrilled with the images, and they've been winning awards, so I'm looking forward to continuing this series.

34 BEAUTY STUDY #1299: MODEL NATALIA COSTA | Photographer: Howard Schatz
Client: Self-initiated | Equipment: Hasselblad | Main Contributor: Howard Schatz

35 BEAUTY STUDY #1392: REIKO YAMANAKA
Photographer: Howard Schatz | Client: Self-initiated | Equipment: Hasselblad

36, 37 EDINBURGH GIN - FILLED WITH WONDER
Photographer: Jonathan Knowles | Client: Edinburgh Gin | Equipment: Hasselblad
Agency: Bright Signals | Creative Director: Guy Vickerstaff
Creative Strategist: Victoria McFadyen | Executive Producer: David Moule

Assignment: Inspired by the beauty of the city, Edinburgh Gin commissioned us to create a scenic campaign to launch their new range of unique small batch gins: Classic, Cannonball, 1670, and Seaside.
Approach: The Filled With Wonder line is fulfilled by the clarity of the scene behind as it is seen within the bottle.

38-40 1923 ENVIRONMENTAL PORTRAITS
Photographer: James Minchin III | Client: Paramount+
Equipment: Leica, Leica 24-70mm Lens, Leica 80mm Lens, Phase One Digital Back
Main Contributor: James Minchin III

Assignment: 1923 focuses on the Dutton family's next two generations as they struggle to survive historic drought, lawlessness and prohibition, and an epidemic of cattle theft; all battled beneath the cloud of Montana's great depression, which preceded the nation by almost a decade. The creative strategy was to capture the journey of the Duttons as they protect their land.
Approach: We captured the dramatic, emotional, and romantic tone and manner as they faced the new hardships of the great depression.
Results: Stellar emotional performances from the talent with an epic storytelling, and high cinematic crafts within the authentic settings.

41 THE SPIRIT OF MARILYN MONROE VISITED MY STUDIO
Photographer: Paco Macías Velasco | Client: Self-initiated
Equipment: Hasselblad, Phase One Magazine
Main Contributor: Paco Macías Velasco

Assignment: I produced this photo only as a small tribute to this icon of the 50s and 60s.
Approach: Manolo Tena singing a duet with Ana Bélen the song in Spanish simply titled Marilyn Monroe (Youtube) accompanied me during the session where the Argentine model Patricia Molina, I characterized her as the legendary M.M. with her wig, dress and makeup reproducing the majestic scene from the movie "The itch of the seventh year" (1955).
Results: The setup of my studio with the fan, the lamps and the background that I used framed this photo, which by the way is one of my favorites in more than 5 decades as a professional photographer.

42, 43 DOUGHNUTS | Photographer: Craig Cutler | Client: Self-initiated
Equipment: 4x5 View Camera | Food Stylist: Karen Evans

Assignment: A personal project to shoot handmade doughnuts with color.
Approach: The idea was to photograph donuts as a fine art still life project. The camera used was a 4x5 Toyo view camera along with color transparency film. I wanted it to be a study about shape and color and less about food. The feeling that film creates is still unique and cannot be compared to digital imagery. The food stylist, Karen Evans, created each donut by hand. Silk screened paper from Color Aid was used to complement each image.

44, 45 CUCURUCHOS: THE HOLY WEEK | Photographer: Artem Nazarov
Client: Self-initiated | Equipment: Canon 5D Mark IV | Main Contributor: Artem Nazarov

Assignment: Cucuruchos: The Holy Week series is part of a self-assigned documentary project that explores religious traditions, ceremonies, and syncretism in Central and South America.

46 FRAGRANCE ON FIRE | Photographer: Lindsey Drennan
Client: Self-initiated | Equipment: Canon 5DSR | Photography Studio: Album Studios
Creative Team: Alanna Davey | Photographer's Assistant: Ryan Francoz
Retoucher: Irmina Mikolajczyk | Main Contributor: Lindsey Drennan

Assignment: I wanted to elevate my product portfolio with this creative self-promotional shoot. Showcasing the contrast of fragrance - soft florals to strong woodsy scents.
Approach: We executed everything in camera on the day of the shoot. We experimented with different ways to set the flowers and set on fire to get the perfect image.
Results: This piece was met with great success including new clients.

47 ACCOUTREMENTS | Photographer: John Surace | Client: Self-initiated
Equipment: Sinar P2, Phase One P25, Schneider-Kreuznach Super Angulon 75mm Lens

Assignment: A study of form, texture and space with no gimmicks.
Approach: Photographed on a ribbed rubber mat angled at 45° to off set the curvilinear forms of the lens and loupe. Every item was carefully placed for compositional harmony and to compensate the forced perspective. The triangular shape of the A-clamp comfortably fills the lower right, while the rear of the mechanical pencil breaks from the edge of the lens board for slight visual tension. The yellow cable release creates a visual path through an otherwise monochromatic palette while also shattering the rectilinear structure. The set was backlit with a large, soft bank of light for smooth highlights and graceful falloff. Top to bottom focus achieved in-camera with Scheimpflug principle.

GOLD WINNERS:

49 PADDLING THROUGH THE OREGON BREAKS | Photographer: Per Breiehagen
Client: Self-initiated | Equipment: Hasselblad, DJI Mavic Pro | Model: Lori Evert

Assignment: A birds eye view of the dramatic and graphic breaks on the Oregon coast, as a paddle boarder makes her way to the beach. Image used to promote my location photography. I knew I wanted to capture the incredible breaks that seem to go on forever along the Oregon coast, but it wasn't until we got the paddle boarder in the water for scale that the image came alive.
Approach: A lot of scouting went into this. Safety was a major issue both in the water and access to the water. Some of these locations are at the bottom of steep cliffs and unfriendly terrain. This remote beach offered fairly easy access and a break that was deemed "safe". Flying a drone over the ocean in strong winds is always an interesting challenge...
Results: Sent out as a self promotion mailer and for social media posts.

50 NIKE ZOOM SOLDIER II "SUPERMAN" AKRON LOOK SEE
Photographer: Matt Roppolo | Client: Heritage Auctions
Equipment: Canon EOS R5, Canon 90mm Lens | Retouching: Hayley Tracewell
Main Contributor: Matt Roppolo

Assignment: After finishing up a group of guitar catalog covers I was given the chance to do a few feature shots for the new Collectible Sneakers venue at Heritage Auctions. I was given a couple of pairs of shoes to be featured and only told that they were Superman shoes.
Approach: I had just finished an image that had not gone as planned, but left me with a sweep of sky blue seamless on my set. I was then asked to shoot what I was only told were Superman shoes. My first thought was "Up, Up, and Away!" So, being that I already had half my background I decided to shoot them in the a sky with Poly-fil clouds. I did the first pair in a daytime sky and was then told to do an image for the second pair. I wanted them to be tied together, so I shot the second pair in a night sky.
Results: The Department Director, Arman Salemi, loved the images, as did the retoucher, Hayley Tracewell.

51 STEVIE RAY VAUGHAN MTV UNPLUGGED GUITAR | Photographer: Matt Roppolo
Client: Heritage Auctions | Equipment: Canon EOS R5, Canon 90mm Lens
Retoucher: Colleen Landis | Main Contributor: Matt Roppolo

Assignment: The Director of the Vintage Guitars & Musical Instruments, Aaron Piscopo, asked me to use a photo of Stevie Ray Vaughan in to accompany the Guild 12 string acoustic guitar that Stevie played during his performance on MTV Unplugged. In the past that I have found photos of celebrities with the item they owned or played to be pretty dull and uninteresting. So, I kept brainstorming, looking at images, and racking my brain for some way to represent SRV without showing a photo of him.
Approach: After looking around at images, I was drawn to a still frame of a video where all you could see of Stevie was his hair, hand, hat, and an acoustic guitar. I decided to I needed his hat, or the closest approximation of it. I didn't have time to order and alter a hat. I then remembered a friend and co-worker said that he dressed similar to Stevie back in the 80's. I hit him up on the off chance that he might have a hat similar to SRV's gambler hat, and was ecstatic to find he did have one. I decided to pay homage to that film still, but where Stevie was I just wanted darkness to represent the loss for the beloved guitar hero.
Results: The image was used for the 2023 May 9 Vintage Guitars and Musical Instruments Signature Auction #7313. The guitar sold for $225,000, and the department director was very happy with the image.

52, 53 HOLO FOOTWEAR AD CAMPAIGN | Photographer: Trevett McCandliss
Client: Holo Footwear | Equipment: Canon 5D Mark II, Canon 50mm Lens
Agency: Wainscot Media | Creative Directors: Nancy Campbell, Trevett McCandliss
Digital Director: Marco Scozzaro | Stylist: Mariah Walker
Photographer's Assistant: William Eadon | Models: Julia Neves, Diamond Lyles-James
Makeup: Maya Ling Feero | Hair: Jason Linkow | Main Contributor: Trevett McCandliss

Assignment: Holo Footwear wanted to create a fresh and inventive series of images to promote their new funky, colorful sneaker line.
Approach: Our approach was to create surreal images using photo collage. We shot the models, sneakers and props and added in a few found images, such as the sky backgrounds, creating fantasy environments to showcase the cool sneakers.
Results: People enjoyed the images. We got a great reaction to the work!

54 FENTON | Photographer: Scott Lowden
Client: House of Current | Equipment: Canon EOS R5, Canon 28-70mm Lens
Creative Director: Wendy Lowden | Account Executive: Lisa Maloof

Assignment: I was tasked with creating a campaign for an outdoor mall, Fenton, in Cary, NC. Our goal was energetic lifestyle images that equally capture the spirit of the talent as well as the beautiful environment.
Approach: Using techniques for directing talent to keep the energy level high, as well as dynamic lighting, we created an energy vibe.
Results: Both the advertising agency and the client loved the images. So much that other clients have seen this work and asked to emulate it for other similar properties.

55 MALPRACTICE | Photographer: Jonathan Knowles
Client: ITV | Equipment: Hasselblad | Creative Director: Shane O'Neill
Creative Team: Natasha Bhatia, Gemma Jewell | Senior Producers: Trine Johnson, Simon Sanderson, Natalie Newell | Producer: Emma Harrower

Assignment: We were commissioned by ITV to shoot the promotional campaign for their new medical thriller Malpractice. Demonstrating the idea that 'Everyone has a breaking point', medical items are seen smashing and shattering under pressure, symbolising the extreme stress experienced by hospital staff in the NHS. The campaign included film and still assets for TV teaser commercials, OOH, press advertising, and social channels. Our approach was to capture imagery in camera that was bold, stylised and dramatic, without the need for any CGI, and with minimal post-production and retouching. With a custom-made pneumatic press and filming on our Phantom Flex 4K, we were able to capture these disintegrations in super slow motion. For the stills, it was all about the moment immediately after impact, where the object retains its original form, but is in an obvious state of explosive failure.

56 FLWRS | Photographer: Laurie Frankel
Client: FLWR | Equipment: Nikon D850, Nikon 24-70mm Lens

57 ACCESS TO OTHERNESS | Photographer: Dennis Letbetter
Client: Gallerie Japonesque | Equipment: Nikon D850, Nikon 28-105mm Lens

Assignment: The project was to create an access to nature, here using birds as a vehicle, to guide and console us throughout difficult times. Many in the began to observe birds in their environment during the worldwide quarantine for the first time. The fascination with them has continued and though birds are decreasing in numbers they can serve at once as caveats about our planet and guideposts to a lyrical and bright future.
Approach: The approach first and foremost was to use natural means to photograph the birds. No enhancements or computer arrangements. To let nature speak as itself without adornment. Natural light, birds in flight in the wild being at once their natural and free selves.
Results: The client reaction has been exuberant. The project has been accepted as beyond expectations. The plans are as a publication with an attendant exhibition.

58, 59 CHAMELEON BODYSCAPE | Photographer: Lennette Newell
Client: Self-initiated | Equipment: Canon, Canon 70mm Lens
Photography Studio: Smashbox Studios | Main Contributor: Lennette Newell

Assignment: Image explores the juxtaposition of color, form, and texture between reptile and homo sapien. The pet chameleon explored the warm female body and rested on the female's derrière. I documented the exploration as it took place with no human interaction to direct the chameleon to any part of the body.
Approach: This study emphasizes the lizard's physical beauty and effortless elegance. Each subject is equal, a peaceful coexistence is not exploited, and a joint interaction persists in space and time.

60 THERE IS NO WAY BUT TO THINK OF THIS AND THAT
Photographer: Jang Won Lee | Client: Self-initiated | Equipment: Canon EOS 80D
Main Contributor: Jang Won Lee

Assignment: Sometimes, I find animals that look somewhat similar to human beings. This artwork is about a seagull that I found.
Approach: I met one indeed serious seagull, and I thought maybe the bird was murmuring, "There is no way but to think of this and that..." The calm environment made the seagull look even more severe.
Results: Thanks to the seagull and the calm environment, I could take this serious and excellent photograph for my exhibition.

60 MALLARD | Photographer: Darnell McCown | Client: Self-initiated
Equipment: Canon 7D Mark II, Canon 24-70mm Lens, Canon 100-400mm Lens
Main Contributor: Darnell McCown

Assignment: Photographing in the VanDusen Botanical Gardens in Vancouver while on a brief vacation.

61 LONDON FROM THE AIR | Photographer: Jeffrey Milstein
Client: Rizzoli New York | Equipment: Fuji GFX 100s, Sony A7R IV
Designer: Lori Malkin Ehrlich | Main Contributor: Jeffrey Milstein

Assignment: Photograph London from the air for a book to be published by Rizzoli, in April 2024.
Approach: Following the publication of Paris From the Air, in 2021, Rizzoli wanted to keep the same format for a new book of London aerials. I compiled a comprehensive portfolio of the city with overall wide city shots from directly above, as well as detailed shots of iconic London buildings, parks, museums, palaces, and monuments. Many are shot with a straight-down style which is a type of aerial I am known for. The shoot required coordination with several helicopter companies and the National Air Transportation system for London.
Results: The book is at the printer. The client is extremely happy. As of today, it is the number one new release in aerial photography on Amazon.

62 BEAUTY STUDY #1516: MODEL ISABELLE SAUER
Photographer: Howard Schatz | Client: Self-initiated | Equipment: Hasselblad
Hair: Danielle Cirilli | Main Contributor: Howard Schatz

63 BEAUTY STUDY #1126: MODEL EMILIE ADAMS
Photographer: Howard Schatz | Client: Self-initiated | Equipment: Hasselblad
Hair: Danielle Cirilli | Main Contributor: Howard Schatz

64 REGAL LIPS | Photographer: Lindsey Drennan | Client: Self-initiated
Equipment: Canon 5DSR | Studio: Sorry Studio | Photographer's Assistant: Jason Mortlock
Assistant: Jack Rintoul | Clothing Stylist: Neil Franklyn | Stylist: Rodney Smith
Model: Julie F. | Hair: Kim Creton | Makeup: Kim Creton | Main Contributor: Lindsey Drennan

Assignment: "Regal Lips" is a self-promotional beauty shoot. This project brings together a talented team to showcase the beauty and power of the classic "red lip". The primary goal was to promote my beauty photography and demonstrate my ability to create visually captivating beauty content. Key goals included promoting my photography services and showcasing my expertise in the beauty and fashion industry. To highlight the empowerment and confidence that a classic red lip represents. And finally to attract potential clients and collaborators within the beauty and fashion sector.
Approach: "Regal Lips" explores the elegance, confidence, and timelessness of red lipstick. It merges classic and contemporary elements, creating a series of visually arresting images. A dedicated team of makeup artists, models, wardrobe stylists, and prop stylists worked harmoniously to bring the vision of "Regal Lips" to life. Each team member contributed their unique skills to create a captivating narrative.
Results: This project is a testament to my creativity and dedication to beauty photography. The project was shared on various platforms, including multiple websites and social media, to engage a broader audience. It was part of a successful email campaign and helped in securing multiple meetings with some top beauty brands in the industry. The project achieved its goal of promoting my business and attracting new opportunities within the beauty and fashion industry. The project's success demonstrates the potential of creative collaborations and the impact of compelling storytelling through photography.

65 GEOMETRIC BEAUTY | Photographer: Jonathan Knowles
Client: Getty Images Creative | Equipment: Hasselblad | Model: Cynthia Abdulahi
Stylist: Antonia Grier | Retoucher: Georgie Wilding

Assignment: Beauty shoot with creative colorful edit.

66 BEAUTY: CLEAN | Photographer: Scott Lowden
Clients: House of Current, Self-initiated | Equipment: Canon EOS R5, Canon 85mm Lens
Creative Director: Wendy Lowden | Makeup: Destiny Crukendall

Assignment: This project was a collaboration with the House of Current to create fun clean beauty images.
Approach: We used clean but creative colors for both makeup and wardrobe, and a longer lens with a shallow depth of field to push the viewer's attention to the eyes and makeup.
Results: We've had a great reaction to the images from prospective clients.

67 BEAUTY: MOTION | Photographer: Scott Lowden | Clients: House of Current, Self-initiated
Equipment: Canon EOS R5, Voigtlander Nokton Classic 35mm Lens, Kolari ND Filter

Assignment: This project was a collaboration with House of Current to create moody, organic beauty images.
Approach: I used an uncoated manual lens, as well as a neutral density filter to give us the organic, soft, images to enhance the moody vibe.
Results: We've had a great response to our online delivery, as well as printing these for display.

68 BEAUTY STUDY #1386: SIGAIL CURRIE
Photographer: Howard Schatz | Client: Self-initiated | Equipment: Hasselblad
Hair: Damian Monzillo | Main Contributor: Howard Schatz

69 BENRIACH: THE FORTY YEAR OLD | Photographer: Jonathan Knowles
Client: Benriach | Equipment: Hasselblad | Agency: Southpaw | Art Director: James Newport
Creative Director: Glenn Smith | Producers: Pete Anderson, Emma Harrower
Assignment: Campaign for the launch of Benriach The Forty. Created by Master Blender Rachel Barrie, Benriach 40YO is one of the oldest peated malts to be released from a Speyside distillery.

70 MADIRA BEER APP | Photographer: Jonathan Knowles | Client: Madira
Equipment: Hasselblad | Set Designers: Peter Saunders, Rebecca Rauter, Maya Angeli
Props: Peter Saunders, Rebecca Rauter, Maya Angeli
Assignment: Selection of beers from around the world photographed for Madira beer delivery app.

71 KRONENBOURG 1664 BLANC | Photographer: Jonathan Knowles
Client: Carlsberg | Equipment: Hasselblad | Ad Agency: Fold 7
Creative Director: John Yorke | Retoucher: Gareth Pritchard
Assignment: Drinks commission for Kronenbourg 1664 Blanc beer.

72 VIOLA BELLA AT THE OPERA HOUSE IN CHICAGO | SUMMER 2023
Photographer: Michael Pantuso | Client: Self-initiated
Equipment: Pentax K3, Pentax 18-55mm Lens | Model: Viola Bella Pantuso
Assignment: Viola Bella Pantuso in Chicago on break from the Royal Ballet World Tour.
Approach: Freestyle approach.

73 HUMAN BODY STUDY, PAIRS #128: DANCERS CASEY HOWES & JAKE WARREN
Photographer: Howard Schatz | Client: Self-initiated | Equipment: Hasselblad

74 HUMAN BODY STUDY, PAIRS #106: DANCERS ELIJAH DILLEHAY & HOLLY WILDER
Photographer: Howard Schatz | Client: Self-initiated | Equipment: Hasselblad

75 TEXT TO DANCE | Photographer: Michael Winokur | Client: San Francisco Ballet
Equipment: Fuji GFX 100s, Mid-Journey AI | Wardrobe: Kate Share, Danny O'Neill
Makeup: Thomas Richards-Keyes | Project Manager: Kate McKinney
Other: Anita Paciotti, Rehearsal Director | Main Contributor: Michael Winokur
Assignment: To celebrate their 90th anniversary, San Francisco Ballet had commissioned a series of dances called Next @ 90. The work was meant to show a break from tradition. I was hired to photograph a select group of their dancers. To show the idea of NEXT and the move away from classical staging I choose to combine studio images of the dancers with backgrounds created with the AI tool Mid-Journey. The generated backgrounds all started with the key word "arch". I chose the arch motif to represent the theater's proscenium arch.
Approach: Creating the backgrounds was not as simple as one would imagine. The AI tools and my skills evolved during the process. I found that the ability to iterate was endless but the ability to direct the machine is overstated - the results are more random than most people understand. I also found that the generated images contain artifacts that presented a lot of extra work and cost in the retouching process. The AI tools are evolving so fast that any review of their flaws is instantly outdated.

76, 77 CIRCUS TÄHTI | Photographer: Markku Lahdesmaki
Client: Self-initiated | Equipment: Canon | Art Director: Anne Kauranen
Main Contributor: Markku Lahdesmaki
Assignment: In the little town of Orivesi, nestled in the heart of Finland, the summer season always brings special kinds of experiences. As we were on our routine grocery shopping trip, we couldn't help but be drawn to the colorful circus posters announcing the arrival of "Tähti" (the Star) lining the road. We knew exactly what we were going to do the following Wednesday evening. The prospect of a night under the big top, filled with wonder and awe, had us full of anticipation.

78 LAWMEN BASS REEVES TIN TYPES PORTRAITS | Photographer: Sarah Coulter
Client: Paramount+ | Equipment: Deardorff 8x10 Camera, Pre-Patent Dallmeyer 2B Petzval Lens
Main Contributor: Sarah Coulter
Assignment: The goal with our tintypes was to create authentic, powerful period portraiture of the cast of Lawmen: Bass Reeves. Bass' story dates back to the mid 19th century, the dawn of wet plate photography both on glass and tin (ambrotypes and tintypes respectively). The process was no small task – we created a dark room on site, where we then shot on both black tin and ruby glass, sensitized, developed and fixed images before the talent's eyes. We wanted to elevate this not only in authentic process but with authentic art direction. After studying many authentic tintypes of the era, we landed on an elevated diorama-approach. We utilized a painted scenic backdrop along with period-correct propping from the show to create individual worlds for each character. Additionally, in our character motion pieces we built out gilded frames specific to each actor to really transport us back to the 1800s.
Approach: Rather than shooting digitally and opting to pull off a treatment in post, it was important to us to execute these historical portraits authentically. We utilized the 172-year-old process Wet Plate Collodion to create our tintype portraits. We took this one step further by avoiding opting for a more modern lens, the photographer utilized an 161-year-old lens from 1862 to lend the bokeh of the era and further lend itself to period-accuracy unmatched in modern treatments.
Results: The results were a great success from the day of the shoot the talent loved watching the images develop right before their eyes to the launch of the campaign. We were able to utilize behind the scenes footage of the shoot to put together a great BTS piece of talent reactions that performed well on Tiktok the day of the premiere. Press utilized multiple exclusive galleries of the tintype photography, including the debut in Entertainment Weekly. The tintype gallery posted on Instagram the day of the premiere quickly became the top performing still asset. Overall, the tintype campaign continues to be a great success as it rolls out.

79 LAWMEN BASS REEVES ENVIRONMENTAL PORTRAITS
Photographer: Kwaku Alston | Client: Paramount+
Equipment: Phase One, Phase One 80mm Lens | Main Contributor: Kwaku Alston
Assignment: The series focuses on Bass Reeves, bringing to life the story of a man who escaped slavery to become the first Black U.S. Marshal in the Old West and the most legendary law enforcement officer of his time. The mission is to create a bold and fearless campaign that shines a light on a hidden historical gem and celebrates the most notable. Black lawman in history whose powerful story is largely untold.
Approach: Our creative approach was to capture the essence of an untold legend, a love story between a man and his family, the Wild West, and the prestige talent of the series.
Results: The result was stunning environmental portraits that captured the essence of the series.

80 SPECIAL OPS: LIONESS ENVIRONMENTAL PORTRAITS
Photographer: Lynsey Addario | Client: Paramount+
Equipment: Nikon Z6, Nikon 50mm Lens | Main Contributor: Lynsey Addario
Assignment: The world is a dangerous place. "Lioness" introduces three strong, complex, and compelling lead characters, who toe the razor-thin line between what's right and what's needed to keep the world safe. Leverage stars Zoe Saldana and Nicole Kidman, while introducing Laysla De Oliveira, as they headline a star-studded production with academy-winning and nominated talent both in front of and behind the camera. Our goal is to ground the creative in reality while the stakes and emotions will feel real and big. This chase will take the audience to far-flung locations and highlight the duality between the opulence of this dangerous world and the brutality of the mission.
Approach: We wanted to capture the essence of the war photojournalism style. So we collaborated with Lynsey Addario, an American photojournalist. Her work often focuses on conflicts and human rights issues, especially the role of women in traditional societies.
Results: The result was authentic and had a sense of reality through the lens of a photojournalist.

81 AKOSIA | Photographer: Chris Budgeon | Client: Self-initiated
Equipment: Canon R5, Canon 50mm Lens, Canon 85mm Lens
Hair: Bernie Fiser | Makeup: Bernie Fiser | Clothing Stylist: Steph Hooke
Main Contributor: Chris Budgeon
Assignment: The assignment was to shoot an dditorial portrait of Melbourne singer, songwriter, and artist AKOSIA.

82, 83 DISAPPEARING ROOTS | Photographer: Ariel Freaner
Client: ZEVEN Magazine | Equipment: Nikon D3X

84 A THREAD OF HAIR | Photographer: Nyk Sykes
Client: AhKim Art of Hair | Equipment: Nikon Z6, Nikon 24-70mm Lens | Hair: AhKim Tan
Models: Joanna Gunay, Christina DiemPhuc, Gwen Barcenas-Hensley, Helin Marzuki
Main Contributor: Nyk Sykes
Assignment: I was approached by a leading international avant-garde hairstylist, AhKim Tan, to work on editorial submissions. AhKim is a finalist in London's International Visionary Awards 2023 at the Alternative Hair Show and has won the Intercoiffure Australia award for avant-garde hairstylist 9-times up to 2019.

Approach: We shot over a period of 18 months. Each headdress and accessory is individually designed and hand-made by AhKim. Tools and materials used include beads, fence wire, needle and cotton wool, hair extensions, and knitting on hair. I wanted to keep the handmade feel. I shot each in sunlight, with no flash used. Individual treatment depended on the texture, color, and shape of each piece.
Results: Photos here have been published by magazines in New York, Milan, Dubai, and San Diego.

85 ROBERT WUN - "BETWEEN REALITY & FANTASY"
Photographer: Colin Douglas Gray | Client: Savannah College of Art & Design
Equipment: Canon R5, Profoto Lights | Creative Director: Raf Gomes
Retoucher: Colin Douglas Gray | Main Contributor: Savannah College of Art & Design
Assignment: Photography of Robert Wun's exhibition at SCAD FASH.

86, 87 CARIBBEAN DREAMING | Photographer: Lians Jadan | Client: Hour Media
Equipment: Canon 5DSR, Profoto Strobes | Creative Director: Lindsay Richards
Model: Tiffany Granzow | Stylist: Rebecca Voigt | Makeup: Gabrielle Yanke | Hair: Monica Jadan
Photographer's Assistants: David Dalton, Raymar Patterson | Main Contributor: Lians Jadan
Assignment: I was approached by Hour Publication to conceptualize and execute a bridal fashion shoot. The envisioned theme revolved around a Caribbean-inspired setting in early April, necessitating the shoot to take place in the metro Detroit area due to budget constraints. Despite the usual temperature range of 40s to 50s, my objective was to scout a suitable location and effectively capture the essence of a tropical paradise, thus infusing the shoot with an exotic ambiance.
Approach: Upon receiving the client's brief, my approach involves immersing myself in many days of idea generation. This includes activities such as online research, recent AI creations, walks, going to museums, and exercise, all of which help me achieve mental clarity. Once a well-defined concept takes shape, I proceed to present these ideas to the client— in this instance, the magazine. With the client's approval, my next step is to secure a suitable location. For this particular project, I required an angular and inviting pool setting. Through persuasive negotiation, I successfully convinced The Griffin property to open their pool and have their pool deck prepared a month ahead of schedule, showcasing their commendable accommodation. While scouting locations, I work diligently to assemble the necessary crew and equipment. Prior to the actual shoot, I find it essential to engage in in-depth discussions about the concept with both the crew and talent. This collaborative approach ensures that everyone can contribute their skills optimally. Once the images are captured, I curate a selection of the best shots and present them to the client. This involves close collaboration to determine the layout and potential cover options. After finalizing the chosen images, they are sent off for retouching cleanup. Subsequently, I apply color grading and undertake the final stages of retouching, thus culminating in the polished and refined end result.
Results: Despite encountering an unexpected setback—arriving at the pool only to discover the heater malfunctioned—the model and I were unfazed. Braving the 40-degree water, we embraced the challenge and managed to capture shots that believably conceal the chilly conditions. The resulting images showcase no hint of discomfort, a testament to our dedication and commitment. I am thrilled to share that this series has not only achieved victory but has also secured placements as a finalist in several prestigious photography competitions this year. The recognition is truly exhilarating and serves as a validation of our artistic endeavors. Equally gratifying is the client's reaction to the final product. Their satisfaction is evident not only in their endorsement of the outcome but also in the tangible growth of their ad sales. These images have proven to be instrumental components of their sales deck, contributing to a substantial positive impact. Thinking back, the journey from overcoming the unexpected challenge to achieving recognition and fostering client success has been incredibly rewarding.

88 THE 70S SHOE | Photographer: Trevett McCandliss
Client: Footwear Plus Magazine | Equipment: Canon 5D Mark II, Canon 50mm Lens
Creative Directors: Trevett McCandliss, Nancy Campbell | Model: Miglė Gromnickaitė
Makeup: Maya Ling Feero | Hair: Vera Koumbiadis | Editor-in-Chief: Greg Dutter
Editor: Kathleen O'Reilly | Photographer's Assistants: William Eadon, Marco Scozzaro
Main Contributor: Trevett McCandliss
Assignment: A fashion editorial story featuring 70s-inspired footwear.
Approach: We used bright mod sets using geometric patterns. The photos were shot with crisp light and a bit of grain to create a retro feel.
Results: Everyone loved the story!

89 LIPS - ZADIG AND VOLTAIRE | Photographer: Michael Winokur
Client: Self-initiated | Equipment: Fuji GFX 100s | Model: Kiara Benioff
Makeup: Natasha Loudermilk | Main Contributor: Michael Winokur
Assignment: We were doing a beauty focused shoot with candy-colored makeup looks. The dress's lip print and the makeup were so fun together I started playing with how to make a picture pairing them. This image came from that exploration and triggered a new idea for me creatively.
Results: Inspired on set by the model's lips and the dress' print this image came from a moment of fun and games on set. In this case encouraging spontaneous exploration created a new idea which will generate future shoots and creative collaborations. The new series is called WRONG the plan is to explore fashion by dressing models incorrectly e.g. against the function of the garment.

90, 91 HOMER CAMPAIGN | Photographer: TC Reiner
Client: Terry R. Pillow | Equipment: Hasselblad
Assignment: Homer is a new luxury leather goods brand founded by Terry R. Pillow, former CEO of Tommy Bahama, and Coach. Pillow wanted to capture the feeling of living in Montecito, California, his newly adopted home, after retiring from a busy life in New York City.
Approach: The photographer put together a storyboard and scouted a variety of locations in and around Santa Barbara and Montecito. When he met with Pillow at his home, he was inspired by the beautiful silk wallpaper in the designer's living room. The model, Tiana, was a local girl just starting her modeling career, that the photographer knew because he had worked with her older sister for Vogue Magazine.
Results: The client loved the images and felt they captured both the flavor of Montecito and a powerful image for his brand.

92 GHOST GIRLS | Photographer: Harry Rifkin | Client: Self-initiated
Equipment: Leica SL2 | Hair: Alysha Marcantonio | Make-up: Alysha Marcantonio
Models: Alina Lee, Abby | Main Contributor: Harry Rifkin
Assignment: Bring to life the concept of Ghost Girls, two ladies who are spirits by day and night.
Approach: To explore the intersection of character with concept, to play with a clichéd depiction of a ghost.
Results: The result was a playful set of images that accomplish the goal of character and performance.

93 INSTALLATION #248: MUSEUM OF FINE ARTS, BOSTON + CIRQUE DU SOLEIL O #83 | Photographer: Howard Schatz | Client: Self-initiated
Equipment: Hasselblad | Main Contributor: Howard Schatz

94 ARES CONTEMPLATES THE COST OF COURAGE | Photographer: PJ Fugatze
Client: God | Equipment: Sony A7R IV, Zeiss Lenses, Profoto Flash
Photographer's Assistants: Aaron Tyler, Christopher Wray-McCann
Model: Jayson Glick | Hair: Barbara Velasco | Makeup: Barbara Velasco

95 ANDROMEDA REARS PEGASUS | Photographer: PJ Fugatze
Client: God | Equipment: Sony A7R IV, Zeiss Lenses, Profoto
Photographer's Assistant: Aaron Tyler | Model: Ariel Laxton
Makeup: Sooyoo Kim | Hair: Barbara Velasco | Main Contributor: PJ Fugatze

96 ALL-AMERICAN COWBOYS | Photographer: Ted Wright | Client: Self-initiated
Equipment: Canon 5D Mark III, Canon 85mm Lens, Epson Enhanced Matte Print, Epson Printer
Clothing Stylist: Amy Bollinger | Illustrator: Ted Wright | Designer: Ted Wright
Main Contributor: Ted Wright
Assignment: Fine Art images for a cowboy show. Photographs of my beautiful grandsons. I have 5 boys and I've been documenting their lives for over 12 years now. My new twins Miles and Marshall will be my next new victims of beautiful images. :)))
Approach: Wrangle the boys together, grab my camera, and shoot some kick-ass cowboy pics. So much fun!!!!
Results: Sold out show. Big images and that makes the difference.

97 SCARLETTE 1960 | Photographer: Harry Rifkin | Client: Self-initiated
Equipment: Leica SL2 | Hair: Alysha Marcantonio | Make-up: Alysha Marcantonio
Model: Alina Lee | Set Design: Tiffany Gabrus, thesweetzerlife | Main Contributor: Harry Rifkin
Assignment: Scarlette 1960 is one in a larger series of a character whose presence in multiple time periods is reflected in place, style, and performance. For this image, the concept involved being in an artificial garden overflowing with flowers.
Approach: Critical to the concept was the construction of the space in which the character would live and deliver on the narrative. Stylistically the wardrobe, hair, and makeup also need to connect to the period.
Results: The final result is a vibrant world for Scarlette to temporarily be in before she is off to another time and place.

98 SOMEDAY | Photographer: Harry Rifkin
Client: Self-initiated | Equipment: Leica SL2 | Hair: Alysha Marcantonio
Make-up: Alysha Marcantonio | Model: Alina Lee | Main Contributor: Harry Rifkin
Assignment: The objective was to explore the interaction of the flowers, the water, and Alina.
Approach: A look at the hair and makeup provides depth to the character all coupled with the romanticism of the flowers, veil, and water.

Results: The mix of elements produced the desired results, allowing for the stark nature of her skin to be offset by the pops of color and blood.

99 UNDERWATER STUDY #980: MODEL SHAWNEE FREE JONES
Photographer: Howard Schatz | Client: Self-initiated | Equipment: Hasselblad

100 SO FAR AWAY | Photographer: Craig Bromley | Client: Self-initiated
Equipment: 1960 Film Camera | Main Contributor: Craig Bromley
Assignment: Photograph two people searching.
Approach: Use a vintage 1960 film camera to add mystery.
Results: Image used for the band Between The Two.

101 SILENT DIALOGUE | Photographer: Carlos Caicedo
Client: Self-initiated | Equipment: Nikon Z9, Nikon 28-75mm Lens
Main Contributor: Carlos Caicedo
Assignment: In my continuous exploration of light, color, and form, I consider every form I create unique. They have a life in themselves.
Approach: Paper has always been my companion for life. After all, they've been part of our lives since childhood. Now I take those familiar forms and see them from a different perspective, always with the interest a child would see it.
Results: I'm my own client, and my audience helps my work survive. They take ownership of my work, and I find satisfaction in the process.

102 DE SADE PORTFOLIO 2 | Photographer: Barry Barnes
Client: Self-initiated | Equipment: Canon EOS 7D, Canon 18-135mm Lens
Model: Emily Bee | Main Contributor: Barry Barnes
Assignment: New work for my nearly 20-year portfolio project of art inspired by the writing of the Marquis de Sade. These pictures combine photography, traditional art and design to show off the many types of work I do in an edgy and creative way.
Approach: Ideas are sketched out and shown to the model before a photo shoot, to give her a general idea of the direction I have in mind. All digital work was created in Photoshop and Illustrator.
Results: My de Sade Portfolio pieces have been some of the most published and award-winning work I have ever produced.

103 DE SADE PORTFOLIO 1 | Photographer: Barry Barnes
Client: Self-initiated | Equipment: Canon EOS 7D, Canon 18-135mm Lens
Model: Lorna Lynne | Main Contributor: Barry Barnes
Assignment: New work for my nearly 20-year portfolio project of art inspired by the writing of the Marquis de Sade. These pictures combine photography, traditional art and design to show off the many types of work I do in an edgy and creative way.
Approach: Ideas are sketched out and shown to the model before a photo shoot, to give her a general idea of the direction I have in mind. All digital work was created in Photoshop and Illustrator.
Results: My de Sade Portfolio pieces have been some of the most published and award-winning work I have ever produced.

104 PAPER THIN | Photographer: Harry Rifkin | Client: Self-initiated
Equipment: Leica SL2 | Hair: Alysha Marcantonio | Make-up: Alysha Marcantonio
Model: Alina Lee | Main Contributor: Harry Rifkin
Assignment: The goal was to explore the interactions of paper materials applied to the nude form.
Approach: The process includes experimentation with a variety of paper materials to get the desired level of interaction.
Results: A delicate balance of all the elements into a single frame.

105 PAPER THIN | Photographer: Harry Rifkin | Client: Self-initiated
Equipment: Sony | Hair: Alysha Marcantonio | Make-up: Alysha Marcantonio
Model: Alina Lee | Main Contributor: Harry Rifkin
Assignment: The goal was to explore the interactions of paper materials applied to the nude form.
Approach: The process includes experimentation with a variety of paper materials to get the desired level of interaction.
Results: A delicate balance of all the elements into a single frame.

106, 107 HUMAN BODY STUDY, PAIRS #117: DANCERS EMILY ARDEN JONES & JOSHUA LEON EGUIA | Photographer: Howard Schatz
Client: Self-initiated | Equipment: Hasselblad

108 GHOST GIRL ~ ALINA | Photographer: Harry Rifkin | Client: Self-initiated
Equipment: Leica SL2 | Hair: Alysha Marcantonio | Make-up: Alysha Marcantonio
Model: Alina Lee | Main Contributor: Harry Rifkin
Assignment: Bring to life the concept of Ghost Girls, two ladies who are spirits by day and night.
Approach: To explore the intersection of character with concept, to play with a clichéd depiction of a ghost.
Results: The result is a playful set of images that accomplish the goal of character and performance.

109 HUMAN BODY STUDY #1555: KENDRA REPKO | Photographer: Howard Schatz
Client: Self-initiated | Equipment: Hasselblad

110 PIGMENT OF MY IMAGINATION | Photographer: Harry Rifkin
Client: Self-initiated | Equipment: Sony | Hair: Alysha Marcantonio
Make-up: Alysha Marcantonio | Model: Alina Lee | Main Contributor: Harry Rifkin
Assignment: The goal of Pigment of My Imagination was to experiment with the layering of pink paint over Alina's body.
Approach: We kept it simple, the materials and her performance are the driving forces of this image.
Results: Remarkable. The interaction of character and materials produced the desired image.

111 ODALISQUE | Photographer: PJ Fugatze
Client: Self-initiated | Equipment: Sony A7R IV, Zeiss Lenses, Profoto Flash
Photographer's Assistant: Aaron Tyler | Model: Sharon Le Berthon
Hair: Barbara Velasco | Makeup: Barbara Velasco | Main Contributor: PJ Fugatze

112 PERSEPHONE IN WINTER | Photographer: PJ Fugatze | Client: God
Equipment: Sony A7R IV, Zeiss Lenses, Profoto Flash | Main Contributor: PJ Fugatze
Assignment: Daughter of Mother Earth (Demeter), Persephone was kidnapped by Hades and taken to the underworld. After eating 4 pomegranate seeds in the underworld, Persephone was forced to return to Hades for 4 months every year. We call these months winter.

113 VALPINÇON BATHER | Photographer: PJ Fugatze | Client: Self-initiated
Equipment: Sony A7R IV, Zeiss Lenses, Profoto Flash | Model: Grace Gordon
Makeup: Sooyoo Kim | Hair: Barbara Velasco | Photographer's Assistant: Aaron Tyler
Assistant: Alana Torres | Main Contributor: PJ Fugatze

114 FLY BY NIGHT | Photographer: David Moenkhaus
Client: Self-initiated | Equipment: Fuji GFX 50s, Canon 100mm Lens
Assignment: A recent hike through a forest preserve took me right back to a moment of wonder when I was a little kid. A recent rainstorm passed through my area and when the temperature quickly dropped below freezing, all vegetation became completely covered in a thin cover of clear ice. It was beautiful and reminded me of that sense of wonder the first time I had seen it. I wanted to really plug into that wonder more, so I decided to replicate the effect back in my warm studio.
Approach: After freezing flowers, sticks, leaves, acorns, grasses, berries, and every other small piece of vegetation I could find I decided I wanted to concentrate on color so I simply froze every flower I could find (over a 1 year period) in varying compositions photographed them with a medium format digital camera in order to get razor sharp detail corner to corner and edge at the size I'll eventually print at which will be 34" x 22". I manipulated the freezing process in order to change the composition or create more or less air bubbles. The series is at 50 now but I'm still making the final edit.
Results: Since I'm still editing the images down to around 40, it's hard to stop. Photographing flowers every day through the Chicago winter was a joy. Feeling the ice in my hands was a joyful thing too, believe it or not. But I grew up in northern Michigan and we were always outside in winter, playing around and getting cold so that when we finally went back inside, we'd feel that warmth, and our bodies and our hearts melted.

115 LAST BLOOM | Photographer: Darnell McCown | Client: Self-initiated
Equipment: iPhone 14 Pro | Main Contributor: Darnell McCown
Assignment: I like the contrast of the old compost with the newer additions.....I also liked the idea that the flowers still had a beauty to reveal even after they were "retired".....I thought it had a kind of still life aspect.

116 BOTANICALS: LIGHT AND SHADOW | Photographer: Beth Galton
Client: Self-initiated | Equipment: Sinar 4x5, Phase One Digital Back
Assignment: It is the ephemeral quality of constant change in the natural world that interests me. I'm drawn to the wild nature of decaying flowers and leaves, which continue to evolve, past the freshness and familiarity of the bloom or bud, into other, unpredictable, often unfamiliar shapes and forms. This duality of freshness and decay–the necessity of both, the perennial march of time and of transformation, is mimicked in the natural light and shadow that I employ in my photos. While many cultural associations of shadows are negative, the presence of light necessitates the presence of shadow. While light illuminates the details and dimensions of our world, shadows allow us to see the nuances and subtle textures of what is illuminated. As time passes, shadows quickly move through our vision–physical reminders of the impermanence and transience of our world, our lives, and our bodies. My series is about the interaction of these evolving natural shapes and forms with the daylight in my studio. A kind of kinetic dance between the botanical and the shadow that it casts. My series explores the beauty to be found in change, in growth and decay, in shadow and in light.

117 DRINK, DESSERT, AND DECONSTRUCT | Photographer: Michael Alberstat
Client: Self-initiated | Equipment: Canon R5, Canon 50mm Lens | Stylist: Emily Nolan
Food Stylist: Janette Mitchell | Main Contributor: Michael Alberstat

Assignment: I wanted to create a fun, colorful narrative for my portfolio that was seasonal, fresh, and eye-catching. Not a typical recipe, but something playful using graphic elements and current lighting trends.
Approach: Working closely with the food and prop stylist we came up with the idea of two images that were food-based and a third that was a deconstruct of those shots. The image of the meringue with melon balls was graphic, seasonal, and interesting, the drink shot also incorporates the use of the fruit but is more elevated as a mocktail, and then the deconstruct using all the elements including the props with some human interaction.
Results: We are thrilled with how this turned out. The colors and graphic nature of the images work as individual shots or as a series, which is a great measure of how successful this shoot was.

118 MODULES MOVEMENT AND ASSEMBLY AT GCGV | Photographer: Robert Seale
Client: ExxonMobil | Equipment: Canon R5, Various Lenses
Creative Director: C. Len Shelton | Main Contributor: Robert Seale

Assignment: Document giant industrial modules being moved by ship to port, and subsequent installation at GCGV plant in South Texas.
Approach: Careful scheduling coordination with the creative team (assistants, drone ops, public affairs officials, coast guard, logistics company, security) as many of the module movements took place at off hours so that roads could be closed, etc.
Results: Photos were used on the Exxonmobil, SABIC, and GCGV websites and annual report and CCR publications.

119 NASA STARSHADE | Photographer: Craig Cutler
Client: National Geographic Magazine | Equipment: Leica SL2
Senior Photo Editor: Samantha Clark

Assignment: A cover story for National Geographic based on the principles of origami that relate to science.
Approach: To photograph a larger NASA sunshade like a large work of art.

120, 121 ARCOSA - LIMESTONE QUARRY IN BRITISH COLUMBIA, CANADA
Photographer: Tadd Myers | Client: Arcosa Specialty Materials
Equipment: Canon R5, DJI Mavic 3 | Main Contributor: Tadd Myers

Assignment: These images were captured at a Limestone Quarry & processing facility on Texada Island off the coast of British Columbia, Canada. Arcosa uses our images for their corporate website, social media channels, collateral marketing, & corporate wall displays.

122 PARISIAN TWINS | Photographer: Laurie Frankel
Client: Self-initiated | Equipment: iPhone 12 Pro

Assignment: While helping my old photo professor in class he taught in Paris, I stayed in part of an old carriage house. This is the bedroom in it.
Approach: I very much liked the spartan simplicity of the room.

123 LIBERTY FLOURISHING | Photographer: Ariel Freaner
Client: ZEVEN Magazine | Equipment: Nikon D3X | Main Contributor: Ariel Freaner

Assignment: Editorial.
Approach: Liberty Flourishing in 2022. Freedom Plaza building in NYC.
Results: Dramatic visual results.

124 DAVID AND PATRIC | Photographer: Geoff Story | Client: Self-initiated
Equipment: Canon 5D Mark III | Main Contributor: Geoff Story

Assignment: I was immediately drawn to David and Patric. They had an almost Socratic air about them. At one point during the shoot, Patric cradled David's head in his arm and a modern pietá emerged. They could have been carved from marble. Their statue-like embrace doesn't feel cold to me, but solid, like the life they've built together.
Approach: I've been working on a documentary chronicling gay history for the past five years. Along the way I have met some amazing people, many of whom have agreed to interview for the film and to allow me to photograph them. In this case, I met my subjects by chance at a campground on a weekend getaway. Before taking out my camera, I approached them and we talked for some time. I didn't ask many questions, allowing them to gradually open up on their terms. I then shared my own life experiences.
Results: The documentary is still in progress, but this photograph was very meaningful to these men. It is part of a body of work I am building that documents the elders of the GLBTQ community.

125 CHILDREN WITH WATERFALL | Photographer: Craig Cutler
Client: Self-initiated | Equipment: Leica M10 Mono

Assignment: Found moment of children with waterfall.

126 THE KING OF THE DESERT | Photographer: Gaspar Marquez
Client: Self-initiated | Equipment: Canon AE-1 | Main Contributor: Gaspar Marquez

Assignment: I've always been attracted to the Sonoran Desert in souther Arizona. I don't know, for some reason I think it's such a special, mysterious and magical place on Earth. This body of work I'm showing you is an homage to this unique habitat where I found all these special elements that I'm drawn to, especially the Monarch of the Desert which is Carnegiea gigantea or Saguaro. By 95-100 years in age, a saguaro cactus can reach a height of 15-16 feet, and could start to produce its first arm. By 200 years old, the saguaro cactus has reached its full height, reaching upwards of 45 feet tall.
Approach: I took a plane to Tucson Az., I borrowed my sister's car and drove to the Saguaro National Park west, I found the perfect spot and hiked until I felt I had approached the perfect suspects for my assignment, or let me put it this way, I felt that the Saguaros chose me to take their portraits.
Results: IPA INTERNATIONAL PHOTOGRAPHY AWARDS 2023 Official Selection & Honorable Mention, Category: Analog/Film, Fine Art; ANALOG SPARKS AWARDS 2023 Honorable Mention, Category: Nature/Plant. So far El Gordo is being shown in an online exhibition for Analog Forever Magazine called Elemental in April 2023

127 THE GIRL IN THE WATERFALL | Photographer: Per Breiehagen
Client: Self-initiated | Equipment: Canon R5, Canon 14-35mm Lens | Model: Anja Breiehagen

Assignment: A Norwegian girl in traditional dress announces Norwegian Constitution Day across the valley of Ål, Hallingdal with her lur (ancient signal horn). The photo is inspired by the nostalgic Norwegian romantic nationalism painters of the mid 19th century. Norwegian romantic nationalism emphasized the aesthetics of Norwegian nature and the uniqueness of the Norwegian national identity. I grew up with these iconic paintings in our literature and galleries— they left a lifelong impression on me. Whenever I wandered in our dramatic nature I visualized how life had been back then. Over the years I've pursued a few ideas to re-create scenes from that time period that feel as authentic as possible about life in the mountains and in the fjords. The final image was sent out as a self-promotional mailer and a social media post on May 17, Norwegian Constitution Day.
Approach: Authenticity is the key in an image like this. The clothing has to match the idea of traditional life in the mid 19th century Norway life. The whole outfit and the horn, look just like they did over a 150 years ago. I grew up near this waterfall so I know it well. The water flow had to be just right to be able to access the rocks to shoot, too much water and the rocks are all covered in raging water and very dangerous to access. I have tried to get this scene just right for several years and finally got the right light and flow last year.
Results: I got great feedback on the image.

128 A BREATH | Photographer: Yichen Wang | Client: Self-initiated | Equipment: Fuji XT-10

Assignment: This is Chaka Salt Lake, a clear realm I reached after driving for hours and taking a small train. The sky and the lake here are clear and bright, everything will be reflected by the broad lake. It is a meditative world, where each can breathe cleanses souls.

128 VASE ROCK | Photographer: Clarence Lin | Client: Self-initiated
Equipment: Nikon D850 | Artist: Clarence Lin | Main Contributor: Clarence Lin

Assignment: Vase Rock, Liuqiu Township, Pingtung County, Taiwan.

129 JOURNEY OF DISCOVERY | Photographer: Wolfgang Gast
Client: Self-initiated | Equipment: iPhone 11 | Main Contributor: Wolfgang Gast

Assignment: Journey of discovery: unknown island – surprising landscape – architecture that tells stories.
Approach: Journey of discovery: object, light, mood – momentary shots of unexpected moments.
Results: Journey of discovery: back to photography – rediscovering my passion – united in one photo series.

130 SCAD FILM FESTIVAL 25TH ANNIVERSARY | Photographer: Colin Douglas Gray
Client: Savannah College of Art & Design | Equipment: Phase One IQ4, Profoto Lights
Creative Directors: Hadley Stambaugh, Siobhan Bonnouvrier | Stylist: Mitchell Hall
Retouchers: Colin Douglas Gray, David Field | Props: Darren McWhorter, Kristopher Hegland
Producers: Ryan King, Trey Vereen, Jenny Upperman | Set Designers: Darren McWhorter, Kristopher Hegland | Makeup: Tre Knight | Hair: Tyler Lively, Latecka Moor-Early
Main Contributor: Savannah College of Art & Design

Assignment: The assignment was a campaign for SCAD's 25th Anniversary of the Savannah Film Festival.

131 JO 2 | Photographer: Craig Cutler | Client: Self-initiated | Equipment: Leica SL2

Assignment: Photographing my favorite subject.
Approach: To create dramatic portraits with my dog as my favorite muse.

132 LEATHERCRAFTING, TUCSON AZ | Photographer: Michael Schoenfeld
Client: Self-initiated | Equipment: Sony A-1, Various Lenses
Main Contributor: Michael Schoenfeld

133 BARS AND STRIPES | Photographer: Michael Schoenfeld | Client: Self-initiated
Equipment: Sony A-1, Various Lenses | Main Contributor: Michael Schoenfeld

134 DAVID FAULK, FOLSOM STREET FAIR | Photographer: Howard Schatz
Client: Self-initiated | Equipment: Hasselblad | Main Contributor: Howard Schatz

135 SELF PORTRAIT | Photographer: Craig Cutler
Client: Self-initiated | Equipment: Twin Lens Rollei Camera
Assignment: Personal self-portrait.
Approach: The approach I took was using a twin lens Rollei camera with two mirrors to create a diptych.

136 NEVER FORGOTTEN - IN HONOR OF OUR AMERICAN VETERANS
Photographer: Ted Wright | Client: JCVT (Jefferson County Veterans Tribute)
Equipment: Canon 5D Mark III, Canon 85mm Lens, Epson Heavyweight Enhanced Matte Paper, Epson Printer | Illustrator: Ted Wright | Designer: Ted Wright | Main Contributor: Ted Wright
Assignment: The JCVT organization came to me to produce a poster image for our American Veterans for their Veterans Park. The image was inspired by my Uncle Joseph W. Morrison who was killed in Vietnam. In his letters that he wrote home to his mother Sybil Morrison, he stated that he would get up every morning to pray that God would give him and his platoon the courage and strength to fight in the jungles of Vietnam. He was killed March 17, 1967. I was nine years old when I looked out of my grandma's farm house window when I saw a large black car come down our gravel road. As soon as my grandma saw the car she let out the longest and loudest scream that I still hear to this day. The two dressed men came to give her the tragic news. It was devastating to our family. It's in his honor that this piece is titled "NEVER FORGOTTEN".
Results: Print available for consumers. Proceeds go to the Vietnam Veterans. ©2023 Ted Wright.

136 FASHION IS EXHAUSTING | Photographer: Laurie Frankel
Client: Self-initiated | Equipment: Nikon D850, Nikon 24-70mm Lens

137 GOLDEN BOY | Photographer: Yaniurka Pedroza
Client: Savannah College of Art & Design | Equipment: Canon EOS R5
Creative Directors: Hadley Stambaugh, Siobhan Bonnouvrier | Retoucher: Yaniurka Pedroza
Main Contributor: Savannah College of Art & Design
Assignment: BTS for the SCAD's fashion film promo 2023.

138 WHERE'S JERRY JOSEPH | Photographer: Michael Schoenfeld
Client: Artist Commission | Equipment: Sony A-1, Various Lenses
Main Contributor: Michael Schoenfeld

139 ASYMMETRY | Photographer: Yaniurka Pedroza
Client: Savannah College of Art & Design | Equipment: Canon EOS R5
Retoucher: Yaniurka Pedroza | Creative Directors: Hadley Stambaugh, Siobhan Bonnouvrier
Main Contributor: Savannah College of Art & Design
Assignment: BTS for the SCAD's fashion film promo 2023.

140 PORTRAITS IN COSTA RICA | Photographer: Craig Cutler
Client: Self-initiated | Equipment: Leica M11
Assignment: A collaborative portrait project with my son, photographing local people in Costa Rica.
Approach: I used only natural light in the natural environment and embraced its constant changes.

141 ABOUT YOU | Photographer: Davis Bell
Clients: About You, Max Poscente | Equipment: Sony A7R II, Canon 28mm Lens
Main Contributor: Davis "Winterlamaster" Bell
Assignment: Max and I met in 2020 amidst his recoding sessions in Dallas and the looming lockdowns experienced in the US. The tumultuous atmosphere and psychological havoc the year was exacting upon us was palpable and we both knew we needed an escape. After only having known each other for 72 hours we plotted our excursion. Our intent-leaving the 24 hour news cycle to find something that could reinvigorate and refresh our eyes. I knew of this location, having stumbled across it on one of my many back-road journeys. I knew it need to be spoken about, and with Max on board, it became the perfect pairing.
Approach: During his creative process in the studio at Modern Electric Sound Recorders , Max (About You) , was pushed out of his element and forced to reckon with the internal and external forces of the process. I wanted to showcase Max in a realm that both encapsulated the mystery of a place but also spoke to the importance to exploring the variations of our own hubris. This former settlement represented that in both the seen remnants of the failed municipality, and the unseen residue of the former inhabitants with their intentions and plans.
Results: This series is cherished amongst a small circle of peers and Max.

142 PORTRAIT OF JENNELL JUAREZ | Photographer: Bill Moree
Clients: Book Project, Self-initiated | Equipment: Fuji GFX 100, Fuji 110mm Lens
Main Contributors: Bill Moree, Jennell Juarez
Assignment: This was part of a series of proof-of-concept work for an ongoing book project.
Approach: I've developed a new portraits and still life portfolios using additive (red, green and blue) lighting. The colors delicately morph with the smallest of gestures. The technique references an intersection of Fauvist paintings and chiaroscuro lighting.
Results: This new work from this book project is being very well received by editorial clients, and is currently leading to some lovely commissions.

143 KATI BRUNINI | Photographer: Michael Schoenfeld | Client: Self-initiated
Equipment: Sony A-1, Various Lenses | Main Contributor: Michael Schoenfeld

144 LILY GLADSTONE, 2023 | Photographer: Lindsay Siu
Client: The Hollywood Reporter | Equipment: Canon R5, Profoto
Stylist: Jason Rembert | Makeup: Alannah Bilodeau | Hair: Carly Campbell
Retoucher: Babydoll Studio | Producer: Ava Selbach
Main Contributors: Lindsay Siu, The Hollywood Reporter
Assignment: Portrait of actress Lily Gladstone for The Hollywood Reporter, Cannes Issue 2023.

145 SHOWCASE | Photographer: Aman Shakya
Client: Savannah College of Art & Design | Equipment: Canon R5, Canon 24-70mm Lens
Creative Directors: Hadley Stambaugh, Siobhan Bonnouvrier | Retoucher: Taylor Franco
Producer: Jenny Upperman | Stylist: Mitchell Hall | Hair: Tre Knight | Makeup: Tre Knight
Main Contributor: Savannah College of Art & Design
Assignment: Headshots for Performing Arts Showcase.

146 TATTOOS AT THE PRISON 2, BOISE ID | Photographer: Michael Schoenfeld
Client: Self-initiated | Equipment: Sony A-1, Various Lenses
Main Contributor: Michael Schoenfeld

146 TATTOOS AT THE PRISON 3, BOISE ID | Photographer: Michael Schoenfeld
Client: Self-initiated | Equipment: Sony A-1, Various Lenses
Main Contributor: Michael Schoenfeld

147 TATTOOS AT THE PRISON 1, BOISE ID | Photographer: Michael Schoenfeld
Client: Self-initiated | Equipment: Sony A-1, Various Lenses
Main Contributor: Michael Schoenfeld

148 UPRIGHT | Photographer: Fangqiu Huang | Client: Fong Captain
Equipment: iPhone 13 | Main Contributor: Fangqiu Huang
Assignment: Exploring women's empowerment.
Approach: The Levitated Mass at LACMA.
Results: Powerful and beautiful at the same time.

149 RISING STARS | Photographer: Allison Smith | Client: Savannah College of Art & Design
Equipment: Canon R5, Canon 24-70mm Lens, Profoto Lights
Creative Directors: Hadley Stambaugh, Siobhan Bonnouvrier | Retoucher: Scott Newman
Producer: Jenny Upperman | Stylist: Mitchell Hall | Hair: Tre Knight
Makeup: Tre Knight | Main Contributor: Savannah College of Art & Design
Assignment: Headshots for selected Performing Arts graduates.

150 MATTHEW HEPWORTH | Photographer: Michael Schoenfeld
Client: Self-initiated | Equipment: Sony A-1, Various Lenses
Main Contributor: Michael Schoenfeld

151 SAN MIGUEL CAFE, DAN BULLARD | Photographer: Michael Schoenfeld
Client: Self-initiated | Equipment: Sony A-1, Various Lenses
Main Contributor: Michael Schoenfeld

152 OBSTRUCTED PORTRAITS | Photographer: Craig Cutler
Client: Self-initiated | Equipment: Leica SL2
Assignment: To create a series of self-portraits.
Approach: To be adventurous in creating a series of self-portraits that all have an element of surprise.

153 SI LAS MIRADAS MATARAN | Photographer: Yaniurka Pedroza
Client: Savannah College of Art & Design | Equipment: Canon EOS R5
Creative Directors: Hadley Stambaugh, Siobhan Bonnouvrier | Retoucher: Yaniurka Pedroza
Main Contributor: Savannah College of Art & Design
Assignment: BTS for the SCAD's fashion film promo 2023.

154 CELEBRITIES + SUPER TALENT PRESTIGE INTERNATIONAL MAGAZINE
Photographer: Amyn Nasser | Clients: Prestige International Magazine, Self-initiated
Equipment: Nikon D800, Nikon D810, Nikon 17-35mm Lens, Nikon 60mm Lens, Nikon 85mm Lens, Nikon 105mm Lens, Profoto Lighting Acute, Photek Umbrellas
Art Director: Amyn Nasser | Producers: Nasser.Studio, Neptune Comm
Stylists: Jennifer O'Bannon, Melissa Laskin | Models: Veronica Ferres, James Goldstein, Emanuela Postacchini, Donovan J. Leitch, Taylor Bagley, Sonya Walger, Eugenia Kuzmina, Susie Abromeit | Countries: United States of America, France
Main Contributor: Nasser.Studio
Assignment: The Editorial Stories I shot for Prestige International Magazine were always large stories often 16 pages per story. Very often I would do 3-6 stories which meant the stories had to be impactful and well thought out. The most important factor to me was keeping the strong feminine strength yet showing the Female and Innocence across the full story. In addition, the scope of Kinetic Technicolor I use involved a large

mix of tonalities which meant it had to work with the selection of frocks and garments. My love for the Female Feminine in Style is evident with a mix of East West from Indian FilmFare to the influences of Hollywood and Franco-Italian visualization.
Approach: I work fast. Do not rely in a large way on mood boards as it is cumbersome to stop for such limitations. And, when shooting there is no need to stop after every shot to show the Talent the shot - I find that gets in the way of capturing a split second of many seconds in brief bursts of moments where the innocence is escaping, and I have to catch it before it leaves the Space of Time!
Results: Incredible Success as the issues of Prestige International always sold out. My Fashion Stories were the strongest and had a lot of comments.

155 REDMAYNE | Photographer: Aman Shakya
Client: Savannah College of Art & Design | Equipment: Canon R5, Canon 24-70mm Lens
Creative Directors: Hadley Stambaugh, Siobhan Bonnouvrier | Retoucher: Taylor Franco
Main Contributor: Savannah College of Art & Design
Assignment: SCAD Savannah Film Festival Portrait.

156 STANDING DESK | Photographer: Laurie Frankel
Client: Robert Valentine | Equipment: Nikon D850, Nikon 24-70mm Lens
Assignment: For a day, I followed one of my creative collaborators, Robert Valentine, to document his approach to work.
Approach: I particularly liked this image because it expressed the formalism in his work and the multiple ways he sees things.

157 SACRED PARADOX | Photographer: Nicolò Sertorio
Client: Self-initiated | Equipment: Nikon D850
Assignment: "Sacred Paradox" delves into the enigmatic duality of Oakland, where places of worship abound amidst escalating violence and dwindling attendance. This project navigates the multifaceted identities of the city's spiritual leaders, exploring their transformative potential and connection to the community. Oakland, a vibrant crucible of faith traditions, presents perplexing questions. Why does violence persist despite the proliferation of sacred spaces? Why is attendance at spiritual gatherings waning? Through the symbiosis of portraiture and audio interviews, their personas unfurl. Within their dual portraits, we capture their spiritual depths, drawing inspiration from the sanctuaries that shape their teachings. Intertwined with the imagery, the audio interviews resonate, revealing their insights and ideas. Intimate reflections and impassioned calls for change echo through the narrative. Their collective guidance bridges the chasm between spirituality and community engagement. "Sacred Paradox" beckons viewers to embrace the collective journey of rediscovering spirituality, fostering connections, and shaping a harmonious future. By elevating their voices and experiences, we hope to ignite conversations that inspire meaningful change. This project invites viewers to embrace the sacred paradox of Oakland and envision a world where spirituality and communal engagement intertwine to forge a brighter path forward.
Results: The project is still in launch phase.

158 SPEED | Photographer: Aman Shakya
Client: Savannah College of Art & Design | Equipment: Canon R5, Canon 24-70mm Lens
Creative Directors: Hadley Stambaugh, Siobhan Bonnouvrier | Producer: Ryan King
Stylist: Tre Knight | Makeup: Naomi Hannon | Hair: Naomi Hannon
Photo Retouching: Taylor Franco | Main Contributor: Savannah College of Art & Design
Assignment: Photoshoot for the Athletics Department at SCAD.

159 BOXER ANTONIO MARGARITO AFTER THE FIGHT, COWBOYS STADIUM, TEXAS
Photographer: Howard Schatz | Client: Self-initiated | Equipment: Hasselblad

160, 161 SPEEDO FASTSKIN CAMPAIGN | Photographer: Beetle Rhind
Client: Speedo | Equipment: Canon R5, Canon 28-70mm Lens
Advertising Agency: Pentland Brands | Art Directors: Andrew Ross-Sheeran, Stu Ross-Sheeran
Photo Retouching: The Forge | Main Contributor: Beetle Rhind
Assignment: The brief was to create an abstract image of speed and motion but still to be able to make out the swim ware. It was also required do do am much of this in camera as possible.
Approach: I approached this buy using a mixture of constant and flash lighting, by mixing the do different light sources and setting your camera to a longer exposure you're able to freeze an element of the movement with the flash, but allow the rest of the frame which is lit by the constant light to have movement of the athlete within it. This insures the athlete is sharp at the moment the flash fires and give blur either before or after.
Results: I was super pleased with the results we managed to achieve everything in camera and choosing a higher camera angle cleaned up the background. We then simplified the background slightly in post to give it a really graphic minimal feel.

162 23/24 SEASON STILLS | Photographer: Grant Gunderson | Client: Tampa Bay Lightning
Equipment: Canon R5, Canon 24-70mm Lens, Profoto Pro Heads, Profoto Pro Packs
Chief Creative Officer: Troy Dunn | Creative Director: Stephanie Morrison
Associate Creative Director: Mitch Feickert | Senior Account Executive: Jessica Hall
Main Contributor: Grant Gunderson
Assignment: Every season we photograph the National Hockey League's Tampa Bay Lightning to have fresh content and have the most up-to-date library with new players. This photography is used for all marketing materials throughout the year from stadium graphics to city takeovers, to social. Normally we shoot in a controlled studio and get each player at multiple angles to cover all layout needs. The main goal for this shoot was to do something we had never done before, capturing the players in-movement and on the ice.
Approach: Since we'd never done a full-speed action shoot, we had two stations back-to-back on ice: one to get our action shots, the other to get more traditionally posed shots. A scout helped us figure out the workable shooting space, and allowed us to ensure we could successfully light the players to capture their full motion without drop off, all while keeping the ice free and clear of cables. We utilized 4 Profoto's with Pro Packs to allow us to shoot 12 to 15 frames per second. The new Canon R5 allowed us to lock onto the player's eye and hold it without dropping during their extremely fast on-ice movement.
Results: The results were exactly what we were hoping for. Our agency team, as well as the client, felt energized by having such fresh and interesting content to work with. We've partnered with this client for over 10 years now, and in that time the only action photos our team or the Lightning internal team have ever had to use in creative layouts were from game footage. This sort of photography was much less controlled, and much lower resolution. Now, we have a library of photography for a whole season which uniquely conveys the kineticism and athleticism of our team doing what they do best.

163 WIRED FLOWERS | Photographer: Robert Tardio
Client: Self-initiated | Equipment: Phase One XF IQ3, Phase One Digital Back
Stylist: Linden Elstran | Main Contributor: Robert Tardio
Assignment: The concept was to use different gages of wire to create armatures to support and intertwine with the nature flower forms.
Approach: I worked with Linden Elstran to create the flower supports.
Results: The images are ongoing. So far industry response has been great.

164, 165 SOLE STOPPERS | Photographer: Tatsuro Nishimura
Client: Genlux Magazine | Equipment: Cambo View Camera
Art Director: Stephen Kamifuji | Stylist: Mimi Lombardo
Assignment: Luxury Shoe Story for Genlux Magazine 23 Spring issue.
Approach: Because the theme was Hollywood Red Carpet, I wanted the shoes to be playful yet elegant. I rigged the shoes as if they were walking or dancing and lit them with hard lights to get some bling!
Results: The client was pleased!

166 GLASS STILL LIFE | Photographer: Craig Cutler
Client: Self-initiated | Equipment: Leica SL2
Assignment: Personal project.
Approach: Create a still life series contained inside of a single water glass.

167 AFTERMATH: THE OVERTURNING OF ROE VS. WADE | Photographer: Beth Galton
Client: Washington Post | Equipment: Sinar 4x5, Phase One Digital Back
Art Director: Bette Blau | Producer: Candace Gottschalk
Assignment: In the Dutch still life paintings of the 17th century—with their platters of half-slurped oysters, sweating cheeses, split fruits, and wilted blooms—we spectators are witness to an aftermath. They are compositional fictions, fantasy picnics which have taken place before our arrival on the scene. Who laid out these weird feasts? Who ate? Who knows? Aftermath is also the subject of these still lifes. They investigate the consequences of the Supreme Court's decision to overturn Roe vs. Wade, the consequences on women's reproductive health and freedom. In the months leading up to that decision, information about how to give oneself an abortion surged across social-media platforms. This is the sad, secret knowledge passed from woman to woman in the absence of safe and legal abortion care. On first look, like their Dutch precursors, the images convey abundance: fruits and flowers, herbs and vessels. But these tablescapes are macabre, confronting the viewer with the tools and tactics that desperate women used to end unwanted pregnancies before abortion was an enshrined right, and are once again using in a post-Roe world. These dangerous home abortifacients are now the reality for many women across America. Among the classical Dutch still life style, there is a sub-genre known as vanitas paintings, which serve to remind the viewer of one's mortality through not-so-subtle emblems like burning candles, and human skulls. I evoked this history throughout the series to

underline the few, desperate choices women have to end a pregnancy and the mortal danger that lurks amidst that desperation. Adopting the style of classic Dutch paintings has allowed me to arrange everyday items in a familiar framework, casting a feeling of ease and prosperity over the photos, which, on closer examination, tell a much darker, more perilous story. It is a story of the present plunged back to the past, back to a time when our rights for an abortion were limited and our very freedom rested in the objects, plants and pills that surrounded us. Using the antiquated style of the classical still life in this series of photos sparks a conversation with the past, a world which we thought was long behind us but with the reversal of Roe vs. Wade, is here once more.
Approach: Collaboration with my team.

168 AIR DUCT | Photographer: Craig Cutler | Client: Self-initiated | Equipment: Leica SL2
Assignment: A personal project using industrial air ducts.
Approach: Creating sculptures by shaping air ducts into works of art.

169 WIRED COSMETICS | Photographer: Robert Tardio
Client: Self-initiated | Equipment: Phase One XF IQ3, Phase One Digital Back
Stylist: Linden Elstran | Main Contributor: Robert Tardio
Assignment: The concept was to use armature wire to create sculpture forms to hold and highlight products.
Approach: Different gages of wire were used to create organic shapes to highlight the products.
Results: The series has been well received via promotion and social media.

170 GREEN PRESS JUICE | Photographer: Joseph Saraceno
Client: JSW Green Press Juice | Equipment: Canon, Profoto Lights
Creative Director: Wilson Wong | Stylist: Suzanne Campos
Main Contributor: Joseph Saraceno

171 HEAVY METALS: BRASS | Photographer: Joseph Saraceno
Client: JSW | Equipment: Canon, Profoto Lights
Creative Director: Wilson Wong | Main Contributor: Joseph Saraceno

172 LEBRON'S FRUITY PEBBLES | Photographer: Cheryl Vorhis
Clients: Arman Salemi, Heritage Auction | Equipment: Canon EOS R5
Retoucher: Hayley Tracewell | Main Contributor: Cheryl Vorhis
Assignment: Heritage Auction began a new department in 2022, Sneakers. Arman Salemi was a fresh face to the Studio. Sneakers had a new approach to the new category. Here we are able to approach shooting with new and creative ideas. Each sneaker is sold as a collectible. This particular shoe is from Lebron James' Nike collection, inspired by his favorite cereal, Fruity Pebbles.
Approach: Heritage Auction is different from large budget ad agencies. Here we have only one sneaker, so my approach was simple; learn what the inspiration behind the shoe is and see if it can be incorporated.
Results: The image came out the way I imagined. Arman was super hipped with are Fruity Pebble shoes.

173 TRIFECTA SNEAKERS | Photographer: Andrien Trujillo | Client: Arman Salemi
Equipment: Canon R5, Canon 24-105mm Lens, Prints for Trifecta Sneakers Showcase
Retoucher: Hayley Tracewell
Assignment: Arman Salemi, department director for sneakers, chooses the sneakers that will have beauty shots for the Trifecta Sneakers Showcase. Arman wanted the shoes showcased to stand on their own as well as a collection. Arman gave me full creative freedom.
Approach: As a collection the main lighting was moody and from above to be cohesive. To have the images stand on their own, I picked background colors and/or textures to compliment or contrast with the shoes.
Results: Both Arman and his external clients were pleased.

174, 175 PITCHER AND PROSCIUTTO | Photographer: Laurie Frankel
Client: March | Equipment: Hasselblad H5X, Phase One Digital Back
Assignment: Home decor store March in San Francisco offers high end items. In our projects together, we create clean, elegant settings which show off the product in simple, accessible ways.
Approach: In this image we wanted to convey the size, strength, and versatility of the butcher block without making it the focus.

176 LIMELIFE SKINCARE SERIES | Photographer: Robert Tardio
Client: LimeLife by Alcone | Equipment: Phase One XF IQ3, Phase One Digital Back
Stylist: Megan Krieman | Retoucher: Jason Harrington
Main Contributor: Robert Tardio
Assignment: We were approached by LimeLife to create a series of "cocktails" showing some of the product ingredients exploding out of various cocktail glasses.
Approach: Working from a list of ingredients for each product, stylist Megan Krieman and I built stationary flowers and ingredient collections and mounted them above the various glasses. Separately, my assistants and I shot various splashes emerging from each type of glass. The elements were combined in post to create six different "cocktail" splashes.
Results: LimeLife was very pleased with the results which have been used in digital and print advertising.

177 RACE STUDY | Photographer: Craig Cutler | Client: Self-initiated
Equipment: Leica SL2 | Main Contributor: Craig Cutler
Assignment: A visual narrative on why racism will not go away.

178 STILA DUO STICKS | Photographer: Takahiro Igarashi
Client: Stila Cosmetics | Equipment: Phase One XF IQ380
Creative Director: Amy Fitzgerald | Main Contributor: Takahiro Igarashi
Assignment: Create a dynamic, bold, visual in a minimalistic way to showcase the duo-shaded Stila sticks.
Approach: Finding a solution to showcase the package and the textures in a clean yet raw way.
Results: Loved it!

179 LAUREN HOLIDAY 02 | Photographer: Nicholas Duers
Client: Ralph Lauren | Equipment: Phase One XF | Main Contributor: Nicholas Duers
Assignment: A favorite image from a recent shoot for Holiday 22/23.

180, 181 GREY GLASSWARE | Photographer: Laurie Frankel | Client: March
Equipment: Hasselblad H5X, Phase One Digital Back, Hasselblad 80mm Lens
Assignment: Home decor store March in San Francisco offers high-end items. In our projects together, we create clean, elegant settings that show off the product in simple, accessible ways. Often the images, as in the case of this one, are inspired by a shot from a collection of old photos owned by the creative director. This shot was of grey glassware.
Approach: The smokiness of the glass inspired a feeling of an old tintype. We cut and diffused the light a lot and painted a backdrop specifically to get that feel for the shot.

SILVER WINNERS:
183 INMUSE | Photographer: Florin Gabor | Client: Lithuanian Academy of Music & Theatre
Equipment: Nikon D4, 50mm Tiltshift Lens | Creative Director: Florin Gabor
Director of Project Management: Mantautas Krukauskas | Main Contributor: Florin Gabor

183 MOUNTAIN MIRROR | Photographer: Per Breiehagen | Client: Self-initiated
Equipment: Canon R5, Canon 14-35mm Lens | Model: Lori Evert

184 USMC #1 | Photographer: Patrick Molnar | Client: Marines | Equipment: Canon R5
Creative Director: Haley Kochersperger | Ad Agency: Wunderman Thompson

184 USMC #2 | Photographer: Patrick Molnar | Client: Marines | Equipment: Canon R5
Creative Director: Haley Kochersperger | Ad Agency: Wunderman Thompson

184 USMC #7 | Photographer: Patrick Molnar | Client: Marines | Equipment: Canon R5
Creative Director: Haley Kochersperger | Ad Agency: Wunderman Thompson

184 USMC #5 | Photographer: Patrick Molnar | Client: Marines | Equipment: Canon R5
Creative Director: Haley Kochersperger | Ad Agency: Wunderman Thompson

184 USMC #8 | Photographer: Patrick Molnar | Client: Marines | Equipment: Canon R5
Creative Director: Haley Kochersperger | Ad Agency: Wunderman Thompson

184 USMC #4 | Photographer: Patrick Molnar | Client: Marines | Equipment: Canon R5
Creative Director: Haley Kochersperger | Ad Agency: Wunderman Thompson

185 SUMMER CHERRY DROP | Photographer: Jan Kalish
Client: Self-initiated | Equipment: Fuji GFX 100 | Retoucher: Madeline Murray

185 23193 AUGUST LUXE JEWELS SHOWCASE POSTCARD
Photographer: Darnell McCown | Clients: Jill Burgum, Heritage Auctions
Equipment: Horseman LD Pro, Phase One Digital Back, Rodenstock APO Sironar Digital 135mm Lens, Schneider APO Digitar 210mm Lens, Dynalite | Digital Artist: Todd Hudgins
Main Contributor: Darnell McCown

185 FEATURE IMAGES FROM WATCHES & FINE TIMEPIECES #5550
Photographer: Darnell McCown | Clients: Jim Wolf, Heritage Auctions
Equipment: Horseman LD Pro, Phase One Digital Back, Rodenstock APO Sironar Digital 135mm Lens, Schneider APO Digitar 210mm Lens, Dynalite | Digital Artist: Juan Cruz
Main Contributor: Darnell McCown

186 USMC #3 | Photographer: Patrick Molnar
Client: Marines | Equipment: Canon R5 | Creative Director: Haley Kochersperger
Ad Agency: Wunderman Thompson

186 USMC #6 | Photographer: Patrick Molnar
Client: Marines | Equipment: Canon R5 | Creative Director: Haley Kochersperger
Ad Agency: Wunderman Thompson

186 STETSON LEGEND | Photographer: Tatsuro Nishimura
Client: Stetson USA | Equipment: Cambo View Camera
Vice President of Marketing: Tyler Thoreson | Creative Director: Donjiro Ban
Chief Creative Officer: Oskar Puchalski

186 SIMPLY STRAWBERRIES AND CREAM | Photographer: Jan Kalish
Client: Self-initiated | Equipment: Fuji GFX 100 | Retoucher: Madeline Murray

186 RIVER OAKS DISTRICT | Photographer: Scott Lowden
Client: River Oaks District | Equipment: Canon EOS R5, Canon 28-70mm Lens,
Canon Digital Back | Creative Director: Wendy Lowden | Account Manager: Stefani Demoff
Account Director: Lisa Maloof | Main Contributor: House of Current

186 HEY CHAMP LAUNCH | Photographer: Lucy Schoenfeld
Client: Hey Champ | Equipment: Sony A7R III | Main Contributor: Lucy Schoenfeld

187 ROYAL HAWAIIAN CENTER | Photographer: Scott Lowden
Client: Royal Hawaiian Center | Equipment: Canon EOS R5, Canon 28-70mm Lens,
Canon Digital Back | Creative Director: Wendy Lowden | Account Manager: Stefani Demoff
Account Director: Lisa Maloof | Main Contributor: House of Current

187 THE SUTTON | Photographers: Nathan Bergfelt, Aaron Lee
Client: Lincoln Property Company | Equipment: Variety of Equipment
Art Director: Danielle Breck | Creative Director: Jennifer Bryan
Stylist: Scarlet Chamberlin | Producers: Emilie Beath, Jamie Bourgidu
Hair: Annah Yevelenko | Makeup: Annah Yevelenko | Main Contributor: Aaron Lee

187 THIS IS THE LIFE | Photographer: Scott Lowden
Client: Fenton | Equipment: Canon EOS R5, Canon 15-35mm Lens
Creative Director: Wendy Lowden | Account Manager: Stefani Demoff
Account Director: Lisa Maloof | Main Contributor: House of Current

188 MYSTERIOUS | Photographer: Lennette Newell | Clients: Nutro Pet Food, MARS Pet Care
Equipment: Canon EOS R5, Canon 70mm Lens | Ad Agency: Sterling

188 A COZY YET ELEGANT DAY OUT | Photographer: Jang Won Lee
Client: Self-initiated | Equipment: Canon EOS 80D
Creative Director: Jang Won Lee | Main Contributor: Jang Won Lee

189 KELLOGG-DOOLITTLE HOUSE | Photographer: James Haefner
Client: Kellogg-Doolittle House | Equipment: Canon 5DS, DJI Mavic 3
Main Contributor: James Haefner

189 BEEAH HEADQUARTERS, ZAHA HADID ARCHITECTS, SHARJAH, UAE
Photographer: Victor Romero | Client: Shawati Magazine
Equipment: Hasselblad, Hasselblad 28mm Lens

190 MONTREAL CHURCH ALTAR | Photographer: Ariel Freaner
Client: ZEVEN Magazine | Equipment: Nikon D3X

190 NIAGARA FALLS WHEEL | Photographer: Ariel Freaner
Client: ZEVEN Magazine | Equipment: Nikon D3X

190 MIAMI INTERNATIONAL AIRPORT | Photographer: Cameron Davidson
Client: Prologis | Equipment: Fuji GFX 100s | Retoucher: Jeff Glotzl
Production Partner: HMC Helicopters | Director of Brand Marketing: Julia Solazzo
Brand Creative: Lisette Goyanes | Main Contributor: Cameron Davidson

190 VENICE EVENING LATE ARRIVAL | Photographer: Ariel Freaner
Client: ZEVEN Magazine | Equipment: Nikon D3X

190 ART DECO NIGHTS | Photographer: Ariel Freaner
Client: ZEVEN Magazine | Equipment: Nikon D3X

190 HANA APARTMENTS: ARCHITECTURAL PHOTOSHOOT
Photographer: Nathan Bergfelt | Client: Fore Property
Equipment: Canon, Canon 11-17mm Lens, Canon 24-70mm Lens
Creative Director: Danielle Breck | Main Contributor: Nathan Bergfelt

191 MFD REPAIR SHOP | Photographer: Andrew Feller | Client: Snap-on Tools
Equipment: N/A | Production Artist: Jenni Wierzba | Director of Photography: Andrew Feller
Design Director: David Brown | Copywriter: Tom Dixon | Account Executive: Danny Yadgir
Account Director: Scott Bucher | Main Contributor: David Brown

191 QUESTIONS CONQUERED | Photographer: Traction Factory
Client: Snap-on Diagnostics | Equipment: N/A | Creative Director: David Brown
Art Director: Mike Basse | Project Manager: Pam Sallis | Digital Artist: HacJob
Copywriter: S.J. Barlament | Account Director: Shannon Egan
Main Contributor: Mike Basse

192 HEINEKEN PURE MALT | Photographer: Jonathan Knowles
Client: Heineken | Equipment: Hasselblad | Agency: Publicis Poke
Retoucher: Gareth Pritchard | Creative Director: Garry Munns
Art Director: Gary Roberts

192 CLUB ORANGE | Photographer: Jonathan Knowles
Client: Britvic | Equipment: Hasselblad | Agency: Oliver Ireland
Creative Director: Tom O'Haire | Design Director: Lauren Blake

192 URBAN DANCE | Photographer: Scott Lowden | Clients: House of Current, Self-initiated
Equipment: Canon EOS R5, Canon 28-70mm Lens | Creative Director: Wendy Lowden

193 EDDIE VEDDER | Photographer: Jérôme Brunet
Client: Rock Cellar Magazine | Equipment: Nikon D5

193 FERRIS WHEEL, TOKYO | Photographer: Craig Cutler
Client: Self-initiated | Equipment: Leica M10 Mono

193 NATURE CONSERVANCY | POKOMOKE RIVER OF MARYLAND
Photographer: Cameron Davidson | Client: The Nature Conservancy
Equipment: DJI Mavic 3 Pro | Photo Editor: Alex Snyder
Director of Photography: Melissa Dale | Main Contributor: Cameron Davidson

194 IMPERIAL PALACE TOKYO | Photographer: Craig Cutler
Client: Self-initiated | Equipment: Leica M10 Mono

194 BEYOND | Photographer: Fangqiu Huang | Client: Fong Captain
Equipment: iPhone 13 | Main Contributor: Fangqiu Huang

194 HAWAII THEATER | Photographer: Scott Lowden
Clients: House of Current, Self-initiated | Equipment: Canon EOS R5, Canon 28-70mm Lens
Creative Director: Wendy Lowden | Wardrobe: Kyle Kagamida

195 SQUISH | Photographer: Zoe Adlersberg | Client: Earnshaw's Magazine
Equipment: Canon 5D Mark II, Canon 50mm Lens | Publisher: Wainscot Media
Creative Directors: Nancy Campbell, Trevett McCandliss | Editor-in-Chief: Michele Silver
Hair: Clelia Bergonzoli | Makeup: Clelia Bergonzoli | Set Designer: Mariah Walker
Props: Mariah Walker | Fashion Director: Mariah Walker
Main Contributor: Zoe Adlersberg

195 LEI ZHANG | Photographer: Aman Shakya
Client: Savannah College of Art & Design | Equipment: Canon R5, Canon 24-70mm Lens
Creative Directors: Hadley Stambaugh, Siobhan Bonnouvrier
Retoucher: Scott Newman | Producer: Jenny Upperman
Hair: Tre Knight | Makeup: Tre Knight | Stylist: Tre Knight
Main Contributor: Savannah College of Art & Design

195 THE BLONDS "GLAMOUR, FASHION, FANTASY"
Photographer: Colin Douglas Gray | Client: Savannah College of Art & Design
Equipment: Canon R5, Astera Lights, Aputure Lights, Felix Lights | Creative Director: Raf Gomes
Retoucher: Colin Douglas Gray | Producers: Drew Brown, Amaya James, Trey Vereen
Executive Director: Alex Delotch Davis | Main Contributor: Savannah College of Art & Design

195 FROZEN HIKING BOOTS | Photographer: Yaniurka Pedroza
Client: Savannah College of Art & Design | Equipment: Canon EOS R5
Creative Directors: Hadley Stambaugh, Siobhan Bonnouvrier
Producers: Adam Williams, Jenny Upperman | Retoucher: Scott Newnan
Main Contributor: Savannah College of Art & Design

196 ALWAYS YOU | Photographer: Craig Bromley
Client: Self-initiated | Equipment: Vintage 1960 Film Camera
Main Contributor: Craig Bromley

196 PATRICK TREGENZA | Photographer: Patrick Tregenza
Client: Self-initiated | Equipment: Hasselblad 907X, Canon 70-200mm Lens

196 TERRA NOSTRA | Photographer: Scott Lowden | Client: Self-initiated
Equipment: Canon EOS R5, Voigtlander Nokton Classic 35mm Lens, Kolari ND Filter

196 VENICE | Photographer: Clarence Lin | Client: Self-initiated
Equipment: Nikon D850 | Artist: Clarence Lin | Main Contributor: Clarence Lin

196 HIPPETY-HOP | Photographer: Harry Rifkin | Client: Self-initiated
Equipment: Sony | Hair: Alysha Marcantonio | Make-up: Alysha Marcantonio
Model: Alina Lee | Main Contributor: Harry Rifkin

196 DENVER MUSEUM FOXES | Photographer: Ariel Freaner
Client: ZEVEN Magazine | Equipment: Nikon D3X

197 SCARLETTE 1960 | Photographer: Harry Rifkin
Client: Self-initiated | Equipment: Leica SL2 | Hair: Alysha Marcantonio
Make-up: Alysha Marcantonio | Model: Alina Lee
Set Design: Tiffany Gabrus, thesweetzerlife | Main Contributor: Harry Rifkin

197 SCARLETTE 1960 | Photographer: Harry Rifkin
Client: Self-initiated | Equipment: Leica SL2 | Hair: Alysha Marcantonio
Make-up: Alysha Marcantonio | Model: Alina Lee
Set Design: Tiffany Gabrus, thesweetzerlife | Main Contributor: Harry Rifkin

197 THE GIRLS OF SAINT MARY ELIZABETH PREPARATORY SCHOOL
Photographer: Harry Rifkin | Client: Self-initiated | Equipment: Leica SL2
Hair: Alysha Marcantonio | Make-up: Alysha Marcantonio | Model: Alina Lee
Main Contributor: Harry Rifkin

198 THE NOTION OF CONFUSION | Photographer: Harry Rifkin
Client: Self-initiated | Equipment: Leica SL2 | Hair: Alysha Marcantonio
Make-up: Alysha Marcantonio | Model: Alina Lee | Main Contributor: Harry Rifkin

198 PIGMENT OF MY IMAGINATION | Photographer: Harry Rifkin
Client: Self-initiated | Equipment: Leica SL2 | Hair: Alysha Marcantonio
Make-up: Alysha Marcantonio | Model: Alina Lee | Main Contributor: Harry Rifkin

198 BLOSSOM | Photographer: Harry Rifkin
Client: Self-initiated | Equipment: Sony | Hair: Alysha Marcantonio
Make-up: Alysha Marcantonio | Model: Alina Lee
Main Contributor: Harry Rifkin

198 THE BARE BULB PROJECT | Photographer: Harry Rifkin
Client: Self-initiated | Equipment: Sony | Hair: Alysha Marcantonio
Make-up: Alysha Marcantonio | Model: Alina Lee
Main Contributor: Harry Rifkin

199 PIGMENT OF MY IMAGINATION | Photographer: Harry Rifkin
Client: Self-initiated | Equipment: Sony | Hair: Alysha Marcantonio
Make-up: Alysha Marcantonio | Model: Alina Lee
Main Contributor: Harry Rifkin

199 VISIONS IN MY HEAD | Photographer: Harry Rifkin
Client: Self-initiated | Equipment: Sony | Hair: Alysha Marcantonio
Make-up: Alysha Marcantonio | Model: Alina Lee
Main Contributor: Harry Rifkin

199 GHOST GIRL ~ ABBY | Photographer: Harry Rifkin
Client: Self-initiated | Equipment: Leica SL2 | Hair: Alysha Marcantonio
Make-up: Alysha Marcantonio | Model: Abby
Main Contributor: Harry Rifkin

200 DAISIES FROM BELOW | Photographer: Laurie Frankel
Client: Eat Your Flowers | Equipment: Nikon D850, Nikon 105mm Lens

200 FLORAL PATTERNS | Photographer: Laurie Frankel
Client: Eat Your Flowers | Equipment: Nikon D850, Nikon 85mm Lens

200 FLOWER 1 | Photographer: Craig Cutler
Client: Self-initiated | Equipment: Leica SL2

201 PETALS ON COLOR SERIES | Photographer: Craig Cutler
Client: Self-initiated | Equipment: Leica SL2

201 FLORAL BEETS | Photographer: Laurie Frankel
Client: Eat Your Flowers | Equipment: Nikon D850, Nikon 24-70mm Lens

201 SUMMER VIBES | Photographer: Dylan Swart | Client: Drizzle
Equipment: Nikon D800, Nikon 85mm Lens | Stylist: Brianna Martinkus

201 CHOCOLATE SCULPTURES | Photographer: Craig Cutler
Client: Self-initiated | Equipment: Leica SL2

202 FEAST YOUR SENSES | Photographer: Evi Abeler | Client: Marina Bay Sands
Equipment: Fuji GFX 100s, Fuji GF 120mm Lens | Ad Agency: Forsman & Bodenfors

202 BALSAMIC ACID PARTIES | Photographer: Jan Kalish
Client: Global Gardens | Equipment: Fuji GFX 100 | Retoucher: Madeline Murray

202 TIJUANA EVENING DELIGHT | Photographer: Ariel Freaner
Client: ZEVEN Magazine | Equipment: Nikon D3X

203 COLORFULLY PICKLING | Photographer: Laurie Frankel
Client: Eat Your Flowers | Equipment: Nikon D850, Nikon 85mm Lens

203 ITALY - ROME MIDNIGHT SNACK DELIGHT | Photographer: Ariel Freaner
Client: ZEVEN Magazine | Equipment: Nikon D3X

204 ENGINEER PORTRAIT STANDING ON WINDMILL TOWER
Photographer: Tadd Myers | Client: RWE | Equipment: Canon R5, Canon 28-70mm Lens
Main Contributor: Tadd Myers

204 ALTERNATIVE ENERGY RESEARCH LAB SERIES
Photographer: Robert Seale | Client: Phillips 66 | Equipment: Canon R5, Various Lenses
Art Directors: Andrew Camacho, Efren Cavazos, Elizabeth Capello
Creative Director: Amal Agha | Graphic Designer: Efren Cavazos
Main Contributor: Robert Seale

204 ARCOSA - CONCRETE RECYCLING FACILITY
Photographer: Tadd Myers | Client: Arcosa Specialty Materials
Equipment: Canon R5 | Main Contributor: Tadd Myers

204 NUCLEAR LANDSCAPE PHOTOGRAPHY REIMAGINED
Photographer: Roger Mastroianni | Client: Energy Harbor
Equipment: Phase One XT IQ 4150, Phase One Digital Back, Rodenstock HR 32mm Lens
Main Contributor: Roger Mastroianni

204 TIJUANA AFTERNOON AT WORK | Photographer: Ariel Freaner
Client: ZEVEN Magazine | Equipment: Nikon D3XS | Main Contributor: Ariel Freaner

204 INDUSTRIAL FACILITIES AROUND THE US FOR ANNUAL REPORT
Photographer: Robert Seale | Client: Phillips 66 | Equipment: Canon R5, Various Lenses
Brand Creative: Amal Agha | Main Contributor: Robert Seale

205 SLB ENERGY SERIES | Photographer: Tadd Myers
Client: SLB Energy | Equipment: Canon R5 | Ad Agency: Fleishman
Main Contributor: Tadd Myers

205 44 FARMS - SALE DAY | Photographer: Tadd Myers
Client: 44 Farms | Equipment: Canon R5 | Main Contributor: Tadd Myers

206 44 FARMS - SORTING CATTLE | Photographer: Tadd Myers
Client: 44 Farms | Equipment: Canon R5 | Main Contributor: Tadd Myers

206 44 FARMS - LIFE ON THE FARM | Photographer: Tadd Myers
Client: 44 Farms | Equipment: Canon R5 | Main Contributor: Tadd Myers

207 DREAM HOUSE | Photographer: Lindsay Siu | Client: Self-initiated
Equipment: Canon R5, Contax 645 | Retoucher: Pinter Creative Studio
Main Contributor: Lindsay Siu

207 PEACE AND CHEETOS | Photographer: Laurie Frankel | Client: Self-initiated
Equipment: Nikon D850, Nikon 105mm Lens | Model: Imogen Knudsen

208 INTI: THE SUN GOD | Photographer: Artem Nazarov | Client: Self-initiated
Equipment: Canon 5D Mark IV | Main Contributor: Artem Nazarov

208 PARASOL IN TOKYO | Photographer: Craig Cutler
Client: Self-initiated | Equipment: Leica M10 Mono

208 MONGOLIAN DESERT | Photographer: Craig Cutler
Client: Self-initiated | Equipment: Leica M10 Mono

209 NEW LONDON LEDGE LIGHTHOUSE | Photographer: Jared Leeds | Client: Self-initiated
Equipment: Nikon Z9, Nikon 35mm Lens | Main Contributor: Jared Leeds

209 REDWOODS: ATMOSPHERE | Photographer: David Westphal
Client: Self-initiated | Equipment: Fuji GFX 100s | Main Contributor: David Westphal

210 ALASKA CLIMATE CHANGED | Photographer: Jim Brennan
Client: Self-initiated | Equipment: Hasselblad

210 JOY OF TECHS | Photographer: Nick Collura
Client: Snap-on Diagnostics | Equipment: N/A | Art Director: Mike Basse
Director of Photography: Nick Collura | Design Director: David Brown
Copywriter: S.J. Barlament | Project Manager: Pam Sallis
Account Director: Shannon Egan | Main Contributor: Mike Basse

211 DANCE | Photographer: Yichen Wang | Client: Self-initiated | Equipment: Fuji XT-10

211 GOOD HAIR DAY | Photographer: Michael Winokur | Client: Self-initiated
Equipment: Fuji GFX 100s | Main Contributor: Michael Winokur

211 KATHERINE | Photographer: John Madere | Client: Self-initiated
Equipment: Canon EOS R5, Canon 85mm Lens | Main Contributor: John Madere

211 BUNNY WARD | Photographer: Craig Bromley | Client: Bunny Ward
Equipment: iPhone 13 | Main Contributor: Craig Bromley

211 ESPY IN BALBOA PARK | Photographer: Ariel Freaner
Clients: ESPY, Esperanza Jimenez | Equipment: Nikon D3XS
Main Contributor: Ariel Freaner

211 JANELLE MONAE | Photographer: Colin Douglas Gray
Client: Savannah College of Art & Design | Equipment: Canon R5, Profoto Lights
Creative Directors: Hadley Stambaugh, Siobhan Bonnouvrier
Retoucher: Colin Douglas Gray | Producer: Jenny Upperman
Main Contributor: Savannah College of Art & Design

211 THOSE BLUE EYES | Photographer: Craig Bromley | Client: Actor
Equipment: Canon, Canon 24-70 Lens | Main Contributor: Craig Bromley

211 DON'T MESS WITH MY VINYL | Photographer: Laurie Frankel
Client: Self-initiated | Equipment: Nikon D850, Nikon 24-70mm Lens
Model: Imogen Knudsen

212 COLEMAN DOMINGO | Photographer: Allison Smith
Client: Savannah College of Art & Design | Equipment: Canon R5, Canon 24-70mm Lens,
Profoto Lights | Creative Directors: Hadley Stambaugh, Siobhan Bonnouvrier
Retoucher: Jarred Joly | Main Contributor: Savannah College of Art & Design

212 RODRIGO, VINTAGE RESTAURANT | Photographer: Michael Schoenfeld
Client: Self-initiated | Equipment: Sony A-1, Various Lenses
Main Contributor: Michael Schoenfeld

212 HEALTHCARE/MEDICAL INDUSTRY PHOTOGRAPHY FOR DEVELOPMENT FUNDRAISING | Photographer: Robert Seale | Client: UTHealth Houston
Equipment: Canon R5, Various Lenses | Art Director: Jonathan Lopez
Main Contributor: Robert Seale

212 CAPTURING EXCELLENCE: INTIMATE PORTRAITS OF THE CLEVELAND ORCHESTRA'S FINEST MUSICIANS | Photographer: Roger Mastroianni
Client: The Cleveland Orchestra | Equipment: Phase One XF IQ4, Phase One Digital Back
Main Contributor: Roger Mastroianni

212 LILY GLADSTONE SERIES | Photographer: Lindsay Siu
Client: The Hollywood Reporter | Equipment: Canon R5, Profoto | Stylist: Jason Rembert
Retoucher: Cake Imagery | Makeup: Alannah Bilodeau | Hair: Carly Campbell
Main Contributor: Lindsay Siu

212 NATHANIEL | Photographer: Michael Schoenfeld | Client: Self-initiated
Equipment: Sony A-1, Various Lenses | Main Contributor: Michael Schoenfeld

212 CONVENIENCE STORE, TUCSON AZ | Photographer: Michael Schoenfeld
Client: Self-initiated | Equipment: Sony A-1, Various Lenses
Main Contributor: Michael Schoenfeld

212 YOLANDA | Photographer: Ariel Freaner | Client: ZEVEN Magazine | Equipment: Nikon D3X

213 JOSIAH AND HIS WIFE BIRDIE BENATOR AT THEIR HOME ON THE OCCASION OF HIS 100TH BIRTHDAY, JANUARY 7, 2022, ATLANTA, GEORGIA
Photographer: Ellis Vener | Client: Private Commission
Equipment: Nikon Z9, Nikon 24-70mm Lens | Main Contributor: Ellis Vener

213 JO 1 | Photographer: Craig Cutler
Client: Self-initiated | Equipment: Leica SL2

213 CHINESE NEW YEAR | Photographer: Yaniurka Pedroza
Client: Savannah College of Art & Design | Equipment: Canon EOS R5
Creative Directors: Hadley Stambaugh, Siobhan Bonnouvrier | Retoucher: Scott Newnan
Producer: Jenny Upperman | Main Contributor: Savannah College of Art & Design

214 THE FUTURE IS FEMALE | Photographer: Lindsay Siu
Client: Self-initiated | Equipment: Canon R5, Profoto | Hair: Anya Ellis
Makeup: Anya Ellis | Retoucher: Cake Imagery | Main Contributor: Lindsay Siu

214 STREET PROFESSOR | Photographer: Laurie Frankel
Client: Self-initiated | Equipment: iPhone 12 Pro

214 ALEXI LUBOMIRSKI | Photographer: Allison Smith
Client: Savannah College of Art & Design | Equipment: Canon R5, Canon 24-70mm Lens, Profoto Lights | Retoucher: Jarred Joly | Producer: Jenny Upperman
Creative Directors: Hadley Stambaugh, Siobhan Bonnouvrier
Main Contributor: Savannah College of Art & Design

214 COLSON BAKER | Photographer: Aman Shakya
Client: Savannah College of Art & Design | Equipment: Canon R5, Canon 24-70mm Lens
Retoucher: Colin Douglas Gray | Creative Directors: Hadley Stambaugh, Siobhan Bonnouvrier
Main Contributor: Savannah College of Art & Design

215 ORTHOFIX - PATIENT PROFILE - SURFER | Photographer: Tadd Myers
Client: Orthofix Medical Devices | Equipment: Canon R5, Canon RF Lenses
Main Contributor: Tadd Myers

215 HOOPIN' | Photographer: Eric Melzer | Client: The Play Project
Equipment: Sony A-1 | Main Contributor: Eric Melzer

216 STUNT #1 | Photographer: Patrick Molnar | Client: Self-initiated | Equipment: Canon R5

216 STUNT #3 | Photographer: Patrick Molnar | Client: Self-initiated | Equipment: Canon R5

216 STUNT #5 | Photographer: Patrick Molnar | Client: Self-initiated | Equipment: Canon R5

216 STUNT #4 | Photographer: Patrick Molnar | Client: Self-initiated | Equipment: Canon R5

216 ALEXIS AND ENRIQUE | Photographer: Jared Leeds
Client: Self-initiated | Equipment: Nikon Z9, Nikon Lenses, Hasselblad Lenses
Main Contributor: Jared Leeds

216 LEAP FROG | Photographer: Eric Melzer | Client: The Play Project
Equipment: Sony A-1, Sony 16-35mm Lens | Main Contributor: Eric Melzer

217 MILWAUKEE ADMIRALS/SOWI PROGRAM | Photographer: Scott Paulus
Client: Milwaukee Admirals | Equipment: N/A | Art Director: Brandon Tushkowski
Director of Photography: Scott Paulus | Design Director: David Brown
Copywriter: Tom Dixon | Project Manager: Pam Sallis | Production Artist: Jenni Wierzba
Account Director: Scott Bucher | Main Contributor: Brandon Tushkowski

217 23/24 SEASON MOTION | Photographer: Grant Gunderson
Client: Tampa Bay Lightning | Equipment: Canon R5, Canon 24-70mm Lens, Profoto Pro Heads, Profoto Pro Packs | Chief Creative Officer: Troy Dunn | Creative Director: Stephanie Morrison
Associate Creative Director: Mitch Feickert | Senior Account Executive: Jessica Hall
Main Contributor: Grant Gunderson

218 SHATTERED | Photographer: Eric Melzer
Client: The Play Project | Equipment: Sony A-1, Sony 16-35mm Lens
Main Contributor: Eric Melzer

218 ORIGAMI MASKS | Photographer: Craig Cutler
Client: National Geographic Magazine | Equipment: Leica SL2
Senior Photo Editor: Samantha Clark

218 STILA SHEER RADIANCE | Photographer: Takahiro Igarashi
Client: Stila Cosmetics | Equipment: Phase One XF IQ380
Creative Director: Amy Fitzgerald | Main Contributor: Takahiro Igarashi

219 GLASS AND WATER | Photographer: Craig Cutler
Client: Self-initiated | Equipment: Leica SL2

219 SINGLE GLASS SERIES | Photographer: Craig Cutler
Client: Self-initiated | Equipment: Leica SL2

219 GLASSWARE AT EASE | Photographer: Laurie Frankel | Client: March
Equipment: Hasselblad H5X, Phase IQ 3100 Digital Back, Hasselblad 120mm Lens

220 BACCARAT X KIM SEYBERT | Photographer: Nicholas Duers
Clients: Baccarat, Kim Seybert | Equipment: Phase One XF
Main Contributor: Nicholas Duers

220 MVMT 9YR ANNIVERSARY | Photographer: Nicholas Duers
Client: MVMT | Equipment: Phase One XF | Main Contributor: Nicholas Duers

220 MVMT X KIM ROSE | Photographer: Nicholas Duers
Client: MVMT | Equipment: Phase One XF | Main Contributor: Nicholas Duers

220 ALINK / 2023 REBRAND | Photographer: Nicholas Duers
Client: ALink Jewelry | Equipment: Phase One XF | Creative Director: Emma Peters
Producer: Kate Skolas | Main Contributor: Nicholas Duers

220 MVMT 9YR ANNIVERSARY 02 | Photographer: Nicholas Duers
Client: MVMT | Equipment: Phase One XF | Main Contributor: Nicholas Duers

220 NOBLESSE MAG X TIFFANY / SEPTEMBER 2023
Photographer: Nicholas Duers | Clients: Noblesse Magazine, Tiffany & Co.
Equipment: Phase One XF | Main Contributor: Nicholas Duers

221 LOUIS VUITTON X NIKE AIR FORCE 1 LOW UNIVERSITY BLUE FRIENDS AND FAMILY VIRGIL ABLOOM | Photographer: Andrien Trujillo | Client: Arman Salemi
Equipment: Canon R5, Canon 24-105mm Lens, Print for Signature Catalogue
Retoucher: James Harris

221 NATURAL BALANCE | Photographer: Joseph Saraceno
Client: Scentury Magazine | Equipment: Canon, Profoto Lights
Creative Director: Wilson Wong | Main Contributor: Joseph Saraceno

221 AARKE CARBONATOR 3 PAIR | Photographer: Takahiro Igarashi
Client: Aarke | Equipment: Phase One XF IQ380 | Main Contributor: Takahiro Igarashi

221 AARKE CARBONATOR 3 SERVE | Photographer: Takahiro Igarashi
Client: Aarke | Equipment: Phase One XF IQ380 | Main Contributor: Takahiro Igarashi

222 TABLECLOTH | Photographer: Laurie Frankel | Client: March
Equipment: Hasselblad H5X, Phase IQ 3100 Digital Back, Hasselblad 35-90mm Lens

222 WALMART / FALL23 FASHION | Photographer: Nicholas Duers
Client: Walmart | Equipment: Phase One XF | Art Director: Bryan Kasm
Stylist: Tristine Drews | Main Contributor: Nicholas Duers

222 NKA WORKSHOP | Photographer: Nicholas Duers | Client: NKA Workshop
Equipment: Phase One XF | Stylist: William Brown III | Main Contributor: Nneka Bennett

222 RLX | Photographer: Nicholas Duers | Client: Ralph Lauren
Equipment: Phase One XF | Creative Directors: Amir Mohammady, Yong Choe
Main Contributor: Nicholas Duers

222 TARGA FRAGRANCE | Photographer: Nicholas Duers | Client: Self-initiated
Equipment: Phase One XF | Main Contributor: Nicholas Duers

223 LAUREN HOLIDAY 01 | Photographer: Nicholas Duers | Client: Ralph Lauren
Equipment: Phase One XF | Main Contributor: Nicholas Duers

223 RL X ACTIVE CLUB | Photographer: Nicholas Duers | Client: Ralph Lauren
Equipment: Phase One XF | Main Contributor: Nicholas Duers

223 POLO BAR | Photographer: Nicholas Duers | Client: Ralph Lauren
Equipment: Phase One XF | Main Contributor: Nicholas Duers

223 RL FOOTWEAR | Photographer: Nicholas Duers | Client: Ralph Lauren
Equipment: Phase One XF | Main Contributor: Nicholas Duers

FILM/VIDEO GOLD WINNERS:
225 MY CONCUSSION STORY | Photographer: Lindsay Siu | Client: YWCA
Equipment: Red Monstro 8K, Canon R5 | Ad Agency: Rethink | Art Director: Abrie Miller
Executive Creative Directors: Leia Rogers, Morgan Tierney | Creative Director: Pamela Rounis
Editor: Nick Greaves | Copywriter: Emily Betteridge | Producers: Kerry Bhangu, Jill McLeod
Head of Production: Laura Rioux | Account Supervisor: Nicole Kerrigan
Account Manager: Karin Torn | Account Director: Kennedy Crawford
Main Contributors: Lindsay Siu, Rethink
Assignment: When people think of concussions, they think of sports. But violence by an intimate partner is the cause of at least 290,000 concussions among Canadian woman and girls each year. That's more than 7,000 for each 1 NHL concussion.
Approach: We partnered with Trevor Linden to help bring attention to this staggering statistic as we call for increased research, better pathways for concussion treatment, and more support for people who experience brain injury as a result on intimate partner violence.
Results: The campaign was picked up by the news and social media.

225 ELITE TRAVELER / SKELETON TIMEPIECES | Photographer: Nicholas Duers
Client: Elite Traveler | Equipment: Phase One XF | Creative Director: Kristen Shirley
Main Contributor: Nicholas Duers
Assignment: While shooting a still image of this Skeleton watch editorial, we took a few extra moments to shoot a series of images with varying light passes. Some time after the publication of the still image, I revisited the additional frames and created a stop-motion animation.

FILM/VIDEO SILVER WINNERS:
226 VENICE | Photographer: Clarence Lin
Client: Self-initiated | Equipment: iPhone 14 Pro Max
Artist: Clarence Lin | Main Contributor: Clarence Lin

226 PARIS | Photographer: Clarence Lin
Client: Self-initiated | Equipment: iPhone 14 Pro Max
Artist: Clarence Lin | Main Contributor: Clarence Lin

226 BARCELONA | Photographer: Clarence Lin
Client: Self-initiated | Equipment: iPhone 14 Pro Max
Artist: Clarence Lin | Main Contributor: Clarence Lin

227 Y3 / ADIDAS | Photographer: Nicholas Duers | Client: Y3 / Adidas
Equipment: Phase One XF | Creative Director: Jared Tomlinson
Art Director: Kevin Rosales | Main Contributor: Nicholas Duers

227 RLX | Photographer: Nicholas Duers | Client: Ralph Lauren
Equipment: Phase One XF | Creative Directors: Amir Mohammady, Yong Choe
Main Contributor: Nicholas Duers

Index

PHOTOGRAPHERS

CLIENTS

ART DIRECTORS

CREATIVE DIRECTORS/ASSOCIATE, EXECUTIVE CREATIVE DIRECTORS/EXECUTIVE DIRECTORS

DIRECTORS OF PHOTOGRAPHY/DESIGN DIRECTORS/DIGITAL DIRECTORS/DIRECTORS OF PROJECT MANAGEMENT

PHOTOGRAPHY STUDIOS/STUDIOS/AGENCIES/AD AGENCIES

PHOTOGRAPHER'S ASSISTANTS

PHOTO RETOUCHING/RETOUCHERS/SENIOR PHOTO EDITORS/PHOTO EDITORS

ARTISTS/DIGITAL ARTISTS/GRAPHIC DESIGNERS/DESIGNERS/SET DESIGNERS/ILLUSTRATORS/PRODUCTION ARTISTS

PRODUCERS/EXECUTIVE PRODUCERS/SENIOR PRODUCERS

COPYWRITERS/EDITORS/EDITORS-IN-CHIEF/PUBLISHERS

MODELS

HAIR/MAKEUP

STYLISTS/FOOD STYLISTS/CLOTHING STYLISTS

PLATINUM

Craig Cutler
www.craigcutler.com
418 Euclid St.
Santa Monica, CA 90402
United States
Tel +1 917 744 5036
cc@craigcutler.com

Lindsey Drennan
www.lindseydrennan.com
Ontario
Canada
Tel +1 647 400 1080
info@lindseydrennan.com

Jonathan Knowles
www.jknowles.com
48A Chancellor's Road
London, W6 9RS
United Kingdom
Tel +44 020 8741 7577
jk@jknowles.co.uk

James Minchin III
www.jamesminchin.com
California
United States
Tel +1 323 828 8272
james@jamesminchin.com

Artem Nazarov
www.nazarovphoto.com
880 Glenwood Ave. SE,
Unit 1419
Atlanta, GA 30316
United States
artem@nazarovphoto.com

Peter Samuels
www.petersamuels.com
2180 Bryant St., Ste. 202
San Francisco, CA 94110
United States
Tel +1 415 786 4480
peter@petersamuels.com

Howard Schatz
www.howardschatz.com
31 W. 21st St., #2N
New York, NY 10010
United States
Tel +1 212 334 6667
howardschatz@howardschatz.com

John Surace
www.johnsurace.com
New York
United States
Tel +1 212 203 3183
john@johnsurace.com

Paco Macias Velasco
www.pacomaciasvelasco.mx
Leopoldo Romano 6-1 Adolfo López Mateos
Cuajimalpa Distrito Federal
05280
Mexico
Tel +1 52 55 1498 5864
pacomaciasvelasco@yahoo.com.mx

GOLD

Lynsey Addario
www.lynseyaddario.com
United States
Tel +1 917 907 4747
lynseyadd@yahoo.com

Michael Alberstat
www.alberstat.com
26 Noble St., Studio 2
Toronto, ON M6K 2C9
Canada
Tel +1 416 895 1864
michael@alberstat.com

Kwaku Alston
www.kwakualston.com
Los Angeles, CA
United States
Tel +1 212 796 0411
kastudio@kwakualston.com

Barry Barnes
www.trainedeyegraphics.com
Emmett, ID 83617
United States
Tel +1 208 365 4896
bb@trainedeyegraphics.com

Davis Bell
www.winterlamaster.com
Los Angeles, CA
United States
Tel +1 808 782 5780
winterlamaster@gmail.com

Per Breiehagen
www.breiehagen.com
65 Forest Dale Road
Minneapolis, MN 55410
United States
Tel +1 612 760 2581
per@breiehagen.com

Craig Bromley
www.cbromley.com
1136 Briarcliff Road NE, #2
Atlanta, GA 30306
United States
Tel +1 404 229 7279
craig@cbromley.com

Chris Budgeon
www.chrisbudgeon.com
15 St. George's Road
Elsternwick
Melbourne, VIC 3185
Australia
Tel +613 9523 7711
mail@chrisbudgeon.com

Carlos Caicedo
www.500px.com/carloscaicedo1
243 Union St., Apt. 306
North Adams, MA 01247
United States
Tel +1 917 445 5923
carloscedo@yahoo.com

Sarah Coulter
www.sarahkcoulter.com
New York, NY
United States
studio@sarahkcoulter.com

Craig Cutler
www.craigcutler.com
418 Euclid St.
Santa Monica, CA 90402
United States
Tel +1 917 744 5036
cc@craigcutler.com

Lindsey Drennan
www.lindseydrennan.com
Ontario
Canada
Tel +1 647 400 1080
info@lindseydrennan.com

Nicholas Duers
www.nicholasduers.com
255 W. 36th St., Suite 1102
New York, NY 10018
United States
Tel +1 917 574 2636
nd@nicholasduers.com

Laurie Frankel
www.lauriefrankel.com
401 D St., Suite A
San Rafael, CA 94901
United States
Tel +1 415 282 7345
lga@lauriefrankel.com

Ariel Freaner
www.freaner.com
113 W. G St., No. 650
San Diego, CA 92101
United States
Tel +1 619 870 4699
arielfreaner@freaner.com

PJ Fugatze
www.fugatze.com
6649 Bedford Ave.
Los Angeles, CA 90056
United States
Tel +1 424 625 9655
fugatze@blingimaging.com

Beth Galton
www.bethgalton.com
109 W. 27th St., #6A
New York, NY 10001
United States
Tel +1 212 242 2266
studio@bethgalton.com

Wolfgang Gast
www.gastdesign.de
Feldstrasse 14
Hürtgenwald-Gey 52393
Germany
Tel +49 01 577 28 71 899
info@gastdesign.de

Colin Douglas Gray
www.ilovecolingray.com
Atlanta, GA
United States
Tel +1 912 659 0702
colindouglasgray@gmail.com

Grant Gunderson
www.grantgunderson.com
Bellingham, WA
United States
Tel +1 360 319 8922
grant@grantgunderson.com

Fangqiu Huang
California
United States
fongchou@hotmail.com

Takahiro Igarashi
www.igarashiphoto.com
84 N. 9th St., #410
Brooklyn, NY 11249
United States
Tel +1 917 407 8262
igarashi@igarashiphoto.com

Lians Jadan
www.liansjadan.com
Detroit, MI
United States
Tel +1 212 920 7672
l@liansjadan.com

Jonathan Knowles
www.jknowles.com
48A Chancellor's Road
London, W6 9RS
United Kingdom
Tel +44 020 8741 7577
jk@jknowles.co.uk

Markku Lahdesmaki
www.markkuphoto.com
825 E. Bogert Trail
Palm Springs, CA 92264
United States
Tel +1 310 748 6818
markkuphoto@gmail.com

Jang Won Lee
www.whimsical-studio.com
Suite E-3/6, 12th Floor, 20 Jangchungdan-ro 13-gil Jung-gu Seoul, 04563
South Korea
Tel +050 6759 5801
hello@whimsical-studio.com

Dennis Letbetter
www.studioletbetter.com
1256 Masonic Ave.
San Francisco, CA 94117
United States
Tel +1 415 431 7546
studioletbetter@mac.com

Clarence Lin
www.clarencelin.com
United States
reroutedoutfordelivery@gmail.com

Scott Lowden
www.scottlowden.com
675 Linwood Ave. NE
Atlanta, GA 30306
United States
Tel +1 404 291 2621
scott@scottlowden.com

Gaspar Marquez
www.gmarquezphoto.com
Brooklyn, NY
United States
Tel +1 917 817 8973
gmarquezphoto@gmail.com

Trevett McCandliss
www.mccandlissandcampbell.com
433 N. Windsor Ave.
Brightwaters, NY 11718
United States
Tel +1 631 252 3527
mcandcstudio@gmail.com

Darnell McCown
1230 Westminister Lane
Duncanville, TX 75137
United States
Tel +1 214 421 9333
darnellmc@sbcglobal.net

Jeffrey Milstein
www.jeffreymilstein.com
331 Wall St.
Kingston, NY 12401
United States
Tel +1 845 331 3111
jmilstein.studio331@gmail.com

David Moenkhaus
www.moenkhaus.com
Chicago, IL
United States
Tel +1 773 612 4166
DaMoenk@aol.com

Bill Moree
www.billmoree.com
Hillsboro, NM
United States
Tel +1 917 586 9769
bill@billmoree.com

Tadd Myers
www.taddmyers.com
1527 W. State Highway 114, Ste. 500
Grapevine, TX 76051
United States
Tel +1 214 7522372
tmyers@taddmyers.com

Amyn Nasser
www.amynnasser.com
United States
studio@amynnasser.com

Lennette Newell
www.lennettenewell.com
2340 Pimlico Lane
Placerville, CA 95667
United States
Tel +1 925 930 9229
lennette@lennettenewell.com

Tatsuro Nishimura
www.tatsuronishimura.com
150 Bay St., #804
Jersey City, NJ 07302
United States
Tel +1 646 713 9612
tatsuro.pc@mac.com

Michael Pantuso
www.pantusodesign.com
820 S. Thurlow St.
Hinsdale, IL 60521
United States
Tel +1 312 318 1800
michaelpantuso@me.com

Yaniurka Pedroza
www.instagram.com/yanipho tography
Miami, FL
United States
institutionalawards@scad.edu

TC Reiner
www.tcreiner.com
Santa Barbara, CA 93160
United States
Tel +1 805 963 8817
tcreiner@gmail.com

Beetle Rhind
www.alexanderrhind.com
Wolfgar Barn, Cheriton Bishop
Exeter, Devon EX66HH
United Kingdom
Tel +44 7818 095 219
alexander@alexanderrhind.com

Harry Rifkin
www.theharryrifkin.com
5900 Pat Ave.
Woodland Hills, CA 91367
United States
harry@theharryrifkin.com

Matt Roppolo
www.mjrphotography.com
815 Elsbeth St.
Dallas, TX 75208
United States
Tel +1 214 277 2522
mattr@ha.com

Joseph Saraceno
www.josephsaraceno.com
26 Wolverton Ave.
Toronto, ON M4J 3H8
Canada
Tel +1 416 908 1598
joe@josephsaraceno.com

Howard Schatz
www.howardschatz.com
31 W. 21st St., #2N
New York, NY 10010
United States
Tel +1 212 334 6667
howardschatz@howardschatz.com

Michael Schoenfeld
www.michaelschoenfeld.com
560 W. 200 S
Salt Lake City, UT 84101
United States
Tel +1 801 560 3305
michael@michaelschoenfeld.com

Robert Seale
www.robertseale.com
Houston, TX
United States
Tel +1 832 654 9572
robert@robertseale.com

Nicolò Sertorio
www.nicolosertorio.com
345 Henry St., Studio 2
Oakland, CA 94607
United States
Tel +1 650 430 3268
nicolo@photonicolo.com

Aman Shakya
www.amanshakya.photog raphy
Savannah, GA
United States
amanevan@gmail.com

Lindsay Siu
www.lindsaysiu.com
3628 St. George St.
Vancouver, BC V5V 3Z7
Canada
Tel +1 604 780 4755
lindsay@lindsaysiu.com

Allison Smith
www.allisonrevelle.com
Savannah, GA
United States
hello@allisonrevelle.com

Geoff Story
www.geoffstory.com
St Louis, MO
United States
Tel +1 314 680 0485
geoff@geoffstory.com

Nyk Sykes
www.nyksykes.com
548 Crown St.
Surry Hills, NSW 2010
Australia
Tel +61 425 250 655
nyk@nyksykes.com

Robert Tardio
www.roberttardio.com
118 E. 25th St., #6
New York, NY 10010
United States
Tel +1 212 254 5413
robert@roberttardio.com

Andrien Trujillo
www.andrientrujillo.com
Plano, TX
United States
atrujillo@ha.com

Cheryl Vorhis
www.cvorhisphoto.com
Dallas, TX
United States
Tel +1 214 212 7834
cherylv@ha.com

Yichen Wang
China
ycwangstudio1@gmail.com

Michael Winokur
www.winokurphotography.com
530 Hampshire St., Apt. 406
San Francisco, CA 94110
United States
Tel +1 650 468 3686
mw@winokurphotography.com

Ted Wright
www.twrightart.wixsite.com/portfolio
1688 Ridgeway Trail
Fenton, MO 63026
United States
twrightart@aol.com

SILVER

Evi Abeler
www.eviabeler.com
86 W. 119th St., Apt. 8C
New York, NY 10026
United States
Tel +1 212 625 3861
studio@eviabeler.com

Zoe Adlersberg
www.zoeadlersberg.com
New York
United States
Tel +1 646 272 9111
zoe@zoeadlersberg.com

Nathan Bergfelt
www.nathanbergfelt.com
State College, PA
United States
nathanbergfelt@gmail.com

Per Breiehagen
www.breiehagen.com
65 Forest Dale Road
Minneapolis, MN 55410
United States
Tel +1 612 760 2581
per@breiehagen.com

Jim Brennan
www.jimbrennanphotography.com
15305 29th Lane
East Parrish, FL 34219
United States
Tel +1 813 610 2756
jimbrennanphotography@gmail.com

Craig Bromley
www.cbromley.com
1136 Briarcliff Road NE, #2
Atlanta, GA 30306
United States
Tel +1 404 229 7279
craig@cbromley.com

Jérôme Brunet
www.jeromebrunet.com
West Hollywood, CA
United States
Tel +1 310 908 0009
info@jeromebrunet.com

Nick Collura
www.nickcollura.com
United States
Tel +1 414 324 3231
nick@nickcollura.com

Craig Cutler
www.craigcutler.com
418 Euclid St.
Santa Monica, CA 90402
United States
Tel +1 917 744 5036
cc@craigcutler.com

Cameron Davidson
www.camerondavidson.com
399 Tennessee Ave.
Alexandria, VA 22305
United States
Tel +1 703 625 6890
cameron@camerondavidson.com

Nicholas Duers
www.nicholasduers.com
255 W. 36th St., Suite 1102
New York, NY 10018
United States
Tel +1 917 574 2636
nd@nicholasduers.com

Andrew Feller
www.andrewfeller.com
Milwaukee, WI
United States
Tel +1 414 217 5074
hello@andrewfeller.com

Laurie Frankel
www.lauriefrankel.com
401 D St., Suite A
San Rafael, CA 94901
United States
Tel +1 415 282 7345
lga@lauriefrankel.com

Ariel Freaner
www.freaner.com
113 W. G St., No. 650
San Diego, CA 92101
United States
Tel +1 619 870 4699
arielfreaner@freaner.com

Florin Gabor
www.floringabor.com
55 Louvain St. W, Suite 200
Montreal, QC H2N1A4
Canada
Tel +1 514 267 6887
info@floringabor.com

Colin Douglas Gray
www.ilovecolingray.com
Atlanta, GA
United States
Tel +1 912 659 0702
colindouglasgray@gmail.com

Grant Gunderson
www.grantgunderson.com
Bellingham, WA
United States
Tel +1 360 319 8922
grant@grantgunderson.com

Jim Haefner
www.jameshaefner.com
6740 Birmingham Club Drive
Bloomfield Hills, MI 48301
United States
Tel +1 248 515 2181
jim@haefnerphoto.com

Fangqiu Huang
California
United States
fongchou@hotmail.com

Takahiro Igarashi
www.igarashiphoto.com
84 N. 9th St., #410
Brooklyn, NY 11249
United States
Tel +1 917 407 8262
igarashi@igarashiphoto.com

Jan Kalish
www.jankalish.com
17 Tresillian Road
Toronto, ON M3H1L5
Canada
Tel +1 416 823 2600
info@jankalish.com

Jonathan Knowles
www.jknowles.com
48A Chancellor's Road
London, W6 9RS
United Kingdom
Tel +44 020 8741 7577
jk@jknowles.co.uk

Aaron Lee
www.aaronleephotography.com
265 N. Hancock, #102
Portland, OR 97227
United States
hello@aaronleephotography.com

Jang Won Lee
www.whimsical-studio.com
Suite E-3/6, 12th Floor, 20 Jangchungdan-ro 13-gil Jung-gu Seoul, 04563
South Korea
Tel +050 6759 5801
hello@whimsical-studio.com

Jared Leeds
www.jaredleeds.com
Boston, MA
United States
Tel +1 617 429 2891
jared@jaredleeds.com

Clarence Lin
www.clarencelin.com
United States
reroutedoutfordelivery@gmail.com

Scott Lowden
www.scottlowden.com
675 Linwood Ave. NE
Atlanta, GA 30306
United States
Tel +1 404 291 2621
scott@scottlowden.com

John Madere
www.johnmadere.com
71 Tern Drive
Montauk, NY 11954
United States
Tel +1 212 966 4136
john@johnmadere.com

Roger Mastroianni
www.rogermastroianni.com
1588 E. 40th St.
Cleveland, OH 44103
United States
Tel +1 216 391 3917
rmastro@mac.com

Trevett McCandliss
www.mccandlissandcampbell.com
433 N. Windsor Ave.
Brightwaters, NY 11718
United States
Tel +1 631 252 3527
mcandcstudio@gmail.com

Darnell McCown
1230 Westminister Lane
Duncanville, TX 75137
United States
Tel +1 214 421 9333
darnellmc@sbcglobal.net

Eric Melzer
www.ericmelzer.com
2103 23rd Ave. S
Minneapolis, MN 55404
United States
Tel +1 612 840 8934
eric@ericmelzer.com

Patrick Molnar
www.patmolnar.com
443 Lakeshore Drive NE
Atlanta, GA 30307
United States
Tel +1 404 431 8383
patmolnar@mac.com

Tadd Myers
www.taddmyers.com
1527 W. State Highway 114, Ste. 500
Grapevine, TX 76051
United States
Tel +1 214.752.2372
tmyers@taddmyers.com

Artem Nazarov
www.nazarovphoto.com
880 Glenwood Ave. SE, Unit 1419
Atlanta, GA 30316
United States
artem@nazarovphoto.com

Lennette Newell
www.lennettenewell.com
2340 Pimlico Lane
Placerville, CA 95667
United States
Tel +1 925 930 9229
lennette@lennettenewell.com

Tatsuro Nishimura
www.tatsuronishimura.com
150 Bay St., #804
Jersey City, NJ 07302
United States
Tel +1 646 713 9612
tatsuro.pc@mac.com

Scott Paulus
www.scottpaulus.com
P.O. Box 1985
Milwaukee, WI 53201
United States
Tel +1 414 526 9980

Yaniurka Pedroza
www.instagram.com/yaniphotography
Miami, FL
United States
institutionalawards@scad.edu

Harry Rifkin
www.theharryrifkin.com
5900 Pat Ave.
Woodland Hills, CA 91367
United States
harry@theharryrifkin.com

Victor Romero
www.vromero.com
Zanzabeel 4. 201 Qamardeen District
Burj Khalifa, Oldtown, Dubai 111076
United Arab Emirates
Tel +971 557 288 857
contact@vromero.com

Joseph Saraceno
www.josephsaraceno.com
26 Wolverton Ave.
Toronto, ON M4J 3H8
Canada
Tel +1 416 908 1598
joe@josephsaraceno.com

Lucy Schoenfeld
www.lucyschoenfeld.com
Salt Lake City, UT
United States
lucyschoenfeld@gmail.com

Michael Schoenfeld
www.michaelschoenfeld.com
560 W. 200 S
Salt Lake City, UT 84101
United States
Tel +1 801 560 3305
michael@michaelschoenfeld.com

Robert Seale
www.robertseale.com
Houston, TX
United States
Tel +1 832 654 9572
robert@robertseale.com

Aman Shakya
www.amanshakya.photography
Savannah, GA
United States
amanevan@gmail.com

Lindsay Siu
www.lindsaysiu.com
3628 St. George St.
Vancouver, BC V5V 3Z7
Canada
Tel +1 604 780 4755
lindsay@lindsaysiu.com

Allison Smith
www.allisonrevelle.com
Savannah, GA
United States
hello@allisonrevelle.com

Dylan Swart
www.dylanswart.com
Canada
dylan@dylan-swart.com

Traction Factory
www.tractionfactory.com
247 S. Water St.
Milwaukee, WI 53204
United States
Tel +1 414 944 0900
tf_awards@tractionfactory.com

Patrick Tregenza
www.ptfoto.com
248 Pearl St.
Monterey, CA 93940
United States
patrick@ptfoto.com

Andrien Trujillo
www.andrientrujillo.com
Plano, TX
United States
atrujillo@ha.com

Ellis Vener
www.ellisvener.com
Atlanta, GA
United States
Tel +1 404 803 8335
ellis@ellisvener.com

Yichen Wang
China
ycwangstudio1@gmail.com

David Westphal
www.westphalphotography.com
827 Cresthaven Drive
Los Angeles, CA 90042
United States
Tel +1 818 953 7300
david@westphalphotography.com

Michael Winokur
www.winokurphotography.com
530 Hampshire St., Apt. 406
San Francisco, CA 94110
United States
Tel +1 650 468 3686
mw@winokurphotography.com

Visit Graphis.com to view the work within each Country, State, or Province.

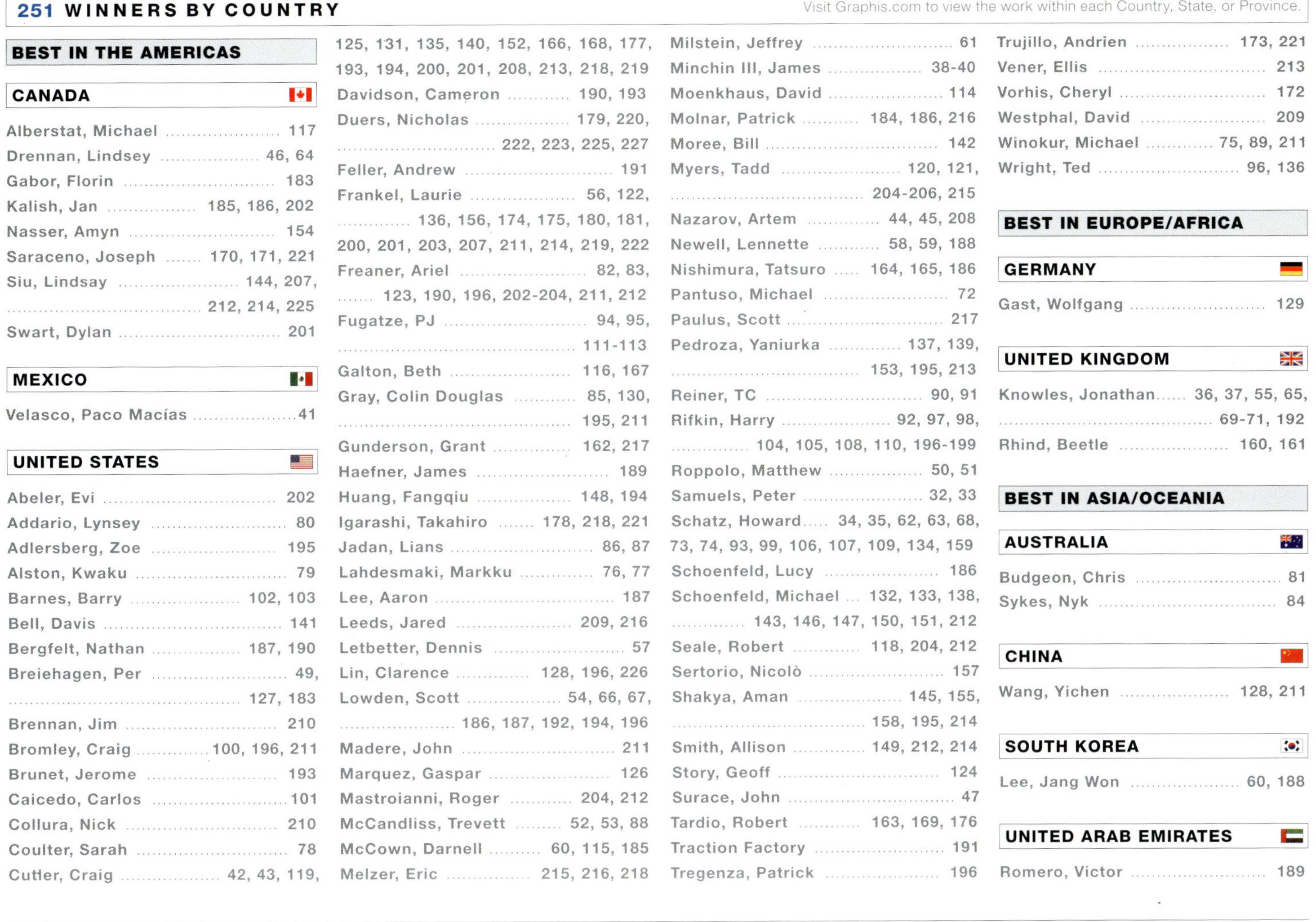

BEST IN THE AMERICAS

CANADA

MEXICO

UNITED STATES

BEST IN EUROPE/AFRICA

GERMANY

UNITED KINGDOM

BEST IN ASIA/OCEANIA

AUSTRALIA

CHINA

SOUTH KOREA

UNITED ARAB EMIRATES

The level of creative talent and awesome photography clearly shows that this is a collection of some of the best in the industry.

It is inspiring to see such fresh and unique images in Graphis from truly talented artists.

Per Breiehagen, *Photographer, Per Breiehagen Photography*

My preferred digital camera is Canon for its expertise in capturing the fine details critical for precise beauty and product photography standards.

Lindsey Drennan, *Photographer, Lindsey Drennan Photography*

I expect my camera to deliver uncompromising high resolution and quality files, and the Nikon D850 does that. I have also always liked the ergonomics of Nikon cameras.

Nicolo Sertorio, *Photographer, NicoloSertorio.com*

I'm currently shooting with Sony's current flagship camera, the A1. That fast sync helps eliminate unwanted ambient light, such as photographing an animal in a barn with daylight spilling in, affecting the design of my light.

Peter Samuals, *Photographer, Peter Samuels Photography*

For Hasselblad, superb camera resolution, wonderfully sharp lenses, and simple software all combine to make a great workflow.

Jonathan Knowles, *Photographer, Jonathan Knowles Photography*

I use Phase One due to its utmost quality in photography. The color, tones, sharpness, and dynamic range are unbeatable.

Takashi Igarashi, *Photograper, Igarashi Photo, LLC*

We sent our Platinum and Gold award-winning photographers a survey to learn what equipment they prefer. The results are below, including which specific models they use. It's no surprise that Canon remains the most popular brand for both cameras and lenses, but Nikon, Phase One, and Sony aren't too far behind.

CAMERAS

1. CANON (32%)
Canon
Canon 5D Mark II
Canon 5D Mark III
Canon 5D Mark IV
Canon 5DS
Canon 5DSR
Canon 7D Mark II
Canon AE-1
Canon EOS 7D
Canon EOS 80D
Canon EOS R5
Canon R5

2. NIKON (13%)
Nikon D3X
Nikon D3XS
Nikon D4
Nikon D5
Nikon D800
Nikon D810
Nikon D850
Nikon Z6
Nikon Z9

3. SONY (11%)
Sony
Sony A-1
Sony A7R II
Sony A7R III
Sony A7R IV

4. HASSELBLAD (11%)
Hasselblad
Hasselblad 907X
Hasselblad H5X

5. PHASE ONE (10%)
Phase One
Phase One IQ4
Phase One P25
Phase One XF IQ3
Phase One XF IQ380
Phase One XF IQ4
Phase One XF
Phase One XT IQ 4150

Other (23%)
1960 Film Camera
4x5 View Camera
Cambo View Camera
Contax 645
Deardorff 8x10 Camera
Fuji GFX 100
Fuji GFX 100s
Fuji GFX 50s
Fuji XT-10
Horseman LD Pro
iPhone 11
iPhone 12 Pro
iPhone 13
iPhone 14 Pro Max
iPhone 14 Pro
Leica M10 Mono
Leica M11
Leica SL2
Leica
Pentax K3
Red Monstro 8K
Sinar 4x5
Sinar P2
Twin Lens Rollei Camera

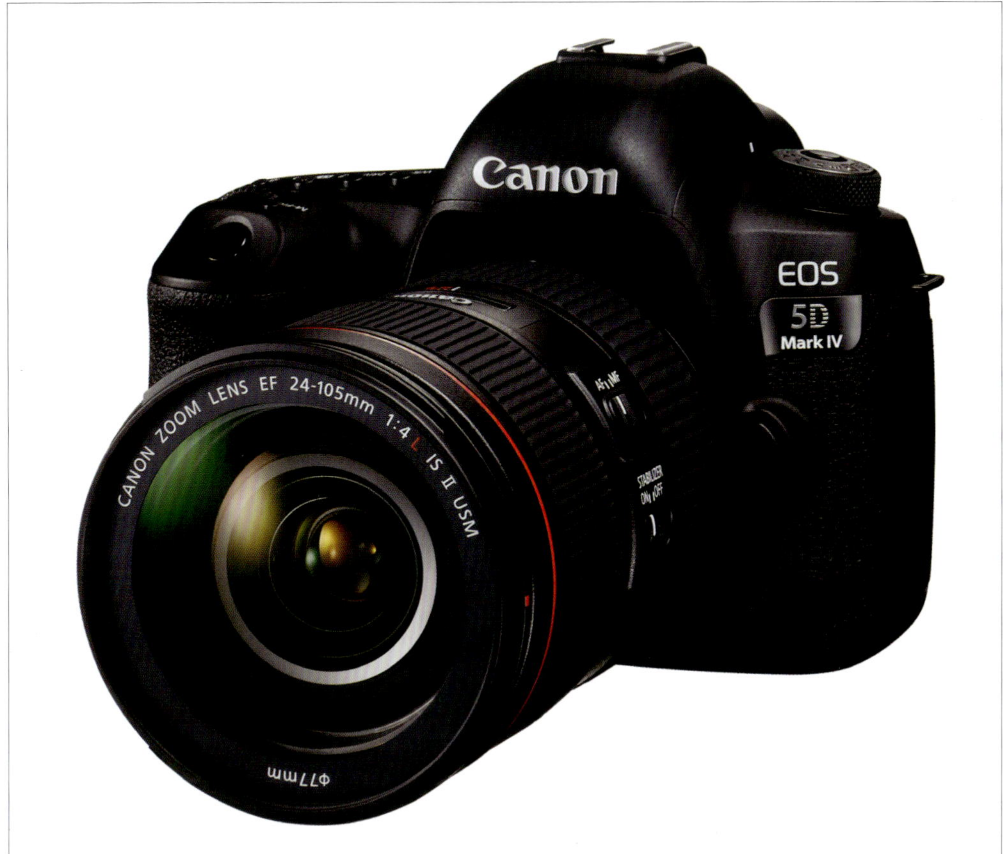

Above: Canon EOS 5D Mark IV | Image from Canon Press Center.

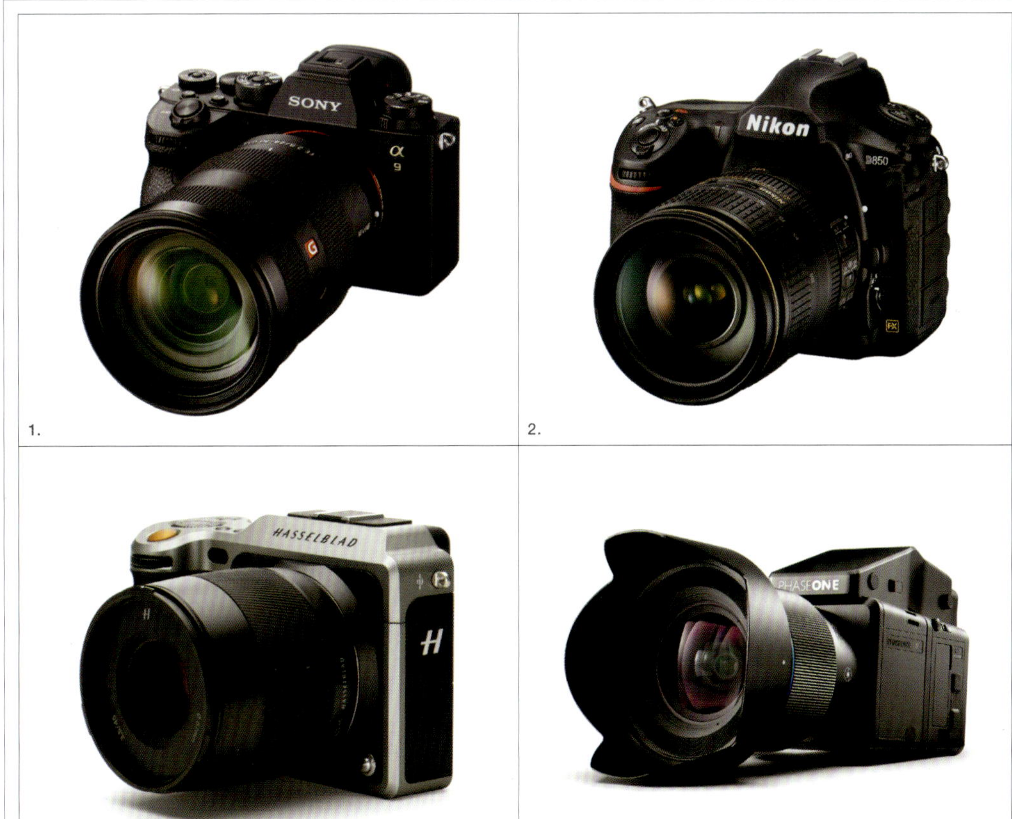

1. Sony A9 II 2. Nikon D850 3. Hasselblad X1D-50C 4. Phase One | All the images are from the brands' press center.

LENSES

1. CANON (47%)
Canon 100-400mm
Canon 100mm
Canon 11-17mm
Canon 14-35mm
Canon 15-35mm
Canon 18-135mm
Canon 24-105mm
Canon 24-70mm
Canon 28-70mm
Canon 28mm
Canon 50mm
Canon 70-200mm
Canon 70mm
Canon 85mm
Canon 90mm
Canon RF

2. NIKON (21%)
Nikon 105mm
Nikon 17-35mm
Nikon 24-70mm
Nikon 28-105mm
Nikon 28-75mm
Nikon 35mm
Nikon 50mm
Nikon 60mm
Nikon 85mm

3. HASSELBLAD (5%)
Hasselblad 120mm
Hasselblad 28mm
Hasselblad 35-90mm
Hasselblad 80mm

4. SONY (2%)
Sony 16-35mm

5. PHASE ONE (1%)
Phase One 80mm

Other (23%)
50mm Tiltshift
Fuji 110mm
Fuji GF 120mm
Leica 24-70mm
Leica 80mm
Pentax 18-55mm
Pre-Patent Dallmeyer 2B Petzval
Rodenstock APO 135mm
Rodenstock HR 32mm
Schneider APO Digitar 210mm
Schneider-Kreuznach Super Angulon 75mm
Sigma Art 85mm
Various Lenses
Voigtlander Nokton Classic 35mm
Zeiss 55mm
Zeiss Lenses

LIGHTING

Profoto (72%)
Kolari ND Filter (8%)
Aputure Lights (4%)
Astera Lights (4%)
Dynalite (4%)
Felix Lights (4%)
Photek Umbrellas (4%)

Advertising Annual 2024

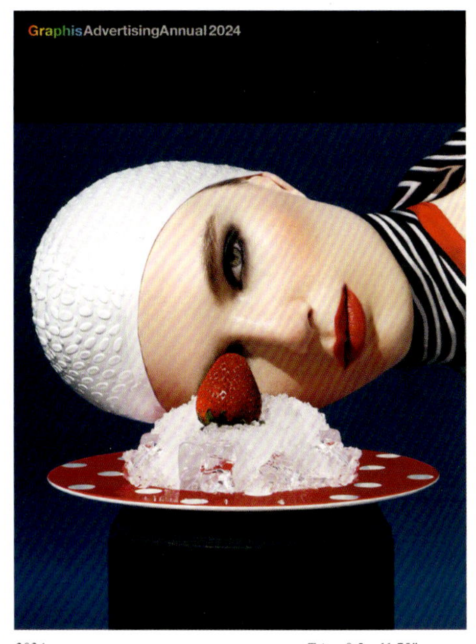

2024
Hardcover: 224 pages
200-plus color illustrations
Trim: 8.5 x 11.75"
ISBN: 978-1-954632-25-7
US $75

Awards: Graphis presents 15 Platinum, 61 Gold, and 99 Silver awards, along with 14 Honorable Mentions.
Platinum Winners: ARSONAL, Brunner, Célie Cadieux, Extra Credit Projects, Freaner Creative & Design, PangHao Art Studio, Partners + Napier, PETROL Advertising, ReThink, Rhubarb, SJI Associates, Sukle Advertising, and SUPERFY.
Content: This Annual includes amazing Platinum, Gold, and Silver Award-winning print and video advertisements from well-established firms and agencies. Honorable Mentions are also presented. Also featured in the annual is a selection of award-winning work from the competition judges and our yearly In Memoriam list of the advertising talent we've lost over the last year.

Design Annual 2024

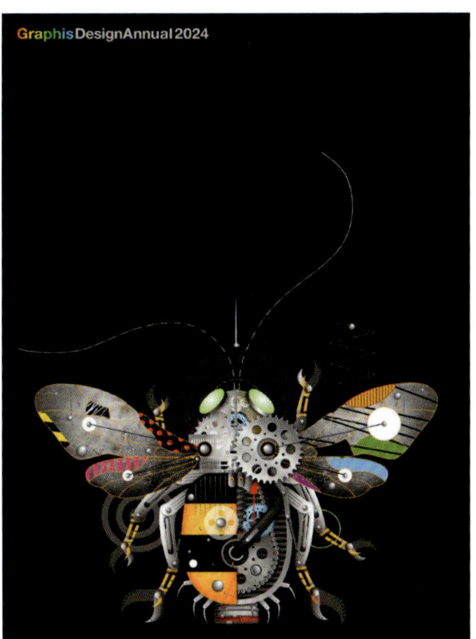

2023
Hardcover: 272 pages
200-plus color illustrations
Trim: 8.5 x 11.75"
ISBN: 978-1-954632-22-4
US $75

Awards: Graphis presents 12 Platinum, 108 Gold, and 436 Silver awards, along with 182 Honorable Mentions.
Platinum Winners: Presenting AV Print, The Balbusso Twins, Carmit Design Studio, Journey Group, Michael Pantuso Design, Namseoul University, Omdesign, PepsiCo Design & Innovation, Studio Eduardo Aires, Sun Design Production, Underline Studio, and Wonderlust Industries, Inc.
Content: This book includes award-winning work from the judges, as well as Platinum, Gold, and Silver-winning work from internationally renowned designers and design firms. Honorable Mentions are presented, and a list of designers that we have lost this past year and a directory of design museums are also included.

Poster Annual 2024

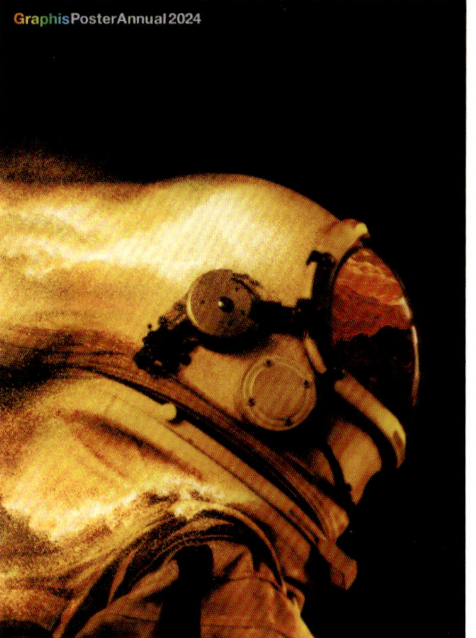

2023
Hardcover: 256 pages
200-plus color illustrations
Trim: 8.5 x 11.75"
ISBN: 978-1-954632-23-3
US $75

Awards: Graphis presents 14 Platinum, 100 Gold, and 266 Silver awards, along with 211 Honorable Mentions.
Platinum Winners: This year's group of international designers include Antonio Castro Design, Atelier Radovan Jenko, Chemi Montes, Holger Matthies, Kashlak, Kiyoung An Graphic Art Course Laboratory, Mirko Ilic Corp., MOCEAN, Peter Diamond Illustration, Šesnić&Turković, Supremat, The Refinery, and Underline Studio.
Content: This book features international Platinum, Gold, and Silver-winning work. Honorable Mentions are also presented. Award-winning work from the judges and a section of Platinum-winning works from 2014 are also included. Platinum and Gold-winning designers discuss their posters and explain the approach they took that resulted in their winning work.

New Talent Annual 2023

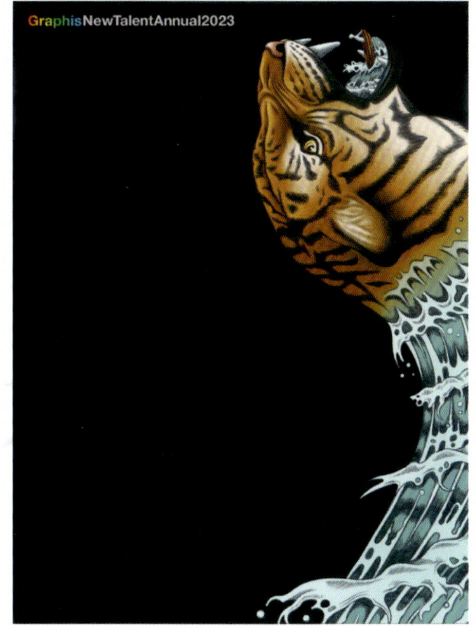

2023
Hardcover: 272 pages
200-plus color illustrations
Trim: 8.5 x 11.75"
ISBN: 978-1-954632-16-5
US $75

Awards: Graphis presents 12 Platinum, 169 Gold, and 344 Silver awards, along with 638 Honorable Mentions.
Platinum-winning Instructors: Advertising: Mark Allen. Design: Elaine Alderette, Brad Bartlett, Brian Boyd, Gayle Donahue, Mads Greve, Seung-Min Han, Réka Holló-Szabó, Miguel Lee, Douglas May, Miles Mazzie, Dong-Joo Park, Søren Patger, Brian Rea, Paul Rogers, Carlos Roncajolo, Simon Sticker, Carter Tindall, Judit Tóth, and Cardon Webb. Photography: Manolo Garcia.
Content: This book contains award-winning entries in Advertising, Design, Photography, and Film/Video. We also present A Decade of New Talent, featuring Platinum-winning works from 2013. All entries are organized by discipline like our professional annuals.

Packaging 10

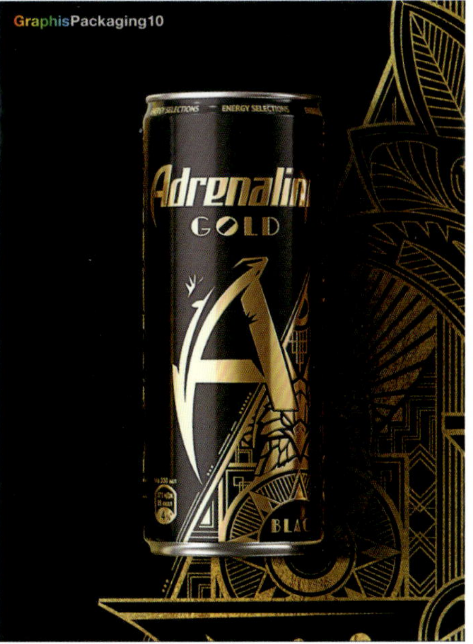

2022
Hardcover: 240 pages
200-plus color illustrations
Trim: 8.5 x 11.75"
ISBN: 978-1-954632-12-7
US $75

Awards: Graphis presents 12 Platinum, 100 Gold, 204 Silver, and 249 Honorable Mentions for innovative work in product packaging.
Platinum Winners: Michele Gomes Bush (Next), Chad Roberts (Chad Roberts Design Ltd.), XiongBo Deng (Shenzhen Lingyun Creative Packaging Design Co., Ltd.) and Lu Chen (Xiaomi), Vishal Vora (Sol Benito), Mattia Conconi (Gottschalk+Ash Int'l), and Frank Anselmo (New York Mets), Ivan Bell (Stranger & Stranger), Brian Steele (SLATE), and the team at PepsiCo Design & Innovation.
Content: This book contains award-winning packaging from the judges, as well as international Platinum, Gold, and Silver-winning packaging designs from designers and design firms from around the world. Honorable Mentions are presented, and a feature of award-winning work from our Packaging 9 Annual is also included.

Narrative Design: Kit Hinrichs

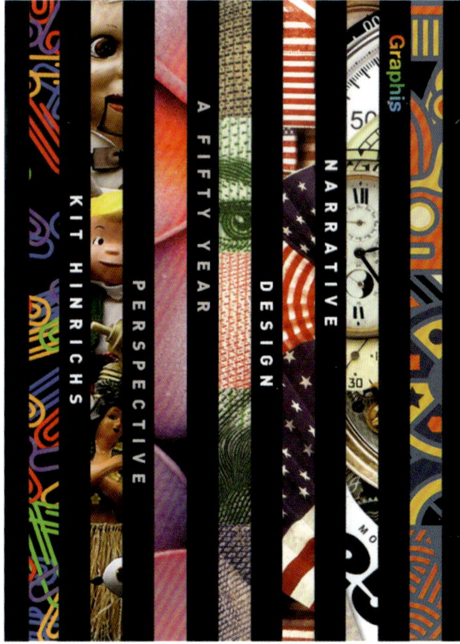

2023
Hardcover: 248 pages
200-plus color illustrations
Trim: 9 x 12"
ISBN: 978-1-954632-03-5
US $65

Narrative Design: A Fifty-Year Perspective is a collection of over 50 years of work from the obsessive graphic designer Kit Hinrichs. To the legendary AIGA medalist, author, teacher, and collector, design is the business of telling a story. It's not just about communicating a product or a corporate ethos—it's about contributing to the collective culture of storytelling. Presented in the book are not individual case studies but rather categories of work and graphic approaches to assignments that have wowed clients and dazzled viewers. The work is arranged to communicate Hinrichs' creative thinking, which always leads to a unique and effective solution to any design conundrum.

Books are available at store.graphis.com

www.Graphis.com